UNDERSEA VICTORY

*The Influence of Submarine Operations on
the War in the Pacific*

UNDERSEA VICTORY

The Influence of
Submarine Operations on
the War in the Pacific

W. J. HOLMES

Garden City, New York
DOUBLEDAY & COMPANY, INC.
1966

c
10-15-69

Charts by Dorothy deFontaine

Library of Congress Catalog Card Number 65–17232
Copyright © 1966 by W. J. Holmes
All Rights Reserved
Printed in the United States of America

940.54
H6
Cop 2

Contents

SPECIAL PROCEDURES USED IN THE INDEX AND GLOSSARY   xi

FOREWORD   xiii

ACKNOWLEDGMENTS   xiii

Chapter I GUDGEON   1

Chapter II S-38   19

Chapter III MEN AND MATERIEL   34

    Commanding Officers – Officer Personnel – Enlisted Personnel – Development of Materiel – Power Plants – The Deck Gun – Radar and Fire Control – Torpedoes – Japanese Submarine Personnel

Chapter IV STRATEGIC PREPARATIONS FOR WAR   45

    Organization – Unrestricted Submarine War – Asiatic Submarine Disposition – Pacific Submarine Disposition – U.S. Anti-Submarine Preparation – Japanese Submarine Organization – Japanese Submarine Strategy – Pearl Harbor Plans – Japanese Anti-Submarine Preparations

Chapter V DECEMBER 1941   56

    Japanese Submarines at Pearl Harbor – U.S. Submarines in Hawaii – Japanese Submarines in the Southwest Pacific – U.S. Submarines in the Philippines – Dutch Submarine Operations – Appraisal

Chapter VI JANUARY–FEBRUARY 1942   72

    Invasion of the Dutch East Indies – *Swordfish* at Kema – Balikpapan – Loss of *Shark* – S-37 and *Natsushio* – Invasion of Sumatra – *Seawolf* in Lombok Strait – British and Dutch Submarines – Approach

to Java – Battle of the Java Sea – Loss of *Perch* – Supply Service
to Corregidor – Submarine Strategy and Tactics in the Southwest
Pacific – Pearl Harbor Submarines – Reconnaissance – Carrier Raids
on Marshalls and Gilberts – *Grayling* at Truk – U.S. Carrier Operations – U.S. Submarine Strategy in the Central Pacific – Japanese
Submarine Operations – Japanese Submarine Strategy and Tactics

Chapter VII MARCH–APRIL *1942*   99

The Second Bombing of Pearl Harbor – Windup of the First Phase
– *Sailfish* and *Kamogawa Maru* – *Seawolf* at Christmas Island – Kido
Butai in the Indian Ocean – Pacific Fleet Submarines – Japanese
Plans for the Second Phase – Tokyo Air Raid – Strategic Movements
of Japanese Submarines – Japanese Anti-Submarine Organization
– U.S. Submarine Operations in April – Carrier Operations in New
Guinea Area – Port Moresby Operation – High Command

Chapter VIII MAY *1942*   113

The Battle of the Coral Sea – Employment of U.S. Submarines –
Pursuit of *Shokaku* – U.S. Submarine Successes in the Central Pacific
– *Triton* in Tung Hai – Submarine Shifts and Command Change –
U.S. Submarines in the Southwest Pacific – S-Boat Operations –
Gun Attacks – Japanese Submarine Operations

Chapter IX JUNE *1942*   132

The Battle of Midway, Japanese Plans – Japanese Sortie – American
Plans – The Japanese Advance – *Nautilus* – Midway Bombed – Mid-
way Planes Attack Kido Butai – Kido Butai – U.S. Carrier Planes
Attack – *Hiryu* vs. *Yorktown* – Confusion in the Kido Butai – Night
Actions – *Tambor* – *I-168* – U.S. Submarines in Pursuit – The Rest of
June – Torpedoes

Chapter X JULY–AUGUST *1942*   152

Fleet Submarines in the Aleutians – Loss of *Grunion* – Southwest
Pacific Submarines – Guadalcanal – Submarine Supporting Opera-
tion – The Battle of Savo Island – *S-44* and *Kako* – Loss of *S-39* –
Japanese Submarines – Air and Surface Forces in the Solomons –
Battle of the Eastern Solomons – Tokyo Express – Japanese Sub-
marines – Submarines in the Aleutians – Makin Raid

Chapter XI SEPTEMBER–OCTOBER *1942*   167

Japanese Submarine Operations in September – American Submarine Operations – *Guardfish* – Battle of Cape Esperance – Battle of
Santa Cruz – Other Japanese Submarine Activity – American Submarines in October

Chapter XII NOVEMBER–DECEMBER *1942*   179

The Battle of Guadalcanal – Japanese Submarines in the Solomons in
November – Japanese Submarine Supply Service – The Battle of
Tassafaronga – Japanese Submarine Losses – U.S. Submarine Orga-
nization in the South Pacific – *Seawolf* off Davao – Solution of the
Puzzle of Palau – *Seal* at Palau – *Albacore* and *Tenryu* – Subma-
rines off Honshu – The Shipping Situation

Chapter XIII JANUARY–FEBRUARY *1943*   193

Submarine Command Changes – New Year's Comparisons – U.S.
Submarines vs. Japanese Escort Forces – Loss of *Argonaut* – Pene-
tration of Japanese Harbors – *Guardfish* at Rabaul – *Wahoo* at
Wewak – U.S. Submarine Special Mission – *Growler* vs. *Hayasaki* –
Loss of *Amberjack* – U.S. Submarine Results – Progress of the War
– Japanese Submarines – *Kiwi* and *Moa* vs. *I-1* – Loss of *I-18* –
Pearl Harbor Submarines

Chapter XIV MARCH, APRIL, MAY *1943*   212

Command Organization – Progress of the War in the South Pacific – Loss of *Grampus* – Battle of the Bismarck Sea – U.S. Subma-
rines in the South Pacific – Loss of *Triton* – U.S. Submarines in
Other Areas – Battle of the Komandorski Islands – Struggle for Con-
trol of the Air in the South – Japanese Submarines in the South
Pacific – Loss of *RO-34* and *RO-102* – *Tunny* and the Japanese Es-
cort Carriers – Death of Yamamoto – *Maru* War in April and May –
Loss of *Pickerel* – Fremantle-Based Submarines – *Gudgeon* and
Kamakura Maru – Loss of *Grenadier* – Submarine Minelaying –
Aleutians Activity – Japanese Submarines in the Aleutians – U.S.
Submarines in the Aleutians – Koga Reacts – U.S. Submarines in the
Carolines and Marshalls – *Pollack* at Jaluit

Chapter XV JUNE–SEPTEMBER *1943*   231

Trigger Torpedoes *Hiyo* – Loss of *Runner* – Japanese Submarines
in the Aleutians – Advances in the South Pacific – Japanese Submarines in the South Pacific – *Scamp* Sinks *I-168* – U.S. Submarines
in the South Pacific – Pearl Harbor Developments – Torpedoes –
U.S. Submarines into the Sea of Japan – *Tinosa* and *Tonan Maru
No. 3* – Progress in the South Pacific – Japanese Submarine Losses
in the South Pacific – Fremantle Submarines – Loss of *Grayling* and
Cisco – Pearl Harbor Submarines – Loss of *Pompano* – Progress
with Torpedo Exploders – New Japanese Defense Plans – *Snapper*
Sinks *Mutsure* – *Trigger* in the East China Sea – Central Pacific Offensive

Chapter XVI OCTOBER–NOVEMBER 1943   252

Skate on Lifeguard – *I-36* Reconnaissance – New Guinea and the
South Pacific – Rabaul Carrier Strike – Battle of Cape St. George –
Brisbane Submarines – *Albacore* Bombed – Fremantle Submarines –
Seawolf and *Akatsuki Maru* – Wolf Packs in the Central Pacific
– Operation Galvanic – Loss of *Sculpin* – Assault of Tarawa and
Makin – *Nautilus* at Abemama – Japanese Defense Moves – Japa-
nese Submarines in the Gilberts – Loss of *Wahoo* – S-44 – *Corvina* –
Capelin – October and November Results

Chapter XVII DECEMBER 1943–JANUARY 1944   273

Japanese Grand Surface Escort Force – Counterattack on *Puffer* –
Gato with Depth Charge on Deck – Grand Escort Force Strength
– *Sailfish* vs. *Chuyo* – Continued Pressure on Japan – *Skate* vs. *Yamato* – December Results – New Year's 1944 – Comsubpac Plans
and Operations – Operation Flintlock – New Guinea – Japanese Submarine Losses – Brisbane Submarines – *Penang* – Fremantle Submarines – Pearl Harbor Submarines – *Swordfish* and the Q-ship –
Flintlock Deployment – Kwajalein Assault – Minefield Intelligence
– Loss of *Scorpion*

Chapter XVIII FEBRUARY–MARCH 1944   293

Eniwetok – Truk Strike – Truk – *Searaven* at Truk – Japanese Sub-
marines and the Truk Strike – Eniwetok Landing – South Pacific –
Brisbane Submarines – Japanese Tanker Sinkings – Pearl Harbor
Submarines – Japanese Convoy System – *Trout* and Matsu No. 1 –
Loss of *Grayback* – Saipan Carrier Strike – New Plans – *Sand Lance*
and Matsu No. 2 – *Tautog* vs. *Shirakumo* – Palau Carrier Attack
– Loss of *Tullibee* – *Tunny* at Palau – *Harder* at Woleai – Japanese
Submarines in March – Strategic Effects

Chapter XIX APRIL–MAY 1944   312

Rotating Patrols – Zone Classification – Hit Parade – *Seahorse* in the
Marianas – *Harder* vs. *Ikazuchi* – *Scamp's* Bomb Damage – Loss of
Gudgeon – Japanese Submarine Losses – *Bluegill* vs. *Yubari* – Hol-
landia Landings – *Tang* at Truk – Convoy Bamboo No. 1 – Tawi
Tawi – *Raton* and *Lapon* – Loss of *Herring* – Wolf Pack in Luzon
Strait – Submarines in the Marianas – Japanese Anti-Submarine
Headquarters – U.S.S. *England*

Chapter XX JUNE 1944   332

Kon Plan – A-Go Operation – Southwest Pacific Submarines –
Harder – *Redfin* – Central Pacific Submarines – *Seahorse* and *Flying
Fish* – *Cavalla* – *Albacore* – Task Force 58 – War against the *Marus*

– Japanese Submarines – Japanese Submarine Communications with
Germany – Japan's Desperate Submarine Situation

Chapter XXI JULY–AUGUST 1944   351

Pacific Submarine Force – British and Dutch Submarines – Submarines in the South China Sea – Convoy College – Submarine Losses
– Japanese Countermeasures – Christie's Submarines – *Rasher* – *Ray*,
Guitarro, *Harder*, and *Haddo* – Loss of *Harder* – Japanese Light
Cruiser Sinkings – Japanese *Maru* Losses – Convoy College – Japanese Countermeasures

Chapter XXII SEPTEMBER 1944   366

Rakuyo Maru – Rescue Operations – *Unyo* Sunk – Outside Convoy
College – Changing Tactics – MacArthur's Approach to the Philippines – Nimitz's Next Move – Submarine Reconnaissance – Third
Fleet Plans – Palau and the Philippines – Japanese Submarines –
Loss of *Seawolf*

Chapter XXIII OCTOBER 1944   377

Third Fleet – Submarine Activities – Attacks on Japanese *Marus* –
MacArthur Returns – Japanese Plans – Lockwood's Submarine Dispositions – Christie's Submarines – *Dace* and *Darter* – Loss of
Darter – *Angler* and *Guitarro* – Battle for Leyte Gulf – The Battle
of Cape Engaño – Lockwood's Submarines – The Battle off Samar –
Japanese Submarines at Leyte – Summary of Japanese Submarine
Results at Leyte – *I-12* and *U-168* – U.S. Submarine Losses – *Salmon's* Escape

Chapter XXIV NOVEMBER–DECEMBER 1944   397

Continued Battle for Leyte – Japanese Submarines in the Philippines – U.S. Submarines in November – *Ray* – Lockwood's Submarines – *Halibut* and the MAD Plane – *Spadefish* and *Shinyo* – *Sealion*
and *Kongo* – *Archerfish* and *Shinano* – Burt's Brooms – November
Submarine Losses – *Growler* – *Scamp* – Japanese *Kaiten* Operations
– Other Japanese Submarine Activity – German and Japanese
Submarines in Malaya – Japanese Submarine Supply Service – December Operations in the Philippines – *Maru* Sinkings in December
– Southwest Pacific Submarines – Japanese Combat Ships *vs.* Submarines in December – *Redfish* and the Aircraft Carrier – Damaged Submarines

Chapter XXV JANUARY–MARCH 1945   422

Lingayen Landings – Third Fleet Operations – Submarines in the
South China Sea – Loss of *Barbel* – Japanese Tanker Movements –
Japanese Combat Ships in the South China Sea – Smaller *Marus* –

Submarine Blockade – Japanese Submarines in the Philippines –
Batfish and the Takao Transportation Operation – End of Japanese
Submarine Operations in the Philippines – Midget Submarine Oper-
ations – *Kaitens* – Japanese Submarine Transportation Operations –
Lockwood's Submarines – Reconnaissance – Loss of *Swordfish* –
Guardfish and *Extractor* – Preparation for Iwo Jima – Carrier Raids
on Tokyo – *Pomfret* as Lifeguard – Japanese Submarines at Iwo
Jima – Japanese Submarines off Okinawa – The Okinawa Cam-
paign – Loss of *Kete* and *Trigger*

Chapter XXVI APRIL–JUNE 1945   444

Lifeguard Submarines – Loss of *Snook* – Okinawa Landing – *Thread-
fin* and *Hackleback* Make Contact – Japanese Submarines at
Okinawa – Temmu *Kaiten* Unit – Continuing *Kaiten* Attacks –
Other Japanese Submarine Operations – Southwest Pacific Subma-
rines – Shallow Water Operations – *Charr, Gabilan,* and *Isuzu* –
Marus and Escorts in Southwest Pacific – Loss of *Lagarto* – British
and Dutch Submarines – German Submarines in the Java Sea –
Awa Maru – East China Sea and Yellow Sea – *Tirante* – Northern
Japan – Into the Sea of Japan

Chapter XXVII JULY–AUGUST 1945   463

End of the Okinawa Campaign – Third Fleet Hits Japan – Subma-
rine Patrols – *Barb* in the Sea of Okhotsk – Lifeguards – Minefield
Reconnaissance – Radar Pickets – Southwest Pacific Submarines –
British Midgets – Loss of *Bullhead* – Japanese Plans to Attack the
Panama Canal – *Kaiten* Operations – End of the War Situation –
Japanese Submarine Preparations – *Spikefish* and *I-373* – High Un-
derwater Speed Submarines – Shore-Based Midgets and *Kaitens*
– End of the War for U.S. Submarines – Japan Surrenders

BIBLIOGRAPHY   483

General Narrative of the War – U.S. Submarine Operations –
British and Dutch Submarine Operations – Japanese Submarine
Operations – Additional Sources for Japanese Operations – Anti-
Submarine Operations – Mine Warfare – United States Strategic
Bombing Survey – U. S. Naval Institute *Proceedings*

INDEX AND GLOSSARY   487

CHARTS

Aleutians – Japan – Hawaiian Is. – Marshall and Caroline Is. – China Seas –
Philippine Is. – Coral Sea – Solomon Is. – East Indies

SPECIAL PROCEDURES USED IN THE INDEX AND GLOSSARY

In order to avoid encumbering the text with excessive footnotes and technical definitions, which could distract and impede the reader's progress, and to provide a central point of reference, a good deal of supplementary information and definitions are included in the index. In some cases, such as definitions, this additional material will not necessarily be followed by page references.

In the index, all ship names are italicized. Australian, British, Dutch, German, and New Zealand ships and personnel are indicated by the abbreviations Aust., Br., Du., Ger., and N.Z., following the name in parentheses.

Class designation abbreviations, in parentheses, follow the name of naval vessels. These abbreviations and other abbreviations used are defined in alphabetical order in the index. U.S. naval class designations are followed by hull numbers. U.S. ships with the same name can be distinguished by their different hull numbers.

Command title abbreviations are defined and explained and other information is listed under the abbreviated title.

Japanese words and phrases are defined in the index.

Maru appended to Japanese ship names ordinarily designates a commercial vessel. However, *Maru* was retained in the name of armed merchant cruisers (XCL), converted escort vessels (XPG), and some auxiliary naval vessels. Such ships are indicated by the class designation in addition to *Maru*.

Last name only of the commanding officer of a submarine generally appears in the text in parentheses after the name of the submarine. Full name and rank is given in the text only when it appears necessary for understanding and continuity. The full name can be learned, and any ambiguity resolved by consulting the index.

The symbol ↓ designates a vessel sunk by a submarine, and the name of the ship in the index is followed by the name of the submarine. Submarines lost during the war are marked * and those sunk by other submarines are additionally marked ↓. The cause of the loss (when known) and the approximate date appear after the submarine names. For complete lists of Japanese vessels sunk the reader is referred to *The Imperial Japanese Navy in World War II*, Military History Section, General Headquarters, Far East Command, 1952 or *Japanese Naval and Merchant Shipping Losses* by Joint Army-Navy Assessment Committee, Government Printing Office, 1947.

FOREWORD

In December 1941 the strength of American submarine forces in the Pacific was as nearly equal to Japanese submarine strength as it was possible for coincidence to contrive. Yet before the war was over Japanese submarines were reduced to comparative impotence while the American submarine force became one of the major instruments of victory. This disparity of accomplishment, with nearly equal initial means, arises from complex causes which make the submarine war in the Pacific a profitable and interesting study.

As submarines were not primarily pitted against each other, but against the seaborne strength of their opponents, it is necessary to consider the contemporaneous progress of all phases of the war to provide the necessary background for an understanding of either American or Japanese submarine strategy. This chronicle is confined to the Pacific, excluding the Atlantic and the Indian Ocean, except where actions there bear directly upon events in the Pacific. Detailed accounts of selected submarine actions and patrols have been included to encourage empathy with those who "dive into the bottom of the deep," without which it is difficult to appreciate the emotional factors involved. Finally, as time was such an important element of the general strategic situation, a strong chronologic arrangement has been adopted despite the temptation to divide the war against Japan into two wars, directed simultaneously from Australia and from Hawaii.

ACKNOWLEDGMENTS

The numerous published sources to which I am indebted are listed in the appended bibliography. In addition, both during and after the war,

I have discussed many of the actions with the participants and so many people have given me assistance that it is impossible to list them all.

I am particularly indebted to Vice Admiral Elton W. Grenfell, U.S.N., Rear Admiral Wreford G. Chapple, U.S.N. Ret., Rear Admiral Karl G. Hensel, U.S.N. Ret., Captain Leslie K. Pollard, U.S.N. Ret., and Rear Admiral F. Kent Loomis, U.S.N. Ret., Acting Director of Naval History; all of whom have read and criticized portions of the manuscript. Dr. Alvin Coox and Captain Toshikaze Ohmae have greatly assisted me in accumulating Japanese materials, portions of which have been translated by Mr. Wilvan van Campen, Mr. Drew W. Kohler, and Dr. Minoru Shinoda.

Finally, I am deeply indebted to my wife, Isabelle W. Holmes, for typing and retyping the manuscript many times, assisting me in the collection of reference material, and without whose help the production of this book would have been impossible.

940.54
Ho
Copy 2

I

GUDGEON

At nine o'clock on the morning of the eleventh day of December 1941, U.S.S. *Gudgeon* backed away from the dock at the Submarine Base, Pearl Harbor, and headed out. She was bound for Japan, there to conduct unrestricted submarine warfare in an assigned area, off Bungo Suido, the passage between the southern end of the Japanese Inland Sea and the Pacific Ocean. She would be the first American ship to enter Japanese waters to exact from Japan a small portion of the retribution due for the attack on Pearl Harbor, just four days before.

As *Gudgeon* rounded the end of Kuahua Island she was pointed directly at Battleship Row, and Lieutenant Commander E. W. Grenfell, from the submarine's bridge, had a comprehensive view of the devastation resulting from that attack. It set a grim tone for this first patrol. At the far right was the shattered hulk of *Arizona*. *West Virginia* had settled nearly upright in the mud but *Oklahoma* had capsized and her bottom bulged obscenely above the black shroud of fuel oil that fouled all Pearl Harbor. *Maryland* was a shambles. *California*, with her main deck under, rested on the bottom, where she had been moored, and at the turn of the channel, opposite Hospital Point, *Nevada* was aground where the Japanese dive bombing attack stopped her in her gallant dash for the open sea.

A few days before, this array of blasted and broken hulks had been battleships, bristling with guns and glittering with spit and polish, before whom *Gudgeon* in her junior and lowly status, kowtowed with military punctilio. Now the survivors of the Battle Fleet looked up from their weary task of salvage and took heart to see a lone submarine going down the channel, a token of defiance, challenging the triumphant sea power of Japan.

Gudgeon was typical of the many submarines that would follow her in first a trickle and then a stream, from this Submarine Base at Pearl

Harbor, to take up their lonely patrols, and each alone, do individual battle with the enemy. Newly commissioned, and due to return to the West Coast for completion of her final trials, *Gudgeon* was at sea on training exercises when the war broke. Hastily she returned to Pearl Harbor to take on torpedoes, ammunition, and provisions, and to top off with fuel for a war mission. Now, four days after the bombing of Pearl Harbor, instead of heading east for Christmas in California at Mare Island Navy Yard, as she was scheduled, she was coming down the channel to head west from Pearl Harbor, embarked upon a long and perilous war.

She was a fleet-type submarine, developed in the peacetime years between two world wars, designed to cope with an aggressive enemy as well as the hazards and logistic difficulties of the vast Pacific Ocean. She was about 1500 tons displacement, 307 feet long, 27 feet beam, with a surface maximum speed of 21 knots and a top submerged speed of 9. At economical cruising speed she had a cruising radius of twelve thousand miles. She carried twenty-four torpedoes and supplies and provisions for fifty-one days at sea without logistic support.

There were fifty-five enlisted men in *Gudgeon's* crew, of whom only seven seamen, four firemen, and two mess attendants were not rated specialists of some kind. Twelve were motor machinist's mates and eight were torpedomen, seven were electrician's mates and five were radiomen. The rest were signalmen, cooks, quartermasters, gunner's mates, fire controlmen; one pharmacist's mate habitually called Doc, and one yeoman to take care of the ship's paper work and records. In addition to Lieutenant Commander Grenfell, the commanding officer, there were three lieutenants in her officer complement: Lyon the executive officer and navigator, Dornin the fire control officer, and Farrell the engineer and diving officer. Lieutenant Junior Grade Bobczynski was the fifth officer in her regular complement. On this patrol there were two additional officers on board; Ensign Robertson, a recent product of the University of California ROTC, and Ensign Sorenson from University of Washington. Embarked for training purposes, these two young officers were shortly handling their full share of work and responsibility.

Gudgeon came slowly down the channel. She turned into the last reach and felt the lift of the long swell of the Pacific. Grenfell noted a flurry of activity ahead at the gate of the channel's torpedo net, halfway down the reach. Almost simultaneously a messenger dashed up the ladder from the conning tower with a message from the radio room. Pearl Harbor was in the throes of another alarm and alert and the channel gate had been ordered closed. There was no alternative but to turn the long submarine around in the narrow channel, backing and filling while the heavy swell and the fresh breeze did their best to push her broadside onto the reef. Hardly had she completed this difficult maneuver when the alert was canceled. *Gudgeon* turned again and ran for the open sea.

Beyond the reef she would be on her own against the world. Once at sea *Gudgeon* could expect every man's hand to be turned against her, and either friend or foe would shoot on sight. *Thresher,* two days before, had been mistaken for a Japanese submarine and depth-charged and bombed from the air as she sought to return to Pearl Harbor from a prewar patrol off Midway. An old four-piper destroyer, *Litchfield,* waited off the outer channel buoys to escort *Gudgeon* clear of the trigger-happy Inshore Patrol. As *Gudgeon* cleared the torpedo net gate Grenfell called Lyon to the bridge.

"Dick," he ordered in terse terms, "go below, secure the radio watch, and put a padlock on that damned radio room door."

Like Nelson putting his blind eye to the telescope, Grenfell determined to stop up *Gudgeon's* radio ears until he had taken her out of reach of Pearl Harbor panic. As Lyon disappeared down the hatch he ordered the officer of the deck, "Secure the channel watch. Station the sea detail. On watch first section," and the word was passed throughout the ship.

Men who had been on deck, standing by the anchor and the lead line as a precaution against further channel maneuvers, now went tumbling down the hatch. Lookouts struggled upward to their accustomed perches on the periscope shearwater, and as they did so Grenfell leaned over the voice tube and quietly gave the order, "Rig for diving."

As soon as the last channel buoy was rounded and the submarine fell in behind the waiting *Litchfield, Gudgeon* must be buttoned up, ready to dive, prepared for any emergency. All the deck hatches, excepting only the conning tower hatch to the bridge, must be firmly seated and drawn down tight in their heavy rubber gaskets, there to remain until the long patrol was over and *Gudgeon* again passed through this point, inbound. After she was rigged for diving, *Gudgeon* and those who were in her became a thing apart from the rest of all creation. Transubstantiation from an inanimate shorebound vessel to a sentient symbiosis of men and machinery accompanied the orderly operations of closing hatches, opening valves, and adjusting circuits.

Two hours later in midchannel between Oahu and Kauai, *Litchfield* sheered off and slowed. As *Gudgeon* passed, semaphore flags fluttered from *Litchfield's* bridge.

"Goodbye. Good luck and God bless." And *Gudgeon* was on her own.

There were no ships of the United States Navy then between her and the coast of Japan, and in that vast stretch of ocean there were no merchant ships to carry the flag of the United States or any of her allies. Search planes flying out their sector to six hundred miles from Oahu would be best avoided. It would be trusting luck too much to depend upon the pilot of a plane at five thousand feet altitude to distinguish an American from a Japanese submarine. Any periscope, excepting *Gudgeon's*, thrusting its one-eyed snake head above the surface, would be enemy, and like any other vessel, when she was on the surface, *Gudgeon's* safety from submarine attack depended upon the sharp eyes of her lookouts, the quick responses of the officer of the deck, and the agile maneuvers of the ship.

The next morning, an hour before dawn, with the island of Kauai astern, *Gudgeon* was trudging wearily westward. It was the better part of valor, and traditional routine, to greet the dawn submerged, and view the new day and the surface of a hostile sea through a periscope rather than risk a surprise at what the sunrise might reveal.

"Lookouts below," Grenfell ordered.

They scrambled down the hatch. For a moment the commanding officer was left alone on the bridge. He stretched up on the step to look over the deck, first forward and then aft. The little ship was wallowing along at about ten knots, in a beam sea, and over the deck the waves broke as they must have on desolate and primitive rocks for eons before the surface of the Pacific Ocean was disturbed by man-made turbulence. The swells, still black with night, came rolling out of the murk, reaching up against the hull to send a splatter of spray against the conning tower fairwater. Above, high-piled cumulus masked the sky, and only an occasional star peeped through as the clouds hurried by. Alone on the bridge, the submarine dwarfed by the sky and the dark expanse of ocean stretching beyond his vision, Grenfell had a feeling of primeval loneliness, as though he were the only man left in the world alive, and everything was as cold and unfriendly as the dark depths of the ocean into which he was about to retreat.

The war had cut straight across his life, as it had across the life of every man on board, dividing it into two unlike parts. For fifteen of his thirty-eight years he had been a commissioned officer of the United States Navy. Most of those fifteen years had been spent in submarines— fifteen years of work and accomplishment and frustrations and disappointments and success, culminating in command of this new submarine. The future was unknown, but judging by many target practices and training exercises, it would be extremely hazardous. The future might indeed be short and never would it resemble the past. Already after only five days of war, even the memory of a normal existence seemed remote and strange. Shaking loose from this moment of introspection, Grenfell dropped down the open hatch, riding the lanyard down to close it after him, and pressed down hard three times on the diving alarm switch.

"Dive. Dive. Dive."

More from habit than for observation, Grenfell stepped carefully across the crowded conning tower to the periscope and reached for the hoist button. As the shining tube flowed past him, bringing the eyepiece up out of the deep periscope well, the captain noted that the quartermaster had completed securing the conning tower hatch, and the helmsman was standing steady at his station in the forward end of the conning tower.

"What's your heading?" he inquired.

"Steady on course three hundred, sir," the helmsman replied.

As he swung the periscope around he noted that the dawn was not yet bright enough to see much through the scope, so he quickly snapped the handles back into their clamps and lowered the periscope back down into its well.

In the after end of the conning tower Dornin, the fire control officer, manned the Torpedo Data Computer. Lyon, the executive officer, stood by him. The Submarine Attack Course Finder, an instrument resembling a circular slide rule and known to a generation of submariners as the "Is-Was," hung around Lyon's neck by a lanyard. With it he could compute a target's course and speed if the electrical computer failed. The chief torpedoman manned the torpedo firing keys on the port side and the soundman, with his earphones over his ears, was attentive to his instruments. A total of eleven men crowded the little conning tower, already full of instruments and gauges so that Grenfell, walking the periscope around with his eye pressed to the eyepiece, had to squinch in his behind each time he passed a station. Farrell, the engineering officer at the diving station, was giving orders to the trim manifold. His voice could be heard coming up through the lower conning tower hatch.

"Pump from after trim to forward trim."

The morning dive, among other things, was intended to give the diving officer an opportunity to "catch a trim," checking and adjusting the ship's weight and balance, in order that she might, at any time later in the day, be quickly submerged and, after the nine seconds it took her ballast tanks to flood, be in good depth control. Shortly afterward the diving officer reported up the voice tube: "Ship has a half switch trim, sir"; indicating that he was confident that he had so balanced the submarine that he could control the depth through any maneuvers at any speed the captain might order.

"Very well," Grenfell responded. "All ahead one-third. One hundred feet."

On this morning it was the captain's intention to make a rapid inspection of the ship from bow to stern, while the crew was mustered at their General Quarters stations. In battle, it was probable that only the captain could see the enemy through the periscope and upon his skill and judgment, more than any others, would depend success or failure; but at any station throughout the ship, a wrong move, a fumbled order, a slow response to an emergency could spell disaster. In a submarine, more than in any other type of ship, the captain, the crew, and the ship formed a team every member of which must function properly without fail, to accomplish their mission and bring the ship home from a successful patrol.

Grenfell dropped down the lower conning tower hatch, half sliding down the familiar ladder, to the control room deck. At that level there was a more or less continuous passageway, from one end of the ship to the other. The captain went forward to the torpedo room to commence his inspection, squatting down and sliding through the watertight doors in each compartment bulkhead, ducking for the hanging valve wheels, and instinctively avoiding shin-menacing protuberances along the familiar route.

At the forward end of the torpedo room, the breeches of six torpedo tubes terminated the accessible portion of the ship. The tubes were loaded and their after doors were closed and ready. In the torpedo racks aft of them the reload torpedoes waited, pre-empting most of the torpedo room space. Up above the racked torpedoes in the small space left between their sleek greased bodies and the arch of the inner hull, the bunks of the torpedomen hung, that they might literally sleep with their temperamental charges day and night. All the torpedomen were busy now with the torpedoes in the racks. Spare torpedoes had been hurried aboard from the Submarine Base, not in the fully ready condition. All the torpedoes had to be made ready and a routine carried out on each torpedo, in the tubes or in the racks, to keep them in perfect mechanical condition. This hour submerged, with no pitching or rolling motion on the ship, was the best time to accomplish the delicate adjustments required.

In the after end of the torpedo room was the hoist and training mechanism of the supersonic transceivers, so that the sensitive sound heads could be extended beneath the ship's turbulence as on an inverted periscope, or raised to a secure recess in the bottom of the outboard hull. The next compartment aft was the officers' country, the tiny wardroom and the three staterooms deserted now that all the officers were manning their battle stations. The electrician's mate of the watch was just disappearing down a hatch in the deck to check the condition of the storage battery, one-half of whose 252 cells (each one sixteen hundred pounds of lead and sulphuric acid) were wedged into the lead-lined forward battery tank below the officers' country.

In the control room, the next compartment, was concentrated much of the apparatus, the meters, the gauges, and devices to control the ship. Every available inch of space along the ship's bulkhead, the sides and the overhead was crowded with gauges, dials, control wheels, valves, and levers. Here was the trim manifold, through which ballast water could be pumped from one tank to another, or to sea, to adjust the balance of the submarine; the air manifold that controlled the ship's reserve supply of air, stored at 3000-pound pressure in steel bottles in the ballast tanks; the vent and blow manifold to control the flooding of the ballast tanks to submerge the ship, or blow them free of water to bring her quickly to the surface. Here also was the gyro compass, and the interior communication switchboard and the emergency steering station. Aft on the port side, separated by a light steel bulkhead from the rest of the compartment for quiet and security, was the radio room. Surveying the situation there, Grenfell wondered where they would find room to install the radar, left behind by the submarine's hurried departure, and waiting for her on the dock at Mare Island. Not in the crowded radio room surely, but somewhere close by.

It was in the control room that the diving officer had his station, standing behind the seated bow planesman and stern planesman, as they faced the two main depth gauges, upon which they glued their eyes as their hands controlled the position of their respective diving planes. Above the depth gauges was the "Christmas tree," an array of red and green indicator lights that told the diving officer the status of every opening in the hull of the ship. Below the deck was the pump room, so crowded with machinery that it was almost impossible for one man to move about.

The crew's space, on top of the after battery, like the officers' space forward, was deserted; the bunks folded up and secure. Only the cooks were busy in the galley, preparing breakfast against the demands of a hoard of hungry men who would shortly be released from General Quarters. The engine room was still warm from the hot engines that had been secured as soon as the diving alarm sounded. Now that *Gudgeon* was submerged, 6500 horsepower of diesel engines stood idle while electric motors drawing current from the storage batteries drove the ship. Beyond the engines was the maneuvering room, where the controllermen on watch followed the signals of the annunciator from the conning tower to control the speed of the main motors beneath them. Before them on the maneuvering board, an array of electric meters indicated the condition of the ship's electric circuits. Aft of the maneuvering room was only the after torpedo room whose four tubes limited the accessible portion of the ship's stern, as their forward counterparts had terminated it in the bow.

Satisfied with his inspection, the captain returned to the conning tower and ordered the submarine brought up to fifty feet. Through the periscope he scrutinized the surface of an empty sea, now gray with the dawn.

"Surface. Surface. Surface."

Through the periscope he watched *Gudgeon's* bow break upward through the sea, like the snout of a blowing whale. Then as he lowered the periscope, he watched the depth gauge until it indicated that the bridge was well out of water.

"Open the conning tower hatch."

The faint woosh of escaping air and the release of pressure in their ears as the hatch popped open told everyone that the inside of *Gudgeon* was again continuous with the earth's atmosphere. Leaving the periscope, Grenfell clambered up the ladder to the bridge to be the first man on deck after the dive as he had been the last man to leave it before *Gudgeon* submerged. The submarine had a new washed look, as she wallowed in the trough of the seas. The seas, rising and falling with a relaxed display of power like the breathing of a sleeping tiger, sloshed through the slatted deck, barely awash. From below came the scream of the low-pressure blowers, as they labored to blow water out of the ballast tanks and give the ship a modicum of buoyancy and freeboard.

"Lookouts on deck. All ahead standard," he ordered.

For the next few days it would be safe to proceed on the surface both day and night and make constant progress toward the distant assigned operating area, but as she neared Japan she would have to be more careful. For eleven more days *Gudgeon* proceeded westward, across the International Date Line, into another hemisphere, diving only for an hour or so each dawn; but as she approached the area where Japanese search planes might be encountered this picnic cruising had to end.

Grenfell had orders from Commander Submarine Force on this first patrol, that as soon as his submarine reached a position within five hundred miles of a Japanese air base, he must dive at dawn and remain submerged until after evening twilight in order that the enemy might have no knowledge of his passage. Marcus Island, a thousand miles from Japan, was believed to be a Japanese air base. In order to reach the operating area, *Gudgeon* would have to creep across fifteen hundred miles of sea patrolled by Japanese planes.

On Christmas morning *Gudgeon* reached the danger line, inscribed upon the chart, that bounded the domain of Japanese search planes. After the dawn dive Grenfell took her down to the calm depth of a hundred feet to celebrate their wartime Christmas. Motor Machinist's Mate Zotti, with his accordion for accompaniment, organized a trio of carolers to sing at each station of the watch from the forward torpedo room on aft throughout the ship. Most of *Gudgeon's* crew were professionals, older but no more warlike than the volunteers who would later swell their ranks. These were men with families who had anticipated being together on this holiday at Mare Island after the long shakedown cruise in Hawaii, and for them Christmas was a grim day of nostalgia and regret.

Less than a month before, the Japanese Kido Butai had crossed these longitudes in the opposite direction, manned by wildly enthusiastic crews headed to attack Pearl Harbor. With a thousand banzais those eager samurais launched a war whose horrors would be returned a thousand-fold by reluctant warriors like these in *Gudgeon* approaching Japan with apprehensive determination.

After that morning the sun never shone on *Gudgeon's* decks or on her crew until she came back across that line. It completely changed the manner of their lives. Lyon, the navigator, who traditionally had placed much reliance upon sun sights, particularly the observation of meridian altitude at apparent noon, must now determine *Gudgeon's* position from the morning and evening stars, while there was not enough light in the sky to drive the submarine under.

Preparing for the morning stars, each night as he came off midwatch on the bridge, Lyon carefully guarded his eyes from bright lights, and before turning in for his brief rest between midnight and dawn, he put two drops of a special eyewash containing adrenalin in each eye. Then, upon being called before dawn, he put on dark glasses with side blinders, and dressed and proceeded to the darkened conning tower. The pupils of his eyes were so dilated that when he came up on the bridge he could clearly see the night with its thousand eyes looking down on him. The horizon under these conditions would be a hazy line between the dark sea and the lighter sky, and only after trial and experience could he distinguish the true horizon, which he had to know to complete his observation. He used an old Indian trick he had read about in a book. Closing his eyes as he looked toward the hazy horizon, he then opened them quickly and blinked rapidly, ending by staring wide-eyed at the true horizon which was then sharply revealed. There were tricks to be learned in this new life for everyone.

This night life on the surface and daytime deeply submerged seriously reduced their rate of progress toward Japan. During the day, running submerged on battery power, speed was nominal (two or three knots) and only during the night could appreciable mileage be gained. Even during the night one engine had to be operated to recharge the exhausted storage battery. When conditions were favorable she could make a hundred and fifty miles a day, but often the day's run fell short of that.

The monotony of the long day dive was boring. With the submarine in perfect trim, she swam through the sea under fingertip control, the bow and the stern planes almost never requiring adjustment; and the depth was so constant that the depth gauge hand might have been painted on the dial. The crew was divided into three watches, one group on watch while the other two rested, or performed minor repairs, adjusted torpedoes, or read or prepared reports or played cards and acey-deucy. Even for the crew on watch (except for the diving officer, the officer in the conning tower on periscope watch, the bow and stern planesmen, the controllermen, and the helmsman) the duties of the rest generally required them to be only in a stand-by status. Meals were served submerged, on schedule, although other submarines sometimes turned night into day under these circumstances in order to cut down on the activity and the food preparation while submerged. In *Gudgeon* baking was done at night to reduce the heat released in the boat submerged. The food was excellent.

Gudgeon had old-type evaporators and distillers. Her new vapor compression stills, along with her radar, were waiting for her on the dock at Mare Island. This meant severe control of water consumption. The showers were filled with provisions and locked. No one was allowed to take a bath until they were nearly home again. Consumption of fresh water averaged 1.8 gallons of water per man per day, including all water for cooking, washing, drinking and redistillation for main storage battery make up water. Radar, vapor compression stills, and air conditioning were the three great boons to American submarines, and of these *Gudgeon* was yet without the first two.

Air conditioning made life tolerable under these conditions. In the older boats without air conditioning the heat and humidity on all-day dives was exhausting and enervating and brought on a myriad of troublesome skin disorders from being constantly bathed in unwashed sweat. Once *Gudgeon* was submerged and the engines cooled off, her air conditioning controlled her temperature and humidity within the comfort zone. She carried chemicals to remove carbon dioxide from the air, and oxygen under high pressure in steel bottles, but these supplies had to be conserved for real emergencies. It was rather stuffy toward the end of the day, so that the first gasp of clear fresh air after she came up was like a draught of cold water to a thirsty man. The atmospheric pressure within the boat had a tendency to build up during the day, but unless the noise was objectionable, the air compressor could be run to keep the pressure down.

While she was submerged she was practically without radio communication. Although she had a vertical antenna that could be exposed while at periscope depth, its successful use required very smooth seas, and only on one occasion while submerged could they copy the FOX (broadcast) schedule sent out from Pearl Harbor. During the night while surfaced she could hear orders and messages broadcast on the FOX schedule, and only on three occasions did she miss copying this nightly schedule, due to poor reception conditions.

The sound gear was kept in constant operation while submerged, but mostly there was nothing to hear but the sound of *Gudgeon's* own propellers. Occasionally they would pick up a noise somewhat like the fast screws of an outboard motor boat but, when periscope observation repeatedly showed an empty sea, these noises were attributed to schools

of fish or some strange and unknown marine life peculiar to this part of
the ocean. There was much to learn about natural noises in the sea in
a new area. As they approached Nanpo Shoto they heard peculiar ham-
mer noises that did not resemble propeller noise or echo ranging, and
these they finally attributed to volcanic noises under the sea.

Several small fishing boats were sighted nearly eight hundred miles
out from the Japanese coast, but it was not until three days before her
arrival in her operating area that *Gudgeon* sighted her first target-size
enemy ship. It happened about ten o'clock in the morning of the last
day of 1941, when in accordance with routine, the submarine was running submerged at periscope depth. The mast tops of what appeared
to be a freighter poked themselves up above the horizon, and the officer
on periscope watch sighted them at this extreme range. Grenfell, called
to the conning tower, tried to close the range but after a chase of
twenty-five minutes he had to give up. The closest he could get to his
first potential target was fourteen thousand yards, far outside the maximum range of his torpedoes.

The top speed of a submerged submarine was eight or nine knots and
after about an hour at that speed the battery would be discharged. The
submarine would then have to come to the surface and charge batteries
before any further submerged maneuvers could be undertaken. To stay
submerged all day, *Gudgeon* had to be very frugal in her use of high
submerged speeds. As even the slowest freighter generally ran at speeds
in excess of eight knots, it followed that *Gudgeon* could expect to make
many contacts with ships she would be unable to close to effective torpedo range. Only if she was fortunate enough to find herself, at the time
of contact, within a reasonable distance from the projected track of her
target, could she maneuver into position for attack.

A submarine commander had to move promptly and correctly as soon
as a ship was sighted or he would be quickly left wallowing in the target's wake, as both enemy ship and opportunity passed him by. If the
ship was sighted hull down, with the mast tops just above the horizon,
the first problem was to determine the general direction of the target's
travel. Usually this could be quickly accomplished by heading directly
at the target and observing it for a few minutes to find out if the true
bearing changed to the right or the left. The general direction of movement thus established, the submarine swung to the *normal approach
course* with the target on the beam, and the submarine's course
at right angles to the target's bearing. On this course she ran for a few
minutes until the situation developed. If the range closed until the target's hull became visible there would be an opportunity to estimate the
angle on the bow (what the relative bearing of the submarine would be
if viewed from the target). The solution of a simple problem in trig-
onometry would then determine the target's course. A couple of range

and bearing observations would add sufficient data for the Torpedo Data Computer (TDC) and the plotting officer to determine the target's speed. The commanding officer could then make further refinements in his approach to come to the *optimum approach course* at a speed calculated to bring him as promptly as possible into attack position, without undue expenditure of battery power. Of course there were infinite variations of this problem, for the target might change course or speed, or be protected by air and surface escorts to be avoided; the periscope observation and estimates required skill and judgments; and the rapid manipulation of instruments and the teamwork required experience, drill, and practice.

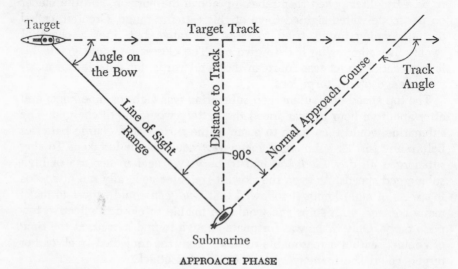

APPROACH PHASE

If after a few minutes' run at a speed as fast as she could afford to go (depending upon the state of the battery and the length of time she might have to maneuver) the submarine pulled ahead of the target; then it was probable that an attack could be made. On the other hand, if the target pulled ahead of the submarine, while the distance to the track was well outside maximum torpedo run, the situation was hopeless—unless the target zigzagged toward the submarine, or slowed down for some reason. So the first ship got clear away without ever knowing it had been tracked by a hostile submarine.

The next morning, long before dawn on New Year's Day, *Gudgeon* encountered a second ship. This time she was on the surface when a darkened ship loomed almost dead ahead, passing from port to starboard. Grenfell estimated the range to be about eight thousand yards, and the relative position of submarine and target was such that *Gudgeon* was silhouetted in the moon's track, where she was certain to be sighted if she lingered on the surface. Under these conditions Grenfell decided to submerge and make a *sound approach*. Once *Gudgeon* was under, he discovered that not only could the target be easily tracked by sound, but in the clear moonlight it could also be seen through the periscope. Unfortunately, the angle on the bow is very difficult to judge in the moonlight, and it had either been misestimated in the first instance, or the target had seen the submarine and turned away as *Gudgeon* was diving, for the angle on the bow was now 135° starboard and the ship was rapidly hauling out of sight.

On the second of January, after 21½ days en route, *Gudgeon* arrived on station in her assigned patrol area. There was little activity and Japanese shipping seemed almost unaware that there was a war going on. The navigational lights on Kyushu and Shikoku were burning. Sampans carried running lights, and although merchant vessels were running darkened, they were proceeding singly, not zigzagging, and had no escorts of any kind. There appeared to be no air patrol or air search and the only planes that *Gudgeon* saw were two naval planes proceeding down the coast of Kyushu on business of their own. There was little traffic of any kind, in or out of Bungo Suido and the only ships sighted were apparently small coastal freighters.

The next contact was on 4 January 1942 at about three o'clock in the afternoon, with *Gudgeon* again submerged. The masts and stacks of a freighter were sighted, with the ship hull down beyond the limited periscope horizon. Grenfell immediately came to the normal approach course at full speed. At the next periscope exposure he could see enough of the target to realize that the angle on the bow was 90° starboard and that therefore there would be little time for maneuver or for closing the range. Nevertheless he succeeded in getting in to twenty-six hundred yards, with a track angle of 120° starboard. The target was disappointingly small, a coastal freighter of about fifteen hundred tons, and the range was long. Grenfell decided it was better to fire two torpedoes, with their tracks spread apart by a small angle to cover any inaccuracies in estimate of target course and speed and promptly the torpedoes were running down the range, hot, straight, and normal. They both missed.

To say that the crew of *Gudgeon* was disappointed would be to state it mildly. This had been the kind of an approach and attack offered to the newest neophyte beginning his training on the Submarine Attack Teacher. The solution had been conventional and correct, like a kindergarten exercise. *Gudgeon* was equipped with the newest TDC, and her fire control party had been drilled and trained and honed to a fine edge. Although it had been impossible to close the range to the optimum thousand yards, Grenfell had maneuvered the submarine into a position for a favorable track angle and a small gyro angle, as attack doctrine required, and still they had missed.

When a submarine's approach succeeded, the captain maneuvered the submarine into the best position, and on the best attainable course, from which to deliver the attack; constantly weighing in his mind the risk of ruining the attack by being discovered against the possible gain of improving the submarine's attack position. Torpedoes were launched from the tubes on the submarine's course (or reversed course if fired from stern tubes). An angle could be applied to the torpedo mechanism before firing it, to cause the torpedo to change course through this set angle (gyro angle) if the torpedo was required to run on a course different from the submarine's course.

Torpedoes running toward the target from nearly ahead or nearly astern had a narrow target to hit, and the enemy ship could generally evade them more easily. Other things being equal it was best to fire so the *track angle* (the angle between the torpedo course and the target's course) was between 70° and 120°. The best position for a submerged submarine was one from which the torpedo run was about a thousand yards, with a zero or nearly zero gyro angle, and with the track angle approximately 100°.

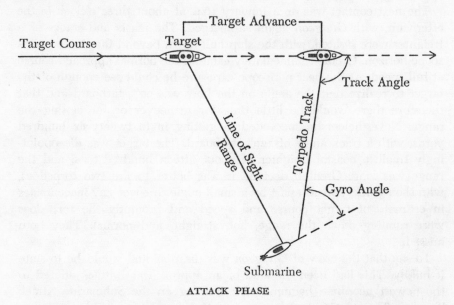

ATTACK PHASE

The torpedoes, launched along the submarine's axis, from either bow or stern tubes, turned through an angle determined by the gyro setting, and then ran at their known design speed, adjusting their own set depth and course, along the torpedo track. If all the computations were cor-

rect, and the torpedoes ran as anticipated, and the target did not successfully maneuver to avoid, and no one made any mistakes, the torpedoes would intersect the target track at the moment the target arrived.

Despite the new mechanical and electrical devices, however, the commanding officer still had to estimate the angle on the bow and the target's
range at each periscope exposure so that the target's course and speed
could be computed by the TDC. When the range was great, a small
error would cause a wide miss and Grenfell came to the conclusion that
that was what had happened, despite his precaution to cover any error
by firing a spread. There was no use crying over spilled milk. The only
thing to do was wait for the next target and do better.

It was five days, however, before *Gudgeon* encountered another ship,
and then she was unable to get closer than five thousand yards. About
midnight on 9 January they had better luck. The moon was just rising
and *Gudgeon* was on the surface when she encountered a five-thousand-
ton freighter, coming down on opposite course to *Gudgeon*, darkened;
but this time the target rather than the submarine was silhouetted
against the moon. Night contacts like that one always developed suddenly. *Gudgeon* as she patrolled at night always had her finger on the
trigger ready to shoot, two tubes forward and two tubes aft always
flooded, outer doors open and the torpedoes ready to go at the touch
of the firing key.

This time she had a few minutes to improve her position and get more
tubes ready for firing. Grenfell worked her in to twenty-five hundred
yards, and fired three torpedoes from the stern tubes, on 100° track. He
was sure that at least one torpedo hit. On *Gudgeon's* bridge they felt
the shock of the underwater explosion. The torpedomen in the after torpedo room were positive that two of the three torpedoes hit. The soundman heard the explosion, and described it as a continuous reverbera-
tion with little directional quality, heard clear around the dial.

Later in the war, this evidence of a hit would be considered very thin,
but this first time everyone in *Gudgeon* felt certain they had sunk their
first enemy ship. Nothing bolsters the morale of a submarine crew better than the sound of their torpedoes exploding against the hulls of enemy ships, and *Gudgeon* was elated. It was compensation for all their
trials and tribulations, all their failures and misses.

The sound of exploding torpedoes was something new for everyone
in *Gudgeon*, even for Grenfell, the "old man" of thirty-eight, who had
long submarine experience behind him. It would be a new experience
for any American submarine crew, for the torpedoes submarines fired in
target practice carried non-explosive exercise heads, and no war heads
had been tested in practice. The explosion *Gudgeon's* people heard may
have been defective torpedoes or other submarine noises but the target

probably was not sunk, for there are no Japanese records of a sinking corresponding to that time and place.

This was the last contact *Gudgeon* made before she pulled out of her patrol area. It had taken 21½ days to come, and Grenfell reasoned that it would take as long to get back. So on 14 January 1942, after twelve days in the operating area, he started the long, weary trek home. Under ordinary circumstances, excepting fishing sampans about six hundred to eight hundred miles from Japan, he could expect no surface contacts. For six days on the homeward journey *Gudgeon* remained submerged in accordance with instructions for operating in an area possibly searched by Japanese patrol planes. Not until 20 January, after a period of twenty-six days of submerged patrol, did *Gudgeon* venture to operate on the surface in the daytime. From then on it should have been smooth sailing.

On the twenty-fifth of January, however, *Gudgeon* intercepted a radio message that put her on her guard. Midway Naval Air Station reported having sighted three Japanese submarines. Japanese submarines, about to conclude their patrols, and ready to start homeward, frequently bombarded the most available shore targets with their deck gun just before departure. When a submarine executed this bon voyage gesture and shelled Midway on the night of the twenty-fifth, Commander Submarines put two and two together. By dispatch he informed Grenfell that a Japanese submarine might be headed in his direction and that there were no United States submarines in his area.

On the morning of 27 January 1942, Grenfell decided that he would run submerged all day and see what happened. In this lethal game of submarine against submarine, like dueling in the dark, the first man to locate his enemy without himself being located is apt to be the only survivor of the encounter. It was nine o'clock in the morning when the soundman reported fast screws on the port bow. Lieutenant Lyon, the executive officer, was on watch at the periscope and trained it to the bearing given. He saw a submarine on the surface, coming up fast on the opposite course.

"All hands General Quarters. Make ready all forward tubes. Down periscope."

Grenfell was in the conning tower almost before the periscope had reached the lowered position. In less than a minute the fire control party was in its place and Dornin had taken over the TDC. Things began to happen fast.

"Up periscope."

"Bearings. Mark."

"Three one two."

"Range. Mark."

"Four two five zero."

"Down scope."

"Angle on the bow forty-five port."

All this information Dornin cranked into the TDC. Sound counted the propeller turns making 240 revolutions per minute. This, according to the best information, would give the target a speed of 16.5 knots, but the Japanese submarine was running into a fairly heavy head sea and Grenfell estimated the actual speed through the water at 15 knots. The TDC showed the distance to the track to be two thousand yards, and Grenfell decided to change course twenty degrees toward the target, to close the range a little. There wasn't time for any more maneuvering. He made two more periscope exposures, checking the range and bearing against the generated data in the TDC, and then just seven minutes after the first contact:

"Final bearing and shoot!"

As the periscope went up he could clearly see six men on the submarine bridge. She was tooling along, in the bright sunlight, headed home as *Gudgeon* was, after a long patrol. She had a gun forward, and her clearing line and conning tower in strange arrangement.

"Bearings on."

"Shoot!"

"Fire One. Fire Two. Fire Three."

Grenfell watched the torpedoes go out, and turn through their gyro angle to the proper track. They looked good.

It is always a greater emotional strain to fire torpedoes at another submarine than at any other type of ship. There but for the grace of God go I, and an alert enemy might even now have his torpedoes in the water racing down the range with my number on them.

There was a tight little knot in the guts of every man in *Gudgeon*. The sea was running high and it was difficult to maintain a steady depth. Grenfell watched the torpedoes through three-quarters of their run and then the tension was too much for someone in the control room, and they lost depth control long enough to duck the periscope under. At the proper interval for the torpedo run, eighty-one seconds after firing, everybody on board felt two distinct shocks, and thirty seconds later when Grenfell succeeded in getting the periscope head above the surface there was no submarine in sight. As the reverberations of the explosion rolled away, there were no propeller noises either. Mindful of the other Japanese submarines in the area *Gudgeon* stayed submerged for the rest of the day. Grenfell was sure he had sunk a Japanese submarine.

The evidence of hitting the submarine was not much better than the evidence of hitting the freighter, but Japanese records are quite complete with regard to combat ships. *I-73* had been on patrol in Hawaiian waters and was missing after 27 January. There can be little doubt that it was sunk by *Gudgeon*.

When *Gudgeon* arrived back at Pearl Harbor, without further adventure, they learned much about the progress of the war. They were avid for war news that had not reached them in their isolated area of the ocean. The news of the Philippines and the East Indies was uniformly bad, except that there were many reports that everyone then believed, of big losses inflicted upon the advancing Japanese. Against this background, the accomplishment of *Gudgeon* seemed insignificant, and the higher echelons of command, in proportion to the height of the echelon, were inclined to be critical of *Gudgeon's* performance.

Gudgeon was credited with sinking a submarine and a five-thousand-ton freighter. There is no Japanese record to substantiate the freighter sinking, and it probably was not hit. American submarines had sunk four *marus* in the Philippines and three off Japan by the time *Gudgeon* returned to Pearl Harbor, but it was either not realized or not appreciated that *Gudgeon* had made history. *I-73* was the first combatant ship ever to be sunk by a United States submarine.

II

S-38

S-class submarines were obsolescent coastal submarines known only by class letter and number, and very different from transoceanic fleet submarines, all of which had names. For S-38, based on Manila, and for her commanding officer, Lieutenant Wreford G. Chapple, the beginning of the war was as different from Grenfell's as S-38 was from *Gudgeon*. S-38 did not have three thousand miles to cruise to find targets. The targets came to her in abundance.

At 0345 on the morning of 8 December, East Longitude date (0915 on 7 December at Pearl Harbor), Admiral Thomas C. Hart, Commander-in-Chief, U. S. Asiatic Fleet, broadcast his command: "JAPAN STARTED HOSTILITIES. GOVERN YOURSELF ACCORDINGLY." Fourteen minutes later he amplified these instructions in a second message: "SUBMARINES AND AIRCRAFT WILL WAGE UNRESTRICTED WARFARE."

For S-38, as for most of the twenty-nine submarines based at Manila, "govern yourself accordingly" meant to proceed immediately to operating areas already assigned. Some were already on patrol. For S-boats these areas were in the coastal waters of the Philippine Islands. As S-38 passed Corregidor, outbound for her first war patrol, the high slopes of the fortress island loomed ominous and foreboding above the channel. Once out into the South China Sea, Chapple set a southerly course for Verde Island Passage, between Luzon and Mindoro. It was this passage that S-38 was assigned to patrol, an area only a short run south from Manila Bay, in familiar seas where she had often conducted torpedo practices and engine trials; where the chatter of snapping shrimp making love along the reef was as familiar to her listening watch as the traffic noises of Manila; and where the phosphorescent fire in her wake at night, beautiful in peacetime, became menacing now that her safety depended upon concealment.

For several days war was much like peacetime patrols. The radio brought disturbing news of the disintegration of the defenses of the Philippines; Manila bombed, Cavite Navy Yard destroyed, Japanese amphibious forces making landings, the ominous and disastrous loss of H.M.S. *Repulse* and H.M.S. *Prince of Wales* off the Malay coast. It was doubtful that Manila would ever again be a haven for rest and replenishment, but for a time the war stayed out of the area assigned to S-38. Even the most peaceful patrols, though, were endurance contests in S-boats.

S-38 had been authorized by Congress in 1918 but she was not built and commissioned until 1923. She therefore incorporated all the lessons of the First World War, and had all the conveniences and devices that were modern some eighteen years before. According to the formula for comparison of naval strengths adopted by the Naval Disarmament Conference of 1922, a submarine over thirteen years old was obsolete. Five years past this arbitrary retirement age S-38 was going strong.

S-38 was 219 feet long, with 20-foot beam, and she displaced all of 800 tons on the surface. Her two 600-horsepower diesel engines were built when diesel engines were rarities. Heavy and slow, they would give her a maximum speed of 14 knots on the surface, with a clean bottom and a fair wind, but 11 or 12 knots were about all that could be counted on consistently. She could make 11 knots submerged though, at the one-hour battery rate, and *Gudgeon,* more modern and more powerful, but with a greater mass to push through the water, could only make about 8 knots submerged. Obviously S-38 was not designed to cross the Pacific Ocean, conduct long, aggressive war patrols and return. It was generally agreed that thirty days at sea was about the limit of her endurance, and endurance it was to keep her there, for the limit of her sea-keeping ability was not fuel, nor food, nor water, but the ability of her crew to endure.

Gudgeon, on her first patrol, did not have radar or vapor compression stills, but she did have air conditioning, and S-38 lacked all three. S-38 also lacked a modern Torpedo Data Computer and automatic gyro setting devices, but of all the things she did not have, the lack of air conditioning was hardest to endure. An all-day dive in an S-boat was an ordeal, peace or war. In the tropics, both the heat and the humidity climbed to oppressive heights and the hull dripped condensed moisture. It was customary during a long dive for officers and men alike to strip to their underpants, with a sweat rag for wiping draped around their necks. Some compartments in the boat were hotter than others. On high-speed runs submerged or on long battery charges the temperature in the crowded motor room at the extreme after end of the ship sometimes reached 135° F. Under these conditions it was necessary to relieve the watch in the motor room every fifteen minutes, and a man coming off watch there, moving to the torpedo room for a blow, would shiver from the chill in that normally oppressive heat and humidity.

With limited refrigeration, the menus were reduced to canned goods after the first few days, and for all practical purposes the fresh water that she took to sea with her would have to last her until she could return because her fresh water distilling capacity was extremely limited. Washing was a rare luxury, despite the salt-caked sweat and the prickly heat. There were two toilets below decks, but the complication of flushing them to sea with high-pressure air, through double valves as a precaution against one leaking, was so discouraging that constipation became a serious occupational hazard, and when the opportunity was available, officers and men alike preferred to answer ordinary calls of nature over the rail, when the submarine was on the surface.

The people in fleet submarines knew what it was like to cruise in S-boats, for most of them had been schooled and trained and served an apprenticeship in the older submarines. S-boats were no worse than the older Japanese submarines, or more crowded than the modern German, whose shorter Atlantic distances made small submarines more practical than they were in the broad Pacific. For all the common ability of submariners the world over to endure hardship, the effectiveness of any submarine depended upon its ability to do damage to the enemy.

S-38 carried a 4-inch gun on deck, a weapon of very limited usefulness. She had four torpedo tubes up forward but none aft, and in addition to four torpedoes in the tubes she could carry eight spares in the torpedo room racks. The torpedoes she carried were an older type than those supplied to fleet submarines. The Mark 10 torpedoes carried in S-boats were nearly as old as S-38. They were ten knots slower than the torpedoes *Gudgeon* carried and their maximum range was thirty-five hundred yards, rather than the forty-five hundred yards the Mark 14 torpedoes could run at full speed. But unknown to anyone then, S-boat torpedoes had an inestimable advantage over their newer rival. S-boat torpedoes, if they hit the target, could be depended upon to explode; the newest Mark 14 torpedoes with the secret magnetic exploder frequently would not meet this very elementary requirement.

On the night of 12 December Chapple got his first look at a target. S-38 was on the surface when they sighted a ship, which he identified as a transport. The ship was silhouetted against the horizon, and S-38 had the dark mass of an island at her back, so Chapple decided to make a surface attack. It was impossible to see much through an S-boat's periscope at night. On the other hand there were no satisfactory instruments for taking ranges and bearings from the darkened bridge of S-38 at night, either. The range could only be judged by "seaman's eye," and every experienced seaman knew that his eye was very deceptive in estimating distances to dark masses of unknown magnitude.

Fortunately the fire control problem turned out to be elementary. The target appeared to be stopped and lying to off the island. Chapple worked the submarine in until he felt there was real danger that S-38 would be sighted by the enemy despite the background advantage. Then he swung her under gentle rudder until the submarine was pointed at the enemy ship, coaching the quartermaster on until he could look down along the clearing line, out over the stub mast, and see the target on steady bearing dead ahead of the torpedo tubes.

"Fire One."

He felt the characteristic thrusting grunt of the submarine as the torpedo left the tube. A faint phosphorescent wake appeared deep in the velvet water, and scribed a glowing line toward the target. Suddenly a bright red explosion burst at the end of the line.

"Dive! Dive!" Chapple ordered as he swung himself down the hatch.

S-38 sought the safety of submergence until the situation cleared. When there was no effort at retaliation and no other ships could be detected in the vicinity, Chapple brought the submarine again to the surface. They ran through the flotsam of a sunken ship, and there was no doubt in anyone's mind that the first shot that S-38 had fired had accounted for a Japanese ship, although postwar information reveals no record of a ship sunk in that position and at that time.

The next real excitement came to S-38 on the evening of 21 December. Stingray, who had been ordered to observe the entrance to Lingayen Gulf, reported that the Japanese invasion forces were arriving and crowding into the Gulf. For forty years, it had been axiomatic that when invasion came to the Philippines, an amphibious landing would be made at Lingayen, bypassing the forts guarding the entrance to Manila Bay through which Dewey had sailed. An invasion force, landing at Lingayen, was on a broad fertile plain leading directly from the beachhead to Manila. Now that the Japanese were there at last, right where they had been expected for years, there was little there to meet them. Their transports and amphibious forces were backed up and protected by the strength of the Japanese Second Fleet, against which it would be useless sacrifice to oppose the weak surface forces of the U. S. Asiatic Fleet or, now that H.M.S. Repulse and H.M.S. Prince of Wales had been sunk, any or all of the Allied surface forces in the Far East. The air force that had been counted on to attack the invaders at the beachhead had been shot out of the skies or destroyed on the ground, and the only force that could interfere with the well-laid Japanese plans was the submarines of the Asiatic Fleet.

There were, besides Stingray, four submarines that could reach Lingayen in time to be of any use to oppose the landing, and Commander John Wilkes, Commander Asiatic Submarine Force, in Manila, ordered all five submarines to penetrate into Lingayen Gulf and attack the invasion forces at the beachhead. It was a forlorn hope and Wilkes knew it, but S-38, S-40, Saury, and Salmon responded to the call. Lingayen was not well adapted for submarine warfare. It is shallow, restricting a submarine's movement in its own third dimension, and too narrow for maneuvers, and fouled with shoals and reefs. Its mouth was easily guarded by patrol craft. The Japanese fully expected to encounter submarine opposition and had made elaborate arrangements to counter it.

At 1930 in the evening of 21 December 1941, Lieutenant Chapple received his orders by radio to leave his assigned area and proceed to Lingayen Gulf and attack Japanese transports making a landing there. It was not necessary for Chapple to consult the chart to learn what sort of a task had been given him. He knew Lingayen and its approaches. His first problem was to get inside the Gulf before daybreak. Northeast from Cape Bolinao for ten miles there extends a coral reef. This foul ground was avoided by ships entering the Gulf, who usually confined their navigation to the safe eastern half of the entrance. S-38 had to run north along the coast of Luzon, past Manila Bay and Subic, and around the end of the reef before the sunrise drove her under.

Chapple had 160 miles to go, and a little computation told him he would be fortunate if he could make it. It was a fine clear night, and the battery charge had been completed and the air banks replenished. S-38 was ready to go. The visibility was good. The low black hull of S-38 was harder to see, against the background of the black sea, than would be the silhouettes of any of her higher freeboard enemies. Like a shadow she crawled up the coast of Luzon, with the mountains of Zambales rising high and black against the eastern sky and the South China Sea stretching out flat and oily to Indo-China on the port side.

S-38 pushed on northeastward until Chapple thought he was clear of the reef. Then he turned and ran due south into the baited trap. All navigational lights on Luzon had been extinguished. It was impossible to be accurate about navigational positions, and it is probable that Chapple took S-38 over the northeast end of the reef which it was quite possible to do—provided he was lucky enough not to hit any pinnacle or high coral heads. In doing so he may have outflanked the Japanese destroyer patrols. At any rate his was the only submarine to get into the Gulf. Three others encountered patrolling Japanese destroyers that effectively barred their entrance.

Before dawn S-38 submerged and came snooping down the Gulf to see what she could find. At 0615 in the morning it was light enough to see through the periscope. Four Japanese transports were moving down the Gulf to the beachhead. They were escorted by destroyers and were surrounded, as they slowly steamed to their anchorage, by a number of large motor launches, carrying depth charges. From the periscope eye view, the depth charges, racked up on the sterns of the motor launches, looked as big as houses, and it was obvious that S-38 would be lucky to get inside this tight screen unchallenged.

In one respect, however, all this activity was in Chapple's favor. With all these escorts milling around, there was so much noise in the water that the Japanese would probably never detect the slow pulse beat of S-38's propellers. The transports were steaming at dead slow speed. The approach problem was elementary, provided the escorts didn't see the periscope. Many target practices, with drastic penalties for being sighted, had made Chapple adept at this stalking game.

"Forty-five feet, and hold her steady," he cautioned the diving officer.

In the S-boat there was no separate conning tower. The commanding officer in the control room, walking his periscope around, literally rubbed shoulders with the diving officer on one side of the control room and the assistant approach officer on the other. The electrician's mate at the main motor controller was within easy reach of his hand. The telephone talker, in communication with the torpedo room, trailing his tail of telephone cord, did his best to keep out from under foot and out of the way of the machinist's mates at the vent and blow manifold, and at the trim pump. The chief of the boat, the senior chief petty officer, stood in the middle of the melee, holding in his hand the periscope switch, raising and lowering the periscope in response to spoken or gestured commands. It was a post of honor, and a central position from which he could exercise a steadying influence on all the crew. When the moment came he would punch the firing key, to send each torpedo on its way.

Observing the needle of the depth gauge steady at its mark, and the bow planesman with his planes set stationary, Chapple watched the diving officer nervously tap the rim of the depth gauge, to induce the reluctant needle to predict which way it would next move. The diving officer caught the eye of his commanding officer and reported,

"Steady at forty-five feet, sir."

A quick glance at the main motor rheostats above the controllers assured the captain that S-38 was at dead slow speed, and that the periscope as it broke the surface of the sea would show no telltale feather.

"Up periscope," he ordered and knelt on the deck before the periscope, as though in prayer.

The chief of the boat responded with a sensitive thumb on the hoist motor switch, and the sleek steel tube flowed upward between Chapple's hands, outstretched as though in benediction, until the periscope handles reached his shoulder level. He snapped the handles down into their operating position and pressed his right eye to the rubber eyepiece. Green water—dark green water—as it should be at forty-five feet, if the depth gauge was correct, but it was better now to be sure than sorry. Without taking his eye away he turned his left palm up and gestured upward. The chief of the boat responded with another foot rise in the periscope. Chapple followed the movement of the eyepiece in deep knee bends. Still dark green water. Foot by foot and inch by inch the chief raised the scope, with his commanding officer unfolding his full height as he followed up the eyepiece. The shade of the green water grew lighter, and then, as a wave rolled lazily over the periscope head topside, a flash of startling sunlight was reflected down the tube to Chapple's eye.

With less than a foot of periscope exposed, like a fishing stake, but like a fishing stake with a glass eye if the sun caught it right, Chapple swung the scope around to the right. There were the transports. He hardly paused to note their formation, and moved on around through full circle to observe the entire surface of the sea to guard against surprise.

"Down periscope," he ordered and then checked its descent after a couple of feet movement.

"Squadron of four transports headed for the beach," he told his approach assistant. "They are at dead slow speed, looks as though they are coming in to anchor. Two destroyer escorts. One on each bow. Motorboats in the inner screen. I'll take a quick look now and give you the setup."

Guardedly he made another periscope exposure and estimated the range and the angle on the bow. Briefly he risked a four-foot periscope exposure to get a complete view of the target beyond the limited horizon of a one-foot height of eye. Then he ducked the periscope well under.

"All ahead two-thirds," he ordered.

He wanted to close the range a little, and move as quickly as possible into firing position. The longer he diddled around the greater were the chances that something would happen to spoil the setup. It was best to get the attack over in the shortest possible time but a thousand things ran through his mind before they coagulated into a battle plan.

"There are four transports," he informed his assistant approach officer, "in line. Coming in at about five knots speed. I'll fire one torpedo on 110 starboard track; at the first one, swing left and fire one torpedo at each transport in natural sequence. You compute the new periscope angle for each torpedo between firings. Depth settings on all torpedoes twelve feet. That should get under the screen and knock the bottom out of the transports. All tubes ready for firing."

He made another observation to check the setup, and then knew he would fire on the next exposure. It would take nimble action on the part of all hands to fire four torpedoes in quick succession at four separate targets but S-38 could do it. And four transports on the bottom would put quite a crimp in the Japanese plan for invasion of Luzon.

He realized that a lot would depend on the confidence he could instill into these men so closely packed around him, depending so much on his eyes alone to see the enemy. How did the Navy Regulations state it? "Or fails to encourage in his own person, his inferior officers and men to fight courageously." The palms of his hands were wet and the back of his throat was dry. Radiating from his stomach was a feeling of emptiness. It transmitted tangible weakness in his knees. He felt as though he was about to vomit.

"Periscope angle 12 degrees," the assistant approach officer coached and for a second that calm report infuriated him. Did this assured young squirt realize that this was not a target practice? Or was he putting on an act?

"Up periscope." He was surprised to find his own voice sounded as calm as did that of his second officer. Maybe they were both putting on an act. The familiar routine procedure sustained him. He checked the upward run of the periscope, and together the chief and he set the periscope angle. When the periscope handles reached his wet palms, the rate of expenditure of time abruptly slowed down and everything fell into place. He could feel his nerves extended along the telephone cord to the torpedo room, and the slow beat of the propellers was attuned to the beating of his heart. The calculating brain of the second officer was a segment of his own mind, and his eye was a part of the periscope as it broke water. He could see the first transport in the left field. He looked up at the periscope setting and gently slapped the periscope handle to adjust it a microscopic hair's breadth.

"Stand by." The target was marching slowly and deliberately across the cross wires. They reached the stack.

"Fire One! Left twenty degrees rudder."

He would have to swing toward the next target or it would never get to the cross wire, even though it was generally bad to fire on the swing. Slowly the first transport was swimming by. He could see masses of Japanese soldiers on deck, ready to disembark.

Damn. Damn. Damn. The target was coming up too slowly. A glance at the compass repeater told him that the submarine had not commenced to swing. S-38 was always a stubborn old bitch. At slow speed she was reluctant to obey her rudder. His eyes snapped back to the target. She was coming up faster now.

"Fire Two."

The chief held the stopwatch up for him to see. Fifteen seconds.

"Rudder amidships."

In a little less than a minute he fired four aimed shots, with the periscope sticking up like a beacon. Then when the last torpedo left the tube he ordered one hundred feet, while the second hand of the stopwatch kept going around. It reached sixty seconds and started down. The time of the torpedo run of the first torpedo was sixty-two seconds. It went on past. Their hearts sank with the tip of the second hand. Four shots. No hits!

"High-speed screws to starboard!"

They were about to find out what it was like to be depth-charged. Very few American submariners had ever heard a depth charge explode, an educational omission the Japanese were eager to remedy. A destroyer was coming up like an express train. It was unnecessary for the soundman to report the sound of screws. The enemy destroyer passed overhead like a train going over a trestle. She went on by and didn't drop. A depth charge exploded, not close, over on the port side. Some deluded escort vessel had picked up a phantom to take S-38 out of the spotlight. The depth charges started going off like Chinese firecrackers, but not close enough to S-38 to worry her, and when they paused in their wild attack, the Gulf was so full of echoes and swirls and turbulence that no one could hear anything. The Japanese were searching for S-38 with supersonic. The eerie pings went out into the water from the searching destroyers, and the echoes bounced off the bottom, and off the turbulence and reverberated through the Gulf like the sound of stones thrown down a deep well. Through it all S-38 slipped silently away.

As the baying pack faded off into the distance, Chapple decided to reload the tubes, an operation that might entail noise that an alert escort could possibly pick up. After his unbelievable four misses Chapple had to get in another attack, although he knew it would be harder the second time against a fully alerted enemy. He reasoned that the Japanese, for amphibious landings in the shallow Gulf, in order to get as close as possible to the beach for disembarking troops, had selected or constructed vessels of shallow draft. This would account for the misses, and as he remembered the easy potshots at the slow-moving transports, it seemed to him to be the only explanation for his failure. His torpedoes had to hit the side of the ship to actuate the impact exploder, and if they were set deeper than the target's draft, they would run harmlessly underneath the keel. So they loaded four new torpedoes into the tubes, with depth settings for nine feet this time, and turned S-38 around and came back to attack again.

This time he had to go all the way in to the transport anchorage area before he found a target. A little before eight o'clock in the morning he found what he identified as an anchored transport. A flotilla of depth-charge-carrying motorboats were running around and around the transport and there were knots of men upon her decks standing by, after the manner of navies since time began. Chapple came creeping in close, so close he couldn't miss. At 0758, from a range of six hundred yards off his target's beam, he fired two torpedoes.

He watched them go down the range, leaving their white bubble tracks, straight and true. Thirty seconds. He saw a geyser of water erupt alongside the target and engulf it. The blast could be heard in every compartment of the submarine.

"Take her down. Eighty feet." They heard the second torpedo explode as she headed down. It wasn't necessary to tell anyone in S-38 that the torpedoes had hit, or that retribution would be on their heels.

S-38 was now in a difficult position. Chapple had brought her into the shallow part of the Gulf, in his pursuit of a target. There was scant water for maneuvering beneath them, and two destroyers overhead, calling plaintively with their supersonic beams, listening for a solid echo from the hull of S-38. Chapple maneuvered to put his pursuers astern and crept silently away, riding as close to the bottom as he dared. For a couple of hours they played this grim game of hide-and-seek.

"Flood from sea to auxiliary," the diving officer ordered, to give S-38 negative buoyancy, and curb her tendency to come up. Chapple watched the diving officer struggle to hold her down. Despite his efforts S-38 seemed determined to come slowly upward. The bow planes were on hard dive and still she persisted in rising. It was a situation so unique that it took some time to solve. S-38 was riding along the shelving mud bottom, her screws pushing her along, plowing the mud, and as the bottom inclined upward, raising the submarine up with it. There was no room there to maneuver. The depth gauge already read forty-seven feet, and S-38 was trapped in the mud at periscope depth. Hastily Chapple ordered auxiliary flooded full, to give her enough negative buoyancy to pin her to the bottom, so that tides and currents would not wash her, like a dead whale, into even shallower water.

Impotent to do anything for their own salvation, stuck in the mud on the bottom, afraid to move, while a myriad of enemies above searched for them, as helpless as a slug under a rock if they were discovered, the crew of S-38 waited for something to happen for their deliverance. Small boats went over them at irregular intervals. A larger ship passed overhead, fortunately missing the conning tower, but fouling the clearing wire with such force that the forward stub mast was bent with a noise that sounded as though S-38 was being rendered plate from plate.

They stopped all machinery. They talked in whispers. They took off their shoes so that their bare feet would make no noise against the floor plates. Like trespassers hiding in a dark closet, they feared to cough or sneeze. The slight trickle from the stern tube gland accumulated water in the motor room bilges. They would not dare to start a pump. On S-boats the vents were operated by pneumatic rather than hydraulic pressure, and the little leaks that occurred around the packing, and past the stems of many air valves, slowly built up the atmospheric pressure in the boat. They did not dare to run the air compressor to bring the pressure down.

With all the machinery shut down, and no current through the main motors, the temperature came down to a comfortable eighty degrees, but the carbon dioxide percentage crept up as the oxygen was used up, and to the oppressive effect of these inexorable chemical changes, the increased atmospheric pressure contributed. They had some soda lime to absorb the carbon dioxide *in extremis,* and some bottled oxygen for emergencies, but their best action was inaction, to move about as little as possible, to decrease their metabolic rate to its minimum, by lying inert and waiting. The pinging destroyers continued searching—sometimes far in the distance, sometimes coming nearer, like a game of lie low sheep.

The sun went down. The moon set early. By the time the moon set, the pinging had died down. When the last pinging destroyer had gone, S-38 backed slowly off the beach, making as little noise as possible. By nine o'clock that night she was proceeding submerged to a secluded and little frequented portion of the Gulf, on the west side, by Hundred Islands. At eleven o'clock Chapple thought he could risk surfacing.

There was then eleven inches of pressure in the boat, over a third of an atmosphere greater than the pressure outside. As soon as the boat was on the surface it was imperative for the captain to get on the bridge and have a look around. Chapple came up the lower hatch while the ballast tanks were still being blown. The quartermaster above him was standing by the conning tower hatch to the bridge with a soft mallet in one hand, to knock the latch clear, and the pull down toggle in the other.

"Open the conning tower hatch."

The quartermaster swung once at the latch, and the hatch blew open with all the excess pressure in the boat behind it. Fortunately the toggle pulled from his grasp, as both he and Chapple clutched tight to the ladder to keep from being blown out the hatch and overboard, like sandhogs blown out of a caisson rupture. In one mighty belch the vertical hurricane expended its force, and the pressure equalized between the inside of S-38 and the earth's atmosphere. Chapple came up on the bridge and peered anxiously out into the surrounding darkness.

As soon as he found the surface clear, they started charging the deeply discharged battery. Along about two o'clock in the morning a motor launch came snooping along in their vicinity and Chapple stopped the charge to still the throbbing of the laboring diesels. They got under way on the silent main motors and stole quietly in closer to Hundred Islands. About a mile off the beach in eighteen fathoms, Chapple anchored with the submerged anchor.

The submerged anchor was a gadget that was omitted from fleet submarines. It was a mushroom anchor on a wire cable, housed in a vertical hawse pipe through the forward trim tank. It could be operated submerged or while on the surface. Unfortunately it had no more holding power than a salad fork in warm butter, but S-38 did not need much to hold her against the weak current of Lingayen, and Chapple used the anchor to good advantage.

By dawn the battery was still not fully charged, nor were the air banks replenished. Moreover the crew was exhausted. So Chapple decided to make a stationary dive down the anchor cable and stay where they were rather than risk new battle for which S-38 was unprepared. They lay there all day, in the mud, alongside their own anchor, resting the exhausted crew. Shortly after sunset S-38 surfaced again and renewed the battery charge. They were forced down once by an approaching patrol boat, and it was nearly five o'clock in the morning before the battery was fully charged and the air banks full.

Some time after 5 A.M. S-38 ventured out toward the center of the Gulf, once more looking for a target. To say that the Japanese were alerted against submarine attack would be an understatement, but for a while there was only one destroyer in sight and that one at a distance. Six transports appeared headed down the bay and Chapple headed for the transports.

He still had five torpedoes, four in the tubes and one spare in the racks. He knew he would have to run the gantlet to get in. He made a short periscope exposure, checked his target, and went boring in. The surface was clear of escorts. Suddenly without warning of any kind there was a terrific explosion close aboard. S-38 went down to ninety feet and slowed, and rigged for silent running. It was probably a stick of bombs from an enemy plane that may have spotted them when they made the periscope exposure. Whatever it was, the patrol boats came running up to exploit the contact and they lost no time in picking up S-38's track.

Careful check showed that the submarine had sustained no apparent damage, except that both control room main depth gauges were temporarily out of commission and the magnetic compass tube was flooded. From noon until sunset, though, the patrol boats dogged S-38's tail. At intervals they dropped a pattern of depth charges, either when a patrol boat thought it had contact, or possibly just as a general harassing measure. Fortunately there was much more water in this part of the Gulf. The submarine sought bottom at 180 feet, but the patrol boats found her out. After one depth-charge attack, uncomfortably close, Chapple backed S-38 clear of the bottom and crawled off to find a safer hideout. When the sun had set she got under way and headed back to Hundred Islands, running submerged at 120 feet. About an hour before midnight she ran aground at 120 feet, and surfaced off Hundred Islands.

Shortly after surfacing, Chapple gave the order to ventilate the inside of the ship's hull outboard, drawing fresh air down the auxiliary induction and distributing it to all compartments in the ship. In order to have as few openings as possible to secure in case of an emergency, he ordered the battery ventilated into the engine room. As this order was carried out the after battery exploded.

A battery explosion is one of the haunting dreads of men who go down to the sea in submarines. Under certain conditions, usually only toward the end of a battery charge, lead acid storage batteries give off hydro-

gen. To keep the hydrogen below explosive limits, the battery is ventilated with copious quantities of air during a charge, but with gentle
zephyrs of positive ventilation at all other times to avoid pocketing of
any hydrogen that might be given off under abnormal circumstances. If
hydrogen accumulates it might be touched off by the spark of any electrical machinery, even from the ventilating blower itself, and then the
atmosphere inside the submarine explodes. This was apparently what
happened in S-38.

When Chapple arrived in the control room from the bridge, two badly
burned men had already escaped from the exploded after battery compartment, but a hasty check showed that Chief Machinist's Mate Earl
Harbin was still in there. In an S-boat the battery was covered with
loosely fitted wooden planks, covered in turn with a rubber and then a
canvas battery deck cover, held down by clamps. This formed the working deck of the after battery compartment which served as galley, the
crew's mess compartment, two officers' staterooms, the main power
switchboard, and for miscellaneous other uses. When the battery exploded this deck was blown helter-skelter, in a wild tangle of gear and
splintered planks and canvas and rubber.

When Chapple peered into the after battery compartment from the
control room watertight door, he could not see all this. The room was
filled with smoke; but he knew what it would be like in there. If Harbin
was still alive he would have to be pulled out somehow before he suf-
focated or was burned to death. Chapple turned to the man beside him.
It was Buck, electrician's mate. Chapple said "Let's go!" and shouldered
his way through the door with Buck right behind him.

They could feel their way along the passageway made by the officers'
stateroom partitions and it was all so familiar they could do it blind.
The footing was the worst. The battery deck planks were heaved up
like pack ice, and beneath them were the electrically charged bare battery connections, and the thin hard rubber tops of the battery cells,
through which a misstep might plunge their feet into strong sulphuric
acid. The air was dense and choking with the smoke of burning rubber.
For all they knew the battery might go off again like a dormant volcano.
Along the bulges of the deck cover little blue flames of burning hydrogen
danced, like the imps in an old print of *Inferno*. They found Harbin
and somehow pulled him out into the control room.

Ventilation slowly cleared the smoke away and they restored some
kind of order. A message arrived over the radio from Manila. When it was
decoded Chapple learned that S-38 was ordered to evacuate Lingayen
Gulf and return to Manila Bay. With these orders he was in complete
agreement. Although he still had five torpedoes, he had only half a
battery he could use. He had three badly wounded men on board.
Harbin's spine was broken. One propeller had been damaged in one of

the groundings. The Japanese seemed to be on top of him every time he moved. Chapple got under way and headed north for the exit from the Gulf.

Two Japanese destroyers were hunting across his track. S-38 submerged to let them pass. They went on over to the east. Then about four o'clock on Christmas morning a more inquisitive or more attentive enemy patrol picked up the sound. It passed over the top of them with a roar of high-speed propellers and dropped a pattern of three depth charges very close. S-38 kept headed north. It seemed to be impossible to round the end of the reef, but Chapple was willing to take his chances running across it, if he could only get out of the Gulf.

The destroyer kept after them, pinging dolorously and following every turn and twist that Chapple tried. The damaged propeller made a thumping noise each turn of the screw. So at nine-thirty in the morning Chapple searched for a spot to run to earth and lay on the bottom again.

The bottom was uneven in this part of the Gulf, with steep pinnacles and ridges. When S-38 laid herself on the bottom she inadvertently picked a bank so steep that she kept sliding down into deeper water. Occasionally she used her motors to hoist herself back up the bank again. But this was apt to bring on unpleasant attention from the destroyer hunting above her. About noon Chapple decided to get under way again, and at 180 feet depth, creep up northward. An hour later they ran aground again.

This time they seemed hard and fast and did not want to be that way. S-38 struggled to get free. As she broke loose she slid on down into deeper water. She went down until the depth gauge registered 350 feet and then hung there for some time, Chapple not daring to use violent and noisy methods to extricate her. S-boats were tested to two hundred feet depth. Eighteen years before, S-38 had passed her first deep submergence test to that depth, and a few times since, after extensive repairs or big navy yard overhauls, she had been retested. When they took her down to two hundred feet in peacetime they made quite a fuss about it, with compression battens rigged and naval constructors stationed throughout the ship to observe the stress and strain of her single-strength hull. Now she was at nearly twice her test depth. The sides of the battery tanks, which were also the main ballast tank tops, compressed under the strain until the wooden deck bulged upward in the middle; but she didn't rupture, she didn't weep. Integrity had gone into the construction of that hull, and eighteen years of tender loving care to keep pits and corrosion from her plates and frames.

By two o'clock Chapple thought she had had enough, and desperate measures were justified. The supersonic destroyer had lost the scent and gone off baying in the distance. S-38 blew tanks and surfaced in the bright afternoon sunlight.

They were northeast of Cape Bolinao, almost on the reef, and rather than take a chance on an attempt to round it in deep water, Chapple decided to bull right straight across. A little later they sighted what appeared to be two destroyers in column, hull down on the horizon, about twelve miles away on the ocean side of the reef, toward which they were going. They dove again to avoid detection, but this time they were in shallow water and S-38 bounced down hard on coral before the conning tower was fully under. There wasn't anything to do but get up and run for it.

The formation on the horizon changed course and dissolved into the high poop and forecastle of a well deck freighter. The freighter did not see, or it chose to ignore, the submarine. S-38 continued on across the reef. At four-thirty in the afternoon they were clear of the reef, and in the deep water of the South China Sea. S-38 submerged and headed for the entrance to Manila Bay.

On 5 January 1942 the Bureau of Ordnance sent a radio dispatch from Washington informing Commander Submarines Asiatic that S-boat torpedoes would run four feet below their set depth. This was caused by the difference in weight and balance between the exercise head and the warhead of the Mark 10 torpedo. This information was a little late to affect the action in Lingayen Gulf, and the four torpedoes S-38 fired at the four transports probably ran under their targets. The 5445-ton *Hayo Maru* was sunk by the torpedo hit Chappel observed. Harbin was transferred to the hospital ashore and became a prisoner of war when Corregidor fell. He died of his injuries while a prisoner on 2 October 1942. It took some time for the submarine tender *Canopus* to repair S-38, but eventually she was patched up and headed south for the Malay Barrier.

III

MEN AND MATERIEL

Commanding Officers

The commanding officers of U.S. submarines that went to war in the Pacific had behind them a common experience of graduation from the Naval Academy at Annapolis, and from the Submarine School at New London, Connecticut. The S-boat commanders were lieutenants, from ten to twelve years out of the Naval Academy, and the fleet submarine skippers were lieutenant commanders with from fourteen to seventeen years of commissioned service, usually about half of it in submarines.

This uniformity of education and experience did not produce a uniform product. There was a great variety of personalities among submarine commanders, no one of which could be selected as typical. Some were tall and lean, and some were short and stout. Some had been outstanding athletes and some had comparatively frail physiques. Some were boisterous extroverts, and some were quiet and studious; and although all of them had successfully worked up to peacetime command through the Navy's rigorous selection system, not all of them were successful as wartime captains.

In peace and in war, a good submarine commander had to be a good ship handler and a good tactician, but war required different characteristics than peace for the successful command of submarines. Peacetime experience tended to develop a commander with high technical competence, with sound theoretical and practical knowledge, capable of personally manipulating most of the ship's complicated apparatus. The skipper might acknowledge the superior skill of the regular gun pointer or stern planesman, but secretly he cherished the conviction that, with a little practice, he could do the job of almost any man on board, and perhaps do it a little better. The responsibility for every important decision made on board was his, and under the Navy's system of selection for promotion one serious mistake could ruin his career.

In wartime the skipper who felt he had to spend every minute on the bridge, directing everything, soon wore himself out and failed to develop subordinates capable of independent action. A wartime captain had to learn to use creative leadership to indoctrinate his officers with the principles he expected them to follow, and then delegate responsibility and authority to go with it. Submarine training exercises attempted to develop this attitude, but no exercises were as rigorous as the crucible of war.

To send submariners, who had spent their professional careers in developing submarine methods and machines, to sea to fight a war, was to some extent like sending the design section of General Motors out to drive their cars in the Indianapolis Speedway races. That some would turn out champions could be expected, and their intimate knowledge of the machines they drove would be an asset, but it would be pure coincidence if the best designers also turned out to be the best drivers. There was nothing really new in this. John Jervis, the Earl of St. Vincent, built up the British Navy to the superb fighting organization that Nelson led to victory, and though it is probable that St. Vincent could never have realized the peak of leadership that Nelson achieved, it is equally probable that Nelson could not have done St. Vincent's job either.

Finally, there was little in the American way of life to psychologically prepare men for war, even men trained and drilled for that job since their early teens. The sword, the spear, the corvus, and the ram; the gun, torpedoes, atom bombs, and missiles; these are the changing instruments of war. In peace their construction and employment is talked about and practiced, but what goes on in the mind of a man in battle was old when Themistocles' triremes put to sea, and yet it was new to each captain, when for the first time he saw an enemy ship through his periscope. Moreover, no one really knew how he would meet the test until he met it, and for all the selection, and the peacetime training, and the psychological examinations, no one for sure could pick the successful wartime skippers from those who were still untested by war.

Officer Personnel

At the beginning of the war, most of the officers of the submarine service were graduates of the U. S. Naval Academy. Those who had not yet achieved command were working up the ladder a few years behind their seniors. A short time before the war started, young reserve officers began to arrive in the submarine service. Many of these were products of collegiate Naval Reserve Officer Training Corps programs. Like their Naval Academy contemporaries all of them were volunteers who had been selected for submarines. Some commanding officers preferred these young reserves to young regulars, feeling that what they

lacked in Navy background they more than made up in adaptablity to
new and different situations. In truth there was little to distinguish one
group from the other. Very few of the young officers who entered the
submarine service after the war started achieved sufficient seniority for
command before the war was over.

Submarine officer personnel had not always been wholly volunteers.
During the 1920s many officers were ordered to submarines who would
have preferred some other type of duty. Informed opinion in the British
as well as in the American Navy held that submarines had seen the peak
of their development in the German Navy of World War I. Since that
time, they believed, the improvement in supersonic devices for locating
submarines, longer range aircraft for searches, and better anti-submarine
weapons had relegated submarines to a very minor role in war. As a result there was a nadir of prestige for the submarine service during that
decade. A young officer might welcome submarine duty for a single tour
because it gave him an early opportunity to assume responsibility and
exercise authority, but after one tour an ambitious officer thought it best
to seek a service of higher prestige.

By 1930 a change came about. Although there had been little submarine construction, the new "V-boats" showed capabilities of speed,
habitability, and endurance, indicating that the depreciation of the submarine was premature. Sonar, developed as an anti-submarine weapon,
proved also a potent tool for submarine operation, and in several fleet
maneuvers the potential worth of submarines was dramatically demonstrated. There had always been a hard core of devoted young officers
who had been attracted to submarines by the challenge of their technical
problems. In 1928 Congress voted extra pay for officers on submarine
duty in recognition of its greater hazard and hardships. It is doubtful
that the extra pay directly induced many into submarines, but its recognition as an extra pay service increased the submarine's prestige. Very
shortly the submarine service was not only wholly volunteer; there was
keen competition for assignment to Submarine School at New London,
through which all submarine personnel were required to pass.

Enlisted Personnel

For enlisted men, submarines had always been wholly volunteer and
an extra pay service. The crew of a submarine was small. A man, no matter what his rate was an individual, not one of the faceless mob. Generally
in a submarine a good man had more responsibility, more privileges,
and a better chance for promotion than he could obtain in a large ship.
Cooks were respected men in a submarine, and submarine crews ate
better than the rest of the Navy. There was a permanence about sub-

marine enlisted personnel that gave the whole service stability and strength. While other services were often harassed by short-time enlistments and changing personnel, it was rare indeed in prewar submarines that a man did not "ship over" when his enlistment expired, until he had completed twenty years of service and transferred to the Fleet Naval Reserve. The quality of the submarine force enlisted personnel is well exemplified by *Gudgeon*. Over 50 per cent of the enlisted men in the crew that took *Gudgeon* out on her first patrol were commissioned officers by the time the war was over.

An aspirant for submarine service, enlisted or officer, had to undergo searching psychological and physical examination, as well as pass a stiff course of instruction at the Submarine School before he was assigned to a submarine. After that his "in-service" training continued until, regardless of his rate or rank or speciality, he passed a written and practical examination in submarines before he was permitted to wear the coveted dolphins. When the war began, the U.S. submarine service was truly a *corps d'élite*.

Development of Materiel

For materiel as for men, the only adequate test for war is combat. It is not surprising, therefore, with a weapons system whose development made tremendous progress during twenty-three years of peace, that the first months of submarine warfare revealed defects. It is perhaps more surprising that so much submarine materiel was so uniformly excellent.

During World War I Congress authorized the construction of a number of submarines, and during the succeeding decade fifty-one S-boats were built in accordance with that building program. Differing in many details, these submarines were about eight hundred tons surface displacement, with a designed surface speed of fourteen knots, which most of them could maintain for only short periods of time. Lacking the endurance, speed, and habitability for cruises with the fleet, they nevertheless preceded and accompanied the fleet in maneuvers off Panama and Hawaii; but by 1925 it was officially reported that "experience in maneuvers indicate that these vessels cannot be considered as a satisfactory type of fleet submarine." Obsolete and overage as they were, twenty-three S-boats saw active duty in the Pacific before the war was over and many of them did hard and valiant service.

Although the Disarmament Conference in 1922 practically brought U.S. submarine construction to a standstill, six V-class submarines were constructed between 1924 and 1930, culminating in size in *Argonaut*, *Nautilus*, and *Narwhal*, whose 2730 tons surface displacement gave them sufficient range, endurance, and habitability, but brought with it slow submerged speed and clumsy diving characteristics that limited their usefulness. Succeeding fleet submarines were smaller. The development of high-speed diesel engines and refinements in compactness of equipment facilitated a design of higher surface and submerged speed, while retaining the habitability and endurance essential for submarine war in an ocean with the dimensions of the great Pacific. By the mid-1930s, when it became apparent that the previous war to end war had not achieved its purpose, a type of submarine had been developed worthy of production in quantity.

Gudgeon, the first submarine to sortie from Pearl Harbor on patrol after December the seventh, was the 211th U.S. submarine to be built since *Holland,* the first submarine in the U. S. Navy, was accepted in 1900. *Gudgeon* was the forty-eighth fleet submarine to be laid down. Thirty-nine of these fleet submarines were on duty in the Pacific when the war began, and seventy-three more were in various stages of construction, trials, and training.

The hulls of the S-boats had been designed to withstand submergence at two hundred feet. A service, in which the lives of everyone might depend upon a single rivet, must develop meticulous techniques and rigorous integrity in the building and repair yards, and this the U.S. submarine service enjoyed in both government and private shipyards. The S-boat hulls, in fact, had a factor of safety that permitted them to dive to well below their test depths. The larger fleet submarines were tested at three hundred feet submergence. Constant improvement in metallurgy, welding, and design paid bonuses of increased factors of safety for these ships also, and on numerous occasions fleet submarines were forced to over twice their test depth. Many fleet submarines deliberately sought these depths in hard-pressed evasion tactics, and survived to bring home the ship and its crew to fight another day. This rugged construction enabled them to withstand depth-charge attacks which would otherwise have been lethal, and contributed immensely to the superiority of U.S. submarines.

Power Plants

Most S-boats were equipped with air injection diesel engines, heavy and slow, and subject to a myriad of minor infirmities, but relatively immune to casualty beyond the capacity of the crew to repair. Fleet submarines were powered with high-speed solid injection engines, evolved by research and development that also produced the diesel locomotive. This engineering advance had not been completed when the war started, and some of the experimental engines of U.S. submarines had to be replaced; but the best American submarine engines were as good as any.

What improvements were made in underwater power plants between two world wars were the consequence of minor refinements. There were no major breakthroughs in submerged propulsion until the Dutch invented the snorkel, which the German Navy adopted and improved. Snorkels were not used by submarines of either side in the Pacific during the war. Vapor-compression stills for the distillation of salt water were adapted to U.S. submarines' use just before the war began, and this solved one of the serious logistic problems of long patrols. Air conditioning was another boon to U.S. submarines, not only for the health and comfort of the crew, but because of the resulting improvement in the reliability of electronic gear.

The Deck Gun

Submarines in all navies carried deck guns, which, of course, could be fired only when the submarine was on the surface. The gun could thus be used only on an unarmed or lightly armed opponent. A submarine is a poor gun platform. The requirements for submersibility seriously handicapped ammunition supply and fire control. Moreover, one good hit with a medium-caliber shell in a submarine would destroy her ability to dive and, if she were so damaged while on patrol deep in enemy territory, this could easily mean the loss of the submarine. The submarine commander who deliberately sought gun engagements with vessels of approximately equal gun power was foolhardy rather than courageous. Submerged, with torpedoes, a good submarine was a David for any Goliath. On the surface she was weak.

Without a deck gun, a casualty that might bring a submarine to the surface would put her at the mercy of any spitkid armed with anything larger than a hand gun. For this reason the gun was a morale factor that had to be considered. It was a weapon of last resort. This probably justified the installation of a three-inch gun on the after deck, the weapon with which most fleet submarines were originally equipped, but many submarines carried heavier armament than that. The S-boats were equipped with a four-inch gun on the forward deck. The forward deck was enlarged for the service of the piece, and S-boats had to accept lower submerged speed because of the battery power required to push this extra bulk through the water. *Argonaut*, *Nautilus*, and *Narwhal* each carried two six-inch guns, one forward and one aft of the conning tower. The broad deck necessitated by this armament contributed to the clumsy diving characteristics of these ships.

Despite these theoretical considerations the gun was a popular weapon. The crew often preferred a gun action full of sound and fury in the bright sunlight to a stealthy torpedo attack submerged. There were many stirring gun actions, against ship or shore target, but probably in the balance U.S. submarines would have been better off without the gun. The torpedo was the weapon of decision.

Radar and Fire Control

In radar, U.S. submarines were clearly ahead of all competition. The naval use of radar had been discovered in 1933 at the Naval Research Laboratory, but it was not practical for shipboard use until the British invented the magnetron. As a result radar was just being installed in U.S. submarines when the war broke out.

Torpedo fire control systems, between wars, passed through a radical change. In S-boats it was essentially necessary to aim the submarine in the direction of the torpedo run. Angle fire was available in S-boats, but had to be preset by hand. In fleet submarines the Torpedo Data Computer (TDC) computed the correct gyro angles and an ingenious system of servomechanisms automatically set the gyro angles on the torpedoes in the tubes while the submarine maneuvered to the attack position. In these submarines it was usual to keep the torpedoes aimed by this system, decreasing the necessity of undertaking the slower and more difficult task of aiming the whole submarine in the direction of the torpedo run. This system was superior to the torpedo fire control system of any other navy.

Torpedoes

All this excellence was very nearly nullified by poor torpedoes. How this could happen deserves more searching investigation than has ever been made; for something very much like it could easily happen again. It is apparent that responsibility was broadly distributed and that the problem was deep and fundamental rather than something superficial that could easily be corrected. It is probable that all of the factors will never be known.

Between two world wars emotional and political factors combined to heap anathema on munition manufacturers as "merchants of death" accused of causing war for personal gain. Responsible commercial organizations were reluctant to become involved in the manufacture and supply of such a purely military device as torpedoes. As one consequence the Naval Torpedo Station at Newport, Rhode Island, operating under the Bureau of Ordnance of the Navy Department, acquired a monopoly for the manufacture of all naval torpedoes. This monopoly became politically entrenched, and every effort of the Bureau of Ordnance to procure torpedoes elsewhere met with violent political opposition. Despite accurate prediction of torpedo shortages, political action was effective in maintaining Newport's monopoly until Alexandria (Virginia) Torpedo Station came into production about a year before the war started. Because of this monopoly, torpedo design did not profit by participation in industrial research and development such as supported the progress of electronics and diesel engine designs.

A small number of naval officers were educated and trained as torpedo experts. Members of this group rotated between jobs at Newport Torpedo Station, the Bureau of Ordnance, and torpedo jobs in the staffs of large submarine and destroyer commands. The monopoly thus became vertical as well as horizontal, with a closed group of naval and civil service experts responsible for research and development, manufacture and test, service supervision of torpedo operation, and evaluating results. An almost parallel situation existed in the German Navy and lead to very nearly identical results.

The Mark 10 torpedo which the S-boats took to war was little improvement over the torpedo U.S. submarines used in World War I. It was 21 inches in diameter, and when fully loaded for a war shot weighed 2215 pounds and cost approximately $10,000. Torpedoes were driven by steam, generated by burning alcohol in air which was carried under high pressure in the torpedo air flask. In the combustion chamber water was sprayed into the hot gases of combustion and the resulting mixture of gas and steam passed through a turbine which turned the torpedo's propellers. Ingenious devices automatically controlled the torpedo to run at a set depth and at a preset course at 36 knots for a maximum distance of 3500 yards. Mark 10 torpedoes carried a warhead with 415 pounds of TNT to be detonated by a simple contact exploder which would operate upon impact of the torpedo with the target.

Fleet submarines carried Mark 14 torpedoes which were longer, heavier, and more powerful, but were otherwise similar to the Mark 10. Mark 14 torpedoes could make 46 knots for 4500 yards or could be preset to run 9000 yards at 31½ knots. The larger warheads of Mark 14 torpedoes were fitted to carry Mark 6 magnetic exploders.

Unknown to each other, in close secrecy and almost simultaneously, the navies of Germany, England, and the United States each developed magnetic torpedo exploders. Magnetic exploders had a great potential advantage over the simpler contact exploders. The armor belt of armored ships minimized the damage of a torpedo hit against the sides of such vessels. For maximum effectiveness a contact exploder torpedo would have to hit such a ship at the turn of the bilge under the armor belt. This was a very narrow target. Magnetic exploders were designed to be triggered by changes in the earth's magnetic field under the hull of steel vessels and explode the torpedo's warhead between one and ten feet beneath the bottom of the target. Torpedo explosions under the bottom of ships were believed to be two or three times as damaging as explosions of the same magnitude against the vessel's side.

The Mark 6 exploder was 92 pounds of complicated electronic and mechanical devices inserted in a cavity in the torpedo warhead. It was designed to function magnetically if the torpedo ran under the target's keel, or to function by impact if the torpedo hit the target's side. The exploder and the warhead incorporated a number of safety devices. When lying in the torpedo tube aboard a submarine the warhead was "unarmed" and safe against accidental detonation by shock or by depth charge explosions. When the torpedo was fired the warhead was automatically armed after the torpedo had run a safe distance. During the very early part of its run the torpedo was subject to violent changes of speed and direction. The shock of these changes might be sufficient to detonate an armed torpedo prematurely. Arming was therefore delayed until these perturbations smoothed out and the exploder's electronic circuits had time to warm up, although during this portion of the run the torpedo was impotent.

In the Mark 14 torpedo this distance was selected as 450 yards. The exploder also had an anti-counter mining device designed to prevent the torpedo from detonating by an explosion close to it, such as might happen if two or more torpedoes were fired and hit in rapid succession. In such an event the pressure wave of the first explosion actuated the countermining device of the following torpedoes to lock their firing pins and prevent their explosion for the duration of the pressure wave. This device would also lock the firing pin if the torpedo ran excessively deep. Unfortunately, the magnetic exploders did not work as intended, and although this was only one of the concatenation of torpedo defects, it was a most troublesome one.

Torpedoes with magnetic exploders were not as dependent upon accurate depth control as those with contact exploders. This turned out to be an inverted advantage. Depreciation of the importance of depth control by both German and American torpedo designers resulted in slipshod engineering of the depth control mechanism. American difficulties with exploders so closely paralleled similar German trouble that Doenitz's castigation of the German Torpedo Experimental Institute would need very little change to be applicable to American torpedo designers.

The depth control performance of torpedoes or the operation of torpedo exploders could not ordinarily be checked by submarine crews. Torpedoes fired in target practice carried exercise heads without explosives or exploders, and the torpedoes were set to run safely under the target to avoid damage to the torpedoes and the target vessel. Exploder and depth control performance tests were made by the Torpedo Station.

Primarily for reasons of economy these were all simulated tests. War-head-carrying torpedoes were not fired in tests to sink target hulks. A generation of submariners grew up without ever having seen or heard a torpedo explode.

Excessive security compounded this situation. It was intended that the magnetic exploder would be a "black box" mechanism, to be adjusted in accordance with cookbook instructions for submarines with a minimum of knowledge on how the apparatus worked. It was not until submarines began intensive preparation for war that magnetic exploders were put aboard submarines and commanding officers were given some instruction in their use. Ironically the Germans, by that time, had discovered grave deficiencies in the magnetic exploders. Knowledge of these German difficulties reached the U. S. Navy Department before the war in the Pacific started, but nothing was done to relieve the secrecy under which magnetic exploders were introduced to the submarine service.

In 1940 Lieutenant Commander E. C. Craig was sent by the Bureau of Ships to England to study the technique of sweeping magnetic mines. He then learned that the British had developed a magnetic exploder, and abandoned it after it had proved to be unreliable. He also learned that British Intelligence had acquired extensive information about German difficulties with a similar exploder and that the emasculation of German submarine torpedoes by malfunctioning exploders had given the British a vital breathing spell to correct some of the deficiencies in British anti-submarine defense. Craig's report was classified Secret and very little of this vital information reached submarine forces. There can be little doubt that such unnecessary secrecy prolonged the time required to discover and correct torpedo defects. In wielding the two-edged sword of secrecy, the U. S. Navy inflicted upon itself more grievous wounds than it did upon the enemy.

Other than the dubious magnetic exploder there were no major breakthroughs for American torpedo design between two world wars. Research on the substitution of oxygen for compressed air in the torpedo was successfully completed at the Naval Research Laboratory in the early 1930s. A few years later the same institution pioneered the use of hydrogen peroxide in torpedoes. However, neither of these advances survived through the development stage at Newport Torpedo Station, whose energies were absorbed in production of its own more conventional design of steam torpedoes. Thus the Japanese Navy, with much smaller research and technical potential, went to war with far better torpedoes than the United States Navy.

The Japanese were farther advanced than any other navy in the use of seaplanes and submarines in cooperation. Eleven large Japanese submarines were fitted to carry light seaplanes, which were used for reconnaissance purposes. Several older submarines were specially equipped to refuel large seaplanes. The Japanese were also farther advanced than any other navy in their use of midget submarines carried on the deck of large submarines. Five I-class submarines were fitted to carry midgets.

In other material respects the Japanese submarines were not so well off. Their RO-class, like the American S-class, were short-ranged but their I-type submarines were capable of crossing the Pacific, conducting a patrol off the West Coast of the United States, and return to port without refueling. Japan started the war with fourteen RO-class submarines and forty-six I-class submarines. Some of the older type RO's were limited to 150 feet diving depth, a fragility that cost them dearly under depth-charge attack. Although their more modern submarines were tested to three hundred feet submergence, they could not compare with the Americans in strength and ruggedness of hulls. They had no radar until near the end of the war, and even then it was crude in comparison with American design. Considering their torpedo superiority, however, it might fairly be said that in balance at the beginning of the war, the Japanese submarines had a material advantage.

Japanese Submarine Personnel

The commanding officers of Japanese submarines were graduates of their Naval Academy at Eta Jima. Although the U. S. Naval Academy at Annapolis was no girls' finishing school, it was a bed of roses compared to Eta Jima. From their Spartan training at Eta Jima and afloat, young officers of the Japanese Navy acquired the Spartan virtues of devotion to duty with a passion to fight valiantly and die for their Emperor. About the Japanese enlisted men little is recorded. Between them and their officers there was a gulf. Very few enlisted men ever succeeded in reaching commissioned rank, but they appear to have been equal to their officers in devotion to duty. The Japanese counted heavily on their Bushido spirit. They believed that their courage and ability to endure the hardships of submarine life gave them an advantage over the Americans who, they believed, were too soft and luxury-loving for submarine service. The Japanese, who relied so heavily on their warrior code of courage, had shortly to admit that the Americans could match their fortitude.

The Americans were certain of their superiority in technology, but very shortly they learned that Japanese materiel and equipment was adequate, and in some important respects was superior to American. The submarine services of the two navies were about as equally matched as they could be, yet there was a tremendous disparity in their accomplishments; and the why and wherefore of this disparity is a most interesting study.

IV

STRATEGIC PREPARATIONS FOR WAR

Organization

United States submarines were generally organized into submarine divisions of from four to six submarines. The division commander was usually an officer of the rank of commander. He was responsible for the training, materiel readiness, and administration of the ships of his division. He rarely went to sea on a patrol in a submarine of his division or exercised tactical control over his ships, except in the unusual situation in which he might go out as a wolf pack commander.

When two or more divisions operated from the same base or submarine tender these divisions were frequently organized as a submarine squadron, and an officer of the rank of captain was assigned as squadron commander. Shortly before the war the two squadrons at Manila were consolidated into a single force and the squadron commander echelon was eliminated for the Asiatic Submarine Force.

In 1941 the United States Fleet was organized into three fleets; Atlantic Fleet under Commander-in-Chief U. S. Atlantic Fleet (Cinclant), Pacific Fleet under Commander-in-Chief U. S. Pacific Fleet (Cincpac), and Asiatic Fleet under Commander-in-Chief U. S. Asiatic Fleet (Cincaf). Each of these fleets had a submarine force which, after a few minor changes, became designated as: Submarines Atlantic Fleet (Sublant), Submarines Pacific Fleet (Subpac), and Submarines Asiatic Fleet (Subaf). The three fleets were coordinated by the Chief of Naval Operations in the Navy Department, Washington. Shortly after the war started Admiral Ernest J. King became Commander-in-Chief, U. S. Fleet (Cominch) and a few months later King became Chief of Naval Operations also. His office, then, had general direction of the three fleets and of the Navy Department.

There was no over-all type commander of submarines. The commander of each submarine force was responsible to his own fleet commander-in-chief. Agreement among the three submarine forces, in the best solution of a wide range of problems, was essential. This was obtained by cooperation rather than by any formal organizational provision. Submarines Pacific Fleet and Submarines Asiatic Fleet (which later became Submarines Southwest Pacific) were entirely independent of each other. Each force commander, within the limits of directives issued by his fleet commander-in-chief, exercised direct control over the submarines of his force. He issued patrol orders to his submarines and sent out radio orders and instructions to individual submarines with no intervening command echelon. A submarine proceeding from one force to another always had definite orders specifying the time or place that the submarine left one force and joined the other.

In addition to this fleet and type organization, naval forces were frequently organized into task forces for the purpose of carrying out a specific operation or mission. Task forces were generally designated by number, and might include many types of ships. A few were largely composed of submarines as was Task Force 7 in June of 1942. Task forces might be subdivided into task groups (Task Group 7·2) and further subdivided into task units (Task Unit 7·2·3). Such assignments were temporary.

Unrestricted Submarine War

Prewar concepts of submarine strategy in the Japanese Navy differed little from those in the United States Navy. Both navies planned to use their submarines primarily as adjuncts to their fleet. Reconnaissance, scouting, and screening ahead of the fleet were high in their priority of tasks. Submarines were expected to carry out these missions aggressively, establishing offensive screens through which enemy units must pass, lying in wait off enemy bases, and patrolling areas along enemy fleet supply routes to torpedo enemy heavy units or fleet auxiliary vessels. In neither navy was war against commerce expected to be a major mission of submarines.

The United States was signatory to the Treaty of London, which forbade submarine attacks on non-combatant ships, except under conditions virtually impossible to meet. Many submarine officers believed that under circumstances of war, especially against an enemy disregarding such niceties of conduct, this policy would erode, but cynically they expected that the approach to reality would take time, during which a submarine commander would be in an ambiguous position; damned if he allowed important enemy vessels to escape because of inability to establish their true character, and damned again if he did not oberve treaty restrictions. Then, on the seventh of December, Chief of Naval

Operations sent out a dispatch declaring unrestricted air and submarine war, demonstrating that political and military leaders were prepared to take bold and decisive action on such an issue, rather than allow junior officers to hold the sack. This was a great boost to morale.

U.S. submarines were not ready for unrestricted warfare. Prewar submarine training had been based on the assumption that treaty provisions would be scrupulously observed (and no one could wish it otherwise), but submarines had therefore adapted their tactics to attacks on high-speed, well-screened combat ships. It might be assumed that maneuvers developed to meet this difficult situation could easily be modified to the task of attacking slower and less agile merchant ships, but the caution that was essential in the former case was unnecessarily restrictive in the latter, and when U.S. submarines were diverted to war against commerce it took time to develop effective tactics for the new task.

In peacetime target practices it was frequently observed that submarines at periscope depth were clearly visible to airplanes flying above them, and that it was then an easy matter for the planes to direct surface escort vessels to the attacking submarine. It therefore appeared that a maneuverable force, protected by both air cover and an anti-submarine destroyer screen, was in a strong defensive situation against submarine attack. For several years prior to the war, U.S. submarine practices stressed attack by sound from deep submergence as the best solution to this problem. A submarine conducting an approach at periscope depth against such a force, it was believed, had little chance of surviving long enough to deliver an effective torpedo attack. *Report of Gunnery Exercises* for 1940–41 stated it was bad practice and contrary to submarine doctrine to conduct an attack at periscope depth when aircraft were known to be in the vicinity. It was considered that under these conditions an undetected attack could be delivered only by sound while the submarine was submerged to a depth of one hundred feet or more. One division commander who permitted his submarines to use their periscopes under such conditions was admonished to see that in the future the vessels under his command would more properly conduct their approaches, and if practicable fire by sound. In the Asiatic Submarine Squadron, commanding officers were threatened with instant relief from command if they exposed their periscopes and were sighted during torpedo practice.

Even when attacking blind at depths of over a hundred feet, the odds were considered to be not very favorable to the submarine. When conducting such an attack by sound bearing alone, one out of eight attacks was expected to end in fatal damage to the submarine. Once a supersonic-equipped destroyer made sound contact with an attacking submarine the odds went down. It was estimated that depth-charge attacks which would surely follow such a contact would result in a submarine kill in one attack out of four. On the other hand, when the submarine succeeded in making undetected sound contact with the target under good sound conditions it was expected that one-half of the submarine sound attacks would be successful, despite zigzags or maneuvers of the target.

It is easy to see, with the advantage of clear hindsight, how the effectiveness of both air screen and anti-submarine sound screen came to be so greatly overestimated. Target practices were usually conducted in clear weather, with the initial location of the submarine known to the protecting aircraft. In the waters around most submarine bases the sound conditions were excellent, and the destroyers who frequently acted as sound screen for the targets became much more proficient at it than the larger number of destroyers without so much experience. How the submarine sound approach could come to be so highly regarded is difficult to understand, but it should be an object lesson in the danger of drawing sweeping conclusions from target practices necessarily conducted under artificial conditions. Of the 4873 U.S. submarine attacks that it was possible to analyze after the war, only thirty-one could be described as sound attacks and none of these was successful.

The United States Navy was deficient in training for night battle. The Submarine Force was reluctant to accept peacetime losses of submarines and their crews in maneuvers. Realistic night battle practices were exceptionally dangerous for blacked-out submarines operating on dark nights in close proximity to large, high-speed, darkened ships. Collisions between surface ships and submarines usually resulted in rapid sinking of the submarine with most of the crew trapped inside. As war came closer, and as the object lesson of German submarine night attacks in the Atlantic became clearer, more attention was paid to this phase of submarine training.

The beginning of the war, however, found most U.S. submarines with no means for taking accurate target observation from a darkened bridge at night and transmitting the information into the torpedo fire control system. Mare Island Navy Yard had invented a *Target Bearing Transmitter* (TBT) designed to facilitate taking target bearings through binoculars from the bridge and electrically transmitting the information to the conning tower. Those few submarines that had this instrument were much better off than the many that had only crude homemade apparatus for the purpose. Most submarine commanders were inexperienced in night attacks and did not, at first, realize the tactical advantage their surface speed gave them at night when attacking slow-speed merchant vessels; an advantage which, of course, was nonexistent against higher speed combat vessels, toward which submarine training had been directed.

Asiatic Submarine Disposition

The tasks and disposition to be undertaken at the outbreak of war were laid down in Rainbow Five, the Allied war plan. The largest segment of U.S. submarine strength (twenty-three fleet-type submarines and six S-boats) was based on Manila under command of Commander Submarines Asiatic Fleet (Captain John Wilkes). Thirteen Netherlands submarines based in Surabaya, Java, would also oppose the Japanese under conditions assumed in Rainbow Five. In December 1941 there were no British submarines in the Far East.

Upon receipt of a dispatch from Commander-in-Chief Asiatic Fleet that hostilities had commenced, U.S. submarines would attack Japanese sea communication in accordance with detailed plans, establishing patrols off strategic locations in the northern Philippines and in the vicinity of Japanese bases. It was expected that submarines would continue to base on their tenders (*Holland, Otus,* and *Canopus*) in Manila Bay. A striking force of eight submarines would be concentrated in the northern Philippines, to throw against any Japanese invasion force once its location was learned. The priority of targets was first capital ships, then loaded transports, and then enemy light forces and transport and supply vessels in ballast. War was to be conducted in accordance with *Instructions for the Navy* (the Treaty of London) unless otherwise instructed.

In late November 1941, it was known that Japan had large forces, including invasion troops in transports, en route to Southeast Asia. The U. S. Asiatic Fleet had been in a state of readiness for a long time. Two submarines (S-36 and S-39) were already on war patrol. *Sealion* and *Seadragon* were under overhaul in Cavite Navy Yard. *Porpoise* was at Olongapo, Subic Bay, in the middle of a battery overhaul that had been long delayed by the threat of war. The remaining submarines of the Asiatic Fleet were in the vicinity of Manila.

At half-past three on the morning of 8 December (Manila time), about an hour after the Japanese struck Pearl Harbor, submarines began topping off with fuel and provisions and leaving singly on their lonely patrols. The fleet submarines were assigned areas off Takao, the Pescadores, at the eastern entrance to Hainan Strait and off southern Hainan, off French Indo-China and Camranh Bay, and off Cochin China (South Vietnam), fairly boxing the South China Sea. The S-boats were assigned areas in the northern Philippines. Shortly only the two cripples at Cavite, the submarine tenders, and the striking force of eight submarines remained in the Manila Bay area.

Pacific Submarine Disposition

When the war started there were twenty-two submarines under command of Rear Admiral Thomas Withers, Commander Submarines Pacific Fleet. Six of these were S-boats based at San Diego and sixteen were fleet-type submarines based at Pearl Harbor. There were additional S-boats at the Panama Canal, under command of Commander Submarines Atlantic. In accordance with Rainbow Five, two of the San Diego S-boats (*S-18* and *S-23*) were scheduled to leave for Dutch Harbor, Alaska, at the outbreak of war. Six of the Panama S-boats started for Australia soon after the war began. The S-boats remaining at San Diego and Panama assisted the surface forces in their anti-submarine training, and by a system of rotation most of them made war patrols when their times came.

In accordance with war plans, the fleet submarines based at Pearl Harbor, at the outbreak of the war, planned to establish patrols in designated areas off Japan, and conduct reconnaissances in the Marshalls and the Carolines. For some time, during the last months of peace, Submarines Pacific maintained two submarines off Wake, and two more off Midway on defensive patrols. The primary purpose of these patrols was to afford realistic experience to submarines in maintaining lengthy patrols without logistic support of any kind. They did not communicate with the nearby bases in any manner, and by operating submerged during daylight, avoided being sighted. The areas they patrolled had been selected because of the strong possibility that the war might begin with a Japanese attack on the outlying American bases. Submarines on these patrols kept their tubes constantly loaded with warhead-carrying torpedoes in the fully ready condition, but they were instructed not to attack unless attacked first, before a declaration of war, even if Japanese ships came into their areas, close to Midway or Wake.

The first patrols of both Asiatic Fleet submarines and Pacific Fleet submarines were planned as area patrols similar to the practice patrols of Pearl Harbor submarines. Each operating submarine was assigned an area within which it was expected to confine its operations, except when en route to and from the area. This reduced communications to a minimum, and radio communications were always both difficult and dangerous for submarines. Area patrols also gave submarine commanders a high degree of independence and reduced the probability of interference between submarines and surface or air operations.

On the other hand, while operating independently in independent areas, submarines were "weapons of opportunity." They might damage the enemy out of all proportion to the scale of submarine effort, but only if chance gave them the opportunity to make contact. The success of the area-patrol method depended upon the probability of making contact, and that in turn depended partly upon the ability of an intelligence organization to produce information about routes and density of shipping, and to project enemy movements into the future in order that the most productive areas might be occupied. It was difficult or impossible to coordinate widely dispersed submarines in defense against enemy operations, or to coordinate submarines in support of offensive operations unless these operations were planned long in advance.

Essentially, when dispersed on area patrol, submarines were committed to a war of attrition. By slow degrees they could help to whittle down the total enemy potential for conducting war. They could not hope to win decisive victory in a few dramatic actions, and only with the greatest difficulty could their actions be coordinated with the actions of others. They could not deny the use of the sea to the enemy, nor could they guarantee the conduct of commerce, convoys, and expeditions over the surface of the sea; but each ship they sank, anywhere or any time, brought Japan closer to defeat.

On 7 December 1941, *Argonaut* and *Trout* were on defensive patrols off Midway. *Tambor* and *Triton* were similarly employed off Wake. *Thresher*, returning from a forty-five-day defensive patrol off Midway, was south of Oahu, under escort of *Litchfield*, about to enter Pearl Harbor. *Plunger*, *Pollack*, and *Pompano* were northeast of Oahu, en route to Pearl Harbor from San Francisco, and *Gudgeon* was at Lahaina, in the Hawaiian Islands, conducting training exercises. *Nautilus* and *Tuna* were under overhaul at Mare Island Navy Yard in San Francisco Bay. *Cachalot*, *Cuttlefish*, *Dolphin*, *Narwhal*, and *Tautog* were at Pearl Harbor in various stages of overhaul. These submarines at Pearl Harbor contributed their mite to the anti-aircraft defense of the fleet, and *Tautog* claims to have shot down a Japanese torpedo plane on its run in.

U.S. Anti-Submarine Preparation

The capabilities of Japanese submarines were by no means underestimated by the American Navy. It was generally expected that war would open with a Japanese submarine attack on the U.S. fleet in Hawaiian waters and that an intensive submarine campaign would then attempt to disrupt communication between Hawaii and the mainland. In preparation for this, the operating areas of the fleet were covered by careful and frequent air searches, and major ships were protected by anti-submarine screens whenever they were at sea. Capital ships no longer were permitted to use the open anchorages in Lahaina or off Honolulu, but berthed in Pearl Harbor, the only harbor judged safe from submarine attack. Prior to the war, important ships moving westward of Hawaii were escorted, and plans were complete to establish a convoy system between Hawaii and the mainland at the outbreak of war. The Hawaiian Sea Frontier maintained an Inshore Patrol to guard the approaches to Pearl Harbor and Honolulu. Considering the demands currently made by anti-submarine war in the Atlantic, preparations to counter Japanese submarine attacks were in fairly good shape. It was by no means an accident that *Ward*, a Hawaiian Sea Frontier Inshore Patrol destroyer, commenced hostilities on 7 December 1941 by sinking a Japanese submarine just outside the entrance to Pearl Harbor over an hour before the air attack developed.

Japanese Submarine Organization

Japanese submarines were also organized in divisions, and the divisions were organized into squadrons. Japanese division commanders and squadron commanders usually accompanied their command to sea, riding in one of the submarines as a flagship. The newest type of Japanese submarines (1st, 2nd and 3rd Squadrons), were organized as the Sixth Fleet under a single commander. The mission of the Sixth Fleet was the destruction of the U.S. fleet in the eastern Pacific. When operating in direct support of a big operation, Japanese submarines were organized as a task force and designated the Advance Expeditionary Force.

Japanese Submarine Strategy

Japanese strategy for the conduct of the war, complicated in detail, was simple enough in over-all concept. In the first phase their objective was the conquest of Southeast Asia, the Philippines, and the East Indies, in a blitz campaign that would strike with full fury at the war's beginning. This would insure access to oil and other natural resources to support their war economy. In the second phase they would build up a defense perimeter that they hoped would defeat the counterattack they knew was coming. Admiral Yamamoto considered the U.S. fleet to be the major obstacle to obtaining these objectives. He therefore planned the surprise attack on Pearl Harbor, with aircraft carriers and submarines, before the declaration of war to knock out the U.S. fleet and gain time to realize the first and second phase objectives before counterattack could be mounted. There is some evidence that the attack on Pearl Harbor was originally planned as a submarine operation and that the carrier attack was added at a much later date.

The Japanese believed that the best strategic use of submarines was as an auxiliary to their main fleet. The Japanese Navy was modeled after the British Navy, so much so that Eta Jima, their Naval Academy, was built as a copy of Dartmouth, with bricks imported from England, and with a lock of Nelson's hair enshrined in its memorial hall. Traditionally, the British Navy depreciated war against commerce as an effective use of naval force. The American strategist Mahan, in his studies of the naval wars of the seventeenth, eighteenth, and nineteenth centuries, very clearly demonstrated that *guerre de course*, however much damage it inflicted on the enemy, if unsupported by a navy that could defeat the enemy and control the sea, never won wars. His studies, highly regarded by the British, undoubtedly affected strategic thinking of the Japanese. Somehow the Japanese failed to note the important conditional clause of the Mahan doctrine or to profit by the object lesson of Britain beset by German submarines in two world wars of the twentieth century. In their assignment of submarine tasks, therefore, the Japanese ascribed a minor part to commerce destruction, and perhaps as a corollary they neglected the anti-submarine protection of their own commerce. The initial disposition of Japanese submarines was in direct support of their fleet.

With exact knowledge of when and where the war would start, the Japanese were able to make efficient distribution of their submarines. Only five were left behind in Japan, in training or under overhaul. Nine RO-class (medium-size submarines) were in the Marshalls and Carolines. Eighteen submarines were assigned to the Southern Force invading Southeast Asia and the Philippines. Three of these planned to lay mines in the Philippines on the first day of war, but the primary mission of Southern Force submarines was observation and scouting ahead of the Japanese invasion forces and attacks on targets of opportunity.

Pearl Harbor Plans

One submarine equipped with a light seaplane reconnoitered Fiji and Samoa and another searched the Aleutians before the Pearl Harbor attack. Three more plane-carrying submarines patrolled in advance of the Carrier Striking Force. They would join with twenty other Sixth Fleet submarines concentrated around Hawaii when the war started.

Four submarines of the First Squadron patrolled off northeast Oahu. The Second Squadron with seven submarines was in the channel between Oahu and Molokai. The Third Squadron with nine submarines was south of Oahu. Two of these submarines had the specific task of searching Lahaina Roads, a U.S. fleet anchorage seventy miles southeast of Pearl Harbor. The Third Squadron was also assigned to rescue downed Japanese aviators. Each squadron was commanded by a rear admiral embarked in the flag submarine of his squadron.

A Special Attack Unit of five submarines (*I-16, I-18, I-20, I-22,* and *I-24*), under command of Captain Sasaki, was assigned a specific task upon which great hopes were pinned. Each of these five submarines carried piggyback, a two-man midget submarine. The midgets were battery-powered for submerged operation but carried no engine for recharging batteries. They were able to attain the phenomenal speed of twenty knots submerged, but of course were very short-ranged, and hence had to be carried almost to the point of their attack. Each one carried two torpedoes. Although not a suicide weapon in the sense that it was not intended that the crew be blown up with the weapon in a successful attack, it was generally recognized that once launched there was small hope of successful recovery, and each midget was fitted with a demolition charge with which, *in extremis,* the crew could destroy themselves with their vessel.

The plan of operation called for release of the midgets off the entrance of Pearl Harbor prior to the scheduled air attack. Each midget would then penetrate Pearl Harbor, running submerged up the long channel, and circumnavigate Ford Island, timing their run to be off Battleship Row at the time of the scheduled air attack. In the confusion of the air attack it was hoped that each midget would torpedo a capital ship. Torpedoes expended, the midgets would then be free to run back out the channel and rendezvous with their mother ships.

Japanese Anti-Submarine Preparations

An island empire, Japanese economy was dependent on sea communication. Moreover, each succeeding step in her planned expansion made her more, rather than less, dependent upon the sea. The war in the Pacific was a struggle, on the surface and beneath the surface and in the air above, for power to control the movement of men and materiel by sea. With that control the sea became a broad highway to tie together all the elements of national strength. Without it the sea was a barrier dividing defenses into isolated units destined for defeat in detail. Japan planned to sweep the western Pacific clear of all surface and air opposition, and her means and her plans to do this were adequate and excellent. She would then establish and support a defense perimeter behind which she would be free to move by sea. For this her logistic resources and her logistic planning were weak, and she failed to appreciate the threat of submarine warfare, with a submarine's unique ability of operating beneath the surface of a sea Japan otherwise controlled.

Japan entered the war with 1703 *marus* of over 500 tons burden. Of these 94 were tankers totaling 570,000 tons, and 1609 were dry cargo and passenger vessels totaling approximately 6.0 million tons. All this shipping passed under government control before the war but the control was divided. To the Japanese Army was assigned about 2.2 million tons, the Navy controlled 1.9 million tons, and the Ministry of Munitions had 1.9 million tons of general shipping.

V

DECEMBER 1941

Japanese Submarines at Pearl Harbor

The First and Second Japanese Submarine Squadrons were the first forces to leave Japan for Hawaii. They left Yokosuka on 20 November. The five midget-carrying I-boats left Kure about the same time. The Third Submarine Squadron staged through Kwajalein, all due to be off Hawaii on the appointed day. On 26 November the Kido Butai (the Japanese carrier striking force) under Admiral Nagumo sailed from the southern Kuriles for Hawaii. With Nagumo in the Kido Butai were six carriers *Akagi, Kaga, Soryu, Hiryu, Shokaku,* and *Zuikaku*) and two fast battleships (*Hiei* and *Kirishima*), two heavy cruisers, one light cruiser and nine destroyers, and a fleet train of eight tankers. Three submarines (the Advance Patrol Unit) screened ahead.

This mighty fleet was the strongest naval force ever assembled in the Pacific until then (and for many months thereafter). There was no force afloat in the Pacific, no land-based air force, or any combination of forces ashore and afloat that could possibly be concentrated in time, between the east coast of Africa and the west coast of the United States, that could meet the Japanese Kido Butai in equal battle. With the additional factor of surprise in his favor, Nagumo launched an all-out air strike from a position two hundred miles north of Oahu, and was completely successful in knocking out the air defenses of Oahu and sinking or damaging every one of the battleships in Pearl Harbor. He then withdrew, having lost a total of twenty-nine planes, with the Kido Butai never having been sighted by an enemy.

To the triumph of the Japanese carrier forces, submarines contributed very little. The five midget-carrying submarines arrived off Honolulu on schedule and launched their incubi shortly after midnight of December 6–7. At 0342 on the morning of the seventh *Condor*, a small minesweeper engaged in a routine sweep of Pearl Harbor approaches, sighted one of the midgets and alerted *Ward*, an Inshore Patrol destroyer. The

Japanese submarine was in an area forbidden for submerged operation to U.S. submarines, so when *Ward* made contact at 0633 in this area, she attacked and sank the Japanese submarine. This was the first action of the war. *Ward's* report of the sinking set in motion proceedings for reinforcing the Inshore Patrol, and alerted the senior commanders at Pearl Harbor. In the nature of submarine warfare there are many more false than true submarine contacts, and as Hawaii had had its fair share of false contacts in the preceding weeks, only the routine precautions were taken to meet *Ward's* emergency. Presumably safe from submarine attack inside Pearl Harbor, the fleet was not called to General Quarters. A little over an hour later it was caught flat-footed by the air attack.

About the same time another Japanese midget submarine was having better luck. It succeeded in entering through the opened gate in the anti-torpedo net guarding Pearl Harbor entrance, and then made its perilous way down the long channel to the inner harbor, undetected. It was in East Loch of Pearl Harbor on its way around Ford Island when the air attack hit Battleship Row. This midget was sighted and fired upon by the seaplane tender *Curtiss* at about 0830. *Monaghan,* the ready destroyer of the Inshore Patrol, proceeding to sea in accordance with standard operation procedure to reinforce *Ward* in her encounter, was under way in the vicinity of this contact. The midget submarine fired both her torpedoes and missed. *Monaghan* rammed and attacked with depth charges and demolished the submarine. A few weeks later this midget was lifted from the bottom of Pearl Harbor, with the crushed bodies of the crew still aboard.

One other midget missed the Pearl Harbor entrance, due to a faulty compass, and ended up aground on the opposite side of Oahu. Ensign Sakamaki, commanding officer of this submarine, became the first Japanese prisoner of the war. The hulk of a fourth midget was discovered off southern Oahu nearly twenty years afterward. It was raised and returned to Japan. The fate of the fifth is still unknown, but it disappeared and apparently made no attacks. The net result of the midget submarine attack was nil. The Japanese Navy thought otherwise and credited the midgets with some of the damage done by aircraft torpedoes in Battleship Row. They knew only that none of the midgets or their crews made their scheduled rendezvous with the mother ships. The crews of the midget submarines were deified as national war heroes and posthumously promoted two ranks. This recognition was denied the fifty-five Japanese aviators who were killed in their spectacularly successful air attack—a very sore point with Japanese naval aviators for many years.

The large Japanese submarines in Hawaiian waters were hardly more successful. *I-71* and *I-72* reconnoitered Lahaina Roads and reported their negative findings. No Japanese submarine succeeded in approaching to within torpedo range of a combat ship. SS *Cynthia Olsen,* a 2140-ton lumber freighter under Army charter, plying between Hawaii and the West Coast, was caught by *I-26* about a thousand miles northeast of Hawaii, and became the first victim of the Japanese submarine force. Many submarine contacts were reported by U.S. planes and patrol vessels. Some of these were real enough, but most were false and one was the U.S.S. *Thresher*, bombed and depth-charged by so-called friendly forces as she tried to make a scheduled entry into Pearl Harbor.

Japanese submarine operation around Oahu was coordinated by the embarked Squadron Commanders and directed over-all by Vice Admiral Shimizu, Commander Sixth Fleet, in his flagship *Katori*, anchored at Kwajalein. This arrangement filled the air each night with Japanese radio communications. Port authorities in Hawaii were thus made conscious of the magnitude and to some extent the location of the Japanese submarine menace. They were consequently cautious in routing ships, and this had some bearing on the Japanese lack of success. *I-6* in Kauai Channel sighted and reported an aircraft carrier and two heavy cruisers headed northeast. Commander Sixth Fleet assumed that these ships were fleeing to the West Coast and he ordered the entire First Submarine Squadron off in hot pursuit. Carrier planes from *Enterprise* caught *I-70* on the surface about two hundred miles northeast of Oahu and sank it. The Japanese knew only that *I-70* disappeared.

About this time *I-69* had a very harrowing experience. She was operating in the vicinity of Barbers Point, in southern Oahu, when she became entangled in what she thought was an anti-submarine net. Unable to move, and in the vicinity of hunting patrol vessels, she sank to the bottom where she remained for fifty hours, while using up the oxygen in her air supply and increasing the carbon dioxide to the point of suffocation. At the end of their endurance, the officers and crew prepared and ate a banquet of their best food and then made a last desperate attempt to break loose by going full speed astern with a nearly exhausted battery. At last *I-69* fought free, and bobbed to the surface in the darkness, lying helpless a few miles off the beach. A patrol boat appeared, and the Japanese crew prepared to sell their lives dearly in final battle, but the patrol vessel sailed serenely by without sighting the helpless submarine lying on the surface. There is irony for both sides in this episode. The frantic Inshore Patrol, which had been shooting up and depth-charging everything that moved, including its own submarines, innocent whales, and numerous ghostly sound contacts, steamed blindly by a real Japanese submarine lying helpless under its guns. The diabolical anti-submarine net that trapped *I-69*, however, was a harmless drill minefield planted with dummy mines before the war started to give district minesweepers practice in sweeping mines. Probably it was one of the most effective defensive minefields laid by the United States in the Pacific, for minefields laid in home waters were usually more effective blowing up friendly vessels than they were in trapping enemy submarines.

The Japanese First Squadron, after pursuing the carrier task force without success, continued on to operate off the West Coast of the United States. Joined by the submarine that had reconnoitered the Aleutians, they made a group of nine I-class submarines in a cordon stretching from the coast of Washington to Los Angeles. They sank four merchant ships in West Coast waters before they had to retire to Kwajalein to refuel about the end of December. Japanese submarines remaining in Hawaiian waters sank SS *Lahaina* about seven hundred miles northeast of Oahu on 11 December, and SS *Manini* and SS *Prussia* about a week later.

On 17 December *I-7* launched its seaplane for a dawn reconnaissance of Pearl Harbor. Despite the tightened defenses of Pearl Harbor this operation was entirely successful and furnished the Japanese with accurate information of the damage caused by the air attack. As Japanese submarines withdrew from their operating areas many of them bombarded nearby areas of the islands. It was impossible to do much about target selection, for the firing usually took place at night and ranges had to be determined very inaccurately by navigational plot. Submarines of the Second Squadron bombarded Kahului, Maui, on 15 December. *I-22* and *I-16* were assigned to bombard Johnston Island on the sixteenth but only *I-22* succeeded in locating this small island. Palmyra Island was shelled on the twenty-third, Hilo, Hawaii on the thirtieth, and Kauai, Maui, and Hawaii on the thirty-first. None of these bombardments caused much damage. A bombardment was a fairly reliable indication that the submarine was departing from the area, and this information was useful in ship routing.

The RO-boats based on Kwajalein did their best to contribute to the Japanese war effort. *RO-63*, *RO-64*, and *RO-68* bombarded a mythical seaplane base on Howland and Baker Islands on the ninth of December. Three more RO-boats were patrolling off Wake. On 17 December *RO-62* collided with *RO-66* off Wake, and *RO-66* was sunk. Two weeks later *RO-60*, returning from operations off Wake, ran aground on the reef at Kwajalein and was lost.

U.S. Submarines in Hawaii

U.S. submarines, being on the defensive, were not so advantageously placed as the Japanese were for the kickoff of the war, but they were not long in meeting the enemy. *Trout* and *Argonaut* were on patrol off Midway. *Trout* learned about the Pearl Harbor attack early in the morning of 7 December, but *Argonaut* was submerged and out of communication with the world until she surfaced that evening. She then quickly found out what had happened. A few hours after sunset gun flashes lit up the horizon to the southwest. Midway was being bombarded by two Japanese destroyers, *Akebono* and *Ushio;* they were mistaken for a much larger force of cruisers and destroyers by both the Marine defenders of Midway and by the submarine patrol.

Trout was on the wrong side of the atoll and unable to close. *Argonaut* decided that she should go to deep submergence and make a sound attack in accordance with standard doctrine. This she did, and as she was apparently sighted by the attacking destroyers before she submerged, she was easily avoided by the Japanese, who completed their mission of bombardment and retired, after causing considerable damage to the installations of Midway. Even if *Argonaut* had been more aggressively handled it is doubtful that she could have accomplished much. Destroyers were very agile targets for slow and clumsy old *Argonaut.* So despite her fortuitous disposition, this first contact between the U.S. submarine force and the Japanese accomplished nothing.

At Wake, *Tambor* (Murphy) was patrolling north of the island and *Triton* (Lent) was to the southward. A few hours after Pearl Harbor was hit, a force of land-based naval bombers flew in from Kwajalein and bombed Wake, doing extensive damage to the meager shore installations. Both submarines were submerged at that hour, and Murphy in *Tambor* did not learn that there was a war on until *Tambor* surfaced that evening and intercepted messages between Wake and Pearl Harbor. He then learned that Wake had been bombed and that it was expected that the attack would be renewed the next morning. He could see large fires raging on the little island but there was nothing *Tambor* could do to render assistance. Both *Triton* and *Tambor* had to stand by impotently, within sight of Wake, while the Japanese bombers came over about noon each day to soften the defenses.

Just before midnight on 10 December (Wake date) Lent, patrolling in *Triton* south of Wake, made out a destroyer on the horizon. He dove and attempted to evade, but the destroyer continued to close. About an hour later he fired the first submarine torpedoes of the war for U. S. Pacific Submarines. After a run of fifty-eight seconds *Triton* heard dull explosions. The submarine command gave her credit for damaging a ship, but none of the ships of the Japanese invasion force then approaching Wake was damaged in this first encounter. *Tambor* had a false contact early that morning, north of Peale Island, and submerged. At seven o'clock Murphy, in *Tambor,* saw gun flashes across the island and immediately moved southward to close them. It appeared to be three ships bombarding Wake but he was never able to get close enough to deliver an attack.

The Marines did much better. Early on the morning of 11 December a Japanese force consisting of three light cruisers, six destroyers, two patrol craft, two submarines, and two transports arrived in the vicinity of Wake from Kwajalein, with the intention of landing and occupying Wake. At 0530 in the morning the cruiser *Yubari* opened negotiations by bombarding the southernmost point of the larger island. Major Devereux on Wake held his fire until 0615. He then opened up with his five-inch guns to such good effect that the destroyer *Hayate* was sunk, and hits were scored in all of the cruisers and several of the other vessels. The whole force retired. As they turned away Marine Wildcat planes got in their innings, further damaging the cruisers, and scoring a direct hit among *Kisaragi's* depth charges. These blew up, sending that Japanese destroyer to the bottom with all hands. The Japanese then withdrew to Kwajalein to await reinforcements to crack this tough nut. Submarines did nothing effective to aid the gallant Marine defenders of Wake.

The day after the Japanese withdrew from Wake was still 11 December at Pearl Harbor. *Gudgeon* (Grenfell) and *Plunger* (White) departed from Pearl Harbor that morning for patrol off Japan. *Gudgeon* continued on and carried out her mission but *Plunger* found a leaking hatch on her initial post-overhaul test dive and returned to Pearl for repairs. On 13 December *Pollack* (Moseley) was ready to go and shoved off alone to take up patrolling off Tokyo Bay. The next day *Plunger*, with her hatch repairs completed, made her second departure. She still had trouble with leaks but by heroic means made her own repairs and continued on her way to Japan.

On 16 December *Tambor*, patrolling off Wake, developed a serious leak from number one main ballast tank into the forward torpedo room. This might endanger the ship on a deep dive, and repairs were almost equally dangerous at sea. Murphy decided to leave patrol station and return to Pearl Harbor for repairs. This left *Triton* as the only naval vessel in the vicinity of Wake.

Admiral Kimmel was relieved of all naval duty by order of the President of the United States on 17 December. Admiral C. W. Nimitz was ordered to relieve Kimmel as Commander-in-Chief Pacific Fleet, but he could not reach Pearl Harbor for a week or more. In the interregnum between Kimmel and Nimitz the United States Navy sank to the lowest ebb of confusion and indecision in its history. Vice Admiral W. S. Pye, Commander Battle Force, succeeded to command temporarily. Kimmel had organized and set in motion a plan to relieve Wake. Three carrier task forces, each built up around a single carrier, were at sea for this purpose.

The Japanese carriers *Soryu* and *Hiryu* (detached from the homeward-bound Kido Butai) moved in to a position two hundred miles northwest of Wake on 21 and 22 December to soften up Wake's defenses for the forthcoming invasion. The *Lexington* task force was loitering five hundred miles northeast of Wake refueling while the Japanese carriers accomplished their mission and withdrew. On 23 December a greatly re-inforced Japanese Wake Island Invasion Force arrived in the vicinity, and early in the morning landed in overwhelming force. Wake surrendered on 23 December (Wake time), but even before this news reached Pearl Harbor Pye had recalled the carrier task forces. That date, not 7 December, was the nadir of the Navy. *Triton* had been patrolling off Wake, but she was recalled earlier, for fear of interference with the projected movements of the carrier task forces. Commander Cunningham on Wake, during the final assault, tried to inform *Triton* of the location of Japanese ships, but the last submarine had already pulled out to leave the Wake defenders to their fate.

On Christmas Day, Nimitz arrived at Pearl Harbor. He found everything in confusion. Kimmel had departed under orders to appear before the Roberts Commission investigating the reason for the defeat at Pearl Harbor. The Chief of Naval Operations, shortly after the Pearl Harbor attack, had advised Kimmel that the Japanese would probably occupy Midway, Maui, and Hawaii before attempting to storm Oahu, and that only submarines and patrolcraft should be based at Pearl Harbor until the defenses were improved. The Commandant Fourteenth Naval District was preparing to evacuate construction crews from Midway, Palmyra, and Johnston. Into this black mood of defeat Nimitz interjected his calm and stubborn determination to fight; to forget the post-mortem of Pearl Harbor, cease worrying about reinforcements, and get on with the war with the men and materiel he had available.

Comsubpac's staff, in offices adjacent to those of Cincpac's on the second floor of the submarine base supply building, planned the submarine operations. Three submarines had departed for patrol off Japan. *Pompano* set out on 18 December to reconnoiter the Marshalls. *Tautog* followed on the same mission on 22 December, and *Dolphin* was in her wake a few days later. On 30 December, the day Nimitz formally assumed command, *Thresher* also departed for the mysterious Marshalls. Although Submarines Pacific had so far accomplished exactly nothing, they were moving into battle position and girding up their loins for a long hard war.

Japanese Submarines in the Southwest Pacific

The war in Southeast Asia and the Philippines was a different war. 8 December East Longitude Date, designated X-day by the Japanese, found their submarines snugly disposed waiting for the radio news of the attack on Pearl Harbor to touch off the war. *I-123* and *I-124* laid mines in Balabac Strait the first day. *I-121* was assigned to a mine-laying mission off Manila Bay but was driven off by anti-submarine patrols. The remainder of the eighteen submarines assigned to the Japanese Southern Force were stationed off the Malay coast, off Manila, the east coast of Luzon, off Leyte Gulf, and off Davao.

Early on X-Day amphibious landings were made on the Malay Peninsula. Planes of the Japanese 21st and 23rd Naval Air Flotillas struck the air bases on Luzon, and by the end of that day one-half of the bomber forces and one-third of the fighter strength of the U. S. Far Eastern Air Force had been destroyed. The direct contribution of Japanese submarines to these successes was nil, but the cooperation between submarines and the Naval Air Flotillas in Malay paid big dividends.

Early air reconnaissance had spotted two British capital ships at Singapore, but bad weather on the ninth precluded Japanese air searches. *I-65* was on station about three hundred miles to the north of Singapore at three o'clock that afternoon when she spotted two British ships which she correctly identified as *Prince of Wales* and *Repulse*. They passed outside torpedo range but *I-65* succeeded in getting out a contact report.

During the night of the ninth, contact with the big British ships was lost, but before dawn the next morning they were sighted again by another Japanese submarine. *I-58* fired torpedoes and missed. Her contact report, however, brought out the Japanese 22nd Naval Air Flotilla in force. Before the end of the day both *Prince of Wales* and *Repulse* were at the bottom of the sea, the first capital ships to be sunk at sea by air attack alone. It was a severe blow to Allied morale and prestige, and it cleared the way for the rapid invasion of Malaya and the Philippines.

U.S. Submarines in the Philippines

Surface combat vessels of the U. S. Navy had been dispersed in southern Philippine harbors before the war, to preserve them from any surprise bombing attacks on Manila. It had been hoped that submarines and patrol craft could continue to base in the Manila area to operate in defense of the Philippines, but when the devastating attack on Clark Field virtually destroyed the air defenses of Manila, it was apparent that Manila Bay was very vulnerable. The eight submarines that had been retained there as a striking force reserve were ordered out to patrol areas in the Philippines on 9 December. The next day Manila Harbor and Cavite Navy Yard were clobbered by Japanese bombers.

Sealion, with her engine dismantled for overhaul and alongside the dock at Cavite, was hit by two bombs and damaged beyond hope of repair. *Seadragon*, moored alongside her and also immobilized, might have suffered the same fate, but the submarine repair vessel *Pigeon* (Hawes) towed her clear of the holocaust under fire. *Seadragon* lived to take her place in the thin defense line but *Sealion* became the first U.S.

submarine lost by enemy action. *Sealion* and *Seadragon* lost five of their people in the attack, the first submarine casualties of the war.

This bombing removed any hope that Manila Bay could be used for submarine service and supply. A total of 232 submarine torpedoes were lost in the Cavite bombing, a crippling blow to Asiatic submarines who had to operate with a deficiency of torpedoes for months to come. The tenders *Holland* and *Otus* cleared out of Manila for the Malay Barrier the next day, rather than risk the loss of submarine spares and reserve torpedoes which they carried. *Canopus*, the oldest tender, was left behind moored and camouflaged alongside the dock at Manila.

As nothing was known of Japanese anti-submarine weapons and tactics, submarine commanding officers had been advised that in their first patrols they should use caution, feel out the enemy, and learn everything possible about their countermeasures. It was planned to limit the first patrol to about three weeks, to enable collection and dissemination of firsthand information as soon as possible. The war in the Philippines moved too fast for this sensible plan to be carried out. After *Holland* departed, submarines on patrol were advised that if they could no longer hear the naval radio station at Cavite, they should not return to Manila. They should stay on station as long as fuel and food held out and then head south for the Malay Barrier. Under these circumstances many of the first patrols of the Asiatic submarines were neither short nor particularly noteworthy for their caution.

Swordfish (Smith) was one of the first Asiatic submarines to make contact with the enemy. En route to her patrol area, she encountered a Japanese convoy on the night of 9 December. The convoy was screened by destroyers. In a night surface attack Smith penetrated inside the screen and fired one torpedo at a cargo vessel. The escorting destroyer counterattacked and *Swordfish* dove deep to evade. In *Swordfish* they heard loud sounds of an explosion and believed that this, their first torpedo of the war, had found its mark. As soon as Smith could shake off the attacking destroyer, he came up to periscope depth and fired another torpedo at his target to make sure. He was confident that the cargo ship sank, but there is no Japanese record of damage or sinking to correspond to this attack.

The next day the Japanese landed at Aparri, at the northern end of Luzon. The U. S. Army Air Force put up effective opposition to this landing despite their losses on the first day of the war. Two minesweepers were destroyed and two transports were so heavily damaged they had to be beached. The Air Force thought they also sank the Japanese battleship *Haruna,* but they were mistaken. December 10 was the day the Japanese sank *Prince of Wales* and *Repulse* and destroyed Cavite Navy Yard. Against this background of disaster, any real Allied successes were minor and ephemeral. The Japanese continued with their blitz amphibious operations without much effective opposition from anyone.

A number of U.S. submarines made contact with Japanese invasion forces, and several of them made torpedo attacks. Like Smith in *Swordfish,* some of them were deluded by timely sounds of explosions into thinking they had torpedoed Japanese ships, but gradually the conviction spread that there was something definitely wrong with the torpedoes. At least one commanding officer became so despondent at his inability to get hits in easy targets that he asked to be relieved by someone who could do better. Shortly afterward this officer left the submarine service, and continued the war with distinguished service in PT boats.

On 13 December *Seawolf* (Warder) reached Aparri. Warder sighted a destroyer patrolling outside a protected bay, and deduced that there must be something more important inside the bay. He let the destroyer go by in order to investigate further. The next morning *Seawolf* penetrated into the bay submerged, and sighted the big Japanese seaplane tender *Sanyo Maru* at anchor. He fired two torpedoes which missed. Warder then swung *Seawolf* to head out and fired two more torpedoes from the after tubes. All these torpedoes were Mark 14 torpedoes with magnetic exploders. *Seawolf's* soundman reported explosions but Warder, observing through the periscope, knew there had been no serious damage to the target. One of his torpedoes did hit *Sanyo Maru,* but it failed to explode. Whether or not the Japanese recovered any of *Seawolf's* torpedoes from this attack is unknown but it was not long, in any event, before the Japanese had recovered U.S. submarine torpedoes for study. They were wise enough not to copy the magnetic exploder.

In *Swordfish,* Smith continued to pursue Japanese convoys. Arriving at her patrol station off Hainan Island, *Swordfish* made three successive attacks on a convoy. *Kashii Maru,* an 8407-ton cargo ship, was damaged in this area on 15 December. The next day *Swordfish* fired three torpedoes at a ship Smith identified as a transport. *Atsutasan Maru* was torpedoed and by Japanese records was "disabled or run aground." She was the first enemy ship ever to be destroyed by a torpedo fired from a U.S. submarine. Generally U.S. submarine attacks at this period of the war were much more frustrating.

Sargo (Jacobs) made her first contact with the enemy on 14 December 1941. Her first target was a 4000-ton cargo vessel, and Jacobs set his torpedoes to run at fifteen feet depth, intending the magnetic exploder to blow up under the target's keel. Eighteen seconds after firing, after a torpedo run of only about 450 yards, there was a violent explosion felt by everyone in *Sargo.* The torpedo had exploded prematurely after running about the distance necessary to arm the exploder, and less than halfway to the target. This was the first premature that had been experienced, or perhaps more accurately the first premature to be recognized as such, for many of the explosions identified as hits by hopeful listeners may well have been torpedoes exploding prematurely before reaching the target.

Information on magnetic exploders was still Secret in the U. S. Navy, and its dissemination was very restricted. Although not a torpedo expert, Jacobs had received two years of postgraduate instruction in naval ordnance, and in addition had completed a short course in torpedoes. He therefore probably had more knowledge of magnetic exploders than most other commanding officers, who had only recently been sketchily briefed on this secret device. Observing that his torpedoes exploded before reaching the target, Jacobs reached the conclusion that possibly the secret of the magnetic exploder had been compromised and that the Japanese might have invented a counter device to explode magnetic torpedoes at safe distances from their ships.

After talking the matter over with his torpedo officer, Lieutenant C. D. Rhymes, he decided to inactivate the magnetic feature. This required removing the exploders from the warheads, cutting certain electric circuits, and returning the same exploder to its recess, sealed against the entry of sea water with a compressed rubber gasket. When this was properly done, this exploder would act as an ordinary contact exploder and it would have to actually hit, not just pass under the keel, to explode and blow up the target.

Ten days later Jacobs found an opportunity to test the performance of the modified exploders. He fired three torpedoes set for fifteen feet at two cargo vessels. *Sargo* was sighted at firing. The targets took evasive action and there were no hits. Shortly afterward he got another shot at one of the same ships, and fired two torpedoes set at ten feet, launched from a range of 1900 yards. No hits. But targets were thick in his area, and on 27 December he had another chance. He fired two torpedoes with 30° gyro angles from a range of 900 yards, and missed with both.

Jacobs was baffled. He realized that even more important than sinking a *maru* or two was the solution to the enigma of torpedoes which when fired under conditions that seemed bound to produce hits, missed enemy vessels sailing blithely by unscathed. A torpedo attack welds a submarine and its crew into a unit, the failure of any element of which can cause disaster to the whole; but the commanding officer is the central character, and only through him can success be achieved. His eye alone sees the target. He alone judges the target's course and measures the range. His skill maneuvers the submarine into firing position, nicely balancing the risk of discovery against gain by improving his position. He makes the decision when to fire the torpedo. Everyone on board is aware of this but none more poignantly than the commanding officer himself. Sixty men have followed him into jeopardy, and it is their due that he should cap their joint effort with success. It would take internal security like the Rock of Gibraltar not to entertain doubts as to his own judgment and skill, not to fear the potential loss of morale, that is the heritage of repeated failures. Jacobs determined to do everything possible to eliminate the factor of possible error in his own judgment as a cause for the mysterious misses.

Toward evening of the same day (27 December) *Sargo* sighted two more ships. They were making nine knots, and *Sargo* was in a favorable position from which to make a deliberate approach. Moreover, the visibility conditions were such that almost unlimited periscope exposure could be made without serious risk of being sighted. Jacobs suspected the accuracy of the tactical data for torpedoes fired with large gyro angles. To eliminate this as a possible source of error he sought and obtained a firing position and course to give his torpedoes a zero gyro angle.

Every element of the approach was checked and rechecked. On every periscope exposure Jacobs called his executive officer to the periscope and each made independent observations of angle on the bow, bearing, and range. The approach dragged on for fifty-seven minutes. During the last fifteen minutes the observed range and bearing checked right on with the generated range and bearing of the TDC—proof that the problem of target's course and speed had been correctly solved. At a range of 1200 yards *Sargo* fired two torpedoes with zero gyro angles, set for ten feet depth, at the first target. A little later the second ship glided across the periscope wires and Jacobs fired at her two more torpedoes with the range now reduced to 1000 yards. They all missed.

Both Jacobs and Rhymes, his torpedo officer, were then convinced that the only possible remaining reason for misses was that the torpedoes were running deep. Jacobs probably knew of the costly British blunder, during World War I, of not allowing for the difference in weight between the warhead and the exercise heads of their submarine torpedoes, causing their torpedoes during the early part of that war to run four feet deeper than set. At any rate, Jacobs reasoned that the warheads of his own torpedoes, being heavier than the exercise heads they had carried in target practice, were causing the torpedoes to run deeper than set. He believed this defect could be overcome by changing the rudder throws of the torpedoes, so he and Rhymes, from theoretical reasoning, proceeded to compute what the new rudder throws should be, and then set them on the torpedoes.

The next evening *Sargo* sighted a good target and trailed it all night, deferring the attack until daylight in order that they might be sure of the target data. In trying to obtain ideal conditions to observe an experiment, their target got away from them and escaped. There were still plenty of targets, however, and on the fourth of January 1942 a slow-speed tanker came lumbering by, vulnerable and alone. Jacobs fired one torpedo at this juicy target, set at ten feet depth, with a firing range of 1300 yards. It missed.

Even Jacobs had now exhausted all means at his command to find and correct the trouble. He sent a dispatch to Commander Submarines Asiatic (Captain Wilkes), then at sea in *Swordfish* en route to Surabaya, reporting that in six attacks under ideal conditions he had fired thirteen torpedoes and scored no hits. He also told Wilkes that he believed his misses were caused by torpedoes running deeper than set, and that in an attempt to correct this difficulty *Sargo* had changed the prescribed rudder throws of her torpedoes.

Sargo's message had been addressed for information to Commander-in-Chief Asiatic Fleet. All submarines that happened to be on the surface had probably intercepted this message and been influenced by it. The ordnance expert on the Commander-in-Chief's staff disagreed with Jacobs' analysis of the torpedo difficulties. He therefore originated a message defending the torpedo and the magnetic exploder. His theory was that the torpedoes ran under the target without exploding because the exploders were flooded. In order to inactivate the magnetic feature of the exploder, the exploder had to be withdrawn from its watertight recess in the warhead, and then replaced and resealed. To insure that the gasket was tight against sea pressure was very difficult with the limited facilities and the poor working conditions on board a submarine on a war patrol, and there was more than a little possibility that some, at least, of the exploders had flooded from this cause.

It was the day after this Asiatic Fleet message went out that the Bureau of Ordnance informed Submarines Asiatic that Mark 10 (S-boat) torpedoes ran four feet deeper than set when carrying a warhead, and that this could be corrected by changing the rudder throws. This of course did not mean that *Sargo's* torpedoes were running deep, for she was equipped with the newest Mark 14 torpedoes, but it may have contributed to Wilkes' loss of faith in torpedo experts.

The other U.S. submarines on patrol in the Philippines were not much more successful. The history of the Asiatic submarines' attempt to check the Japanese invasion is a tale of torpedo misses too depressing to record in detail. Perhaps it is just as well that some of the commanding officers were deluded into thinking they were making hits and sinking ships. Faced with an almost identical sequence of torpedo troubles, German submariners suffered severely from loss of morale. At one time Doenitz seriously considered withdrawing all German submarines from active service rather than expose them further to the hazards of anti-submarine warfare, without compensating opportunity to damage their enemies.

On 21 December *Stingray* made first contact with the main Japanese invasion force headed for Lingayen Gulf on Luzon. This was the battle for which war plans had provided a concentration of submarines. The necessity for submarines to abandon Manila Bay had broken up the striking force, which had been held in reserve for the occasion. It was possible, however, for Wilkes to order four submarines into the area to reinforce *Stingray*.

In the absence of effective air scouting, the contact with the invasion forces was made too late to develop submarine attack on amphibious forces while they were in deep water, where the submarines had sea room to maneuver in three dimensions. Wilkes ordered *Saury, Salmon, S-38, S-40*, and *Stingray* to penetrate into Lingayen Gulf and attack the Japanese landing forces at the beachhead. Although Japanese anti-submarine operations held no surprises, they were able to hold off all but one of the attacking submarines and keep them outside the Gulf. The Japanese landing operations were badly fouled up, and must, at times, have presented many excellent targets, but Chapple in *S-38* was the only submarine to get close enough to the landing beaches to profit by it. He sank *Hayo Maru* as has been recounted. *Seal* (Hurd) sank the 856-ton freighter *Soryu Maru* off the northwest coast of Luzon on the twenty-third. These two ships, and two hits by shore batteries in the seaplane tender *Sanuki Maru*, were the extent of the damage sustained by Japan's amphibious forces in or near Lingayen Gulf.

With the Japanese Army ashore at Lingayen, Manila was indefensible. MacArthur declared Manila an open city and *Canopus* cleared out on short notice. She moved from Manila to Mariveles on Christmas Day. Submarine spares and torpedoes were transferred to Corregidor, and until that beleaguered fortress fell, each submarine calling at Corregidor on other business took out a load of submarine spares and torpedoes.

On 31 December *Swordfish* left Manila Bay for Surabaya with Wilkes and part of the submarine staff aboard. Captain James Fife had already gone to Darwin, Australia to establish a logistics base there for submarines with *Holland* and *Otus*. Admiral Hart embarked in *Shark* for Surabaya and arrived there on New Year's Day. Submarine operating headquarters moved to the Dutch submarine base at Surabaya.

Dutch Submarine Operations

The British believed that American submarines were committed to fall back on Singapore and operate under the British Commander-in-Chief in the event that Manila became untenable. Had they done so, the British believe, they might have executed great destruction upon the Japanese amphibious forces off Malay. This opinion is difficult to justify in view of the experience of seven Dutch submarines who operated under the British Commander-in-Chief in defense of Singapore.

Dutch submarines *K-11, K-12, K-13, K-17*, and *O-16* were stationed off the Malay coast, under British control, before the outbreak of the

war. On 11 December *O-19* and *O-20* were also placed under command of the British Commander-in-Chief, and left Balabac for Singapore. The British planned to counter an expected Japanese landing by
an attack with heavy surface forces, and follow it up with a submarine
attack on the transports. The destruction of *Prince of Wales* and *Repulse*
put an end to the surface attack, but the Dutch submarines followed
the Japanese landing forces into the beachhead and attacked in accordance with the plan.

O-16 (Bussemaker) attacked four loaded Japanese transports in shallow water on 11 December. The Dutch Navy credited *O-16* with sinking
them all, and the U. S. Army-Navy Assessment Committee, from sources
compiled after the war, credit her with sinking *Toro Maru*, a 1932-ton
transport, but Japanese postwar records acknowledged only damage to
Toro Maru and one other small Army auxiliary. The next day *K-12*
(Coumou) attacked a large merchant vessel and a tanker in shallow
water and believed that both were sunk. Japanese sources credit her
only with damage to the 3500-ton cargo vessel *Taizan Maru*. After her
gallant attack of 11 December on the Japanese transports, *O-16* was lost
on 15 December by running into a British minefield near Singapore.
There was only one survivor. *K-17* did not return from her first war
patrol and nothing certain is known of her fate. She may have been a
victim of *I-66*, who claims to have sunk an enemy submarine about the
time *K-17* disappeared. *O-20* also disappeared. Much later it was learned
that she had been disabled by Japanese destroyers on 19 December and
scuttled by her crew to avoid capture.

On 17 December the Japanese attacked Sarawak, a British protectorate
in northern Borneo. There they encountered Dutch naval air forces and
Dutch minefields. The Japanese destroyer *Shinonome* was sunk on 17
December by a Dutch mine off Miri.

On 23 December the Japanese landed at Kuching, Sarawak. *K-14*
(van Well Groeneveld) attacked a convoy in cooperation with Dutch
naval air forces. The 9800-ton cargo ship *Katori Maru* was sunk, and
Hiyoshi Maru, Hokkai Maru, and *Nichinan Maru* were all damaged.
K-14 escaped without damage. The next day *K-16* (Jarman) sank the
Japanese destroyer *Sagiri* with a torpdeo. *K-16* did not long survive her
triumph, for she was sunk in turn by a depth-charge attack.

Appraisal

All Japanese losses from all causes during this first month of the war
added up to a very small price for their victories. U.S. press and official
communiqués abounded in reports of great damage done to the Japanese forces and many ships sunk. Sometimes these reports were the

result of snowballing rumors, but often they were based on the eyewitness account of reliable observers. U.S. combat intelligence officers had not yet learned that an eyewitness account by participants in a confused battle is a most unreliable source of information, but as they developed the professional cynicism to doubt statements of their own comrades, it became apparent that force commanders had to devise a system to appraise reports in order to avoid misestimates that might have serious consequences.

It was difficult for the Americans to comprehend that the human trait of seeing what one hopes to see is universal, not confined to one's enemies. Military history had not prepared them for it. Historians do their best to dispel "the fog of war" by concocting logical and consistent accounts, forgetting that war itself is illogical and inconsistent and that the best historical accounts of actions probably have little relation to the actual happenings. For the Japanese, deeply indoctrinated in tradition and their own accounts of history, it was impossible to comprehend that a samurai warrior could be mistaken when he reported that his enemy had been destroyed "at one stroke." When their turn came to make objective appraisal of defeat, the Japanese, likewise, were unprepared and for their improvidence paid dearly. That was much later in the war. When the new year of 1942 came in, everything was going their way.

VI

JANUARY–FEBRUARY 1942

Invasion of the Dutch East Indies

When the new year started the Japanese were in occupation of large territories in the Malay Peninsula and were pushing rapidly toward Singapore. They held air supremacy over all the Philippines, the South China Sea, and Malaya. MacArthur's forces, sealed off in the Bataan Peninsula, were the only real resistance in the Philippines. The Japanese held the Sulu Archipelago and the west coast of Borneo, and everywhere they were advancing aggressively.

On 7 January Admiral Hart divided the Asiatic Fleet into four task forces. Submarines Asiatic became Task Force Three, with Captain John Wilkes as Task Force Commander. Until then the submarines had operated independently, generally in fixed areas, although an attempt had been made, at Luzon, to effect a tactical concentration against the Japanese invasion forces. After 7 January, Commander-in-Chief Asiatic Fleet took a more direct part in the direction of submarine warfare in an attempt to concentrate and coordinate the counterattack of the various components of ABDA (American, British, Dutch, and Australian) naval forces.

This only added new frustrations for the submarines. With four separate navies, each with its separate interests, loosely bound together, without effective air search and against a background of defeat and retreat, it was in the nature of things that there would be more misinformation than there was good information of enemy movements. Submarines had very limited mobility, and an aggressive enemy with command of the air could practically immobilize them during daylight hours. Authentic information of enemy movements usually arrived too late for slow-moving submarines to get there in time to be effective.

A Japanese landing force appeared off Tarakan, in Dutch Borneo, on 10 January. *S-37*, *S-41*, and *Spearfish* were ordered to penetrate into the beachhead and attack. They arrived too late to inflict any damage. Dutch shore batteries at Tarakan sank two Japanese minesweepers but forces afloat played no part in that action. On 11 January the Japanese landed at Menado and Kema, in the northeastern Celebes, and again submarines were dispatched to the landing area but arrived too late to accomplish anything.

Some of the other submarines, when they were not being chevied around the East Indies trying to beat the Japanese to their next beachhead, were having a limited success. The Netherlands submarine *O-19* (J. W. Bach Kolling) reported sinking two cargo ships in the Gulf of Siam on 10 January. The Japanese lost three ships to submarines that day, but none was in the Gulf of Siam according to their records. *Stingray* (Moore) torpedoed *Harbin Maru* off Hainan, and *Pickerel* (Bacon) sank *Kanko Maru* off the Gulf of Davao. *Akita Maru* was torpedoed and sunk in the Sulu Sea. *Sculpin* (Chappell) reported torpedoing a ship that could have been *Akita Maru,* but the positions do not agree by over 250 miles. Despite these minor losses the Japanese were pressing hard in the decisive strategic area. There were indications that the next line of enemy advance would be down Makassar Strait, between Borneo and Celebes, or through Molucca Passage to the eastward of Celebes. Six submarines were therefore stationed in Makassar Strait and three more were stationed off Ambon south of Molucca Passage.

Information was then received that the Japanese were assembling an invasion force at Kema, in Celebes. It was planned to hit them at their assembly point in a night attack with the surface striking force. Two submarines (*Pike* and *Permit*) were sent ahead to reconnoiter. On 17 January they reported that the harbor at Kema held no large concentration of shipping, and the attack of the surface striking force was called off. Yet this was an occasion when the information was essentially accurate, but off only in timing. When a few days later *Swordfish* observed Kema and found the port overflowing with shipping, the striking force was otherwise employed; but *Swordfish* was later able to profit from her own reconnaissance.

The frustrating experience with torpedoes continued. During January *Seadragon* (Ferrall) fired fifteen torpedoes for only one hit. Her single success severely damaged *Fukuyo Maru* off the north coast of French Indo-China on 23 January. Many other submarines reported torpedo hits without confirmed sinkings or damages to correspond. Lieutenant Commander W. L. Wright in *Sturgeon* reported hits in a "heavy screw ship" off Balikpapan, Borneo. *Sturgeon* had had a succession of exasperating misses, and when at last Wright thought he could report a success, he paraphrased a well-known bawdy song and reported by dispatch "*Sturgeon* no longer virgin" for the edification of the whole Asiatic Fleet who, despite communication instructions to the contrary, were intercepting and decoding every submarine dispatch they could copy. Unfortunately, although *Sturgeon* remained "a very fine fish," she was technically still a virgin, for her torpedoes that night did not find their mark.

For others, even though they escaped "fire and foe," there was worse than frustration in store. *Tarpon*, surfacing in a typhoon with an exhausted battery after a long submerged run, was badly mauled by the sea while she was in the unstable equilibrium a submarine must pass through in surfacing and submerging. She was lucky to limp into Darwin for repairs. On 20 January S-36 ran aground on Taka Bakang Reef in Makassar Strait. A Dutch ship came out from Makassar City to help her, but conditions became progressively worse and the Japanese were coming down the strait. McKnight decided to abandon and destroy his ship. All the crew were saved and taken to Surabaya in the Dutch ship *Siberote*.

Swordfish *at Kema*

Not all the news was bad. On 24 January, Smith in *Swordfish* was still loitering around Kema. He observed two freighters anchored in a roadstead north of that port. There had been persistent anti-submarine patrol activity in this area but this failed to interdict *Swordfish*. The depth of the water was such that a submerged approach was feasible, and Smith believed that it was unlikely the enemy would foul his own anchorage with mines. To get at the target Smith had to pilot *Swordfish* submerged through the lower part of Lembeh Strait. There was no boom or net defense that he could see.

Swordfish proceeded north at slow submerged speed, making periscope exposures every twenty to thirty minutes and running deep in between to avoid air observation. It was impossible to determine the force and direction of the current (necessary for accurate shooting at anchored targets), so Smith decided to expend two precious torpedoes on each ship and fire a spread. He fired his two torpedoes at the first target and, with that maddening obstinacy of a submerged submarine, swung left to aim at the second. After a minute and a half an explosion was heard. Two torpedoes were then fired at the second ship, and these also were heard to explode. *Swordfish* then retired at 180 feet depth. Minor explosions which may have been gunfire, but might have been light air bombs, were heard overhead near the submarine. Small boat propellers also buzzed around and distant depth charges exploded, but *Swordfish* got clean away. *Myoken Maru* was sunk in this attack and apparently the second ship escaped.

Balikpapan

While all this was going on the center of attention was shifting to
Makassar Strait. On 21 January sixteen Japanese transports, escorted by
three patrol boats, left Tarakan headed south. The next day *Porpoise*
and *Pickerel* made contact with this force and reported a major Japanese
movement toward Balikpapan. Both American and Dutch submarines
attacked the Japanese. *K-18* reported torpedoing a cruiser and a destroyer, and *Sturgeon* was credited with sinking a large warship, but
the Japanese credit submarines with only damage to one patrol boat.
The major attack on the Japanese occurred on the night of 24 January
when four old U.S. four-piper destroyers charged into the transport
anchorage off Balikpapan, fired all their torpedoes and most of their
gun ammunition, and sank three transports. It was the most effective
counterattack of the whole campaign.

Allied Intelligence estimated that the next attack would be on Timor,
to cut the communication lines between Java and northern Australia,
and the submarines were disposed accordingly. The Japanese, however,
did not conform to the Allied plans. They moved down Molucca Passage
and landed at Kendari, in southeastern Celebes, on 24 January. On the
thirty-first they landed at Ambon, southwest of Ceram, with overwhelming force.

Loss of Shark

Shark (Shane) had been ordered to Ambon to oppose the Japanese
landing. She arrived there on the first of February and fired three
torpedoes at transports moored near the mouth of the harbor. They
missed. The Japanese destroyer *Amatsukaze,* on anti-submarine patrol
off port, answered the transports' call for help and after five hours' sonar
search made contact. She dropped one pattern of eight charges right
over where she had located a submarine. There was a strong smell of
diesel oil, and no further submarine contacts. Commander Hara of
Amatsukaze was sure of a kill, but *Shark* escaped and reported the
incident the next day. Five days later Shane reported contact with an
empty Japanese cargo vessel, and was chided by submarine headquarters at Surabaya for making unnecessary radio reports and thus revealing his position. It was the last radio report *Shark* ever made, and
what happened to her is conjecture; but it appears most probable that
she never had an opportunity to report a depth-charge attack off Menado
a week later. She went down with all hands.

On 3 February the Japanese had the airfields of Kendari in operation. They were then able to dominate the Flores Sea and to bomb Surabaya. After that Surabaya was no better as a submarine base than Manila had been, and as the submarine tenders *Holland* and *Otus* were no longer safe in Darwin they were moved to Tjilatjap, Java. Dutch Rear Admiral Doorman, with a force of Dutch and American cruisers and destroyers, attempted a surface sweep of Makassar Strait, but the Japanese shore-based naval air forces based on Kendari attacked them with disastrous effect. *Marblehead* was so badly damaged she had to be sent halfway around the world to the East Coast of the United States for repairs, and *Houston* had her after turret knocked out. Both ships had severe personnel casualties. Two Dutch cruisers were also damaged. The surface forces withdrew from the Flores Sea, leaving it clear (except for S-37) for the Japanese to mount an amphibious force at Kendari and send it around through the Flores Sea to attack Makassar City, in southwestern Celebes.

S-37 *and* Natsushio

On 8 February 1942 S-37 (Dempsey) was patrolling submerged off Makassar City. In the last remaining daylight Dempsey observed several ships proceeding in a northwestward direction, but he was unable to get close enough to attack. Under cover of darkness, after the sun had set, he surfaced and pursued. At about a quarter to eight he encountered four destroyers steaming in column, and beyond them he could see other ships. Dempsey found, however, that the destroyers were so disposed, between him and the convoy, that with his slow S-boat surface speed it was impossible for him to outflank the escorts and get in. He therefore decided to attack the destroyers.

He had four torpedoes in his tubes forward and fortunately they were old Mark 10 torpedoes, slow and short-legged, but with reliable contact exploders. The only fire control instrument he had that could be used during a surface attack from the bridge was a dummy pelorus, not designed to be read in the dark. But his executive officer, Lieutenant Hazzard, had ingeniously rigged up this instrument with brass brads (tacked into the bridge rail) around its perimeter so that it could be read by a kind of Braille system. It worked. Dempsey fired one torpedo at each of the four destroyers in column. The third ship in line was hit. The target buckled in the middle and went down in flames. This was the 1900-ton destroyer *Natsushio*. S-37 submerged to evade counterattack and to reload torpedoes. *Natsushio* was the largest combatant ship to be sunk by U.S. forces during the whole East Indies campaign.

The day after S-37 sank *Natsushio*, the Japanese landed at Makassar

City. They were then in full control of Karimata Strait, Makassar Strait, and Molucca Passage—all the northern entrances into the Java Sea; and through their lines only submarines could hope to pass. Japanese amphibious and covering forces were marshaled for the last assault on the Malay Barrier and pushed forward with an energy that allowed the Allies no time to consolidate their defenses.

Invasion of Sumatra

The Japanese Southern Expeditionary Force under Vice Admiral Ozawa sailed from Camranh Bay, Indo-China. On 12 February they were joined by amphibious forces and transports which the Japanese no longer needed for the destruction of Singapore. Allied search planes, flying practically suicide missions in the face of Japanese command of the air, discovered these forces coming down the South China Sea, and it was soon evident that Sumatra was their destination. The Allied striking force came through Sunda Strait between Java and Sumatra to fight for Sumatra, but on 15 February they were attacked by successive waves of Japanese high-level bombers. The ships were successfully maneuvered to avoid all but minor damage, but it was evident that in the face of such overwhelming air superiority it would be impossible to close an agile enemy, and there was little a surface force alone could do to defend Sumatra. Admiral Doorman withdrew. That was the day Singapore fell. The Japanese landed the next day (16 February) near Palembang, and the rich Sumatra oil fields were soon in their hands.

Down at the other end of the Malay Barrier, at Darwin, Australia, the Allied cause fared no better. *Houston*, with two Australian corvettes and a few transports, set out to reinforce Timor on 15 February. They were attacked by land-based bombers from Kendari and escaped serious damage; but it was evident that the reinforcement of Timor was too little and too late and the whole force returned to Darwin. The busy bombers of the Japanese 11th Air Fleet went methodically about the business of reduction of the defenses of Java. On 17 February, in bombing Surabaya, they hit the Dutch submarine *K-7* as she lay on the bottom of the harbor and destroyed her. The Dutch destroyers *Van Nes* and *Banckert* were also hit by horizontal bombers and sunk.

This slow erosion was severe enough, but when the Japanese Kido Butai took a hand the destruction was swift and total. Nagumo, with four of his six carriers, hit Darwin on 19 February. When this attack was over, twelve ships had been sunk, eighteen planes destroyed, the dockside installations and military stores destroyed, the airport demolished, and the town itself abandoned.

Seawolf *in Lombok Strait*

Allied Intelligence had information of a landing on Bali, near the eastern end of Java, several days in advance, but it was difficult to bring a striking force together to oppose the Japanese. Only submarines were waiting in Lombok Strait, between the islands of Bali and Lombok. At two o'clock in the morning *Seawolf* (Warder) encountered the escorts of a Japanese task force coming through the strait. In the darkness Warder successfully took *Seawolf* through the Japanese screen on the surface before being forced down. Navigation was hazardous, submerged in Lombok Strait, with its strong and tricky currents. When dawn came, *Seawolf* had been so buffeted about by the current that Warder could not fix his navigational position by anything he could see through the periscope, but he could see the masts of the transports evidently at anchor, so he came in to attack. *Seawolf* went aground and Warder backed her off only to go aground again, and the second time at periscope depth. She was then unable to back off submerged, so in desperation Warder surfaced although he knew he was within visual range of Japanese forces. Fortunately he came up in a rain squall which gave him an opportunity to close the Japanese anchorage at surface speed for half an hour before he had to dive again. By skillful and courageous ship-handling he worked *Seawolf* into torpedo range of the anchored targets and swung her around to head out to deep water while he attacked with the stern tubes. The soundman heard the torpedoes hit before the pinging destroyer was on top of them. *Seawolf* received a terrific depth-charging but got out with only minor damage. There were no real torpedo hits. What the soundman heard was probably prematures again.

On the night of 19–20 February an Allied surface force attacked the Japanese at the Bali beachhead. The Dutch destroyer *Piet Hein* was sunk, and a Dutch cruiser and a U.S. destroyer were damaged. The Japanese destroyer *Michishio* was disabled but made it back to Makassar City. Bali was occupied on schedule by the Japanese.

British and Dutch Submarines

Unknown to Warder there was a British submarine in his area of operations. Two British submarines had been ordered to the Far East in January. *Trusty* (King) operated for a time in the Gulf of Siam and then had to return to Colombo to repair underwater damage. *Truant* (Haggard) was ordered to oppose the Bali landing. Haggard was given very little intelligence on the area or of the Japanese and he had no knowledge of American submarines in the area. Arriving off Bali, *Truant* found many ships. She fired six torpedoes at a Japanese cruiser but made no hits. Fortunately *Seawolf* and *Truant* did not encounter one another off Bali.

Surabaya was abandoned to the approaching Japanese early in March. *K-10*, *K-13*, and *K-18* were at the Dutch submarine base, disabled and under repairs. They were scuttled to prevent them from falling into the hands of the Japanese. The remaining Dutch submarines joined *Trusty* and *Truant* at Trincomalee. Eight Dutch submarines had been lost in the defense of Malaya and the Netherlands East Indies.

Approach to Java

On 20 February Japanese amphibious forces anchored off Dili, on the island of Timor. Only *Pike* was there to receive them. *Pike* fired one torpedo at an escort vessel and missed. Meanwhile powerful amphibious forces were converging on Java. Fifty-six transports left Camranh Bay for Java on the eighteenth. The next day forty-one transports left Jolo in the Sulu Archipelago for Java via Balikpapan under escort of a cruiser and six destroyers. *Seal* (Hurd) made contact with one of the elements of this armada.

Seal was patrolling north of Lombok submerged at eight o'clock on the morning of 24 February when the soundman reported pinging to the northward, and shortly afterward Hurd saw smoke in the same direction. *Seal* came to normal approach course and soon sighted four cargo vessels, escorted by three destroyers. Hurd went deep and came in as fast as he could go. Ten minutes later he made a periscope exposure and found the range 5800 yards, the angle on the bow already 50° port, and the estimate of the enemy's speed thirteen knots. *Seal* went deep to 110 feet to avoid detection and kept boring in. If she came up to periscope depth and slowed down to take an observation, she would lose distance, and increase the chances of the target getting by before she could get inside torpedo range. Hurd decided to stay deep, maintain best speed, and attack by sound. The sea was like glass and any periscope exposure created a grave risk of being sighted. Although he had not detected air cover there was a good chance of its presence. Prewar doctrine mandated a sound approach from deep submergence in such situations and Hurd, with some misgivings, elected to attack in the prescribed manner. *Seal* fired four torpedoes on sound, and the soundman heard explosions, but the commanding officer was more skeptical. An hour later *Seal* came up to periscope depth and nothing was in sight. None of the Japanese amphibious forces approaching Java was torpedoed by any submarine.

In advance of the approach to Java the Japanese occupied Bawean Island, 150 miles north of Surabaya, and set up a radio station. S-38 was patrolling in the area, and when enemy activity on Bawean was discovered, S-38 (Munson) was ordered to bombard the island. This she did, expending all seventy-two rounds of her 4-inch ammunition. Fire was returned by one small gun on the beach which was silenced by well-directed fire from the submarine. Several large fires were started but nothing that looked like a radio station was observed.

Battle of the Java Sea

The Battle of the Java Sea was fought on 27 February. The Japanese had one destroyer badly damaged. The Netherlands cruisers *Java* and *DeRuyter* were sunk, going down with Admiral Doorman on board. The British destroyers *Electra* and *Jupiter* and the Netherlands destroyer *Kortenaer* were sunk. U.S.S. *Houston*, whose after turret was still out of action, was further damaged, and the only other Allied heavy cruiser, H.M.S. *Exeter*, was severely damaged. On the same day the seaplane tender *Langley*, attempting to ferry planes into Java, was caught and sunk in the Indian Ocean south of Tjilatjap by shore-based bombers of the Japanese 11th Air Fleet.

Japanese Long Lance oxygen-charged torpedoes, fired at extreme ranges, played an important part in the Battle of the Java Sea. Hit by torpedoes, when all Japanese surface ships were well outside maximum normal torpedo range, the Allies believed that they had been attacked by submarines; but Japanese submarines did not take part in this battle.

The next night, attempting to retire from the Java Sea through Sunda Strait, *Houston* and the Australian light cruiser *Perth* ran into one of the main Japanese invasion forces at the critical moment when the landing force was astride the beachhead. In a night melee four Japanese transports were destroyed, but the Japanese covering force moved in and both *Perth* and *Houston* were sunk after a gallant defense. The next morning (1 March) *Exeter*, and the destroyers *Encounter* and *Pope*, attempting to escape from Surabaya, were intercepted by Japanese cruisers and destroyers and all three Allied ships were sunk south of Borneo in the Java Sea.

All this gallant action scarcely delayed the Japanese schedule for the invasion of Java, and although there were still submarines in the Java Sea they were no more effective than the air and surface forces in stopping the Japanese. S-38, after her gun attack on Bawean, picked up fifty-four survivors of H.M.S. *Electra*. S-37 rescued some and assisted other survivors of *DeRuyter*. *Perch*, under command of Lieutenant Commander David A. Hurt, was in the area but she was in no condition to rescue anybody.

Loss of Perch

Perch had had a frustrating series of torpedo failures, so on the night of 25 February when she encountered a large freighter under escort of one destroyer Hurt decided to close to point-blank range and make sure of this one. While *Perch* was firing torpedoes she was sighted by the destroyer, who immediately opened fire and charged. The destroyer scored one hit in *Perch's* antennae trunk on the first salvo, before the submarine could get under. The torpedoes missed and *Perch* went deep to avoid the destroyer's depth charges, which fortunately were set too shallow.

When the submarine surfaced two hours later she found the antennae trunk ruptured and other minor damage. She made repairs and sent a radio report to Commander Submarines Asiatic. Wilkes (at Surabaya) never acknowledged the message and it was apparent that the damage to the antennae trunk interfered with radio transmission although reception was still possible. On the night of 28 February Hurt received a message directing all submarines to disregard area assignments and converge on Java to attack Japanese convoys at the landing points.

In obedience to this directive, *Perch* was on the surface on the night of 1 March steering a westerly course, approximately twelve miles northwest of Surabaya, when she sighted two destroyers. Hurt took *Perch* down to periscope depth. It was a moonlit night and he could see the destroyers through the periscope. They were apparently patrolling, and shortly their maneuvers brought them into a nice position to be attacked with the stern tubes. The range was down to about a thousand yards when apparently the hunted either heard or saw the hunter, for the destroyers suddenly changed course right for *Perch* and charged full speed.

The inaccurate chart showed plenty of water. Hurt went deep. He knew that the Japanese had a tendency to set depth charges shallow. When *Perch* was at a hundred feet a destroyer passed right overhead and dropped a string of charges. Suddenly, when there should have been plenty of water under the keel, *Perch* hit bottom hard; the motors still going ahead. Fortunately there was no damage either from the depth charges or the accidental grounding, but *Perch* had buried herself so deep in the mud that it would be a noisy operation to extricate her. The destroyer came back for another run.

On the second run four accurate depth charges were dropped. Maximum damage was in the motor room and engine room. Electric circuits were knocked out. Power was lost on the port shaft. Ninety per cent of the engine room gauges were broken. Valves were jammed. One high-pressure air bank was leaking badly, sending telltale bubbles to the surface. The hull was dimpled about two and a half inches deep in places over the after battery. The crew's toilet bowl, which in those days was ceramic like its civilian counterpart, was shattered by the shock.

Relentlessly the destroyer came back to make sure of her kill, no doubt guided by oil and air leaks. The third attack was concentrated amidships. A section of the exhaust duct was flooded, and salt water sprayed the fire control panel. The battery exhaust valve jumped off its seat but fortunately reseated itself. Number Two periscope was jammed tight. Number One periscope would raise but it required the combined efforts of four men to turn it. Hatch gaskets were leaking, and the air conditioner water supply valve was cracked and leaking badly.

Shortly after the attack *Perch* managed to get out of the mud and try evasive tactics. It was probably the Japanese destroyers *Hatsukaze* and *Amatsukage* who made this attack on *Perch,* although there are many discrepancies between the two accounts of the action. Commander Hara of *Amatsukage* reported a gun action with a submarine, which dove after receiving several hits. *Amatsukage* followed up with depth-charge attacks which brought up copious quantities of oil. Sure of a kill, Hara abandoned the search. *Perch* maneuvered to evade for two hours after she pulled out of the mud and then surfaced to assess damages.

All the ceramic antennae insulators were broken. Depth-charge fragments littered the deck. The blinker light was compressed flat. The governor of Number One engine was broken and the engine ran away on starting. The camshaft of Number Four engine was broken, but they succeeded in getting Number Two started on a battery charge and Number Three on the screw. *Perch* was not in first-class shape, but this was an all-out defense against a major landing. She had been ordered to "penetrate" the Japanese anti-submarine defenses. She could still fire torpedoes, even though handicapped by disabled periscopes. Hurt headed toward the reported position of the Japanese landing.

About two hours before dawn they sighted two enemy destroyers who simultaneously sighted them. *Perch* dove. Hurt felt she had a better chance on the bottom, even though he realized from recent bitter experience that it put an extraordinary psychological strain on everybody to lie supine upon the bottom and absorb punishment. *Perch* was leaking badly, and to keep her in depth control would require almost constant running of the noisy trim pump. This would be enough to give a good soundman all the sound source he needed to track the submarine constantly. *Perch* found bottom at two hundred feet and lay doggo.

The destroyers were on top of her immediately. The first string was wide of the mark, but the second one found her. It was bad. As soon as Hurt realized that the destroyer had located *Perch,* he tried to raise her off the bottom. He could not do it short of blowing ballast tanks. *Perch* kept accumulating additional damage.

New leaks appeared in the hull connections, and the older ones increased in amount. Number One main ballast tank was cracked, for it would not hold air. There were leaks in the high-pressure air lines. The toilet bowls in the maneuvering room and after battery compartment were shattered. The damaged antennae trunk leaked.

The Japanese destroyer laid its third string of five charges directly overhead, from stern to bow. The bow planes, which were rigged out on 20° rise, were rigged in by the concussion, burning up the bow plane rigging motor. The sound head went out of commission. Two torpedoes made hot runs in their tubes; that is, the concussion tripped the torpedo starting levers so that the torpedo turbines made full power runs with a good deal of attendant racket and heat, without leaving the tubes. Under such circumstances nobody could be quite certain that the exploders had not been armed by the same shock, or that the next concussion would explode the warhead and put an end to the whole fracas. The next run was also close, and spread additional damage throughout the ship. The officers' toilet bowl, by virtue of rank reserved until the last, was shattered and blown clear out into the passageway.

The last run was worst of all. This came about eight-thirty on the morning of 2 March. The depth gauge reading, which had been steady at two hundred feet with the ship resting on the bottom, showed 228 feet after the blast. A big area of the hull up forward was bulged in a couple of inches. The after battery had one cracked cell, and the forward battery had nineteen cracked cells. This flooded the battery sumps with concentrated sulphuric acid. It also introduced the danger of fire if a heavy load was drawn from the battery and, with all the salt water leaks, it aggravated the danger of generating chlorine gas. All the interior communication circuits were knocked out, and most of the instruments had been blasted off their bulkhead mountings by concussion. Two air banks were empty from leaks. The destroyer steamed triumphantly away, again underestimating *Perch's* resilience, but Hurt decided not to attempt surfacing during daylight. The loss of high-pressure air from leaks left the supply of this precious commodity so low that he might have only enough to make one attempt to bring *Perch* to the surface of the sea.

During the day they made what repairs were possible. They lifted grounds on the port main motor, which restored power to both shafts. They pumped the bilges to avoid flooding electrical machinery. They pumped the variable ballast tanks to lighten her as much as possible for the final effort to bring her up.

At nine o'clock at night on 2 March they finally got her to the surface after an hour of trying. The main ballast vents would not hold so the emergency vents had to be operated by hand. The barometer was broken so nobody knew how much pressure there was in the boat. There were full grounds on both main batteries, causing imminent danger of a battery fire, but with a stiff upper lip Hurt called for maximum power on both shafts and broke her loose from the bottom.

They tried each main engine in succession and finally got Number Three started on the screw to give them a surface speed of five knots. One auxiliary engine was started on a battery charge. Half the holding down studs of the operating engine had been broken by the inertia effect of the depth-charge explosions, and the engine vibrated so violently that it seemed only a matter of time before the rest of the studs would go. There were numerous short circuits caused by spray from salt water leaks. The concussion of the depth charges had forced the escape trunk doors so hard against their knife edges that strips of rubber had been neatly cut out of the gaskets. The port reduction gear was cracked and leaking lubrication oil. The steering gear was damaged and the rudder control was very erratic. Number Two main ballast tank leaked badly. They were unable to elevate the gun. There were so many hull leaks that the pumps had to run at full capacity. Hurt then decided that his primary mission was escape, and he headed *Perch* south and east at her maximum speed of five knots.

Before daylight it was necessary to make a trim dive to see if she could be controlled submerged. In spite of every effort to make her light, she was heavy going down, and plunged to sixty feet before anything could be done to check her. Lieutenant Schacht, the diving officer, with a good diving officer's sixth sense of how she feels going down, started blowing everything as soon as the deck was under, and then only with difficulty brought her back to the surface. By that time the engine room bilges were flooded nearly up to the sensitive and vital generators. With all Schacht's skill, he could only get her far enough up to expose the forward deck.

While she lay there waterlogged the repair party attempted to stop the major leaks. With the conning tower hatch closed as tight as they could get it there was still three-eighths of an inch between the gasket and the knife edge. The hatch was sprung. While they were working on it, handicapped by inadequate tools for such a major job, frustrated by the cramped space and the groping blindness of a blacked-out bridge in a darkened ship, the officer of the deck reported three Japanese destroyers in sight.

The nearest destroyer opened up with fire from one gun. The first shell was three hundred yards short. The next was also short but right on in deflection. None of *Perch's* torpedoes could be fired. The gun was out of commission. She could not dive and hope to come up again. It was hard enough to hold her on the surface. She could not fight and she could not run. Hurt ordered abandon ship and scuttled *Perch*. All hands got into the water safely. *Perch* went down quickly with the conning tower hatch open, and the Japanese picked up the crew as prisoners of war.

Supply Service to Corregidor

After the Japanese blitz fell on the Philippines, communication with Manila by surface ship was practically cut off. Air traffic soon dried to a trickle. By the end of January, shortages in the military supplies of Corregidor had developed. On 27 January *Seawolf* arrived with thirty-seven tons of .50-caliber ammunition she had transported from Darwin, in the first run of a submarine supply service. She took out twenty-five Army and Navy pilots and submarine spares and torpedoes. *Seadragon,* on regular patrol off western Luzon, sank a Japanese transport and damaged another on 2 February and two days later called at Corregidor to evacuate critical personnel and take out torpedoes and spare parts. *Sargo* performed a similar service for isolated troops in Mindanao a week later.

A unique supply mission fell to the lot of *Trout* (Fenno). Anti-aircraft ammunition was in short supply on Corregidor and there was little replacement available in the Orient. *Trout* loaded 3500 rounds of 3-inch AA ammunition at Pearl Harbor on 12 January and set out on the long run to Manila. She was routed by way of Midway where she topped off with 20,000 gallons of diesel fuel to permit her to make the run across the Western Pacific at 13 knots. Fenno was briefed that there were no Allied ships of any kind between him and the Philippines except one westbound freighter, manned by volunteers, attempting to sneak across the Pacific on the surface and evade the Japanese blockade. Before leaving Midway *Trout* was informed that even this lone adventurer had been recalled and *Trout* had the only relief in sight for Corregidor.

Trout arrived on 3 February, and after discharging her cargo found that she was light and needed ballast to improve her diving trim. The Asiatic submarines running ammunition into Corregidor had no such problem. They came out loaded with precious torpedoes. Fenno, however, planned to patrol the East China Sea on his way home, and in preparation *Trout* had nearly her full complement of torpedoes on board with room for only two more. High Commissioner Francis B. Sayre had another problem. The reserves of the Bank of the Philippines had been transferred to Corregidor when Manila was evacuated, and Sayre was deeply concerned lest they fall into the hands of the Japanese. *Trout's* dilemma was the opportunity to solve the problem. The submarine was ballasted with gold bars and silver bullion rather than the conventional lead pigs, and *Trout* departed on patrol with twenty tons of gold and silver in her bilges.

Swordfish made a trip to Corregidor on 20 February to evacuate President Quezon to Panay. She returned four days later to pick up High Commissioner Sayre and his party. S-39 made a landing on a small island in the South China Sea where a party of forty British refugees from Singapore were reported, but found no British on the island. *Permit* was placed at the disposal of General MacArthur, but the general elected to come out by torpedo boat. *Permit* took out a load of naval personnel and torpedoes instead.

Submarine Strategy and Tactics in the Southwest Pacific

The history of the Allied defense of the Philippines, Malaya, and the Dutch East Indies is a history of disaster, frustration, and defeat for every arm of the defending forces. In this the submarines shared fully, for despite the many romantic contemporaneous accounts of submarine operations during this campaign, the real results were very disappointing. During the first three months of the war four of the twenty-nine U.S. submarines in the Southwest Pacific were lost. They sank one Japanese destroyer and eight *marus*. Eight of the thirteen Dutch submarines were lost in the same period, during which they sank one Japanese destroyer and three or four *marus*. Allied submarines also torpedoed three other Japanese combat vessels and twelve other non-combatant ones with varying degrees of damage. The total damage submarines inflicted upon the Japanese amphibious forces added up to more than the Allied air forces or the surface navies accomplished, but all of it together was insufficient to have a serious effect on the Japanese conduct of the war. Before the war, Allied submarine forces in the Southwest Pacific had been relatively strong, and much had been expected of them in a campaign that gave them a strategic advantage by bringing many prime targets into their home operating areas.

Torpedo failures had much to do with the discouraging accomplishments of U.S. submarines, but it was not the only factor. The effectiveness of anti-submarine air screens, and of Japanese anti-submarine warfare in general had been greatly overestimated. As a result initial tactical doctrine was too cautious. The effectiveness of a cautious deep approach with torpedoes fired by sound bearings without periscope exposure was highly overestimated. Night tactics were undeveloped. Many submarine commanders jettisoned the prescribed cautious tactics immediately. Submarine personnel were ingenious in adapting fire control instruments to be used from a darkened bridge. Submarine skippers, particularly Wright in *Sturgeon,* were quick to learn new night tactics and to pass on their knowledge to others, but this was an educational phase that should have preceded rather than followed the outbreak of the war.

The Dutch were committed to strategy of concentrating their submarines at threatened beachheads for all-out attack on Japanese amphibious forces. As the Japanese rolled ahead against all resistance, Admiral Hart directed a similiar strategy for U.S. submarines. In the absence of continued and effective air search it was difficult to develop the intended submarine concentration at the proper time and place. The result was often aimless and futile dashing about. Moreover, when the submarines did arrive on time they found themselves opposed by a concentration of anti-submarine forces, in restricted waters that limited the submarines' maneuverability.

Captain Wilkes was quick to see the disadvantage of this strategy and urged a return to a war of attrition, with submarines operating in assigned areas where they had better opportunity to maneuver and attack. It is most probable that Admiral Hart fully appreciated that in the long run the submarine would inflict more damage on the Japanese by the strategy that Wilkes recommended, but the Allied navies in the Southwest Pacific did not have a long run. In the short run he had as Commander-in-Chief Allied Naval Forces in the Southwest Pacific, Hart had to use every weapon he had available to delay the Japanese conquest of the Malay Barrier as long as possible.

Wilkes abandoned the peacetime doctrine of cautious tactics almost immediately. His radioed exhortation to "Penetrate. Penetrate. Penetrate." was in sharp contrast to his peacetime insistence for deep running approach with torpedoes fired on sound bearings. To his everlasting credit Wilkes backed up his submarine commanders in their condemnation of the Mark 14 torpedo. He was ready to do battle both with the torpedo experts on Hart's staff and with the Bureau of Ordnance on the issue. Although the Bureau of Ordnance maintained that the torpedo depth control was accurate and affirmed their undying faith in the magnetic exploder, Wilkes directed his submarines to favor shallow depth setting for contact hits. He tried to measure the depth of torpedo runs by test firing through fish nets, but the Japanese advanced so rapidly that submarine headquarters could never stay long enough in one place to arrange the tests. Wilkes was also apprehensive of the diversion of submarines in Corregidor supply runs, for he saw with great clarity that the submarines' best contribution to victory was sinking Japanese ships, and on this task he proposed to concentrate their efforts.

Pearl Harbor Submarines

The month of January, in the Central Pacific, was a time for the United States to consolidate and reinforce its defenses. The surface forces of the Navy were occupied with escort and protection of the convoys involved. Through most of December, after the initial contacts off Midway and Wake, submarines from Pearl Harbor were plodding wearily westward to their operation areas. When *Gudgeon* left Pearl Harbor she had four thousand miles to go to her assigned area, and no American submarine had ever before operated that far from its base. To get there and come back was a logistic achievement of considerable magnitude, but it so rapidly became a commonplace operation that it passed unnoticed. By January three U.S. submarines were stationed in Japanese waters. The Japanese Navy had a secure fleet anchorage and training area in the Inland Sea, nearly surrounded by Shikoku, Honshu, and Kyushu, and safe from hostile submarines. *Gudgeon* was stationed off Bungo Suido, the western entrance to this haven, and *Plunger* picketed Kii Suido, the other exit of the Inland Sea into the Pacific. *Pollack* was off Tokyo Bay.

When *Pollack* arrived in her operating area, she had expended 32,405 gallons of diesel fuel on the outward voyage and Moseley, her commanding officer, estimated that she could burn only about 12,000 gallons in operation within her area before she had to start back with sufficient fuel to insure her reaching home. As it turned out, fuel oil was not the factor determining the length of her patrol. Moseley found many targets in the area. The night he arrived off Tokyo Bay he attacked a destroyer and missed. Merchant vessels were proceeding unescorted, and many of them carried running lights at night. *Pollack* fired several torpedoes at cargo ships and Moseley was puzzled and exasperated at missing easy targets. On the night of 7 January he sank *Unkai Maru No. 1*, and two days later he torpedoed and sank *Teian Maru*. With only one torpedo remaining he made a night periscope attack at a destroyer patrolling at slow speed in the moonlight and missed again. Then with empty torpedo racks, he headed back to Pearl Harbor.

Plunger (White), off Kii Suido, found few prime targets in her area. She carried the first submarine air search radar on patrol but White found the device a disappointment. The Japanese seemed to be waiting for White and he had more contacts with submarine-hunting destroyers than anything else. On her very first night in the area *Plunger* made contact with a sonar-equipped destroyer. *Plunger* made a fast dive but the Japanese destroyer located her by echo ranging and proceeded to give her a thorough going-over with depth charges. This was the first time anyone in *Plunger* had heard a depth charge explode but from this experience they escaped with minor damage. On 18 January White got his revenge. He fired two torpedoes at the 4702-ton *Eizan Maru*. Both these torpedoes hit. They were the only torpedoes fired by *Plunger* before she had to start back because of fuel exhaustion. With them White sank the third Japanese ship to be torpedoed within sight of Honshu. This may have caused the Japanese some concern about their unprotected merchant marine, but all three U.S. submarines in Empire waters had to return in early January, leaving the area vacant for the rest of the month.

Reconnaissance

A major task for Pearl Harbor submarines was reconnaissance of the Marshall, Caroline, and Marianas Islands. Four fleet submarines left Pearl Harbor on this mission in late December. Since the end of World War I, when the ex-German Islands in these groups were mandated to Japan, they had been *terra incognita* to the United States. No American ship had visited them since the islands belonged to Germany. There was little to tell commanding officers of the submarines, sent out to explore, when they reported to Combat Intelligence for pre-patrol briefing. Jaluit in the Marshalls was reported to be an important base for Japanese air and submarine operations, and Kwajalein was believed to be of minor importance. Truk, in the Carolines, was recognized as an important potential base, and major Japanese fleet units were thought to be operating from there. Many of the atolls were believed to be heavily fortified, including 16-inch guns on Ponape and Yap. Much of this turned out to be misinformation.

Although submarines were the only spies that could penetrate into this area beyond the range of shore-based aircraft, they were poorly adapted and prepared for this kind of reconnaissance. With an uncomfortable four feet of naked periscope exposed, their horizon was only two miles distant. They could see nothing beyond the immediate beachhead, and it was difficult or impossible to make observations with the necessary accuracy. Periscope photography was in a rudimentary stage of development. Charts of the mandate islands were notoriously inaccurate, and currents were of unknown force and direction. Despite these difficulties, submarines operated within five hundred yards of the beach, ignoring the possibility of minefields and the certainty of coral heads. Many of the atolls were so large that a submarine keeping one atoll entrance under close observation would completely miss busy traffic through another channel a few miles distant. Much of the information collected with such difficulty was not worth the effort it had cost, but on 27 January *Dolphin* (Rainer) returned from observing Maloelap, Wotje, Kwajalein, and

Jaluit. She had found very little activity at Jaluit, while Kwajalein appeared to be very busy. This was important information to Vice Admiral Halsey in *Enterprise*.

Carrier Raids on Marshalls and Gilberts

U.S. carrier task forces, occupied in covering troop convoys, had a difficult time mounting any kind of an offensive. On 11 January *Saratoga* was torpedoed by a Japanese submarine about four hundred miles south of Oahu, and had to return to the West Coast for repairs. On 23 January another Japanese submarine sank the tanker *Neches* a few hours after she sailed from Pearl Harbor to refuel a task force accompanying *Lexington* en route to bomb Wake. As *Neches* was the only tanker then available, it was necessary to cancel the whole operation. This was the day the Japanese landed at Rabaul, in northern New Britain. The Japanese Fourth Fleet, after taking Wake, had turned its attention to New Britain. They were supported by four carriers from the Kido Butai. No Allied ships were there to oppose them, and the strategic harbor of Rabaul fell easily into Japanese hands.

In late January, however, two carrier task forces (Halsey in *Enterprise* and Fletcher in *Yorktown*), with five cruisers and ten destroyers, were available for a strike. Halsey originally planned a carrier strike and cruiser bombardment of Wotje and Maloelap, but because of the information supplied by *Dolphin*, a carrier strike on Kwajalein was included in his plan. The strike was made as planned on 1 February. *Yorktown* simultaneously hit Jaluit and the Gilbert Islands. Most of the damage was done at Kwajalein. *Katori*, the light cruiser serving as submarine force flagship, was damaged and had to return to Japan. *Tokiwa*, a minelayer, was heavily damaged. *I-23* was slightly damaged but left port the same day. Two *marus* were sunk and eight others damaged, including an 11,000-ton passenger vessel and a 10,000-ton tanker. This was a very daring raid, as Kwajalein was very deep in the Marshall Islands, and its success was a very great boost to American morale.

During January and early February five new submarines reported to Commander Submarines Pacific: *Grayling, Grenadier, Gar, Grampus,* and *Grayback*. These were sent out on patrol along with *Cachalot, Cuttlefish,* and *Tuna,* on their first patrol, and *Triton* and *Narwhal* on their second. Before the end of February *Pollack* and *Gudgeon* had made their turn around and were out again on patrol. The patrol areas spread from the area south of Truk, up past Saipan and Tinian to the Bonins and Nansei Shoto. *Triton, Pollack,* and *Gudgeon* followed one another into the East China Sea. *Tuna* and *Gar* patrolled the area south of Honshu, vacated in early January when the three pioneers completed their patrols there.

On 10 February *Trout*, taking a roundabout way home with her cargo of gold and silver, sank *Chuwa Maru* northeast of Formosa. She then briefly entered the southern end of the East China Sea before starting back to Pearl Harbor by way of the Bonin Islands. *Triton*, in the northern part of the East China Sea, sank two ships in the latter part of February. With a dozen submarines at sea, in their patrol areas and en route, this was little enough to show for all the efforts. In the Central Pacific submarines averged only about one-third of their time at sea in the operating area, the other two-thirds being spent en route to and from station. A considerable portion of the submarine effort was expended on reconnaissance in the Mandates, and many of the patrols in that area were fruitless because of lack of knowledge of routes and harbors.

Grayling *at Truk*

Submarines, particularly those without air search radars, were, in accordance with doctrine, timid about conducting patrols on the surface where plane contacts might be frequent. On 14 February *Grayling* (Olsen) was patrolling in the Truk area when Commander Submarines Pacific sent her a dispatch warning her that a Japanese aircraft carrier was thought to be headed for her area. Olsen changed station to cover the approach to Truk between Hall Island and Namonuito Atoll. On 17 February a small gunboat came by, en route to North Pass of Truk. *Grayling* attacked but missed. On 18 February *Grayling* was due to leave the area. She was patrolling at deep submergence, relying on the sound gear for contact. At about two o'clock in the afternoon sound picked up a contact, but by the time *Grayling* was brought to periscope depth and had her tubes ready for firing, Olsen was just in time to see a Japanese aircraft carrier steam by at eighteen knots. With the carrier, over the horizon disappeared the best opportunity Submarines Pacific had had until then to inflict serious damage on the enemy.

U.S. Carrier Operations

On 21 February *Lexington* attempted to raid Rabaul, but was discovered by the Japanese 25th Air Flotilla. A hair-raising air battle followed, with *Lexington* fighters shooting down the attacking bombers. Nevertheless, the raid on Rabaul was called off because surprise had been lost. Three days later, on 24 February, Halsey with the *Enterprise* task force bombarded Wake. The same force completed a much more daring raid on 4 March on Marcus Island, only a thousand miles south of Tokyo. These *Enterprise* raids were planned as diversions to take pressure off the hard-pressed southwest. They had no apparent effect, and the Japanese steamroller rolled on with crushing effect. Appearances were deceptive, however, because Yamamoto (Commander-in-Chief of the Japanese Combined Fleet) was very concerned about these carrier raids. He detached two new carriers (*Zuikaku* and *Shokaku*) from the Kido Butai to guard the vulnerable homeland from carrier raids, and retained one of the most powerful Japanese Navy shore-based Air Flotillas on Honshu for the same purpose. There was a flurry of Combined Fleet activity and considerable movement of forces within the Fourth Fleet area. The Kido Butai, then in Truk, sortied when Halsey attacked Kwajalein, and made a fruitless dash fifteen hundred miles in pursuit, delaying the participation of this powerful force in the conquest of the East Indies. Halsey's raid also had important long-range effect on Yamamoto's plans, and some immediate ones on the employment of the Japanese submarine force.

U.S. *Submarine Strategy in the Central Pacific*

In the Southwest Pacific targets came to the submarine operating areas, but Pearl Harbor submarines had thousands of miles to go before they could find Japanese ships. In the Southwest Pacific, the sudden shift from "restricted" to "unrestricted" submarine war made little difference. Most of the ships a submarine might encounter south of Formosa Strait were directly connected with Japanese amphibious forces. It is significant that of the ships sunk by Allied submarines in the Southwest Pacific during the first phase, all were either "Army" or "Navy" and none were "civilian" even in nominal designation. In the Central Pacific many of the ships encountered were Ministry of Munitions vessels, frequently unprotected by escorts. These differences generated corresponding difference in submarine strategy and tactics.

Although Pearl Harbor submarines on patrol were often depth-charged and pursued, the anti-submarine activity they encountered in the first three months of the war was not as intensive as that which opposed Allied submarines in the Southwest Pacific. In January S-26 was lost, with only three survivors, as a result of a night collision in the Gulf of Panama, but in the whole of the broad area under Commander Submarines Pacific no submarine was lost due to enemy action during the first three months of the war. To a considerable extent the most formidable opponent of the Pearl Harbor submarines was the great Pacific itself, with its vast stretch of open sea.

Out of Pearl Harbor in the first three months of the war, twenty-five submarines went on patrol. By the time they all returned they had totaled 1229 days at sea, and steamed 163,214 miles, surface and submerged. Only 480 submarine days of this time had been spent in the operating areas, and the remaining 749 days were expended en route. An efficient intelligence service, capable of selecting the most profitable areas to patrol, was a prime prerequisite for submarine warfare in such a great ocean, but there was little information specifically organized for submarines, and to a large extent submarines were initially depended upon as producers, rather than consumers of naval intelligence. Even with due allowance for the time spent in necessary though unprofitable reconnaissance of the Mandate islands, however, submarine results were small in comparison with the effort expended. In the first three months Pearl Harbor submarines sank one Japanese submarine and six *marus*, and three or four other *marus* were damaged.

The unprotected state of Japanese commerce, and the shift to "unrestricted submarine warfare" called for rapid development of new tactics. Commander Submarines Pacific (Withers) was quick to perceive this. The strategic and tactical concepts of Commander Submarines Pacific, and his staff, have been documented in endorsements to submarine patrol reports. The wide dissemination of these reports undoubtedly assisted in development of a new doctrine of submarine tactics, but it was often disconcerting for a submarine captain to find that his orders going out on patrol were so inconsistent with the new doctrine expounded in the endorsement on his patrol report, when he returned two months later.

When *Gudgeon* left on her first patrol, Grenfell had positive orders to proceed at one-engine speed to conserve fuel, and to operate submerged when within range of possible Japanese air bases during daylight. The time she would have to spend en route and return were therefore a matter of rather simple calculation, but the endorsement of division, squadron, and force commanders criticized the length of time spent submerged en route and noted that "with efficient lookouts" more time could be spent on the surface. The force commander also remarked that in the night surface attack Grenfell should have used *Gudgeon's* superior surface speed to pursue the enemy vessel on the surface.

When *Grayling* returned from patrol after allowing the carrier to get by without attack, the endorsements on her patrol were scathing. The division commander noted that despite intelligence reports of a carrier headed toward her area, *Grayling* was running at deep submergence and relying on the sound gear entirely for contact. Too much reliance can not be placed on the sound equipment and the soundman, he affirmed. Whenever possible, search must be conducted from either the surface or at periscope depth. The eye gives a much broader horizon than the sound gear, he noted, and sound observation must be considered a secondary means. The force commander, commenting on the same subject, was bitter. *Grayling* missed an opportunity for fame and glory on February 18, he said. This failure he attributed to unnecessary deep submerged running.

Grayling's patrol did not result in any damage to the enemy, and this may account for some of the sharpness of the patrol report endorsements. *Triton*, however, on her second patrol, penetrated into the East China Sea and sank two of the six *marus* sunk by the entire Pearl Harbor submarines in the first three months of operations, yet the force commander's endorsements were still very critical. He acknowledged that *Triton's* patrol was aggressively conducted, but *Triton* should have spent more time on the surface patrolling the East China Sea. True the East China Sea was covered by Japanese air search, but British experience in combatting German submarines with planes, he noted, indicated very little damage to a submarine, even if sighted, unless there were surface anti-submarine vessels at hand that could be summoned by the plane. Even with surface forces in the vicinity, the force commander asserted, with the reported poor anti-submarine measures used by the Japanese, the risk incurred was no greater than that which must be demanded of our submarines in all-out war.

These comments were correct, but it might have been more charitable for force and squadron commanders to have accepted their responsibility for developing prewar tactics contrary to those later advocated by their patrol report endorsements. Preparation of the force commander's endorsement was a staff function and, although the force commander signed them, it was probable that the comments on torpedoes were prepared by the force torpedo officer. Unfortunately these comments were more often wrong than right. *Gudgeon's* torpedo performance was analyzed very critically. Only one, rather than two or three torpedoes, should have been fired at *Gudgeon's* targets, the patrol endorsement affirmed, and until the supply of torpedoes could be assured, it would be essential to conserve torpedoes for more appropriate targets. On *Triton's* report it was noted that twelve torpedoes had been expended in four attacks. The extreme shortage of torpedoes would not allow such large expenditures of torpedoes for the results obtained. One good hit, it was asserted, using a magnetic exploder, should be sufficient to sink a 5000-ton ship.

Although the confidence of the force commander in the magnetic exploder was misplaced, his concern with torpedo shortage was understandable. At the rate the torpedoes were being expended it appeared that the Pearl Harbor submarines would shoot themselves out of torpedoes in the next two or three months, and the situation in the Southwest Pacific was even more critical. The reason that such a shortage existed was political, and deeper than anything the force torpedo officer could control. The experience of the war proved him wrong in his confidence in the solo torpedo salvo, which more often than not resulted in a wasted torpedo except in the unusual circumstances of a cold setup with a target unable to maneuver after the torpedo was sighted. But the sins of omission of the torpedo experts at Pearl Harbor, and in the Bureau of Ordnance, were more important than the sins of commission. In the Southwest Pacific the enemy effectively denied the submarine command any opportunity to investigate the many reports of torpedo failures. Torpedo men at Pearl Harbor and at Newport had no such problem, yet they contented themselves with reaffirmation of divine faith in their torpedoes, rather than conduct rigorous tests.

Japanese Submarine Operations

Japanese submarines contributed very little to the conquest of the East Indies. The Fourth Submarine Squadron (*I-53, I-55, I-56, I-57, I-58, RO-33,* and *RO-34*), based at Camranh Bay, Indo-China, operated in the Java Sea and the waters south of Java during January and February. They claimed sinking several ships. *I-57* was incapacitated most of this time, and remained in port because of dysentery in her crew.

The Fifth Squadron (*I-59, I-60, I-62, I-64, I-65,* and *I-66*) moved into the Indian Ocean and the Bay of Bengal. On 17 January *I-60* was sunk by H.M.S. *Jupiter* in Sunda Strait. During February this squadron sank several Allied merchant ships operating between Rangoon and Sumatra.

The Sixth Squadron (*I-121, I-122, I-123,* and *I-124*) based at Davao, Mindanao, and operated in the Flores Sea and Torres Strait north of Australia. They sighted U.S.S. *Houston* and other Allied forces several times but were unable to attack. *I-124* was sunk by U.S.S. *Edsall* and Australian minesweepers *Deloraine, Lithgow,* and *Katoomba* on 20 January while the Japanese submarine was laying mines off Darwin.

In the Central Pacific they were much more successful. During the first part of January most of the submarines operating off the West Coast of the United States had to leave their areas to return to Kwajalein to refuel. Returning through the Hawaiian Islands, *I-9* launched her seaplane for a succcessful reconnaissance of Pearl Harbor. *I-25* (Tagami), en route home between Johnston and the Marshalls on 7 January, sighted a seaplane carrier with planes on deck. She fired four torpedoes at the phantom and claims she sank it, but the Americans had no seaplane carrier of this description and lost no ship on that day. The incident remains a mystery. The next contact between Japanese submarines and an American carrier, however, was no phantom. On 11 January *I-6* attacked *Saratoga* and reported sinking *Lexington,* a mistake that complicated Japanese strategic computations for some time. *Saratoga* was not sunk as had been noted, but she was out of the war undergoing repairs on the West Coast, reducing the carrier power of the United

States in the Pacific by 25 per cent during the next few critical months.

Their other efforts during January and February added little to the score. A Japanese submarine shelled Pago Pago on 11 January causing a little flurry of concern that it might be a prelude to invasion of Samoa. This bombardment seems to have had nothing more behind it than its nuisance value, however. *I-18* and *I-24* were involved in a similar incident at Midway. Approaching the atoll, *I-24* sighted a large merchant ship at anchor but the ship was inside the reef, safe from the submarine's torpedoes. On schedule on the night of 25 January *I-24* surfaced and opened up with her deck gun. She intended to fire seven rounds, but the Marines on Midway returned the fire so prompty and so accurately that she submerged with one round still on deck. *I-18* was brought under fire so quickly that she submerged without firing a single shot. This incident had other unfortunate effects for Japanese submarines. Because of it, and the attendant radio traffic, *Gudgeon,* coming back from patrol, was warned of hostile submarines in her area. Grenfell was put on guard and on 27 January sank *I-73* as has been recounted. Nothing daunted, *I-69* bombarded Midway again on 8 February.

Before the Japanese invaded Rabaul, their submarines were stationed in accordance with their standard pattern for cooperation with their fleet. Submarine patrol lines were established in the Coral Sea to intercept any Allied ships that might come boiling up from the south to interfere with the invasion. No Allied ships came boiling up from there, for there were no ships to boil. Japanese submarines retired without incident.

When Halsey raided Kwajalein, Japanese submarines swarmed out after him, but they were unable to catch up with Halsey hauling out. *I-23*, which suffered slight damage in this raid, continued right on to her assigned patrol station off Oahu. She had a mission in an intricate air-submarine operation scheduled for early March, but before that time she was sunk with all hands. No one knows what happened to her, but her disappearance complicated things for the Japanese.

Ranging far and wide, *I-25* made a seaplane reconnaissance of Sydney on 13 February. The next week her plane was over Melbourne, and on the twenty-fourth over Hobart, Tasmania. On 23 February *I-17* (Nishino) shelled Ellwood, California near Los Angeles, causing little damage but much consternation all along the West Coast.

Japanese Submarine Strategy and Tactics

At the beginning of March 1942, Japan had good reason to be complaisant. The Greater East Asia Co-Prosperity Sphere was practically under her control, and the end of the first phase was in sight. Optimistic planners, before the war, had estimated this would take a year and cost one-third of her Navy. It had been done in three months, and Japan had lost five destroyers, seven submarines, nine minor vessels, and 170,000 tons of merchant shipping.

Japan's initial submarine strategy had been to use her submarines primarily as an auxiliary arm of her fleet, and secondarily for commerce destruction. Although their accomplishments may not have matched the prewar dreams of their submariners, the accomplishment had been real enough. Without submarine scouting, *Repulse* and *Prince of Wales* might have completed their mission, and the submarine contact reports may well have been the difference between a Japanese defeat and a spectacular victory. They thought *I-6* sank *Lexington,* and although she had only damaged *Saratoga,* this was better than any Allied submarine could boast.

Like other navies, they credited their submarines with a number of illusionary sinkings but, on the other hand, they were unaware that a single submarine had turned back a full strike on Wake by sinking one tanker. Fringe operation of submarines with midgets and seaplanes demonstrated imagination and daring but did not accomplish very much. It is probable that the submarines involved might have been more profitably employed in conventional operations. The secondary submarine mission of commerce destruction, counting the ships sunk in the Indian Ocean, had results to show greater than Allied accomplishments in the same field. The Germans were anxious to have Japanese submarines expand their commerce destruction in the Indian Ocean, for any Allied ship sunk there was one less for the Battle of the Atlantic. The Japanese submarine force thus became the only direct link between the Axis partners.

For a nation so dependent upon sea communication, it is remarkable that Japanese shipping was not better organized and protected. There was little cooperation between the separate shipping pools of Army, Navy, and Ministry of Munitions. Civilian ships went out in ballast and returned loaded with raw materials. Army and Navy ships went out loaded with troops and military supplies, and returned empty. It was not unusual for empty ships of this nation desperately short of shipping to pass one another going in opposite directions on a long and hazardous voyage. Tanker tonnage, which later would become critical, was practically idle during the first phase, until the oil wells of the Dutch East Indies could be seized and brought into production.

The protection of shipping was also poorly organized. There was no over-all escort command, no standard communication plan, no convoy or escort doctrine. The Combined Fleet had first call on all destroyers and hoarded them jealously, reluctant to detach any of them for convoy protection. Not infrequently fleet destroyers steamed idly between ports, while important convoys moved independently over the same route unprotected. Moreover, fleet destroyer commanders were contemptuous of escort duty. Their major mission was night battle and torpedo attack (and in this they were superb as the United States Navy was to learn at great cost), but in anti-submarine operations they were not the equal of U.S. destroyers. This was probably, in the end, just as expensive for the Japanese as U.S. destroyers' relatively poorer night battle training was for them.

VII

MARCH–APRIL 1942

The Second Bombing of Pearl Harbor

The Japanese Navy learned by submarine-launched seaplane reconnaissances of Pearl Harbor that the U. S. Navy was making rapid progress in fleet repairs. A few well-placed bombs could disrupt salvage operations, but Pearl Harbor was out of reach of bombing planes taking off from any Japanese bases. Their aircraft carriers were busy elsewhere and, besides, Yamamoto was not disposed to risk the Kido Butai in another Pearl Harbor raid unless a major fleet action might ensue under conditions favorable to the Japanese. The first units of a new type four-engine flying boat (later known to the U. S. Navy as Emily) were about ready for service. Pearl Harbor was out of range of even these long-range planes, but refueling of seaplanes from submarines had been developed and tried out in the Japanese Navy to meet just such a situation. Lieutenant Commander Suguru Suzuki, at Japanese Naval General Headquarters in Tokyo, had a plan for using submarines in cooperation with the new Emilies for a second bombing of Pearl Harbor.

There was some delay because all available submarines had dashed out to intercept *Lexington* after her abortive raid on Rabaul on 20 February but by 3 March a group of Japanese submarines were on station and ready, between Hawaii and the Marshalls. *I-15*, *I-19*, and *I-26*, each with ten tons of aviation gasoline were off French Frigate Shoal, about five hundred miles to the northwestward of Pearl Harbor. *I-9* was seven hundred miles southwest of French Frigate to act as radio beacon. Two RO-type coastal defense submarines were three hundred miles northeast of Wotje to assist in navigation on the return flight. All submarines were to make weather reports on schedule.

I-23 was supposed to be stationed ten miles south of Pearl Harbor as lifeguard and weather reporter. She reached her area early, but sometime after 14 February she disappeared with all hands. The first indication to the Japanese that something had happened to *I-23* was her failure to transmit weather information on schedule. Other events made this failure very significant. The Japanese cryptanalysts had broken the U.S. weather code, and Japanese meteorologists depended upon the daily coded weather report of Midway, Johnston, and Hawaii to predict the weather at the target. Then on 1 March the Americans made a routine change of their weather code and the Japanese were suddenly left without their enemy's weather reports. When I-23 failed to transmit her observations, the information the meteorologists had for predicting the weather was extremely thin.

The refueling took place on schedule. Two big flying boats took off after refueling from the submarines at French Frigate Shoal, and came in along the Hawaiian chain. At 0014 on the morning of 4 March they were picked up by the radar station on Kauai. While the Japanese planes were still two hundred miles from their target, Hawaiian Sea Frontier went to General Quarters. At 0115 Navy patrol planes took off armed with torpedoes, to attempt to locate and attack a Japanese seaplane carrier, a mysterious type of naval vessel possessed only by the Japanese—one of which, it was believed, had launched these "bandits." Shortly afterward Army night fighters took to the air to receive the night visitors.

It was an overcast and drizzly night over leeward Oahu, a situation which the Japanese had been unable to predict because of the disruption of their weather-reporting service. The two bombers lost their bearings in the murk and dropped their bombs miles from the target—one salvo in the sea and the other in the hills back of Honolulu. The defending fighters aloft (at that time without airborne radar or effective fighter directors) were blinded by the same weather and never saw the bombers, who returned unharmed to Wotje in the Marshalls.

The next day on Oahu, there was a tendency to discount the whole thing as a bad nightmare, each branch of service tacitly assuming that the bombs, seen and heard exploding in the hills, had been jettisoned by planes of the other service and that in the thick weather some bombardier had scored a near miss on the Pacific Ocean he had aimed at, and hit Oahu instead. But Lieutenant Commander Layton, Fleet Intelligence Officer, had read a story titled "Rendezvous," by Alec Hudson, in the August 9, 1941, issue of *The Saturday Evening Post*. This story was a fictional account of the bombing of an out-of-range naval base by seaplanes refueled from submarines. With this on his mind, and with the information direction-finders gave him about unusual submarine radio activity in the vicinity of French Frigate Shoal, Layton concluded that the plane that bombed Oahu had come from French Frigate and had there been refueled by Japanese submarines. In this conclusion Alec Hudson, then on duty as an Intelligence officer in Hawaiian Sea Frontier, concurred. To forestall any future such raids, Mine Division One steamed out of Pearl Harbor and planted minefields around French Frigate. As it later turned out, this action and the subsequent guarding of this location was of more importance than the whole bombing raid itself.

Because of these peculiar circumstances, the story grew up that the Japanese had copied the strategy of *The Saturday Evening Post* story when planning the second bombing of Pearl Harbor. This unflattering estimate of the originality of Japanese planners was far from the truth. The Japanese were further advanced in the use of seaplanes operating with submarines than were the Americans. Suzuki, who had planned the whole operation from beginning to end, had never heard of Alec Hudson or, for that matter, of *The Saturday Evening Post*. From the Japanese point of view this operation was unfortunate. Because of it, when they needed to use French Frigate Shoal as a refueling station for seaplane searches in connection with a much more important operation, they found the tiny atoll closely guarded by American vessels.

Windup of the First Phase

There was very little other Japanese submarine activity in the Pacific. *I-6* was still off the West Coast of the United States, but she departed before the end of March. *I-25* was operating off eastern Australia and sent her busy seaplane over Wellington, New Zealand, on 7 March. *I-53*, *I-54*, and *I-55* returned to Japan from the East Indies. *RO-33* and *RO-34* were sent from the East Indies to Truk. In early April these two submarines advanced from Truk to a new submarine base at Rabaul; portent of things to come.

The Japanese Second Submarine Squadron (*I-1*, *I-2*, *I-3*, *I-4*, *I-5*, and *I-7*) returned to Japan from the Eastern Pacific in February, and after overhaul sailed for the East Indies. They left Kendari, Celebes, in late February to deploy in the Indian Ocean three hundred miles south of Soemba Island in support of Japanese surface force operations. *I-5* ran aground off southeast Celebes, and it was not until late March that salvage operations got her off the reef. The Main Body of the Japanese Second Fleet, plus two carrier divisions, came through the Malay Barrier in early March to intercept Allied naval forces fleeing from the Java Sea and Tjilatjap. In this they were terribly effective. Japanese naval shore-based bombers assisted in the slaughter.

There was nothing to oppose the Japanese but American submarines, and they were operating under handicaps. On 1 March Captain Wilkes was forced to leave Tjilatjap to make the long jump down to Fremantle on the southwestern corner of Australia to establish a new submarine base out of reach of the Japanese bombers. With Java in Japanese hands, submarines on station would have to head south for Australia when their fuel supplies ran low. Until then they kept busy.

Both *S-38* and *Seal* reported hits in light cruisers (for which there are no corresponding Japanese damage reports). *Seawolf*, after her attack on the Bali landing force, withdrew briefly to repair damages sustained in grounding and in depth-charge attacks. She was back again in Lombok Strait by 1 March to intercept another convoy headed for Bali; Warder with his usual skill worked *Seawolf* into beautiful position between the convoy and the escorts, and fired torpedoes at the two leading transports. He then attacked an escorting destroyer with his stern tubes. He was sure of hits in all three targets, but it must have been prematures again. *Seawolf* then again endured the punishment of prolonged depth-charging.

Sailfish *and* Kamogawa Maru

The next day, 2 March 1942, *Sailfish* (Voge) encountered another Japanese force in busy Lombok Strait. He attacked a destroyer and missed, but that night he got in a long-range attack on a big ship he identified as an aircraft carrier from her characteristic flat-topped silhouette. He saw flashes of his torpedoes exploding against the side of the enemy. For a long time it was believed that *Sailfish* had damaged the big Japanese carrier *Kaga*, one of the Kido Butai that had spread havoc throughout the Pacific. This estimate seemed to be verified by the absence of *Kaga* from the March and April operations of the Kido Butai. Actually *Kaga* had been damaged by brushing against one of the strictly neutral East Indian coral heads. She was sent back to Japan for drydocking, causing a flurry of excitement among the Pacific submarines. Voge's observations were accurate, however. In that night attack on 2 March, *Sailfish* sank the flat-topped *Kamogawa Maru*, one of the fast merchant ships Japan had converted into aircraft ferries.

On 3 March, *Salmon* (McKinney) who, up until then had made four unsuccessful attacks on ships he identified as light cruisers, got in his fifth attack on a similar ship. This time he was sure of hits and reported sinking a light cruiser. The Japanese destroyer *Suzukaze* was severely damaged by a submarine torpedo at about the time and place he reported, and was probably *Salmon's* target. In the meantime diminishing fuel supply was rapidly reducing the number of submarines on patrol. *S-39*, under command of Lieutenant James Coe, was the last S-boat north of Java. On 4 March Coe torpedoed the naval tanker *Erimo*, which burned in suttee for the last S-boat's departure from the Java Sea. On 15 March Wilkes ordered his five S-boats to proceed from Fremantle, around the bottom of Australia, and come up the east side to Brisbane to join S-boats coming down from Panama heading for the same port. This left twenty fleet submarines operating out of Fremantle directly under Wilkes' command.

Seawolf *at Christmas Island*

The Japanese Navy was still busy in Malay and the East Indies securing their positions. In order to protect the flank of their Burma operation they occupied the Andaman Islands on 23 March, and about the
same time routed an expeditionary force through Lombok Strait for
Christmas Island, about two hundred miles south of Java in the Indian
Ocean. *Salmon,* which was still patrolling Lombok, sighted this force. Mc-
Kinney broadcast its position, course, and speed, although there was little
likelihood that there was anything south of Java to interfere with a Japanese force of that character.

Seawolf, running out of fuel, food, and torpedoes, and whose crew
was reduced to smoking coffee grounds rolled in toilet paper, had been
ordered to reconnoiter Christmas Island and then head for Fremantle.
So far as Warder knew, Christmas was still in Allied hands, and when he
received *Salmon's* message he correctly guessed the expedition's destination and lay in wait for the Japanese. Early in the morning of 31 March
Seawolf and the Japanese task force came together off Flying Fish Cove
on Christmas Island.

Warder identified his contact as four light cruisers in line, apparently
taking station for a preliminary shore bombardment. He picked out the
flagship and fired a salvo of torpedoes from the forward tubes. As well
as he could, with a destroyer counterattack coming his way, making each
inch of periscope exposure as sensitive as a sore thumb, he watched his
torpedoes explode on target. All day long the destroyers hunted *Seawolf,*
pummeling her occasionally with well-placed depth charges. That night
Seawolf surfaced and charged batteries, but before dawn the next morning she had contact again.

When Warder got a look at his new target, one ship appeared identical to the ship he had sunk the day before, including the personal pen-
nant flying from the main truck. Again he selected the flagship and fired
a salvo of torpedoes. The soundman heard the torpedoes run down the
range to the target, and then heard the explosions timed for the torpedo
run, after which there were convincing breaking up noises, before silence
again settled in the ocean.

Later in the same day, 1 April, a Japanese force sortied from Flying
Fish Cove. Warder, with his usual good luck and good management, was
in proper position. His target was a cruiser, carrying the flag of a Japanese
rear admiral, and again *Seawolf* fired, this time his last torpedoes, at
this flagship. The soundman followed them right down to the target for
a perfect hit. This time the destroyers' counterattack was vicious, accurate, and persistent. *Seawolf* had learned through hard experience to

take punishment, and from four o'clock in the afternoon until one o'clock the next morning, she took it. By the time Warder dared to bring *Seawolf* to the surface, *Seawolf's* crew were about at the end of their rope.

Seawolf was credited with sinking three cruisers, as indeed she deserved to have done. The Japanese were very much impressed by the American submarine's persistence in penetrating into their well-screened task force, but the records show no cruisers sunk. The light cruiser *Naka*, flagship of Rear Admiral Nishimura, was hit by a torpedo which flooded two compartments and brought down her foremast. *Naka* was lucky to make port but she did, although she was out of the war for a year while under repairs.

Kido Butai in the Indian Ocean

All this was prelude to the Japanese Indian Ocean operation. The Kido Butai, under Nagumo, left Kendari on 26 March and steamed through Lombok into the Indian Ocean. Five of its carriers were with Nagumo. *Kaga* was in drydock in Japan, and Yamamoto had released *Zuikaku* and *Shokaku* from home guard for this operation. The Kido Butai was headed for Ceylon. Two days later Vice Admiral Somerville, Commander-in-Chief of the British Eastern Fleet, learned they were coming.

With this ample warning the British cleared the harbor of Colombo by eight o'clock on Easter Sunday morning 5 April, when the Japanese attack struck. The British losses in the harbor were light, but the Japanese discovered two heavy cruisers at sea and promptly sent them to the bottom. Four days later they hit Trincomalee, the British Naval base in northeastern Ceylon. Again the British were successful in getting out of the harbor everything that could move. The Japanese, however, found the aircraft carrier *Hermes* and her escorting destroyer at sea and sank them both in short order.

Japanese submarines were operating in the Indian Ocean, and simultaneously the light carrier *Ryujo* with six heavy cruisers were raiding commerce in the Bay of Bengal. In this one week, the Allied losses in the Indian Ocean area totaled 130,000 tons of merchant shipping, one aircraft carrier, two heavy cruisers, and a destroyer. Moreover, practically all the R.A.F. planes in Ceylon had been lost, and the British Eastern Fleet was forced to retire to East African bases.

Their job well done, the Kido Butai retired from the Indian Ocean through the Strait of Malacca; past Singapore, now a Japanese port; through the South China Sea, practically a Japanese lake; and out through Luzon Strait unchallenged. Although its omnipotence was about to be blasphemed, the Kido Butai was at the peak of its power when it entered the Pacific Ocean, with plausible pretensions of control over that prodigious domain also. The first phase had ended. There were a few worries for Naval General Headquarters planners working up the second phase. Logistics were inadequate and reserves thin. There were not enough merchant ships to go around. Japanese carriers had lost more planes and pilots in the Indian Ocean operation than they had ready replacements for. Hard-worked ships needed upkeep and training. Nimitz, at Pearl Harbor, was not content to wait for the Japanese to get ready for phase two. American carrier raids in the Central Pacific and submarine operations everywhere promised future trouble, but these were solvable problems for a victorious navy.

Pacific Fleet Submarines

By the first of March the pattern of Pacific Fleet Submarine operations was fairly well established. The islands of the Central Pacific had been scouted and the location of important Japanese naval bases determined. There were five submarines on stations in the vicinity of Japan, one in the Carolines, and eight more en route to and from patrols—enough for Commander Submarines Pacific (Withers) to attempt a concentration against an important target.

Fleet Intelligence learned that a damaged Japanese carrier was leaving Palau, in the Southwest Pacific, for Yokosuka, the naval base in Tokyo Bay. It was probably *Kaga*, which they believed had taken one of *Sailfish's* torpedoes in Lombok Strait, but which was actually homeward bound to repair underwater damage from her encounter with rocks and shoals. Withers made a vigorous attempt to put submarines on her track, but the information was vague, the sea is broad; and the area to be covered, which looks so small and clear upon the chart, is a vast and rolling ocean veiled by storm and fog and dark of night.

Pollack made a high-speed run from her assigned area to lurk along the great circle course she assumed the carrier would take. *Gar* searched along a probable route for several days. *Narwhal*, en route to her Nansei Shoto operating area, loitered for three days on the great circle course between Palau and Yokosuka. *Kaga* got by unsighted.

By 4 March all the submarines were back guarding their assigned areas. *Narwhal* (Wilkins) sank a ship near Amami O Shima that day and *Tuna* (DeTar) sank another south of Kyushu. Five days later Wilkins, in the big and clumsy *Narwhal*, was patrolling his Nansei Shoto area on a moonlit but overcast night. There was a black squall to the northward and when two destroyers suddenly emerged from the murk, *Narwhal* attempted to evade on the surface to retain the initiative—but the destroyers were too close and coming up too fast.

Narwhal was a cranky ship to dive while carrying rudder, and this forced Wilkins to accept a submerging course that put *Narwhal* down almost in the path of one of the oncoming destroyers, in order to get her under at all. One destroyer crossed the track right astern of *Narwhal* at a range of only nine hundred yards, while the submarine was pumping and blowing like a wounded whale, to catch a difficult trim. Fortunately the Japanese listeners were all asleep or otherwise occupied. The other destroyer had passed out of sight, and while Wilkins was trying to locate it with the periscope, a carrier came out of the squall, range three thousand to four thousand yards, and almost dead astern of the submarine. There was nothing to do but accept the clumsy position *Narwhal* was in. Wilkins fired the two stern tubes, in a snap shot, with the best information he had. Under the circumstances it is not surprising that he missed. This was not the northbound *Kaga* that Wilkins had been searching for, but it would have served as well, if he had been able to torpedo her.

Japanese Plans for the Second Phase

From Marcus to the Coral Sea U.S. carriers had raided, hit and run, and supplementing what the carriers had done, submarines sank ten Japanese *marus* and damaged four others during March. The total tonnage of Japanese merchant shipping sunk added up to over a hundred thousand tons in that month. This was less than the Allied tonnage sunk by the Japanese during the Indian Ocean campaign alone, but the disparity between Japanese and Allied resources was large, and the smaller Japanese losses had greater economic import. At the end of the first phase the Japanese Army and Navy were expected to return a considerable portion of their shipping to control of the Ministry of Munitions, and the Army did actually return some ships. The Navy, on the other hand, found it necessary to requisition more. When Rear Admiral Tomioka, the Japanese planner at Navy General Headquarters, began planning for the second phase, he found logistics to be one of his most vexing restraints.

The dream of blasting across the Indian Ocean to join up with the Germans in the Near East was clearly within the capacity of the Combined Fleet, and just as clearly impossible to support logistically. Navy General Headquarters considered briefly a plan to invade northern Australia, to prevent buildup of a massive air offense they believed was coming from that continent. The Japanese Army calculated they would need ten divisions for the job. There was insufficient shipping to lift half that force, even if the Army would make the troops available. For essentially the same reason invasion of Hawaii was out, and a move toward Hawaii would also result in maximum exposure of Japanese shipping to U.S. submarine attack, a hazard toward which Tomioka was becoming very sensitive. With Japanese logistic limitation to consider, Tomioka decided that the best plan was an island-hopping advance through the Solomons, Fiji, and Samoa to cut American communication with Australia.

The staff of the Combined Fleet, under Yamamoto, reached an entirely different conclusion. Yamamoto, the creator of the plan to attack Pearl Harbor on 7 December, was deeply concerned with the vulnerability of Japan to a return carrier raid from the Central Pacific. He considered that eastward expansion of the Japanese perimeter was essential to protect the Japanese islands. The Combined Fleet Staff came up with a plan to capture Midway, the westernmost American base in the Central Pacific. A serious schism in the Japanese Navy resulted from these divergent views, but in the end Yamamoto won. The plans for the attack on Midway received the Emperor's seal of approval on 16 April.

Tokyo Air Raid

Thresher (Anderson) was on patrol that day, just south of Tokyo. She had been there for several days, making weather observations for which she carried two aerographer's mates on that patrol. The Japanese knew she was there because while she was waiting she sank a ship in her area. On the night of 16 April Anderson had a special mission to perform. He pulled *Thresher* out of her area to deceive the Japanese direction-finder net, and sent a long message, broadcasting the special weather observations they had made. This message was of vital interest to Halsey who, with *Hornet* and *Enterprise,* was several hundred miles to the eastward. Early on the morning of 18 April sixteen U. S. Army B-25 bombers, led by Lieutenant Colonel Doolittle, flew off *Hornet's* deck, to bomb Tokyo, as though to prove that Yamamoto was well justified in his concern for the Emperor's safety from carrier air raids.

The damage to Japan from this first air raid in her history was small in comparison with the many other air raids destined to come later; but all hell broke loose when the Japanese realized that their sacred soil had been violated by enemy bombs. The Second Fleet, just back from the strenuous first phase, came boiling out of the Inland Sea through the Bungo Suido. Bombers took off from Honshu. Every available submarine sortied in futile pursuit. The Kido Butai, entering the Pacific through Luzon Strait, spread out to search the southern areas, delaying the detachment of *Shokaku* and *Zuikaku* for a new venture, and cutting short the time the remaining carriers of the Kido Butai would have to get ready for the Midway operation. Halsey got clear away.

Strategic Movements of Japanese Submarines

At the end of first phase operations all Japanese submarines were withdrawn from the Indian Ocean and the East Indies and submarine operations in these areas were temporarily suspended. In the middle of April a task force consisting of *I-10, I-16, I-18, I-20,* and *I-30,* accompanied by the converted cruisers *Hokoku Maru* and *Aikoku Maru*, departed from Japan for Penang, where three of the submarines would load midgets to operate off Diego Suarez, Madagascar, where a part of the British Eastern Fleet was based. Taking advantage of the refueling opportunity this operation afforded, *I-30* would proceed from Madagascar around the Cape of Good Hope, and up through the Atlantic to Germany.

About the same time *I-22*, *I-24*, *I-28*, and *I-29* left Japan for Truk. They expected to operate in the Coral Sea and then load midgets at a Solomon Islands anchorage for further operations off eastern Australia. *I-21* and *I-27*, with reconnaissance missions in Australia and the South Sea islands, accompanied them. On 18 April these submarines were four hundred miles south of Honshu when Halsey raided Tokyo. They were immediately diverted to a scouting line east of the Bonin Islands, but they saw nothing of Halsey. As they were urgently needed in the Coral Sea they quickly abandoned this search and continued on for Truk. The majority of the rest of the Japanese submarines during April were preparing for the Midway operations. *I-121* left Japan with a cargo of aviation gasoline for the French Frigate Shoal refueling rendezvous with seaplanes.

Japanese Anti-Submarine Organization

Increased shipping losses during March and the shortage of shipping for military operations forced Japanese attention to neglected anti-submarine warfare. On 10 April the 1st Escort Groups, consisting of ten old destroyers and seven smaller vessels, was organized for escort duty between Singapore and Japan. The 2nd Escort Group of four old destroyers and three lesser ships took over escort work between Yokosuka and Truk. These forces were wholly inadequate.

Deficiencies in American torpedoes gave the Japanese an opportunity which they failed to grasp. The Japanese had seen many premature explosions of enemy torpedoes. Some of their ships made port with dud torpedoes sticking into their hulls. They believed that even if a tanker was torpedoed it would not sink. Expecting these conditions to continue, shipmasters preferred to sail unescorted rather than be bothered with convoy operations that would cut down on efficiency of shipping operations. The Combined Fleet resisted every effort to assign fleet destroyers to escort duty.

To the Japanese, it must have appeared that their anti-submarine operations were effective. In April, after their organization of the escort forces, their ships seemed to be almost immune to U.S. submarines. Only four Japanese ships were sunk by submarines during that month, and two of these were torpedoed by H.M.S. *Truant* in the Indian Ocean outside the sphere of the newly organized escort force. The dramatic reduction from the heavy March losses, however, was purely coincidence, having little to do with new Japanese anti-submarine activities.

U.S. Submarine Operations in April

In the Southwest, the move to Fremantle greatly increased the distance between submarines' base and the operating area, and drastically reduced the number of submarines that could be maintained on station north of the Malay Barrier. These few submarines could most profitably be employed against Japanese supply lines, particularly the oil supply routes from Borneo and Sumatra. Humanitarian and other considerations frequently intervened, however. During April, as the situation of Corregidor and Bataan grew desperate, more submarine efforts were directed to support the beleaguered forces. Five submarines made runs to Corregidor during April bringing food, ammunition, and critical supplies and taking out Army and Navy personnel and torpedoes.

Not all the rescue efforts were directed toward Corregidor. *Searaven* (Cassedy), en route to Corregidor with ammunition, was directed by radio to attempt rescue of Australian evaders on Timor. This was a desperate business of close inshore work in Japanese-patrolled waters, landing through surf to establish contact with the Australians while avoiding Japanese traps, and heroic work bringing sick and disabled men through high surf to the submarine. Thirty Australians were rescued. Later in the month *Sturgeon* made an unsuccessful attempt to rescue a party of R.A.A.F. men who were reported as evading the Japanese on a small island off Tjilatjap.

These activities diverted submarines from their normal business of sinking Japanese ships, but it is not always wise to fight a stoic war. Emotional resources are often more important than material ones. It is possible that in operations for the relief of Corregidor and other dramatic special missions submarines were most profitably employed, although it was certain that their efforts could not affect the outcome on Bataan, and pulling submarines out of their operating areas eased the pressure on Japanese shipping.

The Japanese respite from submarine warfare in the Southwest Pacific, by coincidence, extended to the Central Pacific also. During most of April there were only two submarines off the coast of Japan and in the East China Sea. The retreat from Java put both Formosa and Palau outside the effective range of Fremantle-based submarines, and Central

Pacific took over responsibility for those areas, although during April there were no submarines available to send in there. Japanese buildup in Rabaul drew increased attention to the South Pacific. *Tambor* was sent to reconnoiter Truk in the Carolines and Kavieng, on New Ireland, but April patrols throughout the South Sea islands were unproductive.

April was a month of movement, with many submarines en route to and from operating areas and many S-boats being shifted between strategic zones. S-34 and S-35 arrived in Dutch Harbor, Alaska, on 3 April to join S-18 and S-23, which had been hurriedly sent there from San Diego when the war broke out. S-boat patrols in the Aleutians during this stage of the war were of a cold, defensive nature.

Six S-boats (S-42, S-43, S-44, S-45, S-46, and S-47), with the tender *Griffin*, all under command of Captain Ralph Christie, were en route from Panama to Brisbane. This was an epic voyage of twelve thousand miles by submarines designed for coast defense. On April 15 they all made it after a forty-five-day trip, with only one stop at Bora Bora in the Society Islands for fuel. After his arrival Christie was given tactical command of all submarines at Brisbane.

S-38 arrived at Brisbane on 15 April from Fremantle. She was sent out promptly to patrol in the Gulf of Papua, near Port Moresby. On 21 April, with only five days in port after the trip from Panama, S-47 left Brisbane to patrol St. George's Channel, between New Ireland and New Britain. A few days later she was followed into that general location by S-42 and S-44. The need for all the haste was amply justified.

Carrier Operations in New Guinea Area

To counter the threat of the Japanese at Rabaul, Nimitz sent two carriers into the Coral Sea. On 8 March the Japanese extended their perimeter to the north coast of New Guinea and occupied Lae and Salamaua. *Yorktown* and *Lexington* ran up into the Gulf of Papua and sent their planes over the Owen Stanley Range to hit the Japanese beachhead two days later. Although the damage done to the Japanese was overestimated, it was a successful raid. Two large *marus* were sunk and a light cruiser, two destroyers, and several other vessels damaged. The Japanese schedule was delayed, although they went right ahead with the invasion of Finschhafen, New Guinea, on 10 March.

After this raid *Lexington* returned to Pearl Harbor, leaving *Yorktown's* task force to plow sterile furrows back and forth across the Coral Sea. As pelagic as a pod of great gray whales, they kept the sea, nursing from the tankers with which they rendezvoused in midocean. On 20 April *Yorktown* put into Tongatabu, to the southeast of Fiji, to anchor for the first time since early February.

·

Port Moresby Operation

The Japanese had a plan to take Port Moresby, on the south coast of New Guinea, with an amphibious operation similar to those that had been so successful during the first phase. As soon as Yamamoto was convinced that the Tokyo raiders had escaped, the Japanese went ahead with the Moresby operation. Radio intelligence kept them cognizant of an American carrier operating in the Coral Sea. They therefore knew that before the Fourth Fleet could attempt this operation it would have to be reinforced by carriers from the Kido Butai. This reinforcement was delayed by the hunt for Halsey.

About the middle of April Nimitz learned that the new carrier *Shoho* had joined the Japanese Fourth Fleet in the South Seas. He also learned that *Shokaku* and *Zuikaku*, from the Kido Butai, would join up about the first of May to cover powerful invasion forces setting out from Rabaul to capture Port Moresby. This was a direct threat to communications with Australia and it had to be stopped. The Japanese operation also presented a strategic opportunity to the Pacific Fleet. The Kido Butai, so long as it stayed together, was too powerful a force to be tackled; but a detachment of three carriers was of manageable size. Unfortunately, in addition to information and opportunity, Nimitz needed carriers. *Lexington* sailed from Pearl Harbor on 17 April to join *Yorktown* in the Coral Sea, but *Saratoga* was still under repairs on the West Coast, and Halsey with *Hornet* and *Enterprise* was up at the northern end of the long Pacific lunes of longitude staging a grandstand play, while the Japanese were preparing to make an end run around the tail of New Guinea to make a touchdown.

High Command

In early April the Joint Chiefs of Staff in Washington divided up the Pacific Theater of the war. General MacArthur became Commander-in-Chief Southwest Pacific Area in command of all Allied armed forces in the area. The defunct Asiatic Fleet was succeeded by the Southwest Pacific Force, and Vice Admiral H. F. Leary became Commander Southwest Pacific Forces. Wilkes at Fremantle and Christie at Brisbane were Submarine Task Force Commanders under Leary.

Admiral Nimitz at Pearl Harbor became Commander-in-Chief Pacific Ocean Area in addition to being Commander-in-Chief Pacific Fleet. Withers as Commander Submarines Pacific was the next echelon in the submarine command under Nimitz. The Pacific Ocean Area was subdivided into the North Pacific Area and the Central Pacific Area (for which no subordinate commander was appointed); and the South Pacific area, under Vice Admiral R. L. Ghormley with the title Commander South Pacific. Ghormley did not arrive in the South Pacific until the middle of May.

In this division of areas, the Solomons, the Bismarcks, and New Guinea fell to MacArthur's side of the line. The defense of Port Moresby was MacArthur's problem, but the problem of meeting the Japanese fleet belonged to Nimitz. There were three hundred shore-based planes in northern Australia and eastern New Guinea under MacArthur, but the Army pilots were unskilled in naval scouting, and the high-altitude bombing upon which they relied was ineffective against high-speed naval ships with plenty of sea room to maneuver. To check Japanese fleet forces Nimitz had to send a task force into the Coral Sea. The submarines at Brisbane were under MacArthur and his subordinate naval commanders. Before any of Nimitz's submarines penetrated into the Southwest Pacific Area their plan of operation had to be carefully coordinated with Southwest Pacific Forces in order to avoid mutual interference. As the cooperation of air forces, surface forces, and submarines, all operating in the same area is complicated enough when they are all under the same command, the divided command gave promise of many snafus to come.

On 1 May *Yorktown* and *Lexington's* task forces rendezvoused in the Coral Sea west of New Hebrides, and Rear Admiral F. J. Fletcher became officer in tactical command. Two Australian cruisers and one additional U.S. cruiser joined him later. It was a strong force but not strong enough. *Shokaku* and *Zuikaku* sailed from Truk on the same day as Striking Force for a complicated organization of Japanese Invasion Forces and Support Forces and Covering Forces. Six Japanese submarines took up their screening position in the Coral Sea. Three American S-boats were on station along the route the Japanese forces might take— and the stage was set for the Battle of the Coral Sea.

VIII

MAY 1942

The Battle of the Coral Sea

The Battle of the Coral Sea opened on 4 May, by an American carrier strike on a Japanese Invasion Force at Tulagi, just off Florida Island in the Solomon Islands. The Japanese Striking Force (*Zuikaku* and *Shokaku* with two heavy cruisers and six destroyers), under Vice Admiral Takagi, was too far away to retaliate. They entered the Coral Sea from the eastward on 6 May. The next morning Japanese carrier search planes found the tanker *Neosho* and her escorting destroyer and mistook them for a carrier and a cruiser. The Japanese launched an all-out strike and sank both these ships, but while they were so engaged American carrier planes caught the Japanese Covering Force and sank the new light carrier *Shoho*. It was not until the morning of 8 May that the two main carrier forces found each other. An exchange of carrier strikes took place. *Shokaku* was hit by three bombs and put out of action but survived. *Zuikaku* was not hit but lost most of her air group. On the American side *Yorktown* was hit but was able to continue flight operations. *Lexington* took two bomb hits and two torpedoes. Her fires and her underwater damages were brought under control, but later in the day a gasoline explosion in a damaged compartment turned her into a roaring inferno and she had to be abandoned and sunk.

Submarines did not take an effective part in the Battle of the Coral Sea. Four Japanese submarines (*I-22, I-24, I-28,* and *I-29*) were on a line 250 miles southeast of Guadalcanal and two (*RO-33* and *RO-34*) were on patrol south of Port Moresby. They made no contacts. Four American S-boats were on patrol, after superhuman effort to cross the great South Pacific, to reach the operation theater in time. *S-47* and *S-44* were stationed in St. George's Channel when the Japanese Invasion Force came through, yet American submarines did not sight the Japanese. But submarine operations, preceded by weeks of slow movement over long distances, persisted for weeks after the battle, like reverberations of an explosion in the deep sea.

Employment of U.S. Submarines

By the first of May the tide of U.S. submarine activity was flooding again after the April ebb. In Commander Submarines Pacific's operating room the markers for eighteen submarines at sea dotted the position charts—in the Marshalls, the Carolines, off Japan, in the East China Sea, and coming and going between Pearl Harbor and their patrol areas. Five fleet submarines, out of Fremantle, were in the South China Sea and the East Indies. *Spearfish* made the last run out of Corregidor on 3 May with twenty-five extra passengers. *Sailfish* was en route there with antiaircraft ammunition when Corregidor surrendered. Four S-boats out of Brisbane were on patrol in the Bismarck Archipelago and the Coral Sea.

On the first submarine patrols of the war, although no one said much about it, it was tacitly assumed that half of the submarines would not return from their first war patrol. By 1 May, four submarines had been lost in the Southwest Pacific, yet in the Pacific Ocean Area not a single submarine had been lost to enemy action. It was evident that submarine warfare was not so grim a business as peacetime maneuvers had indicated it would be. Air search radar had proved its value. Although early submarine radar could not pick out a ship on the surface of the sea from "sea return," it was capable of locating planes that were invisible from the submarine's bridge, and along a blacked-out and hostile coast it could distinguish landmarks for use in navigation. Radar operators were still relatively inexperienced and the set required constant attention and adjustment, but it made surface operation much less dangerous.

Commander Submarines Pacific's staff still had an abiding faith in the torpedo despite the known skepticism of Wilkes, who had the submarine command at Fremantle. The Bureau of Ordnance, in reply to one of Wilkes' inquiries, admitted that Mark 14 torpedoes ran four feet deeper than set. Commander Submarines Pacific (Withers) thereupon ordered his submarines to take this into account, but to set torpedoes to run five feet under the keel of targets to obtain influence explosions. To the protests of submarine commanding officers that this practice robbed them of many earned successes, the staff turned a deaf ear.

The shortage of torpedoes was still pressing, yet despite this shortage Commander Submarines Pacific Staff had come around to the view that it was necessary to fire torpedoes in spreads. Because of the error inherent in submarine range estimates, and the agility of Japanese ships in maneuvers to evade, solo shots resulted in a high percentage of misses. Comsubpac therefore canceled previous instructions and directed that spreads of two or more torpedoes should be fired to insure at least one hit. From the earliest patrols Withers had insisted on submarines spending a greater portion of their time at sea on the surface, rather than submerged, in order to cover areas more effectively, and to retain the initiative their higher surface speed gave them. In this he was vindicated by accumulating experience and by technical developments in radar.

Commander-in-Chief Pacific and his staff still dictated the strategic disposition of submarines in the Pacific, and approved each individual patrol assignment. Withers, as Commander Submarines Pacific, had very little freedom in determining submarine dispositions but, through improvement in communications, he had acquired the ability to exercise considerable control over submarines already on patrol. The aftermath of the Battle of the Coral Sea, with a damaged carrier returning to Japan through all his submarine operating areas, gave Withers a good opportunity to lay a submarine trap.

Pursuit of Shokaku

When carrier planes from Yorktown and Lexington last saw Shokaku, the big Japanese carrier was enveloped in smoke and flames, listing heavily, and headed north out of the Coral Sea. She had been hit by dive bombers. The torpedo squadrons also claimed four hits, but aviation torpedoes were no better than submarine torpedoes and despite the gallant attacks of American torpedo planes, Shokaku had suffered no underwater damage. Withers believed she had been torpedoed and slowed down, to make her a prime submarine target. She was just as supple as ever in evading submarine traps, but Withers went after her with energy. His first concern was to cover Truk, into which it was practically certain a damaged Japanese carrier would run for emergency repairs.

Tautog (Willingham) was en route to Fremantle from Pearl Harbor to replace one of the submarines from Southwest Pacific being sent home for navy yard overhaul. Anticipating that the action in the Coral Sea would be reflected at Truk, Withers ordered Tautog to proceed to the south side of Truk atoll to catch any traffic through Otta Pass. On 9 May she was off Ponape, when she received several dispatches concerning the Coral Sea action. Willingham concluded that surface operations during daylight, even in this area of intensive Japanese activity, was justified by the necessity to get on station as soon as possible. With one wary eye on the overcast sky and his trust in the SD radar, he continued on the surface at fifteen knots and on 10 May arrived in his area.

Truk atoll can be entered from the south at either Otta Pass or South Pass. The configuration of the big atoll and the proximity of Kuop atoll made it difficult to cover both passes with one submarine, and the best information then available favored Otta as the more important entrance.

Either because this information was false, or because the Japanese carrier slipped by him at night, Willingham sighted nothing but small sampans the first four days in his position five miles off the reef at Otta Pass. The Japanese carrier must have entered Truk sometime on the eleventh. Just before dawn on 15 May a large darkened ship came up from the southeastward and *Tautog* closed to fire torpedoes. She was in firing range before the increasing light of dawn revealed that her target was a hospital ship, illegally proceeding without lights, and Willingham broke off the attack. That afternoon a large freighter came up from the same direction. *Tautog* hit her with one torpedo. A second torpedo made a circular run and Willingham hastily went deep to avoid being hoist with his own petard. When he came back up to periscope depth, the freighter had beached itself on Kuop atoll. This was *Goyo Maru,* which had been part of the Port Moresby invasion group.

Still hoping to intercept cripples from the Battle of the Coral Sea, Willingham guarded Otta Pass. Early in the morning of 17 May he sighted a Japanese submarine of the I-class on a northerly course on the surface, at about three thousand yards range. *Tautog* went to General Quarters, hurriedly getting the forward tubes ready to fire. The sound operator reported that the Japanese submarine was "pinging" with the supersonic, and then immediately afterward he exclaimed that she had fired a torpedo. Willingham pulled the plug and went deep. Almost instantly he realized that what the soundman heard was *Tautog's* own preparation of the forward tubes rather than Japanese torpedoes, but the opportunity had been lost. When *Tautog* got back up to periscope depth the I-boat was out of range. Within an hour a second I-class submarine came by on the same course. Four minutes after it had been sighted, *Tautog* fired two torpedoes and then ducked down to 150 feet to avoid retaliation by the Japanese. Willingham heard one torpedo detonate. Five minutes later, when he came up to periscope depth, nothing was in sight. These circumstances led him to believe he had sunk that Japanese submarine, but he must have been mistaken.

This should have been enough for one day's work. A submarine commander, after surviving two encounters with enemy submarines in a single day, might be excused for feeling he had used up his allotment of good luck. About eleven o'clock that same morning, however, another Japanese submarine was sighted on the same bearing, same course, evidently coming home over the same track her colleagues had used to return from a patrol line they had occupied in the Battle of the Coral Sea. Willingham had a good look at this one and identified it as *I-28.* *Tautog* attacked with two torpedoes, one of which hit and disabled *I-28* but did not sink her. Willingham closed the range and fired a third torpedo, to which the Japanese submarine responded by firing two torpedoes from her stern tubes. *Tautog* evaded by going deep, and *Tautog's*

torpedo went home to sink *I-28.* Thus, although Willingham did not
sight *Shokaku,* he had plenty of action south of Truk before he proceeded on to Fremantle.

In early May *Gar* (McGregor) was patrolling in the Marshall Islands. On 5 May Withers sent her orders to proceed to Truk and patrol
Piaanu Pass, the western entrance to the big atoll. She proceeded at
periscope depth during the daylight, because of the proximity of enemy
bases and the prevalence of low clouds. As a result, on 11 May, when
Withers sent her more specific instructions for the interception of
Shokaku, McGregor found himself unable to reach the assigned position
by the specified time. He arrived off Piaanu Pass on 13 May, and from
then until 18 May when he departed from Truk for Fremantle, he saw
only one Japanese vessel, and that one he believed to be a decoy ship.

The Japanese were, in fact, using only South Pass and North Pass for
heavy ship traffic into Truk. Most of the other breaks in the fringing reef
were protected by defensive minefields. Piaanu Pass was heavily mined,
and so was Otta and Northeast Pass, although according to the best
intelligence available to Withers these three entrances would be the most
probable routes for returning carriers to take. Thus *Greenling* (Bruton),
which was given Northeast Pass to guard, was in for a frustrating experience.

Greenling had been assigned the Truk area to patrol. On 4 May she
sank *Kinjosan Maru,* a 3262-ton cargo ship, about seventy-five miles north
of North Pass, but in the reshuffle to guard the best entrances to Truk
Greenling was ordered to cover Northeast Pass. She arrived there on
6 May and in the next few days sighted several ships inside the lagoon,
proceeding between North Pass and Dublon Island anchorage. For this
traffic, the fringing reef was the best possible anti-submarine barrier.
Greenling reported these ship movements to Pearl Harbor and was told
to remain on station assigned and report contacts for the benefit of submarines farther north. On 16 May Bruton watched a Japanese carrier,
escorted by four destroyers, move majestically up from the southern
anchorage and steam safely out North Pass. Though *Greenling* moved
in close to the northeast channel, hoping the carrier would change its
route, the Japanese ship stayed completely out of the submarine's reach.
The next day two heavy cruisers followed. All these contacts Bruton
dutifully reported, usually after many retransmissions and vexatious rep-
etitions, and not until after several hours had passed before he could
surface to use the radio.

The carrier *Greenling* sighted must have been *Zuikaku,* for *Shokaku*
had preceded her by a few days. Although all the major Japanese re-
turnees from the Battle of the Coral Sea passed safely through Truk,
they still had the gantlet of the northern submarines to run. *Cuttlefish*
was in the Saipan area, but the Japanese entirely bypassed that vicinity,

so it turned out that only Kirkpatrick, who had put *Triton* on *Shokaku's* estimated route, saw her again during her perilous trip.

Triton, after two successful weeks in the East China Sea, was just to the west of Okinawa on 14 May. She intercepted several messages from Comsubpac to other submarines on patrol, referring to a "wounded bear" coming up from Truk to the Inland Sea. Although these messages were not directed to *Triton,* Kirkpatrick decided to come through the Nansei Shoto into the Pacific, to be in "harm's way" if anything developed.

About five o'clock the next afternoon, after making a radar-guided night run through the island chain, *Triton* sighted the masts of a vessel to the northwest. Closing the range, Kirkpatrick discovered two deep-sea fishing vessels, flying the Japanese flag. He sank them both by gunfire. After this action *Triton* set course to the eastward. She had been somewhat delayed and her radar had been knocked out of adjustment by the shock of her own gunfire, just when she might need it most. Kirkpatrick had picked up more messages to several submarines, spread out from Truk to Japan, instructing them to intercept the "wounded bear." From these messages Kirkpatrick worked out the whole story of the pursuit of *Shokaku.* Without being invited, he decided to take a hand.

Triton left her assigned patrol area to take up a position along the route of the damaged Japanese carrier. Submarine doctrine permitted a commanding officer to deviate from his instructions whenever he had new information not available to his seniors. Kirkpatrick reasoned that Commander Submarines Pacific did not know that *Triton* had left the East China Sea and was thus available for the bear hunt. Although the submarine could copy Comsubpac's dispatches it was difficult for *Triton* to raise Pearl Harbor radio, and the effort to do so would reveal her position to the Japanese direction-finder net. Kirkpatrick decided to keep quiet and take up a favorable position for any adventure that might evolve.

On 16 May *Triton* arrived at the position that Kirkpatrick had selected, and dove before dawn. He had carefully worked this out as a chart exercise, and computed that the earliest possible sighting, assuming a speed of sixteen knots, would be quarter after three in the afternoon. Twenty minutes past the hour, he sighted a destroyer at about six miles' distance. The sea was flat calm, and the weather clear, except for a heavy haze all around the horizon. Almost immediately after sighting the destroyer a carrier popped out of the haze, making sixteen knots on a northerly course. *Triton* was in a very unfavorable position. This was about the end of her patrol and she had only one remaining torpedo forward and four aft. She was out at 6700 yards' range and after less than a minute on the normal approach course Kirkpatrick realized she would be unable to close. He tried to change course to bring the stern tubes to bear, but during this maneuver the range opened out until it was too great to justify even a long chance shot.

The carrier was zigzagging but Kirkpatrick had solved the zigzag pattern during the brief approach. Therefore, despite the fact that it was early afternoon, that air cover was very probable, and the carrier had a destroyer screen which he could only hope was still up ahead, he surfaced *Triton* twelve miles in the carrier's wake. At full power on four engines *Triton* made 19½ knots in pursuit on the carrier's base course until midnight, when even Kirkpatrick was willing to concede that *Shokaku* had gotten clean away.

"To come so far and get so close was hard to take," and perhaps he was entitled to a consolation prize. The next afternoon, while working back toward her proper area, *Triton* encountered a Japanese submarine, probably right after it had surfaced. Kirkpatrick fired one torpedo. He watched it hit and blow pieces of the stern of the Japanese submarine a hundred feet in the air. *I-64* went down in two minutes, with her bow high in the air. *I-64* was on her way from Sasebo to Kwajalein to take part in the Midway operation, and the Japanese never knew what happened to her.

Drum, on patrol off Tokyo Bay, had been ordered south to help cover the entrance to the Inland Sea, and although she sank a ship while waiting she did not sight the carrier. *Grenadier*, patrolling off western Kyushu, was ordered to change station to cover Bungo Suido, through which *Shokaku* entered the Inland Sea on 17 May. *Grenadier* arrived there on 16 May but found the area shrouded in heavy fog, and she made no contacts.

Pollack (Moseley), a veteran of two previous patrols off Japan, was en route to a patrol area off eastern Kyushu on 11 May when she intercepted messages to other submarines indicating that a "wounded bear" was coming up from Truk to Japan. Calculation convinced Moseley that *Pollack* would have difficulty reaching the enemy's probable course and still maintain an economic speed which would leave her fuel enough to remain on station for the duration of her patrol. The next day, while still a thousand miles from her area, she sighted a sampan which, with a good deal of difficulty, she destroyed by gunfire. On May 14 Comsubpac gave Moseley further information and changed *Pollack's* patrol area assignment to enable her to intercept the carrier. Moseley figured he could get there by dawn on 17 May. As this was the day that *Shokaku* arrived in port, it is probable that the Japanese carrier had already passed by *Pollack's* station by the time the submarine arrived.

Moseley continued to patrol his station, submerged during daylight, and plagued by sampans that seemed thick as sardines in that area. There were frequently so many sampans around him that he was prevented from making periscope exposures for fear of being sighted. On the night of 17 May he shot up one sampan in his area, and on the night of 20 May sank two more with the three-inch gun, while two others doused their running lights and escaped in the darkness. This preoccupation with small game while hunting "wounded bear" should have kept the bigger game out of the area. But it did not.

Comsubpac warned Moseley by dispatch that shipping had been observed to hug the coast in his area of operations, so about two o'clock in the morning of 21 May, *Pollack* was close inshore near the eastern coast of Kyushu. They sighted a dark object which Moseley at first thought was a slow-moving ship on a parallel course. As the situation cleared he realized that the target was much faster, and he estimated the speed at fourteen knots. At two thousand yards' range he fired four torpedoes, and only as they left the tubes did he recognize his target as an aircraft carrier. The torpedoes missed, probably because of too low a speed estimate. This must have been *Zuikaku* coming home and she too made port without further adventure.

U.S. Submarine Successes in the Central Pacific

The first half of the month of May was dominated by the effort to knock off *Shokaku* before she carried her damages home for repairs. There were other notable developments during this time, however, and even submarines engaged in the pursuit found that it interfered but little with their regular business. *Drum* (Rice), later diverted to the *Shokaku* gantlet, arrived off Nagoya on 1 May. About midnight that same night she made a contact which she identified as a medium-size ship with considerable top hamper. *Drum* fired two torpedoes, and as the second one left the tube realized that a destroyer was closing at high speed. She made a quick dive to a hundred feet to avoid being rammed, firing another torpedo at the destroyer on her way down. This was *Drum's* first patrol, and for Rice, her commanding officer, it was the first attack on an enemy ship. Under the circumstances the Division Commander, reviewing his patrol, was charitable in his assessment that *Drum* had damaged a medium-size freighter. This, however, was one case in which damage to the enemy was underestimated. *Mizuho*, a 9000-ton seaplane carrier, was sunk in *Drum's* attack, and as of that date it was the largest naval vessel the Japanese had lost in the war.

An interesting contact also occurred in early May down at Kwajalein in the Marshall Islands. While closely patrolling there off Roi Island, on 4 May, *Gato* got in a shot at an aircraft carrier entering the atoll. She fired five torpedoes, and although she thought she had two hits, the next day she sighted the undamaged carrier safely inside the reef. This was *Kasuga Maru*, a light carrier converted from a fast merchant ship, and still identified by the American Navy under her peacetime name. Japan converted five big merchant ships by building flight decks on them. As combat carriers they were nearly useless, and even as escort carriers they were not very successful. Their main use was as aircraft ferries, but in May they were an unknown quantity and when *Gato* got her first sight of one it was believed that they would be a big factor in the Pacific war, where aircraft carriers were the main element in control of the sea. *Kasuga Maru* was renamed *Taiyo* upon her conversion, and when American translators first encountered the Japanese characters used in her new name, they were misread as *Otaka*. Under all three names, she was destined to be shot at by American submarines until probably she had survived more submarine attacks than any other ship in the Japanese Navy, before a submarine finally sank her on 18 August 1944.

Grenadier, whose assigned station was off the west coast of Kyushu, in the East China Sea, had an unusual success. Lent, who had previously commanded *Triton*, took *Grenadier* out on her second run. On 8 May, about the time of evening twilight, he encountered a southbound convoy of six medium-size freighters plus one outstandingly big ship which he identified as *Taiyo Maru* (which should not be confused with *Taiyo*, the escort carrier). He was tempted to trail the convoy until after dark, when his surface speed might give him an opportunity to make repeated attacks, but the situation developed to his advantage so he decided to take a bird in the hand and go for the big ship. No escort vessels were sighted, but with such an important convoy, Lent assumed escorts were present and that there probably was an air cover as well. He made a careful approach, with sparing use of the periscope, and at about seven-thirty in the evening reached the position he wanted, undetected.

Lent fired four torpedoes at the big ship in a spread to hit the bow with the first, and the rest spaced out along her length with the last one aimed to hit her in the stern. The middle two were set at twenty-eight feet depth to go under in accordance with doctrine, but the first and last were set for impact. The soundman heard all four run hot and normal. Two explosions were heard, timed to identify the hits as the first and last torpedoes fired. The middle two missed. These circumstances, coupled with some exasperating misses later in the patrol, caused Lent to complain bitterly about the malfunction of the magnetic exploders when he returned from his patrol.

At the moment though he had his hands full. Two minutes after firing his torpedoes, a stick of bombs exploded close overhead. *Grenadier* went deep, and as she passed ninety feet on the way down, there were several more explosions. Lent did not have an opportunity to observe the effect of his hits, or to evade and come up to the surface to pursue the convoy

either. In a very short time *Grenadier* heard high-speed screws overhead, and depth charges started raining down. *Grenadier* had a defective stern tube bearing that made a loud squealing noise at depths
greater than 150 feet, and this handicapped her evasion. In the next
four hours the Japanese followed the submarine and dropped thirty-six
depth charges, some of them close enough to severely shake up the
submarine, but *Grenadier* was running at 250 feet depth and the charges
were set too shallow to do lethal damage. About two o'clock in the
morning Lent managed to surface and put a quick charge in the battery,
but before four o'clock sound picked up approaching high-speed screws
again, and *Grenadier* submerged to spend another full day as fox for the
Japanese anti-submarine hounds.

This persistent pursuit indicated that the Japanese were unusually
vexed by the attack, as well they might be. Lent had correctly identified
Taiyo Maru. She was a transport of 14,457 tons displacement, one of
Japan's biggest ships, headed south with a task force of Japanese sci-
entists, engineers, and technicians to organize the resources of the con-
quered territory to support the Japanese war effort. Almost all of them
were lost when *Taiyo Maru* went down.

Triton *in Tung Hai*

Before *Triton* became involved in the attempt to intercept the homeward-bound damaged *Shokaku,* she spent two weeks in the East China
Sea, an area known to generations of sailors by its Chinese name, Tung
Hai. Kirkpatrick took *Triton* into Tung Hai through Nansei Shoto on
29 April and spent the next day submerged, observing the flat oily swells
with fifteen feet of periscope above the surface to give her range of
vision. A little after seven o'clock on the morning of 1 May, the officer on
periscope watch saw smoke at about ten miles' distance. Within half an
hour, six freighters and one escort vessel were in plain view.

The sea was glassy calm. The sound conditions were poor. The Japanese ships were about a thousand yards apart, approximately in column,
riding high and light on a northeasterly course, making about ten knots.
One escort was a little ahead and on the starboard bow of the leading
ship, and Kirkpatrick assumed that there would be another on the port
side. This proved to be correct. Both escorts were torpedo boats, and
neither one was using supersonic searches. Kirkpatrick came on in and
fired two torpedoes at the leading freighter, shifted his periscope angle,
and fired two more at the next in line. The first two torpedoes hit, the
second pair missed.

Triton kept a wary watch on the escort. The nearer escort turned toward them full speed. *Triton* speeded up, went down to seventy-five feet, ran down the same course she had fired the torpedoes, and passed under the Japanese column between two freighters. This maneuver confused the escort, which dropped some depth charges harmlessly at a distance.

When her torpedo tubes were reloaded and the excitement on the surface died down, Kirkpatrick came up to periscope depth to look around. The convoy was disappearing over the northern horizon, leaving one damaged ship behind. *Triton* set course for it. The target was abandoned and drifting, and Kirkpatrick maneuvered for perfect position to finish it off. From a range of eight hundred yards, with ninety track, and a cold setup, he fired one torpedo set at thirty feet to pass under the keel for an influence explosion. It went down the range straight and hot, passed under the target, and nothing happened. *Triton* then fired another torpedo and this one exploded under the target and broke the ship's back. It was *Calcutta Maru*. She settled fast as Kirkpatrick took pictures through the periscope.

The next night they were only twenty miles off the ten-fathom curve fringing the continent of Asia. During the day, through the periscope, they watched the Chinese junks creep by, with their high poops and forecastles and their strangely shaped battened sails, as egocentric as they ever were through the centuries they had sailed the Tung Hai. At night *Triton* surfaced and ran down along the coast. Hieshan Tao light was burning as usual, but was difficult to see in the misty weather. Kirkpatrick knew that Japanese traffic must be moving through these waters, carrying supplies and munitions to their conquering southern armies, and bringing back the oil and tin and rice and raw materials of Malay and the Spice Islands. Coasting along China would be their most protected route, and through Tung Hai Japanese freighters must be shuttling back and forth weaving the threads of Empire, but wherever they were Kirkpatrick could not seem to find them.

At dusk on the night of 3 May he sighted a small freighter, poking along just inside the ten-fathom curve. When it was dark, *Triton* surfaced and set course to the southeast at seventeen knots to head it off. The night was dark. The sea was smooth and oily. *Triton's* wake stretched out astern a welt of phosphorescence and the bow wave broke in patches and moons of bioluminescence that glowed across the forward deck. The way was cluttered up with Chinese junks, plodding aimlessly along, completely blacked out as they had always been in peace or war, trusting to the white round eyes painted on their black hulls, and to the mercy of Kuan Yin to keep the foreign devils from running them down. A collision with a big junk might be disastrous for *Triton*, so far from home and so dependent upon her ability to operate submerged, to get back there. As she dodged in and out among the junks, it became apparent that the freighter had somehow evaded them, probably by running in to Wenchow to anchor for the night.

After days and nights of frustration the night of 5–6 May brought swift action. At two o'clock in the morning they sighted a darkened vessel at four miles' distance and changed course to investigate. In a few minutes they had contact with a convoy of several vessels proceeding southwest at ten knots in a disposition so loose it could hardly be called a formation. At first Kirkpatrick could not locate the escorts. Assuming they must be up ahead, he decided to stay on the surface and attack the last ships in the convoy.

About an hour after the first contact he fired two torpedoes at the trailing ship. One torpedo sank immediately after firing, and the other missed ahead of the target. It seemed almost certain that the Japanese would see its broad wake, but when nothing happened Kirkpatrick came in again to attack the same ship. A destroyer came down along the convoy on reverse course, and Kirkpatrick watched it cautiously but persisted in his surface attack. At twelve hundred yards he fired two torpedoes. At least one of them hit and blew up *Taigen Maru*. *Triton* put the destroyer astern and quite easily evaded her.

As there appeared to be no immediate danger from the destroyer, *Triton* stayed on the surface and changed course to the south to run around the convoy and gain position for another attack. They sent a radio to Comsubpac giving the convoy's position, course, and speed, but got no answer. The first faint color was in the eastern sky when Kirkpatrick decided he had gained enough southing, and turned in again toward the convoy. In a few minutes he sighted the destroyer up ahead with the convoy plodding along behind. Although the sky was becoming very bright behind him Kirkpatrick stayed on the surface until he had the position he wanted. At 0524 he made a quick dive, having maneuvered on the surface with the destroyer and convoy in view for thirty-two minutes. A half hour later he fired two torpedoes at the third freighter in line, quickly checked the course and speed of the next ship, and fired two more at her also. One of the torpedoes of the first pair hit. The second target apparently successfully maneuvered to avoid, and thwarted Kirkpatrick's ambition to score a double.

When the torpedo hit, the destroyer turned toward *Triton*. Kirkpatrick went down to seventy-five feet and tried his old trick of running under the convoy, but the destroyer stuck to his trail, searching back and forth, tracked constantly by *Triton's* listeners. Kirkpatrick had no trouble maneuvering to keep the destroyer bearing always astern, but after about twenty minutes of this the destroyer stopped, evidently relying on passive listening to locate the submarine. *Triton* kept opening the range, but after listening for four or five minutes the destroyer charged straight in. While this fencing was going on *Triton's* crew seemed anxious to have the destroyer drop the first depth charge and get it over with. When it came, it was close enough to satisfy everybody, knocking loose nuts and bolts off the bulkhead, but *Triton* suffered no real damage.

The next week Kirkpatrick tacked back and forth across the East China Sea, trying to locate another Japanese convoy. On 14 May *Triton* was just to the westward of Okinawa, looking for enemy shipping, when they picked up Comsubpac's dispatch about the wounded bear.

Submarine Shifts and Command Change

During the latter part of May Central Pacific submarines were being reshuffled to take up station for the Battle of Midway. A plan had been worked out to send fleet-type submarines home from Australia for navy yard overhaul, and replace them by submarines from Pearl Harbor. The prospect of an all-out battle for Midway delayed the plan, for Nimitz pre-empted Southwest Pacific submarines routed through Pearl Harbor to the West Coast, and held up their replacements en route to Australia until the Midway crisis was over.

On 14 May, in a routine command change, Rear Admiral R. H. English relieved Rear Admiral Withers as Commander Submarines Pacific. Wilkes, whose orders home had been received before the war started, and who had been continued on in the emergency, was relieved by Captain C. A. Lockwood on 26 May. Lockwood was promoted to rear admiral three days later. He was given the title of Commander Submarines Southwest Pacific (Comsubsowespac), and as type commander in the area he had administrative command over the Brisbane submarines as well as both administrative and tactical command over the Fremantle-based submarines. Because of the distance between the two bases, the administrative command over Brisbane submarines was limited, and Christie retained complete tactical control of these submarines.

U.S. Submarines in the Southwest Pacific

The number of submarines operating out of Fremantle had been reduced by transfer of S-boats to the eastern coast of Australia. The detachment of fleet-type submarines for the long journey back to the United States for navy yard overhaul further reduced the number of submarines available, but Submarines Southwest Pacific were not idle. *Skipjack* (Coe) was on her third patrol in May and sank three ships in the South China Sea despite great difficulties with torpedoes. Coe, an outstanding submarine commander in action, was also articulate and forthright in his patrol reports. He summarizes his torpedo difficulties with the statement: "To make round trips of 8500 miles into enemy waters to gain attack position undetected within 800 yards of enemy ships, only to find that the torpedoes run deep, or over half the time will fail to explode, seems to be an undesirable manner of gaining information which might be determined any morning within a few miles of a torpedo station in the presence of comparatively few hazards." Lockwood, with little faith in the torpedoes, had instructed his submarines to favor shallow-depth settings, but rather than correcting the difficulty this revealed that the faults with torpedoes were many and complex.

Salmon (McKinney) had a new kind of torpedo difficulty. She was operating out of Fremantle on patrol in the South China Sea in May. On 25 May she sank the 11,441-ton repair ship *Asahi*. Three days later she encountered the passenger-cargo ship *Ganges Maru* in the middle of the South China Sea. She fired three torpedoes and hit *Ganges Maru* amidships. The Japanese ship stopped and lowered boats, but McKinney was not satisfied that the ship would surely sink, so he closed to 750 yards, and fired a straight stern tube shot, aimed to hit the target at right angles and amidships. The torpedo was set to run at ten feet, and it seemed improbable, with a ship in *Ganges Maru's* condition, that the torpedo could miss in depth or otherwise; but it did not explode. He then fired another torpedo under identical circumstances and this also missed or failed to explode. McKinney decided to waste no more torpedoes. *Ganges Maru* sank later anyway, but the mystery of the non-explosive torpedoes remained unsolved.

S-Boat Operations

The S-boats out of Brisbane continued to operate under the direction of Captain R. W. Christie, and during the month of May reaped a delayed harvest from all the effort and hardship that they had expended. On 11 May S-42 (Kirk), southeast of New Ireland, encountered the Japanese minelayer *Okinoshima* that had been part of the Tulagi Invasion Force. He sank it with four torpedoes, and the loss of this 4400-ton ship helped balance the Japanese and American accounts for the Battle of the Coral Sea. The next day S-44 (Moore), in the same vicinity, sank the 5644-ton converted salvage vessel *Shoei Maru*. Up north the S-boats patrolled the Aleutian Islands from their base in Dutch Harbor, and gained nothing but an extensive knowledge of submariners' ability to endure cold, and high seas and fog and Arctic storms.

Gun Attacks

Coming and going to their patrol areas off Japan, Pacific Fleet submarines found a ring of Japanese fishing sampans and picket boats at
six hundred to eight hundred miles' radius from Japan. *Hornet* and *Enterprise* penetrated this line in the Doolittle raid, and the pickets made
radio contact reports on the carriers out at eight hundred miles. Several
of these pickets were sunk by dive bombers and cruisers' gunfire of
Halsey's task force. Prisoners picked up confirmed that these small ships
were part of the organized defenses of Japan. Generally they were too
small to warrant expenditure of torpedoes, but to harass the picket lines
as much as possible submarines were directed to sink these spitkids by
gunfire whenever a good opportunity presented itself.

In *Triton*, Kirkpatrick, who had had a tour of destroyer duty, had much
greater faith in the gun than most submarine skippers, and he carefully
trained and drilled his gun crew for such an occasion. His first opportunity came early on the way out to patrol Tung Hai. On the night of
23 April, 250 miles north of Marcus, *Triton* was tooling along on the surface when the lookout sighted a bright light to the westward. Kirkpatrick
changed course to investigate. The target was illuminated with so many
bright lights that it was difficult to judge its size, but assuming that these
lights must be just as blinding to the target's crew as to the submarine,
Kirkpatrick closed on the surface at eighteen knots. He crossed astern of
the enemy ship (which to complete the mystery was lying to in the middle of the ocean), and fired a torpedo at point-blank range. It missed
but the quarry did not seem alarmed. *Triton* fired another torpedo, and
it missed also. Kirkpatrick then assumed that he had greatly misjudged
the size of his target. *Triton* circled around astern, manned the deck gun
and the machine gun on the bridge, and came in again.

As *Triton* came charging in at eighteen knots, with a white bone of
sibilant seas under her black bow, the gun's crew in a tense group
around the 3-inch gun on her after deck waited for the cue to begin their
formal ballet of service to the gun. The lookouts on their perches on the
periscope shears were swaying silhouettes against the sky as *Triton* responded to the gentle rolling seas. The spotter on the after deck balanced
straddle-legged against the motion, with his binoculars glued to his eyes
to search the target, called out data for the sight setter, at the gun, in a
strident voice that seemed a sacrilege in the solemn hush, waiting to be
shattered by the raucous gun. To Kirkpatrick on the bridge, conning his
new command, submarine warfare seemed not far different from the
gallant dash and speed of destroyer action. Then the target, at last becoming aware of the submarine, doused its lights and got under way at

ten to twelve knots. For the first time Kirkpatrick got a good view of his target, limned against the sky. She was a trawler, probably about a thousand tons' displacement. Two minutes later *Triton* opened fire with the 3-inch gun at a range of twelve hundred yards.

"Commence firing."

There was a blinding flash out of the muzzle of the gun and the first shell was on its way. The gun flash ruined the night vision of everyone topside, but it was worse for the trainer who was using an open sight (because the telescopic sight was flooded) and so met each gun flash wide-eyed. It slowed down the firing and the trainer had to be relieved every third or fourth salvo. Under these circumstances the firing was slow. The target did its best to keep the submarine astern to open out the range. The position of the gun on the after deck of the submarine made this a difficult maneuver to counter, and kept the two ships moving in a circle. As the range closed the fifty-caliber machine gun opened up with its rhythmic stutter, and Kirkpatrick could observe hits in the target from both the 3-inch gun and the machine gun tracers. The last four salvos of 3-inch were at a range of about two hundred yards. The final shot blew a large hole in the trawler's bow and she started sinking. From "Commence firing" to "Cease fire" was eighteen minutes, with nineteen rounds of 3-inch ammunition expended and 675 rounds of .50-caliber machine gun shells.

This was a well-conducted gun action and it gave a tremendous boost to the morale of everybody. Nearly everyone on board was involved in some fashion. Many men who otherwise might spend the whole patrol below decks, were on deck to see the target and observe the enemy being punished for his many sins. It was full of sound and fury, and neither *Triton* nor any of her people were hurt. It was magnificent but it can seriously be questioned if it was effective war. The name of the trawler is unknown. Unlike the sparrows, the fall of many Japanese picket boats that were sunk seems to have been unmarked.

When *Greenling* attacked *Seia Maru* with her 3-inch gun it was largely because Bruton was exasperated with torpedoes. *Greenling* encountered the big cargo vessel near Eniwetok on the evening of 30 April, while the submarine was en route to Truk and before she became embroiled in the *Shokaku* chase. Bruton attacked with four torpedoes, all of which missed. He waited for the target to get nearly over the horizon and then surfaced in pursuit. *Greenling* passed *Seia Maru* about six thousand yards abeam, with the target between the submarine and the moon, and when he had a satisfactory position, Bruton submerged to fire two more torpedoes which also missed. *Greenling* then surfaced, with the Japanese ship only seven thousand yards away. *Seia Maru* opened fire on the submarine with a stern gun, and fired two shells, both of which were short. Bruton closed the range to five thousand yards and opened up with his own 3-inch gun. In ten rounds they scored some hits but could not observe any damage. *Seia Maru* opened up again and one shell landed ten feet off the submarine's beam and ricocheted with a wild scream over the gun crew's heads. Bruton reconsidered the damage he might sustain from a single hit and broke off the engagement. He stayed on the surface, however, passed the Japanese ship at full power, regained attack position, and fired two more torpedoes. The first one missed ahead. The second seemed headed for a hit but about halfway to the target it exploded prematurely. The target turned tail and ran. Shortly afterward, *Greenling's* radar picked up an airplane approaching and Bruton submerged. This ended the action.

Silversides did not get off so lightly. She was on her first patrol, under Lieutenant Commander C. C. Burlingame, when she encountered a 300-ton trawler, on the morning of 8 May, about 600 miles from Japan and 550 miles north of Marcus. Full of beans and ambition, on her first enemy contact, *Silversides* attacked with deck gun and machine guns. The sea was choppy, which made the submarine's fire sporadic and erratic. Several times the gun crew was knocked away from the gun by sea breaking over the deck. Accurate gunfire is difficult to obtain with white water seething around the gun crew's hips and the submarine writhing and rolling in corkscrew motion through the cresting seas. Burlingame closed to finish off the trawler and the Japanese returned the fire with rifles and machine gun directed at the submarine's bridge and gun's crew. Mike Harbin, the first loader, fell, killed instantly by a machine gun bullet. *Silversides* got in at least twelve 3-inch hits and riddled the target with machine gun fire, setting the trawler on fire; but it would not sink. That evening burial services at sea were conducted for Mike Harbin, Torpedoman Third Class. With all the millions of people who lost their lives because of the war, a single man's death did not weigh greatly in the balance, but a submarine's crew is a small unit, conditioned to a mutual destiny. In triumph they expected to succeed together, and in disaster together die. For the crew of *Silversides* the death of Harbin loomed large.

Obsessive resort to gun battle by some submarine skippers is difficult to explain, and impossible to justify. It was supposed to be a great morale builder for the crew, but, as in the case of *Silversides*, it could backfire badly. If sinking sampans ever thinned out the Japanese picket line it was impossible to detect it. It was almost impossible to sink a big ship with a submarine's gun, as the Japanese soon learned, and even the pickets could be punched as full of holes as a Swiss cheese, with a 3-inch gun, and still float.

During the attempt to waylay *Shokaku*, two of the best submarine skippers in the business broke cover to sink spitkids by gunfire—like poorly trained foxhounds yapping after a rabbit in the middle of the chase. Somehow the Japanese were unable to profit by the blatant disclosure of submarine location and both these submarines made contact with carriers. When Japanese submarines indulged their corresponding propensity to bombard shore targets, just before leaving an area, U.S. convoy control officers made good use of the information to reroute convoys, but there seemed to be some flaw in Japanese organization for rapid dissemination of similar information.

The real damage done to the Japanese by submarine gunfire was negligible. In the meantime, U.S. submarines with torpedoes (despite the exasperating defects of these temperamental guided missiles) were becoming a force with which the Japanese would have to reckon. In May they sank twenty-one *marus*, for a loss of 105,000 tons of shipping. In addition, a seaplane carrier, a repair ship, a big minelaying ship, and two Japanese submarines were torpedoed and sunk. In 1942 Japanese commerce was outside the range of other Allied weapons (except when an offensive operation exposed them), yet the total loss of shipping to U.S. submarine torpedoes was more than the Japanese economy could stand.

Japanese Submarine Operations

In May, most Japanese submarines were involved with preparation for the Battle of Midway. These preparations were spread out over half the earth's surface, for certain submarines were assigned to creating diversions at places far from the center of action. Six I-class submarines reconnoitered the Aleutians, in the latter part of May, in preparation for the Aleutian invasion, which was in itself intended as a diversion from Midway. A seaplane launched from a submarine reconnoitered Seattle, Washington and reported no heavy ships. About 30 May *I-25* sent her plane over Dutch Harbor on a similar mission. Two submarines made periscope reconnaissance of Cold Bay and Kodiak, with negative results. These reconnaissances were not without adventure. *I-25* was involved in launching her plane at dawn when she sighted an approaching ship, which she identified as an American cruiser. *I-25* was unable to attack, with her plane on deck, and the cruiser passed without sighting the submarine. *I-19* was surprised by aircraft while preparing to launch her own plane, and had to dive and abandon her seaplane. The Japanese, like the American submarines operating in the same area, found the weather and the short nights in the Aleutians great handicaps for submarine operations.

Five I-class submarines (three carrying midgets and two with seaplanes) were operating off the eastern coast of Australia. On 29 May, *I-21* sent her plane over Sydney and reported battleships at anchor in the harbor. This was probably *Chicago*, which had been mistaken for a battleship before. On 31 May *I-22*, *I-24*, and *I-27* launched midgets at a point seven miles east of Sydney. Two of these penetrated into the harbor, causing consternation and confusion. One was sighted by *Chicago*, which opened fire, with her "overs" falling in Sydney's residential district. A torpedo narrowly missed *Chicago* and exploded against the dock, killing a number of sailors. Two damaged and scuttled midgets were recovered from the bottom of Sydney Harbor the next day. The military damage caused by the raid was small. None of the midgets survived the raid.

On the same day four other Japanese submarines were involved in an attack on Diego Suarez in Madagascar. *I-10* made a pre-raid reconnaissance of the harbor with her seaplane and discovered battleships in the harbor. The midget from *I-18* was unable to participate because of mechanical trouble, but *I-16* and *I-20* both launched theirs. One torpedo hit the battleship *Ramillies* and flooded a compartment. Another sank a tanker. *I-16* could see the flames rising from the harbor. None of the midgets were recovered. This was the most successful raid of the midgets. Both these raids were timed to divert attention from Midway. The air attack on Pearl Harbor had been preceded by a midget submarine attack, and the Japanese expected the Allies to draw the conclusion that the Kido Butai was behind the midgets. Nimitz at Pearl Harbor refused to be diverted.

Six I-class submarines (*I-121*, *I-122*, *I-123*, *I-171*, *I-174*, and *I-175*), were en route to station in the Hawaiian area, to refuel seaplanes at French Frigate Shoal. The submarine plan was almost identical to the 4 March bombing of Pearl Harbor, but the big seaplanes were intended to make a thorough reconnaissance and locate the heavy units of the U.S. fleet. *I-121* arrived on 26 May. Had she arrived three days earlier she could have observed a defensive anti-submarine minefield at work, for the U.S. patrol boat *YP-277* ran on her own minefield that day, and was blown up. This was a casualty the Japanese could understand, for Japanese anti-submarine defensive minefields had accounted for six Japanese ships to date, totaling thirty thousand tons. Minefields were unable to distinguish friend from foe.

When *I-121* arrived off French Frigate Shoal, she discovered a U.S. seaplane tender riding peacefully at anchor, with big seaplanes busily coming and going. As long as this state of affairs continued it was obviously impossible to carry out the refueling operations. *I-121* reported the situation and waited. Eight submarines sortied from Kure on 25 May, to take up battle stations for Midway. The Kido Butai sortied from the Inland Sea on the twenty-seventh, followed through the Bungo Suido the next day by the Combined Fleet. On the thirty-first the seaplane reconnaissance from French Frigate Shoal was called off and the submarines involved reassigned. U.S. carrier task forces sortied from Pearl Harbor undetected.

IX

JUNE 1942

The Battle of Midway, Japanese Plans

Like many Japanese naval plans, plans for the Midway operation were complex, dispersing Japanese forces all over the broad Pacific, providing for "diversionary" objectives in addition to the major goal, and calling for punctual junction of important forces on the field of battle. The "diversion" was an attack on the Aleutians by the Northern Force under Vice Admiral Hosogaya, with two small carriers, five cruisers, and light forces, and with landing forces embarked in three transports. Hosogaya also had six I-class submarines assigned to his force. These submarines conducted reconnaissances in May, and then established a submarine cordon across the 50th parallel at 169° W Longitude. They made no contacts and had little effect upon the operations.

The spearhead of the attack on Midway's defenses was the Kido Butai (the Striking Force) with Nagumo. The two Japanese carriers that survived the Battle of the Coral Sea were under repair and training new air groups and were not available for the Midway operation. Nagumo had four carriers (*Kaga, Akagi, Soryu,* and *Hiryu*), two fast battleships, three cruisers, and twelve destroyers in the Kido Butai for Midway operations.

The Midway Invasion Force, under Vice Admiral Kondo, was divided into three groups, each sailing from a different port and scheduled to rendezvous seven hundred miles west of Midway. The Combined Fleet Main Force, under Yamamoto in his flagship *Yamato* (the mightiest battleship ever built) sortied from the Inland Sea in support. Japanese submarines had a variety of missions. Two seaplane carriers (*Chiyoda* and *Nisshin*), each carrying a number of two-man midget submarines, accompanied the Main Force, but as surface forces never got within sight of each other these midgets were never launched. By the first of June the submarines supporting the seaplane reconnaissance from French

Frigate Shoal had been irrevocably thwarted, and the six submarines involved were directed to take their places for the battle phase.

The Advance Expeditionary Force established two submarine cordons between Pearl Harbor and Midway. Four of the French Frigate refueling group set up Line KO, south of the Hawaii–Midway Island chain in longitude 167° W. Owing to the failure of their seaplane reconnaissance mission, they were late arriving on station. Ten submarines formed Line OTSU north of the chain of islands. Both of these cordons moved westward, principally on the surface, between 3 June and 7 June and ended up to the westward of Midway. *I-168*, delayed in Japan for overhaul, sailed independently. On 1 June she reconnoitered Midway and reported no ships present, but noted numerous aircraft on long-range searches. The OTSU group was supposed to be on station by 1 June but they failed to reach their assigned station until 3 June. By that time it was too late. The American carrier task forces had crossed the OTSU Line.

Japanese Sortie

On 26 May the Japanese Northern Force left Ominato for the Aleutians. The next day the Kido Butai left its anchorage in the Inland Sea and headed out for battle. On 28 May components of the Midway Invasion Force sortied from Saipan and Guam, taking circuitous routes to deceive any spying submarine. *Cuttlefish* (Hottel) was patrolling the Saipan area. She had encountered screening destroyers of part of the Invasion Force two days earlier. In that encounter *Cuttlefish* had been severely depth-charged and sighted no heavy units. By the time the sortie was made, *Cuttlefish* was too far to the northward to witness the maneuver.

Yamamoto's battleships moved out of the Inland Sea through Bungo Suido on 29 May. Radio Intelligence in Tokyo had reported six American submarines in Japanese waters, and destroyers reported sighting two enemy submarines just outside the Bungo. The Kure Naval Base sent additional surface and air anti-submarine forces into that area, and the great fleet moved into the open sea without incident.

This alarm must have been caused by *Pollack* (Moseley), the only submarine then in the vicinity of Bungo Suido. She, and *Silversides*, which guarded Kii Suido, and *Drum* off Tokyo Bay were the only American submarines left in Japanese waters. *Pollack* encountered four destroyers on the night of 27 May, and assuming that they were screening heavy units, tried to penetrate the screen but was unable to do so. Shortly after the twenty-ninth of May began she again encountered Japanese destroyers, which in turn sighted *Pollack*, on the surface with the moon at her back. Moseley was forced to dive and was then depth-charged and pursued for several hours. On the morning of 30 May he sighted another destroyer but through all of this the Japanese anti-submarine effort was successful in holding him down and preventing contact with heavy units of the big fleet movement. Before daylight on 31 May, Moseley made another contact with what he thought was a destroyer. When this turned out to be a trawler, he surfaced and set it on fire with gunfire from the deck gun. The burning ship illuminated a wide area of ocean. *Pollack's* destroyer contacts were the closest any American submarine came to the main Japanese fleet until after battle was joined by the opposing carrier forces.

American Plans

Fortunately, Nimitz was not dependent upon submarine reconnaissance for his information. In April his Intelligence organization told him something big was building up in the Central Pacific, and before the middle of May he knew that the Japanese intended to invade the Aleutians and at the same time seize Midway Island. He also had incomplete information of the Japanese order of battle, but he knew that the Midway attack would be spearheaded by the Kido Butai.

Nevertheless it takes more than information, however good, to win battles, and Nimitz was short of carriers to meet the Kido Butai. *Hornet* and *Enterprise* arrived at Pearl Harbor from the South Pacific on 26 May. They had barely time to refuel, replenish, send Halsey to the Pearl Harbor hospital with a bad case of shingles, and sail again for Midway on 28 May under command of Rear Admiral Raymond A. Spruance. This was less than a dozen hours after the Japanese Fleet left the Inland Sea for the same destination. *Yorktown*, with her bomb damage from the Coral Sea, arrived at Pearl Harbor the same day. She estimated that repairs would take ninety days (in a West Coast yard she hoped), but as she rounded Hospital Point the gates of the great graving dock yawned to receive her. Navy yard workmen swarmed over her. Forty-eight hours later, as sturdy as the day she was built, with a brand new air group aboard, and flying Fletcher's flag, she sailed with her task force to join *Hornet* and *Enterprise*.

There was then in the Pacific not a single American battleship with speed enough to operate with carriers. The remnant of the battleship force that had been clobbered at Pearl Harbor was at San Francisco. They went to sea, without orders, during the Midway campaign but never got within a thousand miles of a Japanese ship. Their slow speed made them liabilities rather than assets. There were thirteen cruisers and thirty destroyers available. On 21 May Nimitz organized the Northern Pacific Force under Rear Admiral Theobald and assigned to it five cruisers and thirteen destroyers. This left eight cruisers and seventeen destroyers to support the three carriers whose planes would be the main strength of the defense of Midway.

On Midway there were fifty-four Marine planes, all of them obsolescent and so overmatched against the Japanese Zeros that it was suicide to fly them in combat. There were thirty-two Navy patrol seaplanes, good for long-range searches but too slow for combat, and six Navy torpedo planes and four Army B-26s adapted to carry torpedoes. There were also eighteen Army B-17s which was as many of these big planes as Midway could accommodate; but more of them could be flown in direct from Hawaii. These were excellent planes but they depended upon high-altitude horizontal bombing, practically impotent against high-speed naval vessels with plenty of sea room to maneuver.

There was a shrill theory that carriers could not penetrate within range of hostile shore-based air forces, but Cincpac was not deceived about the strength of Midway's shore-based air defenses. Nimitz knew that a battle between opposing carrier forces would decide the issue. He had three carriers carrying 230 planes. The Japanese had eight carriers at sea. Nimitz knew that four of the most powerful ones with 280 planes would be in the Kido Butai spearhead. He hoped that Midway's shore-based air could inflict enough damage on the Japanese carriers and their planes to even the odds, but the outcome of the carrier battle would decide the fate of Midway and the course of the war.

With ample warning there was plenty of time to dispose American submarines to the best advantage. Combined surface, air, and submarine operation demanded close coordination in the Midway area, and Cincpac tightened his already tight control over submarines. With Cincpac and Comsubpac (Rear Admiral English) both at Pearl Harbor, most of the directives English received were informal and many of them oral. There is no record of the origin of the submarine plans of operation, but it is most probable that English had little to say about the strategy of submarine employment. Whoever created the submarine plan, it was bad. Most of the submarines were disposed for a concentrated defense close in to Midway, instead of being offensively placed farther out where they may have had an opportunity to torpedo a Japanese carrier before the decisive carrier battle.

English did achieve practically full employment for his submarines during the Midway campaign. There were six S-boats in the Aleutians. All of them were at sea. One was strafed by Japanese carrier planes and forced to submerge. Otherwise American submarines in the Aleutians, like their Japanese counterparts, were busy battling their common enemy, the weather. They made no contacts and took no significant part in the action until after Midway was decided.

There were twenty-nine fleet submarines in the Central Pacific. Two were dismantled in Navy Yard overhaul. *Triton*, returning from patrol in the East China Sea, was too low on fuel and torpedoes to extend her patrol any longer. *Silversides* on patrol off Kii Suido was directed to stay there, like a lone cat, watching the northern portal of the Inland Sea. Other submarines on distant patrol stations were directed to close in on Midway, traversing waters through which the Japanese fleet might pass, before or after battle.

Four submarines were assigned station patrol three hundred miles north of Honolulu to guard against the contingency that the Japanese fleet would slip around the American carriers and attack Pearl Harbor. They made no contacts. Three others were placed on a line north of the Hawaiian chain, about halfway between Pearl Harbor and Midway. Japanese submarines of their OTSU Line in their westward movement must have run right through this line, but neither Japanese nor American submarines made contact. Improbable as this "passing in the night" might appear to be as a chart exercise, it was likely enough to occur, as could be attested by anyone who has groped through a black night on a darkened submarine bridge.

Eleven submarines were grouped close around Midway. Six were on the arc of a 150-mile circle with Midway as a center, from southwest around through north. Three more were out at the 200-mile line from Midway in a westerly direction. Two were roving in the backfield between the 150-mile circle and Midway. Intelligence anticipated some kind of action seven hundred miles west of Midway, and *Cuttlefish*, returning from patrol, was directed to maintain a station patrol in that area.

The Japanese Advance

The advancing Kido Butai and the Main Body encountered dense fog, which effectively concealed them from hostile air observation. The Midway Occupation Force on the southern route was in clear weather. On 30 May *Yamato's* radio intelligence picked up a long coded message which they could not read, but which they could identify as from a submarine directly in advance of the transport group. Yamamoto assumed that the Occupation Force had been sighted. It is probable that this message was from *Cuttlefish*, who sent a message to English on that date. The next morning *Cuttlefish* saw three Japanese Navy heavy bombers and submerged to avoid detection, surfacing about an hour later. Within two hours *Cuttlefish* was attacked by another bomber, who dropped bombs on the submerging submarine but caused no damage. That night Hottel surfaced and sent in a contact report. He assumed the attacking planes were from Wake. He had not seen any of the advancing Occupation Force.

The next day *Yamato's* radio Intelligence heard radio transmission from aircraft and submarines in both the Hawaiian and Aleutian areas. The Navy General Staff in Tokyo sent out their estimate that the American carriers were still in the Solomons. A day or two later, however, Imperial General Headquarters in Tokyo reported that radio Intelligence located an American carrier force at sea in the vicinity of Midway. As this message was also addressed to Nagumo, Yamamoto decided not to break radio silence to pass the information on to the Kido Butai.

Early in the morning of 3 June Japanese carrier planes hit Dutch Harbor. Nimitz had informed Theobald that the Japanese invasion forces intended to land at Kiska and Attu, but Theobald did not trust the information. He believed that Nimitz was being deceived by a Japanese ruse and that the true objective of the Japanese was Dutch Harbor. The bulk of Theobald's surface forces was concentrated four hundred miles south of Kodiak. They never made contact with the Japanese fleet. Hosogaya hammered the installations at Dutch Harbor with his carrier planes. U. S. Army and Navy planes attacked the Japanese ships but made no hits. The Japanese landed at Attu and Kiska on 7 June unopposed.

At 0900 on 3 June a patrol plane out of Midway made contact with the Midway Occupation Force seven hundred miles west of Midway. B-17s attacked the force in the afternoon but made no hits. Patrol planes made a torpedo attack on the same force at two o'clock the next morning, and made one hit in *Akebono Maru,* which did not prevent her from continuing on with the formation. *Cuttlefish* made contact with a ship Hottel identified as a tanker, and which was probably one of the Midway Occupation Force. English ordered him to trail, but *Cuttlefish* lost contact when she was forced to dive by approaching daylight.

At 0430 on the morning of 4 June the Kido Butai reached its planned position unsighted and commenced launching search planes. Almost simultaneously Midway and American carriers put their search planes in the air. By 0445 the Japanese strike on Midway had formed up over their carriers and took off for their target. These planes were sighted and reported by a Navy patrol plane while they were en route, and at 0545 the same patrol plane sighted the Kido Butai. Midway launched an attack against the Japanese carriers and put all its defensive fighters in the air.

When English learned of the location of the Japanese carriers he ordered his submarines to go after them. This was easier said than done. The Japanese carriers were about two hundred miles from Midway, approaching from a northwesterly direction. Carriers, in action, moved at nearly twice a submarine's surface speed and, generally, long before a submarine came within a carrier's horizon the submarine would be attacked by angry planes, either friend or foe; forced down, and slowed to a crawl. By the geometry of the Midway disposition there were only two of all the defending submarines that had any chance of getting into action. *Grouper,* on the surface and trying to close the reported position of the Japanese task force, was strafed by Japanese planes. She submerged, went deep and stayed there, taking no further part in the battle.

Nautilus

Nautilus, under command of Lieutenant Commander W. H. Brockman, had better luck and was much better handled. She submerged about sunrise but stayed at periscope depth and raised her vertical antenna to pick up all the gossip. At 0544 she intercepted a patrol plane report of many Japanese planes approaching Midway. The position reported was on the boundary of her sector, and Brockman set course in that direction at the best speed he could make and conserve sufficient storage battery capacity for the demands that might be made upon it before the day was done. In *Nautilus* this was about three knots, about the speed a man can row a boat.

Midway Bombed

At 0635 the Japanese planes arrived over Midway. The Marines in their obsolescent planes put up a stiff battle. Most of the defending fighters were destroyed and Midway bombed, but Lieutenant Tomonaga, leading the Japanese strike, reported to Nagumo that another strike would be required. At 0702 *Hornet* and *Enterprise,* whose presence was still unknown to the Japanese, launched a strike against the Japanese carriers. Three minutes later Midway's ten torpedo planes arrived over the Kido Butai and attacked. Defending Japanese fighters shot down seven of the attacking torpedo planes, and the few torpedoes launched were easily evaded by the Japanese carriers.

Responding to Tomonaga's call for a second strike, and under attack by shore-based planes, Nagumo ordered a second strike against Midway. The planes were spotted and ready, but armed with torpedoes and armor-piercing bombs for use against ships. For a strike against Midway these planes had to be rearmed. While the rearming process was in progress Nagumo received a message from a Japanese search plane that American ships were sighted to the northeast. These ships were at first reported as cruisers and destroyers.

Nautilus

At 0710 *Nautilus* sighted smoke and the black bursts of anti-aircraft fire over the Japanese task force. Brockman changed course to close this action and went to battle stations submerged. He sighted masts sticking up above the horizon, and while making this observation his periscope was strafed by a low-flying plane. A destroyer up ahead was searching for submarines with its supersonic gear. *Nautilus* kept creeping in, making occasional periscope observations. At 0800 Brockman sighted a formation of four ships, a battleship and a cruiser in column, with what he took to be a light cruiser on either bow of the formation—although these outriders were undoubtedly destroyers. A few minutes later the destroyers attacked with depth charges and *Nautilus* went to ninety feet to evade. *Nautilus* had been equipped with "deck torpedo tubes" outside the strength hull, under her high gun deck. Torpedoes in these tubes could be fired from below, but the tubes could not be reloaded or the torpedoes serviced with the ship submerged. No good ever came of this bastard arrangement, and on this occasion concussion of the depth charges tripped the starting lever of one of the torpedoes and the torpedo made a "hot run" in the tube. Until the torpedo's fuel and compressed air was exhausted *Nautilus* made a noise like a garbage grinder and left a trail of air bubbles to point the way to her location. Despite these handicaps *Nautilus* plodded on in.

Midway Planes Attack Kido Butai

The Japanese were having plenty to distract them. At 0755 sixteen Marine dive bombers attacked. Eight of these planes were shot down by the Zeros. There were no hits. Fifteen minutes later fourteen B-17s dropped their bomb loads. The Army aviators, deceived by the forest of splashes from near-misses, reported the Japanese carrier destroyed but there were no hits. Ten minutes later eleven Marine bombers delivered their attack and also failed to damage the Japanese ships.

Nautilus

At 0824 Brockman raised the periscope to find himself in the middle of the Japanese formation. His position was no secret from the Japanese. One of the destroyers had just passed over him. A battleship was on the port bow firing its entire broadside at the submarine periscope. Searchlights were trained on the periscope to point it out, and signal flags were breaking from every yardarm. The range to the battleship was 4500 yards. *Nautilus* fired two torpedo tubes but one of the tubes misfired and only one torpedo got off. The battleship changed course and the torpedo missed. A destroyer came charging in and *Nautilus* went to 150 feet, listening to the depth charges going off above her.

Kido Butai

About this time Nagumo learned that there was an American aircraft carrier to the northeast. He immediately stopped rearming for the second Midway strike and ordered re-rearming with torpedoes and armor piercing bombs. The Midway strike was due back. Many of those planes were damaged and the fighters were low on fuel. The Japanese carriers came up into the wind to receive their returning planes.

Nautilus

Nautilus raised her periscope at 0900 and saw a Japanese aircraft carrier for the first time. The range was sixteen thousand yards. The carrier did not appear damaged. It was maneuvering at high speed and black pompons of anti-aircraft fire bloomed high above it. This must have been the anti-aircraft fire from a Japanese destroyer, which fired briefly at their own returning planes in mistaken identity. A destroyer maneuvered close to *Nautilus*. Brockman seized a favorable opportunity and fired a torpedo at it, still thinking it was a cruiser. The torpedo missed. The destroyer retaliated with depth charges and *Nautilus* went down to two hundred feet to evade at slow speed, still crawling toward the Japanese carrier.

U.S. Carrier Planes Attack

Shortly after nine o'clock Nagumo turned northward to reform his carriers, scattered by evasion maneuvers and recovery operations, and to spot his flight decks for an attack on the American carrier. This northward turn left *Nautilus* astern. It also threw the whole American strike out of kilter. *Hornet, Enterprise,* and *Yorktown* had all launched their planes and several different attack groups were coming in to intercept the Japanese carriers. Their approach courses were based on the reports of the first patrol plane contacts. No one observed the radical change of the Japanese base course. *Hornet's* dive bombers and fighters, arriving at the predicted position and finding no enemy, turned south, and were out of the battle. Lieutenant Commander McClusky, leading *Enterprise's* dive bombers, arriving later at approximately the same position, made one of the most fateful decisions of the day. He decided to turn north, on the assumption that the Japanese carriers were behind schedule. This decision brought *Enterprise* dive bombers, by a circuitous route, over the Kido Butai at a most critical moment.

In the meantime *Hornet's* torpedo planes were the first carrier planes to locate the Kido Butai. At 0928 fifteen planes of this group attacked without fighter cover, and the Zeros swarmed to meet them. Every plane of the attack group was shot down, and only one man (who was picked up out of the water the next day) survived that gallant charge. A few minutes later fourteen *Enterprise* torpedo planes attacked, also without fighter protection. Ten of these planes were shot down and no torpedo found its mark. *Yorktown's* torpedo planes, launched later, reached the Kido Butai shortly after. Twelve *Yorktown* planes came in at 1016. Ten of these were shot down, the Zero fighters following them right down to the water. Still there were no torpedo hits.

At 1020 the slaughter of the American torpedo planes was over, and Nagumo was ready to launch against the American carrier. Another great victory for the Kido Butai seemed certain. The attack of the shore-based Midway planes had been easily beaten off. A submarine attack had left them unscathed. The carrier torpedo attack, which Nagumo most dreaded, had been pressed home with determination despite wholesale destruction of the planes, but the torpedoes were slow, erratic, and easily evaded. The giant B-17s had dumped their bombs and departed and the Kido Butai was without a scratch. It needed only the destruction of the American carrier for another great victory. At 1024 Nagumo gave the order to launch the strike. On board the flagship *Akagi,* the air officer snapped down his signal flag and the first Zero fighter sped down the deck and into the air. At that moment a Japanese lookout shouted "*Bakugekiki.*"

High up above, the dive bombers from *Enterprise* had pushed over into their dives. Almost at the same instant *Yorktown's* dive bombers reached the Japanese carriers and attacked. The Zeros, having a field day with the slow torpedo planes, had followed their victims right down to the deck, leaving the dive bombers unopposed upstairs. Down through the clouds they came in almost vertical dives, with only the popping anti-aircraft fire to distract them from their aim. It was over almost as soon as it started. Within three minutes what had been a Japanese victory became a Japanese disaster. *Akagi, Kaga,* and *Soryu* were in uncontrollable flames. The Kido Butai would roam no more unchallenged in the Indian Ocean and the Pacific, and whatever chance Japan had of winning the war was gone.

Nautilus

At ten o'clock *Nautilus* found herself deserted, the Japanese carrier out of sight and the destroyers departed over the horizon. At 1029 Brockman raised the vertical antenna and intercepted a radio message reporting a damaged Japanese carrier. He could see four large clouds of smoke on the horizon. *Nautilus* changed course to steer for the nearest one. It would be a long, slow run and much would happen before she arrived.

Hiryu *vs.* Yorktown

Hiryu had become detached from the other three carriers and was to the northward during the dive bomber attacks. *Hiryu* was the flagship of Rear Admiral Yamaguchi, Commander Carrier Division Two. While Nagumo was shifting his flag from the doomed *Akagi* to a cruiser, Yamaguchi launched all the planes *Hiryu* then had ready (eighteen dive bombers and six fighters) to attack the American carriers. They found *Yorktown* at 1220 and hit her with two bombs, paying for their hits with thirteen of the eighteen bombers and three of the six fighters. *Yorktown* lost all power and lay dead in the water, belching smoke. It was Fletcher's turn to shift his flag from *Yorktown* to a cruiser.

About this time the Japanese learned that they had three American carriers, not one, to deal with. When this alarming news reached Yamaguchi, he responded by launching all his remaining planes (ten torpedo planes and six fighters) to attack the American carriers. In the meantime *Yorktown's* repair party had brought her fires under control and partially repaired the damage. *Yorktown* was under way again at eighteen knots by 1340.

Nautilus

All this time *Nautilus* was approaching the smoke cloud. About noon she was close enough for Brockman to identify the source of the smoke as a burning carrier. He decided he could be more spendthrift with his battery power and still last until nightfall, so he increased speed to two-thirds (in *Nautilus* about four knots) and kept boring in. Even at this dashing speed (almost as fast as a man might walk) the approach was a long one. It gave everyone in the conning tower of *Nautilus* an opportunity to take a look at the enemy through the periscope. They identified it as a *Soryu*-class carrier, and noted that there were two cruisers apparently attempting to pass a tow line. The carrier's fires appeared to be under control. After carefully weighing the alternative, Brockman decided to attack the disabled carrier rather than the undamaged cruisers. Between 1359 and 1405 *Nautilus* fired three torpedoes, from a range of 2700 yards, and Brockman watched them through the periscope making their run all the way to the target. A destroyer charged down on *Nautilus*, dropped depth charges, and *Nautilus* went down to three hundred feet.

Confusion in the Kido Butai

In the Kido Butai, quite naturally, confusion reigned. There is an inertia of victory, which had sustained the Kido Butai since the war began. There is also an inertia of defeat—and this was new for Nagumo. Disaster rapidly following disaster overwhelmed him. He seemed incapable of decision, and his messages to Yamamoto were confused and conflicting. On board *Kaga* at 1410, Lieutenant Commander Kunisada saw three white torpedo wakes approaching his ship. Two torpedoes missed. The third one struck solidly amidships. It did not explode. The warhead broke off and sank. The air flask, freed of the weight, floated for a while and several of *Kaga's* crew, swimming in the water, clung to it. Brockman was sure it was *Soryu* they attacked. However, the torpedo behavior reported by the observer on *Kaga* is so entirely plausible for the U.S. submarine torpedoes of that time that it leaves little doubt that *Kaga* (with destroyers alongside transferring Nagumo's flag) was *Nautilus'* real target. All the skill and determination, as it had been in many other submarine attacks, was frustrated by defective torpedoes.

Hiryu vs. Yorktown

Hiryu was still in the fight, separated from her three burning consorts, launching her strikes and recovering her planes, undiscovered and unmolested. At 1442 *Hiryu's* torpedo planes found what they took to be a new undamaged carrier. It was *Yorktown*, valiantly getting ready to continue in the battle. *Hiryu's* planes came in against all defenses the damaged carrier and her cruiser escorts could muster. Half of the attacking planes were shot down, but the survivors launched four torpedoes, two of which hit *Yorktown*. She was stopped again, without power, and took a twenty-seven-degree list. For fear that she might capsize with great loss of life, at 1500 Captain Buckmaster ordered abandon ship.

For this victory *Hiryu* was about to pay the price. At 1445, search

planes that had flown off *Yorktown* found *Hiryu* and accuratedly reported her position. At 1530 Spruance launched a strike of twenty-four
dive bombers from *Enterprise* (ten of them were *Yorktown* planes, led by
McClusky). They dove on *Hiryu* at 1704, hit her with four bombs, and
left her a flaming wreck. Yamaguchi deliberately chose to go down with
the ship rather than be rescued.

Night Actions

On board *Yamato,* when news of Nagumo's disaster reached Yamamoto, the two light carriers in the Aleutians were called south and with
the two carriers from the Midway Invasion Force and the Main Body
were ordered to reinforce the Kido Butai. Cruiser Division Seven was
directed to make a night bombardment of Midway. At 1755, after *Hiryu*
too had been lost, these plans were modified and the concentration of
the carriers canceled. *I-168* was directed to bombard Midway to keep
the defenses off balance until Cruiser Division Seven could give it a good
shellacking. Kondo was ordered to assemble all available cruisers and
destroyers and bring the American fleet to night action. Spruance, however, had no intention of being trapped into a night action with a Japanese fleet greatly his superior in gunpower. He turned east, and did not
again come to a westerly course until after midnight, while the Japanese
searched for him in vain.

Tambor

In Pearl Harbor there was considerable apprehension that the Japanese would still go ahead with their invasion plans. All submarines were
ordered to return to their original defense sectors and close Midway to
the twelve-mile circle. The genesis of this order is obscure, but it
effectively removed all but one submarine from the battle. Only *Tambor,*
returning to her sector, made contact. Her path crossed that of Cruiser
Division Seven, which continued to close in on Midway on its bombardment mission until two o'clock in the morning, when Yamamoto called
off the bombardment.

Early on the morning of 5 June *Tambor* (Murphy) was on the surface
about ninety miles west of Midway when she sighted four large ships.
She had been warned that U.S. ships might be west of Midway, and it
was difficult enough to recognize her contact as cruisers let alone establish
their nationality. Murphy decided to fall in with the cruiser formation
on a parallel course until he could identify them. At 0300 he sent a
report to English, vainly hoping that Pearl Harbor could identify the

ships. At 0412, as dawn increased the illumination, Murphy recognized the cruisers as Japanese, but it was then too late. *Tambor* was forced to dive by the approaching dawn and was unable to reach an attack position submerged. Through the periscope Murphy observed that the bow of one of the cruisers was damaged.

When Yamamoto called off their bombardment, Cruiser Division Seven had reversed course. Shortly afterward they sighted a submarine. By blinker tube signal the division commander ordered an emergency turn to avoid the submarine. *Mogami* failed to get the word and crashed *Mikuma's* port quarter. *Mogami* lost her bow, back to the forward turret, and was slowed to twelve knots. *Mikuma* suffered only slight damage and stood by *Mogami* while the other two cruisers continued retiring at twenty-seven knots. The next morning planes from Midway and from the American carriers found the damaged ships. Both ships were bombed. *Mogami,* badly battered, finally made it back to Truk. *Mikuma* was sunk. Thus *Tambor,* without firing a torpedo, brought about more damage to the Japanese than all the other American submarines together.

I-168

Both KO and OTSU lines advanced westward from their original positions during and after the battle of Midway. *I-121* sighted an American submarine on the surface southwest of Lisianski Island shortly after sunset on 6 June. The American submarine remained unaware of the contact, and owes its continued existence to the circumstance that *I-121* was loaded with gasoline for the seaplane reconnaissance and had no torpedoes aboard. The OTSU Line made no contacts. Lieutenant Commander Yahachi Tanabe in *I-168*, however, had plenty of action.

At 0130 on the morning of 5 June, *I-168* surfaced off Midway and in accordance with her orders, opened up a bombardment with her deck gun. She was supposed to keep Midway under fire until two o'clock when Cruiser Division Seven was due to arrive and complete the destruction of Midway's facilities. *I-168's* fire was returned so promptly and so accurately by the Marine shore battery that Tanabe was forced to submerge and withdraw. He had picked up a radio report of a damaged and abandoned aircraft carrier 150 miles northeast of Midway, and *I-168* set out to find it. After daylight in the morning she was bombed by a patrol plane, but escaped without damage and continued working her way steadily toward the reported position of the damaged carrier.

Yorktown, abandoned on the afternoon of 4 June, lay dead in the water during the night, guarded by only one destroyer. By noon of 6 June, however, the tug *Vireo* had the battered carrier in tow and six more destroyers were screening her. The destroyer *Hammann* was alongside supplying power and portable pumps. A salvage party was aboard making progress in reducing the list, and the prospects of towing *Yorktown* back to Pearl Harbor appeared to be good.

Early in the morning of 6 June *I-168* arrived at the reported position and sighted *Yorktown*. For nine hours Tanabe maneuvered to gain position, dodging the seven destroyers that guarded the carrier, and at 1331, undetected, he achieved a position 1900 yards from his target. *I-168* fired four torpedoes. One of them hit *Hammann* amidships, breaking the destroyer's back, and sending her to the bottom almost instantly. Two others hit *Yorktown*. She stayed afloat until the next day but finally sank as the result of her accumulated damage. This attack made Tanabe the hero of the Japanese submarine service, and by a very close margin he survived to enjoy his just acclaim.

The Japanese submarine was located by American destroyers fifteen minutes after the attack. A barrage of depth charges shook *I-168* as a terrier shakes a rat. Some of the storage battery cell jars were broken. The submarine lost all power and the leaking electrolyte generated poisonous chlorine gas. *I-168* lay helpless, and slowly took an up angle of twenty degrees, while the crew kept her submerged by using high-pressure air to adjust her trim. The big angle complicated the task of the electricians in cutting out the damaged cells, but eventually they succeeded and power was restored. Conditions inside the submarine were so bad by that time that she had to surface. The hunting destroyers happened to be out at ten thousand yards when *I-168* came up, but a destroyer soon saw her and came in to attack. When the range fell to five thousand yards Tanabe was forced to dive again, but the short time on the surface had given *I-168* enough fresh air to last until nightfall. The destroyer passed overhead, dropped a few more depth charges, and withdrew. About 2000, after the sun set and the sound of propellers faded out, Tanabe brought *I-168* to the surface and thankfully set course for Japan.

U.S. Submarines in Pursuit

Tambor's contact with Cruiser Division Seven was the last U.S. submarine contact with Japanese surface ships at the Battle of Midway. When it was apparent that the Japanese fleet was withdrawing, submarines were sent out in pursuit, but by 5 June all Japanese ships were outside the reach of the Midway group of submarines. English continued hopefully to send information and estimates of position of Japanese ships to submarines then closing Midway from their patrol areas off Japan and in the Carolines. Such contact reports on fast-moving surface ships are useless to distant, slow-moving submarines, unless it is possible to make accurate estimates of the enemy's course or destination. Reports of damaged Japanese ships came in, but these were mythical or inaccurate. Other than *Mogami* there were no severely damaged Japanese ships afloat. Despite considerable scurrying about, therefore, there were no further submarine contacts with the Japanese fleet.

On 7 June a group of B-17s mistook *Grayling* on the surface for a Japanese cruiser, and dropped a full pattern of bombs. The aviators reported in dramatic detail the sinking of a Japanese cruiser, but the only damage was to the nerves and temper of the crew of the hurriedly diving *Grayling*. Japanese planes bombed *Cuttlefish* the same day and they also missed. *Cuttlefish* ran through the flotsam and jetsam of *Mikuma*, and on 9 June *Trout* rescued two survivors of *Mikuma's* crew. By 10 June there was nothing for English to do but proceed with the redeployment of his submarines to carry on with their war of attrition against Japanese shipping.

American submarines were poorly disposed at the Battle of Midway. Had they taken full advantage of the information available they would have been out several hundred miles from Midway, where they would have had an opportunity to attack the Japanese forces before the critical carrier battle. Whether more attacks by submarines, with malfunctioning torpedoes, would have resulted in greater damage to the Japanese is conjectural. Japanese submarines were properly placed, but their timing was off—and time was the most important dimension in four-dimensional submarine warfare, so Japanese submarine results, too, were disappointing.

There was a War College theory that it was not the business of Intelligence to estimate the enemy's intention and that command decisions should be based upon the enemy's capabilities rather than estimates of what he planned to do. The seven U.S. submarines on station patrol north of Oahu and between Pearl Harbor and Midway, was a bow to this theory, as an attack on Pearl Harbor was within the enemy's capabilities. An attack on the West Coast was also within the capability of the Kido Butai, and for this reason many Army planes were held in readiness there rather than being committed to the defense of the Aleutians. Had Nimitz fully accepted the War College theory, the Battle of Midway would have been lost. It might easily have been lost, even after the Japanese carriers were sunk, if Spruance had charged pell-mell after the retiring Japanese, as some of his critics would have had him do. Midway is acclaimed as a triumph of Naval Intelligence, but more properly the victory might be attributed to the fortuitous circumstances that put Nimitz and Spruance in position to make the crucial decisions—and to the work of fifty-five dive bombers during those three fateful minutes of history that turned a Japanese victory into a crushing Japanese defeat.

Midway changed the course of the war. It also changed the opinion of the opponents with regard to each other. Americans thought Japan was fighting a shoestring war with materiel that were inferior copies of the products of superior American economy. Yet Japan brought to Midway a great superiority of materiel, in both quantity and quality. Her planes and her weapons, particularly torpedoes, were markedly superior to what Americans had to fight with.

The Japanese had been conditioned to consider the Americans soft and effete. To these connoisseurs of courage the ineffective torpedo attacks were eye-openers. They could be complacent about the inferior performance of American planes and torpedoes, but they were impressed with the persistence of the attacks. Very few of the torpedo planes survived, and in the attack of *Hornet's* torpedo squadron every plane was shot down, yet none was deflected from its objective. History holds few examples of such determined charges. A considerable fraction of the six hundred rode back from the charge of the Light Brigade; and Thermopylae was a Spartan defensive action. The Japanese learned that courage was not a Japanese monopoly. It was going to be a hard war, and many of the high Japanese naval commanders knew, after Midway, that Japan would not win it.

The Rest of June

The rest of June was anticlimax for both American and Japanese submarines, although there were several developments that affected the future. In Mozambique Channel, between Madagascar and South Africa, four Japanese I-class submarines, supported by two auxiliary cruisers, followed up their raid on Diego Suarez with a successful campaign against merchant shipping. Five other I-class submarines were operating off eastern Australia. They sank one ship off Tasmania and another off Nouméa. *I-21* shelled Newcastle, Australia and *I-24* shelled Sydney on 7 June.

The occupation of the Aleutians made considerable difference in the pattern of Japanese submarine operations. About the middle of the month the Japanese First Squadron was ordered home from the northern waters, leaving only the Second Squadron with seven submarines remaining. Before departing their areas off the northwestern United States, *I-26* and *I-25* sank a supply ship. On 20 June *I-26* shelled Estevan Point, Vancouver, and the next day *I-25* shelled Fort Stevens, Oregon. About the end of the month the Japanese brought home from Truk five RO-boats, (*RO-61, RO-62 RO-63, RO-64,* and *RO-68*) and reassigned them to the Aleutian areas. These old RO-boats were about the same age as the S-boats that the U. S. Navy had operating in the same area.

The extension of Japanese supply lines to Kiska and Attu opened up an opportunity for U.S. forces to exact a toll of Japanese ships supporting exposed occupation forces. U. S. Navy and Army Air Forces commenced bombarding Kiska Harbor as soon as they discovered the Japanese occupancy. Before the end of the month U.S. air attacks had severely damaged a destroyer and sank one supply ship. The S-boats moved out along the Aleutian chain to do their part, but their limitations for operating in Arctic conditions were soon apparent.

On 19 June S-27 (Jukes) was off Amchitka on a reconnaissance mission before taking up patrol off Kiska. After eighteen hours submerged during a June day in high latitude she surfaced about ten o'clock at night to charge batteries. To do this at the maximum rate, in order to get the charge in before daylight, she had to lay to and put both engines on the charge. About an hour later she was able to put one engine on the screw, but in the meantime the fog had set in and she had drifted five miles. Without radar she was unable to determine her position in the thick weather. As she got under way she went hard and fast aground on a rocky reef and very soon was in a bad situation, unable to back off, the torpedo room flooded, the after battery generating chlorine gas, and the ship lying at an angle of about ten degrees down by the bow. Jukes decided to abandon ship. All hands were taken ashore on Amchitka in a rubber life boat, and six days later were rescued by patrol planes. S-27 was later destroyed to prevent her from falling into the hands of the Japanese.

English decided to send seven fleet-type submarines into the Aleutians to reinforce the S-boats during the period of Japanese activity. The first of these to arrive, about 1 July, was *Growler*. There thus developed a strange similiarity between the patterns of American and Japanese submarine deployments in the Aleutians. Both navies kept five or six older type submarines more or less constantly assigned to the northern area. For both navies this duty was a grim business. The damp condensation dripped constantly from the interior of the steel hulls so that nothing ever dried out. High cold waves swept over the exposed submarine bridge, and cold wind froze the lookouts' hands to their binoculars as they strained their eyes against the blinding fog to sight the enemy or the almost equally dangerous rocks and shoals. On special occasions each navy sent more modern and better equipped submarines into the area for swift action while the older boats for the most part hung on and endured.

Elsewhere the war against Japanese shipping slowed to a stall in June. During the whole month U.S. submarines sank only five *marus*, two in the South China Sea, one in the Carolines, one in the East China Sea, and one in the Solomon Islands. It was late in the month before the submarines engaged in the Midway operation could be refueled, supplied, and redeployed. On 25 June, *Nautilus* was on patrol off Tokyo. She torpedoed *Yamakaze*, and took one of the best periscope pictures of the war, showing that Japanese destroyer looking very much like the cruiser Brockman took it for, going down by the stern, with its bow high in the air and the rising sun painted on top of its forward turret, just about to sink beneath the waves.

Torpedoes

It was June, of course, before submarines from the successful May patrols arrived back in Pearl Harbor, bringing with them a number of very angry skippers complaining about defective torpedoes. Against each of these complaints, the Force Torpedo Officer presented counterarguments, well documented in Comsubpac endorsement to patrol reports.

The system of patrol reports was excellent, and undoubtedly was an important factor in the rapid correction of faulty strategic and tactical submarine operation. During the war, patrol reports became choice reading for the esoteric few who had access to them. The dogma of the torpedo experts, however, was sharply revealed in Comsubpac's endorsements to these reports, which reflect a curious concept that the staff torpedo officer was an apologist for the torpedo, with the function of explaining away all complaints rather than of searching out defects and improving performance. Fortunately this concept did not extend to the Southwest Pacific, where Lockwood followed Wilkes with a healthy skepticism about torpedoes and kept up an open-minded investigation of reported defects, despite the handicap of enemy pressure and inadequate facilities.

A really ingenuous analysis of torpedo exploder failure was reserved for *Grenadier's* report of the *Taiyo Maru* attack. *Grenadier* had fired four torpedoes: two set for twenty-four feet had hit, and two set to run under the target at twenty-eight feet for influence explosion had not exploded, although they had been aimed within the hitting bracket of the other pair. The staff torpedo officer rejected the evidence, arguing that the first torpedo hit aft, stopping *Taiyo Maru* and causing the other three to miss ahead. The second hit reported, he decided, must have been an internal explosion. He then proceeded to tabulate eight different reasons for torpedo misses—and six of them were faults committed by commanding officers.

This patrol report must have caused considerable embarrassment to English. It was dated 18 June. Two days later Lockwood reported by dispatch to the Bureau of Ordnance the result of tests conducted in Australia which proved beyond reasonable doubt that the torpedoes were running on the average ten feet beneath their set depth. English must have been shaken, for on 24 June he informed the Bureau that his submarines also had experienced depth discrepancies. The Bureau of Ordnance responded to Lockwood's report with a statement that no reliable conclusion could be reached from the tests he had used. Lockwood patiently replied that the test would be repeated, and requested that the Bureau, with the infinitely greater resources at their disposal, try some tests of their own.

About this time Admiral King, Commander-in-Chief of the United States Fleet, who had been reading the exchange of dispatches, ordered the Bureau of Ordnance to conduct tests to recheck the tactical data of all torpedoes. On 1 August the Bureau of Ordnance informed all interested parties that tests conducted at Newport Torpedo Station showed the submarine torpedo did indeed run ten feet deeper than set. About a month later the Naval Torpedo Station issued a letter that can best be summarized as an admission that the depth control of torpedoes had been incompetently designed and inadequately tested. Equipment and instructions for correcting modifications would be sent out from Newport, and these modifications would make the torpedo run within three feet of the set depth. If this had been even the beginning of the end of torpedo failures the war would have been much shorter, but unfortunately there was more to come.

X

JULY–AUGUST 1942

Fleet Submarines in the Aleutians

With the arrival of American fleet-type submarines in the Aleutians, business picked up. *Triton* (Kirkpatrick) arrived on 3 July in a dense fog and, guided by her air search radar, groped her way into her patrol area off Agattu Island. The charts were grossly inaccurate, adding to the natural apprehension on the bridge in a fogbound submarine expecting momentary contact with the enemy. Early in the morning of 4 July the fog lifted slightly and Kirkpatrick caught a glimpse of a Japanese destroyer patrolling off McDonald Cove. He stalked the destroyer all day, in and out of the fog, and around the rocks. It was well along in the afternoon when the fog lifted briefly, disclosing the destroyer so close that Kirkpatrick refrained from sounding the General Alarm, and quietly passed the word for General Quarters, lest the Japanese destroyer pick up the submerged submarine by the sound of the alarm gong. A few minutes later he fired two torpedoes, one of which hit amidships.

The destroyer listed heavily to port, and Kirkpatrick watched its crew crawl down over the starboard side as the ship rolled over and went under. This was *Nenohi*, who capsized two minutes after being hit and went down with two hundred of her crew. Japanese destroyer captains characterized destroyers sunk by submarines as "a cat being eaten by a mouse." Yet it is a matter of record that many more Japanese destroyers were sunk by American submarines than there were American submarines sunk by Japanese destroyers—although happily for the submarines the Japanese destroyer captains remained unaware of this throughout the war, and credited themselves with sinking many more U.S. submarines than were actually lost from all causes.

The very next day *Growler* (Gilmore) was patrolling off Kiska Harbor, hampered by the same conditions of fog and current that had inhibited

Triton. Growler also was equipped with only air search radar, which was good enough for navigating by fixes on the high mountain peaks but not sensitive enough to pick up ships upon the sea. With air search radar and fathometer, Gilmore was working in to the entrance of Kiska Harbor about four o'clock in the morning of 5 July when he sighted three vessels he believed to be leaving Kiska, although the fog made all observation uncertain. Continuing to approach for nearly two hours, he found three destroyers at anchor. He fired torpedoes at all three targets, and saw the third destroyer fire torpedoes back at *Growler.* He went deep to avoid the Japanese torpedoes, but before the periscope went under he watched his own torpedoes hit. On the way down *Growler* heard the swish of Japanese torpedoes passing over, speeding alongside both port and starboard.

Gilmore's original contact had been with a Japanese destroyer division escorting a transport into Kiska with reinforcements for the garrison. After their transport made harbor the destroyers stood out again, but because of the fog they anchored just outside Kiska and *Growler* caught them unprepared. The Japanese destroyer *Arare* was sunk. The destroyer *Kasumi* had its bow blown off but about a month later it was successfully towed to Japan for repairs. The third ship was *Shiranui.* It was missed by *Growler's* first torpedo but hit amidships by the second. Its back was broken just abaft the stack but it also was patched up later and towed back to Japan for repairs.

A few days later *Growler* played a return engagement at Kiska, with somewhat different results. Again there was shifting fog, and patrol vessels off Kiska Harbor. The small patrol vessels seemed inefficient in their listening watches and did not inhibit *Growler* greatly. When Gilmore caught a glimpse of a large ship, he commenced a hide-and-seek game, surfacing whenever possible in low visibility to broaden his horizon and reduce his dependence on the sound gear under sound conditions that were very uncertain. He was on the surface about six o'clock in the evening when the fog lifted suddenly, revealing a Japanese destroyer patrolling less than a mile away. *Growler* made a fast dive but the destroyer saw her first. Although the destroyer was conducting a listening patrol, and *Growler's* listeners were on intense watch, neither the submarine nor the destroyer had heard the other and the contact was a sight contact on both sides. It was a close call for *Growler,* who was depth-charged and pursued for four hours. Her sound gear was crippled before it could be rigged in and one periscope was damaged but was still usable. When she finally shook off her pursuer, *Growler* eased into Dutch Harbor for repairs, Gilmore reproaching himself for unjustifiably risking his ship and crew by surface operation so close in to Kiska.

Loss of Grunion

Grunion (Abele), a brand new submarine on her first patrol, was not so fortunate. A few days after she arrived in the Aleutians she also was patrolling off Kiska. On 15 July she was attacked by a patrolling destroyer. Abele fired three torpedoes at the Japanese ship and missed. Later on the same day she attacked three other ships which she identified as destroyers but which were actually submarine chasers. *Submarine Chasers Nos. 25* and *27* were sunk in this attack. On 28 July *Grunion* fired two torpedoes at an unidentified ship and missed. On the thirtieth she was off Kiska again where she reported heavy anti-submarine activity. This was the last ever heard from *Grunion*, and what happened to her remains a mystery. There is nothing in the Japanese official records to account for her loss.

The fog was impartial, hampering the operations of Japanese and American submarines alike. The Japanese had no radar at all to help them. On 14 July the Japanese submarine *I-7* encountered the U. S. Army transport *Arcata* in Unimak Pass and sank her by gunfire, discovering in the process that it took a great many 14-centimeter gun hits to destroy a ship. The submarines of the Japanese Second Squadron were withdrawn at the end of July and replaced by old RO-type submarines which, as it turned out, had an even rougher time of it than the American S-boats of about the same size and vintage.

Southwest Pacific Submarines

Seadragon (Ferrall), in the South China Sea, had a very successful patrol in July. She sank three big *marus* and damaged a fourth off the Indo-China coast. *Sturgeon* (Wright) sank another northwest of Luzon. The Southwest Pacific submarine force was not yet back to strength after the depletion indirectly caused by the Midway operation. It required a month or more for a submarine from Pearl Harbor, scheduled to replace a Southwest Pacific submarine, to work its way to Fremantle, conducting patrol or reconnaissance missions en route.

Thresher (Millican), en route from Pearl Harbor to Fremantle, patrolled for a few days off Kwajalein. There on 9 July she sank the motor torpedo boat tender *Shinsho Maru* and became involved in a nerve-shattering episode with the Japanese anti-submarine forces. Right after sinking her target *Thresher* was attacked by aircraft bombs, two of which exploded uncomfortably close. Apparently, in the clear waters of the Marshalls, she could be easily tracked from the air. Surface patrols, guided to her position, promptly proceeded to securely hook onto

Thresher with a grapnel. Millican, listening to the rattle of chains outside the hull, knew his ship was in a desperate situation and ordered his secret encoding devices destroyed. He then went ahead full speed, with full right rudder and hard dive, and took *Thresher* down fifty feet below her test depth before he succeeded in shaking the Japanese hook out of her. Thankfully leaving Kwajalein astern after this experience *Thresher* proceeded to Truk, where she found considerable traffic coming through North Pass. This was an observation that other submarines would later exploit after Millican moved on to Fremantle.

Plunger sank a ship in the East China Sea. *Narwhal* sank one *maru* and several picket boats in the Kuriles. *Silversides* sank a ship south of Tokyo. S-37 sank the only Japanese ship to be destroyed in the South Pacific area in July. The total loss to the Japanese during July, combat and cargo, was well within the rate of loss that would be made up by shipbuilding. The storm was about to break, however, for both Japanese and American surface and air forces were gathering their resources for the next encounter, which was coming in August, in the sunny seas and steaming jungles of the Solomon Islands four thousand miles south of the cold and foggy Bering Sea and the treeless tundra of the Aleutians.

Guadalcanal

The Japanese, in their planning, were well aware of the strategic importance of the Solomon Islands, and so were the Americans. Although a decision had been made to give first priority to the war in the Atlantic, the Allies could not afford to permit the Japanese to entrench themselves firmly in a position from which it would be costly to dig them out or to let them stay and threaten American-Australian communications. On 2 July the Joint Chiefs of Staff issued a directive to occupy the Santa Cruz Islands, Tulagi near Florida Island in the Solomons, and adjacent positions, with a target date set for 1 August.

Most of July was devoted to scratching together the necessary forces and preparing for the first Allied offensive in the Pacific. On 21 July several thousand Japanese troops were landed at Buna and Gona, on the north coast of Papua, to commence an almost impossible march across the Owen Stanley Range to attack Port Moresby from the land side. It was touch and go who would get there "firstest with the mostest" in the Solomons or New Britain, and the Allies had no time to lose in preparation. Early in July Nimitz learned that the Japanese had moved across the channel from Tulagi to Guadalcanal. The Marines planned to seize the unfinished airfield there, and the resulting "meeting engagement," like the Confederate encounter with Union forces near Gettysburg, decided the site of the next great test of strength in the Pacific.

Submarine Supporting Operation

To the best of their ability submarines contributed to Allied preparations. The S-boats out of Brisbane helped to establish and supply a system
of coastwatchers, which became invaluable before the issue was finally
decided. These boats also patrolled off Rabaul and Kavieng. In addition,
five fleet submarines were sent from Pearl Harbor to patrol the waters off
Truk. This use of submarines in support of pending fleet actions was
well conceived and paid handsome dividends. The submarines were so
far removed from the area of fleet operations that their movements were
not restricted, yet Japanese supplies and reinforcements going into the
Solomons had to run the submarine gantlet.

Gudgeon (Stovall), en route from Pearl Harbor to Fremantle, was assigned an area west of Truk. She sank one ship there and damaged two
big oil tankers before proceeding to her destination. *Tambor* (Ambruster), also en route to Fremantle, sank two ships on her way through
the Caroline Islands. *Greenling* (Bruton) found busy Japanese traffic in
the area previously explored by *Thresher,* north of Truk.

On the night of 4 August at about ten o'clock, *Greenling* made a surface attack on a large unescorted ship, and apparently missed with four
torpedoes. The target continued on a northerly course and Bruton, swal-
lowing his disappointment, continued on the surface in the same direction. Three or four hours later, in the early morning of 5 August he made
contact with what he took to be an entirely different vessel. This time he
saw his torpedoes hit. After the ship went down he ran through the
wreckage and picked up a prisoner. The prisoner revealed that the ship
was the 12,000-ton *Brazil Maru,* carrying four hundred soldiers and two
hundred other passengers. She was the same ship Bruton had attacked
earlier, and she had then been hit by torpedoes which failed to explode.
Brazil Maru was scheduled to be converted to an escort carrier right after
she finished this emergency transport run. Bruton's persistent attacks prevented a lot of future trouble.

Continuing to patrol north of Truk, *Greenling* sank *Palau Maru,* another passenger-cargo ship, on 6 August. This was the day before the
Marines landed on Guadalcanal and Tulagi and all hell broke loose in
the Solomon Islands.

The Battle of Savo Island

The landings were a complete success. Before the end of the day the
Marines had captured the airfield on Guadalcanal and had the situation
well in hand. The Japanese reaction was violent. Shore-based airplanes

from Rabaul attacked within hours the same day and again the next. Despite heavy losses inflicted on them by carrier fighter planes they pushed home their attacks and damaged two destroyers and two transports. One of the transports burned throughout the following night, acting as a beacon for a Japanese cruiser attack, which was on its way.

When the Japanese Admiral at Rabaul (Mikawa) learned of the landing, he embarked all available troops in six transports and ordered them to proceed to Guadalcanal. In the meantime, with five heavy cruisers, two light cruisers, and a destroyer, he set out from Rabaul, flying his flag in the heavy cruiser *Chokai.* Around eight o'clock on the night of 7 August this force charged out into the Solomon Sea through St. George's Channel between New Ireland and New Britain. S-38 (Munson) was on patrol there. Munson was unable to deliver an attack against the speeding cruisers, but they passed right over him, and after they were gone he radioed a contact report on heavy ships moving southeast at high speed. The Japanese transports with reinforcements for Guadalcanal followed after the cruisers. They came through S-38's area at considerably slower speed the next day, and Munson torpedoed the 5600-ton transport *Meiyo Maru.* It went down with the loss of 342 lives. As *Meiyo Maru* was the key vessel of the expeditionary force, the other five transports were recalled to Rabaul, giving the Marines on Guadalcanal a little more time to consolidate their defenses.

The Japanese cruisers continued on toward Guadalcanal anchorage. They were sighted at ten o'clock the morning of 8 August by an Australian search plane, but due to a communication foul-up the information did not get through to the American and Australian surface forces in time to do much good. Fletcher had withdrawn his carrier forces. The Japanese force arrived at Savo Island, off the northwest end of Guadalcanal, about half-past one on the morning of 9 August, to find the Allied cruisers and destroyers badly deployed and unready. Four Allied heavy cruisers were sunk, one heavy cruiser and two destroyers were heavily damaged, and later in the day a previously damaged destroyer was sunk by a Japanese air strike. Two Japanese cruisers and three destroyers suffered minor damage. It was the most brilliant Japanese naval victory of the war and for the Americans it was a correspondingly black defeat. The remnants of the defeated surface forces withdrew the next day, leaving the Marines unsupported ashore on Guadalcanal and Tulagi.

S-44 *and* Kako

Against this pattern of naval defeat the submarines contributed the only bright spot of victory. The old S-44, under command of Lieutenant Commander J. R. Moore, was patrolling off Kavieng, New Ireland. On

10 August, four heavy cruisers of Japanese Cruiser Division Six, returning in triumph from the action off Savo Island, passed through this area.
At 0750 on the morning of 10 August, Moore saw them come, in two
sections of two cruisers each, with the ships of each section in column
and the sections in line bearing forty-five degrees, an impressive display
of Japanese power and might. When the range came down to nine thousand yards, S-44 found herself with a five-degree angle on the bow of
her target. This was too close to the track, so Moore ran out on a divergent course to open out a little and give S-44 more room to maneuver
and her torpedoes time to arm. Then he turned and came in on a course
for an eighty-degree track with zero gyro angle. He let the first ship go
by and five minutes later fired four torpedoes from a range of seven hundred yards. The second cruiser had no time to maneuver with such a
short torpedo run. The first torpedo hit thirty-five seconds after firing.
Three more hit in rapid succession. The Japanese heavy cruiser *Kako*
went to the bottom in five minutes.

That S-44 was there at all was a triumph of endurance, competence,
and logistics. This seventeen-year-old crock had made the epic transpa-
cific voyage from Panama, arriving at Brisbane in the middle of April.
She was on her third war patrol, and during the previous 180 days she
had been 127 at sea despite the worn-out condition of her machinery
and the stress and strain S-boat war patrols imposed upon her crew. With
obsolete fire control equipment and the slower but more dependable
S-boat torpedoes, Moore conducted a brilliant approach, and fully deserved his success which, like Sir John Jervis' victory at Cape St. Vincent,
was greatly needed.

Loss of S-39

After this auspicious start, submarines' contribution to the American
war effort in the Solomon area petered out, and not another Japanese
ship was sunk in that area by U.S. submarines for the remainder of the
month of August. On 14 August, S-39 (Brown), on patrol off Rossel Island, down by the tip of New Guinea's tail, ran aground on a submerged
reef. All efforts to back her off failed. Brown called for help, and the Australian corvette *Katoomba* was sent to his assistance. Before the corvette
arrived twenty-foot-high breakers rolling over S-39 pushed her farther up
on the reef and the ballast tanks were ruptured. On 15 August Brown
made a final desperate effort to get her off, but the ship took a sixty-
degree list and lay on her side on the rocks. Fearing that she would roll
completely over, Brown sent two swimmers in to the reef to secure a line
over which thirty men were evacuated to the reef, on which they spent

a most uncomfortable night, leaving twelve men still on board S-39. The next day *Katoomba* arrived and embarked the entire forty-four men of the crew of the submarine, leaving S-39 to be destroyed by the sea.

Japanese Submarines

Japanese submarines responded to the Guadalcanal landings by concentrating two RO- and three I-class submarines in Indispensable Strait, between Florida and Malaita Islands, to ambush American ships approaching the Guadalcanal and Tulagi anchorages. *RO-33* made contact with the Japanese defenders of Guadalcanal and landed medical supplies. She thought that she sank a transport but she was mistaken. In the first two weeks after the landing, Japanese submarines contributed very little to the series of skirmishes and brutal battles that went on almost constantly.

Air and Surface Forces in the Solomons

The initial Japanese victory at the Battle of Savo Island on 9 August was followed by months of intensive war on land and sea, and in the air, and in the waters under the sea—to decide who would control the island of Guadalcanal, which nobody wanted, but whose possession would determine the direction in which the war would move. On shore, the Marines (who were later reinforced by the Americal Division of the U. S. Army) fought a succession of bloody battles through the jungles to hold Henderson Field. The possession of the airfield was necessary to control the air over the southern Solomons, for if it were lost the Japanese would be able to swarm "down the Slot" through the Solomon Islands in sufficient numbers to push the Marines off Guadalcanal. So long as planes could take off from Henderson Field, Army, Navy, and Marine aviators scrambled at the approach of enemy planes or ships. In the daytime, with the airfield in good operating condition, a Japanese ship entered the waters surrounding Guadalcanal only at the risk of almost certain damage or destruction. The Japanese persisted in their attempts to knock out the airfield by bombing raids. Usually these were tipped off in advance by coastwatchers, and this resulted in almost daily air battles over the southern Solomons.

At night the Japanese sent destroyers and sometimes submarines down the Slot, loaded with supplies and troops to reinforce their forces on Guadalcanal. On occasion Japanese heavy combat ships came down to bombard the airfield at night. During the day American ships moved supplies and reinforcements to the Marines in a very thin trickle, occasionally retaliating for the Japanese bombardments by bombarding Japanese-held positions along the coastline. Japanese planes countered with bombing and torpedo attacks against these American forays. In general the Japanese more or less controlled the waters around Guadalcanal at night, and the Americans in the daytime. This situation was satisfactory to neither party and on repeated occasions the ordinary level of constant struggle erupted into the wildest and most desperately fought sea battles of this or any other war.

The Japanese and American forces were nearly evenly balanced. If the first Japanese victory had been followed up in force it is probable that the Marines could not have held out. There were insufficient Allied surface forces then in the South Pacific to contest a determined Japanese thrust. Fletcher's timorous use of the carrier forces left Guadalcanal virtually unprotected against a Japanese buildup. For various reasons the Japanese were unable to exploit the situation.

The Combined Fleet and the Second Fleet had retired to Japan after the Battle of Midway. Yamamoto was unwilling to commit the main Japanese fleet in a do-or-die effort in the far Solomon Islands. The carrier fleet was short of planes and trained pilots and Nagumo was reluctant to send his half-trained air groups into battle so soon after Midway.

The Japanese have a proverb which might be roughly translated that he who chases two rabbits will come home empty-handed. Despite the wisdom of this saying, the Japanese frequently found themselves charging in all directions at once. In August 1942 they still had the Aleutian bear by the tail. They were also committed to the attack on Port Moresby over the Owen Stanley Range, and this they considered their main objective for which Guadalcanal was initially only a sideshow to protect their eastern flank. Their estimate of the situation, based on intelligence picked up in Moscow, placed the Marine strength on Guadalcanal at about two thousand (an underestimate by a factor of about ten), and they believed that they were confronted with only a raid, in which the Marines would destroy the airfield and then withdraw. All this contributed to the Japanese error of committing their forces piecemeal, at a level of effort that the Americans, deeply involved in the Atlantic, could just barely manage to balance.

On 15 August the Americans had recovered sufficiently to send supplies, ammunition, and Marine planes in to Guadalcanal. The Japanese, still considering New Guinea as the main objective, landed two large convoys at Buna, bringing their strength there to over eleven thousand men. In contrast, they had less than a thousand troops to spare to reinforce Guadalcanal. This was the "Ichiki Detachment," originally intended as part of the Midway Occupation Force. They were still at Guam where they were quickly loaded into destroyers for a fast run to Guadalcanal, and landed there on the night of 18 August. The transporting destroyers lingered after daybreak and one of them was damaged by bombs dropped from a B-17 flying out of Espíritu Santo, in the New Hebrides. Three U.S. destroyers escorting ships into Tulagi waited until after nightfall to oppose Japanese destroyers spotted coming down the Slot. Japanese night optics proved superior to American search radar. *Blue* was torpedoed and sank without ever seeing her antagonist.

Battle of the Eastern Solomons

The Marines wiped out the Ichiki Detachment less than four days after it landed. Yamamoto, who had already sailed from Japan with a strong force of carriers, battleships, and cruisers, then decided to strike in force. On 23 August the main force of Japanese carriers and battleships was descending on the Solomons from the north. Fifteen hundred troops were embarked in the auxiliary cruiser *Kinryu Maru* and four ex-destroyer transports, protected by the light cruiser *Jintsu* and eight destroyers. To the westward were the four heavy cruisers from Rabaul that had fought the Battle of Savo Island so brilliantly, standing by for a repeat performance. Six I-class submarines were in scouting line in advance of the main Japanese force, and six more were disposed in the area south and east of the Solomons.

Fletcher, with the carriers, a new fast battleship, seven cruisers, and eighteen destroyers, was at sea about 150 miles due east of Guadalcanal. Patrol planes made contact with the Japanese transport force on 23 August. The next day the third big carrier battle of the war was fought. The Japanese light carrier *Ryujo* was sunk. *Shokaku* and the seaplane carrier *Chitose* were damaged. *Enterprise* was severely damaged but remained operational. Both carrier forces pulled back. That night Japanese destroyers bombarded Guadalcanal. The next day Marine planes from Henderson Field attacked the Japanese transport group, damaging *Jintsu* and sinking *Kinryu Maru*, which had a large share of the troops on board. While Japanese destroyers were rescuing troops from *Kinryu Maru*, B-17s from Espíritu Santo bombed them. The Japanese destroyer *Uzuki* was damaged. Her sister ship *Mutsuki* received a direct hit and was sunk. This was the first Japanese combat ship to be sunk by a B-17.

Tokyo Express

The remaining Japanese troops were taken in to Shortland Island. Four days later they were loaded into destroyers for a fast run to Guadalcanal. Marine dive bombers caught this force in Indispensable Strait on the evening of 28 August. One Japanese destroyer was sunk, three others badly damaged, and the whole force turned back to Shortland Island. About this time a brigade of Japanese troops originally intended for New Guinea was diverted to Bougainville and these troops also were run down the Slot to Guadalcanal in fast destroyer night runs. The Marines dubbed these destroyer operations the "Tokyo Express." The Tokyo Express succeeded, against all opposition, in building up the Japanese forces ashore on Guadalcanal.

Japanese Submarines

Early in August plans for an extensive Japanese submarine campaign in the Indian Ocean were canceled and two squadrons of submarines intended for that operation were rushed south for action in the Solomons. A pattern of operation in the Solomons developed that greatly favored Japanese submarines. Japanese surface forces had the initiative and picked the time for their sorties to relieve Guadalcanal. In between times they holed up in Rabaul or Truk, safe from American submarines. When they emerged, they operated mainly at night, and at high speed, which rendered them relatively immune to undersea attack. The American carrier task forces, on the other hand, without protected harbors in the area, stayed at sea within striking distance of Guadalcanal, where their unimaginative tactics made them very vulnerable to Japanese submarine attack.

The Japanese made strenuous efforts to exploit their opportunity. Seven I-class submarines of the Advance Expeditionary Force, operating in advance of the Japanese fleet, arrived in the Solomons on 24 August and remained after their surface forces retired. These submarines were frequently sighted and attacked by anti-submarine patrol planes from the carriers. Despite optimistic reports of sinkings, however, the carrier planes succeeded only in damaging *I-17* and *I-121*. The old light minelayer *Gamble* was the first to sink a Japanese submarine in the Solomons area. While she was acting as anti-submarine screen for a task group off Guadalcanal on the morning of 28 August she sighted the conning tower of a large submarine. Her depth-charge attack brought up convincing evidence of a kill. This was the end of *I-123*. The next day *RO-33*, having safely completed her Guadalcanal mission and been sent to patrol off Port Moresby, was sunk by the Australian destroyer *Arunta*.

On 31 August the concentration of submarines against the American carrier forces gave *I-26* her opportunity for fame and glory. For several days Fletcher, with three carrier task forces, had been standing by southeast of the Solomons, patrolling a small area while he waited. This was an invitation for a torpedo attack. Several submarine contacts were made by search planes in the circumscribed rectangle in which the carriers moved. Early on the morning of 31 August *I-26* fired six torpedoes at *Saratoga*. *MacDonough*, a destroyer in her screen, saw them coming and signaled a warning but it was too late. *Saratoga* was hit by one torpedo and had to be sent back to the navy yard for repairs.

From January to June of 1942 *Saratoga* had been in the navy yard recovering from a submarine torpedo. She had missed the Battle of Midway where she was sorely needed. At the end of August she was headed back to the West Coast for new surgery for the old disorder. It was a real accomplishment for Japanese submarines. The heavy cruiser *Kako* was the largest ship to be hit by an effective American submarine torpedo up to this moment in the war. Japanese submarines, in a war in which carrier strength was critical, had sunk the disabled *Yorktown*, and kept *Saratoga* in the navy yard for the greater part of the time. *MacDonough* came very close to ramming *I-26*. She scraped alongside the Japanese submarine as it went deep, but *I-26* escaped without damage.

In the rest of the Pacific the balance was in favor of American submarines for August. During the month a total of 114,000 tons of Japanese merchant shipping went to the bottom, and of the twenty-one *marus* sunk, U.S. submarines accounted for eighteen. Five *marus* were sunk in the Caroline Islands. Four more went down in the Southwest Pacific area and five off the coast of Japan. *Growler* and *Haddock* sank two apiece near Formosa.

Haddock (Taylor) was the first submarine to carry the new SJ radar on patrol. Taylor came back with reports that the new radar required constant nursing by a skilled technician, but it was far superior to the old air search radar. With it, at night he could literally run rings around the Japanese.

When *Haddock* made contact with a freighter in the East China Sea, just before two o'clock in the morning of 26 August, Taylor found the moon too bright in a cloudless sky to permit him to make an undetected surface attack. His radar gave him contact at twelve thousand yards, far outside visual range. He went ahead full speed, and ran around his target to get ahead of his victim by dawn. Radar gave him continuous contact to track his unseen target, and when the sun came up he submerged to make a normal submerged approach with the periscope. Taylor fired four torpedoes from the stern tubes and they all missed. He then swung *Haddock* under hard rudder to bring her bow to bear and fired two torpedoes from the forward tubes. One of these hit and *Teishun Maru* went down in thirty minutes. Taylor watched as *Teishun Maru's* crew, all in clean white uniforms, abandoned ship in good order, forming their boats in column under oars until their ship sank. Then they hoisted sail and headed west.

Submarines in the Aleutians

Up in the Aleutians, *Finback* (Hull) landed a surveying party on Tanaga Island on 11 August and took it off again the next day without casualty. On this brief Aleutian patrol *Finback* sighted several ships but generally was unable to attack because of drifting fog. Hull fired torpedoes at two destroyers on one occasion and thought he had one hit. *Triton* was also still in the area. Kirkpatrick fired torpedoes, in poor visibility, at a "ship larger than a destroyer." He observed a hit with a tremendous explosion but there are no corresponding Japanese records of damage from either attack.

August operations of Japanese submarines in the Aleutians were also unrewarding. *I-25* came through the area about the middle of August, on her way to an operating area off the Oregon coast. Otherwise only three or four old RO-boats were left by the Japanese to operate in the Aleutians. These submarines had a test depth of only 125 feet and their thin skins made them very vulnerable to depth-charge attack.

An American task force moved in to occupy Adak on 30 August. *RO-61*, *RO-62*, and *RO-64* were ordered to attack. *RO-61* succeeded in torpedoing *Casco*, and reported that she had sunk a seaplane carrier. *Casco* was a seaplane tender, but her 1700 tons was a far cry from the 10,000-ton Japanese seaplane carriers; and *Casco* was not sunk. Five men were killed by the torpedo explosion and she had to be beached but she was later refloated and repaired. *RO-61* did not long survive her success. The next day (31 August) she was sighted and bombed by patrol planes. This attack was followed up by depth charges from the destroyer *Reid*. The depth-charge attack forced *RO-61* to the surface, where she was destroyed by gunfire. Five of the survivors of the submarine crew were picked up as prisoners of war.

Makin Raid

Nautilus and *Argonaut* found employment during August, for which their large size made them well suited, and for which their slow speed submerged did not unduly handicap them. On 8 August these two submarines left Pearl Harbor with 222 Marines of "Carlson's Raiders" embarked to raid Makin in the Gilbert Islands. This operation was intended to divert Japanese forces from the Solomons area, to secure intelligence material, and to gain experience in amphibious operations against a reef-protected Micronesian atoll. Lieutenant Colonel Evans F. Carlson commanded the Marines, with Major James Roosevelt second in command. Commander John M. Haines was task force commander embarked in *Nautilus*. Commander William H. Brockman commanded *Nautilus* and Lieutenant Commander J. R. Pierce commanded *Argonaut*. The submarines arrived off Makin on 16 August after an overcrowded and uncomfortable trip, particularly during all-day dives when there was barely standing room on board for both passengers and crew.

The sixteenth of August was spent in reconnaissance. This was too short a time for the careful reconnaissance which should have preceded the operation. In retrospect, Haines believed that with more extended reconnaissance a better landing beach could have been discovered. Even this much observation established the fact that the nineteenth-century charts, the best available, were grossly inaccurate. Recent aerial photographs taken by the U. S. Army were much better, but these had necessarily been taken of a Japanese-occupied island without ground control panels, and they were incorrectly oriented. The fathometer showed that the water shoaled from over a thousand fathoms to 145 fathoms within a quarter of a mile approaching the beach. Accuracy in navigation was essential to rendezvous with small boats, and poor charts were a major headache.

About two o'clock on the morning of 17 August preparations were made to disembark the Marines into rubber boats, and at four o'clock all boats were clear and en route to the beach. An hour later the Marines landed. The submarines remained on the surface, attempting to maintain communication with the Marines through portable radios. Communications were poor. At about seven o'clock *Nautilus* picked up parts of a message asking for fire support in a designated area.

Arrangements had been made to receive fire correction spots from an observer on the beach, but these arrangements failed completely. *Nautilus* opened up with her pair of 6-inch guns and pumped shells into the general area. She had no special bombardment ammunition, but apparently her fire had good effect. A few minutes later she received a message that there were two Japanese ships in the harbor, and Brockman shifted fire to these targets. The ships were out of sight on the other side of the island, with numerous trees in the line of fire, and there was still no communication with the spotter. Firing from fourteen thousand yards' range *Nautilus* attempted to cover the lagoon by shifting range and deflection using indirect fire. After expending sixty-five rounds of ammunition Brockman ceased fire, because he considered further expenditure of ammunition unjustified in this method of blind firing. Unbelievably, when the Marines came back to *Nautilus*, they reported that both the Japanese ships had been sunk.

The Marines were due to leave the beach at seven that evening. About eight-thirty the two submarines picked up seven of the nineteen boats, and maneuvered the rest of the night trying to find the others. The returning raiders reported that it was almost impossible to get through the surf from shore to sea in a rubber boat, so Brockman decided to close the beach by daylight and offer his assistance. *Nautilus* came in to within a half mile of the reef about seven in the morning and located several boats apparently making preparations to come out through the surf. Two or three boats finally made it to the submarine and one of these was sent back, manned by volunteers, with a line-throwing gun and other equipment, and a message for Colonel Carlson that even if the submarines were forced to dive they would stand by indefinitely until all the Marines were off the beach. About eight o'clock a plane contact sent both submarines under. Two bombs exploded at a distance and both submarines stayed down all day.

After sunset *Argonaut* and *Nautilus* rendezvoused and came back in to the beachhead. Colonel Carlson signaled from the beach, directing the submarines to pick up the remaining Marines at a designated point near the entrance to the lagoon on the leeward side of the atoll. By midnight this had been accomplished. Thirty Marines were unaccounted for and a number were wounded. It was believed that every live Marine had been taken off the island, but this was not the case. Nine Marines had been left on the island, and were captured by the Japanese. These were shipped to Kwajalein with the intention of later sending them to Tokyo as prisoners, but on 16 October 1942 Vice Admiral Koso Abe, the Marshall Islands commander, decided they would all be executed. They were all beheaded on his orders. After the war Abe was tried for this atrocity, convicted, and hanged at Guam.

The raid was acclaimed a success. About eighty Japanese had been killed. The Makin garrison was wiped out and for a time the Marines were in actual control of the island. Two planes were destroyed, in addition to the ships *Nautilus* sank, and a quantity of aviation gasoline and other stores destroyed. It is doubtful that any Japanese forces were diverted from Guadalcanal. The intelligence material obtained was immaterial. Some interesting Japanese charts of the Gilbert Islands were recovered, but these turned out on translation to be Japanese copies of the original American plates that had been given to the Japanese Navy after the Tokyo earthquake. The experience helped to indicate difficulties that would later be encountered on a large scale, when the time came for landings in earnest. The Japanese reinforced the Gilberts until they became tough nuts to crack when Tarawa was taken fourteen months later.

XI

SEPTEMBER–OCTOBER 1942

At the end of August 1942 the main objective of the Japanese in the South Pacific was still the capture of Port Moresby. On 26 August they landed an amphibious force at Milne Bay to establish a base through which they could stage troops in landing barges around the end of New Guinea to approach Port Moresby from the sea side. Australians and Americans from MacArthur's forces defeated this invasion attempt in the Battle of Milne Bay. On 5 September the Japanese had to evacuate the remainder of their shattered forces. As a result of this reverse the Japanese decided to concentrate on Guadalcanal, and for the time being to leave Papua on the defensive. Unfortunately the Allies were not informed of this decision, and as Japanese troops had pushed over the almost impossible mountain route to within a few miles of Port Moresby, none of the meager forces of MacArthur could be spared to help out in the defense of Guadalcanal.

As long as Henderson Field remained in operation Yamamoto was unwilling to risk Japanese capital ships in the Solomons, but destroyers continued the night runs of the Tokyo Express, bringing in supplies and reinforcements. The Japanese planned to build up sufficient forces to capture Henderson by assault. Yamamoto would then move in with a full-scale amphibious operation, backed up with heavy naval forces held in readiness at Truk, and "at one stroke" clean the Marines out of the Solomons. The Marines did not cooperate. The Japanese Army staged its assault on 12 September and was badly defeated at the Battle of Bloody Ridge.

Surface naval activity during the first part of September was limited largely to transport operations. Both navies lost light forces in these actions. The destroyer transports *Gregory* and *Little* were sunk in a night action off Guadalcanal. The Japanese destroyer *Yayoi* was sunk by U. S.

Army and Australian Air Forces off Goodenough Island. Army bombers damaged three larger ships. *I-11* took a potshot at *Hornet* on 6 September and missed. The Japanese submarine was damaged in the counterattack and barely escaped.

Japanese Submarine Operations in September

After the Battle of Bloody Ridge, Turner embarked the 7th Marine Regiment in six transports and set out with them from Espíritu Santo to reinforce Guadalcanal. *Hornet* and *Wasp* with their cruisers and destroyers were at sea to guard this convoy against Japanese heavy forces. On 15 September the carrier task forces ran into Japanese submarines who had been patiently waiting east of the Solomons for just such an opportunity. *I-19* (Kinashi) fired four torpedoes at *Wasp*, and three of them hit. Seven minutes later *I-15* (Ishikawa) fired torpedoes at the *Hornet* task force. *Mustin*, a destroyer in the screen, saw them coming, broke the torpedo flag, and shouted the alarm by voice radio, but it was too late for *North Carolina* to get out of the way. This new battleship was hit by one torpedo but was able to carry her wounds stoically. Two minutes later another torpedo from *I-15* hit destroyer *O'Brien*.

O'Brien made it into Espíritu Santo with her bow blown off. She foundered later en route to the West Coast for permanent repairs. *North Carolina* was able to continue with this operation but *Wasp* was done for. She was gutted by fire and an hour after she was hit had to be abandoned. At nine o'clock that night it was evident she was beyond salvage and she was sunk by torpedoes fired from *Lansdowne*. It was a spectacular achievement for Japanese submarines. Within little more than a fortnight they had retired *Saratoga* and *North Carolina* for repairs and sunk *Wasp*. Together with the dive bomber damage to *Enterprise*, these submarine successes had reduced the operational American carriers in the Pacific to one (*Hornet*). Moreover, the gunpower of *North Carolina* and *O'Brien* would be sorely missed before the issue was decided. Near the end of the month *I-4* torpedoed and damaged the supply ship *Alhena*, southeast of the Solomons.

In the Aleutians Japanese submarines were far less effective. U. S. Army Air Force continued to harass Kiska and incidently shoot up the submarines in the area. *RO-63* and *RO-64* were damaged by air attacks on 15 September. On 28 September an Army Air Force raid on Kiska sank the 8000-ton cargo vessel *Nojima Maru*. *RO-67* was damaged in the attack and *RO-65* had a diving casualty while submerging to avoid attack. She hit the bottom so hard that she never came up again, although many of her crew succeeded in escaping. Shortly after this the remainder of the RO-class submarines were withdrawn from the Aleutians, leaving no Japanese submarines at all for a time in the North Pacific.

I-25 (Tagami) arrived off the coast of Oregon in September on a romantic mission proposed by her warrant flying officer, Fujita, to exact vengeance for the Doolittle raid. The Imperial Naval Headquarters had approved his proposal to bomb the United States mainland and assigned the forests of Oregon as a target. On 9 September Fujita took off from *I-25* in his light plane and dropped four incendiary bombs with which he hoped to start devastating forest fires. The air raid was repeated on the night of 29 September but practically no damage resulted from either bombing.

On 5 October Tagami reported sinking a tanker off Seattle and the next day torpedoed another. *I-25* then had only one torpedo remaining and Tagami started back for Japan. About ten-thirty on the morning of 11 October, while on the surface, the lookout reported masts on the horizon. *I-25* submerged and identified the target through the periscope as two submarines running on the surface. Tagami fired his last torpedo and saw it hit. Everyone in *I-25* prayed for the souls of the crew of the American submarine they had sunk.

No American submarine was lost at that time and place and the incident was unexplained until long after the war. In October two Russian submarines, *L-15* and *L-16*, were proceeding south along the West Coast of the United States en route from Vladivostok to Panama. On 15 October only *L-15* arrived at San Francisco and reported that *L-16* had been sunk by an internal explosion off the coast of Washington. Postwar Russian statements infer that the Russians believe *L-16* was sunk by an American S-boat, but data from several Japanese sources prove beyond reasonable doubt that Tagami mistook *L-16* for an American submarine and sank the Russian with *I-25's* last torpedo. As Japan and Russia were then not at war this might have had serious diplomatic consequences had the facts been known at the time.

American Submarine Operations

The accomplishments of American submarines in September were much less spectacular. *S-47* reported sinking a *Kako*-class cruiser in St. George's Channel on 12 September but she was mistaken. The limitations of S-boats in the tropical waters of the Solomons were all too apparent. It was decided to retire them from the South Pacific and replace them with fleet submarines detached from Pearl Harbor. There were then only eight submarines operating out of Fremantle. Twenty submarines were assigned to Brisbane to operate under Commander South

Pacific for the duration of the Solomons campaign. This buildup was not completed until later in the year.

In the Aleutians American submarines accomplished nothing during the month. U.S. submarines sank no Japanese combat ships in the whole Pacific during September. Only twelve *marus* and one naval auxiliary, totaling less than fifty thousand tons, were sunk during the whole month. The outstanding performance of the month was that of *Guardfish* (Klakring), which was sent to an area off the northeast coast of Honshu for her first patrol.

Guardfish

This area had been relatively undisturbed since the war began. *Guardfish* had a stormy trip out, for the roaring forties, even in August, were not comfortable latitudes for submarines. Before she reached her area, she crossed the traffic route between northern Honshu ports and the Aleutians and made her first contact with the enemy. Klakring fired his first torpedoes of the war at a naval auxiliary and missed. The escorting destroyer counterattacked and held *Guardfish* down until the larger ship had safely cleared the area.

Guardfish arrived in her assigned area on 20 August, and finding it infested with sampans, trawlers, and small patrol vessels, sank two by gunfire. Four days later she sank *Seikai Maru* as it came out of the outer harbor of Sendai. The bow of the ship was blown almost completely off and it went down with the screws still turning over, as several of *Guardfish's* officers took turns watching it sink. This ship was part of a convoy, and the rest turned around and ran back into the harbor.

The next morning before dawn *Guardfish* made contact with another ship, but the submarine was sighted and her intended victim changed course toward the beach and sent out a radio submarine warning. Inshore work was very unnerving for *Guardfish* in this area. Accurate navigation was a difficult matter. The coast of Honshu was generally obscured by fog, and nearly 40 per cent of the time the visibility was less than three miles. Offshore the Black Japan Current set northward at two knots, but inshore there was a countercurrent setting southward at nearly the same speed, and until *Guardfish* learned to distinguish between the two by keeping track of the water temperature, dead reckoning was by guess and by god. There appeared to be a system of lights arranged on the beach to guide local pilots. This was no help to Klakring, who did not know the system. Search radar could take ranges on the mountain peaks, but without one good look at the land to identify the peaks, that was little aid to navigation. Nevertheless *Guardfish* submerged and went in after the target, with her trust in luck and her faith in the fathometer.

About six o'clock in the morning she had a Japanese freighter in view.

Klakring fired two torpedoes and watched them run. The first torpedo leaped vertically out of the sea and porpoised repeatedly a few yards off the *maru's* bow. The second torpedo hit under the target's bridge, and sent a plume of spray as high as the main deck but did not explode. The target slowed and changed course. Klakring fired another torpedo and this one either passed under or ran very close alongside the target. There was a loud explosion. The ship headed toward the beach and disappeared in the shoreward mist. Klakring decided to surface and pursue, but on the way up the radar picked up four planes approaching and he thought better of it. A few minutes later *Guardfish* passed within four hundred yards of one of the torpedoes she had fired, floating vertically and minus its warhead. The executive officer and the torpedo officer were called to the periscope to observe this phenomenon.

This indisputable evidence of exploder failure would have been valuable information if it had been followed up. Before the depth control difficulties were corrected many torpedoes ran so deep beneath their targets that exploders did not function, but there was evidence that this was not the sole difficulty. A prisoner reported that some of *Greenling's* torpedoes hit *Brazil Maru* and failed to explode. Although the accumulating of such evidence under battle conditions is most difficult, other incidences strongly indicated dud torpedoes. Klakring's verified observation provided rare evidence that a torpedo had hit the target with such force that the warhead broke clear off the torpedo—and still failed to explode. This could not be explained by deep running or by misadjustment of sensitive magnetic exploder circuits. It could have been the result of a flooded exploder, which might be prevented by proper torpedo maintenance. It was easier to assume that this was the case than it was to conduct competent investigations at a torpedo station under test conditions. Had it been otherwise the war would have been over sooner and many more men would have survived it.

Torpedo exploders did not always fail, and what happened later helped to obscure the evidence. On 2 September *Guardfish* sank *Teikyu Maru* with two torpedoes from a three-torpedo spread. This was a 2000-ton freighter (estimated by Klakring to be much bigger), and the torpedoes functioned perfectly. *Teikyu Maru* broke in two and very promptly sank.

Two days later *Guardfish*, submerged about eight miles offshore, sighted three freighters coming up along the coast, scraping along the beach only a half mile offshore. The current set against the submarine, and Klakring was unable to get closer than five thousand yards, but the overlapping target of the two leading ships was so tempting that he fired one torpedo, set on low speed, and watched it go down the 120-degree track. In the conning tower he could hear no explosion, but the forward torpedo room reported a concussion three or four minutes after firing.

The target emitted a quantity of black smoke, headed toward the beach, and disappeared behind a cloud of smoke.

With traffic running so close to the beach, Klakring decided the best place for *Guardfish* was between the Japanese ship route and the shore, where he could attack from an unexpected angle, and cut off retreat of damaged ships. Close study disclosed a jutting cape named Benten Bana, that would force a knuckle in the track of northbound traffic. Klakring eased *Guardfish* into the tight nook in Benten Bana's lee. His analysis was correct.

He let a small oiler go by, unwilling to disclose his ambush for such small game. Then about four o'clock in the afternoon two large ships came up over the horizon to the south, and their route carried them right by *Guardfish's* position. Klakring fired one torpedo from a stern tube at the leading ship from a range of five hundred yards. Twenty-seven seconds later there was a tremendous explosion, but Klakring at the periscope didn't have time to look. He fired two torpedoes at the second ship from a thousand-yard range. At least one hit. Both ships were so badly shattered that they went down within a few minutes. Most of the officers and many of *Guardfish's* crew filed by the periscope to look. The officers were in agreement that these were big ships, from ten to fourteen thousand tons, but actually they were *Tenyu Maru* and *Kaimei Maru*, of 3738 and 5254 tons respectively.

Even as this brace of ships was sinking, another pair of freighters came over the southern horizon. When they saw what had happened to their predecessors, they fled into a small and shallow bay just south of Benten Bana. Klakring ran south to investigate, skirting just to seaward of the rocks off the cape. One of the freighters had anchored in the harbor, while the other was moving nervously about inside the bay. *Guardfish* worked herself around the rocks until the fathometer indicated twenty-five fathoms and she had a clear shot at the anchored target. She fired one torpedo in low power. Seven and a half minutes later the torpedo hit and the freighter went down stern first, reaching a final resting position with her stern on the bottom and her bow a hundred feet in the air. This was *Chita Maru*, a 2276-ton cargo ship.

Klakring's tactics disturbed the Japanese very much. The next month they planted a minefield along the coast where *Guardfish* had operated. This minefield was designed to protect the seaward flank of freighters running close along the coast. All the mines were anchored mines but some of them were planted in water over 250 fathoms deep, which was much deeper water than American mine intelligence officers expected to find them. The first victims of this Japanese minefield were their own *marus*, but this was the beginning of the northeast minefield that was eventually very costly to U.S. submarines.

Battle of Cape Esperance

Meanwhile, in the South Pacific, the Solomon's pot was beginning to boil again. Guadalcanal was initially a Japanese Navy show but in September the Japanese Army decided to take over the land fighting in earnest. The infamous Japanese Army 2nd Division, that had raped Nanking, was moved up to Rabaul from comparatively soft billets in Java. The Army called on the Navy for a joint amphibious operation to transport the division and land them near Cape Esperance, the northwestern tip of Guadalcanal.

The Japanese Army Air Force was greatly inferior to the Japanese Navy Air Force, and the Navy had to furnish the air support for this operation. The Navy was hard pressed for air strength. They had five carriers, but after the Battle of Midway they were chronically short of carrier pilots. Pilots were being trained for carrier operation in the Inland Sea but they were not yet ready for a carrier battle. Eighty bombers and a hundred fighters were brought down to Truk in escort carriers, and from there ferried into Rabaul. These were fed into the insatiable maw of Henderson Field, and when they were lost they were followed by others, down the same route, until the loss of carrier planes and pilots compromised the whole future conduct of the war. Nevertheless the Tokyo Express continued to run.

It was impossible to stop the night-prowling Japanese destroyers. On the night of 9 October they landed a large contingent of troops, practically completing the transfer of the Japanese 2nd Division to Guadalcanal. That same day the Americal Division of the U. S. Army set out from Nouméa, New Caledonia, to reinforce the Marines. *Hornet* and the new battleship *Washington* were at sea in support. Rear Admiral Scott, with four cruisers and five destroyers, sortied from Espíritu Santo with orders to "search for and destroy enemy ships and landing craft" in an effort to stop the Tokyo Express.

In accepting the challenge for night action, the American Navy was leading into Japanese strength. The Japanese Navy had concentrated on training for night action as the best recourse of a numerically inferior Navy. Their night tactics were well developed, their optics were superior, and their torpedoes were greatly superior to the Americans'. The oxygen-charged Long Lance torpedo, carried by Japanese cruisers and destroyers, gave them a margin of superiority difficult to overcome. One advantage held by the Americans was radar, with which the Japanese cruisers and destroyers were not equipped in 1942.

Scott's cruisers and destroyers met a Japanese force of cruisers and destroyers in the Battle of Cape Esperance on the night of 11–12 October.

Radar enabled the Americans to catch the Japanese by surprise and a confused night battle ensued. The Japanese lost the cruiser *Furutaka*. The American destroyer *Duncan* was sunk. The next day dive bombers from Henderson Field sank two Japanese destroyers trying to pick up survivors of sunken ships. The Japanese submarine *I-2* fired torpedoes at *McCalla* while that American destroyer was also trying to pick up Japanese survivors. The torpedoes missed. Many ships on both sides were damaged. It was a clear-cut victory for Scott, but he had to withdraw his damaged ships to Espíritu Santo and the Tokyo Express resumed its runs.

Battle of Santa Cruz

Nagumo sailed from Truk on 11 October with the strongest Japanese force assembled since the Battle of Midway. As a curtain-raiser the battleships *Kongo* and *Haruna* bombarded Henderson Field with 14-inch shells on the night of 13–14 October and destroyed over half the planes and nearly all the aviation gasoline. The October plan of the Japanese was similar to the September one; interdiction of Henderson Field by air attack during the day and bombardment by night while the troop strength built up until the Japanese Army could carry the field by assault; then move in with the surface Navy and transports to protect, reinforce and consolidate their position. Fifteen Japanese submarines were deployed in Torpedo Junction, between Espíritu Santo and the Solomons. D-day was set for 22 October but had to be postponed because of the hard fighting ashore. Both sides lost light naval forces and air strength in constant minor conflicts.

On 18 October Vice Admiral W. F. Halsey relieved Vice Admiral Ghormley as Commander South Pacific. Halsey sent a force of two carriers, two battleships, six cruisers, and fourteen destroyers to the northward of Santa Cruz Islands to counter Nagumo's southward thrust. On 25 October an optimistic Japanese observer reported that Henderson Field was in Japanese hands. Nagumo, who was waiting for this to happen, sent a contingent of carrier bombers and fighters to land at Henderson Field, while he moved south for the kill with five carriers, four battleships, eleven cruisers, and twenty-seven destroyers. The Japanese planes arrived over Guadalcanal to find the capture of Henderson Field to be greatly exaggerated. American fighters took off from the mud and shot down every one of the Japanese planes. The Marines and the Army pushed the Japanese back away from the airfield, and in the fighting the Japanese 2nd Division was practically destroyed.

On 26 October the two fleets came together in another great carrier battle. In the Battle of Santa Cruz the Japanese lost no ships. The carrier *Hornet* was sunk. The destroyer *Porter* was torpedoed by a Japanese submarine during the battle. Her crew was rescued, but the destroyer was so badly damaged that it had to be sunk by gunfire. Many ships on both sides were damaged, but most important at that moment, the Japanese lost over a hundred carrier planes and pilots.

The battle ended with both sides retiring with their damaged ships. It was a tactical victory for the Japanese but Nagumo recognized it as a strategic disaster. He was relieved of command of the Japanese Third Fleet and went back to Japan for a shore job. All the Japanese carriers except *Junyo* returned to Japan for repairs. *Enterprise* was the only American carrier left in the South Pacific. The American and the Japanese carrier forces had fought each other to a standstill. The surface forces took the center of the stage in Ironbottom Sound to decide the issue of control of the Solomon Sea.

Other Japanese Submarine Activity

In these struggles both American and Japanese submarines were auxiliary forces. Japanese submarine strategy continued to be close cooperation with the Combined Fleet in preparation for the decisive fleet action which they expected would some day decide control of the sea. In this their accomplishments during September had been very effective, but in October they were less spectacular. *I-26* served as a refueler for seaplanes making searches out of the Shortlands during the first part of the month. On 14 October *I-7* bombarded Espíritu Santo as a diversion for the battleship bombardment of Guadalcanal. She tried the same diversion on 23 October, the day the Japanese had scheduled to capture Henderson Field. These diversions did not divert. *I-22* arrived in the southern Solomons on 21 September and reported sighting a convoy on 1 October. Sometime after 5 October she disappeared.

The first solid success in October was made by *I-176*. On 20 October she encountered a task force of heavy ships in "Torpedo Junction" halfway between Espíritu Santo and San Cristóbal. In a night attack she torpedoed a big ship and reported sinking a *Texas*-class battleship. She was mistaken. There were then no old American battleships in the South Pacific. Her target was the cruiser *Chester*. *Chester* was not sunk but she was so badly damaged she had to be sent back to the United States for repairs and was out of the war for several months.

After the Battle of Santa Cruz, the Commander of the Japanese Advance Expeditionary Force ordered all fifteen of his submarines then in the Solomons area to concentrate between Santa Cruz and Espíritu Santo. Only *I-21* and *I-24* made contact. *I-21* fired a salvo of torpedoes at the battleship *Washington*. A torpedo exploded prematurely four hundred yards from its target, demonstrating that Japanese exploders were not perfect either. This narrow escape in a brand-new battleship convinced Halsey that capital ships could not be kept constantly at sea in an ocean infested with enemy submarines.

On 26 October *I-1* succeeded in evacuating Japanese troops from Goodenough Island, over in the New Guinea area. The Japanese destroyer *Yayoi* had been sunk by bombers in a previous unsuccessful attempt to carry out the evacuation. The isolated success of this Japanese submarine, when the destroyer had failed, received little notice, but it was prophetic of the type of employment which would absorb much of the effort of Japanese submarines.

Outside the South Pacific area Japanese submarines were less effective. The Aleutians area was temporarily inactive. Their war against merchant shipping in the Indian Ocean had modest success. *I-30* arrived in Singapore, returning from the long haul around the Cape of Good Hope, into the Atlantic to Germany and back, loaded with technical equipment of German origin. On 12 October, after leaving Singapore on the last leg of her long and perilous journey, she hit a British mine and sank. Many of her crew survived, but all the precious technical equipment was lost.

American Submarines in October

The buildup of American submarine forces at Brisbane kept the Japanese and American undersea strength nicely balanced in the South Pacific, but Japanese combat ships remained immune to submarine attack. Auxiliary vessels were not so fortunate. On 1 October *Sturgeon* (Pieczentkowski) torpedoed and sank the 8033-ton aircraft ferry *Katsuragi Maru*. *Sculpin* sank two ships and *Gudgeon* sank another in the same general area. One of the busiest submarines in the South Pacific was *Amberjack*.

On 6 October, *Amberjack* (Bole) was sent to reconnoiter Greenwich, a lonely atoll between Truk and the Solomon Islands. This task accomplished, she set out for New Ireland. On the way she sank the 2095-ton passenger-cargo ship *Senkai Maru*. Arriving off Kavieng on 10 October she discovered two Japanese ships in the harbor. Bole fired four torpedoes to run 3500 yards down the channel to the target. *Tenryu Maru* was damaged and the 19,000-ton ex-whale factory *Tonan Maru No. 2* was sunk in shallow water. *Tonan Maru* had been converted to a tanker, so the Japanese later salvaged her and towed her to Japan to be repaired and sent to sea again. Clarey, *Amberjack's* executive officer, was fated to meet her again much later in the war.

On 16 October *Amberjack* was sent to reconnoiter Ocean Island, and shortly afterward was sent to Espíritu Santo to prepare for a special mission. The gasoline situation on Guadalcanal was acute. Surface transportation was having a hard time getting through, and flying in aviation gasoline was a shoestring business of constant shortages and emergencies. At Espíritu Santo two of *Amberjack's* fuel tanks were cleaned out and converted to gasoline storage. She was loaded with nine thousand gallons of aviation gasoline, two hundred bombs, and a number of Army aviation personnel, and set out to relieve Guadalcanal.

Amberjack arrived in Ironbottom Sound, between Savo Island and Guadalcanal, on 25 October, almost simultaneously with three Japanese destroyers making a daring daylight raid. Two old four-piper destroyer minelayers beat a hasty retreat out of Sealark Channel under a rain of shells but a tug and barge, discharging supplies off Lunga Point, were caught and sunk while Bole watched through the periscope. The Japanese were too far away for submarine torpedo fire, and at thirty knots they had come and gone before *Amberjack* could do anything to close the range. The next day Bole discharged his passengers and cargo at Tulagi.

Outside the South Pacific American submarines continued their relentless pursuit of Japanese shipping. *Skipjack* sank a 6800-ton freighter in the Carolines. In the Aleutians the Army Air Force was the main agent to keep up the pressure on Japanese supply lines to Kiska. They sank one large *maru* and a destroyer and damaged another. *S-31* added to the Japanese difficulty by the first confirmed success of an S-boat operating out of Dutch Harbor. Working her weary way the length of the Aleutian chain, she sank a *maru* near the southern end of Kamchatka.

In the Southwest Pacific only two ships were sunk by submarine torpedoes during October. Torpedoes were in short supply for the eight submarines working out of Fremantle. Five submarines were sent out on mining missions to piece out. *Thresher* laid a small minefield in the northern part of the Gulf of Siam and *Gar* laid another in the same general area. *Grenadier* and *Tambor* laid minefields in the Gulf of Tonkin, and *Tautog* laid mines off French Indo-China. Like most submarine minefields laid in enemy waters, the success of these fields was difficult to determine.

Whale, operating out of Pearl Harbor, also laid mines off Osaka Bay on the coast of Japan, but for the most part the Pearl Harbor submarines, closer to torpedo supply, continued to go to sea with nearly full racks of torpedoes. This was very fortunate, for during this month the Pearl Harbor submarines sank twelve *marus* off the coast of Japan and four more in the East China Sea.

This made October the blackest month so far for Japanese merchant shipping. They lost 176,997 tons from all causes, and of the thirty-one *marus* sunk, submarines accounted for twenty-six. The bloody battles in the jungles of Guadalcanal and New Guinea, and the violent night actions in Ironbottom Sound were hammering out a hard-won victory. Their impact was dramatic and direct. But the influence of the steady pressure on Japan's line of communication was almost equally important, and Japan's shortage of shipping eventually had a great deal to do with the decision in the South Pacific.

XII

NOVEMBER–DECEMBER 1942

The Battle of Guadalcanal

The Japanese Army had to move up another division to replace the 2nd Division, cut to pieces in the October battles. Between 2 November and 10 November the entire 38th Division was landed on Guadalcanal by repeated runs of the Tokyo Express. On the American side, Turner brought in artillery, supplies, and reinforcements in transports protected by cruisers and destroyers. These operations resulted in clashes between light naval forces and air forces, but minor ones in comparison with the storm that was brewing.

The Tokyo Express could not carry tanks, heavy artillery, or supplies in sufficient amounts to support all the Japanese troops on Guadalcanal. Twelve transports were gathered together at Buin, on Bougainville, and major surface forces rendezvoused at Rabaul and Truk to support their run down the Slot. Reconnaissance was so well organized that both sides were well informed of what the other was doing.

On 11 November Turner brought two convoys in to Guadalcanal protected by an escort of cruisers and destroyers under Rear Admiral Callaghan. The convoys had a brush with Japanese air forces on the way in, and Turner received word from coastwatchers that major forces were approaching. The transports were hastily unloaded and pulled out. Callaghan remained behind to meet the Japanese in a violent night action, most of it at point-blank range. The Japanese lost the battleship *Hiei* and two destroyers. The Americans lost the cruiser *Atlanta* and four destroyers. Both sides had many damaged ships. Callaghan and Scott were both killed in action.

On the night of 13–14 November Japanese cruisers returned to bombard Henderson Field. Planes from there and from *Enterprise* clobbered the withdrawing Japanese cruisers the next day, sank the cruiser *Kinugasa*, and damaged several other ships. Nevertheless the twelve transports pushed on down the Slot. Planes from Henderson Field sank eight

of them, but four badly damaged ships managed to run themselves
aground off Guadalcanal and unload at least part of their cargo.

In support of the transports, the remainder of the Japanese bombardment group, which had been turned back by Callaghan's sacrifice
on the night of 12–13 November, came in again. *Trout,* on patrol near
Santa Isabel, made contact with this Japanese task force on the afternoon
of 14 November. She fired torpedoes but missed, and later sent a contact report which added to the information search planes had reported
of the approaching Japanese. Two U.S. battleships and four destroyers met the Japanese in Ironbottom Sound in another wild night battle,
with battleships slugging it out with each other at close range. The Japanese battleship *Kirishima* and a destroyer were sunk. Three American destroyers were sunk. These four days of battle convinced the Japanese Navy that it was impossible to supply Guadalcanal by transport
runs, but the Japanese did not know how to give up, so they continued
to attempt reinforcement and supply operations by other means.

Japanese Submarines in the Solomons in November

Japanese submarines were active in support of their surface forces. Seaplanes operating from submarines scouted Scott's task force approaching
Guadalcanal on 8 November. *I-122* refueled flying boats off Indispensable Reef. Three Japanese submarines (*I-16, I-20,* and *I-24*) were ordered to Indispensable Strait to launch midget submarines against ships
anchored off Guadalcanal. The transport *Majaba* was torpedoed at anchor on 7 November, but was successfully beached and later salvaged.
I-20 was damaged in the counterattack of U.S. destroyers. The Japanese
claim sinking a transport and a destroyer. Only one midget returned.
I-16 launched midgets again on 28 November. The freighter *Alchiba*
was torpedoed and so severely damaged that she had to be beached
where she burned for four days. This operation was the most successful
Japanese midget submarine operation in the Pacific during the war.

Another force of five submarines (*I-15, I-17, I-26, I-172,* and *I-175*)
operated in Torpedo Junction to intercept American reinforcements. On
the night of 10 November, the old four-piper minesweeper *Southard,*
carrying supplies to Guadalcanal, surprised a Japanese submarine on the
surface near San Cristóbal Island. *Southard's* gunfire drove the submarine
under, but the minesweeper had played target for U.S. submarines many
times and was an old hand at the game. Her sonar quickly picked up the
target and she delivered a depth-charge attack. In the resulting turbulence she lost sonar contact, but *Southard* kept hunting until after daybreak, when her sonar again located the target. Repeated depth-charge

attacks brought a submarine to the surface, where it was finished off by gunfire. There were no survivors.

The remaining four Japanese submarines were still waiting on the morning of 14 November when the badly mauled American cruisers pulled out of Ironbottom Sound after a night of hard and bloody battle. Two destroyers were out at four thousand yards ahead of the damaged cruisers to counter Japanese submarines, but the destroyers too had been damaged in the night action and they were not at the peak of their efficiency. About ten o'clock in the morning *Sterett* made a sound contact and delivered a depth-charge attack with no results. An hour later *I-26* fired torpedoes at *San Francisco*. The torpedoes passed ahead of their target but kept running straight for *Juneau's* bridge. The already damaged cruiser went down immediately. Nobody stopped to pick up survivors and all but ten of *Juneau's* crew perished with the ship. Both *I-15* and *I-172* were missing after this operation. The Japanese assume that *I-15* was sunk by *Southard* on 11 November, but American accounts usually identify *Southard's* victim as *I-172*.

Three Japanese submarines (*I-9*, *I-19*, and *I-21*) picketed Nouméa in November. They reported sinking a transport, but this cannot be confirmed. *I-31* carried out a reconnaissance of Samoa with her float plane. *I-9* and *I-19* sighted a task force but were unable to attack.

Japanese Submarine Supply Service

Two days after the eminent success of *I-26* in sinking *Juneau* a new order, far-reaching in its cumulative effect, was issued by Yamamoto to the Japanese submarine force. Transports failed to supply Guadalcanal. Brilliant and successful as were the Tokyo Express runs of Japanese destroyers, their accomplishments were insufficient, the effectiveness of their opposition increased, and destroyer losses became intolerable. Admission of failure was unthinkable. Yamamoto had to use every means available. He ordered the submarine force to organize a supply system for Guadalcanal. In a conference held on the submarine flagship at Truk in November all the submarine captains were opposed to this plan, but Vice Admiral Teruhisa Komatsu, Commander-in-Chief Sixth Fleet, announced that it was the Imperial command and that settled the matter.

Experiments had been in progress for months to find the best method of landing supplies from submarines, without requiring them to surface at the delivery point. The Japanese tried firing rice in bags from torpedo tubes. When that did not work they constructed plywood dummy torpedoes, loaded with rice to be ejected from the tubes. This was no better. Tanker-like auxiliary submarines were built to be loaded with fifty tons of supplies, and towed astern of a submerged submarine. When the unloading point was reached this device could be released and it would come to the surface. A simpler method was the most effective. Rice was loaded into steel drums on deck. If a submarine was prevented from surfacing at its destination these drums were released from below to bob up to the surface and be retrieved by boats from the shore. Submarines were modified for this trade. One gun and all but two torpedoes were removed. This greatly reduced the submarine's offensive strength. Handicapped with a deckload of rice, Japanese submarines proved to be much less agile in evasion under attack.

New Guinea was also shortly to become a customer for Japanese submarine transport and freighter service. During September and October, the Japanese Army had been pushed back from the vicinity of Port Moresby, through the jungles of New Guinea, in some of the most difficult fighting of the war. On 19 November the Allied attack on Buna began. On 24 November the Japanese destroyer *Hayashio,* on a supply run to Lae, was bombed by U. S. Army aircraft and sunk, and by the year's end Japanese submarines were desperately engaged in supplying and evacuating forces cut off in northern New Guinea.

Submarines were withdrawn from commerce raiding in the Indian Ocean and Australian waters to augment the number available for supply runs. Eleven submarines were on the Guadalcanal freight line in December, and by January twenty submarines were similarly engaged. Supply of bypassed areas was a duty destined to occupy a considerable part of the Japanese submarine force for most of the remainder of the war, and from the moment of the decision to so use them, Japanese submarines declined in importance and effectiveness.

The Battle of Tassafaronga

The use of fast destroyer runs did not cease, and this led to the Battle of Tassafaronga on 30 November, the last big battle in Ironbottom Sound. On 29 November an American task force of five cruisers and six destroyers under command of Rear Admiral Wright entered this cock pit for the purpose of intercepting a Japanese landing operation which was expected to take place at Tassafaronga, near Lunga Point on Guadalcanal. During the night of 29 November eight Japanese destroyers under command of Rear Admiral Tanaka left Buin and headed for Guadalcanal. The two task forces thus came together almost as though by appointment. Radar enabled the Americans to catch the Japanese by surprise, fire torpedoes and open fire with the cruisers' guns before the Japanese ever sighted their adversaries. Nevertheless Tanaka's well-disciplined destroyers promptly fired torpedoes, executed a simultaneous turn to the left, and retired at twenty-four knots, without disclosing their position by answering gunfire. Their "Long Lance" torpedoes turned the tide of victory. *Northampton* was sunk and three other cruisers heavily damaged. The Japanese lost one destroyer.

Even with this clear-cut victory, the Japanese were unable effectively to supply troops on Guadalcanal by means of destroyer runs. Aircraft from Henderson Field continued to search out and harass surface ships by day, and fast torpedo boats from Tulagi became increasingly a menace to Japanese night operations. Eight destroyers made a run on 3 December, and although they were attacked by bombers and torpedo planes, managed to land a week's supply of rice on Guadalcanal at the cost of one destroyer damaged. Despite occasional successful runs like this the Japanese Army on Guadalcanal was reduced to a miserable state—first on one-third ration and finally one-sixth ration of rice, and each day finding a larger number of ineffectives from disease and starvation. On 7 December Tanaka brought down ten destroyers with supplies, but these were met by both air and torpedo boat attacks. Two destroyers were damaged and the Japanese turned back without accomplishing their mission. When the next run was attempted on 12 December one destroyer was sunk by PT-boat torpedoes and the rest turned back. Torpedo boats had also been moved up into attack position in New Guinea, and were making life miserable for Japanese supply efforts there. Under these conditions increasing dependence was placed on the Japanese submarines to run supplies to the starving Japanese troops.

Japanese Submarine Losses

The offensive efforts of Japanese submarines were gradually diverted to the service of supply. One submarine arrival was planned for each night. If it was completely successful it would keep the Army on Guadalcanal supplied with rice on a day-to-day basis. Almost from the beginning the submarines encountered trouble. On 10 December *I-3*, on a supply run, encountered *PT-59* near Cape Esperance. Two torpedoes from the PT boat hit *I-3* and she sank with only one survivor, who swam ashore to join the Japanese Army.

On 14 December *Wahoo* (Kennedy), while submerged in the vicinity of Shortland, sighted a Japanese submarine on the surface. Kennedy fired three torpedoes and observed one hit. The Japanese submarine went down with men still on the bridge. This may have been a premature torpedo explosion alerting a Japanese submarine into a dive to safety, but it may have been an actual sinking, for it is impossible to be positive about the cause of loss of some of the Japanese submarines missing in the Solomons.

On 20 December *Seadragon* (Ferrall), while patrolling submerged near New Ireland, sighted a Japanese submarine on the surface. *Seadragon* fired three torpedoes for one observed hit. *I-4* was returning from an aborted transportation run about this time. She was last heard from sending a message to Rabaul, and was probably *Seadragon's* victim. On 25 December *Sailfish* (Moore) made a night attack on a Japanese submarine south of New Britain and claimed a hit. The same night *PT-122*, operating off the coast of New Guinea, attacked a Japanese submarine with torpedoes and observed hits, but neither of these reported sinkings coincide with Japanese records. In the Solomons-New Guinea area, however, five Japanese submarines disappeared during the two months ending in December. The Japanese submarine service of supply was an expensive operation.

U.S. *Submarine Organization in the South Pacific*

Fleet submarines sent out from Pearl Harbor to augment the submarine strength of the South Pacific were based at Brisbane. When they crossed the equator into south latitude they came under Christie's operational control. Recognizing the need for close coordination of surface, air, and submarine operations, Nimitz designated Christie as a task force commander under Commander South Pacific (Halsey). All submarines operating out of Brisbane were under Christie's command. This left Southwest Pacific Force (MacArthur's navy) without any submarines directly under its control on the eastern coast of Australia. MacArthur had a healthy regard for submarines and insisted on having a group of submarines which he could deploy in defense of New Guinea. Six submarines were returned to his over-all command, but operational control remained with Christie. These six submarines were not specifically designated, but MacArthur had the right to direct the deployment of six submarines at all times.

In December 1942 Captain Christie received orders as Officer in Charge Naval Tropedo Station, Newport, Rhode Island. Captain James Fife relieved him as Commander Task Force 42 (the Brisbane Submarine Command) on 23 December 1942. Fife was responsible both to Nimitz, through Comsopac (Halsey), and to MacArthur, through Comsowespac, a unique relationship which Fife was able to handle with sound satisfaction to both commanders. In his dual capacity he could shift submarines between South Pacific and Southwest Pacific with a minimum of formality, but his situation also had unique difficulties. Because of the distance between Brisbane and Comsopac headquarters at Nouméa, Fife often found himself without adequate information for optimum control of the submarines in the Solomons. Because of the number of echelons of command between Army Air Force in New Guinea and the submarine command at Brisbane, air force bombers were often inadequately briefed on submarine disposition off New Guinea.

MacArthur, concerned with the defense of northern New Guinea, assigned to his submarines the primary task of attacking the Japanese destroyers in night supply runs to the vicinity of Buna. This was a difficult task, particularly for those submarines still without SJ radar. In an effort to accomplish their mission, submarines were assigned close-in positions off Buna, Gasmata, and in the vicinity of Vitiaz and Dampier Straits. In December their areas were moved farther out to avoid interference with air and surface forces. Their assigned primary mission was the defense of New Guinea, and their secondary mission was destruction of enemy shipping. In January 1943 this directive was happily changed, and they were given offensive missions on Japanese traffic routes.

November was a poor month for American submarines in the South Pacific. While the air and surface forces were engaged in their desperate struggle for control of the sea, U.S. submarines in this area were unable to sink a single combat ship during the month, and damaged only one *maru*. In the whole Pacific Theater only nine *marus* were sunk by submarines in November. There was no letup of pressure on Japanese logistics, however, for the air forces rose to the occasion and in the same month sank sixteen *marus*, more than in any previous month, and for the first month during the war exceeding the number sunk by submarines. As these sinkings included twelve big transports on the Guadalcanal run, the total loss of Japanese shipping came to over 165,000 tons. The most successful submarine patrol was that of *Seawolf* (Warder), which sank three ships in the Gulf of Davao, and the story of her patrol exemplifies some of the difficulties confronting submarines at this stage of the war.

Seawolf *off Davao*

Seawolf left Fremantle in early October on her seventh war patrol. She was headed home for navy yard overhaul after a long hard year of war, although only Warder knew this as she worked her way up along the western coast of Australia, through Lombok Strait into the Flores Sea. This area seemed to have been changed but little by wiping out three and a half centuries of Dutch rule. In native vintas inherited from Malay pirate ancestors whole Moro families calmly sailed the Flores Sea while the world went mad around them.

Off southern Celebes, *Seawolf* made an unsuccessful attack on a freighter coming out of Makassar City, expending two of her precious torpedoes for no hits. Torpedoes were in short supply at Fremantle and *Seawolf* had been outfitted for this patrol with the new Mark 14 tor-

pedoes forward and only ancient Mark 9 torpedoes aft. Commander
Submarines Southwest Pacific, harassed by the torpedo shortage, kept
statistics on percentage of torpedo hits made by all commanding officers.
Seawolf's next encounter was with a 5000-ton tanker, escorted by one
submarine chaser, northeast of Balikpapan. The closest Warder could
get was 3200 yards with a 130-degree track. Weighing his chances of
success at such long range (with a flat calm sea through which the torpedoes would leave a smoking white wake to direct the target's evasion),
Warder decided he had little chance of improving his batting average
and he let her go by on the chance of better targets to come.

At dawn on 2 November Seawolf dove at the entrance to Davao
Gulf, the deep indentation into southern Mindanao. That afternoon a
freighter came out headed right past Seawolf's position. Warden intended to fire bow tubes but the target zigzagged widely and he found
himself committed to a stern tube shot with the old Mark 9 torpedoes.
The ancient fish did their duty and Gifu Maru went down in nine minutes, while Warder watched the Japanese abandon ship down a cargo
net rigged over the port side. All this took place within full sight of a
lighthouse and Warder expected a destroyer to come charging out of
Davao after him. He waited around, hoping for a potshot at an eager
beaver, but when this did not develop by nightfall, Seawolf surfaced
and stood up the Gulf of Davao. Just before dawn on 3 November she
dove about twelve miles south of the harbor entrance.

There were two small freighters in Davao Harbor but Warder spotted
a larger ship (Sagami Maru) at anchor in nearby Talomo Bay, loading
hemp from barges alongside. By ten-thirty he had maneuvered into an
ideal position to attack with his good torpedoes in the bow tubes. He
measured the range by bouncing a supersonic ping off the helpless target's side, and from a thousand yards fired a carefully aimed torpedo.
This first torpedo was set at eighteen feet depth for a target with estimated draft of twenty-five. The torpedo went under the ship and exploded on the beach beyond. The next torpedo Warder set for eight
feet, and this one made a bull's-eye at the point of aim. The ship took
a large list, then righted itself without much change of draft. The third
torpedo ran under but did not explode, and the fourth one did the same.
The Japanese ship opened fire with bow and stern guns. Warder could
hear the shells smack the water above Seawolf. The freighter was not
badly hurt. Japanese colors were bravely flying from the fore, the main,
and the staff, and she was shooting for all she was worth.

Warder withdrew Seawolf to reload tubes. A half hour later he came
in again. Both guns on the maru opened up on the periscope. Seawolf
fired one torpedo and this hit aft. When the smoke and spray and debris
cleared away, Sagami Maru's deck had been cleared of people who had
been watching the battle. Her forward gun was still manned but no

longer firing. The Japanese colors were down, but Warder believed this was due to the halyards being carried away in the explosion. Five boats were carrying people from ship to shore and the ship seemed doomed. Warder wanted to be sure of this, however, so he swung *Seawolf* and expended one old Mark 9 from the stern tube. This hit and *Sagami Maru* promptly sank.

A few minutes after the last attack three planes zoomed in on the periscope. *Seawolf* went down to 120 feet. Two subchasers came out and dutifully dropped depth charges, but Warder was not yet ready to leave. The motor ships in Davao Harbor had departed in the excitement, but about three-fifteen another ship came standing in and *Seawolf* went back to battle stations.

The sea was flat calm and *Seawolf* had difficulty making an undetected approach. In his zeal to cut down periscope exposure Warder found himself too close for a bow tube attack. He swung around and fired three Mark 9 torpedoes from the stern tubes. One of these started to make a circular run and *Seawolf* hurriedly went deep to avoid her own torpedo. They heard an explosion timed correctly for the torpedo run but there is no record of a Japanese ship sunk or damaged on this attack. Two escorts gave *Seawolf* a prolonged depth-charging and kept her on the run until after nightfall.

The next day they patrolled submerged at the Gulf's entrance. After dark *Seawolf* surfaced and ran down toward Borneo to deceive the Japanese direction-finders while she transmitted a message. The message off, the submarine returned to the southwesterly approach to Davao. Tokyo Rose reported the sinking of an American submarine and Warder hoped they had chalked off *Seawolf* so that the Japanese around Davao could relax. He surfaced and headed up the Gulf to dive at dawn on the Davao traffic route.

About ten o'clock on the morning of 8 November a freighter came out, escorted by a minesweeper, zigzagging wildly. Just as Warder reached firing position a new zigzag leg brought the target right over the submarine and *Seawolf* had to go deep to avoid a collision. This one got away, but almost immediately there was an inbound target in view.

Shortly after noon Warder fired two torpedoes from the bow tubes at the inbound ship. Both torpedoes hit. The ship appeared to hog upward in the middle. The bow gun was blown overboard, but there was no panic and both stern gun and anti-aircraft gun on the bridge opened fire on *Seawolf's* periscope. The ship settled to the hawsepipe but would not sink, so Warder swung the submarine's stern around and expended his last Mark 9 torpedo. This hit, and when the smoke cleared away *Keiko*

Maru had sunk. *Seawolf* surfaced after dark and set an easterly course for Palau. The Philippines fell astern and Warder announced to the crew that they were headed home at last.

Solution of the Puzzle of Palau

Palau was an enigma to the submarine force. They were certain that the Japanese were using Palau as a base. It should have been a lucrative patrol area for submarines, but it had not turned out so. The Japanese were indeed making extensive use of these handy islands, but their effective deception was wholly inadvertent. When a Japanese task force set out from Palau on 6 December to capture Davao, they had lively encounters with phantom submarines. There were no real submarines then off Palau and had there been they would have been guarding the wrong channel. The best American charts showed Malakal Passage to the eastward as the major entrance through the reef, and it was here the submarines patrolled when they were in the area. In October a secret Japanese chart was captured on Guadalcanal. This disclosed that Toagel Mlungui (West Passage) was the best channel for big ships. *Seawolf* was sent to investigate.

Arriving there by sunrise on 11 November, she dove and headed into Toagel Mlungui, intending to take some pictures. Her photography was repeatedly thwarted either by rain squalls or by a busybody patrol vessel snooping around. About five o'clock in the evening it was raining heavily. Someone dropped one depth charge off the channel entrance. *Seawolf* stayed at periscope depth and watched. Two destroyers came out of the channel headed northwest. *Seawolf* went after them. Fifteen minutes later while busily engaged in making an approach on the leading destroyer, Warder made a sweep around with the periscope, and there was a big carrier coming out of the rain and twilight. The range was about four thousand yards. He ordered full speed and tried to close, but it was hopeless. The carrier went on past and ten minutes later changed course for the southwest.

It was hard luck and not much could be done about it. As soon as it was dark, Warder surfaced and went off in pursuit at full speed on four main engines. Desperately he tried to raise Pearl Harbor by radio to report this contact, but he was denied even this satisfaction, for Pearl Harbor would not answer. A few hours later an electrical casualty put *Seawolf* definitely out of the carrier pursuit, and Warder decided to call the whole thing off and head for Pearl Harbor. No ships were sunk, but he had solved the puzzle of Palau. After *Seawolf* succeeded in getting a report through to Pearl Harbor, *Seal* was ordered to guard Toagel Mlungui and profit by the discovery.

Seal *at Palau*

Seal (Hurd) had left Fremantle only a week after *Seawolf*. She also headed for Pearl Harbor and home, but by a different route. On 11 November she was 150 miles to the south, between Palau and Rabaul, when she intercepted *Seawolf's* contact report with the carrier. Hurd had hopes of getting in an attack on the carrier if it was headed for Rabaul, but in this he was disappointed. Pearl Harbor sent *Seal* a message directing her to move up to cover Toagel Mlungui, left unguarded by *Seawolf's* departure. She arrived on station on 15 November.

Seal had two contacts the first day in the area, but she could not reach firing position on either of them. After dark she surfaced and ran off to the southward in pursuit of a tanker that had just eluded her. For this reason, the next morning at dawn she was a considerable distance south of her area when she submerged. About two o'clock in the afternoon a convoy of several ships, guarded by one destroyer, popped up over the horizon. *Seal* moved in to attack.

It was Hurd's ambitious intention to fire one torpedo at the leading ship in the near column, from a range of about six hundred yards, and then the other three bow tubes at ships in the far column, before swinging inside the destroyer and firing the stern tubes. The destroyer was pinging with its supersonic, but with no indication of contact. Just as *Seal* reached firing position the lead ship of the near column changed course toward the submarine, either at the beginning of a left zig or because of contact with *Seal*. Hurd had a good setup on the ship in the far column, so he ignored the nearer ship and fired two torpedoes at the far one from a range of about eleven hundred yards. The destroyer was then on *Seal's* starboard quarter passing aft rapidly and would have to make a wide circle to attack the submarine.

Twelve seconds after firing there was a loud bang and a crash in the conning tower. The periscope went black and vibrated violently. *Seal* rose from sixty-one feet to fifty-five feet and hung there for a minute before starting down. The control party abandoned the conning tower and closed the lower hatch. They heard what they took for torpedo explosions, but due to the understandable urgency in getting out of the conning tower, the quartermaster was a little uncertain of the timing of these explosions. *Seal* went down to 250 feet while the destroyer up above made a prolonged depth-charge attack. After dark *Seal* surfaced to find No. 2 periscope bent over at right angles, the radar antenna broken off, and No. 1 periscope sprung so that it could not be raised. There was a good sample of Japanese bottom paint on No. 2 periscope and small quantities of uncooked rice between deck boards of the cigarette deck and the bridge. *Seal* reported her blind condition and was directed to proceed to Pearl Harbor. Commander Submarine Force Pacific considered the evidence of a successful attack very slim and was irked at the necessity of early termination of *Seal's* patrol. Nevertheless *Boston Maru*, a transport of 5477 tons, had been hit and sunk by *Seal's* torpedoes, and considering the paucity of submarine successes in November this should have been cause for congratulations.

Albacore *and* Tenryu

Since S-*44* sank *Kako*, Japanese cruisers had been often attacked but never hit by submarines. This immunity was finally broken by *Albacore* (Lake). She was patrolling off the north coast of New Guinea in December, attempting to intercept supply runs to Lae. On 18 December she made a submerged attack on a *maru* but missed. That night she encountered a destroyer and missed again. Shortly thereafter Lake sighted a larger target and fired two torpedoes, both of which hit. He was unable to identify his target. It was not until later that it was learned that *Albacore* had sunk the light cruiser *Tenryu*.

Tenryu was small and old for a light cruiser (3300 tons and built in 1918), but she and her twin sister ship *Tatsuta* were busybodies, and in the South Pacific they pulled more than their weight. *Tenryu* had taken part in the first attack on Wake where she had been bloodied by the Marine shore battery when that early Japanese amphibious attack was turned back. She was back again with the support forces when Wake was finally overwhelmed. She was with the Occupation Force at the Battle of the Coral Sea. She was with Mikawa's victorious cruisers at the Battle of Savo Island and she fought valiantly at the Battle of Guadalcanal. *Tatsuta* lasted a year longer. In sinking *Tenryu*, *Albacore* rid the north New Guinea coast of one of its most bothersome gadflies.

South Pacific submarines were more successful in December, when they sank four *marus* and damaged three more in addition to the cruiser and the Japanese submarine which they destroyed. The Fremantle submarines were still suffering from a shortage of torpedoes, but they managed to add a couple of *marus* to the score. In the Gulf of Tonkin, *Fukken Maru* was sunk by a mine on 29 December. This was probably one of the mines laid by *Tambor* the previous month.

Submarines off Honshu

Drum, Sunfish, and *Trigger* laid minefields off Honshu during December. While *Drum* (McMahon) was en route to her minefield plant on 12 December she encountered an escorted southbound carrier with a deckload of planes. *Drum* was in the unfortunate condition of having two of her forward tubes loaded with mines. McMahon fired four torpedoes at the carrier (which he identified as *Ryujo*) and got one hit. Escorting destroyers drove him deep before he could bring his stern tubes to bear on the damaged carrier. The carrier was not *Ryujo*, which had been sunk at the Battle of the Eastern Solomons. It was *Ryuho*, a converted carrier which had been bombed during the Doolittle raid and capsized in Tokyo Bay during her conversion. A hard luck ship, *Ryuho* had just managed to get to sea when *Drum* put a torpedo into her to send her back to the navy yard, and if McMahon had had all six torpedo tubes loaded he may well have ended her career then and there.

Trigger (Benson) had the unique experience of seeing a ship hit one of the mines that had just been laid. On the night of 20 December *Trigger* moved in close to Inubo Saki, the eastern point of Honshu just north of Tokyo, with her torpedo tubes full of mines. She submerged in the moonlight and began laying her planned minefield. Before the second line was finished a freighter and a small escort came around the bend. Benson hurriedly completed his mining mission and had just pulled clear when the freighter ran square into one of the mines. When the explosion cleared the ship lay wallowing in the low swell, with its back broken. The escort, assuming that a submarine had torpedoed its consort, raced around through the minefield to locate the culprit. Benson discreetly withdrew. As *Trigger* was going deep he heard another explosion and believed that the escort had located another mine the hard way. If the escort hit a mine that night, however, there is no record of it. While this was going on near Tokyo, *Halibut* (Gross) moved in to the busy area off northeast Honshu. Gross sank five *marus* there and damaged another during the month of December.

Kingfish (Lowrance) made a December patrol off Formosa. She was plagued by poor torpedo performance, but the new SJ radar functioned perfectly to help make up for it. En route to the area, on 7 December, *Kingfish* encountered *Hino Maru*, and when defective torpedoes spoiled his attack, Lowrance used his radar to run around his target by day and come in during the night to make three separate attacks spread out over thirteen hours before he could sink the *maru*. On 28 December *Kingfish* sank *Choyo Maru* in the northern end of Formosa Strait in an attack which the Japanese credited to a mine.

The Shipping Situation

In December submarines sank fifteen *marus*. Although the total tonnage lost dropped below 100,000 for the month, this was more than Japan could afford to lose. Japanese planners had estimated that they would lose 800,000 tons during the first year of the war. This estimate was reasonably accurate, for Japan lost about a million tons from all causes. However, planners had also estimated that after the first year the situation would be under control and the rate of loss would decrease. On the contrary, the rate of sinkings was increasing. Shipbuilding could not keep up with the losses. Japan would have to draw in her belt even tighter than she expected.

The Japanese Army, deeply committed on Guadalcanal, was, if anything, less conditioned than the Navy to get out of such a situation. The Army simply did not know how to give up. They were having a very bad time in New Guinea also but this they rationalized as a temporary setback to be redeemed later. The Army high command insisted that Guadalcanal must be held. They made a firm requisition upon the War Ministry for three hundred thousand tons of shipping for the supply service of this operation. The strategists did not explain how with three hundred thousand tons of shipping, or ten times that amount, they would be able to unload transports at Guadalcanal. That was Navy business.

It was unusual, in Japan, for the War Ministry to deny a pre-emptory request by the Army high command, but Tojo, the War Minister, was up against it. There simply was not three hundred thousand tons of shipping to feed into the Solomons sinkhole. Frequent discussions between Army and War Ministry staff could not resolve these difficulties. On occasion staff officers came to blows over the arguments. On 31 December a final conference was held at the Imperial Palace in the presence of the Emperor. It was decided to evacuate the troops from Guadalcanal by early February. A new defense line in the northern Solomons was agreed upon. In New Guinea, troops at Buna would pull back to the Salamaua line and the reinforcement of Lae and Salamaua would continue.

Shipping shortage was a major factor of this first Japanese retrograde movement in modern history. Tojo was overly optimistic about the establishment of a defense perimeter in the northern Solomons. Events were too recent for perspective. With the advantage of hindsight the crisis is clearer. At Midway Japan's forward movement stopped. At Guadalcanal she started moving back. The inertia of her early victories had been spent, and Japan was destined to continue strategic retreat with ever-increasing momentum.

XIII

JANUARY–FEBRUARY 1943

Submarine Command Changes

In early 1943 a series of changes in high submarine commands became necessary. On 19 January a plane carrying Rear Admiral R. H. English and several members of his staff to a mainland conference crashed in foggy weather north of San Francisco. Rear Admiral C. A. Lockwood was ordered as Commander Submarines Pacific on 10 February to fill the vacancy caused by the death of Admiral English in this unfortunate accident. Rear Admiral Ralph Christie, who had just arrived in the United States from Brisbane, was ordered back to Australia to relieve Lockwood as Commander Submarine Southwest Pacific at Fremantle. Fife remained in command of the Brisbane submarine task force. When these changes were effected, the top U.S. submarine command became stable for a long time.

New Year's Comparisons

The Japanese Navy started the war with sixty submarines. During the first thirteen months of war they lost nineteen and retired two more for overage. There were fifty-one American submarines in the Pacific on 7 December 1941. During the same period thirty-seven new American submarines entered the Pacific war and eight were lost, to give the Americans a total of eighty submarines to start 1943. The growing ascendancy of the American submarines was not, however, a matter of numbers alone.

A major factor in the relative effectiveness of submarines was the difference between two philosophies of undersea warfare. The Japanese regarded their submarine force as a weapons system by means of which they hoped to reduce the strength of the American fleet to a level at which Japan could win a climactic fleet action. To that end in the first year of war, Japanese submarines generally operated as a distant offensive screen for their own fleet movements, or they were deployed in areas where American capital ships might operate.

Their accomplishments reflected their employment. During the first year of a war in which aircraft carriers were the decisive weapons of sea warfare, Japanese submarines sank two American carriers and twice torpedoed another. During the same period the largest Japanese combat ship to be sunk by a U.S. submarine was a heavy cruiser.

American peacetime philosophy of submarine employment generally agreed with that of Japan. American submarines were trained and equipped to attack combat ships. The big advantage of the magnetic exploder (if it worked) was against heavily armored vessels. Even after the dramatic declaration of unrestricted submarine war at the war's beginning, a positive doctrine of commerce destruction would be difficult to document. Target priorities continued to put carriers and battleships at the top of the list. Nevertheless, American concepts of submarine employment underwent a profound change. Almost from the beginning American submarines patrolled along Japanese commerce routes.

Results reflected this employment. By the end of December 1942, American submarines had sent 142 *marus* to the bottom. Comparative figures for Japanese submarines are difficult to compute. In the Indian Ocean a group of Japanese submarines cooperated with the Germans in a destructive submarine campaign, but in the Pacific not more than a score of noncombat Allied vessels were sunk by Japanese submarines in the first year of war.

While Japanese submarines' efforts were concentrated against American capital ships, they made weighty contributions to their Navy's objectives. Assignment of large numbers of submarines to supply missions helped to change this. American submarines were also diverted (often profitably) to special missions, which exploited their unique characteristics. Occasionally there was short-lived confusion of objectives on the part of some high commanders, but American submarines persistently kept after the seaborne commerce of Japan, with the instinct of a bulldog going for its antagonist's throat.

In 1942 shortage of shipping limited Japan's offensive potential. The destruction of ten *marus* a month during 1942 was not a great accomplishment for American submarines, but it was sufficient to keep Japan from improving her unsatisfactory situation. The rate of shipping loss was increasing, and from the beginning of 1943 the attrition of Japan's merchant shipping was an increasingly important factor in her downfall.

By January 1943 most U.S. submarines had the new SJ radar. The Japanese too had radar in their heavy ships by the end of 1942, but it was a long time before it became available to their submarines, and Japan lagged far behind in electronic weapons. The Japanese later tended to attribute the superiority of American submarines to radar, and it certainly was an important factor. To offset this, however, the Japanese had superior optical instruments and greatly superior torpedoes. Materiel superiority was not the whole explanation of the increasing effectiveness of American undersea warfare. The American submarine force was a great deal better all around than the Japanese ever expected it to be.

In the first year of war Japanese anti-submarine warfare improved very little. The organization of the weak and ineffective First and Second Escort Forces still left commerce protection largely in the hands of the naval districts and the area fleet commanders. After passing out of the limited area of responsibility of the local commanders, Japanese merchant ships were frequently on their own on the high seas, depending only on diverse routing, their own guns, and zigzagging for anti-submarine protection. Only the oldest and least efficient destroyers and small vessels were assigned to convoy escort duty. The Combined Fleet jealously conserved the best destroyers. Major fleet units were well screened, but Combined Fleet destroyers scorned escort duty for non-combat ships.

U.S. Submarines vs. Japanese Escort Forces

At first destroyers were low on the priority list of targets for U.S. submarines, but destroyers and submarines in their mutual search for each other came into frequent contact. During 1942 U.S. submarines sank four destroyers, damaged three others, and sank two old destroyers that had been reclassified as submarine chasers. One of the eight U.S. submarines lost in 1942 was certainly sunk by Japanese destroyers and two of the others may have been victims of Japanese light surface forces, but the balance of battle was certainly in favor of U.S. submarines. In the first month of the New Year clashes between U.S. submarines and Japanese light naval forces increased in frequency.

Trigger (Benson), after laying her minefield in December, moved down to the entrance of Tokyo Bay to finish her patrol. On 10 January the Japanese destroyer *Okikaze* came out to hunt down the American submarine. Benson was not content to play mouse for the prowling Japanese. *Trigger* caught *Okikaze* at an unguarded moment despite the destroyer's cautious zigzag approach. Benson fired three torpedoes, two of which hit, and *Okikaze* promptly sank.

Loss of Argonaut

On the same day *Argonaut* (J. R. Pierce), patrolling southeast of New Britain, was not so fortunate in her battle with Japanese anti-submarine forces. More than usual is known about this action because a passing

U. S. Army plane, which was out of bombs, witnessed the encounter. The plane crew saw a Japanese convoy of five *marus*, protected by destroyers, under submarine attack. They reported that one destroyer was hit by a torpedo and there appeared to be explosions in two others. The destroyers retaliated with a heavy depth-charge attack which brought the bow of the submarine to the surface at a steep angle. The Japanese ships then circled around, pumping shells into the stricken submarine until it sank.

This encounter took place in *Argonaut's* assigned area, and subsequent efforts to make contact with her by radio were fruitless. Japanese records list a depth-charge attack followed by gunfire which finished off a submarine at approximately the time and place reported by the plane. None of the Japanese ships was reported as sunk or damaged. This was undoubtedly the end of *Argonaut*. There were no survivors. She was the first U.S. submarine to be sunk since the loss of *Grunion* in the Aleutians in July.

Penetration of Japanese Harbors

January was a month for submarines to go in after targets they could not reach on the high seas. *Trout* (Ramage) was patrolling off Miri, in northwestern Borneo. Ramage found a tanker at anchor in water too shallow to navigate submerged. Pondering the situation, he decided to take *Trout* in on the surface at night. That night he surfaced after dark and crammed a charge into the battery to the limit of its capacity. Ramage then brought *Trout* in on the surface with the silent main motors on the battery. This stealthy approach was undetected. *Trout* fired four torpedoes, two of which hit, and the target erupted in brilliant flames. Ramage then got out of there with *Trout* at full power on the engines until they reached deeper and more comfortable water. The torpedoed ship was the 17,500-ton *Kyokuyo Maru*, which was severely damaged. The Japanese later salvaged her and put her back into service.

Guardfish *at Rabaul*

Guardfish (Klakring) was patrolling off New Hanover on the night of 12 January when she encountered a patrol boat which Klakring identified as a destroyer. After sighting the target, *Guardfish* submerged to forty-five feet and with only the SJ radar antenna exposed, made a perfect approach to seventeen hundred yards with radar data to guide him. Klakring fired three torpedoes, one of which hit *Patrol Boat No. 1* (an old destroyer). It sank so quickly that when *Guardfish* surfaced thirty minutes later the sea was empty.

The bight of the sea between New Ireland and New Britain swarmed with Japanese ships and planes, most of them hunting for American submarines. Several *Guardfish* attacks were frustrated by anti-submarine forces. A properly marked hospital ship passed by close aboard. Early on the morning of 23 January Klakring received a radio tip-off from Brisbane that there were good targets coming around the west end of New Ireland. *Guardfish* set off full speed on the surface to intercept them.

En route she encountered a large ship guarded by two destroyers. While Klakring was maneuvering to gain position to attack, the escorts opened up with accurate gunfire that dropped a full salvo in *Guardfish's* wake. The submarine made a quick dive and then took a number of close depth charges before the Japanese destroyers went on about their business. That afternoon Klakring had revenge. The destroyer *Hakaze* came out hunting for submarines. Klakring watched her closely and when *Hakaze* made a wrong zigzag he quickly seized his opportunity and fired three torpedoes. *Hakaze* saw them coming too late. She turned away and two torpedoes passed up along her starboard side, but the third one hit right under the stack. The destroyer laid over on her side and presented her bright red bottom while all hands in *Guardfish* filed by the periscope to see the Japanese abandon ship.

After sinking *Hakaze*, *Guardfish* patrolled a glassy sea for several days, encountering many patrol boats and planes but no worthwhile targets. Klakring decided that the time was ripe to have a look into Rabaul Harbor, where good targets were sure to abound. That Rabaul was the bastion of the South Pacific ringed with Japanese defenses of every description did not deter him. On the night of 26–27 January *Guardfish* made a high-speed run on the surface to St. George's Channel, to approach Rabaul from the Bismarck Sea side. This first attempt was thwarted by a chance encounter with two small boats, which forced the submarine to break off the surface run and submerge.

The next night *Guardfish* started out again. This time Klakring evaded several echelons of echo-ranging patrols and came on in. He passed up a freighter as too unimportant to warrant revealing his presence in Blanche Bay, the approach corridor to Rabaul. He could see a mass of ships in Simpson Harbor, Rabaul's inner harbor, and decided to try a long-range slow-speed shot. The sea was flat calm but strong, and variable currents necessitated occasional periscope exposure. As *Guardfish* worked in to 8000-yard maximum range of her torpedoes Klakring raised the periscope to check his position. It was instantly zoomed by a small plane and all hell broke loose. A shore battery opened up and shell explosions close aboard could be heard in *Guardfish's* conning tower. Two patrol boats raced toward the submarine. The torpedo room reported that *Guardfish* had been hit by a projectile over the wardroom (a false alarm it later proved). Klakring decided to get out of there.

Wahoo *at Wewak*

On 16 January *Wahoo* left Brisbane under a new commanding officer, Dudley W. Morton, who was destined to link the names *Wahoo* and "Mush Morton" in a saga of the submarine service. *Wahoo* carried a full load of twenty-four torpedoes, sixteen forward and eight aft. She was ordered to patrol off Palau (though she never got there) and, en route, to reconnoiter the harbor of Wewak, on the north coast of New Guinea. Ordinarily the reconnoitering assignment could be considered fulfilled by observations through the periscope from a mile or so off the reef, noting the density and direction of enemy traffic and spotting defense installations that might be visible. On 19 January, when *Wahoo* was at sea, the Japanese landed at Wewak, and this gave an urgency to the reconnaissance assignment that it had not had before.

The new commanding officer interpreted his instructions as requiring him to go inside the harbor to look around. It then developed that Wewak did not appear on the small-scale charts of New Guinea with which *Wahoo* had been provided, and the name was definitely absent from the New Guinea Sailing Directions. Motor Machinist's Mate Keeter, however, had purchased a school geography of Australia while in Brisbane, and this showed Wewak at Victoria Bay, on the back of the New Guinea bird. His objective determined, Morton then enlarged a tracing of the small-scale chart of Victoria Bay by improvised optical methods, and transferred to it all the Sailing Direction information. With this unorthodox method of making a large-scale chart out of small-scale information, Morton decided that penetration into the harbor was feasible.

At three-thirty on the morning of 24 January *Wahoo* dove two and a half miles from the entrance to Victoria Bay, and ran in submerged, making careful and frequent periscope observations to guide her entrance. At first the results of this daring move were disappointing, and it was not until 1318 that O'Kane, the executive officer who manned the periscope, picked up the masts of a ship. This turned out to be the destroyer *Harusame* (as later identified from Japanese records). Morton decided to keep *Wahoo* in deep water and fire a long-range shot at the stationary target. This plan was upset, when on the firing observation O'Kane found the destroyer underway and standing down toward the submarine. Making a quick change in plan of battle, *Wahoo* fired three torpedoes from a range of eighteen hundred yards, and in the rapidly changing situation underestimated the target speed, so they missed astern. Morton then fired a fourth torpedo set for a target speed of twenty knots, and this one the alerted *Harusame* avoided by turning away.

Harusame then circled right and charged the periscope. O'Kane watched her come, boiling mad and out for vengeance. Morton held fire until the range was twelve hundred yards and then fired one torpedo, which missed. *Wahoo* then had one torpedo left in the forward tubes and it was impossible to bring the after tubes to bear. *Harusame* and *Wahoo* were headed directly at each other, with *Harusame* coming in for the kill. Morton waited until the range closed to eight hundred yards, just enough to give his torpedo time to arm, and then fired "down the throat," about as subtle a tactic as a duel with shotguns at five paces; for if the submarine missed, the destroyer attack would almost certainly be lethal, but if the torpedo hit, the destroyer was probably doomed. It had the sole advantage from the submarine viewpoint that anything the destroyer did after the torpedo was fired would probably be wrong—and few destroyer captains had the fortitude to do nothing. *Harusame* tried to avoid with full rudder and took the torpedo amidship. This broke her back, and pictures taken by *Wahoo* showed a destroyer beached and sunk. *Harusame* was later salvaged, to be sunk again by Army Air Force planes eighteen months later.

Wewak Harbor was soon aswarm with searching small boats, and planes from overhead dropped bombs. *Wahoo* went down to ninety feet and felt her blind way out, guided by sound bearings on the varying reef noises. After sunset she surfaced and ran north at four-engine speed. In the *Harusame* attack Morton attributed his success against a narrow, shallow-draft high-speed target to the proper functioning of the magnetic exploder. To magnetic exploders *Wahoo* owed her continued existence, and Morton was ever afterward a defender of this unpopular device.

If the startled crew of *Wahoo* thought that the audacity of this attack was an isolated incident in their lives, they were soon to learn otherwise. *Wahoo* set off across the open sea to Palau, and early on the morning of 26 January encountered two unescorted freighters on an easterly course. *Wahoo* dove and moved in to attack, O'Kane at the periscope again, while Morton analyzed the data flowing in to the conning tower and made tactical decisions. When he had the position he wanted he fired two torpedoes from the after tubes at each freighter. The first two torpedoes both hit, but the second ship was hit by one torpedo and was only damaged.

Four minutes later the periscope went up to see what they could see and O'Kane reported three ships, not two, in view. The first target was sinking. The second one was making six knots in a ponderous yawing charge at the periscope. The newcomer was a big transport that had somehow appeared while *Wahoo* was busy making her attack. Morton fired three torpedoes at the undamaged transport, two of which hit. He fired two more torpedoes at the damaged freighter and then had to duck deep to avoid being rammed. They heard so many explosions on the surface that it was impossible for *Wahoo* to tell what happened there. She loaded her remaining torpedoes into the tubes. Five torpedoes were then in the six forward tubes and the four after tubes were full.

Eight minutes later *Wahoo* came back to periscope depth and fired one torpedo at the damaged transport. It ran under the target without exploding. Morton then fired another torpedo with the same setup. This one hit and blew the midsection "higher than a kite." Troops went over the side. The transport's stern went up and the bow pointed for the bottom.

Wahoo then set out after the cripple, which was making six knots away from there. Twenty minutes later it was apparent *Wahoo* could not catch up submerged. She must have chanced upon a convoy rendezvous, because O'Kane picked up the masts of a fourth ship, joining the cripple over the horizon. *Wahoo's* battery was low and she had to surface to charge batteries. The transport had managed to launch a number of boats and barges into which troops were loaded. These were headed for New Guinea, two hundred calm sea miles away, and Morton knew that left alone these same troops would soon be in merciless battle with MacArthur's army in the jungle. *Wahoo* surfaced close to the troop-loaded barges. One of them opened up on the submarine with ineffective machine-gun fire. Morton replied with 4-inch and 20-millimeter and sank the largest barges. There is no doubt that this remarkable man became intoxicated with battle, and when in that state of exhilaration he was capable of rash action difficult to justify under more sober circumstances.

When the batteries were charged *Wahoo* set course at flank speed to overtake the two ships that had disappeared over the horizon. When he found them he had to make a long end around run to gain position ahead for attack, keeping the tops of the masts of his targets in sight through the fully extended high periscope. Finally he reached a position ahead along their track and *Wahoo* submerged. The new ship was a tanker. It was getting too dark for good periscope observation before Morton reached his attack position. He fired his last three bow torpedoes at the tanker for at least one good hit. The freighter had turned away again and was out of range.

Sometime later in a dark and moonless night they surfaced and were surprised to find both ships still together and struggling along at slow speed. The freighter was firing her deck gun at every phantom, making a difficult target for *Wahoo*, who had only stern tube torpedoes remaining.

Eventually the *marus* made a wrong zig and Morton fired two torpedoes at the tanker for what he felt sure was the finishing shot.

The crippled freighter was still going, still firing at *Wahoo*, at every opportunity, much of it wild but when they found the range, accurate enough to force the submarine into a hurried dive. The *maru* was using flashless powder superior to anything *Wahoo* had, and often the first indication that the Japanese ship had fired would be the rise of splashes close aboard. The courage and persistence of this ship aroused the admiration of *Wahoo*, but when a searchlight beam of an approaching Japanese escort stabbed above the horizon, the *maru* turned toward rescue and exposed herself. *Wahoo* fired her last two torpedoes, both of which hit. The submarine then turned east, leaving only the belated escort sweeping a clear horizon where the last ship went down. About midnight Morton got off a dispatch to Pearl Harbor reporting that in a running torpedo- and gunfight he had sunk four ships and expended all torpedoes. Japanese records identify only two ships sunk in this battle with the convoy.

A submarine without torpedoes has nothing left to do but return to base, and *Wahoo* headed for Pearl Harbor. The next morning they sighted smoke and found another four-ship unescorted convoy. Morton had no torpedoes but the magazine was still filled with four-inch gun ammunition. This was a challenge to his resourcefulness. Examining the convoy, he discovered one tanker without the deck guns so conspicious on the others, and Morton concocted a scheme to separate the unarmed tanker from her consorts. He ran out several thousand yards, then surfaced in the broad daylight and charged the convoy full speed. Sure enough, the three armed ships opened up with inaccurate gunfire and headed for a nearby rain squall at best individual speed, leaving the slower tanker to fall behind.

When the range to the tanker was down to seventy-five hundred yards, however, an escort, which Morton identified as a corvette but which his officers insisted was a destroyer, came dashing out of the rain squall and headed for the submarine. Morton estimated he could outrun a corvette on the surface. He called for more power out of his engines than their designer had built into them—and got it. The corvette-destroyer continued to close, and when a broadside salvo whistled overhead to raise a forest of white splashes from the sea, even Morton had to recognize the better part of valor, and submerge. That night he reported by radio, "Another running gun battle, *Wahoo* running destroyer gunning."

It is difficult to account for a phenomenon like Morton. There was nothing in his pre-*Wahoo* record to indicate he would rise to the summit of leadership. Kennedy, who preceded him in command, made two mediocre patrols with the same ship and the same crew, yet almost any rational system of selection would pick Kennedy rather than Morton. In

Kennedy's long peacetime submarine service he had a well-earned reputation as one of the Navy's most accomplished submarine approach officers. Without Kennedy's meticulous and exacting training of *Wahoo's*
crew Morton's unconventional methods might not have worked. It is
probable that Kennedy had to precede Morton as Sir John Jervis first
steeled the heart of the British Navy for Nelson to fashion into a band of
brothers.

Morton's methods of leadership were certainly unconventional. Very
few submarine skippers could or would turn over the periscope to a
second officer in a tight attack, but with the Morton-O'Kane combination
this worked smoothly. The discipline in *Wahoo* was hardly recognizable
as such by more conventional officers, but in action *Wahoo* and her crew
responded perfectly to their captain's will and for him reached peaks
beyond their anticipated maximum performance or their ordinary capabilities. They would follow "Mush" Morton through hell—and most of them
did go with him in *Wahoo* into the Sea of Japan never to return.

U.S. *Submarine Special Mission*

U.S. submarines were also involved in many special missions. It was
neither profitable nor proper to avoid all missions of mercy, or in support
of clandestine war, or many other special tasks for which submarines were
best suited. The trick was to maintain a balance which did not divert
too much submarine effort from their major job. Insofar as possible special missions were combined with combat missions so that a U.S. submarine was usually diverted from her patrol for only a day or two.

Searaven landed seven Allied agents on Ceram in the East Indies on
New Year's Eve. On New Year's Day *Nautilus* evacuated twenty-nine
civilians, including fourteen nuns, from a small island near Bougainville
in the Solomons. *Grayback* acted as a beacon ship for bombardment of
Munda, New Georgia. She also rescued six crashed Army aviators from
Rendova Island in the same locality. *Gudgeon* landed personnel and
equipment on Negros Island in the Philippines, and a month later on her
way home evacuated twenty-eight refugees from Timor. *S-18* reconnoitered Attu and the Semichis in the Aleutians. *Greenling* landed coastwatchers on New Britain. *Tambor* landed guerrillas and ammunition on
Mindanao in the Philippines. *Tautog* laid mines off Borneo. *Grouper*
rescued aviators in the Solomons. *Thresher* reconnoitered Christmas Island in the Indian Ocean and *Pompano* reconnoitered Bikini and Eniwetok in the Marshalls. All of this aided the war effort, but the true objective of the submarine force was to sink enemy ships. Pursuing their
main objective more often brought the submarines into close conflict, but
very rarely as close as *Growler* and *Hayasaki*.

Growler *vs.* Hayasaki

Growler, under command of Lieutenant Commander H. W. Gilmore with Lieutenant Commander A. F. Schade as executive officer, patrolled in the Bismarck Sea approaches to Rabaul during January and February. Information on enemy ships from plane and other submarine sightings was plentiful, and *Growler* was chevied about on radio information from Brisbane trying to head off important Japanese ship movements. On 16 January she torpedoed *Chifuku Maru,* but alert patrol boats by day and flare-dropping planes by night prevented her from completing several attacks. She sighted and approached marked hospital ships on three separate occasions and watched them proceed on their way unmolested.

On 31 January *Growler* made an attack on a 2500-ton converted gunboat, firing one torpedo which ran under the target without exploding. At 800-yard range Gilmore could see the crew of the Japanese ship man the rail to watch the torpedo go under. A week later on a night of poor visibility, *Growler* encountered a ship which her lookouts thought resembled the gunboat that had been spared by their defective torpedo, but which was actually the naval auxiliary *Hayasaki,* a 900-ton provision ship. Trusting to the poor visibility, *Growler* closed on the surface. When the range was 2000 yards and the track angle 130 degrees starboard, *Hayasaki* sighted *Growler,* came about, and charged in to ram the submarine.

In poor visibility, and with a ship less than half the size they estimated, *Growler's* bridge party did not immediately detect *Hayasaki's* change of course. The radarscope below very quickly indicated that the range was too close for torpedo fire. "Let full rudder!" Gilmore shouted down the hatch to the helmsman, and sounded the collision alarm. By this maneuver *Growler* rammed *Hayasaki* halfway between the bridge and the bow. The submarine was making seventeen knots and the impact was terrific. *Growler* heeled over fifty degrees and everybody was knocked off his feet. *Hayasaki* opened up on the submarine's bridge with accurate machine-gun fire.

"Clear the bridge!" Gilmore ordered. The quartermaster and the officer of the deck scrambled down the hatch, pulling two wounded lookouts with them. The commanding officer, the assistant officer of the deck, and one lookout were still up there.

"Take her down!" Gilmore ordered from the bridge. Schade hesitated for thirty seconds, then carried out the last order of his commanding officer and pulled the diving alarm. Schade still had his hands full saving *Growler.* Her bow was crushed back for thirty feet. Bullet-hole leaks in the conning tower were uncontrollable. Two depth charges went off, not close. Water in the pump room was several feet deep. Half a foot of water was slopping to and fro across the control room deck. Schade assumed command and brought the damage under control.

Thirty minutes after the collision he brought *Growler* up to make battle surface. There was nothing in sight. Schade believed that the Japanese ship had been sunk by the impact, but *Hayasaki*, though damaged, survived over two more years of war before she was sunk by a mine in the Java Sea. For ordering his ship to dive to safety and so sacrificing his own life while he lay wounded on the bridge, Gilmore was awarded a posthumous Congressional Medal of Honor.

Loss of Amberjack

Not as fortunate as *Growler* was *Amberjack* (Bole), which left Brisbane on 26 January to begin a patrol in the Shortland area just south of Bougainville. This hot spot was an assembling area for Japanese forces operating in the Solomons, and the area was under almost constant Allied observation. Brisbane therefore had many radio orders and instructions for *Amberjack*, with considerably more than usual radio traffic. *Amberjack* no sooner arrived off Shortland than she was ordered to Buka. She was then ordered south to cover Vella Lavella. She reported sinking a schooner by gunfire and sighting an enemy submarine. On 4 February she reported that she sank a 5000-ton freighter in a night action. A two-hour surface engagement ended with the torpedoing of the enemy ship and a spectacular explosion, but there is no corresponding Japanese record of a ship sunk. Chief Pharmacist's Mate Beeman was killed by machine-gun fire from the Japanese ship during this engagement and one officer was wounded.

Amberjack was then ordered to keep south of 7°30′ South and cover the Rabaul traffic. A few days later these orders were changed. On 14 February she reported having been forced down by two Japanese destroyers the night before, and that she had rescued a Japanese aviator from the water. She was then ordered to stay north of 6°30′ South. All further messages to her were unanswered.

Japanese records report a patrol plane attack on a submarine in *Amberjack's* area on 16 February. This attack was followed up by depth-charge attacks made by torpedo boat *Hiyodori* and *Submarine Chaser No. 18*. A large amount of oil and wreckage came to the surface. On 10 March *Amberjack* was due to make a routine homeward-bound report estimating the time of her arrival. When that time passed every effort was made to communicate with her by radio but she remained forever silent.

It is difficult to understand why all the chasing around to which *Am-*

berjack was subjected was necessary. Submarines ordered into tight spots like Shortland were sometimes pulled out and rotated to quieter areas to give the crew an opportunity to recover from days of constant tension. It was also necessary to clear submarines out of areas scheduled for night blind bombing, or for surface operations in which they might be mistaken for enemy submarines. Sometimes it was possible to move submarines on to projected tracks of important targets that had been sighted, but this required more time than staff officers usually appreciated. Submarines were not free to run from place to place at maximum surface speed in areas through which important targets moved. They could count on being forced down by planes or anti-submarine forces. The attempt to shift submarines quickly to counter fast surface ship movements more often led to wild goose chases.

U.S. Submarine Results

Alabacore (Lake) made a patrol in Bismarck Sea in which she also endured a good deal of chasing around and patrol area changes. The Task Force Commander at Brisbane and Commander South Pacific severely criticized Lake, in their patrol report endorsements, for firing twenty-one torpedoes for only three reported hits. It appears probable that two of these recorded hits may have been close prematures, for there is no Japanese report of ship damage to correspond, and *Albacore* observed at least one definite premature. The one torpedo that surely hit sank the destroyer *Oshio* on the night of 20 February, north of the Admiralty Islands—the second Japanese combat ship to be sunk by Lake in two successive patrols.

This made three Japanese destroyers and one patrol boat sunk by submarines during the first two months of the New Year, plus two additional destroyers damaged. Twenty-six *marus* were sunk in these two months, and thirty additional *marus* and four naval auxiliaries were damaged. The large proportion of damaged ships indicates that the high command might well have been more concerned with poor exploder performance than with inaccurate torpedo fire.

Progress of the War

Meanwhile the Solomons campaign went on. A task force of cruisers and destroyers went up the Slot to bombard Japanese airfields at Munda, New Georgia on 5 January. On the twenty-third they again went in to bombard Japanese installations at Kolombangara. The Japanese retaliated with a major air attack against the task force, and on 30 January in the Battle of Rennell Island *Chicago* was sunk by an aircraft torpedo. Tokyo Express runs of the Japanese destroyers continued, and as the Allies did not know of the Japanese high-level decision to abandon Guadalcanal, it was assumed that violent action in Ironbottom Sound might break out again at any moment. A number of casualties to destroyers and light naval forces were suffered on both sides, but the Tokyo Express was running in reverse. On 7 February the last Japanese destroyer runs were made to complete the evacuation of 11,706 men from Guadalcanal despite American control of the air and sea. On 9 February all organized resistance ceased on Guadalcanal.

In New Guinea the Americans and Australians pressed forward. Lae and Salamaua were soon depending partly on Japanese submarine supply services. In the Aleutians U. S. Army Air Forces continued to pound Kiska, and the U. S. Army occupied Amchitka on 12 January. A task force of cruisers and destroyers moved in to the Aleutians, bombarded Kiska on 18 February, and further disrupted Japanese communications.

Japanese Submarines

The Japanese decided to send four I-class submarines back to the Aleutians to attack targets of opportunity. *I-21* was sent on a commerce raid off Sydney. In an attempt to divert attention from the Solomons during the Guadalcanal evacuation, *I-165* bombarded the Cocos Islands in the Indian Ocean and *I-166* bombarded Port Gregory in western Australia. *I-8*, with the cruiser *Nara*, bombarded Canton Island in the Central Pacific for the same purpose. These bombardments caused little damage and failed completely as diversions. Japanese submarines also scouted American forces at the Battle of Rennell Island on 29–30 January, but most of the Japanese submarine effort was devoted to supply runs. On 29 January *I-1*, in a supply run to Guadalcanal, encountered the New Zealand corvettes *Kiwi* and *Moa* and a confused battle ensued.

Kiwi *and* Moa *vs.* I-1

Kiwi (Bridson) made sound contact on *I-1* at 2105 and shortly afterward sighted the submarine's wake. Bridson called for full speed and rammed the submarine in the port quarter. *Kiwi* opened up with every gun that would bear, and Japanese soldiers began going over the side. Landing barges on the submarine's after deck caught fire and illuminated the battle. Bridson rammed again and swept the submarine bridge and deck with 20-millimeter fire from ranges never exceeding 150 yards. The third time the corvette rammed she backed off, with *I-1* spouting oil. *Kiwi's* guns became too hot to fire and *Moa* took over, pounding the submarine until it ran aground in a sinking condition. Both corvettes stood by until dawn and rescued the submarine's wounded gunnery officer.

As so often happened in night action the battle narrative of the belligerents differed greatly. According to Japanese accounts *I-1* (Sakamoto) was first attacked while making a periscope observation before running in behind the reef to discharge cargo. American torpedo boats opened fire from ranges of 2000 yards with machine guns and torpedoes. Sakamoto ordered ninety feet but it was too late. Depth charges exploded immediately overhead. The main circuit breaker blew, leaving *I-1* without power. The high-pressure air line was ruptured. The submarine went down out of control at an angle of forty-five degrees with all loose gear tumbling into the forward ends of the compartments. The depth gauge, which had been damaged by the depth-charging, registered 450 before the submarine's plunge was stopped. She then shot upward, still out of control, and broached. The next time she went down she hit the bottom.

Sakamoto then determined to surface and fight it out. With difficulty *I-1* came up for battle surface and opened fire on the destroyers and torpedo boats which surrounded her. The submarine's decks were swept by machine-gun fire that killed everybody but the navigator. He dashed below shouting "Swords! Swords!" The officers rallied and swarmed up the ladder swords in hand. The navigator, a famous swordsman, tried to board an enemy torpedo boat that ranged alongside but this attempt to return to the tactics of the cutlass-armed boarding parties of yore failed. The navigator was unable to make it over his enemy's rail, and was left dangling by one arm as the ships swung apart.

The torpedo boat's fire ignited the gasoline in the landing barges on the after deck of *I-1*. With this illumination the torpedo boats poured in a storm of shells. *I-1* returned this fire, but the submarine's after gun had been removed to carry cargo and the torpedo boats came around astern where the forward gun would not bear. The torpedo boats fired three torpedoes but these all missed. The first lieutenant spurred the gun crew to heroic action. They scored a hit on a torpedo boat which sank as the submarine's crew cheered. The enemy's fire slackened and it appeared that the submarine might win the unequal battle, when one of the torpedo boats rammed and mortally wounded *I-1* after she had been desperately fighting for an hour and a half. The first lieutenant decided to run the submarine aground. As the bow hit, the stern sank, trapping those left below, so that thirty men went down with the ship while fifty made it to shore on Guadalcanal.

The survivors found themselves ashore armed only with two swords and three rifles. With them they brought the code books, as there had been no opportunity to destroy classified material when the ship was abandoned. The code books posed a problem. If they were burned, the smoke would disclose the refugees' position, so the code books were torn in shreds and the shreds buried in the sand. As there was grave risk that other secret material left aboard might become compromised, four volunteers waded out and destroyed the hulk with explosives. Another submarine was later ordered to complete the destruction of *I-1*, and planes went out also on this mission, but they were unable to find the submerged wreck.

News of the unorthodox disposal of secret codes did not reach the horrified communications security section in Tokyo until a month later. A commando landing on the American-held island was then ordered to recover the buried code books, but they could not be located, and it could only be assume that they were compromised. *I-1* had been carrying not only the codes then in use but the reserve issue that would be put into effect after the next code change. A total of 200,000 items of codes and ciphers had been compromised and had to be replaced as soon as possible. Ironically the U. S. Navy recovered valuable intelligence material from the hull of the sunken submarine, but the buried codes were never found.

The wounded prisoner (who was not the gunnery officer) was transferred to Pearl Harbor where he was interrogated by a language officer and another intelligence officer with submarine experience. The two submariners met as though at sword's point, but as the Japanese described the end of *I-1* this antagonism broke down. Although they could not understand each other's language, the Japanese often responded to the question put in English in such fluent Japanese, with gesture and facial expression, that it was unnecessary for the translator to translate. Details of the loss of *I-1* had little intelligence value, however, and more important information was solicited. Intelligence had recovered considerable information from enemy sources about American torpedo defects and they were anxious to learn more. When adequate rapport had been established the American submariner subtly put the question through the interpreter, "Do Japanese submarines have difficulties with explosion of their torpedoes before they reach the target?" and the Japanese responded with a smirk, "We don't but you do!"

Loss of I-18

I-18 was lost near Guadalcanal about two weeks later. This Japanese submarine left Truk with a cargo of provisions for Cape Esperance on 22 January. She successfully completed her supply mission and was then ordered to intercept American reinforcements east of Guadalcanal. On 11 February she reported sighting an American task force and was never heard from again.

Her destruction was the result of nice cooperation between anti-submarine patrol planes from *Helena* and the destroyer *Fletcher*. The planes sighted a Japanese submarine about nine miles from the task force and dropped a bomb and a smoke pot to mark the position. *Fletcher* was directed to take over the attack. She picked up sonar contact very quickly and dropped a pattern of nine depth charges. A few minutes later there was a terrific explosion which brought up a large quantity of debris. A big Japanese submarine surfaced briefly, rolled over, and sank. Japanese submarines accomplished very little in the first two months of 1943, other than delivering supplies to beleaguered Japanese forces. This service did not effect the final outcome.

Pearl Harbor Submarines

During the Solomons campaign Nimitz maintained the strength of the Brisbane submarines at twenty or more by detachments from the Pearl Harbor submarines. In addition, one submarine patrolled in the Marshalls, one or two off Truk, and one off Palau, where their patrols exerted a direct leverage on the South Pacific operations. This left few submarines for patrol of the productive areas off Honshu and in the East China Sea, but in February *Tarpon* was on patrol in the area south of Tokyo Bay.

Tarpon (Wogan) was one of the older fleet submarines. She had been at Manila when the war broke out, and in May 1942 was sent back from Fremantle to Mare Island for overhaul. It was not until October 1942 that she returned to service and was sent on patrol in the South Pacific. On that patrol *Tarpon* made only one contact with a convoy, made a single attack which the division commander and the force commander criticized as lacking in aggression; and she sank no ships. In February *Tarpon* was on her sixth patrol, having yet to sink an enemy ship.

During the last days of January *Tarpon* encountered gales with seas running so high she could not maintain depth control at less than 120 feet. The weather moderated on 1 February, and that night at 2132 she was on the surface when SJ radar reported a pip. Wogan closed at full speed on the surface and at 7000 yards sighted a large ship. *Tarpon* submerged with only the radar antenna above the surface and worked in to attack position. The target could be dimly seen through the periscope when *Tarpon* fired four torpedoes for one hit.

The *maru* turned away and Wogan surfaced and pursued. About an hour later he hit her again with two torpedoes and then circled the stricken ship until it disappeared on the radar. It was the 10,935-ton *Fushimi Maru*. Japanese records are vague about what happened to *Fushimi Maru* that night, but the evidence that she sank is strong.

A week later on 8 February, while on the surface at night in a rough sea with a high wind, *Tarpon* again picked up a radar pip and closed at full speed. Torpedo data computer and navigational plot both tracked the ship at 17 knots on course 155. At that speed *Tarpon* could barely keep up. At 6500 yards Wogan could see the amorphous mass of a big ship, and at 5000 yards he went down to radar depth. He closed until the target could dimly be seen in the periscope for a check bearing and then fired four torpedoes, all of which exploded at the proper interval.

Wogan's description of this week's work was perfunctory and accurate. He thought his second target was an *Asama Maru*-class ship. In this and his other estimate he was correct. It was *Tatsuta Maru*, Japan's 16,975-ton liner, en route to Truk. In one week *Tarpon* had sunk 27,910 tons of Japanese shipping.

Total tonnage sunk is often used as a measure of relative submarine effectiveness, possibly because the exact registered tonnage of an identified merchant ship is one statistic to which everyone can agree. Frequently, however, known registered tonnage is added to estimated tonnage of unidentified ships and to displacement tonnage of combat ships to yield a figure of very dubious value, but by this criteria *Tarpon* had risen, in a week, from the bottom to near the top of the list. *Greenling*, *Drum*, *Guardfish*, and *Triton* were the only U.S. submarines then with higher scores.

One night in the following October, with Wogan still in command, *Tarpon* had a dramatic battle with a mysterious vessel, but *Tatsuta Maru* was the last Japanese ship that *Tarpon* sank during the war, although she made a total of twelve patrols before the war ended. On her later patrols she was relegated to quieter areas for reconnaissance and rescue missions, in deference to her age and growing infirmities. Her history exemplifies that submarine warfare, like any other kind, can be months or years of hard, tedious, exacting, dangerous work, with possibly only a few minutes of stirring action.

In one respect U.S. submarines sank too many ships in February. *Sawfish*, a new submarine, was on her first patrol south of Kyushu at three o'clock on the morning of 17 February when she sighted a light several miles to westward. She closed to investigate this most unusual occurrence and found two ships in company. Suspecting some sort of a booby trap, *Sawfish* opened up the range and dove ahead of the strange ships to investigate further at dawn. About sunrise a small freighter came along. *Sawfish* fired three torpedoes and observed one hit. The ship went down. The ship matched the description of a decoy ship *Trigger* had encountered some time earlier, so *Sawfish* discreetly remained submerged to see what would happen.

About noon smoke was sighted on the horizon and *Sawfish* turned toward it. An hour later, when she was about in firing position, *Sawfish* identified the stranger as a Russian and let her go by. The skipper was not altogether convinced that this was not a ruse. All the Russian markings could have been rigged in an hour and no Russian ships had ever been reported in this area. That night *Sawfish* sank another freighter. Four more ships with Russian markings were sighted during this patrol and all of them proceeded safely by. Upon *Sawfish's* return, Commander Submarines Pacific disclaimed any information of Russian ships in the area.

The mystery was cleared up later when the Russians protested that two Soviet merchantmen were torpedoed and sunk en route from Vladivostok to the United States through the Strait of Tsushima and south of Japan. The usual route for this traffic was through La Pérouse Strait and north about Japan, but that route became icebound about 15 January although the Russian liaison office reported that Russian ships were using it until 3 March. Following this unfortunate occurrence improvements were made in recognition markings and the Russians furnished better information of individual ship movement and general traffic routing.

XIV

MARCH, APRIL, MAY 1943

Command Organization

On 15 March a new fleet numbering system went into effect. The old South Pacific Force under Admiral Halsey became the Third Fleet. The Central Pacific Force became the Fifth Fleet under Vice Admiral Spruance, and Naval Forces Southwest Pacific became the Seventh Fleet under Vice Admiral Carpender. In this system the Fremantle submarines became Task Force 71, with Christie as Task Force Commander, under Carpender, who in turn reported to General MacArthur, the Area Commander. The Brisbane submarines became Task Force 72, and Fife was Task Force Commander under Carpender, but also was under the administrative command of Christie. As Commander Submarines Pacific, Lockwood reported directly to Nimitz, Commander Pacific Ocean Area. He had neither tactical nor administrative responsibility for Christie's submarines, but under Nimitz's orders was required to keep the number of Seventh Fleet submarines at twenty by rotating Pearl Harbor submarines to replace Seventh Fleet submarines sent home for overhaul or lost by enemy action. The major portion of Seventh Fleet submarines still operated out of Brisbane, where they had a number of special missions to perform, but their opportunities to sink Japanese ships decreased as air and surface forces encroached upon the areas where previously only submarines had operated.

Progress of the War in the South Pacific

After losing Guadalcanal, the Japanese redoubled their effort to save New Guinea, but they had no intention of allowing the Americans to push into the northern Solomons. The Japanese reinforced their position in New Georgia and worked diligently to expand their air bases at Munda in New Georgia. Merrill with a task force of cruisers and destroyers ran up the Slot to Kula Gulf, between New Georgia and Kolombangara to bombard Munda, and Vila on Kolombangara, to discourage the Japanese. He caught two Japanese destroyers (*Murasame* and *Minegumo*) on a supply run to Vila and promptly sank them both.

Loss of Grampus

When Merrill started up the Slot *Grampus* and *Grayback* were ordered into Blackett Strait to catch any Japanese ships trying to escape through that exit from Kula Gulf. *Grayback* had only one contact. She believed that this was *Grampus* and turned away to avoid her. If it was *Grampus* it was the last contact U.S. forces ever had with her.

Grampus (Craig) was out of Brisbane on her sixth war patrol. On 2 March she was ordered to leave her area off the north end of Buka, come down along the west coast of Bougainville, and take station in Blackett Strait. There is no assurance that she received these orders, for she was not heard from after 12 February. There was nothing unusual in this. A wise submarine commander in a hot spot like the Solomons generally maintained strict radio silence unless he had a message of compelling importance to transmit. *Murasame* and *Minegumo* went through Blackett Strait on their way to be sunk by Merrill's task force, but there is no real evidence that they made contact with *Grampus* en route. There was a large oil slick in the Strait the next day, and this plus the contact made by *Grayback* gave rise to a conjecture that *Grampus* may have made contact with the Japanese destroyers and come off second best in the encounter. It is pure conjecture. Both destroyers were later sunk that night. What happened to *Grampus*, and when, remains a mystery.

Battle of the Bismarck Sea

Encouraged by a successful convoy run to Wewak, the Japanese at Rabaul organized a convoy of eight transports with eight destroyer escorts to take 6900 troops and supplies to Lae. They greatly underestimated the Allied air strength in Papua. Moreover, Kenny's bombers had abandoned high-altitude bombing of ships at sea in favor of a newly developed tactic of skip bombing. This was a disastrous surprise to the Japanese. All eight transports and four of the escorting destroyers were sunk. U.S. torpedo boats moved in that night to mop up the cripples. Of the entire convoy only four Japanese destroyers escaped, and these together with submarines rescued 2700 troops. From then on supply to northern New Guinea was confined to destroyers and submarines, with Japanese submarines carrying an increasing share of the burden.

U.S. *Submarines in the South Pacific*

The Battle of the Bismarck Sea was an epoch, marking the end of *maru* traffic south of Rabaul. What traffic the Japanese had with their forces in Papua and the Solomons was carried on, after that battle, by fast destroyer night runs and by submarines. Dominated by U.S. air and surface forces, the New Britain and Solomons areas became increasingly difficult and unprofitable for U.S. submarine operation. Submarines continued to perform a variety of special missions in these areas, particularly landing coastwatching parties and taking them out again if the area became too hot to hold, but after the first of March no Japanese ship of any kind was sunk by submarines in the area south of Rabaul.

The Japanese had a system of sending destroyers north from Rabaul to the equator to reinforce the anti-submarine screen of convoys coming down from Truk or Palau. American intelligence officers finally figured out what was happening, and submarines were sent up to the line to exploit the situation and catch the convoys before their escorts joined up. Some of the submarines were Brisbane submarines and some came out of Pearl Harbor and moved south from patrol areas in the Carolines. In March, *Triton, Trigger, Tuna, Snapper,* and *Greenling* were so employed. Together they sank a half dozen *marus* and damaged a couple more. The Japanese responded to this attack by arranging the rendezvous between their convoys and escorts farther north. This was the undoing of *Triton,* which was lost in March in that area.

Loss of Triton

Triton (MacKenzie) came out of Brisbane in February and was given a patrol area in the Rabaul-Shortland area. From there she was sent up to the equator, where she was assigned an area between areas already occupied by *Snapper* and *Trigger,* lying in wait for Japanese Rabaul-bound convoys. On 6 March MacKenzie found a convoy and chased it into *Trigger's* area to sink a ship. The next day he made a radio report of his return to his own area. A few hours later *Triton* made another radio report of a night action with another convoy and claimed four hits, although MacKenzie could not observe results because *Triton* was driven down by gunfire from the escorting destroyer. The 7000-ton *Mito Maru* was torpedoed in this attack.

Triton was last heard from on 11 March, when she again reported course and speed of a convoy she was chasing. On 13 March Fife warned MacKenzie of three Japanese destroyers that had been observed headed toward his area. The destroyers were assumed to be an escort en route to pick up a convoy, or a hunter-killer group attracted to a new area of submarine activity. These three destroyers were responsible for the loss of *Triton*. Japanese reports describe an attack made by destroyers slightly north of the equator on 15 March. Their report of great quantities of oil and pieces of wood and cork coming to the surface leaves little doubt that a submarine was sunk there.

The position reported by the Japanese was in *Trigger's* area, but she survived to bring home a story generally confirming the Japanese reports. *Trigger* (Benson) encountered a Japanese convoy in her area on 15 March and made a successful attack which sank one *maru*. *Trigger* was then depth-charged by the escorts, but their counterattack was neither severe nor long continued. For an hour or more thereafter, however, Benson heard many distant depth-charge explosions. The Japanese reported that a big *maru* was damaged in addition to the ship that Benson sank. *Triton* had probably followed this convoy into the area adjacent to her own, ignoring boundaries as she was permitted to do in hot pursuit. By chance the two submarines made almost simultaneous attacks, and *Triton* called down on herself the brunt of the Japanese counterattack. She was never heard from again.

U.S. Submarines in Other Areas

U.S. submarines sank a total of twenty-one *marus* in March and damaged fifteen others. These sinkings were spread over a wide geographic area—from the East Indies where *Gudgeon* sank two big ships, to Wake Island where the 10,000-ton *Suwa Maru* beached herself after being hit by one of *Tunny's* torpedoes. Up off the northeast coast of Honshu *Permit* sank one ship. The Japanese credited submarines with sinking another in that area and damaging two more; but it is more probable that these losses were caused by their own mines, with which the area had been sowed to trap unwary submarines.

March would have been less than an average month for U.S. submarines had it not been for *Wahoo* (Morton) in the Yellow Sea. "Mush" Morton at sea in *Wahoo* was enough to tip the scales against the Japanese. *Wahoo* made the entire run from Midway through the Nansei Shoto into the East China Sea without sighting a single Japanese ship or plane. Finding few targets in the Tung Hai, Morton continued on into the shallow and easily mined Yellow Sea. Despite the unattractive characteristics of the Yellow Sea *Wahoo* penetrated deeper and deeper until Morton found himself a few miles off the breakwater at Dairen. There he found plenty of targets.

On 19 March *Wahoo* sank two ships, despite premature explosions of some of her torpedoes and one definite dud. On the twenty-first she sank two more *marus*. The Japanese were entirely unprepared to handle the unexpected situation created by Morton's audacious move. Most of the crews of the sunken ships perished in the freezing water. *Wahoo* sank one ship each day on the twenty-third and twenty-fourth, still plagued by poor torpedo performance. On the twenty-fifth Morton resorted to the use of his deck guns to sink two small ships, remarking that anyone who hasn't been on a submarine's bridge at battle surface with a 4-inch gun and three 20-millimeter guns all at rapid fire, in the morning twilight on a calm sea in clear, crisp weather, "just ain't lived." With *Wahoo's* last two torpedoes on 29 March, Morton sank the ninth Japanese ship for that patrol and headed home, torpedoes expended.

Battle of the Komandorski Islands

During the month of March both American and Japanese submarines continued their cold, miserable, and unprofitable northern patrols and contributed nothing much to the approaching crisis in the Aleutians. To harassed combatants on both sides in the Solomons and New Guinea, the Aleutians seemed as remote as the other side of the moon, but what happened in one theater had an inevitable influence on the other. As American naval, air, and ground forces were built up in the Aleutians it became increasingly difficult for the Japanese to supply their outlying garrisons. What ships they lost in the effort subtracted from their resources to fight the war in the South Pacific. In this respect the Japanese occupation of Attu and Kiska was to the advantage of the Americans. On the other hand, it was a shorter distance from Truk to Japan to the Aleutians than it was from Espíritu Santo to Hawaii to Dutch Harbor, and interior lines of communication gave the Japanese an opportunity to affect strategic concentrations against divided American naval forces.

American intelligence officers estimated that the Japanese had two cruisers and several destroyers under Hosogaya in the far north, and the arrival of two more cruisers to reinforce him went undetected. On 22 March Hosogaya set out for Paramushiro with four cruisers and four destroyers to escort three transports to Attu. Rear Admiral C. H. McMorris, at sea with two cruisers and four destroyers, encountered Hosogaya's force en route. When McMorris sighted the tops of Japanese ships over the horizon he closed at full speed, eager for battle with what he was assured were equal forces. The Japanese heaved up over the horizon with four cruisers. McMorris was overmatched two to one and had to fight a difficult retiring action. Army Air Force planes were unable to take off from Adak in time and were no more help to him than were the submarines. From this difficult situation he was fortunate to escape with heavy damage to *Salt Lake City* and the destroyer *Bailey*, while inflicting minor damage on two Japanese cruisers. Without losing any of his ships he turned back the Japanese reinforcement of Attu.

Struggle for Control of the Air in the South

At the beginning of April Yamamoto opened up intensive air operations, first directed against the Solomons to interdict American forces there, until he later shifted his attention to Papua. Japanese aviators were very optimistic in their reports of results in these actions. They did sink three Allied ships and damaged several others, but contrary to their belief they suffered far more losses of planes and pilots than they inflicted on their opponents. Kenny's bombers over New Ireland evened the score for ships lost in the South Pacific. Ainsworth took his task force of cruisers up the Slot again to stop fast night runs of Japanese destroyers to New Georgia.

Japanese Submarines in the South Pacific

There were no outstanding successes for Japanese submarines in the South Pacific in the spring of 1943. *I-6* and *I-26* left Truk in March to operate off the east coast of Australia, and *I-6* laid magnetic mines off Brisbane en route. Over a dozen submarines were engaged in making supply runs, and the trade often ran into difficulties. *I-176*, with a picked crew under command of Tanabe (who commanded *I-168* when she sank *Yorktown*), made one supply run to Lae which she survived by a scant margin.

I-176 surfaced at dusk at the prearranged disembarkation point off Lae. The impatient landing craft from ashore approached immediately, and the submarine crew hurriedly unloaded the cargo of rice. The work was about half completed when signal rockets were fired from ashore, followed by machine-gun fire. Tanabe gave the order to dive, but before the deck could be cleared three B-25s were over them strafing with machine guns. One plane dropped a bomb which hit aft in the deck cargo of rice drums. The crew came tumbling down the hatch as the submarine started down with a heavy port list. The conning tower and radio room leaked like sieves. The pressure hull was punctured aft. Many men were killed on deck. The quartermaster was dead at the wheel. When the diving officer turned to Tanabe at the periscope for instructions he found his commanding officer still standing but critically wounded.

Despite her damage they succeeded in beaching *I-176* in a nearby river, where overhanging trees gave some protection from observation. The engineering officer was in favor of abandoning the submarine and taking the crew ashore, but they patched the holes with wooden plugs and made the hull more or less watertight. The landing craft from ashore came out, surprised to find *I-176* perched on the beach rather than blasted to the bottom. They took off her supplies and ammunition and the wounded and the dead. Tanabe refused to be taken ashore. On the night of the twentieth they backed the submarine off the beach, with diffi-culty, and eventually they made it to Rabaul where she was repaired.

Loss of RO-34 and RO-102

RO-34 was sent out from Rabaul on 2 April to search for ships in the Guadalcanal area. In this she was too successful for her own good. Early in the morning of 5 April she made contact with Ainsworth's task force of cruisers and destroyers on one of its runs up the Slot to try to intercept Japanese landing barges and destroyers trading with New Georgia. De-stroyers *Strong* and *O'Bannon* in the cruiser's anti-submarine screen made radar contact with a surfaced submarine. *O'Bannon* opened up with her 5-inch guns in radar control and crippled *RO-34* on the opening salvo. She then closed to visual range and hammered the Japanese sub-marine with machine-gun fire and deck guns, followed by salvos of depth charges as the submarine went under. The next day the Japanese ordered *RO-34* to make weather reports and act as lifeguard for a Japanese air strike, but they never heard from her again.

Later in the month *RO-102* departed from Rabaul to operate against the supply lines to Milne Bay. She reported on 9 May that there were no enemy vessels in her area. Six days later she was ordered to with-draw from her position and return to Rabaul. No reply to this message was received. *RO-102* was sunk by *PT-150* and *PT-152* on 14 May.

Tunny and the Japanese Escort Carriers

To beef up the air strength of Rabaul, Yamamoto sent his carrier air groups to operate from Rabaul airfields. The Japanese were reluctant to operate their carriers south of Truk, so escort carriers and even some combat carriers were reduced to acting as airplane ferries running planes from Japan to Truk. From Truk these planes were flown down to Rabaul.

Lockwood was aware of this traffic and made strenuous efforts to stop it. It was much more efficient to sink a carrier full of planes and pilots than to shoot them down later one by one in aerial combat. It was also easier said than done. Truk had many passes and they were all hard to

guard. Although Lockwood could not know, Piaanu Pass and Northeast
Pass were closed by defensive minefields, so submarine strength was
wasted off these passes when it could have been better employed off
North Pass, and Otta Pass in the south, had the intelligence been better.
Otta Pass was so protected by Kuop atoll that it required two or three
submarines to guard it properly, and at North Pass was assembled the
elite of the Japanese anti-submarine forces.

Tunny (Scott) was patrolling southwest of Truk. She had already sunk
two *marus* on this patrol in addition to torpedoing *Suwa Maru* at Wake
on her way to work. On the night of 9–10 April, when she made radar
contact at 14,000 yards, she knew immediately it was different. It was a
formation of three large pips with an escort on each bow. Plot soon estimated the speed at eighteen knots. *Tunny* went to four-engine speed
to gain position ahead.

Ten minutes later the formation zigged toward her and *Tunny* found
herself right ahead of the Japanese. With their combined speed the range
closed rapidly and soon the formation was visible from the bridge. There
was one big aircraft carrier in the starboard column and two escort carriers in the port one, with fifteen hundred yards between, and a destroyer
on each bow of the formation. *Tunny* was highballing right down in
between. Scott flooded *Tunny* down until her decks were awash to reduce the silhouette and slowed to two-thirds speed to cut down the visibility of the boiling wake, but he kept on the surface to maintain maneuverability. He intended to get between the columns and fire bow tubes
at the two ships in the port column and stern tubes at the big one.

At this critical moment three small pips appeared in the formation
(possibly motor torpedo boats) in between the columns, one point on
Tunny's bow, and with a range of only five hundred yards, forcing Scott
to change his plan. He changed *Tunny's* course to the right, went down
to forty feet, and shifted the Torpedo Data Computer to the leading ship
in the left-hand column for a stern tube shot. It took fast work. The
targets were not yet visible in the periscope, so he had to fire the first
salvo by radar, with a wide spread, and lead the target a little to offset
the tendency of radar bearings to lag. Scott fired four torpedoes. The
range was only 800 yards and at the end of the busy minute of the
torpedo run, while they were lining up on the next target, they heard
four hits.

Keithly, the executive officer, tried to pick up the second target
through the periscope, but it was very dark and the Japanese formation
was a little ragged from the recent zig, with the target behind its proper
position. Maybe the position keeping was not up to Japanese Navy standard for a blinker signal opened up. Keithly saw it and made a check
bearing by periscope just before firing the bow tubes. *Tunny* fired six

torpedoes, longitudinal spread, with initial range 650 yards. The first three hit.

Depth charges followed immediately, probably from the motor torpedo boats, because the destroyers' screws could be heard in the distance. *Tunny* turned to parallel the formation's course and went deep. Two depth charges were close as they passed a hundred feet, and then there was a very heavy explosion in the distance, but everybody in *Tunny* was too happy to care. She surfaced shortly after midnight and got off a message to *Pike*, to alert her for cripples or the remnants of the Japanese formation that was headed her way.

Tunny went on up to North Pass, where the anti-submarine activity was so intense it kept her busy dodging pickets, patrols, and flare-dropping planes. Despite these efforts to discourage him Scott was on the spot when the Japanese submarine *I-9* came out the channel. *Tunny* fired three torpedoes at it, but the Japanese submariners were alert, and swung ship to comb the track; so all three missed. *Tunny* went deep to avoid two torpedoes *I-9* fired down the track, and in this perilous thrust and riposte no one got hurt.

No Japanese carrier had been torpedoed in *Tunny's* attack on 10 April either. Scott's attack on the carriers was one of the most skillful submarine attacks of the war. *Tunny* had an unusual opportunity. Never before or since did a submarine succeed in reaching a position from which to fire both bow and stern tubes at multiple aircraft carrier targets in one single attack. *Tunny*, her skipper, and her crew met every test superbly. Submariners post-mortemed each other's attacks like Monday morning quarterbacks but no one ever came up with a suggestion that would have improved Scott's approach on the carriers. It was art for art's sake. The hits they heard must have been prematures again, and all the planes those carriers carried had to be shot down the hard way.

Death of Yamamoto

Yamamoto turned his main attention from the Solomons to New Guinea on 11 April and made several big air attacks. In all these attacks the Japanese aviators greatly exaggerated the damage done, deceiving Yamamoto into thinking that Allied advances were stopped in their tracks. He sent the Japanese carrier air groups back to the carriers and the Japanese defense relaxed.

The tendency to be overoptimistic about results of attacks was not confined to aviators or to the Japanese. After night surface action in particular, the number of ships reported sunk nearly always exceeded the actual count. Submarines on both sides frequently reported sinking ships that never went to the bottom. Kenny's Fifth Air Force repeatedly reported the destruction of Rabaul, only to have it arise vigorously from its ashes. It was the unpopular duty of a responsible staff to deflate reports to prevent making tactical and strategic decisions based on false information. In many cases the truth was learned too late. Rather than being knocked flat, the Allied forces were about ready to surge forward.

Yamamoto did not live to see it. On 18 April he made an inspection trip to Buin on Bougainville. His plane was shot down by U. S. Army fighters. Yamamoto and several of the Combined Fleet staff were killed. This was as severe a blow to the Japanese as the loss of a major engagement. Reserves for high command were thin in the Japanese Navy. It was generally believed that Yamaguchi, who went down with *Hiryu* at Midway, had been marked to succeed Yamamoto. If so, the Japanese may have paid dearly for the samurai tradition that inspired Yamaguchi to lash himself to the bridge of the sinking carrier. Koga succeeded to command of the Combined Fleet. His tenure was destined for another tragic ending, and he was never the leader that Yamamoto was.

Maru *War in April and May*

In April and May U.S. submarines sank forty-nine *marus* and three Japanese escort vessels, a monthly average equal to the best previous month of the war. One of the most productive areas was off northeast Honshu. *Flying Fish, Scorpion,* and *Pickerel* were there in April to sink seven *marus. Wahoo* and *Pogy* relieved them in May. Ship sinkings in the area prompted the Japanese to reinforce the minefields they had laid there the previous October. In May three thousand additional mines were laid off northeast Honshu and Tsugaru Strait.

Loss of Pickerel

Pickerel (Alston) failed to return from her patrol in this area. She left Midway on 22 March for northeast Honshu and was never heard from again. The Japanese record an anti-submarine attack on 3 April which could conceivably have had *Pickerel* as a target, and they also record that *Submarine Chaser No. 13* was sunk by a submarine torpedo on the same day. *Pickerel* was the only submarine that could have been there. It is possible that she was involved in a "sea disaster" on 7 April to which the Japanese attribute the loss of two *marus.*

Pickerel was due to leave her area to return home at sunset on 1 May just before the Japanese sowed the area so heavily with mines. There were two mine lines in her area, however, laid off shore in deep water the previous October, after *Guardfish's* field day off northeast Honshu. American submarines did not know about these mines, although in deference to the possible existence of such a field they were directed to stay in water deeper than 60 fathoms. These Japanese mines had been laid in 250 fathoms, deeper than any American submarines expected to encounter moored mines, and *Pickerel* may have run into the field.

Japanese mine lines were often laid to present a 10 per cent threat; that is, a submarine crossing a single line once had only a 10 per cent chance of hitting a mine, but of course if *Pickerel* operated very long in the area she may have crossed either or both of these mine lines many times. Moored mines at the end of 250 fathoms of cable, dipped and swung at the end of their long tether in a wholly unpredictable fashion, and might rarely watch at the depth they were set to operate, but even with the probabilities in favor of *Pickerel* she may well have hit a mine.

Standing orders required a returning submarine to report the expected time of entering Midway's 500-mile circle, in order that she might be recognized and protected. As *Pickerel's* report was not received on time, planes were sent out from Midway as far as they could search along her route, in hopes she had suffered only a radio casualty or was coming home damaged; but no one ever saw or heard of *Pickerel* again. Whatever the unknown public relations officer had in mind when he dubbed submarines "The Silent Service," it was frequently descriptive of their end.

Fremantle-Based Submarines

Although most of the Southwest Pacific submarines were still operating out of Brisbane in the spring of 1943, the Fremantle-based submarines managed to keep the Japanese occupied in the Philippines and the East Indies. *Grayling* sank *Shanghai Maru* in the Philippines on 9 April. That same day Lieutenant Commander W. B. Sieglaff, in command of *Tautog*, had a very busy day in the Celebes Sea. *Tautog* attacked a convoy of five ships with a destroyer escort and sank *Penang Maru*, Sieglaff fired torpedoes at the destroyer also but missed. *Tautog* then swung around to present her stern tubes and fired two more torpedoes at another freighter and missed again, but the destroyer ran into the torpedo track and an influence explosion close aboard crippled her thin hull. The destroyer headed for the beach, but Sieglaff followed her into shallow water and hit her again with *Tautog's* last torpedo. This was the end of the Japanese destroyer *Isonami*.

Gudgeon *and* Kamakura Maru

Gudgeon (Post) also had a profitable patrol in the Philippines. She left Fremantle on 15 April to undertake a special mission of landing personnel and equipment for guerrillas on Panay, and then proceed to Pearl Harbor for refit. Late at night on 27 April *Gudgeon* encountered a large unescorted ship on a southerly course, making 17½ knots and zig-zagging forty degrees each side of the base course every five minutes. Post identified his target as *Kamakura Maru,* a familiar prewar visitor to Honolulu. He tried for an hour and a half to gain position ahead on this high-speed target, but finally had to accept a large track angle and fired four torpedoes while still on the surface.

Gudgeon submerged after firing the torpedoes and heard three timed hits on her way down. Post was not satisfied that the big ship was sinking, so he closed to fire torpedoes from the stern tubes. His first look through the periscope showed the target stopped and on an even keel, but at the next look the bow was rising in the air and she was sinking fast by the stern. He had correctly identified his target. It was the 17,526-ton passenger liner *Kamakura Maru.*

Kamakura Maru was on her way to Java with military government personnel. She was the pride of the Japanese merchant marine but she had been routed through the Sulu Sea without escort, depending on her speed and her zigzag course for submarine protection. At seventeen knots and at night the Japanese considered her safe enough from submarines. In fact, most of them believed that she could not have been sunk by a submarine and that she must have hit a magnetic mine. Survivors were picked up by destroyers. There was no attempt to keep her loss a secret. Newspapers described the arrival of survivors at Surabaya, with the military government typists looking very sexy in their wet dresses. There was no overt criticism of her lack of escorts.

Loss of Grenadier

Grenadier (Fitzgerald) was lost off the west coast of the Malay Peninsula on 22 April. This was ordinarily an area patrolled by British submarines, but the British submarines had been withdrawn to the Mediterranean leaving only Dutch submarines at Ceylon during the first half of 1943. The Dutch submarines were fully occupied patrolling Malacca Strait, and the Burma traffic up along the Malay coast had been unmolested for some time. Under these circumstances arrangements were made with the British to permit *Grenadier* to occupy the area with the intention of throwing Japanese anti-submarine defense off-balance.

Grenadier found poor hunting in the area, but on the night of 20 April she made contact with two ships, that turned away before she could attack. Estimating their base course, Fitzgerald ran for position ahead at dawn. About fifteen minutes before planned diving time a plane came in on *Grenadier*. She made a quick dive but as she passed 120 feet a bomb went off right over the maneuvering room. The submarine was badly damaged. The stern was twisted and leaking. The main motor cables were severed and the maneuvering room was on fire. She lost all power and settled to the bottom in 267 feet of water.

The crew patched up the damage, a task that required tremendous labor, with a bucket brigade bailing the maneuvering room bilge to keep the main motor from flooding. Many men lost consciousness from heat prostration and physical exhaustion. That night they got her to the surface. Some of her auxiliary machinery and her radio were patched up, but her stern had been so twisted in the explosion that she had no propulsion. The gun was out of action. An attempt to sail her to the nearest land failed in a dead calm. Fitzgerald sent a message describing her condition, destroyed all classified publications, destroyed the radar and radio equipment, and prepared to scuttle *Grenadier*.

There were two ships in sight at dawn. A single engine plane came over but *Grenadier* opened fire with 20-millimeter and machine guns, scored several hits, and the airman dropped his bomb two hundred feet wide of the submarine. As the ships approached, however, it was apparent that the submarine could neither fight nor run away, and Fitzgerald gave the order to abandon ship. As the crew took to the water, with the sick and non-swimmers in rubber boats, the Chief of the Boat below decks pulled the vents and dashed up the conning tower ladder to go over the side with his commanding officer. All of them became prisoners of war. Fitzgerald was subjected to the most sadistic torture imaginable to induce him to give information on submarine operations and technical equipment. Despite the brutal treatment they received all but four of *Grenadier's* crew survived to be rescued at the end of the war.

Submarine Minelaying

In the Southwest Pacific Christie's submarines continued quietly planting mines in places where he thought it would do the most good. Usually these mining missions were part of a regular patrol, and commanding officers liked to plant their mines as soon as possible to get them out of the way. Thus *Tautog* sowed mines off Borneo before Sieglaff went on to sink *Isonami* and *Penang Maru* on the same patrol. During April and May *Trout* also laid mines off Borneo. *Silversides*, one of Fife's submarines operating out of Brisbane, laid mines in Steffan Strait, New Ireland, but most of the mines laid in these months were planted by Lockwood's submarines operating out of Pearl Harbor.

The location of early minefields in Japanese waters and the East China Sea was decided in rather haphazard manner. When Nimitz set up an analyses section for mine warfare, better locations for submarine minefields were indicated, and Lockwood was directed to prepare a mining plan for submarines. *Stingray* was sent to lay mines off Wenchow, China. *Runner* mined the entrance to Hong Kong. *Scorpion* and *Steelhead* planted mines off Honshu, and *Snook* planted a field off the Saddle Islands, near the mouth of the Yangtze River.

Minelaying was not an easy task as *Snook* (Triebel) discovered before she relieved herself of the evil eggs she carried. Fog, haze, and poor visibility and uncertain currents made exact navigation difficult, and the area was infested with Chinese junks that complicated the problem of laying the field unobserved. The approach was made submerged. *Snook* stuck in the mud at sixty-five feet, and when she planed up and scraped over that shoal, she ran in the mud five or six more times before she found a hole seventy-five feet deep in which she could lie until dark. When she blew up to the surface at night she nearly ran her periscope through the bottom of a Chinese junk silently sailing along in its own Tung Hai. After *Snook* arrived at the prescribed location, the plant was completed in two hours and she was free for a short patrol, feeling light-hearted after unburdening herself of the mines. In the next twelve days Triebel sank three ships with torpedoes. No one knows what the Japanese did about the Saddle Islands minefield.

It is difficult to determine the effectiveness of submarine-laid minefields. Mines laid by surface minelayers in water frequented by Japanese supply missions in the South Pacific had some dramatic successes. Much later in the war, mines laid by the Army Air Force in Japanese waters were an important factor in the final destruction of remnants of Japanese seaborne commerce. But minefields laid by submarines were small and scattered. This caused the Japanese to disperse their minesweepers and thus may have contributed to the success of other mining operations. Postwar analyses indicate twenty-seven Japanese ships may have been sunk or damaged by submarine mines, but the Japanese themselves were often confused as to the cause of their ship losses. Minelaying was not popular with submariners and it is probable that an equal effort spent in torpedo attacks would have been more productive of results.

Aleutians Activity

In late April the center of activity shifted back to the Aleutians. Although occupation of Attu and Kiska was more of a strategic liability than an asset to the Japanese, it was a constant worry to American strategists (particularly the amateurs) who wanted the Japanese to be driven out. Attu had been occupied by Japanese troops in June 1942, then evacuated, and later reoccupied. In April 1943 it was held by about two thousand Japanese Army troops. McMorris, with three cruisers and six destroyers, bombarded their positions on 25–26 April.

Nautilus and *Narwhal* had worked on an Attu project earlier in the month, when they transported an Army Scout company to Dutch Harbor. On 1 May these two big submarines re-embarked these troops and set out for Attu, arriving on 4 May. D-Day was progressively postponed from 8 to 11 May because of the weather. The submarines stood by, observing the beach when visibility permitted, but mainly concerned with the air supply for a hundred troops in each submarine, in addition to their crews. In these latitudes at that time of year the daylight dives lasted from 0500 to 2300, and the air became very thick before the hatch could be opened when the submarine surfaced at night. Finally on 11 May the submarines successfully landed their Scouts at 0300 in the morning and withdrew.

Troops from the submarines were first ashore, but they were followed by others from destroyers and transports until four thousand were ashore at three landing beachheads by nightfall, and eleven thousand were eventually landed at Attu. The landings were supported by three old battleships and nine destroyers under Rear Admiral F. W. Rockwell, while McMorris with his cruisers and destroyers patrolled the western Aleutians. The concentration of heavy ships around Attu (until they were withdrawn on 17 May) presented an opportunity for Japanese submarines.

Japanese Submarines in the Aleutians

There were a half dozen I-class submarines in the Aleutians in April, and when the situation became hot at Attu four more were dispatched to reinforce them. *I-31* happened to be on a supply run to Kiska on D-Day. She hurriedly discharged her cargo at Kiska on 10 May and shoved off for Attu. Very shortly she was in the thick of things. On 12 May she fired torpedoes at a warship, and claimed two hits. She also reported damaging another vessel of unknown class. The next day she reported that she torpedoed and heavily damaged a light cruiser. After that report she was silent, and what happened to her is uncertain. On 15 May *I-35* reported that she had attacked and heavily damaged a light cruiser. Both *I-34* and *I-35* were depth-charged and damaged near Agattu, but both survived.

Two submarine torpedoes were fired at *Pennsylvania* on 11 May, but that old battlewagon managed ponderously to avoid them. Two destroyers depth-charged the submarine and brought it to the surface under gunfire. It must have managed to escape that counterattack, however, for *I-31* (the only Japanese submarine sunk during the period) was heard from two days later. On 15 May two more torpedo wakes passed astern of *Pennsylvania*. Torpedoes were fired at the transport *J. Franklin Bell* on 15 May and they also missed. Despite the Japanese submarines' report of successes no U.S. ship was torpedoed during the Attu landings.

U.S. Submarines in the Aleutians

United States submarines had a little better luck in the northern area. On 28 May *S-41* (Hartman) sank the 1036-ton *Seiki Maru* near Paramushiro, the second sinking by an S-boat during the long and arduous arctic patrols. On 11 June *S-30* (Stevenson) sank the 5228-ton *Jinbu Maru* in the same area, but the fighting on Attu was all over by then. On 29 May Colonel Yamazaki led a thousand of his men in a suicide charge that ended Japanese resistance on Attu.

Koga Reacts

The Japanese Navy reacted vigorously to the Attu landings. Koga, the new Commander-in-Chief, sortied from Truk on 16 May with a carrier, three battleships, and light forces. His intention was to join with other forces at Tokyo and then fall upon the American Aleutian task force with overwhelming superior force. By the time everything was ready to depart for the Aleutians, it was too late to affect the issue. Koga's abortive northward move left Turner free to take his first step up the Solomons ladder unopposed by heavy Japanese naval forces. It also, indirectly, gave *Trigger* an opportunity which she exploited early the next month.

Kiska had been isolated by the fall of Attu. A conference at Imperial General Headquarters had already decided that Kiska would have to be evacuated, but it would be some time before this could be undertaken. In the meantime, Kiska became a customer for the Japanese submarine supply service. This kept a number of Japanese submarines harmlessly employed and exposed them to the American anti-submarine forces.

U.S. Submarines in the Carolines and Marshalls

By May of 1943 nearly as many new U.S. submarines had entered the Pacific as were there when the war began. Incorporated in these new submarines were improvements in design and new equipment that frequently made the prewar submarines seem antiquated in comparison. Yet there was plenty of service still in the older ships, as demonstrated by *Plunger* and *Pollack,* which had both been at sea off Honolulu when the war began.

Plunger (Bass) was on patrol in the Carolines on 8 May when she made contact with a northbound convoy of five ships with two escorts. Unable to close during daylight, Bass observed the convoy's base course and speed and was off in pursuit on the surface as soon as the sun set. About three o'clock the next morning Bass made a night periscope and radar attack. Two hits were heard as *Plunger* went deep to evade the escorts, and subsequent prolonged observation showed only four ships remaining with the convoy after this attack.

The convoy stuck to its old course, zigzagging with short legs, thirty-five degrees each side of the base course. *Plunger* surfaced and ran full power for position ahead again, but was unable to gain position before sunrise. The convoy was within easy air range of both Truk and Saipan, but as no plane came out to force him down Bass continued on the surface, running around the convoy's flank. At four o'clock in the afternoon he achieved attack position and fired four torpedoes at two large freighters. Before the escorts forced him under, Bass observed that both targets had been hit.

It was sunset again before *Plunger* could surface. There were then three ships in sight, two hull down to the northward and the third left behind and apparently sinking. Bass went after the undamaged ships which were still on the old base course, taking no radical evasive action, and behaving as though the submarine was fate which could not be avoided. It was nearly dawn before *Plunger* had attack position again. She fired four torpedoes for what appeared to be three hits.

At sunrise on 10 May Bass looked through his periscope to observe a big ship stopped and listing with the escort standing by. While he was making an approach on this ship, he saw the last and biggest vessel of the convoy lying to, at a range of about four thousand yards. Incredibly this ship, after the convoy had been a day and a night under repeated submarine attack, was still standing by and stopped only a short distance from a torpedoed ship. There had still been no augmentation of the escorts, and no air cover had been sent out although by this time they were only a little over a hundred miles from either Guam or Saipan.

Bass abandoned the attack on the cripple and went after the big un-damaged ship. It got under way before *Plunger* reached attack position, but Bass fired his stern tubes at her for two observed hits.

Plunger was running out of torpedoes, and the escort standing by robbed her of freedom of action. About ten in the morning, planes finally arrived on the scene to hunt for *Plunger*. Bass maneuvered for position and fired two torpedoes from the stern tubes at the stopped and dam-aged ship. Both hit and both were duds. A few minutes later he fired his last torpedo and saw it hit underneath the stack. The escort came down and dropped one depth charge. The ship did not sink. It appeared to be abandoned.

Plunger stood by all day, and so did the escort. Bass was determined to finish off the ship by gunfire if he could evade the escort. About seven o'clock at night *Plunger* surfaced and made a radio report of the situation to Lockwood. Without torpedoes Bass could only wait for a favorable opportunity to use the gun. About dawn he got the break he wanted. The escort disappeared some place off the radar screen.

Plunger closed to three thousand yards and opened up with the 3-inch gun. There were several guns on the target but none of them were manned, so *Plunger* continued to close until the range was seven hun-dred yards and Bass could read the target's name (*Asaka Maru*) across her stern. *Plunger* continued to fire until she had expended all her am-munition (180 rounds including one round of target practice ammuni-tion). This was quite a feat of strength, requiring relief of all the ex-hausted ammunition passers except James McGuire, the muscular Negro cook, who stuck it out all the way through, working his way up from the magazine as the others dropped out until he was finally serving the gun. *Asaka Maru* was riddled with holes, through which fires could be seen raging inside her. After all the ammunition had been fired, radar picked up an approaching plane, and *Plunger* submerged.

Japanese records show that on 10 May *Kinai Maru* and *Tatsutake Maru* sank in the position reported for *Plunger's* action. No mention is made of *Asaka Maru*, and it is possible that Bass may have read Osaka, the home port of *Kinai Maru* painted on her stern. It is equally pos-sible that Japan's records are inaccurate and that more than the two ships recorded were sunk in *Plunger's* attacks.

Pollack *at Jaluit*

In deference to her age, *Pollack* (Lewellen) was assigned a quiet area in the Marshalls for patrol in May, with a mission that was largely recon-naissance. It proved anything but quiet, for the Japanese air activity and their traffic in reinforcing the Gilberts kept *Pollack* on the jump. On 18

May Lewellen sank a small freighter at Wotje after watching it inside the lagoon for three days before it would come out to be sunk. The next day *Pollack* ran on down to Jaluit and arrived on 20 May just in time to meet *Bangkok Maru* coming in. *Pollack* demolished *Bangkok Maru* with multiple torpedo hits, and thus racked up two *marus* for the patrol—not bad for an old ship in a quiet area.

It was actually an achievement greater than anyone knew at the time. *Bangkok Maru* was carrying twelve hundred troops to Tarawa. They never made it. Most of them were rescued and taken to Jaluit. Equipment and armament intended to reinforce Tarawa went down with the ship. The troops stayed on Jaluit for the duration of the war. Had they finished their journey they would have all died at Tarawa a few months later, and by statistical averages they would have killed or wounded an equal number of U. S. Marines.

XV

JUNE–SEPTEMBER 1943

Trigger *Torpedoes* Hiyo

When Koga brought his heavy ships up from Truk to Tokyo in response to the attack on Attu, his task force moved through submarine patrol areas off Truk and off Honshu. The risk, however, must have appeared slight to him because American submarines had, until then, managed to sink only one heavy high-speed combat ship. Destroyer screens and high speed apparently had the Combined Fleet's submarine problem under control. Combined Fleet Staff intended to keep it that way by resisting every effort to divert fleet destroyers to convoy escort duty.

Trigger (Benson) was on patrol off Tokyo Bay. On 22 May she sighted a task force of three battleships and a carrier coming up from the south at eighteen knots. Benson succeeded in getting inside the outer screen, but high speed and a fortuitous zig, when the range to the carrier was nine thousand yards, left *Trigger* on the task force's port quarter empty-handed. This was Koga, home safe from Truk.

Imperial Headquarters abandoned their plan to send heavy fleet units into the Aleutians, and the carriers were ordered to the Inland Sea for training exercises. *Trigger* torpedoed and sank a *maru* on 1 June so the Japanese knew there were submarines operating off Tokyo Bay, but high speed still seemed adequate protection. On the night of 9–10 June *Trigger* picked up radar contact with two carriers at twelve-mile range. *Salmon,* patrolling the adjacent area, had already contacted this task force and sent out a contact report, which *Trigger* did not receive. *Salmon* was still trailing, unknown to Benson, but she was hopelessly behind. Benson bent on all four engines at full speed, but the carriers sped past him out of torpedo range.

The next night *Hiyo* came down the bay at twenty-two knots, with a destroyer escort on each bow. This was the carrier whose speed and lucky zig, coming up from Truk with the battleships, had carried it right by *Trigger*. This time *Hiyo's* luck had run out, and speed only brought her more quickly to within range of *Trigger's* torpedoes. Benson watched it come, zigzagging radically. He maneuvered *Trigger* at her best speed inside the nearest screen. The submarine fired six torpedoes from a range of twelve hundred yards. With the last one off *Trigger* was right ahead of the nearest destroyer. Benson took *Trigger* deep, and heard four hits on the way down, before the depth charges started falling.

Hiyo was not sunk. Four of *Trigger's* torpedoes prematured close aboard the carrier, but one hit in No. 1 boiler room. The light cruiser *Isuzu* towed *Hiyo* into Yokosuka and she made it into drydock with her main deck awash. At a time when Japan desperately needed flight decks to train carrier pilots, *Hiyo* was out of action, but because of *Trigger's* malfunctioning torpedo exploders the carrier survived to fight again another day.

Loss of Runner

The Japanese lost seven *marus* and two picket boats off the coast of Honshu in June, but their busy minelaying off the northeast coast of the island paid off, and saved them from greater losses. *Runner* (Bourland) was the victim of one of their mines. She was a new submarine with less than five months of war service when she left Midway on her third patrol. *Runner's* patrol instructions eventually brought her right into one of the newly laid minefields. She was never heard from after leaving Midway and she undoubtedly hit a mine.

Japanese Submarines in the Aleutians

With the Aleutians closely invested by American air and surface forces, the Japanese attempted to communicate with Kiska and evacuate the garrison by submarine. *I-9* made one successful round trip between Paramushiro and Kiska. She left Paramushiro on 9 June on her second trip and was never heard from again by the Japanese. *I-9* was sunk by the destroyer *Frazier* by gunfire and depth-charge attack near Kiska on 13 June.

I-24 left Paramushiro late in May with orders to rescue Japanese survivors evading American forces on Attu. After three unsuccessful attempts to contact survivors these orders were canceled, but *I-24* was never heard from again. On 11 June she encountered *PC-487* near Attu Island. The submarine chaser made sonar contact on a submerged submarine and attacked with depth charges, which brought *I-24* to the surface. *PC-487* deliberately rammed at nineteen knots, and then backed off and rammed again. *I-24* sank and *PC-487*, battered by her own ramming tactics, made it back to Attu with difficulty.

Without radar, Japanese submarines had difficulty in navigating through the prevailing fog and low visibility in the Aleutians. On 16 June *I-157* ran hard aground on Little Sitkin near Amchitka Island, while making fourteen knots in foggy weather. The submarine jettisoned everything heavy and movable; lubricating oil, torpedoes, and fuel oil went over the side without budging her off the rocks. Finally the captain ordered the cells of the main battery to be broken up and wrestled up the hatch, dripping sulphuric acid, to lighten the ship. After disposing of over a hundred of the big battery elements in this manner *I-157* finally broke loose. She was then too light to compensate for diving under any circumstances. She had to stay on the surface, where she was at the mercy of any air patrol or surface vessel that found her but, under cover of the fog, she cleared out and made it back to Kure.

I-2 also ran aground southeast of Kiska but was refloated with minor damage. Without radar, Japanese submarines sometimes found themselves suddenly under fire without ever seeing their assailant. On 20 June *I-7* had a surface engagement with a patrol boat a short distance from her anchorage in Vega Bay on Kiska. A hit in the conning tower killed five persons (including the commanding officer and the division commander) and *I-7* ran aground. She was unloaded and refloated the next day and that night headed back toward Yokosuka. Apparently because of her damage she was unable to dive.

Ten miles south of Kiska she encountered the destroyer *Monaghan*, early on the morning of 22 June. *I-7* thought she was engaged with three enemy ships, and understandably so, for she never saw her assailant. The submarine fought as best she could, firing back at gun flashes flickering in the turbid night.

Monaghan had made radar contact at 0135 on the morning of 22 June at 14,000 yards' range and closed to 2300 yards. At that range the destroyer opened up at the unseen target with the guns in full radar control. The submarine answered the gunfire and remained on the surface to continue the unequal struggle. After eight minutes of firing, the destroyer saw brilliant flashes of hits in the darkness. Shortly after this *Monaghan's* radar warned her of rocks ahead and she broke off the action. *I-7* ran aground. Forty-three of her survivors were taken off the ship and the submarine was later destroyed by the Japanese.

The destruction of a ship by gunfire while neither combatant could see the other caused consternation in Japanese submarine headquarters. Submarines had evacuated some eight hundred men from Kiska, and landed 120 tons of provisions during June, but at a terrific cost. Three submarines had been lost and three others damaged. It was decided that evacuation of Kiska by submarines was entirely too expensive, and the operation was called off.

Despite the American occupation of Attu at the western end of the Aleutian chain, and the continued observation of Kiska by air and by sea, the Japanese decided to run the risk of evacuating the remainder of the garrison by surface ships. On 28 July, making good use of the Aleutian fog, a task force of three cruisers and about a dozen destroyers steamed into Kiska Harbor. In one of the neatest operations of the war, they picked up every Japanese on Kiska and returned to the Kuriles without a single enemy contact. Unaware of this evacuation, the Americans stepped up the tempo of their bombings and bombardment, and on 15 August landed on Kiska with overwhelming force to find it completely abandoned.

The whole Aleutian adventure was expensive for Japanese submarines. In the year of Japanese occupation they lost six submarines in the Far North. Five midget submarines transported to Kiska and based there were also lost and accomplished nothing. Japanese submarines counted as their successes four transports, two light cruisers, one seaplane carrier, and an unknown vessel in the Aleutians. Their actual accomplishments were far less than that. They sank the Army transport *Arcata* and damaged the small seaplane tender *Casco*. The rest were imaginary victories, and their final balance sheet was decidedly in the red.

Advances in the South Pacific

Meanwhile, in the Solomons, Army troops and Marines landed at Segi Point, New Georgia, on 21 June. The next day MacArthur's forces landed at Woodlark Island to protect the eastern flank of his communications for his advance up the New Guinea coast. On 30 June the Army and Marines of Turner's Third Amphibious Force landed at Rendova and other islands near New Georgia. The same day MacArthur moved ahead to land at Nassau Bay in New Guinea.

The advance in the Solomons brought renewal of night runs of Japanese cruisers and destroyers to reinforce New Georgia. U.S. cruisers and destroyers went up the Slot to stop them. The Japanese and American light forces met in the Battle of Kula Gulf on 6 July and in the Battle of Kolombangara on 13 July. In these two night actions each side lost a light cruiser and two destroyers. The Japanese had the best of it in damaged ships, but their reinforcement runs to New Georgia were disrupted and Munda fell to the Americans on 5 August. The growing domination of the air by Allied air forces over the whole South Pacific made it hazardous for any Japanese surface ship to be in the area during daytime. During July the Japanese lost five destroyers and the big seaplane carrier *Nisshin* by bombing.

Japanese Submarines in the South Pacific

Three Japanese submarines were operating off the east coast of Australia in May and June of 1943. Two PT boats were sunk by submarine torpedoes on 23 May off New Caledonia. *I-178* did not return from her patrol in the Tasman Sea. She disappeared some time late in May or early June.

There were several Japanese submarines engaged in making supply runs to Lae, New Guinea in June and July. Four submarines were patrolling off San Cristóbal in the Solomons in June. *RO-103* torpedoed and sank two cargo ships returning from Guadalcanal on 23 June.

When the Third Amphibious Force was sighted off Rendova the Japanese sent submarines into the restricted water of Blanche Channel to intercept them at the beachhead. *RO-107* penetrated into Blanche Channel on 4 July but apparently never got out. She was missing after 4 July. *RO-103* left Rabaul on 11 July for New Georgia. *LST-342* was torpedoed and sunk by a submarine torpedo southeast of New Georgia on 18 July. If this was the work of *RO-103* she did not long survive her success. She reported sighting enemy forces on 24 July and from then on was silent.

Scamp *Sinks* I-168

One other Japanese submarine was lost in the South Pacific in July. On 26 July *I-168* left Truk for Rabaul. She reported her noon position on 27 July and after that was missing. This probably was the submarine sunk by *Scamp*. Although most Allied authorities identify *Scamp's* target as *I-24*, that Japanese submarine definitely made her last departure for the Aleutians and was lost there.

Scamp (Ebert) was patrolling submerged off New Hanover on 27 July. At about six o'clock in the evening sound reported high-speed screws, and a high periscope exposure disclosed a submarine on the surface. Ebert started his approach and made another periscope exposure when the range was 4200 yards. Immediately after this exposure sound reported that the enemy submarine had fired torpedoes. *Scamp* went deep and sound tracked the torpedoes across her stern. Six minutes later Ebert brought her up to periscope depth for another look, and discovered the Japanese submarine still on the surface. The Japanese flag was clearly painted on the conning tower, reassuring to Ebert, who noted that the enemy submarine closely resembled the U.S. *Permit* class. *Scamp* swung left to cut down the gyro angle and fired four torpedoes. They heard one hit. Two minutes later Ebert had another look through the periscope and saw a 500-foot pillar of brown smoke to mark where the submarine had been. Gruesome noises of heavy deep explosions followed, and that night Ebert found large quantities of diesel oil on the surface but no survivors. *I-168* disappeared about that time and place. It was a quick end of the submarine that sank *Yorktown*.

U.S. Submarines in the South Pacific

It was expected that the attack on New Georgia would bring out heavy Japanese forces from Truk to oppose the move. A group of U.S. submarines were stationed on patrol between Truk and Rabaul to intercept and report the expected enemy task force. Koga, with his battleships and carriers, was still in Japan, where he had hastened to oppose the Attu landing. The submarines positioned to intercept a Japanese task force therefore made no contact with combat ships, but they were in excellent position to intercept traffic between Rabaul and Truk. These submarines sank half a dozen *marus* in the area during June and July and damaged at least three others. Submarines also continued their special missions in the South Pacific, most important of which was a reconnaissance of Empress Augusta Bay on Bougainville Island.

Pearl Harbor Developments

Fostered by the close proximity of the two headquarters, cooperation between Submarines Pacific and Commander-in-Chief Pacific was very close. Lockwood operated under a general letter of instructions from Nimitz, who required only that two submarines be constantly on patrol off Truk and two more off Palau to keep tabs on movement of major Japanese fleet units. In addition, submarines were required to be prepared to undertake special missions on request. Pressures of the Solomons campaign and the Aleutians operation, however, afforded the submarines little leeway for independent operations. It was not until June 1943 that these pressures eased so that Lockwood could consider a coordinated submarine campaign. On 24 June Lockwood issued his first Operation Plan.

No startling changes were brought about by this Operation Plan, but it marked changes in the command relations between Commander-in-Chief Pacific and Commander Submarines Pacific. One of the features of the new plan was a higher place given to tankers on the priority list for submarine targets. Analysis indicated that the number of tankers available to Japan was insufficient and that the loss of tankers would have greater effect on Japan's economy than the loss of dry cargo ships. While this analysis seemed logical enough, Japanese tanker construction was, in fact, keeping well ahead of losses. Submarines had not been very successful in sinking tankers. Minelaying continued to be an assigned task, but in practice the minelaying days of Lockwood's submarines were behind them. Submarine Force Staff started planning the invasion of the Sea of Japan. This almost landlocked sea, entered only by three narrow straits, had so far been a safe area for Japanese traffic with the Asian mainland.

Torpedoes

On the same day that Lockwood issued his first Operation Plan, Nimitz sent out a dispatch directing all submarines and destroyers in the Pacific Fleet to inactivate magnetic exploders on all torpedoes and to fire all torpedoes for impact hits. Lockwood was wholly in accord with this move. Actuated by acceleration forces of violent speed and course changes, or by pitching in a heavy sea, or from other causes not fully known, magnetic exploders had a propensity to function prematurely. Largely because of this, magnetic exploders had already been discarded by the Germans and the British. The deep running of American torpedoes, until discovered and corrected, not only caused the torpedoes to miss, it masked the exploder defect. In the very early months of the war very-deep-running torpedoes were probably locked on safe by the action of hydrostatic pressure in the anti-countermining device. This device was suspected early and removed from torpedoes. Even after that, deep-running torpedoes ran smoother than those at proper depth, and their magnetic exploders were less liable to premature. When deep running was corrected, premature explosions became much more frequent.

The Bureau of Ordnance asked Nimitz by dispatch what reason had led to the decision to inactivate, although the performance of exploders had been the subject of much correspondence. Two months before the Bureau had admitted that the exploder was liable to premature if the torpedo ran at less than twelve feet deep. They also outlined conditions which would adversely affect the operations of the exploder, including factors of magnetic latitude, target course, condition of degaussing and the beam of the target, and the depth of the torpedo. The Bureau recommended that under certain conditions the exploder should be inactivated, but once the torpedo was loaded into the tube this was impossible, and it was never an easy adjustment to make in a submarine at sea. Inactivation of all exploders removed the cause of prematures and placed complete reliance on the simpler contact exploder. Torpedoes would then have to hit the target's side rather than merely run under the keel, but most submariners were prepared to accept this. Unfortunately, inactivation of the magnetic exploders only unmasked even more serious defects in the Mark 6 exploder.

Commander Submarines Seventh Fleet also questioned the reasons that led to inactivation. On 11 July he reaffirmed his decision to retain the magnetic features of the exploders for Southwest Pacific submarines. Christie, who was a torpedo expert, stated his reason for sticking by the magnetics. He said they saved some hits that would otherwise be missed, that it was the only defensive weapon against shallow-draft anti-submarine craft; and as final argument, revealing the conflict between weapon designer and the operational commander, "if it was discarded it was gone forever."

The first electric torpedoes arrived in Pearl Harbor while this discussion was going on. The design of this torpedo was copied from a German electric torpedo captured in 1942, but an exact copy would not function with American submarine torpedo tubes and the Bureau also thought some improvement could be made. The development was contracted out to Westinghouse and Electric Storage Battery Company. It encountered difficulties, not the least of which was lack of cooperation on the part of Newport Torpedo Station. When the first electric torpedoes reached Pearl Harbor there was still a serious problem with hydrogen gas given off by the torpedo storage battery. Methods of controlling this problem were worked out by the Submarine Force at Pearl Harbor, although some risk of hydrogen explosion remained and several such accidents occurred in submarines on patrol. The electric torpedo had almost perfect depth control and a dependable contact exploder. It was cheaper to manufacture and it left no wake to warn the target, but its maximum speed was thirty knots against the forty-six of the steam torpedo. Electric torpedoes were not at first universally popular with submarine commanders, but they constantly gained in acceptance.

U.S. Submarines into the Sea of Japan

The loss of *Runner*, following hard on the heels of *Pickerel*, in the area northeast of Honshu decided Lockwood to give that area a rest until anti-submarine activity decreased there. The submarines that had been scheduled for operation off northern Honshu were thus available for the penetration of the Sea of Japan, a project the submarine staff had been carefully studying.

For planning information, as well as for operational intelligence, Lockwood relied on the Joint Intelligence Center of Nimitz's headquarters, rather than create a separate submarine intelligence organization. This worked out very well. The Joint Intelligence Center had resources and research facilities that the submarine staff could not hope to duplicate, and these were placed freely at the disposal of the submarine operation officer. Lockwood, in turn, kept the Center constantly informed of submarine operations, sent them copies of all patrol reports, and quickly passed on any information his submarines picked up.

It was decided that the Sea of Japan could best be entered through La Pérouse Strait, between Hokkaido and Sakhalin. There were good indications that the other two available straits were heavily mined. Russian ships used La Pérouse enroute between Vladivostok and U. S. West Coast ports. Although this was no assurance that there were no controlled mines, or deeply laid mines to catch submerged submarines, it did indicate that submarines would run little risk of contact mines if they could make the transit undetected on the surface.

In the last week of June, *Plunger* (Bass), *Permit* (Chapple), and *Lapon* (Kirk) assembled at Midway in preparation for a coordinated entry into the Sea of Japan. *Narwhal* (Latta) was assigned a diversionary mission of bombarding Matsuwa To in the Kuriles to cover their retirement.

All three submarines ran through La Pérouse on the same night on the surface. Going through the strait, *Plunger* made contact with a patrol vessel and was forced to dive in water that might have been mined. *Permit* had a similar experience. She hit the bottom at 180 feet when she thought she had 240 feet of water under her, and damaged her sound head. Despite these misadventures all three reached their assigned areas on schedule. *Plunger* and *Permit* remained concealed in their assigned areas until *Lapon*, which had been assigned the southern part of the sea, could reach her operating area.

On the night of 7 July the season opened. *Lapon*, with the farthest to run, found no worthwhile target on her more distant station. Both *Plunger* and *Permit*, in the northern end, had plenty of targets. All Japanese ships were sailing unescorted, carrying running lights and not zigzagging. *Plunger* sank one ship and *Permit* two.

Right after sinking the second ship *Permit* surfaced. While she was blowing tanks, and in that logy and uncertain state with half-filled ballast tanks, she was pooped by an abnormally big wave, which swept green over the bridge and down the conning tower hatch. The conning tower was flooded and two feet of water was slopping to and fro over the pump room floor plates. The most serious casualty, however, was SJ radar, which was knocked out of commission for four days at a most critical time. *Permit*, so far from home and cut off from help, was fortunate to escape so easily. It was a reminder that the sea was a hostile environment, an enemy older than the Japanese, that may well have accounted for some of the submarines that disappeared so mysteriously.

After ninety-six hours of operation in their areas all three submarines raced for the exit through La Pérouse. A few hours before leaving her area *Permit* sighted a small vessel. After observing it for some time, and noting that it had an unusual radio antenna, Chapple decided it was a Japanese picket similiar to those so plentiful in the Pacific. No flag was displayed and no identification marking could be seen. *Permit* came up to battle surface at 1800 yards and commenced firing as she closed the range. Shortly a large white flag was shown. *Permit* ceased fire and approached to learn that she had been firing at a Russian trawler. The trawler had been hit by several shells and was in a sinking condition. One man had been killed and another mortally wounded. *Permit* took the survivors, including several women, on board and that night transited La Pérouse into the Sea of Okhotsk where she made a radio report of the incident to Lockwood. Lockwood ordered her to take her passengers to Dutch Harbor, the nearest American port, where they were landed for repatriation. The Russian vessel had been engaged in fishery research and the Russians, relying on the isolation of the Sea of Japan, had not displayed the large identification marks agreed upon nor notified the United States of the operation. It was a very unfortunate incident, marring a daring and successful operation, and was regretted all around. The relationship between the trawler's crew and the submarine's crew while the Russians were aboard *Permit* was much more cordial than could normally have been expected under the circumstances.

Narwhal, plagued by fog, had to defer her bombardment until the day after it was scheduled. She bombarded Matsuwa airfield and hangars with her two 6-inch guns, firing at a range of 14,000 yards. A battery of several guns returned the fire, and after twelve minutes of bombardment, salvos were landing so close to *Narwhal* that Latta broke off the engagement and submerged. There is no evidence that any Japanese forces were diverted because of *Narwhal's* attack. She escaped without damage, but the anti-submarine drill she gave to Matsuwa was profitable to the Japanese battery and in their next submarine encounter they were much more efficient. All submarines returned safely from the adventure with or without the help of diversion. The Japanese ships they sank were few and small, but the operation served to further disperse inadequate Japanese anti-submarine forces.

Tinosa *and* Tonan Maru No. 3

Inactivation of the magnetic exploders did not bring about a great change in the number of ships sunk by submarines. In the first eight months of 1943 submarines sank an average of twenty-two ships per month. In June, July, and August they sank twenty-four, twenty-three, and twenty-one respectively. The Japanese could have told why, for in July they knew of at least eight ships totaling 75,000 tons that had been struck by dud torpedoes. Some of these were damaged even by duds, but it is difficult to sink a big tanker with non-explosive torpedoes as *Tinosa* (Daspit) very methodically demonstrated.

Tinosa was on patrol in the Carolines, southwest of Truk, about six o'clock on the morning of 24 July, when *Tonan Maru No. 3*, a big 19,000-ton whale factory converted into a tanker, came by; unescorted, heavily loaded, on an easterly course, making about thirteen knots. When first observed the tanker was out at 35,000 yards range with an angle on the bow of 90 degrees, so Daspit went on an end run for three hours to gain position ahead, and then submerged to wait for the big ship to come by. About half past nine in the morning he had the position he wanted and fired four torpedoes. At least two of them hit, for Daspit saw large splashes of water arise between the foremast and the mainmast, and sound heard slight explosions, but the target did not appear to be damaged. *Tonan Maru* changed course, giving *Tinosa* a large track angle. Daspit fired the remaining two torpedoes from the forward tubes, and these both hit, one of them aft, with a heavy explosion and much smoke. *Tonan Maru* stopped and settled by the stern but evidently was not sinking. Ironically, as it later turned out, the unfavorable track angle she presented in evasion had been the tanker's undoing.

Tonan Maru was practically helpless, and impotent as long as Tinosa stayed submerged. The Japanese ship fired off some depth charges but these were intended for intimidation, and Daspit was not easily excited or intimidated. The tanker had a formidable battery of deck guns which prevented *Tinosa* from surfacing, so Daspit selected a perfect position 875 yards off the tanker's beam and fired one torpedo from the stern tube. He watched it run down the range, leaving a track of bubbles and smoke, to hit the target squarely amidships. There was a splash of water as high as the main deck, similiar to those he had witnessed in the first salvo, but no real explosion, and the target was undamaged. Daspit correctly interpreted this shot as a dud hit, with such impact that the torpedo air flask ruptured and sent up the splash, while the warhead remained unexploded.

Daspit was a careful observer, of an inquiring mind, and he was determined to get to the bottom of torpedo failures. At the beginning of the attack *Tinosa* had on board sixteen torpedoes, that had cost the United States over $160,000 f.o.b. Newport Torpedo Station, but their only function was to sink enemy ships, and they were worthless if they could not do it. Moreover, a ship missed by several torpedoes remained just as valuable a target as she was before the attack, so Daspit continued to fire deliberate, well-aimed single torpedo salvos. He took his time (over five hours from the first salvo to the last one), carefully examined and checked all torpedoes, obtained perfect position for each shot, and through the periscope watched each one run down the range and hit. He fired a total of fifteen torpedoes. All but two of the first salvo were observed to hit. The crew of the tanker watched them come, and fired 4-inch guns and machine guns at the periscope and at the approaching torpedoes, but they were helpless. The eleventh torpedo hit aft, jumped clear of the water, and dropped back into the sea. There were no first-order explosions except of the one torpedo in the second salvo—the chance impact that had disabled *Tonan Maru*.

A destroyer escort arrived while *Tinosa* was firing the thirteenth torpedo, but Daspit continued the exercise until he had only one torpedo left. This he decided he would take back to Pearl Harbor as an exhibit for the torpedo overhaul shop. The destroyer dropped some depth charges (which were not duds) and passed right over *Tinosa* but, fortunately for the submarine, the destroyer was not aware of it. There was a good negative temperature gradient at 180 feet and this blacked out the destroyer's listening apparatus. With the experiment concluded, *Tinosa* withdrew, and that night headed back to Pearl Harbor. The Japanese came out and towed *Tonan Maru* in to Truk. In this experiment, carried out in enemy waters, with the unwilling cooperation of a big Japanese tanker, Daspit pretty well proved that the contact exploders were defective. It might have better been done at Newport, where observation could have been taken on the target, and the torpedoes examined after their runs, and it should have been done before any submarine or any destroyer went to sea armed with such torpedoes, to do battle with the enemy.

Progress in the South Pacific

Allied forces moved forward with increased momentum in the South Pacific. On 6 August Japanese destroyers attempting to supply Kolombangara encountered U.S. destroyers, out to stop them, in the Battle of Vella Gulf. U.S. destroyers, firing torpedoes with the magnetic exploder inactivated, sank three Japanese destroyers and damaged a fourth in their first clear-cut destroyer victory in the South Pacific. Nine days later the Third Amphibious Force landed Marines and Army troops at Vella Lavella, bypassing the Japanese on Kolombangara. On 24 August the U. S. Army occupied Bairoko Harbor on the Kula Gulf coast of New Georgia. This brought to an end the bloody New Georgia campaign.

On the New Guinea flank the Japanese were forced out of Lae on 15 September, and the next week Australian troops were landed at Finschhafen, New Guinea. Submarines supported these advances both in the Solomons and New Guinea by special missions. *Greenling* transported Marine raiders to the Treasury Islands off Bougainville on 1 September. *Guardfish* and *Gato,* late in September, landed reconnaissance parties on the east coast of Bougainville and re-embarked them after they had surveyed the vicinity of Cape Torokina. *Sculpin* and *Grouper* reconnoitered New Britain, and landed and supplied coastwatcher parties there for MacArthur's forces. Except for such special missions U.S. submarines were pretty well crowded out of the area. There were no *marus* south of Rabaul.

Japanese destroyers still made a few supply runs to northern New Guinea but, in fourteen months of operations in the South Pacific, the Japanese had lost forty destroyers and many more had been disabled. More and more the Japanese service of supply was turned over to their submarines. *I-174* made a run into Lae on 9 September with a new Japanese commander to stage a last-ditch defense of that New Guinea port. The next night three U.S. destroyers bombarded Lae and the Japanese decided to fall back to Sio by a forced march of fifty miles through the jungle. *I-177* made the last supply run to Lae on 15 September. After that several Japanese submarines continued supply runs to Sio.

Japanese Submarine Losses in the South Pacific

Japanese submarines operating in New Hebrides and the Solomons sustained disastrous losses in August and September. *I-17* (Harada) and *I-25* (Obiga) were sent out from Truk to reconnoiter Espíritu Santo. On 19 August U. S. Navy shore-based planes and the New Zealand trawler *Tui* cooperated in a successful attack on a submarine near Nouméa. Six survivors were rescued who identified the sunken submarine as *I-17.* What happened to the other Japanese submarines that disappeared in the next few weeks is far less certain. *I-25* reported the results of her aircraft reconnaissance of Espíritu Santo on 24 August. That was her last report. *Patterson,* on station as anti-submarine screen of a task force en route from Espíritu Santo to the Solomons the next night, made radar contact on a surfaced submarine. The pip disappeared at 4000 yards but *Patterson* regained contact by sonar and delivered a depth-charge attack which resulted in several heavy underwater explosions. This may have been the end of *I-25.*

RO-35 reported sighting six transports off Espíritu Santo on 25 August, and then she also was forever silent. On 30 August *I-20* sighted two battleships and an aircraft carrier in the New Hebrides. That was her last report. The destroyer *Ellet* was sent out from Espíritu Santo on 3 September to hunt for a reported submarine. *Ellet* picked up radar contact at 13,000 yards and closed the range. At 3000 yards she had sonar contact and made several depth-charge attacks. Daylight disclosed a large oil slick. On 15 September *Saufley* was escorting a southbound convoy from the Solomons. A Japanese submarine made a torpedo attack on one of the cargo ships in the convoy and missed. *Saufley* counterattacked, and after several depth-charge salvos a Japanese submarine broached in broad daylight at 2000 yards range. The destroyer opened up with all guns. A patrol plane dashed in through the shellfire and planted two depth bombs close aboard the submarine. The Japanese submarine went down leaving scattered wreckage, but no survivors. *Ellet* and *Saufley* probably accounted for *RO-35* and *I-20*.

I-182 sailed from Truk on 22 August to patrol in the New Hebrides and was never heard from again. *RO-101* left Rabaul on 10 September for patrol in the Solomons. She reported making an attack and then disappeared. On the night of 1–2 October *Eaton* was up the Slot with a destroyer task force hunting for Japanese landing barges. Near the entrance to Kula Gulf radar picked up a pip at 3000 yards. *Eaton* illuminated with star shells and identified a Japanese submarine on the surface. *Eaton's* first salvo was right on, and before the submarine could do anything about it she had numerous hits in her pressure hull. Three minutes after this action started the Japanese submarine made her last dive, belly up. This was probably *RO-101*.

The Japanese accomplished very little to balance the loss of six submarines in the South Pacific during August and September. U.S. task forces of cruisers and destroyers sallied up the Slot north of Vella Lavella during August to intercept Japanese landing barges running between Bougainville and New Georgia. The light cruiser *Columbia* narrowly avoided a salvo of submarine torpedoes fired at her on one run. The Americans believed that Japanese submarines lurked along their route and were coached into position by the observations of snooper planes. Such operations were possible but they required very fortuitous stationing of the submarines and a very sophisticated communication net. There is no evidence in the Japanese records to indicate that they were able to effect such close cooperation at a tactical level between planes and submarines. The Japanese more often regarded their submarines as producers of intelligence for the surface task forces. For this their reconnaissance in the New Hebrides proved to be very costly.

Fremantle Submarines

Christie's submarines still used magnetic exploders and had increasing difficulties with prematures. *Silversides*, in the first attack on her sixth patrol, had two prematures out of a four-torpedo salvo. Alerted by the prematures, the target avoided the other two torpedoes. On the very next attack *Silversides* had two more prematures. *Grouper,* returning from an unsuccessful patrol, was bitter about the exploder troubles. *Bonefish, Bowfin,* and *Finback,* however, managed to sink ships. Christie informed the Bureau of Ordnance that since the installation of the latest modification to the exploder, the percentage of prematures had increased from 1.71 per cent to 13.5 per cent. Like all statistics compiled from observations taken under combat conditions these percentages are suspect, but it was apparent the exploder had not been improved. On the other hand it was a moot question whether it was better to endure trouble with prematures or by inactivation end them and suffer the frustration of dud torpedoes.

Loss of Grayling and Cisco

Grayling (Brinker) was lost in the Philippines in August. She left Fremantle on 30 July and went up through Makassar Strait to the Philippines. She delivered a cargo of supplies to guerrillas on Panay on 23 August and then in accordance with her orders patrolled the entrance to Manila. The 5480-ton cargo vessel *Meizan Maru* was torpedoed and sunk in *Grayling's* area on 27 August. On 10 September her operation orders directed her to break off patrol and proceed to Pearl Harbor for navy yard refit. *Grayling* was never heard from again, and none of the reported Japanese anti-submarine attacks in the area seems to account for her loss.

Cisco (Coe) left Darwin for the South China Sea on 19 September. Nothing was ever seen or heard of her after her departure. There was a Japanese anti-submarine attack in the center of the Sulu Sea on 28 September. Oil was reported as bubbling to the surface for two weeks after this attack. The position reported was along *Cisco's* route and the source of the weeping oil may well have been her ruptured fuel tanks.

Pearl Harbor Submarines

Plunger (Bass) and *Wahoo* (Morton), just back from a navy yard refit, set out from Midway on 6 August for another invasion of the Sea of Japan. Morton had quietly decided that this assignment, where targets were reported as plentiful, gave *Wahoo* an opportunity to make a perfect patrol. He decided to shoot the moon and fire only single torpedo salvos to sink a ship with each torpedo fired—twenty torpedoes twenty ships sunk—and thus hang up a record that could not be beaten. That this was contrary to torpedo firing doctrine did not worry Morton.

Wahoo and *Plunger* reached their assigned operation areas without undue adventure. When *Wahoo* fired her first single torpedo salvo it missed. Two hours later Morton fired another single at a medium-size freighter and this hit but was a dud. *Wahoo* had a crack fire control party. Japanese ships in the Sea of Japan were sailing singly, unescorted, and Morton was certain that given good torpedoes he could make every one hit. He fired ten torpedoes and counted ten misses, although he may have had a little more success than he thought, because Japanese records show a tanker and a medium-size freighter damaged at a time and place that could only have been *Wahoo's* doing. As this damage is recorded as slight it was probably caused by duds. In exasperation Morton sent off a message to Commander Submarines Pacific requesting that *Wahoo* return immediately from patrol to reload with electric torpedoes. This request was granted. *Plunger* was also having difficulties with torpedo failures, but she managed to sink two medium-size freighters.

Loss of Pompano

After the loss of *Runner* Lockwood gave the area off northeast Honshu a three-month rest. Before *Pickerel* and *Runner* came to grief this location had been good submarine hunting ground. Lockwood was still unaware that the Japanese had sowed it thick with mines; and by his estimation this busy corner should be ripe again for a profitable patrol. On 20 August *Pompano* (Thomas) left Midway for the fatal area, and like her two predecessors was never heard from again. It was later learned that *Akama Maru* was sunk on 5 September and the heavy cruiser *Nachi* was damaged in a submarine attack the next day in *Pompano's* area. It can only be assumed that some time after these successes *Pompano* hit a mine and was sunk.

Progress with Torpedo Exploders

When *Tinosa* returned to Pearl Harbor after Daspit's efforts to sink *Tonan Maru* with dud torpedoes, the Submarine Base torpedo shop broke down the sample torpedo that Daspit had reserved for this purpose. The torpedo shop could discover no maladjustment of the torpedo's exploder. A long letter from the Bureau of Ordnance dated 31 August urged return to the magnetic exploder. The Bureau seemed resigned to the conclusion that nothing could be done to improve the magnetic or contact exploder. Lockwood was unwilling to accept this conclusion.

Arrangements were made to fire two live torpedoes for impact against a submerged cliff, to duplicate *Tinosa's* duds under experimental conditions. Perversely, the first torpedo functioned perfectly. There was then some discussion of discontinuing the experiment rather than waste a second torpedo. Daspit, recalling the single explosion in his experiment with *Tonan Maru*, argued strongly to continue. The second hit was a dud. In a ticklish diving operation, meddling with an armed torpedo warhead a hundred feet beneath the surface, this dud torpedo was recovered for examination. It was discovered that the firing pin did not hit the primer with sufficient force to explode it.

Under the tremendous deceleration forces created by a forty-five-knot torpedo on impact with a solid body, the firing mechanism was unable to do the job it was designed for. If the torpedo hit the target with a glancing blow, these forces were smaller and the exploder then functioned—which explains why the large track angle shot at *Tonan Maru* was effective. The Bureau of Ordnance was informed, and on 16 September confirmed that they also produced duds under similiar conditions. The slower electric torpedoes did not develop this difficulty. Still frustrated, the Bureau suggested that the exploder might perform properly if torpedoes were fired only at slow-speed settings.

In these tests and trouble, knowledge of the highly secret exploder mechanism became widely spread around Pearl Harbor's many shops and repair facilities. Never was there a more dramatic exposition of the penalties concurrent with excessive secrecy. While the experts at Newport behind an iron curtain of secrecy fumbled for an answer, three perfectly good solutions were proposed by three different repair facilities at Pearl Harbor. The simplest was to lighten the firing pin (and so reduce inertia forces) by cutting away excess metal. This could readily be done at Pearl Harbor. Ingenious tests were devised to prove the modified exploder, and on 30 September *Barb* departed on a war patrol with twenty torpedoes that were reasonably dependable.

New Japanese Defense Plans

On 1 September the Japanese had 5.2 million tons of shipping, nearly a million tons less than the minimum required to run their economy. The Japanese Army argued for a reduction of the Pacific defense perimeter. Finally the Navy agreed to a new perimeter running through the Marianas and then through the Carolines to the head of the New Guinea bird. Rabaul, eastern New Guinea, the northern Solomons, and the Marshalls, left outside, were expected to defend themselves to the utmost in order to delay Allied penetration to the inner perimeter. It was expected that the Allied advance would be long delayed in taking Rabaul. So much Japanese strength had been expended on this bastion that the inner perimeter was practically without fixed defenses. The first requirement was for a quarter of a million tons of shipping to build up the new defense line.

Faced with a demand for an additional quarter of a million tons of shipping for military use, the War Ministry had some hard decisions to make. Japan needed to produce four thousand planes a month to check the rising tide of defeat in the air. Her best production record was less than half that. Increased imports of raw material, particularly oil and bauxite, were needed, and this required more shipping rather than less.

On 30 September there was an Imperial Conference to decide the *General Outline of Future War Direction Policy.* Like many such conferences this one resulted in compromises, and promises to everyone that totaled more than could be delivered. The defense perimeter would be reduced. The military would get its quarter of a million tons of shipping to build up the inner defense line. The War Ministry would boost plane production to forty thousand planes per year. The Navy would reduce shipping losses from sinkings and damages to below a million tons a year and it would improve the turn-around period of cargo ships by providing more escorts.

All this was easier said than done. Rabaul continued to be a drain on resources. It was not easy to disengage without acknowledging defeat and retreat. Koga hoped for a big fleet action, and if he won, that would solve everything. The Combined Fleet had lost many destroyers in the Solomons. It was difficult to muster enough destroyers to send carriers to sea to train pilots. Koga would not part with any of his first-line destroyers for convoy escort duty.

The first *kaibokans* (frigates) were coming into service. The anti-submarine forces wanted 360 of these built as fast as possible, but Koga wanted carriers, submarines, and fast transports. The best compromise the anti-submarine forces could achieve scheduled only forty *kaibokans* for production.

Japan's only solace was the poor performance of U.S. submarine torpedoes. Many ships had miraculously been saved by premature torpedo explosions. Others made port with unexploded dud torpedoes embedded in their hulls. There was a theory that American torpedoes could not sink a Japanese tanker, and brash tanker skippers advocated sailing independently rather than waste time in port waiting for the formation of a convoy. Those who were better informed were less optimistic.

In September 178,000 tons of Japanese merchant ships were sunk. This was a record month for losses, but a record that was not destined long to stand. Despite their torpedo troubles U.S. submarines managed to sink thirty-one of the fifty-two Japanese *marus* sunk in September, and damaged an additional thirteen. Although it was another month before Pearl Harbor submarines found a solution for their dud exploders, the Japanese detected an improvement in U.S. torpedo performance in September. Very early in the month *Mutsure* had a disastrous encounter with U.S. torpedoes.

Snapper *Sinks* Mutsure

Mutsure was one of the first of the *kaibokans* upon which the Japanese depended to solve their escort problem. She was escort for a convoy north of Truk on 2 September when the convoy encountered *Snapper* (Clementson). While *Snapper* was making her approach, the convoy zigged at the wrong moment and Clementson found himself right ahead of the escort. *Mutsure* was industriously pinging with her supersonic, and Clementson realized that if he changed course to close the convoy he must put *Snapper* broadside to the escort's probing supersonic beam. He identified *Mutsure* as a destroyer, a natural mistake, and he decided to take the escort as a target. The *kaibokan* was then dead ahead of the submarine and *Snapper* was looking right down *Mutsure's* throat. When the range decreased to give his torpedoes a 900-yard run, Clementson fired three torpedoes. Thirty-five seconds later he saw *Mutsure's* bow lift several feet in the air, and when the explosion cleared, the forward part of the *kaibokan* had been sheared off clear to the bridge. Two more explosions followed and *Mutsure* went down rapidly.

Trigger *in the East China Sea*

Trigger (Dornin), on patrol in the East China Sea, had serious troubles with dud torpedoes, but it is doubtful that the Japanese appreciated her difficulties. This was Dornin's seventh war patrol, but his first command. As a result of his long experience he was firmly of the opinion that night surface attacks were best. *Trigger* had an experimental radar installation that Dornin found to be very effective for this purpose.

On the night of 18 September, west of Okinawa, *Trigger* encountered two ships and made a night surface attack that resulted in two dud hits. Gunfire drove *Trigger* under, but later the same night she attacked again and made one good hit. All hands in the conning tower witnessed the ship sinking, but it cannot be clearly identified from Japanese records.

On 21 September Dornin had a further opportunity to test his theories. That afternoon he sighted a six-ship convoy with air escort on an easterly base course, zigzagging widely. The air cover was effective in keeping *Trigger* submerged outside torpedo range, and the convoy passed out of sight. At dusk the submarine surfaced and went off in pursuit. By eight o'clock radar had found them. *Trigger* came up along the starboard side of the convoy out at 8000 yards' range, while radar told Dornin that the convoy was in two columns, with three tankers in the starboard column and the three cargo ships in column beyond, not zigzagging, making eight knots on course 080 true. Just before nine o'clock Dornin closed in and fired six torpedoes at the two leading tankers. Both were hit. One torpedo passed through the tanker column and hit the middle freighter in the column beyond.

Both tankers caught fire. The largest one erupted in flames five hundred feet in the air, illuminating the scene so that all six ships of the convoy were in clear view. All the Japanese ships opened up with wild gunfire in every direction. The stricken freighter broke in two and sank. *Trigger* swung left and fired her stern tubes at the third tanker and then submerged to reload.

Forty minutes later she surfaced with all her remaining torpedoes in the tubes and came in to attack again. The surface was still illuminated by burning ships. In a wild melee *Trigger* fired all her torpedoes while the Japanese replied with gunfire at the submarine or anything else that moved. The whole action took three and a half hours, all within distance of 8000 yards of the burning tankers. Three more of *Trigger's* torpedoes were duds and two Japanese ships escaped. This was probably small consolation for the Japanese. The tanker that supplied most of the illumination was the fleet tanker *Shiriya*, and with her was lost *Sanyo Maru* and *Argun Maru*. *Gyoku Maru* was heavily damaged.

When *Trigger* pulled out of the East China Sea with all torpedoes expended she had been just nine days in her area. Her patrol was shorter and more dramatic than most, but many submarines in the Pacific, from Kamchatka to Java and the South Pacific, contributed to the number of *marus* sunk or damaged. When the score for the month was added, the rate of losses was nearly three times the tonnage the Imperial Conference had estimated they could sustain.

Central Pacific Offensive

On 24 August the Joint Chiefs of Staff proposed that Nimitz begin a Central Pacific offensive by capture of the Gilbert Islands and Nauru. By 1 October they promised to have at his disposal five new battleships, ten fast carriers, seven escort carriers, twelve cruisers, sixty-six destroyers, and transport and cargo vessels sufficient to mount a major amphibious campaign. The buildup of American naval strength, which Yamamoto had foreseen, was faster than even he anticipated. It was about to overwhelm Japan.

The Gilberts and the Marshalls were outside the reach of shore-based air forces. For preliminary reconnaissance, submarines were required.

They could spot the strong points of the Japanese defenses and take periscope pictures of the shoreline of important islands. Their periscope pictures were important because the perspective from a periscope was about the same as that of a landing boat's coxswain. However, the comprehensive photographic coverage in depth, necessary to support a major operation, was impossible from a submarine. In August Nanumea and Nukufetau in the Ellice Islands, and Baker, a small island near the equator, were occupied. This gave the U. S. Army Seventh Air Corps bases for air searches and photographic reconnaissance of the Gilberts.

Fast carrier strikes were scheduled to break in new air groups, beat down Japanese shore-based air strength, and obtain photographic coverage. The first of these carrier strikes was on Marcus, nearer to Japan than to the projected area of operation. For this operation the task force commander (Pownall) asked Lockwood to station a submarine near Marcus for the purpose of rescuing downed aviators. *Snook* (Triebel) was sent out for this duty. She made preliminary reconnaissance, made weather reports, and remained on the surface during the air strikes, on call to perform rescue operations. Nothing came of this assignment. *Steelhead* was assigned to similar duty off Tarawa on 20 September when Pownall's task force raided the Gilberts, but she had no call for her lifeguard service either.

The knowledge that a submarine was there to pick them up if they crashed in the sea was of such value to a flier's morale that this task became routine for submarines during carrier strikes. U.S. submarines were not the first ones in this business. For the carrier strike on Pearl Harbor on 7 December 1941 Japanese submarines of Squadron Three were assigned lifeguard stations south of Oahu. Like the first U.S. submarine lifeguards, the early Japanese effort achieved nothing. As the war progressed, however, with bigger and better carrier strikes, the U.S. submarine lifeguard service became highly organized and successful.

XVI

OCTOBER–NOVEMBER 1943

Skate *on Lifeguard*

A U.S. task force of six carriers, the strongest task force in the Pacific since the Japanese attack on Pearl Harbor, hit Wake on 5 October. Battleships and cruisers followed up with a bombardment. *Skate* (McKinney), on her first patrol, was assigned as lifeguard for this strike. She arrived near Wake two days before the strike, and used the time observing Japanese activity and taking pictures through the periscope. At dawn on 5 October she was on her assigned station, on the surface twelve miles west of the island. From there she had a good view of the bombing and the dogfights between American and Japanese planes. She saw several planes fall, and as it appeared to McKinney that "we had control of the air," *Skate* came in on the surface to approach the nearest crash. Suddenly a Japanese fighter plane dove out of a cloud, strafing. *Skate* made a quick dive and it was not until she was safely under that Lieutenant W. E. Maxson reported that he had been wounded by a bullet in his back. The pharmacist's mate administered first aid.

A half hour later when the air was clear, *Skate* surfaced to continue the search for downed aviators. She was forced to dive again and again, but kept trying to perform her mission. After dark she continued searching the area without success. Lockwood, at Pearl Harbor, arranged for *Skate* to rendezvous with a destroyer after the second day's strike to give Maxson early medical attention. If the rendezvous failed McKinney was instructed to proceed full speed to Midway.

The next morning was squally and overcast, but *Skate* had no difficulty recognizing approaching planes as friendly, nor did the planes make any mistake about *Skate*, for they circled around and asked the location of the target. Then they disappeared in the proper direction and shortly afterward Wake erupted in bomb explosions and anti-aircraft fire. *Skate* closed in to six miles, where heavy shells started falling around her. She made a quick dive to get out of there submerged. An hour or so later she surfaced to receive a message reporting the positions of three downed aviators.

Skate trimmed down until the bow was just out of the water. The commanding officer manned the bridge alone. A three-man rescue party clung to the deck in the bow, each man with the knowledge that an unexpected threat to the safety of the ship would force *Skate* to dive and leave him spread-eagled in his life jacket in the pellucid vastness of the sea, as a helpless target for any chance Japanese fighter pilot. *Skate* closed in full speed, despite the splashes Wake's shore battery raised from the sea around her. About noon she went alongside a rubber boat and picked up Lieutenant Kicker, the first customer of the submarine lifeguard service. Fifteen minutes later a swimmer from the rescue party went over the side to help another aviator aboard.

There was still another pilot reported down off Peacock Point and McKinney went after him. About five miles off the beach the shore battery fire became so accurate that *Skate* was forced to dive. She stayed down only half an hour and then tried it again. There were three planes over Peacock Point. McKinney hoped they were friendly, but when one headed for *Skate*, he pulled the plug. With *Skate* going past sixty feet, bombs exploded close enough to cause slight damage.

Toward sunset the submarine surfaced and continued to search the area. Night search was difficult. *Skate* searched the surface of the sea by cautious use of the Aldis signal lamp, and regularly hailed through the megaphone but made no contacts. Maxson remained conscious and repeatedly asked that *Skate* stay on station rather than depart for medical assistance, but as the wounded man's condition grew worse McKinney decided to head for Midway. Shortly after he made this decision, Lockwood at Pearl Harbor received a message from the Task Force Commander (Montgomery) giving the positions of nine aviators in life rafts near Wake. Lockwood had a difficult decision to make, weighing the chances of making further rescues against the risk of Maxson's life. His decision was that *Skate's* mission came first. He passed on the information of the aviators' positions and directed McKinney to return to the area.

About six o'clock on the morning of 8 October Maxson died of his wounds. *Skate* continued the search. About eleven o'clock on the morning of the ninth, they rescued another aviator from a life raft. Shortly before midnight that night they held services below, administered final rites on deck, and committed the body of Willis Edward Maxson III to the deep. The next day they rescued three more aviators. Although they stayed on station until the fourteenth they could find no more.

The loss of one of her best officers deeply affected *Skate*, but her performance of duty cemented a bond between the submariners and the aviators of the Fifth Fleet that endured throughout the war. Captain Felix Stump sent *Skate* a message: "Anything on *Lexington* is yours for the asking. If it is too big to carry away we will cut it up in small parts."

I-36 *Reconnaissance*

This heavy attack on Wake appeared ominous to Koga, who interpreted it to mean the beginning of an offensive at Wake or in the northern Marshalls. *I-36*, with a reconnaissance plane on board, had been off Hawaii nearly a month waiting for an opportune moment to get a look at Pearl Harbor. On each attempt she was thwarted by the radar defenses of the Hawaiian Islands, and an alert Inshore Patrol. Shortly after the Wake attack *I-36* hauled out three hundred miles and in desperation launched her reconnaissance plane in a one-way suicide flight. The plane could not carry enough fuel to perform its mission and return to the mother submarine. The doomed aviator flew safely over Pearl Harbor, reported four battleships, four carriers, five cruisers, and seventeen destroyers in port, and then disappeared somewhere in the Pacific Ocean.

Koga's alarm inspired by the Wake attack was increased by knowledge of this concentration of force. He ordered four more submarines to the Hawaiian area and he himself, in the battleship *Yamato* with powerful elements of the Combined Fleet, moved up from Truk to Eniwetok, trying to catch Nimitz at an unfavorable moment and win the fleet victory upon which he pinned his hopes. No sooner had he moved out of his central location at Truk than action flared up again around Rabaul. Koga was learning the disadvantages of the strategic defensive, an unhappy state in which clever deductions from hard-won intelligence might still be off enough in timing to be worse than no information at all. On 24 October Koga moved back to Truk with the Combined Fleet, thus beginning a series of errors that had far-reaching consequences.

New Guinea and the South Pacific

There were four Japanese submarines in Huon Gulf, where MacArthur's transports were busy plying back and forth to Finschhafen. The transports went unmolested, but a Japanese submarine torpedoed the destroyer *Henley* on 3 October. She went down in fifteen minutes. Most of the crew were rescued. On 2 October Finschhafen fell to MacArthur's forces.

The Fifth Air Force hammered Rabaul all during October with big bomber raids, but failed to knock it out as a Japanese naval base. These raids goaded Koga into sending his carrier air groups down from Truk to reinforce Rabaul's air defenses. His fleet air arm was there destroyed again in the continuous fighting, leaving the Japanese carriers impotent when they were badly needed later.

In the Solomons, nine Japanese destroyers made a run into Vella Lavella to evacuate troops from New Georgia. They were intercepted by U.S. destroyers in the Battle of Vella Lavella and each side lost a destroyer, but the Japanese succeeded in their evacuation mission.

On 1 November the 3rd Marine Division landed at Empress Augusta Bay in Bougainville, the first of many echelons to hack out airfields and a defense perimeter in Bougainville jungles. Four cruisers and six destroyers of the Japanese Eighth Fleet sortied from Rabaul to support a counterlanding. A U.S. task force of four cruisers and eight destroyers met them in the Battle of Empress Augusta Bay on 2 November. The Japanese lost the light cruiser *Sendai* and a destroyer. The Japanese submarines *RO-104* and *RO-105* had also been ordered into Empress Augusta Bay at the first report of the U.S. landings. They arrived just in time to rescue many of *Sendai's* crew.

Rabaul Carrier Strike

Although no U.S. ships were sunk in the Battle of Empress Augusta Bay the Japanese believed they had knocked out the U.S. task force. Koga then thought he saw an opportunity to annihilate the Americans on Bougainville "at one stroke." He sent Kurita with eight cruisers and four destroyers of the powerful Japanese Second Fleet down from Truk to Rabaul, hoping to set them up to repeat a victory like Savo Island. Fortunately Halsey had not been deceived by repeated reports of the Fifth Air Force that Rabaul had been knocked flat. He was expecting a Japanese advance from Truk to Rabaul and made sound arrangements to watch for it.

Five of Fife's submarines had been sent north of the prevailing weather front to intercept any approaching Japanese task force. In this they failed. *Growler*, stationed close to Truk to guard the southern exit, suffered electrical casualties at a critical time and had to withdraw. The others were in a scouting line in the open sea. By chance, or good planning, Kurita skirted this line and the submarines made no contact.

This was a disappointment, but a little careful chartwork indicates that the probability of success of such a submarine disposition was not good against a high-speed force. The configuration of Truk's southern exits is such that it takes three submarines to do the job to which *Growler* alone was assigned. Even if *Growler* and two others had been on station, a high-speed night run out the exits would have had a fair chance of getting by undetected. A scouting line of four submarines in the open sea would also have to be too short or too thin to be anything but a long chance. The long chance was worth taking, but it could not be counted on for sure success. Halsey knew this and did not wholly depend upon the submarines for information of the movements of the Japanese fleet.

Aircraft Solomon Islands (Airsols) maintained intensive air search over Rabaul's approaches south of the weather front. At dawn on 4 November they found Kurita's tankers off Kavieng and crippled two of them with bombs. Kurita detached a heavy cruiser and a destroyer to tow them back to Truk. Around noon of the same day they found Kurita's main force. With Kurita located, Halsey was forewarned of what was coming, but he was still in a precarious position.

Halsey had no battleships or heavy cruisers to oppose the Second Fleet. The South Pacific had been stripped to build up Spruance's forces for the forthcoming Gilberts operation. Fortunately Sherman's task force of two carriers was still under Halsey's command and Montgomery with three more carriers was en route to the South Pacific. Without waiting for Montgomery, Sherman hit Rabaul with a carrier strike. This was a risky operation for two carriers. There were over 150 effective Japanese planes at Rabaul, but it was Sherman's good fortune that the quality of Japanese aviators had greatly declined. The carrier strike caught Kurita by surprise. Fifteen minutes after the Japanese anchored at Rabaul, carrier planes were over Simpson Harbor like hawks over a chicken run. An hour later the harbor was a shambles. Without good torpedoes it was difficult to sink armored ships, but six cruisers and two destroyers were so severely damaged they were not capable of offensive action for many months.

On 11 November both Montgomery and Sherman launched carrier strikes against Rabaul. Two more cruisers and three destroyers were damaged. In attempting counterattacks, the Japanese air forces took severe losses. The destruction of the Japanese carrier air group was practically completed. Koga withdrew the remainder and replaced them with planes drawn from the Marshalls. By these carrier strikes the Bougainville beachhead was made secure and both the Japanese Second Fleet and their carrier planes were removed as a threat to the forthcoming Gilberts offensive.

Battle of Cape St. George

On 25 November, off Cape St. George, five U.S. destroyers under Captain Arleigh Burke met five Japanese destroyers returning to Rabaul with evacuees from Buka. Three Japanese destroyers were sunk and a fourth damaged. No U.S. destroyer was hit or damaged, a convincing demonstration of the ascendency U.S. destroyers had achieved over their Japanese counterparts in the year of hard action since the previous November, when the Japanese destroyers had had it all their own way with their Long Lance torpedoes.

I-177 had just reached Rabaul, returning from a supply run to New Guinea, when news of the Battle of Cape St. George came in. She hurriedly put to sea again and rescued two hundred survivors of the sunken destroyers. When she was forced to dive by a radar-equipped bomber there was barely standing room below. This was the last naval engagement of the Bougainville campaign. Rabaul's effectiveness declined continuously thereafter. Before long the mighty fortress was a customer for the Japanese submarine supply service.

Brisbane Submarines

The decline of Japanese shipping in the Solomons and the Bismarcks reduced the opportunities for Fife's submarines operating out of Brisbane, while the South China Sea and the East Indies teemed with Japanese shipping out of reach of U.S. surface and air forces. The number of submarines at Brisbane was allowed to decline as they became due for overhaul and the strength of the Fremantle group was built up by replacements. A few submarines continued to base in eastern Australia to be available for special missions connected with MacArthur's advance. A guerrilla supply service was organized for trading with the Philippines, and *Narwhal* was permanently assigned to this mission. The large size and slow speed of *Narwhal* and *Nautilus* made this pair more suited to the guerrilla trade then to combat missions. *Nautilus* later joined *Narwhal* when business with the Philippines picked up, and *Nautilus'* services were no longer required in the Central Pacific.

There was considerable ship traffic still between Palau and northern New Guinea. *Peto* (Nelson) sank two ships around the corner of northern New Guinea, beyond the range of intensive air patrols, in early October. *Silversides* (Coye) was sent to patrol this area later in the same month and sank four *marus*, three of them out of the same convoy. In late November *Raton* (Davis) operated on the Palau traffic routes and despite exasperating experiences with prematures, managed to sink three Japanese ships. After her first three attacks were all spoiled by erratic exploders, she inactivated the exploders and notified Fife by dispatch that she had done so. Notwithstanding these troubles, the submarines operating in the open sea on the Palau traffic routes were more effective in whittling down Japanese strength than were Halsey's Truk watchers. In even these distant areas, however, submarines were commencing to conflict with the far-ranging planes of the Fifth Air Force.

Albacore *Bombed*

The identification of a friendly submarine from the air was always a difficult problem, requiring careful indoctrination and briefing and constant practice. It was most difficult in the New Guinea area. *Tuna* had been nearly sunk by an Australian plane in July. On 8 November *Albacore* (Hagberg) was on the surface on the equator at 149° East Longitude, in pursuit of a Japanese convoy, when a Fifth Air Force bomber arrived. The friendly plane ignored the convoy and bombed *Albacore*, fortunately causing no damage. The next night in the middle of the Bismarck Sea, in the bright moonlight, *Albacore* sighted a four-engine bomber ahead about two miles, and made a quick dive. The first salvo of bombs made a near miss off the submarine's bow as she passed sixty feet on the way down. *Albacore* lost all power, and everything movable on board changed location. Control was shifted to hand power but the main induction flooded before the big valve could be closed, and *Albacore* went down out of control to 450 feet before her dive could be checked. For the next two hours *Albacore's* crew battled to save their ship and their lives. This unfortunate occurrence was the consequence of inadequate briefing of Fifth Air Force pilots. *Albacore* was fortunate to be able to make repairs and continue her patrol. On 25 November she sank a *maru* on the Palau traffic route.

Because of *Albacore's* experiences MacArthur imposed a bombing restriction on the Fifth Air Force against all ships north of 2° South. Everything south of that line, except the narrow submarine safety lanes leading to submarine bases, were blind bombing zones in which the Fifth Air Force bombed anything that moved, with or without identification. This arrangement excluded submarines from the areas more accessible from Brisbane. To assist submarines to reach the far out area, a refueling base was established at Tulagi and the tender *Fulton* was moved up to Milne Bay to service submarines, but logistic difficulties, added to the reduction in Japanese traffic, accelerated the shift of submarine strength from the east to the west coast of Australia. By the end of November there were fourteen submarines based at Fremantle and only nine at Brisbane.

Fremantle Submarines

The buildup in Fremantle submarine strength was immediately reflected in increased *maru* sinkings in the South China Sea. *Gurnard* (Andrews) sank two ships off northwest Luzon on 8 October. Two days later

Bonefish (Hogan) sank two *marus* out of a convoy off the coast of Indo-China. *Bluefish* (Porter) sank a big tanker on 8 November, and ten days later sank the destroyer *Sanae* and heavily damaged the fleet tanker *Ondo*. *Bowfin* (Griffith) made the most successful patrol out of Fremantle in November.

Bowfin refueled at Exmouth Gulf and entered the South China Sea through Lombok Strait, Makassar and Sibutu Passage. She sank four small schooners, and possibly two other coasters by gunfire on the way up, but it was not until the night of 25–26 November that she encountered larger game.

That night was no night for man's inhumanity to man. The rain came down in solid sheets through the pitch black night. With the sky indistinguishable from the sea the lookouts clung to their perches as the only solid object in a world of water and peered out into the void. St. Elmo's fire played up and down the radar mast. The radar was erratic but suddenly it picked up pips on both sides at 1000 to 4000 yards. At first Griffith feared he had blundered into a small island, although the fathometer steadily indicated 75 fathoms.

Bowfin came left to clear out to seaward, and had to back emergency to keep from ramming a big tanker. The submarine had run right into the middle of a five-ship Japanese convoy. In the confused situation Griffith first thought the convoy was headed south, and it was only when he had to back his engines again to avoid another ship that he realized that all the Japanese ships were on northerly courses. He extricated *Bowfin* from the entanglement and tracked the convoy for an hour until the situation was entirely clear.

When he had the convoy sorted out Griffith attacked the leading ship with three torpedoes, which blasted off the target's bow and bridge structure. As *Bowfin* turned to fire at another target her first victim swung broadside to the submarine. There was time only to fire one torpedo before Griffith had to back again to avoid collision. The second target was hit with this single torpedo. *Bowfin* swung around and fired three torpedoes to finish off the damaged ships and then withdrew to reload tubes.

It was morning before Griffith was in attack position again, and in the first daylight submerged approach he missed. *Bowfin* then surfaced and made an end around run for another attack, and in that attempt demolished the target with four hits. Japanese records confirm the sinking of two 5000-ton freighters in this series of attacks.

The next day *Bowfin* sank a small ship, which later was identified as S.S. *Van Vollenhoven*, originally a French ship that the Japanese had captured in Indo-China. Early on the morning of 28 November Griffith picked up a radio contact report from *Billfish* which put *Bowfin* on the track of a five-ship Japanese convoy. In a night surface attack *Bowfin* sank two ships out of the convoy, one of them a 9866-ton tanker. As these ships were going down an enraged Japanese vessel bore down on the surfaced submarine and opened up with a dozen guns at close range. One shell hit *Bowfin* in the superstructure and exploded, carrying away the main induction and a ventilation line.

Bowfin was then in a bad way with all hands working to control the leaks. As her damage control party labored, her undaunted commanding officer fired two deliberately aimed torpedoes at her attacker and stopped it in its tracks. With only two torpedoes remaining, Griffith fired them at a large freighter. After they had run about 500 yards one of them prematured, throwing the other off its course so that both torpedoes missed.

The next morning under quieter circumstances *Bowfin* found opportunity to assess her damages, and make emergency repairs that could get her home. But she was not yet through. En route through the Celebes she encountered a Japanese convoy. With all torpedoes expended she was impotent, but she trailed the convoy until she could coach *Billfish* on to the track and repay the obligation which Griffith had incurred when *Billfish* performed the same service for *Bowfin* a few days before.

Bowfin was credited with nine ships, not counting the coasters she had sunk by gunfire, and a total of 70,948 tons on this one patrol. Only five of these, for a total of about 27,000 tons, can be identified. It is of course possible that the incomplete Japanese records fail to list a ship or two, but it is much more likely that the assessment was unduly optimistic. Undoubtedly some of these discrepancies were due to prematures, which frequently exploded close to the target and were indistinguishable from true hits. Such episodes encouraged Christie to believe his magnetic exploders were more effective than they were. *Crevalle* off Luzon, in the same month, thought she sank an escort carrier but was most probably deceived by prematures, for there is no record of a ship sunk or damaged to correspond to her report.

Seawolf *and* Akatsuki Maru

It was difficult enough to assess damages without the confusing effect of premature torpedo explosion, and many ships were reported sunk when they were only damaged or when depth-charge explosions were confused with torpedo hits. Often when Japanese accounts of submarine attacks became available they did little to clarify the situation. A captured document described an unsuccessful attack on *Akatsuki Maru* on 9 November, illustrating that the universal tendency of observers to see things that did not happen.

Akatsuki Maru was in Luzon Strait proceeding alone at 13 to 15 knots that morning, according to her account, when she was set upon by three submarines. Three torpedo tracks were sighted to port and *Akatsuki* maneuvered to avoid them. Then three more torpedoes were sighted coming toward her from another bearing on the port side. Almost immediately two more torpedoes were reported coming at her from starboard. The agile *maru* dodged the first salvo. As it passed harmlessly ahead, one torpedo from the second group ran right under the ship, and a second one hit under the bridge. It failed to explode. Two more duds hit her in the stern but the total damage was slight.

The date and approximate location identifies this as an attack made by *Seawolf* (Gross). *Seawolf* was out of Pearl Harbor, carrying torpedoes with modified exploders. She fired four torpedoes from a range of 1600 yards on a port track. Gross watched them run hot and normal. He was chagrined to see this *maru* sail blithely by undamaged, and he could only conclude that his torpedoes ran deep or were duds. *Seawolf* was the only submarine involved in this attack. She definitely fired four torpedoes, and half of the torpedoes encountered by *Akatsuki Maru* were illusions.

Wolf Packs in the Central Pacific

In October 1943 there were thirty submarines on patrol in the Central Pacific spread out between the equator and the Sea of Okhotsk from the International Date Line to the coast of China. Two or three of the older submarines were kept constantly busy in the Marshalls and the Gilberts gathering information for Nimitz's planners, but in the period of a year the number of submarines employed in the war against the *marus* had doubled. This increase brought some changes in tactics.

On 1 October the first Coordinated Attack Group (or wolf pack) of three submarines (*Cero, Shad,* and *Grayback*) left Midway for the East China Sea. The pack was commanded by Captain C. B. Momsen, who was embarked in *Cero*. On an informal basis there had been many previous instances of cooperation between submarines in adjacent areas, but Momsen's pack was the first one formally organized and commanded by a separate wolf pack commander embarked in one of the submarines. His objective was to coordinate the searches and attacks of the three submarines. They had been drilled and organized in accordance with a definite attack doctrine.

In the Atlantic, the Germans had used such tactics very successfully, but Atlantic convoys sometimes had seventy or more ships, with many escorts. Under such circumstances a single German submarine could sink only a small proportion of the convoy and from a large escort group a single escort could be detached to hold down a single submarine while the convoy proceeded on its way. German wolf packs were the natural counter to large convoys with many escorts. Japanese convoys were small, generally about five ships with one or two escorts. Against these small convoys single submarines were effective in attack, although the pack was more efficient in search.

Momsen's wolf pack was credited with sinking five ships and damaging seven others, but only three *marus* can be identified as sunk and two big ones heavily damaged. On the average, the submarines of this wolf pack were not as effective as three submarines acting singly. Momsen recommended against the use of the coordinated attack as then organized. He acknowledged that the group might be more successful in locating targets, but this advantage was offset by the loss of freedom which individuals had in developing uncoordinated attacks.

Momsen also recommended that a wolf pack commander should not be embarked in a submarine of his group, but should remain at a shore base where he would be better able to collect all information and have better communication services for its dissemination. The Germans used such a system effectively, but communications were easier in the Atlantic where distances were shorter. Momsen's recommendation was not adopted because it was felt that it would necessitate a greater volume of long-range radio transmitting from submarines in their operating areas and therefore give the very active Japanese radio direction-finders more material to work on. To defeat radio direction-finders in the Atlantic, the Germans developed a system of "squirt transmission" in which a long message was electronically compressed for transmission. German submarines were able to broach and get off their messages in one short squirt without call up or acknowledgment. It had to be recognized that U.S. naval communication in the broader Pacific was not that good, for it was a frequent experience of U.S. submarines that they were required to expose themselves on the surface, sometimes for hours in very dangerous situations, while they tried to call up a radio station to accept an important contact report.

A second Coordinated Attack Group under command of F. B. Warder, who had commanded *Seawolf* earlier in the war, went out on 3 November. Warder confirmed Momsen's observations. He recommended that any future wolf packs should be directed by the senior submarine commander rather than embark a separate wolf pack commander. It is interesting to note that a Japanese division commander habitually rode one of his submarines to sea and frequently attempted to operate them in coordinate groups, but that there was strong Japanese opinion that this system had fewer advantages than disadvantages.

Operation Galvanic

As the time for Operation Galvanic (Gilbert Island Operation) drew near, many submarines became involved. Commander Fifth Amphibious Force (Turner) asked for submarine photographic reconnaissance of Tarawa, Makin, and Abemama. Until that time experiments with periscope photography had not been very successful, but Lockwood made a very fortunate choice of *Nautilus* (Irvin) to do this job. Her executive officer (R. B. Lynch) was a camera enthusiast. Due very largely to his skill and special knowledge, *Nautilus'* photographic mission was an outstanding success. She returned from her mission in late October with excellent photographs and the additional information that the charts of Tarawa were aligned eleven degrees out of the correct orientation. This error if left undiscovered would have caused untold confusion in a closely coordinated bombing, bombardment, and landing operation.

Turner was very pleased with the photographs *Nautilus* brought back. Preinvasion photographs of beachheads became essential for amphibious operations from that time on. The methods and equipment developed by Lynch were standarized and adopted for all submarines on photographic missions.

Such missions were usually undertaken in cooperation with the Joint Intelligence Center, which was also charged with collation and dissemination of aerial photographic intelligence. In preparation the Joint Intelligence Center worked up charts, tide and current tables, information on minefields, known enemy installations, and any previous photographs of the objective. The information required from the submarine could then be narrowed down, an important consideration, for on one of these missions a submarine might be required to take between one and two thousand carefully oriented pictures from ranges of five hundred yards to a mile off a hostile coast, where there might very well be minefields that Joint Intelligence Center had not yet learned about.

Shortly after *Nautilus* returned from reconnaissance other submarines began leaving for their stations during Operation Galvanic. *Thresher*, *Apogon*, and *Corvina* were spotted around the perimeter of Truk. *Seal* was off Kwajalein, *Spearfish* off Jaluit, and *Plunger* was directed to first observe Maloelap and then dash down to be lifeguard at Mili. *Paddle* embarked a special party of aerographic personnel and took station off Nauru to observe and report weather, including upper air soundings. This service was of great importance because of the sensitivity of landing operations to weather conditions, and because the direction of movement of atmospheric disturbances from west to east made observation to the westward of the objective essential to good weather prediction. *Sculpin* and *Searaven* were off Oroluk between Truk and Ponape, where they would be in good position to intercept any Japanese fleet movement from Truk toward the area of operation.

Loss of Sculpin

Embarked in *Sculpin* was Captain John Cromwell, as wolf pack commander. Cromwell was Commander Submarine Division 43. Ordinarily as a division commander he remained at Pearl Harbor, charged with the training, overhaul, and maintenance of the ships of his division, and in addition took turns with other division commanders in maintaining a responsible watch at Lockwood's headquarters. In this latter capacity he became acquainted with submarine plans for future operations and with intelligence material and its sources. During Operation Galvanic a senior submarine officer was needed at sea to be on the spot to make strategic decisions in directing submarine operations in case the Japanese sortied from Truk. In preparation Cromwell was fully briefed on the plans for Operation Galvanic and on the present and future location of all submarines in the Central Pacific.

Acknowledging the validity of the comments of Momsen and Warder about the wolf pack system, it was decided that Cromwell's submarines would operate independently until the Japanese made some move that would make it profitable to form the pack under his command. If this happened the pack would be assembled on radio orders from Lockwood. Until then Cromwell was a passenger in *Sculpin*, while she operated north of Oroluk under Commander Connaway, her skipper.

On 18 November *Sculpin* made radar contact with a fast convoy and made an end around run at full power to gain position ahead. At dawn on the nineteenth she submerged in what promised to be a successful attack until the convoy zigzagged toward her, forcing her to go deep. Connaway waited while the convoy passed and then surfaced, to make another end around. The Japanese, however, had left the destroyer *Yamagumo* behind the convoy as a sleeper. *Sculpin* was forced into an immediate quick dive and *Yamagumo* delivered a depth-charge attack which caused some damage.

About noontime Connaway decided to come up to periscope depth and have a look around. The depth gauge stuck at 125 feet and the diving officer accidently allowed the submarine to broach. *Yamagumo* was still waiting for just such a break and she dashed in to drop eighteen depth charges. These caught *Sculpin* before she could get deep, and exploded all around her. The submarine was thrown out of control, with steering and diving gear inoperative, with many leaks, and her hull distorted. Connaway recognized that he could not hope to control *Sculpin* submerged, and he brought her up to battle surface in a desperate attempt to fight his way clear. Almost immediately *Yamagumo* landed a salvo on the submarine, demolishing the conning tower and killing the commanding officer and the executive. Lieutenant Brown, who succeeded to command, decided to scuttle rather than risk having *Sculpin* boarded and captured by the Japanese. He ordered "Abandon ship."

Cromwell was in a bad spot. He well knew that the Japanese had methods of interrogation which sometimes succeeded in wringing information out of the most reluctant prisoner, and he knew he was in possession of most important information which must not become known to the Japanese. He told Brown that he "knew too much" to become a Japanese prisoner, and he refused to abandon ship. With eleven other men of *Sculpin*, dead and alive, he rode her down in her last dive. Forty-two of the submarine crew became Japanese prisoners of war. For his self-sacrifice in order to safeguard the information he held, Cromwell was posthumously awarded the Congressional Medal of Honor.

Lockwood, back in Pearl Harbor, was of course ignorant of these events. On 29 November he ordered Cromwell to form his wolf pack. When nothing was heard from *Sculpin* Lockwood became concerned for her safety. In order to avoid confusion to the other submarines the instruction to form the pack was canceled, and in orders which required acknowledgement *Sculpin* was directed to observe Eniwetok. When no answer came from *Sculpin* they knew she was lost, but her story was not learned until the end of the war.

Assault of Tarawa and Makin

D-day was 20 November at Tarawa and Makin. Upon these two small Gilbert Islands converged a mighty amphibious force, with supporting naval vessels of all kinds and sizes, including thirteen battleships and eleven fast combat carriers. Sailing from widely separated ports in New Zealand, the New Hebrides, Samoa, and Hawaii, 200 ships carrying 35,000 troops and 117,000 tons of cargo met on schedule off the Gilbert Islands and landed troops of the 27th Division of the U. S. Army at Makin and the Second Marine Division at Tarawa. The Japanese garrisons on these islands put up a bitter defense. On Makin the 27th Division suffered 186 casualties in subduing the 600- to 800-man Japanese defense force. Tarawa, which the Japanese had been busily fortifying since the Carlson raid in August 1942, was a tough nut to crack. The Second Marines, in a heroic assault, stormed the island at the cost of 3000 casualties and wiped out 4800 men of the Japanese defense force. Only 146 Japanese prisoners survived.

Most of the submarines involved in this operation made only indirect contribution. *Paddle's* weather reports were unexciting but important and were successfully completed. *Thresher* sank a transport north of Truk on the thirteenth. *Searaven* sank the 10,052-ton tanker *Toa Maru* north of Ponape on the twenty-fifth. *Seal* sighted and reported two cruiser task forces at Kwajalein but was unable to attack. *Plunger,* on lifeguard duty at Mili, rescued one aviator. While performing this service she was strafed by an enemy plane and five men were severely wounded. Fortunately all of the injured recovered from their wounds. The greatest submarine service to the recapture of the Gilberts had been performed six months earlier when *Pollack* sank *Bangkok Maru* with 1200 troops intended to reinforce Tarawa, and who otherwise would have been there to meet the Marines at the beachhead.

Nautilus *at Abemama*

Nautilus (Irvin) was the only U.S. submarine with a direct part to play. After completing her October reconnaissance of Tarawa, she embarked seventy-eight men of the Marine Amphibious Reconnaissance Company and left Pearl Harbor on 8 November. She performed lifeguard service at Tarawa on the eighteenth and nineteenth during heavy carrier strikes, and during which she drew fire from the island's coast defense batteries but was not hit. On the evening of the nineteenth she closed the beach to observe and report surf conditions on the reef, and departed on her primary mission to land the Reconnaissance Company at Abemama.

About ten o'clock that night *Nautilus* encountered "friendly forces." The destroyer *Ringgold* and the cruiser *Santa Fe,* with special assignments for the next day's bombardment, were in advance of the main forces approaching Tarawa. *Ringgold* knew of *Nautilus'* special mission, but information had been received that the submarine had been diverted to the westward to pick up an aviator, and the destroyer assumed that, if encountered, the submarine would dive on contact. When a pip appeared on *Ringgold's* radar, moving south at twenty knots, it was believed to be a Japanese patrol boat. The destroyer opened fire.

Nautilus was in close to a dangerous reef toward which she was being set by a two-knot current and was in a poor position to dive. Irvin fired a recognition flare and dove, but the destroyer fired another salvo, one shell of which hit *Nautilus* in the conning tower just as the hatch was being closed as she went down. Fortunately this shell was a dud. It did enough damage anyway, and the *Nautilus* damage control party had a bad couple of hours, while the submarine maintained depth control with a steep up angle that did little to reassure the passengers.

Nautilus surfaced the next morning and continued to Abemama. A small group of Japanese occupied that island, so Irvin and Captain J. L. Jones, U.S.M.C., who commanded the Marines, spent the daylight hours observing the beach before embarking the landing party that night. The Marines went over the side expressing satisfaction at leaving the submarine for the comparative safety of rubber boats headed for a hostile beach, remarks they had cause to regret before they reached shore four hours later, after battling a choppy sea and a stiff current. *Nautilus* continued to stand by and landed the reserve food, ammunition, and supplies the next night.

The next day Jones came back on board with a map showing the exact location of the Japanese defenses. It was decided that *Nautilus* would try bombardment. On signal from the Marines, the submarine opened up with her pair of 6-inch guns, using quick fuses and high-capacity shells, with radio spotting from the beach. Five minutes later the Marines signaled cease-fire. That night Jones reported that some of the seventy-five rounds the submarine fired made direct hits on the Japanese defenses, killing and wounding fourteen men. The rest committed suicide. The bombardment, in proportion to effort, was probably the most effective naval bombardment of the war. *Nautilus'* 6-inch battery may have been anachronistic for a submarine, but it certainly was lucky.

After Abemama was secured *Nautilus* picked up an escort to guide her through the trigger-happy surface forces and returned to Pearl Harbor. Although *Nautilus* performed valuable service, her experience in being fired on without challenge while in an established safety lane convinced Lockwood that, in the future, close-in work for submarines during a landing operation should be avoided.

Japanese Defense Moves

With the Japanese Second Fleet cruisers damaged and out of action as a result of the Rabaul carrier strikes, and with their carriers practically without planes or pilots, there was little the Japanese Navy could do about the assault on the Gilberts. Their shore-based air strength in the Marshalls had been weakened to defend Rabaul. On 20 November *Independence* was hit by an airplane torpedo and was forced to return to port for repairs, but this was the total accomplishment of Japanese shore-based air forces. On 21 November two light cruisers and two destroyers departed from Truk loaded with troops intended to reinforce the Gilberts, but by the time they arrived at Kwajalein the Gilberts had fallen. Three other cruisers moved up to Kwajalein on 26 November, and then moved back again to Eniwetok. These were the ship movements reported by *Seal*, which had Kwajalein under observation. By far the most effective blow in defense of the Gilberts was struck by a Japanese submarine.

Japanese Submarines in the Gilberts

Four Japanese submarines (*I-19, I-35, I-169,* and *I-175*) were on patrol southwest of Hawaii in November, and these were ordered to the Gilberts at best possible speed. Five more sortied from Truk or were ordered up from Rabaul. *I-175* (Tabata) arrived on 23 November. At about dawn the next morning she fired three torpedoes at the escort carrier *Liscome Bay.* There was a terrific explosion and twenty-three minutes later *Liscome Bay* went down with 644 of her crew. *I-175* was slightly damaged by depth charges in the counterattack, but she escaped and returned to Truk.

For this success the Japanese submarines paid dearly. Of the nine submarines that rushed into action around the Gilberts, only *I-175* and two others returned to port. The U.S. destroyer *Meade* picked up *I-35* by sound contact almost as soon as that submarine arrived in the area, on 22 November. *Meade* was joined by *Frazier* in a depth-charge attack that forced *I-35* to the surface. Both destroyers opened with gunfire and *Frazier* rammed the surfaced submarine. *I-35* attempted to man the deck gun but was prevented from doing so by pistol fire from *Frazier's* deck. *Frazier* backed off and *I-35* sank, leaving four swimmers in the water. The destroyer lowered a boat for their rescue. One of the survivors opened fire on his rescuers. He was killed by return fire. The other three became prisoners of war.

I-19 also hurried down from Hawaii for her last battle. On 25 November, the U.S. destroyer *Radford* made radar contact with a surfaced submarine. The pip disappeared but ten minutes later *Radford* had sound contact. Depth-charge attacks brought up oil and flotsam. *Radford's* victim was probably *I-19*, the submarine which in September 1942 had sunk *Wasp* in the Solomons. Four other Japanese submarines that hastened to the defense of Tarawa did not return and their fate is unknown. *I-21, I-39, I-40,* and *RO-38* were missing when the score was in. In addition *RO-100*, while on a supply run to Buin, struck a mine in Bougainville Strait and was lost. The British submarine *Tarus* (Wingfield), in Malacca Strait off the west coast of the Malay Peninsula, torpedoed and sank *I-34* on 11 November.

This was a greater rate of loss than the U.S. submarines ever suffered. *I-174,* one of those that managed to survive, barely escaped. She was apparently spotted by radar plane patrol when surfaced on the moonless night of 26 November. The plane must have called up destroyers, for *I-174* was suddenly charged by a destroyer coming out of the black night. The first depth-charge attack hit her at ninety feet, knocked out all power and depth control, and flooded the engine room and motor room bilges. The destroyer persisted in the attack until *I-174's* battery and high-pressure air were exhausted and she had to surface. Two minutes after she surfaced an airplane forced her to submerge again, and she managed to stay down under control for a few minutes by bleeding high-pressure air from her torpedoes. A sudden rain squall was her salvation and she escaped. When *I-174* returned to Truk her commanding officer reported that it was plain suicide for Japanese submarines without radar to operate against American anti-submarine forces. Vice Admiral Takeo Takagi, Commander-in-Chief of the Sixth Fleet, did not agree.

Loss of Wahoo

Although U.S. submarines avoided the disastrous losses that Japanese submarines endured, they did not get off lightly in October and November. After *Wahoo's* frustrating experiences with dud torpedoes in the Sea of Japan in August, Morton brought her home to reload with electric torpedoes. He then took her back into the Sea of Japan. *Sawfish* followed her a few days later through La Pérouse Strait. Nothing was ever heard from *Wahoo* after she left Midway.

On 5 October *Konron Maru,* one of the big Japanese train ferries plying between Japan and Korea across the Strait of Tsushima, was torpedoed and sunk. The Japanese, contrary to their general custom, announced the loss of the ship with 544 lives, stating that the ship sank in a few seconds. It raised consternation in Japanese anti-submarine headquarters. The Strait of Tsushima were considered almost sacred Japanese waters, and their freedom was essential to continued communication between Japan and the Asian mainland. The *Konron Maru* attack was undoubtedly the work of *Wahoo*. Morton had taken considerable pains to acquire all available intelligence on the routes and schedules of these ferries before his departure on patrol, and *Wahoo* was the only submarine that could have been in the vicinity.

Wahoo not only penetrated into these dangerous waters, she certainly got safely out, for on 6 and 9 October two Japanese *marus* were sunk in the Sea of Japan to the northward, along a route *Wahoo* would take to withdraw. Through all this Morton maintained a discrete silence. This was good common sense in the Sea of Japan, so no concern was felt for *Wahoo's* safety until after *Sawfish* came out. Then as the date passed for *Wahoo* to report her outbound passage through the Kuriles, her silence became ominous. Planes were sent out from Midway to scout along her homeward route, but finally Lockwood had to admit this gallant ship with her colorful skipper had disappeared forever in the Sea of Japan.

There is no definite attack that can be connected with *Wahoo's* loss. Both La Pérouse and Tsushima were mined, but *Sawfish* came out through La Pérouse on 9 October without encountering mines. Japanese accounts report a plane attack on a surfaced submarine in La Pérouse Strait on 11 October, and this may have been the attack which sank *Wahoo.*

S-44

S-44 (Brown) was on patrol in the northern Kuriles on 7 October when she made contact with what she took to be a small *maru.* Brown approached on the surface in the darkness, with the crew at battle surface. At close range he opened up in a surprise attack with the 4-inch gun. Rather than a small *maru*, S-44 had picked on a Japanese destroyer, which replied with its full battery in rapid fire. S-44 was overwhelmed. She took seven direct hits in her control room and conning tower and sank, leaving several men swimming in the water. The Japanese picked up two as prisoners of war, and they survived forced labor in Japanese copper mines until released at the end of the war.

That was the end of rash old S-44, who for so long had carried the torch as the only submarine that had sunk a major Japanese Navy ship (*Kako*). It was also the end of S-boat patrols in the Aleutians and Kuriles. Lockwood ordered the remaining old S-boats withdrawn and turned over to the training command.

Corvina

Corvina (Rooney) was on her first patrol off the southern entrance to Truk in November. At the end of this assignment she was scheduled to join Southwest Pacific submarines. She was directed by radio to report to Fife on 30 November, but she never acknowledged that message and all attempts to communicate with her failed. On 16 November *I-176* fired three torpedoes at a surfaced U.S. submarine in *Corvina's* area. Two hits were observed. There were no survivors. *Corvina* was the only U.S. submarine to be sunk by a Japanese submarine during the war.

Capelin

What happened to *Capelin* (Marshall), also lost on her first patrol, is unknown. *Capelin* put in to Darwin on 16 November, after only seventeen days of her patrol, with a defective conning tower hatch, noisy bow planes, and a defective radar. These defects were repaired to Marshall's satisfaction and she again departed on patrol. Nothing was heard of her after that. Unknown to the Allies there were Japanese minefields along the northern Celebes, in *Capelin's* area. At least one Japanese anti-submarine attack was reported in a position that could have been *Capelin's*, but there is no real evidence that she was lost to either mines or Japanese anti-submarine attack.

New submarines were coming out of U.S. shipyards thick and fast. At Portsmouth Navy Yard a record was set of 173 days for construction, and a number of submarines, of which *Capelin* was one, were constructed, fitted out, and in service in less than three hundred days. It is possible that this time was insufficient to allow for annealing of hull stress in an all-welded hull. Some of the defects reported by *Capelin* at Darwin are characteristic of hull distortion. It has been conjectured, but with no other evidence, that stress relief distortion of her hull may have contributed to *Capelin's* loss.

October and November Results

In the two months of October and November U.S. submarines sank two Japanese combat ships and seventy-one *marus*. One fleet tanker was sunk and three others severely damaged. Several other large ships were damaged, but the most important Japanese ship to make port after being torpedoed was the carrier *Junyo*.

Halibut (Galantin) was patrolling off the south coast of Honshu in late October and early November. She had made five attacks on convoys, but sank only one freighter when on 5 November she picked up a task force making nineteen knots in a southwesterly course. Initial contact was made by radar at twenty-eight thousand yards at about four o'clock in the morning, and Galantin closed the range at maximum speed on the surface until forced to dive by the approaching dawn. He counted two battleships, a heavy cruiser, a carrier, and several destroyers in the task force. From her silhouette he identified this carrier as *Shokaku* class and naturally picked her as his target.

Shortly after dawn he fired six torpedoes from the bow tubes and observed one hit. The task force scattered, but left destroyers behind to guard the stricken ship. *Halibut* had only one torpedo remaining. This jammed in the tube when Galantin attempted to finish off the carrier and left *Halibut* impotent. The carrier was *Junyo*, which was heavily damaged but made it back to port.

Tarpon (Wogan) also patrolled off the south coast of Honshu in October. On the night of 17–18 October she had an encounter with a mysterious unescorted vessel, making sixteen knots through her area.

Wogan succeeded in achieving a good firing position 1500 yards off the target's port beam and fired a spread of four torpedoes, two of which hit. The target was severely damaged but it charged directly for the submarine and forced *Tarpon* to go deep and under. Coming up to periscope depth astern of his target, Wogan fired two difficult single torpedo salvos "up the kilt" and both missed. The enemy ship opened up on *Tarpon* with furious fire of everything from machine guns to 6-inch guns. Projectiles exploded over *Tarpon* and rattled off her hull at periscope depth. Wogan persisted and hit the narrow stern of his antagonist with the third torpedo fired at it. This put an end to the fireworks, but the ship still floated. Wogan circled around to the port side of the immobilized target and finished her off with a fourth torpedo hit.

Wogan was certain *Tarpon's* antagonist sank. Captain John Cromwell, in what must have been his last official action as Commander Submarine Division 43, before he went out in *Sculpin* for his fatal operation as a wolf pack commander, endorsed *Tarpon's* patrol report crediting her with sinking a Japanese auxiliary naval vessel. Wogan's description fitted no known Japanese ship, however, and even at the end of the war, what went down that night could not be identified from Japanese lists of ships sunk. It was some time after the war before *Tarpon's* account could be matched with the sinking of *Michel,* the last of the German commerce raiders.

Michel was headed for a Japanese port when Wogan clobbered the heavily armed raider. The Germans were wrathful with the Japanese for failing to furnish adequate anti-submarine escort for the raider, and even insinuated that the German ship may have been mistakenly torpedoed by a Japanese submarine. The Japanese, however, were having a hard time with their anti-submarine problem and one German raider was only a drop in their bucket of trouble.

November was a record month, with forty-five *marus* sunk by submarines. From all causes the Japanese lost 320,000 tons of merchant shipping in this one month, making a mockery of their optimistic September estimates that they could hold their losses down to a million tons a year. This rate of loss was disastrous for Japan, and threatened her ability to continue effective war.

XVII

DECEMBER 1943–JANUARY 1944

Japanese Grand Surface Escort Force

The alarming rate of Japanese shipping loss convinced even the hardest headed Combined Fleet zealot that something had to be done. Mobility of the fleet was threatened by the loss of fleet tankers. The rate of plane production upon which everything depended could not be maintained without more imports of raw material. On 15 November the Grand Escort Command was created, with Admiral Oikawa as Commander-in-Chief. Practically all the escort forces were placed under his command, abating to some extent the confusion that had existed because of lack of a uniform escort doctrine and communication procedures.

It introduced nothing new to anti-submarine warfare. Escort vessels depended upon depth charges, of which destroyers carried about thirty, and the new *kaibokans* could carry as many as three hundred. The Japanese had no ahead-thrown weapons. For locating submerged submarines they used both supersonic pinging and passive listening. They were experimenting with magnetic airborne detectors, but by the beginning of 1944 these were not yet in service. Their attack procedures depended largely on seaman's eye and rule of thumb, and they lacked the highly developed mechanical and electronic equipment of the Allies. Beginning in the spring of 1944 some of the escorts were equipped with radar, but it was not until later in the year that either radar or radar detectors were generally available for escorts.

After the Gilberts invasion, captured documents revealed some interesting information on Japanese anti-submarine methods. The Japanese credited U.S. submarines with the ability to make twenty-four to twenty-five knots on the surface and twenty knots submerged, far better performance than they could produce. They believed that radar was being used for the solution of torpedo firing problems (which was correct) and that curved fire was rarely used (which was not correct). Many unusual methods of deception were reported, including the use of dummy periscopes with explosives attached, carrying sail to disguise submarines as fishing boats, and ejection of debris to simulate damage. All of these devices had been considered and rejected as impractical.

Despite some inaccuracies, Japanese technical intelligence was not bad. The Japanese knew all about U.S. torpedoes and their difficulties and had good information on other ordnance. A great deal of torture was endured by submarine prisoners of war to protect information that the Japanese had anyway. The Japanese did lack information on the maximum depth attainable by U.S. submarines, and they credited themselves with sinking about ten times as many submarines as were lost from all causes. Very often depth charges were set too shallow, and overoptimism frequently resulted in breaking off attacks too soon. Until the Grand Escort Force became effective Japanese anti-submarine methods were spotty, but sometimes when an escort was good, it was very very good. Surely *Puffer* had no criticism about lack of persistence in an attack which she endured.

Counterattack on Puffer

Puffer (Jensen) was patrolling the northern part of Makassar Strait on 9 October when she encountered the fleet tanker *Hayatomo,* escorted by a 500-ton torpedo boat of the *Chidori* class. *Puffer* hit the tanker with two torpedoes which did not sink it. Jensen maneuvered to finish it off. The escort, which until then had accomplished nothing, came up and dropped some depth charges. Jensen decided to withdraw temporarily, but stayed at periscope depth to exploit any opportunity that might be presented. About twenty minutes later, without warning, six depth charges went off close aboard.

Puffer was hurt but not badly. There were some leaks which were difficult to control. The rudder and the stern planes were damaged and were noisy in operation. *Puffer* went deep and *Chidori* stayed over her pinging and dropping depth charges at intervals, and always and forever dashing up at high speed in response to any maneuver Jensen attempted. The submarine ran silent and ran deep. *Puffer* shut down her air conditioning to conserve power and reduce noise. The crew bailed the motor room bilges by hand.

They used carbon dioxide absorbent and released oxygen but the air got very foul. *Puffer* had no great difficulty operating at deep submergence. The anti-submarine measures taken against her were unique only in their amazing persistence, and the sureness with which *Puffer* was repeatedly located and attacked. Another escort came up during the evening to help out the first. They stayed over the submarine until afternoon of the next day. After the pinging ceased, Jensen decided to stay down until after nightfall to give *Puffer* a better chance to get clear. About seven o'clock in the evening of the second day, she surfaced directly from deep submergence, in the bright moonlight. Radar showed up one of the patrol in the distance, but *Puffer* worked around it and cleared out. She had been submerged 37 hours and 45 minutes. All her maneuvers had been canceled out by deep ocean currents, and when she surfaced it was approximately in the same position in which she first submerged.

By the time she surfaced many of the crew of *Puffer* were past caring what happened to them, or to her. Those who, while on watch, had something to think about outside themselves, and whose duties gave them a knowledge of the situation, were better off than those who could only stand and wait. The officers on watch attempted to keep the crew informed, but everyone resented the use of the public address system because of the noise it made. To remedy this, officers occasionally went through the boat to inspect and to tell the men what was going on. The physical effort involved in these trips made them quite a task toward the end of the dive. Men were irrational about sound. They resented one man's squeaky sandals. Yet they were all agreed that it was a mistake to shut down the air conditioning. The temperature in the maneuvering room went to 125°, and this together with high humidity contributed greatly to the fatigue. Men spent all the time they could huddled against anything comparatively cool, cuddling water-filled pipes with almost obscene affection.

Officers and crew who survived this ordeal were forever after bound together by an insoluble tie. They learned many things about themselves and about each other. One of the soberest was an appreciation of men's different capacities to endure. Toward the end of the dive most men were too exhausted to stand a watch. Those who kept *Puffer* going were informal volunteers, who did just those things that had to be done. These men were not the normal leaders of the crew. The exuberant extroverts collapsed, leaving the quiet plodders to bring home the ship.

Gato *with Depth Charge on Deck*

Not all Japanese depth charges were set shallow, as *Gato* had cause to be thankful for. *Gato* (Foley) sank a ship out of a convoy about two hundred miles north of the Admiralty Islands on 20 December. The escort made a well-conducted counterattack, dropping nineteen depth charges, all of them close. A rain squall gave Foley an opportunity to surface and head back toward the convoy for another attack, but in low visibility and evening twilight he made visual contact with the escort and turned and ran for it with the escort pursuing. At this critical moment *Gato* discovered that there was an unexploded depth charge lying on deck. *Gato* had been carrying it around both on surface and submerged, but fortunately had not dove deep enough to set it off.

With the escort pursuing, and *Gato* trying to gain position for another attack, Foley had an interesting problem disposing of this embarrassing piece of Japanese ordnance without risking blowing the stern off the submarine. This he solved by lashing the depth charge into a rubber boat, with a slow leak, and gently pushing it over the side in what he fondly hoped was the path of the pursuing escort. This experience was unique for American submarines, but a Japanese submarine had an experience very much like it.

I-176 was on the surface at night off New Britain when a flare suddenly burst overhead, sending the Japanese submarine into a quick dive. As she went under something hit the bridge and at forty-five feet there was a small explosion above her. When she surfaced next morning she discovered that a depth charge dropped from a plane had made a direct hit on the bridge as she was diving. It had hit with such force that it penetrated the bridge structure, breaking open the depth-charge casing. When *I-176* passed forty-five feet the depth-charge exploder functioned, but the main charge had been spilled. It didn't detonate but was plastered all over the bridge as a yellow mud. *I-176's* crew could read "depth charge" in English on the casing and be thankful for the extraordinary accuracy of some bombardier.

Grand Escort Force Strength

The Grand Escort Commander was forced to get along with whatever escorts he could pull together. He had about fifty ships, the best of which were fifteen twenty-five-year-old destroyers. *Kaibokans* were coming into service, but there was not yet enough of them to be effective. Oikawa knew that large convoys with more escorts would help solve his problem, but this meant longer time in port waiting for escorts. Frequently emergency conditions required that ships sail with whatever escorts that could be mustered, or sometimes with no escort at all.

In December the 901st Naval Air Flotilla was organized exclusively for escort duty. Oikawa's force included four escort carriers. All of these were at first engaged in ferrying planes south, and when they could be released they all needed navy yard overhaul. The aviators assigned to the 901st Flotilla were untrained, resulting in many operational losses, and as soon as they achieved acceptable skills they were transferred to Combined Fleet carriers.

Without sufficient escorts Oikawa conceived the brilliant idea of laying a gigantic mine barrier from Japan to Borneo, behind which Japanese commerce could move with relative impunity. This did not receive immediate approval of the Navy General Staff, for Japan's stock of mines was being reserved against the probable emergency of Russia entering the war. In the meantime the Grand Escort Command tried to struggle along with the inadequate means available. In the fall of 1943 they noted that American torpedo performance was improving, and in December they received convincing proof that poor torpedo performance would no longer be their salvation.

Sailfish vs. Chuyo

On 3 December a Japanese task force consisting of the light carrier *Zuiho,* carrying the flag of the officer in tactical command, two escort carriers, *Chuyo* and *Unyo,* the heavy cruiser *Maya* and two destroyers, were en route from Truk to Tokyo. The carriers were returning from a plane ferry trip. There was no standard anti-submarine doctrine. The general attitude of fleet destroyers was that convoy protection was a matter of common sense. A warning was received from Tokyo radio that there was a possible submarine in the vicinity. The task force was in typhoon weather, with mountainous seas, forty- to fifty-knot winds, and torrential rains. *Zuiho* issued orders for a submarine alert, but shortly after midnight, in view of the state of the weather, and the task force speed of eighteen knots, they considered the danger past and ceased zigzagging. The first indication that there was a submarine in the vicinity was a torpedo hit on *Chuyo.*

Chuyo sent out the standard short-form message meaning "we have been torpedoed," but communication broke down and the only ship to receive the message was the cruiser *Maya.* She did nothing about it. The destroyer *Urakaze* figured out from the big ships' maneuvers that one of them had been hit, but as she had no instructions she continued on into the stormy night. It was common sense that this was not a night for a destroyer skipper to borrow additional trouble. About half an hour after midnight *Chuyo* sent an amplifying message to Tokyo that she had been hit by one torpedo, there was a fire in the crew's quarters, but she was able to proceed.

Zuiho first learned that a ship in the formation she commanded had been torpedoed in a message from Tokyo at about four o'clock in the morning. She ordered *Unyo* to tow *Chuyo,* escorted by the two destroyers. This plan was later canceled. At six o'clock *Chuyo* was hit by a second torpedo and stopped dead in the water and helpless. This she reported to Tokyo. *Maya* came to her rescue. *Zuiho* ordered *Unyo* to help *Chuyo.* *Unyo* directed the two destroyers to join *Chuyo* and neutralize the enemy submarine "with concerted effort." At this time *Urakaze* had lost sight of both *Unyo* and *Chuyo*. She sighted *Chuyo* just in time to see her smacked by another torpedo and sunk.

This was the work of *Sailfish,* under command of Lieutenant Commander R. E. M. Ward. The raging typhoon was, of course, much more of a handicap to the submarine than it was to the heavy Japanese ships. When *Sailfish* made radar contact, just before midnight on 3 December, she discovered that she had encountered a Japanese force of several large ships, with a couple of destroyers, making eighteen knots on a northwesterly course. She built up to full speed, but the best she could do in the teeth of the storm was twelve knots. This speed nearly drove *Sailfish* under the great black waves, which pounded her hull and periodically swept completely over the bridge.

It was physical torture for the lookouts to face the wind, for the raindrops driven by the fifty-knot wind stung like buckshot, and each drop that hit an eye was temporarily blinding. Yet look into it they must. "The old man" was on the bridge as exposed as they were, straining all his vitality into his eyes to penetrate into the darkness. This was the night when radar made all the difference; radar and torpedoes that would not premature in the heavy seas, or fail to explode if they hit the target.

About midnight the near ship turned on a searchlight, pointed in *Sailfish's* direction, and Ward went down to forty feet, placing his trust in radar. It was impossible to conduct a methodical approach, and he had to adapt his tactics to the exigencies of each succeeding moment. He estimated he was on the left flank of a formation, with four big ships in line of bearing, with the biggest in the center, and *Sailfish* only four hundred yards from the nearest destroyer track. When the biggest ship closed to twenty-one hundred yards Ward fired four torpedoes and thought he had two hits. Several depth charges went off, none very close and *Sailfish* went deep to reload. For an hour and a half they stayed in the peace and quiet below a hundred feet while the tubes were reloaded, and everything made ready. They surfaced again to be buffeted by the tempestuous seas, as they struggled to regain contact.

Around three o'clock in the morning *Sailfish* had a radar pip, but it was nearly six, with morning twilight coming on, before Ward could close the range to under four thousand yards. The morning twilight would shortly drive him under and he would lose any chance to get closer, so he fired four torpedoes at thirty-one hundred yards' range, and two of them he thought were hits. One erupted in a terrific explosion that sounded like a battleship's full broadside. The Japanese threw up a tantrum of star shells, anti-aircraft traces, and other ordnance, but despite the illumination Ward still could not identify the target. When the tracers started coming his way he submerged.

About nine o'clock he found a damaged carrier dead in the water with a destroyer standing by. Depth control was extremely difficult. At sixty feet he could see only green water and at fifty-five feet *Sailfish* nearly broached as each succeeding heavy sea passed over her. Ward kept coming in, and finally found the position he wanted and finished off *Chuyo* with a three-torpedo salvo.

It was a crucial test for a torpedo to run in such tempestuous weather without premature explosion from the pounding of the bucking sea, and to maintain accurate depth control, and to function properly on impact with the target. The modified Mark 14 torpedo met every test. *Chuyo* went down, the first big Japanese combat ship to be sunk by a submarine since *S-44*, with Mark 10 torpedoes, sank *Kako*.

Ten minutes after he fired the *coup de grâce* Ward took a sweep across the horizon with the periscope. There was nothing in sight on the target bearing, but as he swung around to locate the destroyer he found a heavy cruiser at 3300 yards bearing right down on *Sailfish*. Caught in an impossible position for attack, he could only go deep to evade and lost all chance for a crack at *Maya*. The cruiser must have been behind the stricken carrier when *Sailfish* made the final attack. Ward bitterly anticipated that the Monday morning quarterbacks would take note that he should have looked on both sides of the carrier, which was a dead duck anyway.

The Monday morning quarterbacks on either side had little to criticize in *Sailfish's* performance. The Japanese thought that this was an outstanding submarine attack. They worked up an analysis of it, which circulated among Japanese submariners as an example of what can be accomplished by courage, skill, and persistence. The Americans thought the same. Three days later *Sailfish* was damaged by a surprise bombing from a Japanese plane, but she made ingenious repairs to the damage and continued on patrol to sink two freighters. For this patrol *Sailfish* was awarded the Presidential Unit citation. After the end of the war, it was learned that about half the crew of *Sculpin* were being transported from Truk to Japan in *Chuyo,* and all but one of them went down with the Japanese ship.

Continued Pressure on Japan

Pressure against Japan was continued in all areas during December. On 4 December Pownall, with a task force including six carriers, moved into the Marshalls and bombed Kwajalein and Wotje. The destruction of Japanese naval vessels at Kwajalein was disappointing. The task force of four cruisers that *Seal* had spotted arriving on 26 November got out of there on 3 December, just in time to miss the carrier strike. *Nagara*, a light cruiser, brought in reinforcements and then distributed them to Mili, where she depth-charged *Plunger*. *Nagara* managed to get back to Kwajalein in time to serve as a target for the carrier planes, but she and the light cruiser *Isuzu* and a naval auxiliary were only damaged. Six *marus* were sunk and three more damaged. The U.S. carrier *Lexington* was damaged by a Japanese aircraft torpedo during withdrawal. As soon as Tarawa and Abemama airstrips were ready, Kwajalein was no longer a safe anchorage for Japanese ships.

A day later, in the Solomons, a group of destroyers bombarded Choiseul Island, and on 8 December battleships and cruisers bombarded Nauru. In the New Guinea area MacArthur made a landing at Arawe Peninsula on 15 December. On the twenty-first even the northern area came to life when naval aircraft from Attu bombed Paramushiro in the Kuriles.

The First Marine Division landed at Cape Gloucester, New Britain, on 26 December. Cruisers and destroyers had continued to bombard Bougainville, and on Christmas Day Sherman's task force of two carriers moved in to bombard Kavieng, where they sank a couple of *marus* and damaged two small patrol vessels. There was not much to show for the effort, but Koga became disturbed at these indications of further landings in the Bismarcks and scheduled the mighty battleship *Yamato* herself to carry troops to Kavieng. Apparently they decided on a roundabout approach, for on Christmas Day *Yamato* encountered *Skate* about 150 miles northwest of Truk.

Skate *vs.* Yamato

Skate picked up a nineteen-knot task force of one big ship and two destroyers on a southeast course by radar at twenty-three thousand yards early on Christmas morning. As the submarine closed in she had to dive because of the approaching dawn. McKinney could not see the target clearly enough to identify it, and was unaware that he was the first American privileged to see the almost legendary behemoth of the Japanese Navy. *Skate* fired four torpedoes and one of them hit. The damage was assessed as minor, but it was enough to deter *Yamato* from carrying out her mission.

December Results

On 18 December *Grayback* in the Nansei Shoto got in a night attack on a convoy and sank a freighter. Three hours later she surfaced to pursue the convoy. A Japanese destroyer had trailed behind to catch her in such a maneuver. It came charging down *Grayback's* wake in the moonlight. The submarine submerged and fired a salvo of four torpedoes from the stern tubes which sank *Numakaze* so quickly she was unable to get off a radio message. Japanese records show *Numakaze* as missing from this time in about this locality.

On 20 December *Puffer* exacted revenge for her long ordeal, on Japanese escorts in general, by sinking *Fuyo,* an old destroyer, near Subic Bay in the Philippines. During the month, however, submarines were not as successful as they were in the record month of November. They sank only twenty-nine *marus* in the last month of 1943, as compared with forty-five the previous month. The carrier strikes on Kwajalein and Kavieng, and shore-based air operations in the Marshalls, plus the welcome contribution of Japanese ships sunk in Chinese ports by China-based U. S. Army Air Forces, raised the total of Japanese *marus* sunk to fifty-eight, and the tonnage to about 200,000.

New Year's 1944

New Year's Day 1944 found U.S. submarine forces stronger than ever. There were seventy-three submarines in the Central Pacific. In Australia there were twenty-four more, and the strength of Christie's command was raised to thirty in January. In twenty-five months of war the United States had lost twenty-five submarines from all causes (two in the Atlantic). During the same period the Japanese had lost forty-seven. All U.S. submarines had dependable radar. An answer to their torpedo exploder difficulties had at last been found. A new explosive greatly increased the destructive effect of torpedo warheads. The electric torpedo was in service.

Despite the difficulties with torpedoes, U.S. submarines had more than held their own against Japanese shipbuilders. In twenty-five months U.S. submarines sank thirty Japanese naval vessels and 435 *marus.* Japan, which had started the war with a barely adequate six million tons of shipping, had only five million tons to start the year 1944. In tanker category, Japan had improved her position somewhat, but since the exploder difficulties had been overcome, the monthly average of all Japanese ships sunk by submarines had doubled, and tankers were in for greater trouble.

Comsubpac Plans and Operations

The buildup of the Central Pacific offensive had a profound influence on the planning and operations of Submarines Pacific. In the first twenty months of war, submarine patrols north of the equator could be carried out without much regard to fleet operations. But submarine patrols lasted two months. They had to be planned with due consideration to what the situation would be during the entire patrol. A big offensive operation meant that Japanese traffic would first be drawn to the area of operations, and then probably cease abruptly. The whole pattern of Japanese traffic would be affected, and great opportunities for submarines might be created by predictable Japanese defense moves.

Lockwood attended daily conferences at Cincpac headquarters and participated in the development of plans for future operations. When these were decided he laid the submarine requirement before his own staff at Subpac headquarters. The details were then worked out; the availability of submarines determined in conference with Submarine Squadron Commanders, submarine operating areas laid out, logistic support arranged, communication plan worked out, the patrol orders cut, pre-patrol conferences held with the submarine skippers, and the submarines made ready to depart on the date selected.

Once submarines were at sea communication with them centered in the operations room at Comsubpac headquarters, under the control of Captain Richard Voge, the operations officer. Into the operations room there flowed a wealth of information—from submarines at sea, from Nimitz's headquarters on the hill, from the Joint Intelligence Center— and out of it ran communication circuits that could rapidly broadcast messages to the submarines. Four hours after the sun set in Pearl Harbor the same sun sank below the horizon in the Carolines, and submarines in their operation areas popped to the surface where they could hear Haiku Fox, the broadcast radio schedule out of Hawaii. Voge then would take over in the operations room, there to remain until the sun rose again over the coast of China.

Before him was a great magnetic wall chart of the Pacific, and on it magnetic markers spotted the estimated positions of every submarine at sea in Subpac areas. Through the voice tube to the communications room below messages could be initiated to the submarines, whose status, character, crew, and commanding officer Voge knew as well as he knew the stark environment of the operations room. Out over Haiku Fox went messages of instructions: Lockwood's orders to the submarines, terse commands that might send them to triumph or destruction, commendation and encouragement, information of happenings in adjacent areas, padded out with news of babies born and gossip, and grim esoteric humor to bind this force together. In over the same route came much less frequent messages from submarines at sea.

Operation Flintlock

After the Gilberts operation Nimitz began preparation for Operation Flintlock, the conquest of Kwajalein. The 4 December raid on that center of Japanese strength in the Marshalls quieted all contention that the assault on Kwajalein should be preceded by the seizure of the nearer bases of Mili, Wotje, and Jaluit or the reconquest of Wake. The minor bases could be interdicted and the mobility and power of the U.S. fleet used to leapfrog directly into Kwajalein and Majuro in the center of the Marshalls. Shore-based airplanes flew many photo reconnaissance missions over their objective, but submarines were also called upon for observation and reconnaissance.

As planning progressed, additional information was required, and *Tarpon* was sent in to make photo reconnaissance of Kwajalein to supplement the information already obtained there by *Seal* and *Spearfish*. Close islands to the westward of the Marshalls required examination to locate potential Japanese defense centers. *Seal* was sent to photograph Ponape in January, *Sunfish* reconnoitered Taongi and Kusaie, while *Searaven* gathered important periscope pictures of Eniwetok.

For all carrier strikes lifeguard submarines were stationed at the objectives. During Flintlock the lifeguard organization was perfected and a simple system of communication by uncoded voice radio initiated, enabling pilots to communicate rapidly with the guarding submarines and pass on information of the location of a crash landing. The Japanese had voice radio also. Their air intelligence officers tried to confuse the system by sending out false calls to divert submarines or entice them within range of shore batteries. Voge defeated them by the neat device of assigning voice radio calls like Lonesome Luke, and Lulu Belle, which the Japanese linguists found difficult to pronounce convincingly.

New Guinea

In the Southwest Pacific MacArthur continued moving up the coast of New Guinea. Sherman's carriers made additional raids on Kavieng, and Airsol's planes worked over Rabaul, sinking a number of *marus*. Seaborne communications with Rabaul became very difficult for the Japanese, but they could and did fly in planes.

Japanese submarines damaged two auxiliary vessels in the South Pacific during January, but their major effort continued to be in the service of supply to hopelessly situated forces cut off by advancing Allies. On 3 January *I-177* came in to Sio to pick up General Adachi, commander of the New Guinea Army Forces, and move him to Madang. *I-177* was driven off by torpedo boats, but next day managed to pick up her passenger. She was depth-charged by torpedo boats right afterward. She had similar difficulty at the other end of her run, and it was 8 January before she could complete her mission. Upon her return to Rabaul it was decided there was no longer a safe anchorage in that harbor for a submarine, and on 10 January *I-177* left Rabaul en route to Truk.

Japanese Submarine Losses

Less fortunate was *I-181*. She left Rabaul for transportation operations on 13 January and did not reach her destination. Japanese Army observers reported that a Japanese submarine was destroyed by U.S. surface forces in St. George's Channel on 16 January. *I-171* left Rabaul for Buka on 30 January and nothing was heard from her after 3 February. A Japanese submarine was sunk by U.S. destroyers *Guest* and *Hudson* near Green Island, between Cape St. George and Buka, on 1 February. Except for the slight discrepancy in dates this may well have been *I-171*. *RO-37* departed from Truk on 3 January for operation in the New Hebrides. She scored one of the two successes of Japanese submarines in the South Pacific during January when she torpedoed the fleet tanker *Cache* on the twenty-second. Her triumph was short-lived. The U.S. destroyer *Buchanan,* coming to *Cache's* assistance, picked up radar contact on a submerging submarine and followed up with depth-charge attacks. *RO-37* was destroyed in these attacks.

Brisbane Submarines

U.S. submarines had little direct part in the Allied advances in the Southwest, although they continued their special missions and reconnaissances. The Brisbane submarines found their greatest opportunity to sink Japanese ships along the route between Palau and Truk. To reach this area submarines usually went from Brisbane to Tulagi to top off with fuel before proceeding to the operating area. Three Brisbane-based submarines: *Scamp* (Ebert), *Albacore* (Blanchard), and *Guardfish* (N. G. Ward) went up that way early in January. On 14 January they were concentrated in a narrow lane across the Palau–Truk convoy route, with *Blackfish* four or five hundred miles to the eastward passing them contact reports on convoys she encountered.

About noontime on the fourteenth *Guardfish* made contact with two Japanese destroyers. She started after them but the Japanese ships disappeared to the northeastward. Shortly afterward *Guardfish* heard a heavy but distant explosion, and Ward saw a column of fire and smoke shoot five hundred feet in the air. Twenty miles away, *Albacore* had encountered the same destroyers.

Albacore, whose speciality seems to have been Japanese combat ships, made contact with these destroyers about the time they slipped over *Guardfish's* horizon. Blanchard had a difficult time achieving a favorable position as the destroyers continued radical and erratic evasion tactics, but after an hour of maneuvers he reached a favorable position for a stern tube shot. He fired four torpedoes, which blew up *Sazanami* as witnessed by *Guardfish*. *Albacore* then received a prolonged depth-charge attack, during which a Japanese convoy a few miles to the south-east ran into trouble.

Scamp made contact with this convoy of three large tankers with two destroyer escorts, on an easterly course, shortly before noon, while *Albacore* was busy a few miles to the northward. About an hour after *Sazanami* was hit, Ebert fired two torpedoes from *Scamp's* bow tubes at a big Japanese tanker and heard two solid hits. *Scamp* then had to duck deep to evade one of the other tankers, and did not see the effect of her attack, but again there was a witness. From *Guardfish's* periscope Ward saw a second great column of smoke mushroom above the horizon to mark the end of *Nippon Maru*, a ten-thousand-ton tanker.

Guardfish had a difficult time running around the prolonged counter-attack on *Albacore*, but while the Japanese destroyer was thus occupied *Guardfish* slipped around and got ahead of *Scamp's* convoy. Nearly four hours after *Scamp's* attack, *Guardfish* fired six torpedoes at a big tanker and saw five hit. *Kenyo Maru*, another ten-thousand-ton tanker, went down. The Truk–Palau convoy route was hot all the month of January, as the Japanese moved in oil and supplies for the fleet at Truk. Sub-marines sank eight ships along that line during the month.

Penang

British submarines out of Trincomalee patrolled Malacca Strait and the Indian Ocean. On 10 January H.M.S. *Tally Ho* (Bennington) sank the light cruiser *Kuma* off Penang. H.M.S. *Templar* (Beckley) tor-pedoed and heavily damaged the light cruiser *Kitagami* about a hundred miles from the same place on 28 January. German and Japanese sub-marines shared the use of Penang as a base for Indian Ocean opera-tions, and for both navies this proved to be expensive in the long run. *I-27*, the most successful Japanese submarine in the Indian Ocean opera-tions, left Penang on 4 February and was never heard from again. She was sunk by British destroyers *Paladin* and *Petard* on 12 February. *RO-110* departed from Penang in early February for operations in the Bay of Bengal and also was missing from the day of her departure. She was sunk by the Indian sloop *Jumna* and the Australian minesweepers *Launceston* and *Ipswich* on 11 February off the east coast of India. On 14 February *Tally Ho* torpedoed and sank the German-operated ex-Italian submarine *UIT-23* off Penang.

Fremantle Submarines

Christie's submarines were still plagued by prematures. On 9 January *Redfin* (King) fired three torpedoes at a convoy and all three exploded prematurely in succession. After surfacing later in the morning *Redfin* found pieces of her own torpedoes scattered over her deck. The next day Christie ordered King to inactivate his magnetic exploders. A week later (17 January) *Redfin* encountered the Japanese destroyer *Amatsukaze*. King fired four torpedoes at *Amatsukaze* and was sure he sank her. Although eighty of the Japanese destroyer crew were killed, *Amatsukaze* made it into the nearest port for emergency repairs. She was out of the war for a year.

Bowfin also had serious trouble with prematures, as Christie tried out the latest modifications designed by the Bureau of Ordnance to overcome this difficulty. Notwithstanding exploder trouble, and although Southwest Pacific submarines continued their full quota of minelaying and special missions, Christie's submarines on the average were slightly more successful in sinking Japanese ships this month than were Lockwood's, whose exploders were all inactivated. In the South China Sea and the Indies, submarines sank twelve *marus* and eight of those were tankers.

Pearl Harbor Submarines

With more submarines under his command, off Japan, in the East China Sea, and the Mandate islands, Lockwood's submarines sank thirty-three *marus* in January. This made January another record month with a total of 355,000 tons of Japanese shipping lost from all causes. There was also some notable damage to Japanese combat ships in the Central Pacific. On 16 January, off Bungo Suido, *Sturgeon* hit *Suzutzuki* with two torpedoes, which blew both the bow and the stern off that destroyer, but somehow *Suzutzuki* made it to Kure, where for nine months she was under repairs. A wolf pack of *Tullibee*, *Halibut*, and *Haddock* patrolled the Marianas during January with very few contacts, but on 19 January *Haddock* (Roach) made contact with a task force of two carriers and several destroyers. The task force closed the range so rapidly that three minutes after contact *Haddock* was forced to dive, and her attempt to radio a contact report to her pack mates failed to get through. Roach, who was on his first patrol as commanding officer, made a well-conducted approach and fired six torpedoes at one of the carriers. His target was the escort carrier *Unyo,* who was heavily damaged but survived to have other encounters with submarines.

Swordfish *and the Q-Ship*

Swordfish, under command of Captain K. G. Hensel, patrolled off Tokyo. Hensel was Commander Submarine Division 101, but on this patrol he was ordered to additional duty as commanding officer of *Swordfish.* He was a little old and rank-heavy for command of a submarine. When the war started he was in command of the Submarine School at New London. With the reputation as an expert in submarine attack tactics, earned in many years of peacetime submarine command, he had instructed many of the younger submarine skippers in the prospective commanding officer class at New London. About a year after the war started he broke loose from this academic job, but he was then too old to command a submarine and the closest he could get to action was division commander at Pearl Harbor and Midway. His duties there called for him to supervise the pre-patrol training of his submarines. In this he demanded perfection. He was outspoken and blunt in his criticism even though he was always conscious that he had never commanded a submarine on a war patrol.

Other division commanders went out as wolf pack commanders to share the dangers and observe firsthand the situation a submarine encountered. For Hensel this was an unsatisfactory substitute. Only the skipper feels the weight of ultimate responsibility for the ship, its crew, and its mission. Only he has to make irrevocable decisions, often with incomplete information, and sometimes so nearly instantaneous they have to be instinctive. The long sleepless nights on the bridge, the oppressive environment, the constant frustration, and the physical fatigue that condition men's minds to error are parts of the job that cannot be simulated. Hensel wanted command. When *Swordfish* came in to Midway after an aborted patrol he got it.

Swordfish's ninth patrol had been unproductive and cut short by a myriad of materiel casualties. Her captain reported that she was not in fit condition to patrol off Japan. Hensel, a division commander, was ordered to fly from Pearl Harbor to Midway to take over command.

Swordfish was fixed up to his satisfaction and she shoved off on her tenth patrol on 29 December. Her crew was apprehensive, but they kept their mouths shut. They felt that a four-stripe skipper was too old for this business. Hensel had the reputation of being a stubborn precisian.

The trip out to the operating area demonstrated that the previous

captain might have been right. *Swordfish* passed through four successive storms, one of them a full-blown hurricane. The submarine suffered
a number of materiel casualties. The safety tank was inoperative because
the valve stuck. The radar was undependable. The steering mechanism
was noisy. The Torpedo Data Computer was obsolete. *Swordfish* had a
series of electrical fires, symptomatic of deteriorated insulation, and used
up nearly all her fire extinguisher carbon dioxide. Hensel was undaunted.

On the night of 13–14 January, a little over a hundred miles south of
Tokyo, *Swordfish* found a convoy of four *marus* and three escorts. In a
workmanlike approach and attack Hensel torpedoed and sank *Yamakuni
Maru*. The counterattack was violent and accurate. It shook old *Swordfish's* bones until they rattled. The steering system was so noisy Hensel
set the rudder and maneuvered by varying the speed of the screws.

At 320 feet *Swordfish* found a density layer and managed to sneak
away so she could surface to charge batteries and reload tubes before
dawn. But the old submarine's main motor control panel had been
knocked out of adjustment by the depth-charging. When she dove at
dawn all hell broke loose. *Swordfish* lost all power. The maneuvering
room and the pump room were both on fire. She headed for the bottom
with a steep down angle, and then headed for the surface with a sharp
up angle, and lay helpless in the swell trying to regain power to evade
an inquisitive approaching patrol boat. In the nick of time they got her
under way on one screw, and she went down for the day to pull herself
together. The next night Hensel took her back in close. For *Swordfish*,
after this conditioning for crisis, the Japanese had prepared a surprise.

All through the war American submarine commanders had imagined
they were encountering Japanese Q-ships, diabolically designed to decoy
submarines into attack which could be turned into lethal counterattack.
Any such activity must have been the impromptu work of some local
commander, for *Delhi Maru* was the first Japanese ship specially designed and reconstructed as a Q-ship. She was a 2000-ton merchant
ship converted to a decoy ship at Sasebo, equipped with depth-charge
launchers and masked batteries, with sonar, and with extra watertight
integrity to keep her afloat and fighting after one or two torpedo hits.
She was specially equipped to detonate magnetic torpedoes at a distance from the ship. Everyone on board was trained naval personnel.

Delhi Maru was ready for sea on 14 January, and a favorable opportunity was presented to her when *Swordfish* sank *Yamakuni Maru*
that day. Accompanied by two escorts, she came down the bay on the
night of 15 January with the mission of enticing the submarine into an
attack, and then destroying the enemy in a well-organized counterattack.
She had no means of knowing that *Swordfish* had been set up for her,
but in the first part of her mission she was eminently successful; Hensel

enticed easy. *Swordfish* was waiting. About ten o'clock that night the submarine listeners heard echo-ranging, and shortly afterward they picked up radar contact at fourteen thousand yards. Hensel swallowed the bait hook, line, and sinker, and ran in at full speed on the surface.

The moon was three-quarters full and entirely too bright for a surface attack. Shortly after midnight *Swordfish* submerged to radar depth. When the range closed to six thousand yards Hensel could see his target through the periscope. He identified it as a *maru* with two torpedo boat escorts. He intended to turn out and fire stern tubes, but when the target zigged and presented him with a port track he changed the setup and fired three torpedoes from the bow tubes, so sure of his data that he ignored spread doctrine and fired all three torpedoes to hit. They did.

The first torpedo hit under the bridge and obscured the target in an explosion that sent spray and flame two hundred feet high. *Swordfish* went deep, unsuccessfully searching for a density layer to hide under. As they went down they heard a "Fourth of July celebration" of explosions. Hensel thought the target might have been carrying munitions. The depth-charge attack was prompt and close, but by three o'clock in the morning *Swordfish* was able to surface and clear the area.

The first torpedo to hit blew *Delhi Maru's* captain clear off the bridge and into the sea, and the next two sent the Q-ship after her commanding officer to the bottom. The escorts reported, without too much conviction, that they had annihilated the attacking submarine. *Delhi Maru's* career as a decoy ship lasted less than twenty-four hours. Hensel didn't even know that he had been enticed into that attack.

Flintlock Deployment

Six submarines were deployed in preparation for D-day of Operation Flintlock. Three submarines, *Permit* (Bennett), *Skipjack* (Molumphy), and *Guardfish* (Ward) were off Truk atoll exits. *Seal* (Dodge) was at Ponape, *Sunfish* (Shelby) at Kusaie, and *Searaven* (Dry) at Eniwetok. Their missions were patrol, reconnaissance to detect sorties of Japanese fleet units, and lifeguard for carrier strikes. Operation orders required that in event of contact with an enemy task force approaching the Marshalls their primary mission was to get off a prompt contact report, and they could not attack until such a contact report had been completed.

This order was not popular with submarine commanders, who realized that, if contact with a fast-moving task force was not exploited immediately, a rare opportunity would be gone forever. Fortunately *Haddock* had not been under these instructions when she attacked *Unyo*, or that escort carrier would undoubtedly have escaped unscathed. During

Flintlock this controversy was academic, for no major Japanese fleet units sortied to offer opposition to the U.S. fleet, but such instructions remained in force for subsequent operations.

Skipjack, stationed on the eastward of Truk, sank the converted seaplane tender *Okitsu Maru* and the destroyer *Suzukaze* on 26 January while on Flintlock station. *Guardfish,* off the southern entrances, sank the destroyer *Umikaze* on 1 February. *Permit,* off the northern entrance, watched a Japanese task force containing two battleships sortie from Truk and turn westward toward Palau. *Permit* could only close the range to twenty-four thousand yards, much too great for attack, and as soon as the task force was over the horizon Bennett surfaced sixteen miles from the busy North Pass and attempted to get a contact report through. Seven minutes later Japanese planes came up and forced *Permit* under. When they departed she came up again to get her message through to Pearl Harbor. For an hour and nineteen minutes she called Pearl Harbor, which finally receipted for the message, and *Permit* submerged. This was the longest time since the war began that an American submarine had remained on the surface during daylight that close to North Pass.

Trigger (Dornin), which was not assigned to the Flintlock operation but which was patrolling about three hundred miles north of Truk, torpedoed the destroyer *Michishio* and sank the submarine tender *Yasukuni Maru* on 31 January. The 11,933-ton *Yasukuni Maru* had been overhauled and refitted in Japan to relieve the light cruiser *Katori* as flagship of the Sixth Fleet, because *Katori* was urgently needed in the greatly depleted light surface forces of the Japanese Navy. The big submarine tender with two other large ships and two destroyer escorts were returning to Truk when the convoy encountered *Trigger*. Dornin attacked on the surface on a starlit night. The first attack was partially thwarted when *Trigger's* radar confused one of the escorts with the rear ship in column, which Dornin intended as the target. The escort was badly damaged but did not sink. In a two-hour stern chase *Trigger* overtook the convoy and attacked again. Just before daylight she put at least two torpedoes in *Yasukuni Maru*. The big submarine tender went down so fast that there were only forty-three survivors. It was a severe loss to the Japanese submarine force.

Kwajalein Assault

Four fast carrier task groups of Task Force 58, under Rear Admiral Marc A. Mitcher, commenced working over the Marshall Islands on 29 January, to such good effect that by evening of that day there were no operational Japanese aircraft east of Eniwetok. There were three or four

Japanese submarines then in the Marshalls. *RO-39* was ordered to proceed to Wotje atoll and destroy the enemy. She was never heard from again. On 1 February U.S. destroyer *Walker*, in an area in which no U.S. submarine was scheduled to operate, made contact by radar and illuminated a surfaced submarine by star shell. It was *RO-39*, which made a quick dive but not quick enough. *RO-39* was destroyed on the destroyer's first depth-charge attack. The main Japanese fleet based at Truk was unable to offer any opposition to the Flintlock operation.

Three attack groups moved into the Marshalls in 217 ships with sixty-four thousand Marines and Army troops embarked. They landed at three objectives. Majuro Atoll, 270 miles southeast of Kwajalein, was occupied without opposition. Roi and Namur at the northern end of Kwajalein atoll were completely occupied by 2 February. Resistance ended at Kwajalein Island (the third objective), at the other end of the atoll, on 4 February. The Marshall Islands passed under control of the United States.

Minefield Intelligence

These new conquests brought to the Joint Intelligence Center a mass of captured documents. Among these were Japanese secret "Notices to Mariners" establishing limits of restricted navigation within which mines had been planted. For submarines these were most important finds.

Oikawa had begun to lay his great mine barrier flanking the East China Sea, and if submarines had had to learn about the mines the hard way many of them would have been lost.

Mine warfare posed one of war's difficult dilemmas to the Japanese. If the locations of minefields were kept too secret Japanese ships would be blown up by their own mines. Many of them were. If the locations were widely publicized the submarines the mines were intended for might learn about them. To solve this problem the Japanese issued secret notices to mariners, and to remind their users of the classification printed all secret notices with a red border. This was very useful to Cincpac Joint Intelligence Center. Faced with the difficulty of scanning a mass of captured documents, a translator would pounce on the red border first, and very shortly information on a new minefield would be in the hands of operating submarines.

Loss of Scorpion

This system was not fast enough to save *Scorpion*, who was last heard from on 6 January en route to patrol the Yellow Sea. *Scorpion* (Schmidt) made a midocean rendezvous with homeward-bound *Her-*

ring to transfer a man with a broken arm. The seas were too rough to make the transfer. The two submarines parted and nothing was ever heard of *Scorpion* again.

The Japanese had planted two hundred mines across the shallow mouth of the Yellow Sea in August. The secret notice to mariners restricting navigation around the field was picked up on Kwajalein more than a month later, too late to be of any help to *Scorpion*. Track charts of U.S. submarines that had operated in the area disclosed that many of them had crossed and recrossed the restricted area many times and safely returned to port. Two hundred mines in that broad reach were hardly more than a token threat, but possibly *Scorpion* had been unfortunate enough to be stung by one of them. There were no survivors and the nature of her end is only a conjecture.

XVIII

FEBRUARY–MARCH 1944

Eniwetok

The next object for Spruance's Fifth Fleet was Eniwetok, about three hundred miles northwest of Kwajalein and a thousand miles east of the Marianas. It had been planned that Operation Catchpole, the occupation of Eniwetok, would not be undertaken for about two months, because the carriers would be busy in an assault on Kavieng. As the situation developed it was not necessary to occupy Kavieng. The reserve force for Kwajalein had not been committed, and this provided a nucleus of a force to move into Eniwetok. The very fortunate decision was made to advance the date of Operation Catchpole and forestall Japanese efforts to build up the defenses of Eniwetok. Sherman's fast Carrier Group hit Eniwetok on 31 January, destroying all the Japanese air defenses and a small amount of shipping. Carrier strikes were repeated, and on 15 February the Eniwetok Expeditionary Group sortied from Kwajalein in nine transports, with a fire support group of battleships, cruisers, and destroyers.

To insure against interference with this amphibious operation, a carrier strike on Truk had been planned. Characteristic of the meticulous planning of the Fifth Fleet Staff, detailed plans for such a strike had been worked out prior to their departure from Pearl Harbor. When it was decided to advance the date of the Eniwetok landing, and the simultaneous strike on Truk, it required only a dispatch from Spruance to Lockwood for the submarines to be informed of what was expected of them.

Truk Strike

Ten submarines were deployed in support of Operation Hailstone, the carrier strike on Truk. Three of these came from Fife's Brisbane submarines, and the rest from submarines based at Pearl Harbor. *Searaven*

(Dry) was north of Truk on lifeguard duty and *Darter* (Stovall) was south of that atoll for the same mission. The remainder were spread out on an arc of roughly 150 miles' radius from northwest to southwest of Truk as a net to catch any Japanese ships fleeing from Truk. These were *Sunfish* (Shelby), *Skate* (Gruner), *Tang* (O'Kane), *Aspro* (Stevenson), *Burrfish* (Perkins), *Dace* (Claggett), and *Gato* (Foley).

Truk was deep in the web of Japanese defenses, and to get at it Spruance would have to pass within range of several Japanese air bases. It was assumed that the carriers would be sighted and that they would have to fight their way in and out against Japanese land-based aircraft. Moreover, the carriers would probably be sighted in plenty of time for every Japanese ship afloat in Truk to clear out of there, and it was in this scramble that the submarines were expected to find their opportunity. Accordingly submarines were placed on the various routes Japanese ships might take to Palau or Saipan.

Truk

Koga at Truk realized that Truk anchorage was no longer secure against air attack. It was within range of heavy bombers from Kwajalein or from Bougainville. Soon after the fall of Kwajalein he cleared out some of the Combined Fleet heavy ships and sent them to safer anchorages at Palau. *Permit* saw the first contingent en route and reported their departure but was unable to close to firing range. When Airsols sent a Marine Corps plane from Bougainville to photograph Truk on 4 February Koga knew his flagship had been sighted. He then left Truk in *Musashi* for Japan and sent the remaining carriers and cruisers to Palau. *Permit* attacked two separate task forces en route to Palau but made no hits.

The light cruiser *Agano* was less fortunate. She had been under repairs at Truk for damages received at Rabaul, and it was 16 February before she was ready to get under way. The submarine net had then been spread. *Agano* cleared North Pass, escorted by two destroyers, the day before the sky fell in on Truk, but then her luck deserted her. About one o'clock on the morning of 17 February *Skate* made contact by radar. Gruner made a very neat approach and hit the cruiser with three or four torpedoes. *Agano* was a new light cruiser that had been identified by Allied observers as everything from a pocket battleship to a light cruiser, and Gruner believed he had sunk a heavy cruiser of the *Kako* class. After *Agano* went down her survivors were rescued by her escorts who decided to return to Truk—which was for them a very unfortunate decision.

Since the war began, U.S. submarines patrolling Truk had known that any surface ship they sighted was enemy, and they were free to fire on radar contact in the darkness, or with a few inches of periscope above the surface while the mast tops of the target swam by above the wave crests. With friendly forces entering the area submarines would have to indentify their targets carefully, but Spruance was anxious that submarines retain their freedom as long as possible. *Tambor* had missed an attack opportunity at Midway through uncertain identification, and *Skate* would surely not have sunk *Agano* if, in the short time she had to attack, she had had to confirm identification. For this reason an elaborate signal system had been worked out to periodically broadcast, during this operation, one-word, clear language radio messages that meant the submarine areas were free, until a specific code word was sent which warned that the Fifth Fleet was coming in. So long as the battleships remained with the carriers launching strikes a hundred miles to the northeast there was no danger, and the all-clear signal was rebroadcast.

The carriers launched their first strike before dawn on 17 February. Unbelievably, they had made their high-speed approach undetected by Japanese search planes, and they caught Truk by surprise, a feat more remarkable than the Kido Butai's undetected peacetime approach to Pearl Harbor. Some time before, a submarine had sunk the Japanese ship carrying Truk's new fire control radar, so the anti-aircraft fire was less accurate than it might have been. The first strike was a fighter sweep which knocked out Truk's air power and left the Japanese almost defenseless. The heavy combat ships had departed, but in the lagoon were submarines and light forces and over fifty *marus* and naval auxiliaries. They were like fish in a rain barrel for the dive bombers and torpedo planes that followed the fighters.

Searaven *at Truk*

Searaven, on lifeguard duty off Northeast Pass, had a ringside seat. About half-past six in the morning she had radar contact with planes approaching from the northeast, and ten minutes later carrier planes passed directly overhead. With them she exchanged recognition signals and established communication. Shortly afterward *Searaven* had to dive for an unidentified plane and through the periscope watched a dogfight between opposing fighters. She was down most of the morning, and when she surfaced it was just in time to catch the magic word "Crabapples." The surface forces were coming in. Pearl Harbor radio picked up the cry to rebroadcast it and "Crabapples," "Crabapples" reverberated from pole to pole as a welcome for the surface forces into the waters where for so long only submarines had opposed the Japanese.

Searaven did not have long to wait before she caught sight of friendly battleships, cruisers, and destroyers approaching. For a submarine after many lonely patrols off Truk it was like settlers in a beleaguered stockade seeing the U.S. cavalry gallop across the plains. *Searaven* went down to two hundred feet, as her instructions then required, and the task force went right over her; a destroyer probing with supersonic pings and the screws of the heavy ships clearly heard through the submarine's hull in the torpedo room.

Spruance was on his way to circumnavigate the atoll. Soon his three-star flag, flying from the battleship *New Jersey,* was off North Pass where, less than a month before, *Permit* at the risk of her life had surfaced for an hour to get off a contact report. A small group of Japanese light forces were caught northwest of there. The light cruiser *Katori* and the destroyer *Maikaze* and a trawler were sunk by gunfire, but neither surface ships nor submarine made more than minor contribution to the slaughter by the carrier planes within the atoll. The Japanese struck back to the best of their ability, and that night the U.S. carrier *Intrepid* was hit by an airborne torpedo. The carrier planes went back the next morning to finish off whatever was left at Truk from the previous day's work. The Japanese lost two light cruisers, four destroyers, a number of fleet auxiliaries, four big tankers, and many other *marus,* for a total loss of 200,000 tons of shipping.

Tang, while on Hailstone station on the seventeenth, sank two big *marus. Searaven,* on the morning of the eighteenth, received a call for lifeguard "Daisy Mae" and ran in full speed to the spot designated. She was forced down once by an unidentified plane, but a carrier fighter then gave her air cover and guidance. *Searaven* picked up the entire crew of a *Yorktown* torpedo bomber four miles from Northeast Pass light, and for all practical purposes completed the submarines' participation in the Truk strike.

Japanese Submarines and the Truk Strike

Japanese submarine reconnaissance in the Marshalls and Gilberts failed to reveal the great fleet movements preceding the Truk strike. U.S. anti-submarine action had considerably thinned out their number. *I-11,* which had been observing Samoa, was ordered to the Ellice Islands on 11 January and was never heard from again, decreasing the number of patrolling submarines by one. About that time *RO-39* was sunk off Wotje. *I-175* was then ordered to rush to that island. En route, *I-175* encountered Sherman's carrier task force but probably was never aware of it. The battleship *New Jersey* had radar contact and ordered the destroyer *Charrette* to investigate. The destroyer established sonar contact and was joined in the hunt by the destroyer escort *Fair.* A hedgehog attack made three hits. *I-175* was never heard from again. Less than two months before, she had scored one of the greatest triumphs of the Japanese force by sinking the escort carrier *Liscome Bay*, with great loss of life.

RO-40 left Truk for the Gilberts on 12 February. She ran into the Eniwetok Expeditionary Force on 15 February and was sunk in a depth-charge attack by the destroyer *Phelps* and the minesweeper *Sage* near Kwajalein. These sinkings nullified the reconnaissance of Japanese submarines.

On 15 February *Aspro* (Stevenson) was on station north of Truk as part of Hailstone submarine dispositions when she encountered a Japanese submarine on the surface southbound. *Aspro* was unable to close the range submerged, so Stevenson waited until the Japanese submarine passed by and then surfaced in the daylight and made an end around run, keeping his adversary in sight through the high periscope. *Aspro* finally lost visual contact due to approaching darkness, but closed to twenty-one hundred yards by radar and fired four torpedoes. Stevenson saw two hit. This was *I-43* which had departed from Saipan for Truk the day before, but never arrived.

Headquarters of Vice Admiral Takeo Takagi, commander of the main Japanese submarine force (Sixth Fleet), was at Truk. He flew his flag from *Heian Maru*, an 11,614-ton submarine tender. *Heian Maru* was sunk in the air raids and down with her went all her valuable cargo of submarine spares and supplies. With practically no warning of the carrier raid there was insufficient time for the submarines in port to get out of the atoll. They submerged and lay on the bottom until it was all over. Two of them received minor damage. *RO-44*, en route to Truk, arrived during the holocaust but did not sight any of the attacking task force. She waited outside the reef but eventually received clearance to enter. Coming through the atoll, she had difficulty in navigating between the hulks of capsized and sunken ships. After the raid was over several submarines sortied and took up patrol position northeast of Truk, but Spruance was long gone by then. Takagi must have then known the same frustration that Commander Submarines Pacific experienced on the day of the Pearl Harbor attack.

It was soon apparent to Takagi that the Combined Fleet would never again base at Truk, and it was no longer a good place for repair and overhaul of submarines or a rest area for their crews. Although it was some time before he could leave, he made plans to move Sixth Fleet Headquarters back to Japan. Cut off from support through Truk, and subjected to repeated air raids, Rabaul was impotent. Any kind of communication with Rabaul was difficult and its air defenses were soon abandoned, leaving one hundred thousand men, mountains of supplies, and a fortress of defense installations as useless to the Japanese as though they were on the other side of the moon. It was no longer possible to use Rabaul as an advance submarine base. Seventh Submarine Squadron

Headquarters was pulled backed from Rabaul to Truk. Only four of Rabaul's submarines survived the transfer, leaving behind them a total of twenty-five submarines that in two years of war had been sunk in the Coral Sea, and in the Solomons and off New Guinea. Even the stanchest samurai submariner was shaken.

Eniwetok Landing

The initial landing on Eniwetok was made on Engebi on 17 February, and that island was secured by the next day. The capture of the more heavily defended Eniwetok Island and Parry Island was not completed until the twenty-third, but a fighter strip was in operation on Engebi on the twenty-seventh. The United States was then in possession of a base from which an assault on the Marianas could be launched. Not a single Japanese ship or plane interfered with the occupation of Eniwetok. Mopping-up operations in the Marshalls continued.

South Pacific

In the South Pacific destroyer groups ran rampant, bombarding Kavieng and Rabaul and circumnavigating New Ireland. Green Island, east of New Ireland, was occupied to provide another post in the fence around Rabaul. On 19 February the last big air battle over Rabaul was fought. The next day all the remaining Japanese fighters departed for Truk. On 27 February an amphibious force under MacArthur landed at Manus, in the Admiralties, destined to become a great naval base for further advances. In these operations U.S. submarines played minor parts in reconnaissance and transportation. In the landing at Manus, the local Japanese defense forces were alerted by radio intelligence gained from U.S. submarine communication, and on this occasion submarine participation probably did more harm than good.

Brisbane Submarines

Brisbane submarines were busy helping out the Truk strike during early February, and after that their most lucrative hunting ground along the Truk–Palau route was deserted. Fife's submarines therefore had to reach out clear to the western end of New Guinea. There, near the end of February, they found fruitful employment. The Japanese were trying frantically to build up a new defense perimeter anchored in western New Guinea, toward which MacArthur was advancing. Japanese ship traffic in that area was doubly important and was well outside the reach of Fifth Air Force or the surface forces. This area was nearly as accessible from Fremantle as it was from Brisbane. *Hake* (Broach), *Balao* (Cole), *Gato* (Foley), and *Cod* (Dempsey) worked the stretch between Hollandia and Halmahera and sank eight ships there during February, severely handicapping the Japanese attempt to build up their defenses before the rising tide swept over them.

The guerrilla supply service, with *Narwhal* as its mainstay, was based on the east coast of Australia. *Narwhal* (Latta) made trips to the Philippines with the regularity of an interisland steamer, but many of her runs were far from routine. On 2 March she pulled into Butuan Bay on Mindanao with seventy tons of ammunition and stores for Colonel Fertig's guerrilla forces. She took aboard twenty-eight outbound passengers, two of them women, and sailed on schedule.

The next day, still in the Philippines making her appointed rounds, *Narwhal* encountered an escorted Japanese ship. Latta decided to attack and blew the bow off *Karatsu*, a river gunboat, with a single torpedo. The escort counterattacked with too much accuracy to please *Narwhal's* passengers or crew. Latta remarked that the second depth charge dropped was the closest experienced by *Narwhal* in the two hundred or more depth charges that had been aimed at her in her ten war patrols. It was right overhead and lacked only sufficient depth to have been lethal.

The next port of call was Tawi Tawi, a protected anchorage at the western end of the Sulu Archipelago, well known to all Asiatic submariners, for the Asiatic Fleet had based there in the months before the war when Hart had dispersed the fleet in anticipation of a surprise peacetime attack on Manila. The new breed of submariners were destined to learn more about this spot, and in preparation *Narwhal* was bringing supplies and equipment for a coastwatcher stationed there.

Unloading was a slow job. A submarine's hatches are not good cargo hatches, and there were only two bancas and *Narwhal's* rubber boats into which to discharge cargo. Eight new passengers had arrived on board, and only two more boat trips to the beach would complete the special mission when radar picked up a vessel 8500 yards dead ahead. Almost immediately it was sighted and identified as enemy. Latta cleared the deck, made ready on both main engines, and swung around to put Tawi Tawi astern. There was another vessel in company with the first. Destroyers! Range 5500 yards, and a third one on the radar screen at 12,000 yards coming down the coast. *Narwhal* got under way, with the cold engines smoking heavily under overload, and stood out to sea, salvaging as much of the deck cargo as possible down the engine room hatch. When the nearest enemy ship was at 3100 yards in the bright moonlight, it opened up on *Narwhal* with a broadside. *Narwhal* went down deep. When they counted noses the submarine had two extra passengers who had been unable to disembark in time when *Narwhal* hurriedly pulled out. The depth-charge attack was not too close, but Tawi Tawi was bound to be an unhealthy port for some time and *Narwhal* headed south with her extra passengers.

Japanese Tanker Sinkings

January had been a bad month for Japanese tankers. Any complacency the Japanese may have had about the effectiveness against tankers of the American submarine torpedo was rapidly dispelled. Improvement in the torpedo made it even more potent against tankers than it was against dry cargo vessels or combat ships. Torpedoes with impact exploders ruptured tanker sides and vented their decks, turning those vessels into roaring infernos and death traps for their crews. February was a disastrous month for Japanese tankers.

The Grand Surface Escort Force organized two special convoys to relieve the fuel situation in Japan. The first of these, consisting of *Ariake Maru, Goyo Maru,* and the new *kaibokan Sado,* was making good progress up through the East China Sea on 2 February when it encountered *Tambor* (Kefauver). *Tambor* made radar contact at nineteen thousand yards early in the morning, but being unable to obtain the position he wanted, Kefauver trailed the convoy all day and most of the night until the moon set the following morning. This gave him an opportunity to make a surface attack on both tankers. Kefauver observed hits on both ships before *Tambor* was forced down by the escort.

Sado gave *Tambor* a bad time in the counterattack, forcing the submarine to the bottom in 268 feet of water, and pounding her hull with many depth charges. It was eight o'clock that night before *Tambor* could ease cautiously up to the surface and creep away to repair damages. Both tankers sank, and the Japanese in their disappointment thought that *Sado* had accomplished nothing but to rescue the survivors.

Four big tankers were sunk by carrier planes in the Truk attack, including *Tonan Maru No. 3,* the ex-whale factory *Tinosa* had pelted with dud torpedoes in July. Fremantle submarines had a fruitful month in February, sinking a dozen *marus* in the South China Sea. Several of these were tankers. *Tonan Maru No. 2,* a sister ship to the one sunk at Truk, was torpedoed and badly damaged in the middle of the South China Sea on 9 February. In the meantime, the second emergency tanker convoy with five tankers and the *kaibokan Shimushu* had been organized and was headed north with oil that was desperately needed in Japan.

Jack (Dykers) was patrolling along the Singapore–Japan traffic route in the South China Sea early on the morning of 19 February when the bridge lookout picked up first one tanker and then another, until they counted five, in two columns, on a northerly course. The night was dark, and despite the famous Japanese night lookouts, Dykers elected to remain on the surface and trust the new smoky gray night camouflage Pearl Harbor had worked out after much experimentation. Although the Japanese accounts mention only one escort, Dykers thought he spotted three, one of them a destroyer. Evading the escorts, *Jack* got into attack position and fired four torpedoes at overlapping targets. One of the tankers was hit and erupted in brilliant flames that obscured observation of the effect of the other torpedoes. The escort charged about, firing wildly, and Dykers pulled out to start an end around run to gain position ahead again.

It was afternoon before the submarine regained contact with the convoy. Four tankers, without escort, came up over the horizon and *Jack* dove forty thousand yards ahead and came in on a submerged approach. The sun had set when she reached position to fire torpedoes. Dykers divided his stern tube salvo between two tankers. Both of them were hit, and both of them were incinerated in their own cargoes. The remaining two tankers ran off on diverging courses. One of them did have an escort, and Dykers picked the other. At four-engine speed he slowly overtook it. A salvo of three torpedoes missed and the tanker opened up with a 5-inch gun on the attacking submarine. Some of the shells were close, but Dykers stayed on the surface and worked into attack position again. *Jack's* next torpedo salvo scored three hits and the fourth tanker blew up and sank.

The fifth tanker and the escort escaped. Of the four destroyed there is some confusion about names. Tokyo in consternation received the report that all five had gone down. This attack convinced the Japanese Navy that it was futile to sail important convoys with a single escort. To provide more escorts, from the few available, it was necessary to increase the size of convoys. This they were loathe to do but it was a step they could no longer avoid, and convoys of as many as fifteen ships with three or more escorts began to appear.

Pearl Harbor Submarines

Although a good share of the effort of the Pearl Harbor submarines was expended in support of fleet operations, they did not slight their old operations areas off Japan and in the East China Sea, where some fourteen Japanese ships were sunk by submarines in February. *Pogy* (Metcalf), in a memorable melee with a Japanese convoy off northeast Formosa, torpedoed two cargo vessels and sank the destroyer *Minekaze* for good measure. She followed this by sinking one ship and damaging another on 20 February and sank another *maru* on the twenty-third.

In the Marshalls and the Carolines Pearl Harbor submarines' work was done, and not a ship was sunk by submarines east of Truk in February. To balance this they acquired a new area to patrol. After the S-boats were withdrawn from the northern area, Commander Submarines Pacific was directed to keep one submarine in the Kuriles "on the Polar Circuit." *Sand Lance* (Garrison) was the first submarine to make the patrol. She arrived off Paramushiro on 24 February, encountering hurricane weather en route. On station she found herself surrounded by pack ice, and blinded by snowstorms, which formed ice on the bridge and filmed the periscope. Despite these handicaps she sank *Kaiko Maru* on 28 February before heading south for warmer weather and new adventures.

Japanese Convoy System

The Japanese were faced with a two-pronged advance: Nimitz coming through the Central Pacific to the Marianas, and from there by any of several routes to the heart of the Japanese Empire; MacArthur along the New Guineas to the Philippines. The Japanese high command viewed MacArthur's advance as the greatest immediate threat to their oil supply from the East Indies, but both advances had to be met and they frantically set about bolstering Japanese defenses in Saipan and in western New Guinea.

The Grand Escort Force had plans to reduce losses from submarine attack by organizing large convoys with more escorts, all under direction of experienced naval officers. The convoys into the Marianas were designated Matsu (pine) convoy, and those to New Guinea were called Take (bamboo) convoy, symbolizing that they would be strong as pines and tough as bamboo, and would not yield to any difficulties. Tanker convoys were designated by kana and numerals.

Trout *and Matsu No. 1*

Convoy Matsu No. 1 formed in Manchuria and embarked the crack 29th Division in four transports with three of Japan's best destroyer escorts (*Kishinami, Okinami,* and *Asashimo*). They were en route to build up the defenses of Saipan and Guam when about three hundred miles southeast of Okinawa the convoy encountered a submarine on 29 February. The 11,409-ton *Aki Maru* was damaged and the 9245-ton *Sakito Maru* went down so fast that of the 4000 troops on board only 1700 were saved and all their equipment was lost.

The Japanese believed that the counterattack of the escorts succeeded in destroying the attacking submarine. In this they were undoubtedly correct. *Trout* (Clark) left Midway on 16 February for the East China Sea and was never heard from again. The attack reported by convoy Matsu No. 1 occurred in *Trout's* area, and although she did not live to report it there is no doubt that this brilliant attack was *Trout's* last one.

Loss of Grayback

Farther to the south another gallant submarine was lost at about the same time. *Grayback*, under the veteran commander J. A. Moore, left Midway on 3 February to patrol the area between Formosa and Luzon. On 25 February she made a radio report of several attacks. She had only two torpedoes left and was directed to return to Midway. This was the last report she ever made.

On 19 February she had sunk two *marus*, and on her last attack on 24 February she sank the 10,000-ton tanker *Nampo Maru* and damaged the 17,000-ton liner *Asama Maru*. The Japanese report that on 26 February in a position probably occupied by *Grayback* a carrier plane bombed a surfaced submarine. Surface ships followed up the attack with depth charges at a point where bubbles and oil continued to appear. This was probably the end of the tenth patrol of *Grayback*.

Saipan Carrier Strike

After the Truk strike it was decided to follow up with a carrier strike on Saipan. Photographic intelligence of Saipan was greatly needed, and the quickest way to get it was from a carrier attack. For this strike the submarines were disposed in a pattern similar to the Truk strike plan, and again the one-word warning signals were used. *Apogon, Searaven, Sunfish,* and *Skipjack* were stationed on the arc of a circle thirty miles from Saipan. *Tang* was out at sixty miles as safety man, and *Sunfish* had the additional duties of lifeguard. The carriers were sighted by Japanese search planes, but the task force successfully fought its way in, launched its attack, and retired without damage. Japanese ships, warned of the approaching carrier task force, cleared out of Saipan and ran into the waiting submarines.

Unyo, the escort carrier damaged by *Haddock* the month before, had taken refuge in Saipan, where she had been hungrily watched by patrolling submarines. It was hoped that she would be one of the ships flushed out by the carrier strike, but apparently she had sailed before the submarines were stationed. Early in the morning of 23 February *Sunfish* (Shelby) thought she had *Unyo* on her radar screen, in the dark and misty morning, but it must have been the transport *Shinyubari Maru* that went down with *Sunfish's* torpedoes. Farther out *Tang* (O'Kane), playing safety, sank five *marus* between the twenty-second and twenty-fifth of February. The carrier strike destroyed 120 Japanese planes and succeeded in completing its photographic reconnaissance. In addition they sank two freighters and a number of small craft.

New Plans

The Joint Chiefs of Staff on 12 March decided to bypass Truk and Kavieng. Guam, Tinian, and Saipan were assigned as the next objectives for Nimitz. There were a number of sound reasons for this decision, among which was that on Guam and Saipan, Army Air Force B-29 bombers could be based within range of Japan. In the meantime there was considerable cleaning up to do in the Marshalls and in the South Pacific.

Because of the reduced Japanese activity around Rabaul and Truk, the number of American submarines at Brisbane was reduced to six. Three of these were almost constantly engaged in the Philippine trade with coastwatchers and guerrillas. The other three were available for operations against Japanese traffic with western New Guinea and for special missions for MacArthur's forces. In March, Captain Fife was ordered to duty on the staff of Admiral King in Washington. He was relieved of the submarine command at Brisbane on 15 March by Captain J. M. Haines.

MacArthur was preparing to move farther up the New Guinea coast. *Dace* (Claggett) landed a reconnaissance party at Hollandia on 23 March, but the landing party was discovered by the Japanese, who killed four of them and forced the others to disperse into the jungles. Submarines took little direct part in the next New Guinea operations.

Sand Lance *and Matsu No. 2*

The second big convoy to reinforce Guam and Saipan, Matsu No. 2, left Tokyo on 12 March and on the next day was in hot water with *Sand Lance. Sand Lance* had come down from the cold Sea of Okhotsk, searching for a warmer area south of Tokyo. After her February success near Paramushiro she sank another ship in the southern Kuriles on 2 March. She had bent No. 1 periscope in an encounter with an ice flow and it was jammed in the fully elevated position where it was a serious embarrassment in any daylight approach. She had also lost one sound head and her pitometer log by grounding when she attempted to approach an anchored target. In an unsuccessful attack on what Garrison later believed to be a shallow-draft decoy target she had expended five torpedoes. On 13 March she was south of Tokyo with only six torpedoes remaining.

There was considerable air activity in her area that night and *Sand Lance* was forced down twice by planes. Shortly before three o'clock in the morning the soundman reported two ships pinging. When Garrison raised the periscope in the bright moonlight he found himself in the middle of convoy Matsu No. 2.

In view of the importance of this convoy, Combined Fleet had loaned the light cruiser *Tatsuta* to the Grand Escort Force to beef up the escort. What Garrison saw through the periscope in the moonlight was a light cruiser, a destroyer, five *marus*, and some other ships indistinct in the distance. He greatly regretted the five torpedoes wasted on the decoy *maru*, but made every one of his six remaining torpedoes count. The four torpedoes in the stern tubes he divided, two for the cruiser and the other two for a big *maru*. Both targets were hit. Then he swung ship to bring the bow tubes to bear and fired his last two torpedoes at another *maru*.

Sand Lance was completely surrounded by Japanese ships, but the escort could not find her, so Garrison watched the travail of the burning cruiser, saw one *maru* sink, and another spewing black smoke and down by the bow. The soundman reported two destroyers coming in fast and *Sand Lance* went very deep. For eighteen hours the angry escorts pelted the submarine with 105 depth charges, but they were all set for 250 feet and *Sand Lance* was too deep for them to do much damage.

The surviving escorts of Matsu No. 2 were very much impressed and depressed at the handy way in which Garrison moved into the middle of their heavily guarded convoy and picked off *Tatsuta* and *Kokuyo Maru*. They reasoned that American submarines were waging a deliberate campaign against escort vessels, a type in which the Japanese had a painful shortage. In this estimate they were a month ahead of King's staff in Washington who had reached the conclusion that after Japan's heavy losses in destroyers Koga would be severely handicapped by lack of light forces. King issued instructions to give Japanese destroyers high priority as targets. It was some time in April before these orders reached submarines on patrol, but in the meantime destroyers continued to be sunk because they were continually in harm's way.

Tautog *vs.* Shirakumo

Tautog (Sieglaff) picked off a destroyer in this manner. *Tautog* had followed *Sand Lance* into the Kuriles, and after sinking two *marus* was homeward-bound by way of vacant areas off Hokkaido. Early on the evening of 16 March she had radar contact with a convoy. *Tautog's* battery was nearly discharged, so Sieglaff trailed along with the convoy, tracking by radar while he jammed a few amperes into the battery. A light haze reduced the visibility, and radar reported they had contact with a seven-ship convoy, with at least one escort, in a formation so very loose that it was difficult to keep track of all the ships.

When *Tautog* was ready in all respects Sieglaff came in, using radar as a guide, until he could pick up the target visually as a black amorphous mass. Trusting to his submarine's slim and camouflaged silhouette, he closed on the surface to 1500 yards, with radar and the bridge target bearing transmitter checking each other all the way. Sieglaff fired four torpedoes and heard three of them hit, but an escort closed rapidly and forced him down before he could attack again.

No depth-charge attack developed, so *Tautog* came up to periscope depth to find the night too dark for the periscope to be useful. Easing up to forty feet the radar indicated all clear, so Sieglaff surfaced. Two hours later he again found the convoy and attacked, firing both bow and stern tubes. When the escort charged again, *Tautog* put it astern and remained on the surface making seventeen knots. As the range opened out the ships of the convoy disappeared from the radar screen. The escort depth-charged the ocean astern for *Tautog's* amusement, but its blind tantrum saved the convoy from another attack, for *Tautog* could not run around it to get at the convoy. Sieglaff did not know that one of his targets had been a destroyer. *Shirakumo* sank in the attack along with the 5460-ton *Nichiren Maru*.

Palau Carrier Attack

After Koga evacuated Truk he decided to base the Japanese fleet flagship *Musashi*, with a part of the Combined Fleet, at Palau. One carrier division with supporting forces moved to the Singapore area to continue flight training, and the remaining carriers were similarly engaged in the Inland Sea. In part, these dispositions were forced by the difficulty of supplying oil in Japan for fleet maneuvers, but the presence of powerful fleet units in Palau was a menace to MacArthur's forward movements. To guard MacArthur's flank and to destroy Japanese naval ships and air forces, a carrier strike on Palau was planned. This was a daring plan, with carriers operating 2500 miles from their nearest base, and their route flanked by moribund but still dangerous Japanese air and submarine bases. The attack force consisted of eleven carriers operating in three groups with the customary supporting vessels. Submarines were stationed for attack, for observation, and as lifeguards.

Tullibee (Brindupke), *Blackfish* (Sellars), *Bashaw* (Nichols), *Tang*

(O'Kane), and *Archerfish* (Kehl) were stationed on the arc of a sixty-mile circle with Toagel Mlungui Passage, the main channel into Palau from the west, as a center—covering the western escape routes. *Tunny* (Scott) was close in to Toagel Mlungui and *Gar* (Lautrup) was east of Peleliu on lifeguard. *Pompanito* (Summers) was off Yap, and *Harder* (Dealey) was off Woleai as lifeguards because Spruance planned to include strikes on both these islands.

On the twenty-fifth of March the carrier forces were sighted by Japanese search planes. Spruance pushed ahead as rapidly as possible and advanced the date of the strike one day, but the Japanese were able to clear their heavy naval vessels out before the strike. Carrier planes came in with mines to drop in the escape channels, bottling up the lagoon so that a total of thirty-six Japanese ships large and small, including five big tankers, were sunk. Most of the Japanese air strength was destroyed and Spruance retired without damage.

Loss of Tullibee

On the night of 26 March a group of fleeing Japanese ships came through *Tullibee's* area. The submarine made radar contact on a large convoy and Brindupke came in on the surface, unable to see the target in squally weather. The escort was alert and dropped a number of depth charges. Brindupke fired two torpedoes from the bow tubes on radar data.

Gunner's Mate Kuykendall was on the bridge. A minute or so after the torpedoes left the tubes there was a violent explosion and Kuykendall found himself swimming in the water. He heard voices in the dark but by morning he was the only survivor to be picked up by the Japanese. Kuykendall was sure *Tullibee* was sunk by a circular run of one of her own torpedoes. The loss of *Tullibee* was unexplained until after the war when Kuykendall was recovered from a Japanese prison camp. Through the hole she left in the submarine screen steamed many of the Japanese refugees.

Tunny *at Palau*

Gar rescued six aviators from the sea, but it was *Tunny* which had most of the action. *Tunny* arrived on station off Palau well ahead of time. On 22 March she had a brush with a convoy, and one *maru* was heavily damaged. The next night Scott picked up radar contact on a single ship at thirteen thousand yards making eighteen knots on widely zigzagging courses. About eleven o'clock Scott had the target in view and identified it as an I-class submarine. *Tunny* closed at full speed but was unable to reach torpedo range until the I-boat made a wide zig. *Tunny* quickly closed the range to fifteen hundred yards and fired four torpedoes. *Tunny* swung with right full rudder to avoid possible counterattack and dove.

As the hatch closed there was a terrific explosion. The flash lit up the interior of *Tunny's* conning tower. For an instant Scott was uncertain "what hit who," but *I-42* went down with horrible breaking-up noises. She was en route from Palau to Rabaul on a supply run, and her fate remained a mystery to the Japanese. When the breaking-up noises ceased, *Tunny* surfaced and got out of there, transmitting a message to *Gar*, into whose area she had penetrated in hot pursuit, and to Lockwood reporting the attack. For Scott this was the most nerve-wracking attack of *Tunny's* career. They spent the next day submerged to pull themselves together and Scott prescribed a shot of grog for all hands.

On the twenty-fifth three destroyers came through the area but Scott passed up an opportunity to attack because he thought the destroyers were a screen for larger game. About noontime on the twenty-ninth he also passed up a chance to attack a convoy of motley *marus*, still waiting for an important target. This was contrary to doctrine. Submarines were instructed to take a bird in hand, unless a bigger one was in sight in the bush. In this case Scott seems to have been guided by some instinct.

That evening he picked up sound contact and sighted the masts of two destroyers coming out the passage. Shortly afterward *Tunny* sighted what looked like a floating pile driver and heard a number of depth charges go off. Scott came in and about twenty minutes later identified the pile driver as a *Kongo*-class battleship, screened by destroyers and a light cruiser. Outwitting the screen, he closed to two thousand yards and fired six torpedoes.

The torpedoes passed right under a screening destroyer, who hoisted a great display of signals, and the battleship turned to comb the torpedo tracks. The destroyer charged back down the torpedo wakes at *Tunny*, who went deep. Scott heard two explosions on the way down. Like *Skate* who had nicked *Yamato*, *Tunny* was unaware that her target was one of the world's largest battleships. It was *Musashi*, Koga's flagship. Thanks to the alert escort's warning, *Tunny* only damaged her. One torpedo hit *Musashi*, killing seven men and blowing off part of her bow, but the damage did not disable the big ship and she was well clear by the time the carriers attacked the next day. Koga, who was not aboard his flagship, was not so fortunate. His plane, en route from Palau to the Philippines, encountered a storm on 31 March and crashed at sea. Admiral Soemu Toyoda succeeded to command of the Combined Fleet on 5 May.

After these adventures *Tunny* was lifeguard the next day and watched the carrier planes come in while she steamed in circles on the surface thirty miles from Toagel Mlungui. About noon the bridge watch saw nine torpedo bombers pass. Two of them peeled off and came in on a steep glide. One sheered off but the other continued his run and dropped a two-thousand-pound bomb a few yards from *Tunny's* forward engine room. The plane was clearly identified, with U.S. markings plainly visible, and *Tunny* was on assigned lifeguard station flying a set of No. 7 U.S. colors. Some trigger-happy pilot had been poorly briefed.

There was considerable damage in *Tunny* from the bomb. All the remaining torpedoes in the after torpedo room were damaged, and there were serious short circuits in the main motor controls. *Tunny* submerged to make emergency repairs and then surfaced to send out emergency identification signals and report the incident to Lockwood. She remained on lifeguard station, and early on the morning of 1 April offered her services to a Japanese aviator swimming in the sea thirty miles from Palau, with no life jacket and two hungry sharks in company. He refused to come aboard. Three hours later, however, *Tunny* picked up another Japanese pilot, who gratefully accepted her offer of lifeguard service. That evening listening on the radio they heard *Harder* getting a workout at her atoll to the eastward.

Harder *at Woleai*

After the two-day strike at Palau, the carriers hit Yap, but found no Japanese planes there. On 1 April all three carrier groups hit Woleai and found very few Japanese there to justify the effort. *Harder* (Dealey) was lifeguarding Woleai. A friendly plane contacted the submarine by voice radio and gave Dealey the position of a downed pilot drifting toward the reef. *Harder* started out full speed on all four engines passing down along the Woleai shore two miles off the beach, while carrier pilots put on a show "that made Hollywood colossals seem tame." A number of fighters left off bombing the Japanese installations to form a comfortable umbrella over *Harder* to protect her on her mission. The downed pilot had been swept onto the beach through the surf, and was finally located on the tip of one of Woleai's islands.

Harder flooded down to give herself an opportunity to lighten ship if she hit a coral head, and maneuvered to within fifteen hundred yards of the beach, with white surf breaking on the reef twenty yards off her bow. Japanese snipers opened up on the submarine and the fighter cover strafed the beach to keep them down. From a host of volunteers Dealey selected the three best qualified and launched them in a rubber boat trailing a long line to pull them back against the surf and wind. After many frustrations battling the wind and sea and badly cut by the coral, the rescuers picked up the aviator. The safety line carried away and a volunteer swimmer went in through the surf with another one. Finally, with the planes bombing and strafing the beach to hold off the Japanese, all hands were pulled safely aboard and *Harder* backed away from the reef.

Off Woleai *Harder* combined lifeguard with photographic missions. *Seal* was similarly employed off Ponape, while *Greenling* (Grant) made excellent and important photographs of the beaches of Saipan where shortly the Marines would be locked in desperate struggle.

Japanese Submarines in March

During March Japanese submarines accomplished very little except service of supply. Eight submarines were patrolling and reconnoitering in the Marshalls. One of these was *I-32*. She left Truk on 15 March to carry out a transportation mission to Wotje and then to destroy enemy shipping east of the Marshalls. A U.S. hunter-killer group had been sent out with the specific mission to sink Japanese submarines supplying Wotje. On the moonless night of 24 March U.S. and Japanese forces made contact. The destroyer escort *Manlove* closed a radar contact to three thousand yards when the pip disappeared. *Manlove* promptly picked up sonar contact and was joined by *PC-1135* in attack with depth charges and ahead-thrown weapons which produced deep, heavy explosions. In the morning the sea was covered with oil and *I-32* had disappeared.

When the Japanese discovered the task forces en route to Palau, Takagi decided to leave the Marshall Islands submarines on patrol. Six submarines at Truk were incapable of immediate operation, and only *I-38* sortied in pursuit of the carriers. Seven submarines in training or repair status in Japan were ordered out to take station off Palau. Considering the distances involved this was rather a futile gesture, and they were all recalled before they reached their assigned stations.

Strategic Effects

In February 119 *marus* were sunk, fifty-three of them by submarines, and the total loss of Japanese merchant shipping was a disastrous five hundred thousand tons. Submarines sank or severely damaged twenty-one tankers during the month and four additional tankers were destroyed by carrier planes at Truk. Alarmed at this threat to their oil supply, the Japanese made drastic changes in their shipbuilding program, converting many dry cargo ships to tankers while on the building ways. By this means they succeeded in more than matching tanker building with tanker losses, at a heavy cost to other shipping.

Additional tanker tonnage did not solve their problem. At Truk and later at Palau carrier planes destroyed fleet tankers in sufficient numbers to impose upon the Combined Fleet a strategic disposition depending largely upon oil shortages. Moreover, in the spring of 1944, there was a subtle change in the character of submarine warfare. Prior to that time submarines were most effective in a war of attrition. Shortage of ships kept Japan in a hand-to-mouth existence and severely restricted the scope of her strategy. By 1944 Japan's oil supply routes were crowded up against the coast of China, and in this reduced area U.S. submarine strength was sufficient to impose an effective blockade. Thus, although there was plenty of oil in Japanese hands in the East Indies, and more tanker tonnage than ever to move it, it was impossible to import sufficient oil into the home islands.

The Grand Escort Force did what they could. They increased the size of convoys, at the corresponding cost to shipping efficiency, and increased the number of escorts for each convoy. At first they were encouraged to think this was effective. *Maru* sinkings by submarines dropped from fifty-three in February to thirty-three in March and then to a satisfying twenty-two in April. But hope was short-lived. This temporary reduction in sinkings was due to the coincidence in a number of factors.

Lockwood's submarines were busy supporting fleet operations, and these operations imposed considerable variations in the number of submarines at sea at any one time. Brisbane submarines had been left behind in the back area by the war's forward movement, and it required time for a redistribution of submarine strength. Christie's submarines were having increased difficulty with prematures. *Bowfin,* whose record in sinking Japanese ships was outstanding, had eight prematures in one patrol. Nimitz sent a dispatch inquiring into the circumstances and Christie replied on 13 March that *Bowfin's* patrol was the end of a long effort to perfect the magnetic exploder and that no further experiment would be made by submarines on patrol. After that Southwest Pacific submarines also inactivated their magnetic exploders.

XIX

APRIL–MAY 1944

Many Japanese were convinced that the United States Navy had teams of submarines habitually operating together. They believed that they could count the cost when crack teams took the field. To a certain extent this was true, for the idea of the wolf pack persisted in the Central Pacific, and some of these packs were more successful than others. In the Southwest Pacific groups of submarines often cooperated in patrolling an area and sometimes cooperated in specific attacks, but such associations were informal and were directed by the senior submarine skipper rather than by an embarked separate wolf pack commander. Groups of submarines operating together under either system were transient associations, existing for a single patrol at the most. New operating conditions, however, dictated increased association on patrol.

By April 1944 progress of the war had brought the air and surface forces into control of six million square miles of sea that, when the war began, had been the exclusive operational territory of the submarines. Lockwood moved an advance submarine base into Majuro, in the Marshalls, and the submarine tender *Euryale* was sent to Seeadler Harbor in the Admiralties to ease the logistic problems of Pearl Harbor and Brisbane submarines. Darwin, in northwestern Australia, was already being used for the same purpose by Fremantle-based ships. Japanese surface traffic, and thus U.S. submarine operating areas, crowded into narrower limits and this necessitated changes in patrol procedures.

Rotating Patrols

To meet this changed situation Voge, Lockwood's operations officer, devised the rotating patrol. The first of these, off the Japanese home islands, was organized in April 1944. The areas near Japan were subdivided and grouped together and a group of submarines sent in, not necessarily simultaneously, to occupy the whole territory in accordance with a simple system of rotation, in which each submarine progressed from area to area around the circuit, changing areas every four or five days. This gave each submarine equal opportunity in the hot, close-in positions, and meanwhile covered the whole wide spectrum of converging traffic lanes. Area groups were laid out geographically to facilitate movement without confusion, and safety lanes were provided through which submarines could proceed within the territory without danger of attack from a friendly submarine in an adjacent area.

Zone Classification

To provide for close cooperation between submarines and surface ships and air forces, an oceanwide system of zone classification was established which, with little change, was later extended to the Southwest Pacific and remained standard throughout the war. Submarine havens were reserved for submarine non-combat operations to provide safety lanes for submarine movement and areas for submarine training. In these zones submarines were not to be attacked unless their enemy character was positively identified. Submarine patrol zones were reserved for submarine combat operation into which friendly surface forces would not enter without prior warning. Air surface zones were reserved for air and surface forces into which submarines would not move without previous arrangements. In joint zones under careful restrictions, air, surface, and submarine forces operated simultaneously. Blind bombing zones were added when the system was extended to the Southwest Pacific, and from these zones submarines were excluded in order to permit air attack day or night on any target that moved without necessity for prior identification.

Hit Parade

The rotating patrol off the main Japanese islands was given the code name "Hit Parade," and the submarine schedules in this plan were designated by the names of musical instruments in accordance with a system devised by the imaginative Voge. In April seven submarines were playing in Hit Parade, and the seven Japanese ships sunk in this area in April were evenly distributed among the seven players. Six of these ships sunk were *marus*, but *Pogy* (Metcalf) on the night of 29 April caught the Japanese submarine *I-183* on the surface as it came out Bungo Suido headed south for Truk. The Japanese knew only that *I-183* never reached her destination. A little farther south, in Nansei Shoto, four submarines were operating in old-style independent patrols. *Halibut* (Galantin) was the most successful in this group, sinking two *marus* and the small mine-layer *Kamone*.

Rotating patrols were organized for the Bonin Islands and for the Marianas, later during April. The Japanese Matsu convoys carrying troops and supplies to Saipan and Guam had to run the gantlet of the rotating patrol system. In early April, before the rotating patrol was organized in the Marianas, *Seahorse* (Cutter) was sent on an independent patrol off Saipan. This was her fourth patrol.

Seahorse *in the Marianas*

Japanese anti-submarine activity was intense off Saipan, the southern terminus of their Matsu convoys. Several times *Seahorse* was thwarted by combined air and surface patrols, or untimely movements of convoys, despite her careful watch on the harbor. A convoy of several *marus* entered Tanapag Harbor on 5 April, giving *Seahorse* the slip by using a channel Cutter did not know about. This must have been Matsu No. 3 arriving.

Three days later Cutter torpedoed two *marus* from another convoy. This was Matsu No. 4, which had already encountered *Pollock* up north and lost one transport. On the ninth a big convoy of fifteen or twenty *marus*, with four destroyers and seven other escorts arrived—the largest convoy Cutter had ever seen. *Seahorse* sank one ship out of the assembly. On the twentieth Cutter worked in close to the harbor entrance and arrived just in time to meet an RO-class Japanese submarine coming out. He fired two torpedoes and heard one hit, but *Seahorse* lost depth control when the torpedoes were fired and Cutter could not see the results of his attack. *RO-45* must have been in the Marianas about this time en route from Kure to Truk, and *Seahorse* has generally been credited with its destruction in this attack. Japanese records, however, show that *RO-45* arrived at Truk and was sunk some time later in the month.

Cutter could see many ships, including a light cruiser, inside Tanapag Harbor, but when *Seahorse* had to withdraw to take up assigned station as lifeguard for a strike of Eniwetok planes on Saipan, a convoy slipped out. When next he had an opportunity to view the harbor it was nearly empty. Probably Matsu No. 5 had sailed for Japan, but it did not get clean away, for Matsu No. 5 encountered *Trigger* (Harlfinger) farther north about midnight of 26 April. *Trigger* sank the 11,739-ton *Miike Maru* and heavily damaged another ship.

On the twenty-seventh *Seahorse* picked off a 5000-ton cargo ship and then hurried south to take lifeguard station off Satawan Island, southeast of Truk, for a carrier strike and cruiser bombardment of that island. On the surface there, on station, Cutter exchanged recognition signals with the cruiser *Louisville,* which solicitously inquired if there was anything Cutter needed. *Seahorse* was out of coffee, nearly as necessary as lubricating oil for the smooth running of a submarine, and when the submarine went alongside the cruiser for this necessity, *Louisville* generously added ice cream and fresh bread. Times had changed in the western Carolines for submarines.

Harder *vs.* Ikazuchi

Harder (Dealey) was also still in the western Carolines, after her rescue of the aviators at Woleai. On 13 April orders were issued to submarines to give priority to Japanese destroyers as targets. This order did not have time to reach *Harder* before she complied. A Japanese patrol plane had spotted *Harder* that day and forced her to dive. The plane must have summoned help, for that afternoon the masts of a destroyer were sighted about at the position where the submarine submerged. The Japanese destroyer *Ikazuchi* was definitely on a submarine hunt and Dealey headed in to oblige, at slow speed to conserve the battery, assured that the destroyer would wait for him. At thirty-two hundred yards *Ikazuchi* apparently had sonar contact and charged. She was the first Japanese destroyer, but not the last, to underestimate Sam Dealey and *Harder.* Dealey let the range get down to nine hundred yards and then "expended four torpedoes and one Jap destroyer." *Ikazuchi* went down in four minutes after being hit, its depth charges exploding among the survivors as she went down.

Scamp's *Bomb Damage*

Not all encounters with Japanese anti-submarine forces were victories for the submarines. On the morning of 7 April *Scamp* (Hollingsworth) was patrolling south of Mindanao when she encountered an enemy task force of cruisers and destroyers with an aircraft screen. The sea was glassy calm, and when *Scamp* attempted to approach she was detected and attacked ineffectively with depth charges. When she came up to periscope depth after this attack the task force had disappeared and Hollingsworth surfaced to send out a contact report. For over an hour the submarine's radiomen were unable to establish communication, and while they were trying a float plane came in out of the sun and attacked. *Scamp* dove, but not fast enough. On the way down, at forty feet, the bomb went off.

Scamp was badly hurt. She lost all power, and the hydraulic system went out with the vents still open. The rudder jammed and there was a bad fire in the electric insulation in the maneuvering room, with toxic smoke that made everyone back there deathly sick. The submarine went down to 330 feet out of control. There the diving officer caught her and she started back up for the equally dangerous surface. The plane had only one bomb or it was certain of a kill, for no more bombs came, although *Scamp* must have been trailing oil, commotion, and air bubbles. After a time the electricians in the poisonous atmosphere of the maneuvering room made repairs and restored power. The diving officer performed miracles and regained control and *Scamp* evaded at 150 feet when the surface forces came up hunting for her with depth charges. Through all this travail her crew reacted magnificently, doing everything that had to be done quickly and accurately, quietly and without confusion—although everyone on board well knew that each moment might be their last. A multitude of individual acts of heroism saved the ship. The radio was knocked out but next day they succeeded in getting a message off to Haines, who directed *Dace* to rendezvous and escort *Scamp* into Seeadler Harbor in the Admiralties, the nearest port of safety.

Loss of Gudgeon

Gudgeon (Bonin) left Pearl Harbor on 4 April to patrol the northern Marianas and was never heard from again. On 11 May Comsubpac sent her radio orders to leave her area for a lifeguard assignment. An acknowledgment of this order was required and when none was received another submarine was sent in her place. This was disquieting but not too ominous. *Gudgeon's* radio transmitter may have broken down or some disturbance in the ionosphere may have blacked out radio traffic in her area, but back in Pearl Harbor her radio frequencies were then guarded with particular care.

Each morning when Lockwood came into the Operations Room, before going up on the hill to Cincpac's Conference, he glanced first at the magnetic wall chart to see *Gudgeon's* marker in her assigned area, and then thumbed through the incoming dispatches—although he knew very well that he would have been informed instantly if any news had been received from her. Both he and Voge knew what was foremost in each other's mind but neither would admit anxiety for the silent submarine. Then abruptly on 14 May Lockwood directed Voge to order *Gudgeon* to leave her area and return to Midway without waiting the few more days before the normal termination of her patrol. If *Gudgeon* were in any kind of trouble, he reasoned, he would relieve Bonin of the responsibility for premature termination of the patrol.

The Operations Room watch then advanced *Gudgeon's* marker each morning, by an average day's run along her assigned track, until on 23 May it stood at the five-hundred-mile circle from Midway. A returning submarine would report its arrival there to prevent being mistaken for a Japanese submarine by Midway search planes. When no such report came in from *Gudgeon,* Midway was requested to conduct special searches along her route, and to be prepared to send her help if she were discovered limping home in trouble. As days went by, however, it was apparent she was not coming back. On 7 June she was reported overdue and presumed lost. The next morning, when Voge was alone in the Operations Room, he quietly removed her marker from the chart.

Japanese Submarine Losses

Japanese submarines had a hard month again in April. *I-169* dove to escape an air raid at Truk on 4 April and suffered some sort of casualty that prevented her from ever surfacing again. *I-2* left Rabaul the same day for Truk and was never heard from again. She was sunk by U.S. destroyer *Saufley* in a depth-charge attack near the Admiralties on 7 April. *Pogy* sank *I-183,* as has been recounted. *I-180* was next to go. She left Ominato in late March for the Aleutians, and although she was not heard from again by the Japanese it was not until the night of 25–26 April that the destroyer escort *Gilmore* sank her with hedgehogs and depth charges off Kodiak, Alaska. Thereafter there was only one Japanese submarine (*I-177*) left in the whole northern area, and when her patrol was completed (in July) no more Japanese submarines were assigned to the Aleutians or the Kuriles. *I-174* was sunk on 29 April not far south of Truk by U.S. destroyers *MacDonough* and *Stephen Potter.* *RO-45* left Truk late in April to operate against U.S. carriers. She took her place on the patrol line and was never heard from again.

Bluegill *vs.* Yubari

Although U.S. submarines in April sank only twenty-two *marus,* they sank eight Japanese combat ships. In addition to the sinkings already recounted, *Redfin* (Austin) sank the Japanese destroyer *Akigumo* off Zamboanga. *Flasher* (Whitaker) sank the ex-French gunboat *Tahure.* The minefield laid by *Tautog* off Borneo claimed the destroyer *Amagiri.* The largest combat ship sunk by a submarine in April was the 3000-ton cruiser *Yubari.*

In their haste to fortify the western Carolines, the Japanese pressed *Yubari* into service as a transport. With nine hundred troops on board, and screened by the destroyer *Samidare*, she headed for Sonsorol Island, an isolated atoll between Palau and the Philippines. *Bluegill* was on her first patrol under command of Commander E. L. Barr, also making his first patrol as commanding officer. They were on a reconnaissance of Sonsorol. On 27 April Barr sighted a cruiser and a destroyer, but the cruiser disappeared behind the island. *Bluegill* came in to attack the destroyer. Suddenly *Yubari* reappeared from behind the island, coming down range full speed. Barr quickly changed the setup and fired six torpedoes at the cruiser. He saw the first one hit and heard other explosions as he went deep to avoid *Samidare's* vengeance. *Yubari*, which had often been reported sunk before, was really sunk this time.

Hollandia Landings

On 22 April MacArthur landed at Hollandia and Aitape in a complete surprise to the Japanese. These landings were preceded by intensive land-based and carrier plane air bombardment, and naval gunfire, and came off with practically no casualties. The fast carrier task forces of the Pacific Fleet provided protection against interference from the Japanese fleet, as well as air bombardment and close air support of the landings. On the return journey to Majuro the carriers worked over Truk while the cruisers bombarded Satawan and the battleships bombarded Ponape. Since the attack of 18 February the Japanese had moved about a hundred planes into Truk. These planes were destroyed, shore installations were heavily damaged, and patrol vessels and small craft were sunk. This was really the end of Truk as a naval base. Japanese submarines continued to operate from Truk for a time, but its usefulness as a great naval base had ended. After this raid, until the end of the war, only an occasional submarine succeeded in reaching there again.

Tang *at Truk*

For the carrier strike on Truk, *Tang* (O'Kane) was pulled off patrol at Palau and directed to take lifeguard station off Truk. *Tang* had been assigned as lifeguard on other strikes without being used, and O'Kane resented leaving his patrol station. *Tang* and O'Kane had already established a reputation of being a hot combination. As it turned out they had plenty of action on this lifeguard assignment.

Tang was on the surface at sunrise on the twenty-ninth shortly after arriving on station south of Truk, providing rapt spectators for a large group of carrier planes coming in to blast Truk again. About ten o'clock in the morning O'Kane had his first lifeguard call. A life raft with downed aviators was afloat a few miles from a reef island, upon which was a known Japanese gun emplacement. Carrier planes provided air cover to bomb and strafe the gun emplacement while *Tang* dashed in, picked up three aviators, and retired without interference. That evening there was a call to the eastward, requiring a long surface run around Kuop Atoll. The planes had all been recalled and O'Kane felt naked without air cover. He surfaced and opened up on the Japanese gun emplacement with his 4-inch gun while he ran for it. When the range was around nine thousand yards the Japanese came out of their holes and returned the fire, but *Tang* fortunately escaped without damage.

The next morning they encountered a Japanese submarine on the surface, and O'Kane made a submerged approach to fire torpedoes. Just as *Tang* was about at firing range a group of carrier planes prematurely flushed the quarry. The Japanese submarine dove, leaving O'Kane holding the bag. Two hours later he had to surface to rescue a downed aviator, with the nervous feeling that the Japanese submarine might be making an approach with *Tang's* number on one of her torpedoes. Fighter cover flew anti-submarine screen for *Tang*. It was a busy day.

Task Force 58 lost twenty-six planes in combat during the two-day strike. Nineteen airmen were lost with them, but twenty-eight others were rescued by air-sea rescue teams. On call, the task force flew air cover for *Tang* to permit her to operate within range of Japanese guns. Battleship float planes spotted life rafts and towed them clear of danger until *Tang* could reach them. Of the twenty-eight airmen rescued *Tang* had twenty-two on board by nightfall of the second day. Through this experience procedures were worked out for cooperation between planes and submarines in this kind of work and became standard practice for the rest of the war. It became traditional that if an aviator survived a crash at sea, a submarine would come through both Hell and shallow water, if necessary, to reach him.

Convoy Bamboo No. 1

All this activity hastened Japanese efforts to reinforce western New Guinea and head off MacArthur. Convoy Bamboo No. 1 left Shanghai on 17 April with nine Army transports carrying two Japanese divisions en route to western New Guinea by way of Manila. Rear Admiral Kajioka was in command of both convoy and escorts. He had commanded the Japanese forces that captured Wake, and the Port Moresby invasion force at the Battle of the Coral Sea. Escort vessels were very scarce by this time and Kajioka's flagship was the old coal-burning mine-layer *Shirataka,* whose smoke cloud was a beacon for submarines far and near. Nevertheless, the convoy proceeded without undue difficulty until it ran into *Jack* just north of Luzon.

Jack (Dykers) was on patrol on the surface northwest of Luzon, at dawn on 25 April, when the bridge watch sighted a periscope. *Jack* hurriedly put it astern and evaded at flank speed. A few minutes later a plane came in. *Jack* dove, and the plane's light bomb went off wide of its target. There was no doubt that *Jack's* position had been spotted, and Dykers felt sure that any Japanese convoys would now be routed around him. Much to his surprise, however, at noon he sighted smoke and then the masts of many ships. The Japanese were certainly well aware of the importance of Convoy Bamboo No. 1, and fully cognizant of the submarine danger, but their communications must have been poor, their organization bad, or Kajioka had fatalistically decided to stick to his plan, for he brought his convoy right to *Jack.*

Jack trailed the slow-speed convoy, a procedure greatly facilitated by the volume of black smoke emitted by *Shirataka.* An hour before sunrise Dykers surfaced and began an end around run, but a plane came by and forced him down until after dark. Then *Jack* surfaced and ran along with the convoy at an easy pace, holding off until the moon set, to give the submarine an opportunity to make an undetected surface approach. The escorts on the starboard bow were numerous and alert, charging up at times to interpose between the submarine and the convoy and behaving in general as though they had radar to guide them. *Jack* played this game of cat and mouse for some time and then speeded up and ran around the head of the nine-ship convoy to try out the escorts on the other side.

The port side escorts were active too, and Dykers decided that the best solution was to fire a spread of slow-speed long-range torpedoes under the escorts at the massed overlapping ships of the convoy. He made three separate attacks, and fired nineteen torpedoes. Several of them seemed to hit and Dykers felt sure of sinking two or three ships. Only *Yoshida Maru No. 1* went down. She was a 5425-ton freighter. The Japanese had packed her full of troops and conditions on board were appalling. When *Jack's* torpedoes hit, *Yoshida Maru* went to the bottom and with the *maru* went an entire Japanese Army regiment, regimental commander, sacred regimental colors and all.

Bambo No. 1 rested at Manila for two days after this disaster, trying to do something to improve conditions aboard the transports. South from Manila the Combined Fleet took charge of the convoy, relieving the Grand Escort Force of responsibility. Three good fleet destroyers were assigned to escort, together with a minesweeper and two submarine chasers. Kajioka was still in command, with *Shirataka* as his flagship. Everything went well after leaving Manila until they neared the northern end of the Celebes Sea on 6 May. Then suddenly the sea seemed full of torpedoes coming at the convoy from all directions. Three transports were hit in rapid succession.

This was the work of *Gurnard* (Andrews), which came out of Pearl Harbor to patrol the Celebes Sea and then proceed to Fremantle. She sighted smoke on the horizon shortly after eight o'clock that morning, and to avoid possible detection by aircraft, commenced a long, slow, submerged approach. Checking back afterward with the approach plot, it turned out that *Gurnard* had made sight contact on the smoke at nineteen miles. The slow submerged speed of the submarine and a slow convoy made the approach a very long one. It was noon before Andrews got a good look at Bamboo No. 1, eight transports in three columns, staggering slowly along on a constant helm zigzag plan, herded by escorts cavorting along the edges, like sheep dogs bunching up the flock.

By one o'clock Andrews had worked *Gurnard* into the position he wanted, just astern of the bow destroyer escort, which would then have to reverse course to counterattack; and a longer way ahead of the submarine chaser on the convoy's quarter. Andrews divided his fire between two big ships in the nearest column, three torpedoes at each. He watched one hit his first selected target, and thought he heard another which must have missed the target astern, and then ran through the near column to blast a ship in the column beyond. It had indeed. The submarine's second target was hit by his second group of torpedoes too, but *Gurnard* was then too busy to watch.

The nearest escort came down at *Gurnard* with a brave display of bunting flying from the signal halyards, a white rolling bone in her teeth, and a wisp of brown smoke flat out off the lip of her stack like the picture on a magazine cover. Andrews had to forego another attack and go deep for safety. A couple of hours later he came up and tried to take periscope pictures of the three sinking ships, but a submarine chaser drove him off. That night *Gurnard* searched the area, running through a sea littered with debris, and administered the *coup de grâce* to one cripple still afloat.

The Japanese thought there had been at least three submarines in this attack; one of the U. S. Navy's crack teams, they thought. When they saw a submarine boldly raise its periscope and cruise leisurely around the striken convoy they thought that their arrogant enemy was demonstrating contempt for the fleet destroyers' ineffective anti-submarine efforts. It was *Gurnard* alone and she respected but was not intimidated by the escorts.

Because it was broad daylight, and profiting from their previous experiences, the Japanese were more successful in their rescue operation than they had been the night *Jack* worked them over. Many of the troops in the three sunken transports were saved and even some of the field guns, lashed to rafts, were later salvaged. The Commander of the Japanese Second Area Army asked to have the convoy continued to its original destination, but Tojo, in Tokyo, had had enough. The bight of the Pacific, between the Philippines and New Guinea, was swarming with submarines and the U. S. Army Fifth Air Force was eager for another battle like Bismarck Sea. Japan could no longer expend so many transports.

The surviving troops were landed at Halmahera to be ferried down to northern New Guinea in landing barges by roundabout routes. Most of them never got there until long after the issue was decided. Two submarines had effectively blocked two Japanese divisions from the campaign for northern New Guinea. Many of the Allied soldiers who lived through that campaign, without ever seeing or hearing of a submarine, survived it because of the work of *Jack* and *Gurnard*.

While *Gurnard* was engaged with Bamboo No. 1, *Crevalle* (Walker), not far away off Borneo, sank Japan's biggest commercial tanker, the 17,000-ton *Nisshin Maru*. The Japanese had routed a tanker convoy through Palawan Channel, under very light escort, secure in the belief that those seas were too dangerous for American submarines.

A great stretch of the South China Sea to the westward of Palawan Channel is foul with shoals and coral heads, and on the charts marked "unsurveyed" and "dangerous ground." During peacetime the Japanese had secretly surveyed this area and charted its safe channels. They used their secret knowledge to protect their oil convoys from Borneo. As a further protection of the route they mined Balabac Strait. This was one minefield U. S. Naval Intelligence failed to locate through captured documents. It claimed a U.S. submarine a few months later, and the navigational hazards of Palawan Channel eventually destroyed another. Despite these dangers *Crevalle* was there to send the big tanker to the bottom. She had been there for some time, in fact. Over a week before, she had torpedoed a small net tender not ten miles from the spot she sank *Nisshin Maru* on 6 May, but somehow the word of her first success seems never to have reached the Japanese routing officers.

Much of the action in the Southwest Pacific was in the triangle between Mindanao, Halmahera, and Palau, where Japan continued to send ships, despite the reluctance to trust Bamboo No. 1 out into this area. *Aspro, Bluefish, Pargo,* and *Ray* sank five *marus* there during the month of May. Submarines in the vicinity of Mindanao sighted several Japanese task forces off Davao, and in the Sulu Sea, and it was evident that Japan was building up to some kind of a naval concentration.

Tawi Tawi

On 3 May Admiral Toyoda, the new Commander of the Japanese Combined Fleet, issued his general orders for the A-Go operation. Toyoda's plan was to lure the U.S. fleet into the area between Palau and New Guinea, where the Japanese shore-based air strength from Yap, Woleai, Palau, and Biak could assist the fleet to win the decisive battle upon which the Japanese Navy still pinned it hopes. The action would have to be fought no farther eastward than Palau, because the Japanese Navy no longer possessed sufficient fleet tanker capacity to extend their operations farther from their bases.

In preparation for the A-Go operation a concentration of the Japanese fleet was ordered to Tawi Tawi, the westernmost island of the Sulu Archipelago, already familiar as an operating area to many U.S. submarines. Rear Admiral Jisaburu Ozawa, who was to command the Japanese fleet, departed Singapore on 11 May for Tawi Tawi with Carrier Division One. Two other carrier divisions, battleships, heavy cruisers, thirty destroyers, and other vessels joined him there later in the month.

Some inkling of this operation had reached Admiral Kinkaid of the U. S. Seventh Fleet, through documents captured at Hollandia, and he directed Christie to have his submarines reconnoiter Tawi Tawi. *Bonefish* (Hogan) arrived in the area almost simultaneously with Ozawa's Carrier Division One. Coming down through Sibutu Passage on 14 May Hogan sighted a tanker convoy and sank *Inazuma,* one of its escorting destroyers. The next day Hogan sighted a Japanese carrier and three battleships. *Bonefish* was unable to reach attacking position, but Hogan's contact report confirmed the Japanese concentration at Tawi Tawi. *Ray* (Harral) off Davao sighted a task force of five large ships on 14 May.

The coastwatcher support effort paid off handsomely on 25 May when a Filipino coastwatcher reported the presence of six carriers, ten battleships and heavy cruisers, and many other Japanese ships at Tawi Tawi anchorage. Christie ordered additional submarines into the area. *Puffer* (Selby), which relieved *Bonefish* on 22 May, fired a salvo of torpedoes at the carrier *Chitose.* Two hits were heard and claimed, but *Chitose* suffered no damage. The destroyer *Yukikaze* was damaged at Tawi Tawi on that date and she may have stopped the *Puffer* torpedo intended for *Chitose. Gurnard,* on the twenty-fourth, got into the act by sinking one of the fleet tankers, the 10,000-ton *Tatekawa Maru.* From the very moment he arrived there Ozawa found his fleet at Tawi Tawi bedeviled and hazarded by aggressive submarines.

Raton *and* Lapon

Southwest Pacific submarines were also operating in the South China Sea. *Raton* (Davis) and *Lapon* (Stone) were patrolling adjacent areas. On 24 May *Raton* attacked a convoy and damaged one *kaibokan* (*Matsuwa*) and sank another (*Iki*). Three hundred miles to the northward on this same day *Lapon* sank two large cargo ships. A couple of days later Christie warned *Lapon* that a Japanese submarine had been sighted in her area, and Stone began a cautious submerged patrol in ambush for the enemy. *Raton,* after her action with the *kaibokans,* headed north and the stage was set for tragedy.

On the morning of 27 May, Stone sighted what he took to be a Japanese submarine on the surface, headed northeast. From the silhouette he identified it as a Japanese I-class submarine and turned away for a stern tube shot. At a range of fourteen hundred yards he fired two torpedoes, and then checked fire, for as the angle on the bow increased he was no longer certain of the identification of his target. The target submarine changed course to the west shortly after *Lapon* fired, and Stone went deep, hearing two "end of run" explosions as *Lapon* went down.

Raton, at that time, was headed northeast on the surface. She noted interference on her SJ radar, but that soon ceased. Shortly after six o'clock there were two heavy underwater explosions nearby on the port side. *Raton* turned hard right and got out of there. There can be no doubt that these were *Lapon's* torpedoes which fortunately missed but exploded close enough to shake up *Raton* severely. Although there were numerous occasions when friendly submarines tracked each other, except on this occasion they recognized each other in time. This was the only time during the war when a U.S. submarine actually fired torpedoes at a friendly submarine.

Loss of Herring

Far to the north the Kurile Islands had their usual share of submarine action in May. *Tautog, Barb,* and *Herring* were in the area. *Tautog* (Baskett) was first in the area. She sank two ships there early in May, after which she moved south to Honshu where she sank two more. *Barb* (Fluckey) followed *Tautog* into the Kuriles and also sank two ships. *Herring* (Zabriskie) was last of the three to reach the area. Nothing was directly heard from *Herring* after she left Midway.

Barb picked up a prisoner from a ship she sank on 31 May, who revealed that a submarine had torpedoed and sank the *kaibokan Ishigaki* the day before. This could only have been the work of *Herring*. From postwar information it is possible to piece together more of *Herring's* last few days. She sank a *maru* on 31 May and then on 1 June sighted two more Japanese cargo vessels at anchor off Matsuwa To. Zabriskie came in and sank both these ships with torpedoes, but Matsuwa To's shore battery had engaged a submarine before, when *Nautilus* bombarded them. This time they were alert and opened up so accurately that they scored two direct hits in *Herring's* conning tower. Lockwood knew only that *Herring* did not answer when he sent a message to her requiring acknowledgment. Careful watch was kept for her, and "damaged submarine" proceedings were carried out in early July at Midway, when she was due to return, but there can be no reasonable doubt that *Herring*, on 1 June, was the only U.S. submarine to be sunk by Japanese shore battery.

Wolf Pack in Luzon Strait

Pickings were slim in the home waters of Japan in May. *Pogy* sank a couple of *marus* and *Pollack* sank the destroyer *Asanagi* escorting a convoy northwest of Chichi Jima. Japanese traffic in the East China Sea enjoyed a short holiday. Captured documents picked up in the Marshalls revealed the extent of the mine barrier planned by Oikawa. A vast minefield from Formosa to Kyushu along the Nansei Shoto chain was designed to keep U.S. submarines out of the East China Sea. For a time it was effective, until intelligence could determine the extent to which the plans had been carried out, and locate gates in the barrier. The first of Oikawa's barrier mines were laid in February 1944, and it was sheer good fortune that they were located by intelligence effort rather than the hard way, by submarines running into them. For a while the convoy route along the China coast was vulnerable only between the Philippines and Formosa, and into this area Lockwood sent a wolf pack consisting of *Bang* (Gallaher), *Parche* (Ramage), and *Tinosa* (Weiss), under command of Captain G. E. Peterson.

Lockwood had continued to experiment with coordinated attack groups in target practices, and the contraction of the submarine operating areas afforded a good opportunity to try out some of the new ideas that had been developed. Peterson's group arrived in Luzon Strait on 16 April but nothing exciting happened until the twenty-ninth. *Bang* then made contact with a southbound convoy of twelve to fifteen ships with numerous escorts. Gallaher tracked the convoy as the new coordinated attack doctrine required, and tried to coach his two teammates into position so that there would be one submarine on each flank of the convoy and one trailing when the first attack was made. About ten o'clock at night *Bang* was in position for the first attack when the convoy made a series of wide zigzags that left everyone but *Bang* far astern. *Bang* was the only one to make an attack. She sank one freighter, but an active escort drove her deep to escape a depth-charging.

When Gallaher came back to periscope depth an hour later the convoy was out of sight. *Bang* surfaced and soon regained radar contact and made another attack on a heavily loaded freighter, but missed because of a fire control error. About dawn she was in position again, and this time got two hits on a freighter which sank in a cloud of smoke. All three submarines pursued the convoy next day, as it headed for Lingayen Gulf. Japanese destroyers came down from Takao and the reinforced escort was able to hold the submarines outside attack range during daylight. The convoy made it into Lingayen without further loss.

On 3 May *Tinosa* made contact with a northbound convoy. The three submarines trailed until nightfall and then attacked in succession. In a wild series of night attacks they sank five Japanese ships, *Bang* and *Tinosa* each accounting for one and *Parche* sinking three. This was a Japanese convoy carrying iron ore from Hainan to Takao. There were six freighters in the convoy, with four escorts (a *kaibokan* and three smaller ships). *Bang* thought she sank a destroyer in the night melee but according to Japanese accounts none of the escorts was damaged. The loss of five ships out of a six-ship convoy was a severe blow for the Grand Surface Escort Force. They felt that the escort was poorly trained and uncoordinated. Throughout the night of battle the escorts could hear three submarines talking jubilantly with each other by radiotelephone but the escort was impotent to do anything about it.

Submarines in the Marianas

With seven ships sunk by three submarines in a short patrol Peterson's wolf pack was much more successful than the previous coordinated attack groups in the Central Pacific. In comparison with the best individual ship patrols, however, the performance was not so spectacular. *Sand Lance* (Garrison) during the same month sank five ships in a lone submarine patrol in the southern Marianas, while *Silversides* (Coye) in the northern Marianas sank six *marus*. Moreover, the next coordinated attack group in the Marianas owed much to Coye, who steered them into a mess of Japanese convoys in the first few days of their patrol.

This wolf pack consisted of *Shark II* (Blakely), *Pintado* (Clarey), and *Pilotfish* (Close) under the command of Captain L. W. Blair. The imaginative Voge, for his use in dispatches to a group, initiated a system of giving each coordinate attack group a short title compounded with the wolf pack commander's name. This group he christened "Blair's Blasters." They arrived in the northern Marianas on 29 May while *Silversides*, at the whirlwind end of her busy patrol, was pursuing a Japanese convoy. Repeated carrier strikes in the Marianas had convinced the Japanese that Nimitz's next big amphibious operation would be in this area of the Pacific. Frantically they tried to reinforce Saipan and Guam to resist the expected blow, while Lockwood's submarines preyed on their desperation. On the night of 29 May *Silversides* fired the last of her torpedoes, but Coye continued to trail the northbound convoy he was pursuing, sending out contact reports that brought Blair's Blasters into action to wind up the submarine campaign against the reinforcement of the Marianas.

On the evening of 31 May *Shark* made contact on the convoy that *Silversides* was trailing. Blair attempted to maneuver his Blasters into the classic position, with *Pintado* and *Shark* as flankers and *Pilotfish* as trailer. This disposition never came off, for the enemy convoy continued to make violent course changes so that the port flanker wound up on the starboard side and the trailer never did make contact. Just before dawn on 1 June *Pintado* made an attack and sank a *maru* out of the convoy.

In the meantime *Silversides* made contact with a southbound convoy. *Pilotfish* was in a position to close this convoy and did so, but was unable to get in an attack. *Pintado* also attempted to make attacks but was driven off by a persistent patrol plane. While this was going on *Shark* encountered another northbound convoy and sank one ship on 2 June. This northbound convoy crossed the track of Japanese Convoy No. 3530, which was en route to Saipan with seven thousand Japanese troops and all their tanks and equipment embarked in seven *marus*, with four escorts. As the loaded southbound ships were more valuable targets than the returning northbound empties, Blair directed the attention of all three Blasters to Convoy No. 3530.

At ten o'clock on the morning of 4 June Blair ordered *Pilotfish* to take position ahead, with *Pintado* and *Shark* as flankers. Four hours later all three submarines were in position and dove to attack. Just then the convoy changed its base course, leaving *Shark* as the only submarine in position to attack. Blakely charged in and sank the transport *Katsukawa Maru*.

The next day *Shark* again was the only submarine to get in an attack. She sank two more *marus* while *Pilotfish* and *Pintado* vainly tried to get in. Shortly after midnight on 5–6 June *Pintado* made a torpedo attack with electric torpedoes and Clarey thought he heard hits, but evidentally the convoy escaped from this attack without damage. *Pintado's* opportunity came about noon on 6 June. Clarey fired a salvo of torpedoes at *Kashimasan Maru*, which was loaded with gasoline. *Kashimasan Maru* erupted in brilliant fireworks and burned far into the night, sending up a pillar of smoke and flame in advertisement of disaster. Profiting by the resultant confusion, *Pintado* torpedoed and sank the transport *Havre Maru*. Blair's Blasters followed the broken remnants of Convoy 3530 the next day until they were called off the chase by Spruance, who was then approaching Saipan, and needed to be sure all friendly submarines were clear before his surface forces entered the area.

Japanese Air Flotilla 901 had been organized and equipped with forty-eight land-based bombers (Betties) and thirty-two flying boats for air escort of convoys. The first employment of this flotilla was protection of the Saipan convoys. Air Flotilla 901 considered themselves very successful. They had thwarted some of the Blasters' attacks, but they did not seem to be much help to Convoy 3530, whose remnant was the last Japanese convoy to reach Saipan. The surface escort of that convoy consisted of the torpedo boat *Otori* and three submarine chasers. This escort was detailed by the Combined Fleet and was manned by Combined Fleet officers and men with a Regular Navy commander in command.

There was gossip in Tokyo that the convoy commander was drunk up to the time of sailing and that he did not hold pre-sailing conferences with his captains, so there was much confusion in the convoy. He denied this charge and retorted that it was only because of the good work of the surface escort that two of the seven *marus* got through. Most of the troops in the sunken transports were saved by the escorts, but they arrived at Saipan in confusion, without equipment, and there never was enough time to reorganize them, so they were of little use in the defense of Saipan. Submarines played an important role in holding down the Japanese buildup in the Marianas, and Blair's Blasters definitely softened up Saipan for the hard battle that was coming.

Japanese Anti-Submarine Headquarters

In April, when only twenty-two *marus* were sunk by submarines, the Japanese Grand Escort Headquarters thought that their introduction of large convoys with more escorts had brought the problem under control. In May the submarines sank sixty Japanese merchant ships and compounded their offense by sinking six escort vessels—three of them destroyers. Grand Surface Escort Force then conceded that the submarine problem was as bad as ever.

The Escort command had gathered together a number of naval reservists from the merchant fleet, the universities, and the shipping companies to work as a brain trust and analyze the submarine problem. This section had a small but very active communication intelligence unit.

The voice radio and short-range communications between wolf pack units, which the U. S. Navy fondly hoped the Japanese could not pick up, gave the communication intelligence group a considerable volume of traffic to work on. Piecing all their information together, the communication intelligence section deduced that May was the month when several crack U.S. submarine teams were in the field.

Although their direction-finder fixes on U.S. submarines were quite accurate and numerous, the Japanese seemed unable to profit much from this information, probably for lack of a communication system that could disseminate the information rapidly to those who could use it. Like most navies they classified direction-finder results as secret, to the detriment of their rapid distribution. Each month intelligence drew up and printed an elaborate chart of the Pacific Ocean in several colors, collating all the information on submarine contacts.

A month late, this information, like the observations of the mythical backward-flying phillyloo bird, elucidated where U.S. submarines had been but not where they were going. The charts went out only to the favored few, who were at a loss to know how to use the mass of information. When U. S. Navy Intelligence acquired copies of these charts, through the captured document route, they also were at a loss as to what could be done with them. Nevertheless, the U. S. Navy also continued to highly classify their own less accurate direction-finder information.

U.S.S. England

On one momentous occasion, however, direction-finder fixes enabled the U. S. Navy to profit from a series of errors by the Japanese submarine force. Each time U.S. carrier task forces struck New Guinea, Truk, or Palau, the Japanese submarine command responded by sending every possible submarine to sea in pursuit. In April and early May this cost them two submarines (*I-174* and *RO-45*), although they made no contacts with important U.S. forces. The A-Go operation was planned by Toyoda to have everything in place to clobber the next carrier strike. An important part of the plan was the establishment of stationary submarine patrol lines in position to intercept any American striking force coming and going.

Between Truk and the Admiralties, across the mouth of the cul-de-sac interjacent to New Guinea and the Carolines, the plan called for the establishment of a strong submarine cordon. This cordon was called by the Japanese the NA line. On 15 May seven RO-boats left Truk to take up station thirty miles apart in the NA line. Several other submarines were busy on supply missions and it was planned that, on signal, they would knock off that activity and swarm to attack any American striking force.

The U. S. Navy was aware of increased Japanese submarine activity in the area and stepped up their search and anti-submarine activities. Until about this stage of the war, the Atlantic had had first call on anti-submarine ships and equipment, but by May 1944 the submarine situation in the Atlantic had so improved that some of the new gear could be sent to the Pacific. At Purvis Bay in the Solomons were three new destroyer escorts (*England, Raby,* and *George*), equipped with ahead-thrown weapons (hedgehogs). At Pearl Harbor the Cincpac anti-submarine warfare section was anxious to try out this group.

On 16 May a division of U.S. destroyers moving up along the Solomons made contact with *I-176*. This Japanese submarine was engaged in running supplies into Buka. The destroyers were on a scouting line conducting a supersonic search when one of them made sonar contact. The destroyers attacked with depth charges and brought up a heavy oil slick. Japanese radio intelligence was able to follow this attack through the destroyers' communications and they knew how *I-176* had been sunk. Under these circumstances they were justly nervous when their radio intelligence learned that *RO-104* on the NA line had been sighted by a patrol plane. They immediately ordered that the entire NA line should be shifted sixty miles to the southeast.

The move entailed a considerable amount of radio chatter before the line settled down in its new location, and this gave the U.S. radio direction-finder net some material to work on. With the patrol plane sighting, and the radio fixes, and with considerably theoretical reasoning as to what the Japanese were up to, the Cincpac anti-submarine warfare section figured out the position of the Japanese submarine scouting line. Ordinarily, piling conjecture on conjecture in this fashion resulted in a structure that leaned far out from the truth, but in this case everything fitted. Cincpac anti-submarine section passed on their information to Halsey, who ordered out the new specially equipped destroyer escort group to clean up a Japanese submarine scouting line in estimated position that was quite accurate.

I-16, on a supply run to Buka, was the first to suffer. En route to carry out their orders, the destroyer escort group encountered *I-16* on 19 May. U.S.S. *England* attacked with hedgehogs, and brought much gruesome debris to the surface. *I-16* was never heard from again. Three days later this killer group reached their position at the northern end of the NA line. In five days in a series of brilliant attacks, they worked their way down the line sinking *RO-106, RO-104, RO-116,* and *RO-108* in that order, and on 31 May they destroyed *RO-105*. All of the successful attacks were made by U.S.S. *England,* in the most brilliant anti-submarine operation in history.

About this time Japanese radio intelligence informed the Japanese submarine command that the U. S. Navy seemed to be fully aware of the

Japanese submarine disposition, and Takagi radioed a warning to the NA line. *RO-109* and *RO-112* fled the area and were saved. *I-44*, the first Japanese submarine to be equipped with radar, was then operating to the northward of New Ireland. Despite her constant use of her new radar she was bombed by a patrol plane without warning. Shortly afterward, she was suddenly attacked by a destroyer with depth charges and very severely damaged. Just as she was about to surface in desperation to fight her way out of contact with the persistent destroyer a heavy rain squall saved her and she surfaced and ran for it. She had to return to Kure for repairs.

Through this period the Japanese submarine high command was not functioning at its best. Vice Admiral Takagi, Commander of the Sixth Fleet (submarines), had maintained his headquarters at Truk in order to be as near as possible to his operating submarines. On 6 May, after the last carrier raid destroyed most of his repair facilities, supplies, and communications, he withdrew to Kure. When the fighting around Saipan began to build up he decided he should again be near the center of action, and he moved Sixth Fleet headquarters to Saipan on 5 June. This was a decision he lived to regret—but not for long.

Takagi was very much shaken by the severe submarine losses in May. Sixth Fleet staff made an analysis of the situation and concluded that (a) too many submarines were concentrated in areas where anti-submarine action was intense, (b) there were too-frequent changes in submarine dispositions, (c) submarines were being detected by radar while Japanese electronic defenses were not yet ready for operations. The parallel between the first two of these findings and Wilkes' conclusion from the operations of Asiatic Fleet submarines at the beginning of the war is striking.

The Japanese made a habit of sending their squadron commanders to sea, with one of the submarines of his squadron as flagship. This system also came under scrutiny. It necessitated a large volume of radio communication between submarines, and this was thought to have something to do with the high losses. Statistics proved that the ratio of loss of squadron flagships was higher than for other submarines, which the Japanese suspected might be due to the tendency of the squadron commander to stay on the surface as long as possible in order to keep in communication with his command. Once a squadron flagship submerged, for all practical purposes the squadron commander ceased to function. Ironically, while the Japanese were learning these lessons, the Americans were experimenting with embarked wolf pack commanders who encountered the same problems.

XX

JUNE 1944

Kon Plan

MacArthur continued his advance in Northwest New Guinea, and on 27 May landed at Biak. Biak was tenaciously defended by the Japanese. The capture and development of Biak would put Halmahera and the southern Philippines in jeopardy, as Toyoda well knew. To fend off this disaster he devised the Kon Plan for reinforcing Biak with troops embarked in combat ships, a plan reminiscent of Guadalcanal.

The first attempt aborted on 3 June when the Japanese task force was sighted by a submarine and then trailed by a search plane, destroying all element of surprise. The Japanese cruisers and destroyers returned to Davao, where *Hake* (Broach) was on guard. *Hake* was unable to get at the cruisers, but torpedoed and sank the destroyer *Kazagumo* at the entrance to Davao Gulf.

Six destroyers made the next attempt. They were attacked by the Fifth Air Force on 8 June. *Harusame* was sunk and three others damaged but continued on toward Biak until they were turned back (without landing their troops) by Allied cruisers and destroyers. Toyoda then brought up his big guns to support the next attempt. He sent the super battleships *Yamato* and *Musashi* and three cruisers to back up the next "transportation units" of cruisers and destroyers. This made up a more powerful surface force than the Allies could muster in that area of the ocean. Some very hard naval fighting was in prospect until a more direct threat to the security of Japan caused the cancellation of the Kon operation.

A-Go Operation

Special long-range air reconnaissance had informed Toyoda of a gigantic American naval buildup in the Marshalls and the Solomons, which he hoped meant that Nimitz was about to burst into the trap that had been laid for him between Palau and New Guinea. On 10 June *I-10* and *I-38* were ordered to make an air reconnaissance of Majuro and Kwajalein and *RO-42* and *RO-44* were directed to make a periscope reconnaissance of Majuro and Eniwetok. *RO-42* never arrived to carry out her orders, for she was sunk near Kwajalein on the night of 9–10 June by the destroyer escort *Bangust*. *RO-44* made close observation of Eniwetok on the tenth, however, and found the anchorage practically deserted. *I-10* launched her plane on 12 June to reconnoiter Majuro and found the atoll bare.

Both of these well-conducted submarine reconnaissances were too late. A great surge of Allied military power was being mounted all over the world. On 6 June Allied Expeditionary Forces under General Eisenhower landed on Normandy beaches. The same day fast carrier task forces of Spruance's Fifth Fleet sortied from Majuro. During the next few days one of the greatest armadas of history staged through the Marshall Islands. Japanese search planes did not discover the Fifth Fleet until 11 June. The next day a cloud of carrier planes from fifteen combat carriers hit Saipan, Tinian, and Guam. Hurriedly Toyoda canceled the Kon operation and initiated the A-Go operation for the all-out defense of the Marianas.

Takagi, Commander of the Japanese Sixth Fleet, had moved his headquarters to Saipan to be nearer his submarines during A-Go operations. Although he had lost seven submarines around Truk and the Admiralties in the latter part of May, Takagi had twenty-one submarines still at his disposal. These were operating out of Truk and the Marianas, reconnoitering the Marshalls, making supply runs, or were standing by to sail from Japan on orders. When the first carrier strike hit, Tagaki regretted his impetuous dash to Saipan to set up submarine headquarters in the thick of things.

After that first carrier strike was over all Japanese communications with Saipan were in difficulty. On 13 June Toyoda sent out his estimate that the American objective was Saipan and Tinian. Takagi then tried to place his twenty-one submarines in "ambush" position to destroy the American carriers.

Eight Japanese submarines were stationed east and southeast of Guam. Ten were strung out east of Saipan, and two more were to the westward. Only *I-185*, en route from Japan to Wewak on a supply mission, was allowed to continue, and when high seas carried away the drums of rice she carried as deck cargo, she too joined the Saipan ambush on her own initiative. Even as Takagi's orders went out, however, his forces started melting away. On 10 June U.S.S. *Taylor*, working with a hunter-killer group north of the Admiralties, tracked down an oil slick to a sonar contact. Depth charges forced a Japanese submarine to the surface and gunfire finished off *RO-111*. Three days later the destroyer *Melvin*, approaching Saipan as anti-submarine screen for a bombardment group of battleships, had night radar contact with an unidentified target. She opened up with her 5-inch guns and surprised *RO-36* on the surface with a storm of shells which promptly sank that Japanese submarine. It is probable that Takagi was unaware of these losses, for his communications shortly became so bad that he directed Commander Submarine Squadron Seven, then at sea, to take over control and conduct the battle.

Southwest Pacific Submarines

Meanwhile Christie's Southwest Pacific submarines kept Ozawa's striking force at Tawi Tawi under observation. Submarines were moved through the Sulu Archipelago on schedules that maintained a guard of three submarines off Tawi Tawi. Three more kept station southeast of Mindanao to watch for any movement there of the Japanese fleet. With thirty-six fleet submarines under his command, Christie was able to continue his regular patrols, which also proved costly to Ozawa.

Japanese oil technicians had decided that Tarakan crude could be used for bunker fuel without refining, and this somewhat eased the Japanese fuel situation, but at the expense of greater fire hazard to their ships. There was a shortage of fleet tankers, however, and this had been a factor in the selection of Tawi Tawi as the fleet base for A-Go operations—it was close to the Tarakan source of fuel supply. Despite their short run, the fleet tankers got into difficulties. On 5 June in the Sulu Sea, *Puffer* (Selby) sank the fleet tankers *Takasaki* and *Ashizuri*, and on 8 June *Rasher* (Laughon), in the Celebes Sea, sank *Shioya*, another fleet tanker.

Harder

Probably more irksome to Ozawa was Sam Dealey in *Harder*, a specialist in Japanese destroyers. *Harder* headed north through Sibutu Passage, close to Tawi Tawi, en route to a special mission on the night of 6 June. Radar picked up a convoy of three big ships and two escorts, and Dealey stepped out full speed on the surface to gain position ahead. A fickle moon ducked from behind a cloud to reveal the submarine to the Japanese destroyer *Minazuki* 12,000 yards away. *Minazuki* charged and *Harder* turned away at nineteen knots with the destroyer pursuing in the submarine's broad white wake at twenty-four knots. When the range came down to 8500 yards Dealey dove and turned hard left submerged, to bring his stern tubes to bear on the destroyer's track. *Minazuki* charged blindly on, and when the range closed to 1100 yards *Harder* fired four torpedoes. Two of them hit *Minazuki*, and she went down so fast that *Harder* surfaced four minutes after firing to continue pursuit of the convoy. The second destroyer took up the battle. Dealey maneuvered into position to fire six torpedoes at it, but they all missed and the retaliating depth-charge attack kept *Harder* down until the convoy cleared the area.

Before noon the next day *Harder* was forced deep by a float plane which evidently called up the destroyer *Hayanami* to assist in tracking down the submarine. *Hayanami* sighted *Harder's* periscope at about 4000 yards and attacked, coming down the range fast, with a constant helm zigzag that presented Dealey with an angle on the bow changing from port to starboard and back again. This was Dealey's favorite setup —as dangerous as a game of Russian roulette. Keeping his periscope up, he let the range close to 650 yards and then fired three torpedoes in rapid succession. The fourth one wasn't needed. Fifteen seconds after the first torpedo left the tube it hit *Hayanami* squarely amidships and the second one hit aft. Less than a minute after the torpedoes hit, *Hayanami* sank stern first. That afternoon six destroyers came out and formed a scouting line to search for *Harder* and vengeance, but Dealey recognized the better part of valor and stayed deep.

That night in hazy weather, *Harder* proceeded northward through Sibutu Passage, narrowly avoiding a rocky pinnacle as dangerous in these waters as a Japanese destroyer. On 8 June she successfully completed her special mission by picking up six Australian intelligence officers off northeast Borneo, although the Australians were heard to wish they were back on Borneo before the voyage was finished. Early the next morning *Harder* was forced down by a float plane which dropped a bomb for a jolting near-miss. Two destroyers hurried up. A smooth and glassy sea precluded an undetected periscope exposure, so Dealey elected to remain at deep submergence. When the destroyers departed that afternoon *Harder* came up and headed south through Sibutu Passage on a course that took her very close to the Tawi Tawi anchorage. At nine o'clock that night she encountered two patrolling destroyers in the narrowest part of Sibutu. *Harder* submerged for a moonlight periscope approach. When the two hunters presented an ideal overlapping target at 1000 yards' range Dealey fired a salvo of four torpedoes. Two of them hit the near destroyer and one appeared to miss astern and hit the destroyer beyond. Through the periscope Dealey and his executive officer both saw the two destroyers sink but, like so many night action accounts, not everything that was observed happened, for only *Tanikaze* went down that night.

The next afternoon Dealey, through the periscope, sighted a large task force. It was eight miles to the nearest battleship, which Dealey correctly identified as *Musashi* class. While he watched it, a dense black smoke screen was spread between him and the big ship and a destroyer came charging in at thirty-five knots. The submarine at periscope depth in those clear waters had evidently been sighted by a patrolling float plane. Again Dealey had a "down the throat" shot at a charging destroyer. At 1500 yards he fired three torpedoes. The soundman reported fast screws to starboard and Dealey went deep without pausing to observe results. At fifty-five seconds there were two explosions, like torpedo hits, and after that a deafening series of progressive rumblings and explosions. It seemed certain that another Japanese destroyer had paid the penalty for rushing at *Harder* like a cat pouncing on a mouse, but there is no record of the Japanese losing a destroyer on that occasion.

Redfin

Dealey had witnessed the departure of *Yamato* and *Musashi* on the Kon operation. Two hours later he was on the surface to report this important contact. That night *Harder* closed Tawi Tawi anchorage to count the ships of the Japanese fleet behind the reef. When she reported her reconnaissance Christie ordered her out to a quieter area and sent *Redfin* (Austin) in to relieve her.

On 11 June, as he came through the Sulu Sea to take his station, Austin sank *Asanagi Maru* transporting oil to Tawi Tawi, keeping up the psychological pressure on Ozawa. There is evidence that this constant harassing by submarines inhibited Ozawa from sending his carriers to sea for the flight training his green aviators so badly needed. To the Japanese admiral it appeared that a swarm of submarines dogged every move he made, and his fleet destroyers were impotent to hold them off. The mice had developed a keen appetite for cats.

On the morning of 13 June the Japanese fleet sortied from Tawi Tawi. *Redfin* was there to watch them go. Early in the morning, after numerous patrol plane contacts near Sibutu Passage, Austin watched two cruisers and four destroyers come out zigzagging widely. The destroyers came back to escort the main body of battleships and carriers. At nine o'clock in the morning the main body passed *Redfin*. Austin tried to get in an attack on a battleship but was unable to get closer than 4500 yards and the Japanese fleet safely passed over the northern horizon near Borneo. It was evening before *Redfin* could surface and blow the whistle for the Battle of the Philippine Sea.

Central Pacific Submarines

Lockwood's submarines were ready and waiting. At Pearl Harbor the Submarine Force Staff had worked closely with Fifth Fleet Staff in planning the Marianas operation. The war of attrition against Japanese

shipping, which everyone recognized had such far-reaching and important effect on the ability of the Japanese to wage war, went on with
minimum diminution. Three submarines were in Luzon Strait and five
more were north and west of the Marianas between Saipan and Japan.
Both these groups were so situated they could strike at Japanese traffic
as well as watch for the Japanese fleet. *Flying Fish* (Risser) was off San
Bernardino and *Growler* (Schade) off Surigao. With Christie's submarines south of Mindanao they completed a cordon of submarines at all
the exits from the Philippines into the Pacific, so that no matter what
route he chose, Ozawa would have to risk interception by a submarine.

In the Philippine Sea, west of Saipan and north of Palau, nine submarines were lurking. Neither the number nor the positions of these
submarines were fixed. Submarines moved through the area en route to
their patrol stations, and the desired concentration was maintained by
throttling the flow through the strategic area. Submarine positions were
shifted from day to day as information on the movements of the Japanese fleet was received at the Pearl Harbor headquarters of Submarine
Force Pacific.

The first contact of the Japanese fleet with the Pacific submarine dispositions was a phantom one. The Japanese First Supply Force of four
tankers with destroyer escorts was proceeding from Davao northward,
well off the coast of Mindanao on the night of 14–15 June when the
destroyer *Shiratsuyu* thought she sighted a submarine torpedo coming
at her. Dodging the mythical torpedo, *Shiratsuyu* cut across the bow of
a tanker and was rammed. The tanker cut the destroyer in two, and
Shiratsuyu sank before dawn, the explosion of her depth charges killing
over a hundred of her crew. No word of this occurrence reached the
American submarines, still waiting in silence across the path of the approaching Japanese fleet. On 15 June the Marines landed on Saipan.

Seahorse *and* Flying Fish

When *Redfin* broadcast her contact report everyone was on his toes.
Flying Fish moved in close to San Bernardino, sensing that the Japanese
fleet was coming that way. At four-thirty on the afternoon of 15 June
Risser saw them come out of the channel into the Pacific. He was unable
to get closer than twenty thousand yards but *Flying Fish* tracked the Japanese fleet on course 080 speed 20 and trailed until she lost contact at
sunset. Then she surfaced and made her vital contact report, following
along at two-engine speed hoping to pick up a laggard. At nine o'clock
that night Risser turned back to resume his watch at San Bernardino.
The next day *Flying Fish's* sighting was confirmed by two reports from

Philippine coastwatchers, who also saw the Japanese fleet come out through San Bernardino Strait.

Meanwhile *Seahorse* (Cutter) was proceeding through the western part of the Philippine Sea to a South China Sea patrol area. Almost at the time *Flying Fish* was reporting the Japanese carriers, *Seahorse* had contact with a task force of Japanese heavy ships about two hundred miles east of Surigao. This force was advancing on course 045 at 16½ knots and Cutter could see the masts of battleships and the radar pips of other ships. Slowed down by a main motor casualty, he could not close the range, nor keep up with the Japanese for long to hold the contact.

When Cutter tried to get off his contact report the Japanese jammed the radio frequency and it was three o'clock in the morning before the report got through. The composition, disposition, and objective of this second force was then a mystery to American tacticians; but it was, of course, the Kon operation detachment hurrying north to join up with Ozawa, and its course and speed suggested that the rendezvous would be in the southern part of the Philippine Sea. A naval battle was imminent. The submarines had duly announced the arrival of the main Japanese forces on stage, and robbed them of any opportunity to catch Spruance by surprise.

Back in Pearl Harbor all this information was being plotted and discussed and passed on to Spruance. The Japanese tried valiantly to jam all submarine frequencies. It required twenty-four hours for *Seahorse* to get through her second amplifying report, but vital information got through despite radio interference. By radio orders Lockwood made adjustment in the positions of his submarines. *Cavalla* (Kossler) was en route to San Bernardino to relieve *Flying Fish,* which was low on fuel. Lockwood diverted *Cavalla* to the southward and assigned her a temporary patrol area across the projected route he assumed for Ozawa's carriers.

Cavalla

Cavalla was on her first patrol. It was also Kossler's first patrol as commanding officer. Shortly after *Cavalla* entered the Philippine Sea she ran into a typhoon, and the weather had barely cleared when Lockwood sent her word that the Japanese fleet had sailed, and assigned *Cavalla* a new temporary area to patrol. The next day she was on station. *Pipefish* was also in this area, and the two submarines made contact with each other and coordinated their search plans to cover a wider spread of assumed enemy courses and speeds. At sunset on 16

June the search was negative. Kossler reported that fact to Lockwood and set course for San Bernardino.

Three hours later he had radar contact with a convoy on a southeast course. Kossler pulled ahead and about three o'clock in the morning dove to attack. The convoy consisted of two big tankers with three destroyers as escorts. As *Cavalla* came in to attack position one of the escorting destroyers passed close, and Kossler changed course to let it go by. Suddenly the destroyer turned to charge the periscope and *Cavalla* had to go deep. The destroyer passed overhead and held the submarine down while the tankers got by.

When *Cavalla* surfaced before dawn nothing was in sight. To Kossler it seemed futile to chase the fifteen-knot convoy. He felt he had bungled his first approach on an enemy ship. With the best of luck, and four engines at full power, it would take a full day to catch up. The typhoon they had encountered a few days before had increased *Cavalla's* fuel expenditure until the submarine had barely enough fuel left to complete the patrol mission. *Flying Fish* was waiting for relief off San Bernardino. At 0545 Kossler sent a contact report to Lockwood and changed course for San Bernardino.

At Pearl Harbor the situation looked different. Lockwood knew, and Kossler did not, that *Flying Fish* had already reported the transit of the Japanese fleet through San Bernardino and it was no longer imperative that that spot be kept under continuous observation. *Cavalla's* tankers were in all probability en route to fuel Ozawa's carriers. That was then the hottest contact any one had with the Japanese fleet. At 0704 Kossler received a message to turn around and chase the tankers. This message also went to *Muskallunge, Seahorse,* and *Pipefish;* trail, report, and then attack. *Cavalla* spun on her heel, bent on four engines, and dashed off after the tankers in a chase even more futile than it had been an hour before.

That afternoon she had plane contacts but nothing more. *Cavalla* was up and down all afternoon to avoid search planes, and as a result fell farther and farther behind the tankers. The planes could be shore-based search planes, so it was not certain there were carriers nearby. About five o'clock in the evening Lockwood sent Kossler a message to slow down to two-engine speed to conserve fuel, but to keep his chin up, and continue to search along the course the tankers had taken.

It all seemed a hopeless business. There was no assurance that the tankers had continued on the same course. They could be anywhere in that vast expanse of ocean. Lockwood ordered four submarines to shift their positions a hundred miles south. In retrospect this message seems pure clairvoyance, for it put these submarines right across the path of the Japanese fleet.

Then at 1741 *Cavalla* dove again to avoid a searching Betty and at

1900 she was up again, continuing doggedly on. At 1957 she had radar
contact at thirty thousand yards. Kossler put on four engines and turned
to close. The range closed fast. At twenty-two thousand yards a large
number of pips appeared on the screen, and at 2015 he knew that he
had contact with a big task force.

Kossler had a tough decision to make. As the contact developed he
knew he was in a favorable position to attack. There was a carrier in
the task force, tracking nicely on course 100, speed 19, and Kossler was
confident he could get within torpedo range. With a fleet action imminent
it was doctrine to make a contact report before making an attack. History
holds no instance of a commanding officer court-martialed for sinking
an enemy capital ship in battle, but a timely report of the location of
the Japanese fleet could decide the coming battle which might determine
the course of the war.

Cavalla alone was in contact with a major Japanese task force. If Kossler attacked, successfully or not, the counterattack would hold the
submarine down for many hours; and there was the cold-blooded possibility that *Cavalla* would not survive an attack to make a contact report
at all. In reluctant obedience to doctrine Kossler paralleled the Japanese
task force, went down to one hundred feet, and let them parade by while
he listened to the propeller beat and tried to count the heavy ships. At
2130 the Japanese task force and a historic opportunity had passed
Cavalla by, leaving two high-speed screw ships trailing behind to hold
the submarine down for another hour before she could surface and get
off her contact report. Then she hurried off in pursuit at her best four-
engine speed, but with the task force making nineteen knots it seemed
futile. Lockwood notified all submarines that *Cavalla's* report had relieved them of the necessity to report first. They could now shoot first
and report afterward.

Albacore, Finback, Bang, and *Stingray* moved south in accordance with
Comsubpac's orders. *Stingray* and *Bang* were too far east, as it turned
out, for high adventure. *Bang* saw many planes, some of them Japanese,
but most of them American. *Stingray,* on the surface on the night of 18
June, had a fire in her superstructure and reported this derangement
to Comsubpac by radio. The Japanese jammed the transmission of the
message so industriously that Lockwood was unable to make sense of
what he received, and asked *Stingray* to repeat it. Spruance, knowing
the approximate location of *Stingray,* deduced that the submarine's unreadable message was a contact report, which put his estimate of the
Japanese position much farther east than it was actually. At about the
same time Ozawa broke his long radio silence to send a message to the
Japanese airfields on Guam, arranging the cooperation of land-based
planes, and alerting the shore establishments to be prepared to service
Japanese carrier planes that might run out of fuel on a long-range strike

at American carriers. American direction-finders obtained a fairly accurate fix on this transmission but Spruance, with well-founded distrust of high-frequency direction-finders, placed more trust in *Stingray's* unreadable message.

Finback, too far north for effectiveness, but one hundred miles west of *Bang,* was closer to the Japanese. At about seven o'clock that night she saw flashing signal searchlights below the southern horizon. She tried to close at high speed to develop this contact but was unable to bring the signalers above the horizon where radar could detect them. At 2300 on 18 June she reported what she had seen to Lockwood. *Finback's* report was delayed nearly two hours in reaching Spruance, which reduced whatever value this spectral contact may have had.

Spruance's Task Force 58 had rendezvoused at noon on 18 June and steamed westward to meet the Japanese. At eight-thirty that evening, with no certain information on Ozawa's position, Spruance reversed course to better cover the Fifth Amphibious Force, astride the beachhead at Saipan. Ozawa, whose search planes had located Spruance on the afternoon of the eighteenth, was in position at dawn on 19 June to launch long-range strikes against the American carriers. A half hour before sunrise the Japanese battleships and cruisers launched their float planes for a search. At 0630 these planes made contact with a portion of the American fleet and at 0730 Ozawa launched his first strike.

Albacore

Albacore (Blanchard), about a hundred miles south of *Finback,* had more solid contact. Patrolling a north–south beat thirty miles each side of her station at 12-20N 137-00E, *Albacore* listened to the radio gossip but saw nothing much all day of the eighteenth except Japanese search planes that forced her down repeatedly to escape observation. At 0716 on 19 June Blanchard took her down again to avoid a snooping Betty. About a half hour later he came up for a look around through the periscope, and as the scope broke water, saw a Japanese carrier, then a cruiser, then the tops of several other ships—"range thirteen thousand yards, angle on the bow seventy starboard." From then on things happened fast.

Five minutes later *Albacore* sighted another carrier, and a cruiser with attending destroyers. This carrier had an angle on the bow of ten degrees starboard. As that worked out to only twenty-three-hundred yards from the track, Blanchard selected it as his target, swung right to give his torpedoes a ninety-degree track, and bore in to decrease the firing range. The carrier was making twenty-seven knots. A quick look around showed the cruiser on the submarine's port quarter passing well clear astern. The first carrier and its cruisers were on the starboard quarter eight thousand yards away. Many planes were overhead. At 0808 he had the position he wanted. "Up scope." "Stand by." "Final bearing and shoot."

As the periscope went up, Blanchard noted that the "white light" was dark on the TDC, indicating no solution. Something had gone wrong with the computer, or the follow-up system, on the data. It was too late to shift to the hand-operated angle solver. It was too late to locate the trouble. The target was going by like an express train. Whatever was done had to be done in the space of a few heartbeats. Blanchard ordered the final periscope bearing set in the TDC and commenced firing a wide spread of six torpedoes from the forward tubes.

Planes swarmed angrily above the firing submarine. The screening destroyer that had been loitering on the carrier's quarter bore down full tilt. *Albacore* went deep. There was a heavy explosion timed for the sixth torpedo's run. The first depth charges were close, and knocked cork from *Albacore's* hull. During the next three hours every time *Albacore* poked up above two hundred feet, a destroyer responded with a depth-charge attack. The submarine heard several deep distant rumbling heavy explosions, and Blanchard optimistically estimated that the carrier had been damaged by one torpedo hit. In this estimate Lockwood concurred. Many torpedoes had been fired at Japanese aircraft carriers under more favorable circumstances with better evidence of hits, without much effect upon subsequent Japanese operations; but the new torpedoes were very hard-hitting and this time it was different.

Albacore's target was the new carrier *Taiho,* biggest in the Japanese fleet and Ozawa's flagship. At 0809 *Taiho* was launching her planes for a strike at the distant American carriers. As one of *Taiho's* planes took off the pilot spotted the wake of a torpedo headed for his carrier. Instantly he crash-dove on the torpedo, sacrificing his life and his plane but probably diverting one of *Albacore's* torpedoes. Despite this dramatic episode one of *Albacore's* torpedoes hit the big carrier, just as Blanchard estimated it did. Ordinarily *Taiho* could have carried one hit without greatly impairing her battle efficiency. But *Albacore's* torpedo ruptured gasoline tanks; the volatile fraction of the Tarakan fuel compounded the damage control officer's problem, and at 1532 *Taiho* blew up with a terrific explosion and sank soon after.

Cavalla

After making her contact report on the Japanese task force on 17 June, *Cavalla* continued down the track at four-engine speed. Shortly after midnight 18–19 June Kossler decided the chase was hopeless and turned back to his patrol station, but virtue was about to be rewarded.

Before dawn on 19 June *Cavalla* had several contacts with Japanese search planes, apparently flying out of Yap. These kept the submarine diving and surfacing between contacts. At 0720 Kossler sent a message to Lockwood reporting this situation. About ten o'clock there were more plane contacts that sent *Cavalla* down again, and Kossler sighted four small planes to the northwest circling at low altitude. The sound operator reported water noises on the same bearing, and Kossler kept a careful periscope watch in that direction. At 1048 he saw a ship's masts directly beneath the circling planes. *Cavalla* came to normal approach course and went to Battle Stations.

Four minutes later when the periscope went up again "the picture was too good to be true." Four ships were in sight, a large carrier with two cruisers up ahead and a destroyer about a thousand yards on the starboard beam. The angle on the bow was twenty-five degrees starboard. No time for loitering. The destroyer (*Urakaze*) was going to give him trouble but Kossler decided to take his chances on being detected. He came around for a ninety-degree track. The executive officer and the gunnery officer took a quick look through the periscope to check the identification. They agreed the target was a *Shokaku*-class carrier with a large Japanese ensign flying from its peak. At 1118 Kossler fired six torpedoes in a divergent spread. The first one hit after a fifty-five-second run, and the second and third followed at eight-second intervals. The last three missed astern.

Two minutes later the troublesome *Urakaze* dropped four very close depth charges as *Cavalla* was sounding to deeper depths. The hull ventilation outboard piping was flooded and two of the three sound sets were knocked out. About three hours later Kossler heard terrific explosions in the direction of the attack. It was after sunset before *Cavalla* could surface to report that she had torpedoed a *Shokaku*-class carrier, that *Cavalla* had received minor depth-charge damage which they could handle, and they "believed that baby sank." Kossler was correct on all counts. His target was *Shokaku* herself, fighter of so many battles and survivor of so many attacks. This time she was hit by at least three powerful torpedoes (Japanese credit *Cavalla* with four hits), and about three hours afterward *Shokaku* blew up and sank.

Task Force 58

Unable to locate the Japanese carriers with sufficient accuracy for a strike, Task Force 58 received the Japanese air attack with intercepting fighter planes and anti-aircraft fire from surface ships. A total of 330 Japanese carrier planes were destroyed on 19 June, and at the end of the day Ozawa had only a hundred planes still operational. Two U.S.

battleships, two carriers, and a heavy cruiser were damaged by the Japanese air attack, but the fighting efficiency of the Fifth Fleet was unimpaired.

That night *Finback* again sighted searchlights to the south. Chasing this beacon she made radar contact, but was unable to identify the ships with certainty, as she was required to do before making an attack in a Joint Zone. When the range closed to fourteen thousand yards, four destroyers broke off from the main group and headed for *Finback,* forcing her to submerge. Just before midnight she surfaced but was unable to report this contact because of a breakdown of her radio transmitter. This was the last submarine contact with the Japanese fleet during the battle. The next day, at noon, *Bang* encountered a task force. Submerged, she closed the range to eight thousand yards and recognized U.S. ships. *Bang* went down to two hundred feet and from that depth exchanged recognition signals with a U.S. destroyer.

On the afternoon of 20 June a search plane from *Enterprise* finally found the Japanese fleet. A late afternoon strike at extreme range was launched after the retiring Japanese. *Hiyo* was sunk and four other Japanese carriers were damaged. Two tankers were sunk and one was damaged. The battleship *Haruna* and the cruiser *Maya* were heavily damaged. This ended the battle. The next day the Japanese were out of reach of Task Force 58.

The Japanese credited submarines with sinking the carrier *Hiyo,* after she was damaged by an air attack. It is understandable that they should see phantom submarines, but the Japanese fleet was well outside the perimeter of submarine dispositions when *Hiyo* went down. There were no submarines between Ozawa and Okinawa, for which he was headed. Except for searching the area for downed aviators for several days after the battle, submarine participation in the Battle of the Philippine Sea ended with *Finback's* abortive contact.

They had done all right. From the time Ozawa concentrated his fleet at Tawi Tawi they kept him under observation, destroyed his destroyers, heckled his logistic support, and inhibited him from continuing the carrier training exercises his aviators needed so badly. They gave the alarm when he sortied from his advance base, and they detected the debut for battle of the Japanese fleet into the Pacific. They topped off this performance on the day of battle by sinking two of the biggest Japanese aircraft carriers. For the first time in history submarines had achieved their full potential in a fleet action. It was no accident that Fifth Fleet and Pacific submarines operated in the same waters with mutual confidence and smooth cooperation. They had been doing so for a long time in submarine lifeguard operations. It started many months before with *Skate's* tragic and dramatic rescue operation at Wake.

War against the Marus

The war against Japanese commerce continued unabated all during the Marianas campaign. In addition to the watch on Tawi Tawi and Davao, Christie's submarines in the Southwest Pacific increased their supply runs to the guerrilla forces in the Philippines. *Nautilus* and *Narwhal* were almost exclusively engaged in the trade. Notwithstanding their extra duties, Christie's submarines efficiently continued their main business of sinking Japanese ships in the East Indies and the South China Sea.

Lockwood kept one submarine in the Kuriles during this month and *Barb* sank three ships in this high northern area. From Japan, down through the Nanpo Shoto to the edge of the Fifth Fleet operating areas in the Marianas, submarines continued to torpedo Japanese shipping. Several *marus* were sunk close to the coast of Japan. *Swordfish* sank the Japanese destroyer *Matsukaze,* and *Archerfish* sank *Coast Defense Vessel Number 24* to continue the war against Japanese escorts. It was not all one-sided, however. *Golet* (Clark) left Midway in late May to patrol the area off the northeast coast of Honshu. She was never heard from again. From postwar Japanese reports it appears probable that she was destroyed by anti-submarine patrol vessels in her assigned area on 14 June.

Luzon Strait, between the Philippines and Formosa, built up to a major area of struggle. *Bang* and *Seahorse* left the Philippine Sea after the battle to join *Growler* there and harass Japanese convoys coming up through the northern part of the South China Sea.

By June the Joint Intelligence Center had collected sufficient information on Oikawa's mine barriers to map a safe route for submarines to flank Nansei Shoto minefields and find safe operating areas between these "restricted areas" and the China coast. The East China Sea and the Yellow Sea, which had been allowed to lie fallow for a few months, were fertile ground again for submarine operation. *Tang* (O'Kane), *Tinosa* (Weiss), and *Sealion* (Reich) all entered the area around 20 June. Although they were not operating as a wolf pack they rounded the northern end of the mine barrier and fell upon the unprepared Japanese convoys like wolves on a flock of sheep. In the latter part of June and early July *Tang* sank ten ships, *Tinosa* two, and *Sealion* four in the area that the Japanese had considered relatively safe.

On the Pacific side of the mine barrier, *Sturgeon* (Murphy) was patrolling. With Saipan gone, the Japanese began desperately to reinforce Iwo Jima, the Bonins, and Okinawa. Okinawa, until then in a back area, lay practically undefended. *Sturgeon* was there to meet the first reinforcements sent down from Japan. She sank the loaded transport *Toyama*

Maru on 29 June and another transport, *Tairin Maru,* on 3 July. *Toyama Maru's* cargo must have been exceptionally important, for the loss of this ship caused consternation at Imperial General Headquarters.

In the month of June submarines sank forty-eight Japanese *marus,* in addition to fourteen major and minor combat ships. Carrier raids in the Marianas and the Bonins, and Army Air Forces in New Guinea together knocked off thirty more *marus.* Eight cargo ships were lost by Japan from other causes to bring the total loss of Japanese merchant shipping to 278,000 tons. Moreover, as soon as the Marianas became effective U.S. bases, Japanese commerce was crowded into very narrow lanes vulnerable to both submarine and air attack.

Japanese Submarines

Guam is over five thousand miles from San Francisco. Amphibious war had never before been fought over such great distances. The amount of shipping required for the logistics of this huge effort was unbelievable. Kwajalein, Majuro, and Eniwetok atolls served as staging bases. Eniwetok took a large share of the non-combat shipping. During one month there were 1700 arrivals and departures at Eniwetok, and on one day 414 ships were present in the lagoon. With this vast flow of traffic, over sea areas Japan had so recently considered her own ocean, Japanese submarines were presented with an unprecedented opportunity which they were in no condition to exploit.

Of the twenty-two submarines Takagi threw into the battle for the Marianas thirteen were destroyed. As none of Takagi's staff who were with him on Saipan survived, and as Japanese submarine commanders seemed to have suffered more than the usual number of delusions during this period, it is difficult to piece together a consistent account of what actually happened.

After reporting her reconnaissance of Eniwetok, *RO-44* was ordered to Saipan. Early on the morning of 16 June, however, she encountered the destroyer escort *Burden R. Hastings* about 120 miles from Eniwetok atoll and was destroyed in a hedgehog attack. The same night *RO-114* encountered Oldendorf's bombardment group about a hundred miles east of Saipan. *RO-114* reported that she torpedoed an *Iowa*-class battleship which exploded so violently that the other ships in the task force scattered in confusion. From the American side there is no report of this engagement. This Japanese torpedo attack appears to have been unobserved, but shortly after midnight on 16–17 June the destroyer *Melvin* had radar contact with a surfaced submarine. The submarine submerged. *Melvin* and *Wadleigh* attacked with depth charges and brought up convincing evidence of a kill. *RO-114* was never heard from again. This was *Melvin's* second kill in three days.

RO-117 reported sighting battleships and cruisers on 16 June. Thereafter she was silent. Planes from Eniwetok caught her on the surface on 17 June and sank her. On 18 June Ozawa directed all Japanese submarines north of Ulithi to withdraw westward of 145° E. The Japanese fleet was about to enter the battle area and needed to be sure that any submarine contact was hostile. Some Japanese critics consider that the meager real results obtained by Japanese submarines was partially due to this order, but it does not seem to have prevented contacts between Japanese submarines and U.S. capital ships.

On 19 June *RO-115* reported that she sank a *Wasp*-class carrier. The next day Japanese radio intelligence picked up a message which they interpreted to read that all survivors of *Bunker Hill* had been rescued. Despite these convincing confirmations, no U.S. carrier was torpedoed. On 20 June, after Ozawa had withdrawn, Toyoda ordered all submarines to leave their ambush stations, assigned by Takagi's original order, and move in close to Saipan and Guam to annihilate the armada of American ships crowded off these islands. The parallel between these orders and similar futile orders issued to American submarines at Midway is striking.

In the meantime *I-184*, which had been on a supply mission to Mili, was ordered to rush to Saipan from her Marshall Islands area. She did, and arrived in time to be sunk by carrier planes from *Suwannee* on 19 June. That same day *I-185*, which had interrupted her supply mission to Wewak to get into the battle, reported that she sank a carrier-like ship. No such ship was lost, but three days later on 22 June, destroyers *Newcomb* and *Chandler* had sonar contact in the vicinity of a group of transports they were escorting. Successive depth-charge attacks brought up oil and debris including human remains. This is believed to have marked the end of *I-185*.

When *I-10* finished her reconnaissance of Majuro on 12 June, she too rushed to the area east of Guam to take up her ambush station. Between 24 and 27 June she tried to evacuate Commander Sixth Fleet and his staff from Saipan, but was unable to establish contact at the rendezvous. On 2 July she reported that she sank a warship seventy miles northeast of Saipan. This encounter remains unexplained, but two days later, on 4 July, she encountered the destroyer escort *Riddle* which made sonar contact with a submerged submarine while escorting a refueling group. *Riddle* was joined in a depth-charge attack by the destroyer *David W. Taylor*, and together they finished the long career of *I-10*.

After the failure of *I-10* to rescue Takagi, *I-38* and *I-6* were ordered to evacuate Sixth Fleet Staff from Saipan. These submarines were prevented from approaching the rendezvous point by vigilant anti-submarine patrols. On 30 June *I-6* reported sinking a carrier-like vessel twenty miles east of Saipan. Apparently this was within sight of the waiting Takagi, for he confirmed the sinking. Despite this convincing evidence, no such ship was sunk. *I-38* also reported an attack for which there is no corresponding record of damage.

On 2 July Takagi ordered all effort to rescue him and his staff to be abandoned. Four days later he sent his last message that the Sixth Fleet staff would make a suicide attack on an enemy position. After that nothing more was heard of him. It is doubtful that he would have lived much longer had *I-6* been successful in rescuing him from Saipan. On 13 July a search plane sighted a submarine seventy miles west of Saipan and called up surface escort vessels. Two escorts, *William C. Miller* and *Gilmer*, responded. They established sonar contact and made depth-charge attacks which brought up debris including parts of naval uniforms and human tissue. This was the end of *I-6*. *I-38* survived to return to Kure. On 13 July Vice Admiral Shigeyoshi Miwa, who had been in a Japanese submarine off Pearl Harbor as a Squadron Commander when the war began, assumed command of the Sixth Fleet.

Although Miwa might have been deceived by overoptimistic reports of Japanese successes, he was under no delusion as to the extent of his submarine losses. One by one, his submarines failed to answer to the radio. On 14 July *RO-48* reported that intensive anti-submarine activity had forced her from her station north of Saipan. That was the last ever heard of her. She may have been sunk by the destroyer *William C. Miller* shortly after her last report.

In the midst of this holocaust Japanese submarines were given supply missions for the Marianas' garrisons whose situation was otherwise hopeless. *I-41* picked up 106 flight personnel from Guam and brought them safely to Japan. *I-36*, on a supply mission to Truk, returned with eighty-six flying personnel on 16 July. *I-5*, after a supply mission to Ponape, received minor repair at Truk, and departed for Japan on 16 July. Two days later she encountered the destroyer escort *Wyman* east of Saipan. *Wyman* picked up radar contact shortly after midnight on the night of 18–19 July and ran down to investigate. The pip disappeared from the radar screen about the same time sonar made contact. *Wyman* attacked with hedgehogs and sank *I-5* with all hands.

I-26, *I-45*, and *I-55* were deck-loaded with special vehicles to be transported to the hard-pressed garrisons of Tinian and Guam. *I-26* succeeded in landing hers at Guam on 6 July, but *I-45* was detected by patrol craft and had to destroy her cargo to escape. *I-54* and *I-55* encountered intensive anti-submarine activity at Tinian and could not carry out their mission. Apparently part of the anti-submarine activity these two submarines encountered was the hunter-killer group of which the destroyer *Wyman* was part. On 28 July *Wyman* made a hedgehog attack which brought up debris. Some of the wood brought up was stamped with Japanese *kanji* and was later identified as part of *I-55*.

In three hedgehog attacks, after only two sonar contacts, *Wyman* had destroyed two Japanese submarines. As so often happens when news is bad it is bad all over. *I-33* was lost in training exercises in the Inland Sea in June. *I-166* was torpedoed and sunk by the British submarine *Telemachus* (King) in Malacca Strait on 17 July.

Japanese Submarine Communications with Germany

The month of July also brought to an end Japanese submarine communications with Germany. *I-30*, which made the first attempt at the long voyage in 1942, was sunk on the last leg of the return trip as has been recounted. *I-8* (Uchino) made a successful round trip in 1943 with quinine for the Germans and the latest German anti-aircraft guns for the Japanese. *RO-500*, built in Germany for the Japanese, also successfully reached Japan in August 1943. The other attempts to carry on this trade were disastrous.

I-34 had been en route to Germany when she was sunk by H.M.S. *Taurus* in Malacca Strait in November 1943. *RO-501*, another submarine built by Germany for Japan, encountered a hunter-killer group in the Atlantic and was sunk by the destroyer escort *Francis M. Robinson* on 13 May 1944. The next month *I-52*, returning to Japan from Germany, encountered the same hunter-killer group and was sunk by plane from U.S.S. *Bogue*, 24 June 1944.

I-29 nearly made it. She arrived in Singapore on her return journey in July with a precious cargo of German technical material. On 25 July, while crossing the South China Sea, she reported that she had sighted a hostile submarine. This was her last report. *I-29* had been sighted in turn, and the information on her course and speed passed on to a wolf pack consisting of *Rock*, *Tilefish*, and *Sawfish* operating in Luzon Strait. All three of these submarines lay in ambush for the lone Japanese submarine the next day. On the afternoon of 26 July, *Sawfish* (Banister), lying in wait submerged, saw *I-29* approach on the surface right on schedule. *Sawfish* fired four torpedoes, three of which hit. *Rock* was close enough to see the plume of smoke and water from the torpedoes' explosion. *Tilefish* was even closer. She was starting an approach on the Japanese submarine when *Sawfish's* torpedoes hit and *I-29* blew up and sank.

Japan's Desperate Submarine Situation

At the end of July Miwa had only twenty-six submarines in the Sixth Fleet and only a few more superannuated ones in training assigned to naval districts. Twenty-five Japanese submarines had been lost in the previous three months and Miwa was unable to obtain accurate information as to what had taken place during the A-Go operation. Japanese electronic warfare was in its infancy, but analysis indicated that there were fewer losses among those submarines equipped with radar or counter-radar than among those not so equipped. In view of the disastrous losses Miwa concluded that submarine operations under existing circumstances were impossible. The major portion of the Sixth Fleet was ordered back to Japan for installation of radar and radar warning devices, leaving only three Japanese submarines at sea on special missions.

The Battle of the Philippine Sea completed the destruction of the Japanese carrier forces as an effective fighting force. After this battle Japanese carriers appeared only as a "Diversionary Attack Force." Naval aviation became more and more directed to suicide tactics, using relatively untrained aviators with obsolete equipment but a fanatical determination to die in action. The days of the Kido Butai were gone forever.

The months of June and July also marked the decline and fall of the Japanese submarine force. In August Japanese submarine activity dropped to nearly zero. More than the installation of new electronic devices took place during this period of waiting. When Japanese submarines again became operational they too were oriented toward suicide tactics. Their objectives became ever more firmly fixed on the capital ships of the U. S. Navy as the only targets of sufficiently dramatic appeal to attack with suicide weapons. The vast commerce of the war moved over the broad reaches of the Pacific, escorted lightly in the eastern Pacific, or sometimes escorted not at all, but relatively undisturbed by Japanese submarines. The back of the Japanese submarine force had been broken, but like a rattlesnake with a broken back it could still be deadly if its striking power was ignored.

XXI

JULY–AUGUST 1944

Many Japanese credited U.S. submarines with defeat of the Japanese fleet in the Battle of the Philippine Sea. Submarines made a major contribution, but Ozawa turned back not because two of his carriers had been sunk by submarines, but because Task Force 58 had destroyed most of his planes and Spruance still stood in full strength between the Japanese fleet and the Saipan beachheads. The Japanese and many Americans did not appreciate the genius of Spruance in coordinating the elements of power on land and sea, and under the sea and in the air above, to secure the Marianas and incidentally defeat the Japanese fleet. Organized resistance ceased on Saipan on 9 July, Tinian was secure on 1 August, and organized resistance ended on Guam on 10 August. With the Marianas in U.S. hands wise men in Japan knew that defeat was inevitable, but the Japanese philosophy of death before surrender left them no way out.

Pacific Submarine Force

The vital commerce of Japan with Southeast Asia was then crowded into the East China Sea and the South China Sea. In the next few months U.S. submarines ripped the Japanese merchant marine to shreds. One of the most important points of vulnerability was Luzon Strait and the northern neck of the South China Sea, where Japanese supply lines were squeezed through the Formosa Strait. In June Comsubpac organized this locality into a Rotating Patrol Area. The demarkation line between Southwest Pacific and Pacific submarine operating areas was shifted ninety miles south to give Lockwood undivided responsibility for this area. Five operating sub areas were laid out, with a safety lane thirty miles wide running east to west across the middle. This rotating patrol area was christened "Convoy College" by Voge, but during the summer of 1944 the Japanese came to know it better as "Devil's Sea."

That the downfall of Japanese submarines correlated with the rise of U.S. submarines to new heights of effectiveness was pure coincidence. The two submarine forces, starting out the war so even in strength, had been diverging in growth for some time. Fifty-two new American submarines had reported for duty during 1943. At the rate of six per month new ones continued joining up during 1944. At the end of that year Christie had forty and Lockwood 116 fleet submarines. The advance westward greatly improved logistics for the Central Pacific submarines. Majuro in the Marshalls was in full operation as an advance submarine base. No longer was it necessary to creep through the Marianas. Lockwood solved Kossler's pressing fuel problem by sending *Cavalla* into Saipan for emergency refueling.

Cavalla arrived there on 1 July with the battle on Saipan still in full bloom. She was received like a queen by the Fifth Fleet and the Fifth Amphibious Force for her sterling services during the Battle of the Philippine Sea. While the submarine fueled in Garapan Harbor her crew stared in open-eyed wonder at the power of bombardment groups and the air support mustered to help the Marines and the Army in their desperate battle on shore. Twenty-four hours later *Cavalla* departed full of fuel and admiration. From that moment, the Marianas continued to increase in importance to submarine logistics.

With greater numbers and improved logistics it was no longer necessary to neglect some areas in order to concentrate attention on the most vulnerable spots. *Sunfish* and *Skate* were in the high north where they sank four *marus*, and *Skate* sank the destroyer *Usugumo* for good measure. Two fast carrier groups hit Japanese installations on Iwo Jima and the Bonins on 4 July. They destroyed ten Japanese ships (*marus* and light naval vessels) and left slim pickings for submarines patrolling the area between the Bonins and Japan. The three submarines that had entered the East China Sea during June were still there in early July, profitably employed in sinking Japanese ships.

British and Dutch Submarines

In June 1944 two Dutch submarines (*K-14* and *K-15*) were assigned to Fremantle and used in special missions in the Netherlands East Indies. In August a squadron of British submarines moved from Ceylon to Fremantle. Since the middle of 1943, British and Dutch submarines (under British operational control) had operated out of Ceylon, patrolling Malacca Strait and the coasts of the Malay Peninsula and Burma. With the improvement of the naval situation in the Mediterranean additional British submarines were sent to the Far East. In August the depot ship

Maidstone with nine British and four Dutch submarines moved on to Fremantle, where they were sent out to patrol under the operational control of Christie.

These submarines had been designed for the Atlantic. They were much smaller than U.S. fleet submarines and as a consequence had smaller fuel capacity, could carry fewer fresh provisions, and were much less habitable all around than U.S. submarines then operating. Most serious was the lack of air conditioning, which made a patrol in the East Indies a hellish experience. Temperatures on long dives were often 120° F., and prickly heat was a constant torture. *Surf* suffered five cases of heat stroke on one patrol. Despite this hard lying, they endured. *Tantalus* made a fifty-two-day patrol, thirty-four days of which was north of the Malay Barrier.

Dutch submarines were usually given areas in the Dutch East Indies. British submarines were restricted by their fuel capacity to areas in the southern part of the Java Sea and to the Gulf of Siam. In these areas the usual targets were small merchant vessels and junks carrying supplies and raw materials in interisland trade. Against these ships British submarines were very adept in the use of their deck guns. With the southern areas covered by British and Dutch submarines Christie's big American fleet submarines were released to concentrate up around the Philippines.

Submarines in the South China Sea

One of the most successful patrols in the South China Sea was made by *Flasher* (Whitaker). She entered the South China Sea in late June, coming up from Fremantle through Lombok Strait, the Java Sea, and Karimata Strait. On the way up to her operating area *Flasher* sank one ship out of a southbound convoy. A few days later she sank another freighter but most of her contacts were sailing boats or coastal freighters too small for the expenditure of a torpedo.

Crevalle (Walker) and *Angler* (Hess) were operating in the vicinity and Whitaker had orders to coordinate the search activity of the three submarines in a loosely organized coordinate group in accordance with Southwest Pacific practice. Walker and Hess reported no luck in finding targets, and Whitaker sent a message to Christie reporting that contacts were too few to justify the presence of three submarines in that locality. Then on the stormy morning of 19 July, in poor visibility, the officer of the deck of *Flasher* suddenly sighted a ship at fifteen thousand yards and dove immediately. A few minutes later Whitaker had a look and identified the target as a *Kuma*-class cruiser, with one destroyer escort, making eighteen knots. It was the light cruiser *Oi*.

Flasher came straight in and crossed the target's track for a stern tube shot. Two torpedoes of a four-torpedo salvo hit. *Flasher's* firing position was only five hundred yards from the escorting destroyer and retaliation was immediate. The submarine took fifteen close depth charges, fortunately without damage, and she was held down for an hour and a half before Whitaker could get another look.

Oi was still there, down by the stern with a good port list. Whitaker fired four more torpedoes from the bow tubes and these all missed, probably because the torpedoes were set at ten feet in a very rough sea. A long series of depth charges followed. In the late afternoon, when Whitaker had another peek, the cruiser was gone. The destroyer was still there but it shortly took off at high speed to the southwest. Whitaker considered it possible that the damaged cruiser had been able to get under way. He sent *Angler* a message and told her to search for the cripple on a southwest course. His concern was unjustified. From Japanese accounts *Oi* was hit in the engine room with one torpedo. She sank five hours later and the destroyer rescued about 65 per cent of her crew.

The next day Whitaker organized a scouting line of three submarines and set out across the South China Sea to the vicinity of Luzon looking for greener pastures. Early on the morning of 25 July *Angler* was on the surface. Just as dawn was breaking the quartermaster sighted a convoy twelve miles distant. Hess immediately informed the other two submarines and trailed the target to establish its base course.

There were nine ships in this convoy bound from Manila to Japan with six escorts. The escort carrier *Taiyo* trailed to provide air cover. Air activity kept the three submarines diving and blowing all day, but they hung on to the edges until nightfall. Shortly after midnight all three submarines attacked the convoy. *Flasher* sank a tanker (*Otorisan Maru*), which blew up to illuminate the whole ocean. She also damaged another ship (*Tozan Maru*). *Crevalle* sank the 11,409-ton *Aki Maru* and finished off the ship *Flasher* had damaged. *Angler* torpedoed one ship (*Kiyokawa Maru*) which did not sink. *Flasher* was then out of torpedoes and turned south for Fremantle. Christie credited *Flasher* with seven ships totaling forty-seven thousand tons on this patrol. This was too high, but a light cruiser and 3½ *marus* was a worthy accomplishment for any patrol. A total of thirteen *marus* were sunk in Southwest Pacific areas during July, and the Japanese Navy was also deeply nicked. In addition to the light cruiser *Oi* sunk by *Flasher*, *Paddle* (Nowell) sank the destroyer *Hokaze*, and *Mingo* (Staley) sank the destroyer *Tamanami*.

Convoy College

Convoy College, however, was the scene of the greatest activity. The Japanese recognized that this area was critical, and intensified the antisubmarine activity there so that gradually the area between Formosa and

the Philippines became the cockpit in which the battle of U.S. submarines vs. Japanese anti-submarine forces was fought out. *Bang, Seahorse,*
and *Growler* operated there as a coordinated attack group in late June
and early July. They were followed into Convoy College on 4 July by
a group consisting of *Apogon, Thresher, Guardfish,* and *Piranha* under
command of Captain O'Regan, who was in *Guardfish.* This group sank
eight ships. Most of the action was concentrated into a series of attacks
on one convoy of ten ships and three escorts on 16–17 July. *Piranha*
(Ruble) sank one ship out of the convoy. *Guardfish* (Ward) sank three
and *Thresher* (MacMillan) sank two. Somewhere along the line an escort got in the way and was heavily damaged.

O'Regan's pack was followed by a group consisting of *Rock, Tilefish,*
and *Sawfish.* This group sank *I-29* as has been recounted, but all the
marus got by them. About the same time another wolf pack (*Parche,
Hammerhead,* and *Steelhead*) under command of Commander L. S.
Parks, embarked in *Parche,* entered Convoy College. The patrol of this
group lasted sixty days, about one-half of which was spent in the area.
Most of it was monotonous patrolling with numerous airplane contacts,
a full-blown typhoon, and an occasional picket boat to be avoided.

Parks carried on voluminous radio conversations, assigning tasks to his
group, arranging search plans, exchanging information with submarines
in adjacent areas. Sometimes the three submarines rendezvoused to pass
information back and forth by bottle line, but all their schemes to intercept Japanese convoys were futile. An unescorted aircraft carrier came
through at high speed, causing a flurry like a June bug running through
a duck yard, but the carrier got through without an attack. A cruiser
took *Parche* under long-range gunfire but the submarine quickly submerged to safety. *Marus* were scarce until 30 July.

Then *Hammerhead* made contact with a convoy on an easterly course.
She tried to coach the others in without success. The next morning *Steelhead* picked up the tops of many ships of a slow-speed convoy, and got
off a contact report. This convoy had three or four planes in the air over
it at all times, but despite the heavy air cover *Steelhead* held contact
and trailed, sending reports every hour.

That night both *Steelhead* (Whelchel) and *Parche* (Ramage) succeeded in gaining position ahead of the convoy. One of the wildest night
melees of submarine warfare in the Pacific took place early in the morning of 31 July. Whelchel opened up with an attack on a tanker and a
freighter. The tanker erupted in brilliant flame to illuminate the battle.
Parche was guided in by the fireworks. When Ramage arrived the escorts
were in a tight circle around the undamaged ships. *Parche* came in on
a spiral course at full speed, then cut ahead of one escort and astern of
another to gain position between the escorts and the convoy. Just then
the convoy zigged and headed directly for the submarine.

The range closed so fast that the nearest target was inside torpedo arming distance before Ramage could fire. Dodging this freighter by a scant two hundred yards, Ramage opened out the range and swung to fire two bow torpedoes. The freighter dodged the torpedoes, but *Parche* then fired a stern tube shot at another freighter and this one hit. Illuminated by the light of a burning ship and bursting Japanese colored signal rockets, *Parche* made a good target herself. The *marus* opened up with machine guns and 4- or 5-inch deck guns. Tracers arced across the sky to add to the fireworks, and splashes from the heavy guns plumed the sea around them. Ramage ordered the bridge crew below while, with a volunteer to man the target bearing transmitter, he stayed topside to conn *Parche* through the holocaust. Exhilarated by the excitement of battle, in perfect empathy with a ship and crew responding instantly to every command, Ramage went berserk. For forty-six action-packed minutes he maneuvered *Parche* through the frantic convoy at full speed on the surface, dodging attempts to ram her, swinging ship to fire nineteen torpedoes in succession as the sweating torpedo crews below labored to keep the tubes loaded.

Like most night melees the estimate of the damage inflicted was greater than actual. Lockwood credited *Parche* with sinking four ships and damaging another while *Steelhead* was credited with sinking two. The Japanese lost two dry cargo ships (*Manku Maru* and *Fuso Maru*) and two tankers (*Koei Maru* and *Kokura Maru*), and one was heavily damaged (*Dakar Maru*). In Convoy College during the month of July over twenty Japanese ships went down.

Submarine Losses

The U. S. Submarine Force lost two submarines in the month of July. *S-28* (Campbell) was lost in training exercises off Pearl Harbor on 4 July. Contact was lost with her while she was submerged acting as a sonar target. She disappeared with all hands in fourteen hundred fathoms of water.

Robalo (Kimmel) was on patrol in enemy waters when she went down. On 26 July she was two miles off Palawan Island in the Philippines when an explosion occurred. *Robalo* sank immediately. Four men swam ashore and were captured by the Japanese. From the notorious Puerto Princesa prison camp on Palawan they succeeded in getting out a message through guerrillas about the loss of *Robalo* and their own plight. They attributed *Robalo's* sinking to a battery explosion, but it is more probable that the explosion was of enemy origin. None of *Robalo's* crew survived the Japanese prison camp.

Japanese Countermeasures

On 3 August Oikawa fleeted up to Chief of Navy General Staff and Admiral Naokuni Nomura relieved him as commander Grand Escort Force. At the same time the escort forces were placed directly under the Combined Fleet. While this made it easier to assign some fleet forces to escort duty, it also made it easy for Combined Fleet to divert the escort forces to Combined Fleet operations. Despite the fact that Combined Fleet had irrevocably lost its air arm and the Sixth Fleet submarines had been emasculated, Toyoda still dreamed of a naval battle that would dramatically reverse the situation. He resolutely refused to assign fleet destroyers to the escort forces, although Japanese escort forces had been destroyed in large numbers and there was a serious shortage of surface escorts.

In August the First Escort Force with headquarters at Takao had five old destroyers, thirty-six *kaibokans,* and seven miscellaneous vessels for escorts. They deplored the shortage of destroyers, but as a matter of fact the *kaibokans* were more efficient in anti-submarine warfare than most destroyers. *Kaibokans* carried as many as three hundred depth charges. They were armed with machine guns and two 4.7-inch deck guns in whose use their crews were very proficient. Their sonar was good, but their radar was inferior and they lacked modern ahead-thrown weapons.

A large portion of Japanese anti-submarine air strength was concentrated at Takao, to give protection to their commerce at its point of greatest vulnerability. The 901st Air Group built up a force of two hundred planes in the general locality. Slowly they scraped together some modern equipment until one-third of 901st Air Group planes carried radar and one-third carried magnetic airborne detectors (MAD).

MAD was a device by means of which a submerged submarine could be detected from an airplane flying above it. It was so heavy that it seriously overloaded the plane, which also had to have some of its steel armament removed to improve magnetic sensitivity. All planes were equipped with bombs with delayed-action fuses which could be set to explode at various depths. The Japanese had also developed a circular-run torpedo carried by aircraft for use against submarines. This torpedo was dropped about two hundred yards in advance of the submarine, and ran in a reducing spiral for four complete cycles as it sank to six hundred feet. It was armed with contact exploders. So far as known this weapon had very little success.

The 901st Air Group endeavored to sweep out a path thirty miles ahead of a convoy, using planes equipped with MAD in the daytime, when submarines were submerged, and radar-equipped planes at night when the submarines were on the surface. Due to the shortage of MAD planes, in practice these planes were usually called up after a visual or radar contact had been made. The First Escort Force also had four escort carriers to trail important convoys and provide close air cover. The Japanese thought they were sinking U.S. submarines at the rate of fifteen per month. They were sure at least ten were sunk in Convoy College during the summer and fall of 1944, and 901st Air Group was credited with four or five kills. Actually only one U.S. submarine was lost in Convoy College during the whole war.

The number of *maru* sinkings in Convoy College fell off sharply during the first half of August, but this does not appear to have been due to increased intensity of Japanese anti-submarine efforts. A wolf pack of three submarines entered the area about the same time that Park's wolf pack departed at the end of their successful patrol. The new group seemed never to catch up with Japanese convoys. Although they noted increased air activity they were able to carry out search operations with reasonable effectiveness. However, they completed a patrol thirty-five days of which was spent in Convoy College and sank only one ship, on the eve of their departure. While the Japanese were enjoying a breathing spell in this area, however, the routes from northern Luzon south through the Sulu Sea broke out in a rash of sinkings.

Christie's Submarines

Before the middle of the month in August, Christie's submarines sank fifteen *marus* of assorted sizes. In addition *Guitarro* sank the *kaibokan Kusagaki* and *Cod* sank a special transport, *LSV No. 129*. Not all of this was accomplished without loss.

Flier departed Fremantle in early August about the same time as *Rasher* and *Bluefish*. These submarines were routed by divers passages into the South China Sea and *Flier* (Crowley) came up through the Sulu Sea into Balabac Strait. On the evening of 13 August she was tooling along on the surface when suddenly there was a terrific explosion and a dozen men were swimming in the water. *Flier* and all their other shipmates were gone. Crowley, who had been on the bridge, was one of the survivors. They decided to swim for the coral reefs to the northwest. During the night of swimming several men silently disappeared in the darkness. In the morning Crowley ordered everyone to strike out independently for the nearest land. Only seven of them made it. Friendly Filipinos took them to a U. S. Army coastwatcher unit on Palawan; from there they were later picked up by *Redfin*.

Unknown to the Allies, Balabac had been mined early in the war. Although many submarines had previously used this route *Flier* was the loser by the law of averages and ran into one of the patiently waiting Japanese mines. *Robalo* had been lost near Palawan, most probably on a mine, only a few weeks before. After the loss of *Flier* Balabac was avoided by submarine traffic, and submarines bound for the South China Sea were henceforth routed through Karimata Strait.

Rasher

Rasher (Munson) and *Bluefish* (Henderson) came up from Australia about the same time, by different routes, with plans to rendezvous in the South China Sea. Munson had orders to coordinate the searches of the two ships. They rendezvoused on 8 August with *Hoe* (southbound at the end of her patrol) and transferred an injured man from *Rasher* to *Hoe* for early medical attention. *Rasher* and *Bluefish* headed off across the South China Sea to the coast of Luzon. On 15 August Munson detached *Bluefish* to proceed to Cape Calavite, the northern point of Mindoro, to complete the destruction of a tanker that had run itself aground after being hit by *Puffer* with her last torpedo.

On 18 August *Rasher* was twenty miles south of Cape Bojeador, northwest Luzon, proceeding up the coast to join up again with *Bluefish*. One of Lockwood's wolf packs had broadcast a contact with a southbound convoy and *Rasher* was expecting action. The night was pitch black. The rain came down in blinding sheets. From the drowned bridge of *Rasher* it was sometimes difficult to see her own bow, but through this semi-liquid atmosphere radar could penetrate. Suddenly they had radar contact with a southbound convoy. Munson informed *Bluefish*, eighty-three miles ahead of the convoy, *Raton*, in an adjacent area, and *Spadefish*, chasing the convoy out of Convoy College.

Rasher came on in using radar to guide her, and pinging occasionally with the sound gear to keep track of the escorts and "sort out the convoy." At 2122 Munson commenced firing, having still seen only pips on the radar screen, in a night so black it was impossible to distinguish sea from sky. After firing two torpedoes at what he thought was a tanker Munson checked fire because he was doubtful the gyros were matching properly. He swung around to parallel the convoy and then, after the proper time for their run, both torpedoes hit. A volcano of flame shot up a thousand feet in the air, and with an appalling explosion the ship burst in two, one part separated five hundred yards from the other and both parts burning furiously. The convoy fell apart like a Japanese fan with the rivet knocked out. The near escort opened fire with all its guns in all directions, reversed course, and fiercely depth-charged the inoffensive sea, two miles astern of *Rasher*.

Gunfire broke out all through the convoy. *Rasher* came in again and fired both bow and stern tubes at two more *marus*. The convoy scattered. *Rasher* broadcast a contact report and asked for assistance from any submarine within range. She had only six torpedoes left. When these were loaded in the empty tubes she attacked again. Then she was through. Radar spotted an escort joining up with a cripple to creep off to the south. Munson called *Bluefish* on the voice radio and Henderson replied that he was already busy making an attack on two tankers. *Spadefish* picked up another piece of the convoy to the northward and sank a ship.

This was convoy HI-71 of ten *marus*, mostly fast tankers, which departed from Moji 8 August for Manila. The escort consisted of the escort carrier *Taiyo*, the destroyer *Yunagi*, four *kaibokans* (*Sado, Matsuwa, Hiburi*, and *Mikura*), and *Special Subchaser No. 39*. They came down through Convoy College in typhoon weather, and on the night of 18 August breathed a sigh of relief in the lee of Luzon. Suddenly *Taiyo* exploded with a shocking concussion and an awful eruption of flame. Unable to locate their enemies in the pitch black night the disorganized convoy was attacked again and again until seven *marus* (including the 17,000-ton *Teia Maru*) in addition to the escort carrier had been sunk or damaged.

Munson did not know he had sunk the famous escort carrier *Taiyo*. He thought his first target was a tanker, and that a cargo of gasoline provided the spectacular explosion with which *Taiyo* ended her long career. *Taiyo* had been the first Japanese carrier of any kind to be attacked by U.S. submarines when *Gato* missed her with five deep-running torpedoes on 4 May 1942 off Kwajalein, and she had been target for more submarines than any other Japanese carrier. It seemed the ultimate in ignominy for *Rasher* to shoot her down in mistake for a tanker. Munson facetiously remarked in his patrol report that the escort could go home now, the convoy had reached its destination, but his colleagues were not that magnanimous and a different situation was building up to the southward.

Ray, Guitarro, Harder, *and* Haddo

Ray (Kinsella), on patrol off Balabac Strait, encountered a big convoy on 18 August and in a daylight attack sank one tanker. That night she searched for the convoy along its track but located only the escorts. All the next day *Ray* trailed, bucking the air cover, but she finally tracked this convoy down as it was arriving at a bay on the west coast of Mindoro, where the ships anchored for the night rather than risk the fate of HI-71. *Ray* was then a cat at a mouse hole, but the Japanese tactic of holing up for the night committed the submarine to a daylight submerged attack, in which at the most she could torpedo two ships of the fifteen or sixteen tucked safely in the bay for the night. Kinsella called for help. *Harder* (Dealey) and *Haddo* (Nimitz, Jr.) responded. Dealey, as senior skipper, assumed tactical command on arrival. The three submarines rendezvoused and the skippers held a megaphone conference to work out a plan for the morning. *Guitarro* (Haskins) reported by radio that she was coming down from the north, and Dealey assigned her a position along the convoy track to Manila. The other three took station off the bay. The sea was like glass.

Nimitz took *Haddo* down to deep sounding to get a bathythermograph card to determine the depth of sonic-reflecting density layers so he could plan evasion tactics, and then came up to radar depth and waited. The convoy started out at sunrise. *Harder* came in first and occupied most of the attention of the escorts while *Ray* and *Haddo* stabbed into the convoy. *Guitarro* was waiting within sound of the depth charges. Five big *marus* went down before the Japanese convoy could clear the ambush.

Harder and *Haddo*, as a coordinated attack group, then continued on to the entrance of Manila Bay. They arrived just as the escorts of HI-71, after losing their convoy, were coming in from the north. This was Dealey's dish, and Nimitz was just as eager. They took on the *kaibokans* and annihilated *Matsuwa*, *Sado*, and *Hiburi*. The next day (23 August) Nimitz sank the destroyer *Asakaze* with his last torpedo. *Haddo* then took leave of *Harder*; Nimitz said goodbye to Dealey and headed south for Fremantle. *Haddo's* place was taken in Dealey's wolf pack by *Hake*, which had just joined up with *Harder*.

Loss of Harder

On the morning of 24 August the Japanese got their revenge. *Hake* and *Harder* were operating off the west coast of Luzon. *Hake* sighted the Thailand destroyer *Phra Ruang* and a Japanese minesweeper, but broke off her attack when the destroyer ran into a bay, leaving the patrolling minesweeper outside. As *Hake* pulled out she saw *Harder's* periscope ahead, and turned south to clear the area. Nearly an hour later she heard a series of fifteen rapid depth charges in the direction she had last seen her packmate. *Harder* and Sam Dealey were never heard from again. The Japanese record a depth-charge attack in that area on that day, which brought up wood and cork and it seems certain that *Harder*, after Dealey's many victories over them, lost one last battle with Japanese escorts.

Japanese Light Cruiser Sinkings

August was a hard month otherwise for Japanese light forces. U.S. fast carrier task forces raided the Bonins on 4 August. With the aid of submarine contact reports they intercepted a Japanese convoy and sank the escort, consisting of the destroyer *Matsu* and two coast defense vessels, together with several LST's and four *marus* in the convoy. In the long run, however, submarines accounted for the largest number of Japanese light forces sunk in August.

Croaker (Lee), on patrol just south of Nagasaki, on 7 August sank the light cruiser *Nagara* with one hit out of a four-torpedo salvo. The antisubmarine effort of the escorts was feeble. Lee kept his periscope up while he took color moving pictures of the sinking.

The date of 18 August was a bad day all around for the Japanese Navy. In the Philippines, *Hardhead* (McMaster) was patrolling off Surigao Strait. Radar picked up a target which was identified as a battleship. McMaster made two attacks and fired a total of fifteen torpedoes which blasted his target to the bottom. Several days later *Sturgeon* rescued a Japanese officer and three men from the sea. They identified *Hardhead's* target as the light cruiser *Natori* and confirmed the sinking.

Japanese Maru Losses

The destruction of Japanese light forces was only incidental to the destruction of the commerce between the extremes of the attenuated Japanese Empire. From the Sea of Okhotsk down around the islands of Japan to Nansei Shoto scattered sinkings kept pressure on Japan. Off the Ryukyus *Barbel* (Keating) sank three small *marus* whose importance was greater than their tonnage to Japan's frantic effort to reinforce Okinawa. A little to the westward, in Tung Hai, *Pintado* (Clarey) sank two ships, one of which was a big tanker, *Tonan Maru No. 2*. This was the second time that ship had been "sunk" and the third time it had been torpedoed by submarines. By curious coincidence Clarey had been executive officer of *Amberjack* when she torpedoed *Tonan Maru No. 2* the first time in Kavieng Harbor on 10 October 1942. To Clarey the unique silhouette of the ex-whale factory seemed like a ghost returned to haunt him. *Croaker* was busy in the Yellow Sea, and *Ronquil* (Monroe) was in the southern end of the East China Sea, but despite their slow start in August the greatest successes of Lockwood's submarines in August and September were in Convoy College.

Convoy College

A wolf pack made up of *Spadefish* (Underwood), *Redfish* (Mc-Gregor), and *Picuda* under command of Commander Donaho (who also commanded the pack) moved into Convoy College on the heels of the first unsuccessful August wolf pack. They also had trouble finding convoys at first, but *Redfish* sighted the unfortunate HI-71 convoy. *Redfish* attacked and missed, but the contact report put *Rasher* on the alert for her spectacular night battle with HI-71 and coached *Spadefish* into position to get in on the gleanings after *Rasher's* attack had scattered the convoy. Donaho's wolf pack continued in Convoy College until late September and, as a pack, made one of the most successful patrols on record. *Picuda* sank the destroyer *Yunagi* on 25 August. *Yunagi* had been one of the escorts of HI-71 and her sinking left few survivors of that famous convoy. *Picuda* also sank three *marus* during the patrol, and *Redfish* sank three more, but *Spadefish* topped the pack with six ships sunk during the patrol.

Next to arrive was a wolf pack consisting of *Tunny* (Pierce), *Queenfish* (Loughlin), and *Barb* (Fluckey) with the pack commander (Captain E. R. Swinburne) riding in *Barb*. They pulled into Convoy College on 20 August. The next ten days they spent dodging Japanese search planes, with no other contact larger than sampans. They could generally avoid the planes by the usual up-and-down tactics, but any lack of alertness resulted in a bombing. Some Japanese planes could home on SJ radar transmissions, so submarines risked revealing their own locations by operating this air search apparatus and therefore they limited its use.

On 29 August another pack arrived. The new pack was commanded by Commander T. B. Oakley (who also commanded *Growler*). The other two submarines in his group were *Pampanito* (Summers) and *Sealion* (Reich). Late the next day they had contact with a convoy almost simultaneously with Swinburne's wolf pack. With six submarines after the same convoy the night action which followed resulted in even more than the usual confusion inherent in a night action.

The Japanese air cover was thick, night and day. Moreover, Japanese planes were using radar very effectively. Their radar transmissions could be picked up by the submarines' radar detectors but the problem of approaching a convoy on the surface with such close air cover was complicated and difficult. *Tunny* had five separate air contacts between midnight and seven o'clock the next morning. During this same period *Barb* logged nine airplane contacts. Air cover was successful in holding *Tunny* out beyond attack range, but from the persistence with which she was tracked it seems probable that she absorbed most of the attention of MAD- and radar-equipped planes while the others got in.

As *Barb* came in on the surface a plane came directly at her and forced her down to radar depth. Then just as she worked into an attack position she heard four torpedoes explode. A tanker in the convoy burst into flame and the rest of the convoy changed course, leaving *Barb* out in left field, with a patrolling plane between her and the burning victim of some other submarine's torpedoes. Taking a chance on the plane, Fluckey surfaced and dashed off in pursuit of the convoy. *Tunny* gave him a contact report. Just as dawn was breaking to reveal submarines in every direction, *Barb* sighted the convoy again. Again she crept into position for a submerged attack when sound reported torpedoes running in her direction, so close, Fluckey reported, that he lowered the periscope to let them go by. An escort blew up and sank, and the convoy changed course, spoiling *Barb's* attack position. A few minutes later a freighter presented an opportunity for stern tube shots. Fluckey took it and hit the target with three torpedoes.

Japanese Countermeasures

During the night and the next day five of the six submarines attacked. Twice again *Barb* heard torpedoes from another submarine running by her. A few days before, *Queenfish* had reported a salvo of torpedoes fired at her by a Japanese submarine and *Sealion* sighted what appeared to be midget submarines as she came in to attack that night. There is nothing in Japanese accounts, however, about use of either conventional or midget submarines for anti-submarine work in Convoy College, and it is most probable that *Barb* had the misfortune of repeatedly getting in the line of fire of her packmates.

If there were no Japanese submarines present, practically everything else the Japanese had was there: gunfire from escort and convoy, bombs from MAD planes by day and bombs from radar-guided planes at night, and hundreds of depth charges dropped from surface escorts. From some of the noises described it appears possible the Japanese may have used their spiral run torpedoes. Intense anti-submarine action kept up for two days.

On 1 September *Barb* watched an air attack on *Tunny*, six miles distant. Planes dropped float lights to mark out the submarine's position and then made repeated bombing runs. In this attack *Tunny* received serious damage. She reported to Swinburne that a near miss had dished in the hull over her after torpedo room, causing leaks and other damage that would handicap her in any future action. Pierce decided to terminate *Tunny's* patrol and return to Saipan for repairs. *Sealion*, which had

shot herself about out of torpedoes, also headed back to Saipan for a reload.

The next day a plane gave *Barb* a very close shave. A near miss from
a heavy bomb caused minor damage. When *Barb* surfaced after the attack she found fragments of the bomb, including the tail vanes, on her
deck.

These all-out anti-submarine measures did not save the convoy. It is
quite impossible to determine who sank who in the confused action.
Shirataka, the smoking escort flagship that had led convoy Bamboo No. 1
to disaster in May, went down that night along with *Hinode Maru No.
20*, another escort. *Okuni Maru* and *Chiyoda Maru* were sunk and *Rikko
Maru* was heavily damaged.

XXII

SEPTEMBER 1944

Rakuyo Maru

Swinburne's wolf pack and Oakley's pack both continued to work Convoy College in September. On 9 September *Queenfish* sank two more *marus*. *Sealion* arrived back in Convoy College with a fresh load of torpedoes and rejoined Oakley's group on 11 September. The next night all three of Oakley's submarines got into another convoy. *Growler* sank the *kaibokan Hirato* and the destroyer *Shikinami*. *Growler* was then out of torpedoes and Oakley turned south to report to Fremantle for duty. The other two submarines of his pack sank three *marus* out of the convoy.

That convoy was a six-ship convoy, with five escorts, which left Singapore for Japan on 6 September, to be joined at sea by three ships from Manila. On board *Rakuyo Maru* (one of the Singapore contingent) were 1350 English and Australian prisoners of war. A total of 750 other prisoners were crowded into one of the other ships. These prisoners had been taken in 1942 and used as slave labor to build a railroad in Malaya. Twenty-two thousand of their comrades had died of malnutrition, abuse, and disease, and the emaciated survivors were being shipped back to Japan to work in factories and mines.

The first indication to the Japanese that the convoy was in trouble, on the night of 12 September, was a violent explosion which blew up *Hirato*, the leading escort. *Rakuyo Maru* was one of the ships sunk that night. The Japanese abandoned ship, leaving the prisoners to shift for themselves. The next day the majority of the swimming Japanese were picked up by escorts, while the prisoner survivors were held off at gunpoint.

Rescue Operations

On 15 September, *Pampanito* was doubling back through the area of the attack when she sighted several men on a crudely constructed raft. *Pampanito* picked them up and discovering what had happened, immediately began search and rescue operations for other survivors. She found them in small groups, so exhausted they were unable to help themselves. The strongest swimmers in the submarine crew went over the side to help the rescued men aboard. A work crew on deck stripped the survivors of their rags and washed them down with diesel oil to remove the heavy crude oil with which they were covered. Then they were helped below and packed in the already crowded submarine, two to a narrow bunk, and three on each empty torpedo skid. The pharmacist's mate labored with inadequate means to keep the weakest ones alive.

Pampanito sent a message to *Sealion* for help. When the light failed that evening the two submarines had 127 survivors on board. Both submarines then headed for Saipan full speed, distressed with the knowledge that they must be leaving more dying men behind. Seven of their passengers died before the submarines could reach port.

Back in Pearl Harbor Lockwood had already taken over. He ordered *Barb* and *Queenfish* to the rescue. When these two submarines received their orders they had 450 miles to go to reach the area. Immediately they headed south at full speed.

Unyo *Sunk*

The next night, about ten o'clock as they charged through the starlit night with the throttles hard down, radar picked up a convoy. Both submarines moved in to attack. *Queenfish* had only four torpedoes, all aft. She got in the first attack and reported one hit in a transport. As she turned away with empty tubes the officer of the deck spotted a carrier in the formation. *Barb* was coming in on the other bow of the convoy. She picked a tanker as her target, when suddenly Fluckey saw the carrier. Still on the surface, he swung *Barb* to line up both carrier and tanker and fired six torpedoes from the forward tubes. Five of them hit, two in the tanker and three in the carrier. *Queenfish*, from her side of the convoy, could see the tanker burning bright. *Barb* swung to bring her stern tubes to bear, but the nearest escort was only 750 yards away and the submarine had to submerge to keep from being rammed. The escort carrier *Unyo* went down that night, the second Japanese escort carrier to be sunk in Convoy College within a month. The 10,000-ton tanker *Azusa Maru* joined the carrier on the bottom.

Barb then had one torpedo forward and two aft and an urgent desire to chase the remnants of the convoy to deliver the remaining torpedoes. Swinburne decided that any further delay might prevent reaching the rescue area by daylight, and at 0100 he ordered *Queenfish* and *Barb* to proceed full speed on their rescue mission. At dawn they commenced seeing wreckage and floating bodies, but it was noon before they encountered men still alive in the water. *Barb* picked up fourteen and

Queenfish eighteen additional ex-prisoners. They searched all the next day in rising winds and sea, and on the evening of 19 September in typhoon weather set out for Saipan with reasonable assurance that there were no more men alive on the flimsy rafts in the heavy seas.

Outside Convoy College

Outside Convoy College, the pattern of the war against the *marus* in September was much the same as it was in August. No area except the Sea of Japan was safe from submarine attack. Sinkings occurred everywhere Japanese ships went, from the polar circuit to the Sulu Sea. East of the Philippines the Japanese abandoned their efforts to maintain surface sea communication. When U.S. carrier task forces raided Palau and Yap they found few shipping targets.

Batfish (Fyfe) sank the destroyer *Samidare* north of Palau on 26 August. Half a dozen destroyers and *kaibokans* were heavily damaged, and a number of minor Japanese vessels were sunk by submarines in August and September. All of them added up to a tremendous destruction of Japanese merchant shipping and their escorts. In the three months of July, August, and September submarines alone sank twenty-seven Japanese naval vessels and 165 *marus*.

Changing Tactics

U.S. submarines were fortunate to get through these three months with the loss of only two submarines in combat missions. This was approximately 5 per cent of the submarine sinkings with which the Japanese credited the Grand Escort Force. To a considerable extent U.S. submarines could attribute their good fortune to the rugged construction of their hulls, for if *Barb* and *Tunny* had been no better built than their Japanese contemporaries, these two submarines would undoubtedly have been listed among the missing. But the frantic anti-submarine efforts of the Japanese were too little and too late. The increase in air and surface escorts was more than matched by the increase in numbers of U.S. submarines in the operating areas. The new tactics of the Japanese were met with new tactics by the submarines, and Japanese desperation was offset by the audacity of young submarine skippers.

Bigger convoys and more escorts, and more submarines in the area required more cooperation between submarines than was necessary in the old days of lonely patrols. Lockwood sent out wolf packs under separate commanders embarked in one of the submarines of the pack, of course quite unaware of Japanese skepticism of their similar system. It was soon apparent that the system had its drawbacks. It probably generated more radio traffic. Any effort toward attack cooperation filled the air with yak-yak to which the Japanese listened with a certain amount of awe, but from which they seemed to profit very little.

In the search phase a wolf pack commander had a definite function and communication circuits available to exercise command, but the attack phase cut off communication with the pack, and left him like a hen with one chick. In submarine attacks there are often reasons for two opinions but never room for more than one decision. It is no secret that sometimes there were violent differences of opinion between the pack commander and the flagship's skipper, although what is known is based on rumor for none of these arguments reach the documentation stage. Gradually Lockwood shifted over to the system of having the senior skipper of a group act also as wolf pack commander, except in special situations in which the pack had a complex strategic mission. This worked all right, but *Barb's* experiences definitely indicated that, with or without a separate commander, coordination to prevent submarines from interfering with each other during the attack phase was still an unsolved problem.

In September 1944 the submarine war of attrition approached the stage of a submarine blockade of Japan. Japan had lost so many ships that she probably could not have sustained her war economy if she was free to do so. She was prevented from using the inadequate resources she did possess by a cordon of submarines that sank a large proportion of the ships that put to sea, and detained a larger portion in port waiting for escorts. Singapore and Manila and many lesser ports in the south were crowded with shipping waiting for escorts.

Japanese merchant seamen discerned that the war was lost, and ruefully quipped that they could cross Devil's Sea by stepping on the exposed periscopes of cruising U.S. submarines. Had the situation been allowed to continue it seems probable that this side war of submarines vs. anti-submarines would eventually have resulted in a clear submarine victory and Japanese commerce with Southeast Asia would have dried up from submarine attack alone. But by September, the fast carrier task forces of the Pacific Fleet were ready to prowl. Their operations greatly changed the situation for both sides, and the aim and objective of all American forces was to get the war over as soon as possible, regardless of who claimed credit for the victory.

MacArthur's Approach to the Philippines

While submarines were doing their level best to sever communication between the Philippines and Japan to the north, MacArthur was approaching the Philippines from the south. The direct assistance subma-

rines could give to this advance was slight. *S-47* (Young) put a reconnaissance party ashore near the northernmost point of New Guinea at the
end of June. As a result of the reports of this party, MacArthur selected
Sansapor near the western tip of New Guinea as the next invasion point
and U. S. Army forces under his command landed there successfully on
30 July. On 18 August *S-42* (Glenn) landed three men on Halmahera
Island for reconnaissance. Unfortunately two of these three men were
lost on this mission. On 15 September Southwest Pacific forces landed on
Morotai, off Halmahera, and when the airfield there became operational
(4 October) the Fifth Air Force was within range of Leyte.

As MacArthur moved nearer to the Philippines, service to coastwatchers, to clandestine radio stations, to rescue and evasion missions, and to
organized guerrilla forces placed greater demands upon submarine services of supply. Although submarines on combat missions continued to
lend an occasional hand, most of this duty fell to the lot of *Nautilus*
(Sharp) and *Narwhal* (Latta or Titus). When these two submarines became unable to handle the volume of traffic *Seawolf* (Bontier) and
Stingray (Loomis) were added to the supply group. In the three months
July, August, and September these four submarines completed seventeen
missions in the Philippines. Most of it was routine work of landing men
and supplies and picking up evacuees, but some of it was far from routine.

On the night of 26 September, on a supply mission to guerrillas on
Cebu, *Nautilus* ran hard aground on a coral reef. That this did not happen more frequently was a tribute to the careful navigation of the ships
in the trade. *Nautilus,* however, was in a very precarious position, for if
daylight found her exposed on a reef like a stranded whale, she could
expect a swift end to her career. Sharp did everything in his power to
pull her off—he landed the remainder of his cargo, jettisoned ammunition, blew reserve fuel over the side, and mustered the crew on *Nautilus'*
broad deck to sally the stubborn old lady. Finally, about three hours before dawn, while the erratic tide was supposed to be full but was already
ebbing fast, with full power on her backing screws, *Nautilus* pulled clear
and was free.

Three days later her sister ship *Narwhal* (Latta) rescued eighty-one
ex-prisoners of war. These were the remnants of a shipload of prisoners
the Japanese were evacuating from Mindanao on board *Shinyo Maru.*
That *maru* was sunk by *Paddle* on 7 September. The helpless prisoners
in her hold were shot down by machine-gun fire as *Shinyo Maru* was
sinking. Nevertheless a number of them fought free and jumped over the
side. Boats rescuing the Japanese crew picked up some of the prisoners
and brutally executed them for attempting to escape. A few others swam
ashore where they were later picked up by *Narwhal.* The story of their
experiences did very little to endear the Japanese to the submarine force.

Most of the earlier submarine supply runs were to the southern Philippines, but by October the Philippine Islands were almost completely covered by a network of guerrilla organizations that had to be supported. *Nautilus* and *Narwhal* ranged all the way up to northern Luzon. This service of supply was of the utmost importance to the guerrilla forces, who in turn were a strong support to the reconquest of the Philippines.

Nimitz's Next Move

MacArthur never doubted for a moment that his true objective was the Philippines, but when the Central Pacific forces reached the Marianas they had triple ways to take. They could join with MacArthur in the Philippine venture, or cut straight through to the China coast, or work up the Bonins ladder to Japan. MacArthur expected the Pacific Fleet to join his forces in the conquest of the Philippines, but to Nimitz's planners this was chewing up the dragon from the tail to its head—a slow, expensive, and dangerous process. They favored a straight thrust to Formosa to cut the Japanese Empire into two parts, neither of which could exist without the other. For this they needed more resources than they had available. At Nimitz's disposition there were amphibious facilities to lift four divisions—not enough to take Formosa. Okinawa was practically undefended then, and could easily have been taken but it would require a major effort to hold it after it was occupied. The Japanese, reeling from the loss of the Marianas, had to be kept off balance, and Nimitz needed a four-division objective to keep rolling them back. To gain and maintain control of the eastern approaches to the Philippines, Formosa, and the China coast, Nimitz's next move was planned to occupy Yap, Ulithi, and part of Palau. Where to go after that was still undecided by the Joint Chiefs of Staff in Washington.

Submarine Reconnaissance

Submarine reconnaissance was important in the preparation for the forthcoming amphibious operations. The excellent work of *Greenling* (Grant) in reconnoitering Saipan before the invasion there, and the beautiful periscope pictures of the landing beaches Grant brought back, increased the demand for this sort of work in all future amphibious operations. *Seawolf* (Lynch) made a photographic reconnaissance of the Palau area in July and *Permit* (Chapple) performed the same task for Woleai and Yap, in the Carolines. In August *Burrfish* (Perkins) went out for additional photographic coverage of Angaur and Peleliu in Palau. While this type of reconnaissance was very valuable, the Amphibious

Force was anxious to know as much as possible about depth of water, surf condition, underwater obstacles, and beach defense, and this information could be obtained only by an actual landing on the beach.

Burrfish took with her a beach reconnaissance party from Fifth Amphibious Force for this purpose. After waiting for favorable moon conditions the party went ashore on Peleliu and returned with much valuable information. An attempted landing on Angaur was thwarted by alert Japanese radar. Perkins then moved up to land the party on Yap. They landed once and were safely recovered. On the night of 15 August five men went ashore again in a rubber boat while *Burrfish* stood by offshore to pick them up on their return. The boat returned with only two men. Three others failed to make the rendezvous, even after the men with the boat abandoned all caution and searched the beach with flashlights. It can only be assumed that they were captured. None of them survived the war.

Third Fleet Plans

While this was going on and while the Fifth Fleet under Spruance was tidying up the Marianas, the Third Fleet Staff under Halsey was planning the next operation. Submarine cooperation with the Fifth Fleet had reached the peak of effectiveness at the Battle of the Philippine Sea, but Halsey's planners wanted to change the setup for the Palau–Yap operation. They asked to have a group of ten submarines placed at their disposal. Nine of them were to be spotted in a double "reconnaissance line" (dubbed the Bear Pit) between the Philippines and Palau. A tenth submarine was needed for lifeguard duty off Palau until after the initial strike, when she would join the others in the Bear Pit. These submarines were organized in three wolf packs with Captain C. W. Wilkins riding in *Seahorse* in over-all command. In addition *Gar* was off Yap on lifeguard and Christie had one submarine off San Bernardino, one off Surigao, and others dispersed throughout the East Indies watching the routes the Japanese might take.

Lockwood was not happy with this arrangement for his submarines. It smacked too much of the old days when Commander Submarines Pacific had little strategic control. Since then an organization and communication facilities had been developed for rapid and effective dissemination of information to submarines on patrol. No fleet flagship at sea could perform the function of the Operations Room at Subpac headquarters. Moreover, the probability that the Japanese would respond to a landing in Palau with a sortie of their battered fleet was slight. The Third Fleet plan presaged much shifting of submarines in the futile fashion of the early campaigns. There was no longer any Japanese surface traffic with

Palau, and ten submarines dispersed as planned would have no opportunity to continue the relentless war of attrition or to strengthen the submarine blockade of Japan.

Nimitz based his decision on the principle that Commander Third Fleet (or Fifth Fleet) could have anything reasonable he asked for in a major operation. Although the same ships made up both fleets, the Third Fleet when it went to sea under Halsey had a different character than when it went to sea as the Fifth Fleet under Spruance. When Spruance embarked upon an operation his plan could be read like the timetable of a crack railroad, with the assurance that everyone would be where and when the plan specified, in spite of "rock and tempest, fire and foe." This characteristic facilitated cooperation between submarines and the Fifth Fleet.

Halsey's staff, on the other hand, were splendid opportunists and no one, especially the Japanese, could be sure what the Third Fleet would do next. It was pretty much in the cards that no matter where Halsey planned to place the submarines he would want to move them in a hurry before the operation was over. On that basis, and to give him more direct control of the submarines, Halsey's request was very reasonable, so the ten submarines went out as directed by the Third Fleet to be in position by 13 September and to operate in the Bear Pit until 25 September.

As it turned out both Halsey and Lockwood were right. The Japanese fleet did not come out. The ten Bear Pit submarines made no contacts. The number of Japanese ships sunk by submarines dropped during September to below the August or the October figures. Halsey found a tide in the affairs of war which taken at its flood led on to earlier victory. The location of the Bear Pit was changed not once but several times. Although these submarines were ineffective during this period, the Third Fleet seized its opportunity and advanced the whole conduct of the war by a great leap forward.

Palau and the Philippines

From 6 to 8 September a sixteen-carrier task force blasted Yap, Peleliu, and Ulithi. Halsey then moved over to strike the airfields of Mindanao to keep down air opposition to landings on Peleliu and on Morotai. These strikes, on 8 and 9 September, met with little opposition so Halsey canceled the remaining scheduled Mindanao strikes and hit airfields and shipping in the central Philippines instead. The opposition there was also weak and the harvest was rich in planes and *marus*. One carrier group then sailed south to cover Morotai and another east to cover Peleliu during the landings, while the third group refueled and replenished.

Intelligence gained in the Visayan strike indicated that the Leyte garrison was weak. Halsey therefore sent a dispatch to Nimitz on 13 September suggesting that the Yap, Peleliu, and Morotai and Mindanao landings be called off and that MacArthur and Nimitz join forces to land on Leyte, bypassing all the Japanese strong points in between. Nimitz passed this dispatch on to MacArthur and to Washington. MacArthur agreed immediately, except that the Morotai landing had to go forward to give the Fifth Air Force a staging base into Leyte. Nimitz also accepted the proposal but continued with the Palau operation to give him a base to jump off for the Philippines. The Combined Chiefs of Staff then in session in Quebec agreed, and the target date for Leyte was advanced two months to 20 October. The Yap landing and the Mindanao campaigns were canceled.

Landings took place as scheduled on 15 September on Morotai and Peleliu. Peleliu turned out to be a tough nut to crack and to dig the Japanese out of their defensive caves after the airfield was captured. Ulithi was occupied without opposition on 23 September, and Service Force immediately commenced moving forward its advanced base from Eniwetok to Ulithi.

Light opposition in the Visayas encouraged Halsey to amend and extend his plan of operation. He moved the Bear Pit up to the latitude of Formosa to clear the submarines out of his path and to re-establish their reconnaissance line where it would cover his northern flank. On 21 September he moved in with his all-powerful carrier task force and hit Luzon. Manila was taken by surprise. The harbor was crammed with shipping held up waiting for escorts to cross the Devil's Sea. Carrier planes made a shambles of the harbor. Ships en route to Manila took refuge in Coron Bay in the Calamian Group, and a 350-mile strike pursued them there to spread disaster through all the shipping in the Philippines. Ninety-five Japanese ships were sunk in September by carrier planes, far exceeding the fifty-eight sunk by submarines during the month. Japanese shipping control was thrown into utter confusion from which it never fully recovered.

Japanese Submarines

Since July, when Miwa recalled the Sixth Fleet, Japanese submarines had been inactive except for transportation runs. Obsessed with the necessity to supply the militarily impotent bypassed garrisons, the Japanese Navy designed and built two classes of submarines for this service. Thirteen submarines of the *I-361* class were built; about 1500 tons displacement, armed with 14-centimeter guns but no torpedoes; with a maximum surface speed of 13 knots and a safe diving depth of only 245 feet. Ten submarines of the *HA-101* class, designed specifically to carry aviation gasoline, were only 370 tons but could dive to 325 feet. Even this diversion of submarine effort to transportation did not satisfy the Japanese Army, who proceeded to construct and man their own submarines for their own service of supply; but these abortions (one of which was later salvaged from Lingayen Gulf by the U. S. Navy) never accomplished anything of military value. In August the first four of the *I-361* class were ready for operation and were sent out on transport runs to Wake, Narau, and Truk. *I-364* left Yokosuka on her maiden run to Wake on 14 September. The next day she was torpedoed and sunk by *Sea Devil* (Styles), also on her maiden patrol.

By September Japanese submarines were ready to take a more active part in the war again. The Navy General Staff had promulgated the Sho Plan of Operation, replacing the disasterous A-Go Plan. Sho-1 was a plan for defense against invasion of the Philippines, Sho-2 for defense against invasion of Kyushu, Nansei Shoto, or Taiwan. Either of these called for decisive fleet action in which the Advance Expeditionary Force submarines would sortie for battle. In event of invasion in Palau or Halmahera submarines would cooperate with the local defense forces but the fleet would not be committed. Miwa had about thirty submarines, not including those under construction or superannuated submarines assigned to training duty only. Four were in the Indian Ocean, operating out of Penang. Little is known about the details of the operation of the Indian Ocean submarines during this period. Several I-class submarines were in the navy yards for installation of the new suicide weapons and six were engaged in transport operations.

On 10 September a radio dispatch erroneously reported landings at Davao, and every available Japanese submarine sortied. The next day the operation order was canceled, but the planned advance of five submarines (*I-177*, *RO-41*, *RO-43*, *RO-46*, and *RO-47*) to the Philippine area was continued. They were stationed in a double reconnaissance line in the Mindanao-Halmahera-Palau triangle, suggestive of a half scale mirror replica of the Bear Pit submarines. Very likely they ran through the Bear Pit, undetected and undetecting, to get to their station. On station, like the Bear Pit submarines, they saw nothing. The Visayan carrier strike on 12 September destroyed all diesel fuel at Cebu, making it necessary for submarines to replenish in Japan, and this curtailed their time on station. On 23 September four Japanese submarines were ordered to the vicinity of Palau and one to Morotai, where amphibious forces and bombardment groups offered many attractive targets.

Miwa received a dispatch from the Base Force at Peleliu on 2 October reporting that two U.S. destroyers had been torpedoed and sunk. The next day U.S. destroyer escort *Miles* made a convincing attack on a submarine in the Palau area and brought up debris and oil. Neither *I-177* nor *RO-47* were heard from after this date, and Miwa acting on the theory that they had been unable to report their successes credited them with the sinkings reported by the Base Force on 2 October. No destroyers were, in fact, torpedoed that day. *I-177* and *RO-46* were directed to make reconnaissance of Ulithi on their way home, but *I-177* had been sunk probably before these orders were issued.

Northeast of Morotai *RO-41*, on 3 October, reported sinking an aircraft carrier. A U.S. task force of two escort carriers and four destroyer escorts were in that vicinity. At 0807 the destroyer escort *Shelton* was hit by a submarine torpedo and went down some fourteen hours later. She must have received *RO-41*'s torpedo intended for the escort carrier. Destroyer escort *Richard M. Rowell*, standing by *Shelton*, made a depth-charge attack with a sound contact on *RO-41*. The Japanese submarine evaded and eventually made it back to Kure.

Loss of Seawolf

RO-41 had been operating very close to a U.S. submarine safety lane, used for traffic between Manus and the Philippines by submarines on the guerrilla supply run. There were four U.S. submarines in the safety lane at that time. About an hour before *Shelton* was hit, *Narwhal* exchanged recognition signals with *Seawolf* (Bontier), which was northbound en route to Samar with supplies and an Army reconnaissance party. About three hours after *Shelton* was torpedoed, a plane from the escort carrier *Midway* sighted a submarine well inside the safety lane. The plane dropped two bombs and a dye marker on the submerging submarine. This, of course, was in direct violation of submarine haven restrictions which specifically applied to the safety lane.

Rowell was eighteen miles away, standing by *Shelton*. She came dashing up to cover the plane contact, arrived at the dye marker, picked up sonar contact, and promptly attacked with hedgehogs. She then heard a submarine oscillator sending a confused series of dots and dashes which *Rowell*'s sound operator did not recognize as a U.S. submarine's recognition signal. *Rowell* evaluated this as an attempt to jam her sonar. She attacked a second time with hedgehogs and brought up debris and a large air bubble. That night when Christie tried to raise the U.S. submarines in the vicinity by radio three of them responded but *Seawolf* was silent. There can be little doubt that she was sunk by *Rowell*'s second attack—a very tragic end for a veteran ship which, in her long career, had survived many anti-submarine attacks by her enemies, but was lost with all hands in a more lethal assault by her friends.

XXIII

OCTOBER 1944

Third Fleet

RO-46, which had been ordered to make a reconnaissance on her way home from Palau, was off Ulithi on 7 October. She reported an aircraft carrier (it was *Bunker Hill*), two heavy cruisers, and several other vessels inside the atoll. This report initiated Japanese plans for a submarine attack on Ulithi. Had *RO-46* been a day earlier she would have witnessed the majestic sortie of the fast carrier task forces of the Third Fleet. They left Ulithi to rendezvous under Halsey on 7 October for a campaign to destroy Japanese air and sea communications and isolate the Philippines for the forthcoming invasion.

On 10 October seventeen carriers, supported by battleships and cruisers, bombed Japanese shipping and airfields on Okinawa. The Japanese promptly alerted their Base Air Forces for Sho-1 and Sho-2 operations. The next day two carrier groups hit northern Luzon and on 12 October all the Third Fleet carriers began a five-day attack on Formosa and northern Luzon.

This series of strikes provoked violent reaction from the Japanese shore-based air forces. The Japanese had over six hundred planes in the area and flew in as many more to join in the fray. Japanese pilots reported that a dozen or more U.S. carriers and many other ships had been sunk or damaged. Radio Tokyo joyfully reported that Halsey was defeated and the Emperor proclaimed a mass celebration for the Glorious Victory of Taiwan. The Japanese were carried away by their own propaganda and threw everything into the battle.

Several ships of the Third Fleet were damaged, although none were sunk. *Houston* and *Canberra* were hit by aircraft torpedoes and both these cruisers lost all power. Halsey ordered them taken in tow, hoping the Japanese would send out a task force to destroy them and give the Third Fleet an opportunity to hit heavy units of the Japanese fleet. Their Second Striking Force of three cruisers and a destroyer division did sortie from the Inland Sea for this purpose, but after reaching the latitude of Okinawa they heard reports of very active U.S. forces, thought better of their plan, and retired.

In these battles the Japanese shore-based air forces lost over six hundred planes. Forty or more *marus* and light patrol vessels were sunk. The Combined Fleet, deluded by the overoptimistic reports of Japanese aviators and by their own propaganda, ordered a general pursuit of Halsey and sent the Grand Escort Force out, along with everything else they could muster. Most of the surface escort vessels survived this folly, but the 901st Air Group, which had developed into a potent anti-submarine organization, was sent out to search for Halsey and lost many of its specially equipped planes and skilled pilots. It never regained its full effectiveness as an anti-submarine force.

Submarine Activities

Submarines took little part in these battles. U.S. submarines supplied lifeguard services for the air strike. The most successful on lifeguard was *Sterlet,* which rescued six pilots off Okinawa. *Besugo* (Wogan) with two other submarines formed a coordinated attack group off Bungo Suido with the primary mission of reporting movements of major Japanese forces. Wogan was under orders to report any Japanese task force before attacking it. *Besugo* sighted and reported the sortie of the Second Striking Force on 15 October. The next night she again sighted cruisers and destroyers in Bungo Suido, and fired six torpedoes at a target she identified as a cruiser. Wogan observed one hit. The destroyer *Suzutsuki* had her bow blown off in this attack (the second time a U.S. submarine had done this to *Suzutsuki*). The damaged destroyer succeeded in making it back to Kure to be patched up again.

Of the five Japanese submarines operating in defense of Palau and Morotai only three survived. These were en route home to Kure to refuel and replenish at the end of their patrol when Halsey hit Okinawa. Miwa ordered the returning submarines to intercept but none of them made contact with the Third Fleet. Eight I-class submarines were training in the Inland Sea, three of them with suicide weapons. Toyoda ordered the other five submarines out after Halsey. They straggled out the Bungo, as they became ready for extended operations. Information on the location of the Third Fleet was erratic and Japanese submarines were chevied around as new and contradictory reports reached Tokyo. They made no contacts. *Canberra* and *Houston* were towed with painful slowness across the Philippine Sea all the way to Ulithi, and Japanese submarines never sighted these vulnerable targets.

Attacks on Japanese Marus

Recognizing that the Philippines would be the next point of attack, the Japanese frantically tried to reinforce them, and at the same time import from Malaya and the East Indies the oil and raw material Japan desperately needed. U.S. carrier task forces and submarines nicely supplemented each other in preying on this desperation. To avoid submarine attacks convoys hugged the coast, and anchored in safe ports of refuge. Carrier attacks on the crowded ports were devastating. Air attacks also destroyed patrol vessels and Japanese anti-submarine air forces—the natural enemies of submarines.

In October 1944 submarines topped all previous records for destruction of Japanese commerce, sending seventy *marus* to the bottom while the air forces were sinking an additional forty-seven. The location of submarine attacks took on a curious pattern. Only one *maru* was sunk in the high north and one in the Yellow Sea. Six or eight went down between the Bonins and the coast of Japan. The rest of the sinkings were concentrated in a narrow lane from Formosa Strait, down through Convoy College, along the west coast of the Philippines and on down to Borneo. The chart of Japanese ships sunk by submarines in October looked as though a *banzai* charge of Japanese *marus* had come up out of the South China Sea to be broken on the ramparts of the western Philippines.

MacArthur Returns

On 20 October MacArthur returned to the Philippines. He landed at Leyte with two Army corps, embarked in and supported by 738 ships of the Seventh Fleet under Vice Admiral Kinkaid. Halsey with the Third Fleet had 105 additional combat ships (including eighteen fast carriers) to meet any attack of the Japanese fleet, provide additional air cover, and beat down air reinforcements through Luzon. During the first four days of the invasion air and naval resistance by the Japanese was light.

Japanese Plans

The Japanese fleet was divided. The First Striking Force of battleships, cruisers, and destroyers, under Vice Admiral Kurita, was at Lingga, near Singapore, where the ever-pressing fuel supply problem was most easily met. The Main Body (under Ozawa) of four carriers, two her-

maphrodite carrier-battleships, three light cruisers, and ten destroyers
was in the Inland Sea for flight training, repairs, and aircraft replenishment. Another force, the Second Striking Force, under Vice Admiral
Shima, consisting of three cruisers and four destroyers, was at Bako in
the Pescadores Islands after having made an abortive pass at Halsey off
Formosa. U. S. Seventh Fleet busyness with sweeping channels into
Leyte Gulf and initial landings on offshore islands tipped off Toyoda
that major operations were imminent. On 17 October he issued alert
orders for Sho-1 operations (the battle plan for defense against Philippine
invasion). Kurita sailed from Lingga on 18 October, and arrived at
Brunei, in northwest Borneo, on the twentieth. That same evening,
Ozawa sortied from Bungo Suido with the carriers. Shima, with the
Second Striking Force, left Bako on 21 October.

The Japanese plan of battle was very complicated. At Brunei the
First Striking Force divided. The Southern Force of two battleships, a
cruiser, and four destroyers under Vice Admiral Nishimura split off to
proceed across the Sulu Sea to Surigao Strait, while the stronger Center
Force of five battleships, twelve cruisers, and fifteen destroyers under
Kurita went up through Palawan Channel and across Sibuyan Sea to
San Bernardino Strait. The Second Striking Force came down through
the South China Sea to follow Nishimura across Sulu Sea and Surigao.
The Southern Force and the Center Force were to meet in Leyte Gulf
and destroy the Seventh Fleet. Ozawa's Main Body of carriers (with very
weak air strength) were to serve as a diversion force to draw Halsey
north while Kinkaid was being destroyed.

Lockwood's Submarine Dispositions

To the eastward of Luzon, the whole area of the Philippine Sea south
of the 20th parallel was designated as an Air Surface Zone, from which
submarines were excluded. Lockwood's preparations for the Leyte landings were to maintain submarine concentration off southern Japan, off
Nansei Shoto, and off the northern end of Formosa to guard the approaches from Japan and at the same time sink Japanese ships. Two
wolf packs were in Convoy College and two other wolf packs were en
route there, proceeding along the dividing line between Air Surface
Zone and Submarine Patrol Zone.

Wogan's wolf pack, having spotted Shima's sortie from Bungo Suido
on 15 October, was still there. After *Besugo* torpedoed *Suzutsuki* on 16
October, Wogan informed Lockwood that he considered his instructions
to report first had expired, and thenceforth his pack would consider their
primary mission as attack. He disposed *Besugo* and *Ronquil* in the western approaches to Bungo and ordered *Gabilan* to guard the eastern side.

On 19 October Lockwood sent *Gabilan* instructions to leave Wogan's pack and proceed northward to cover Kii Suido. Ozawa sortied from the Bungo on the night of 20 October, and by chance selected an eastern diversion course, completely avoiding both submarines left on guard off Bungo. No submarine sighted the Main Body (the Japanese carrier diversion force) on its journey to the Philippine area.

Shima's force of cruisers and destroyers came out of the Pescadores Islands on the night of 21 October, with Convoy College to run through. A few hours after leaving Bako the Japanese force encountered *Seadragon* (Ashley), which made radar contact at thirty thousand yards. Closing to three thousand yards on the surface on a dark night, Ashley indentified one of his targets as a carrier (although no carrier was present). He fired four torpedoes from the stern tubes, and reported two hits, but evidently Shima's task force suffered no damage in this attack. Ashley frantically informed his packmates that a Japanese task force was coming down the line. Both *Blackfish* and *Shark* made contact but neither was able to close to firing range. Shima was going through Convoy College at twenty-five knots and a submarine had to be both agile and lucky to get within torpedo range.

At eight o'clock the next morning *Icefish* (Peterson) got a good look at Shimas' force and correctly identified two heavy cruisers and three destroyers, but Peterson also was unable to close to attack range. He surfaced two hours later in a heavy sea to get off the important contact report but was forced down before he could raise a receiving station. That evening, when *Icefish* could come up again, Peterson tried for hours to get any Allied station to receipt for his message but all of them were dumb. Finally an Australian station, copying through interference after many repeats and call-backs, picked up the contact report shortly after midnight. Shima got through Convoy College unscathed but he still had a long road to travel to Leyte Gulf.

Christie's Submarines

Christie had over twenty U.S. submarines on station in the South China Sea and in the Philippines. Some were assigned lifeguard mission for the carrier strikes and several had special missions to perform in connection with the stepped up guerrilla war. Some of these special missions were of such a character that the submarine involved was forbidden to make attacks that would disclose its position and thus possibly compromise the special mission. Other submarines were generally disposed with an eye to cover the routes the Japanese might take from Lingga to Leyte, but generally all their extra duties did not interfere

with the submarines' business of sinking Japanese ships, as their accomplishments during this period eloquently attest.

Off the west coast of Borneo, *Dace* (Claggett) and *Darter* (McClintock) were paired in a coordinated attack group under the direction of
McClintock. On 11 October Christie sent McClintock instructions to
cover the western approaches to Balabac and the southern approaches
to Palawan Passage, and the two submarines moved up around the
corner of Borneo to do so. On 14 October they encountered a convoy of
tankers. *Dace* sank two tankers and *Darter* heavily damaged a big ore
carrier in this attack. Kurita then knew, when he sortied from Lingga
on 18 October, that there were U.S. submarines on his planned route.
Nevertheless he did not deviate from his plan. His supply vessels had
already been deployed and he accepted the submarine hazard rather
than attempt a redeployment. He sent advanced anti-submarine patrols
along his route, and covered the area with the land-based planes of the
901st Air Group. After refueling at Brunei, Kurita set out on 22 October
with his Center Group for San Bernardino by way of the west coast of
Palawan.

Dace *and* Darter

At midnight on 20 October McClintock picked up a news broadcast
and for the first time heard about the landing at Leyte. Anticipating
movements of the Japanese fleet he set out with *Darter* for Balabac,
leaving *Dace* behind in Palawan Passage. Southwest Pacific submarines
seem to have suffered from lack of information during the operation. It
was dangerous to brief submarine commanders on future operations before leaving on a long patrol, as was dramatically demonstrated by
Cromwell's decision to go down with *Sculpin*, and take with him special
knowledge of future operations, rather than risk it in capture by the
Japanese.

But lack of information sometimes meant missed opportunities. *Batfish*
(Fyfe), coming up through Makassar into the Sulu Sea, did not hear
about the invasion until 23 October, after she had wasted a good part
of the twentieth sparring with a small vessel Fyfe identified as a Q-ship.
Arriving in the Sulu Sea on the night of 25 October Fyfe lamented
that he had missed an opportunity to intercept Japanese fleet units by
just about the length of time he had spent on the Q-ship before he
learned about the invasion. McClintock was more fortunate in picking
up the news, and his dispositions turned out to be very sound indeed.

On the night of the twenty-first, lying on the surface, charging batteries, *Darter* picked up radar contact at twenty-six thousand yards.
The target was headed up Palawan Channel at twenty-three knots and

Darter had slim chance of getting in but she dashed off in pursuit, hoping that something might happen to deliver the enemy into her hands, or that she could coach *Dace* into contact. McClintock identified his quarry as three heavy cruisers. This may have been *Aoba*, with destroyer screen, headed north to join Shima's Second Striking Force, or it may have been one of Kurita's anti-submarine sweeps. The pursuit pulled both *Dace* and *Darter* far up Palawan Channel before they gave up the chase, about dawn, and reversed course to head back toward Borneo.

At midnight on 22–23 October *Dace* and *Darter* were within speaking distance of each other, on the surface coming down the Passage. Shortly after midnight McClintock called through a megaphone to Claggett, "We have radar contact. Let's go," and with this as necessary and sufficient plan of action *Dace* and *Darter* set out together in an operation which links their names together in a sister act of almost telepathic cooperation. *Dace* was having trouble with her radar. She fell in astern of *Darter* and followed in her wake until the radar was working well. The target was a task force of eleven heavy Japanese ships, at fifteen knots, steady course, in two columns five thousand yards apart. At four o'clock *Dace* and *Darter* were together ahead of the task force. *Darter* took the western column and gave *Dace* the eastward one.

Both submarines decided to attack at dawn. At 0617 *Darter* submerged ahead of her column, and *Dace* went down on her side. The visibility was better to the east and McClintock could see battleships and cruisers in *Dace's* column before he could make out much of his own target. *Darter* was almost dead ahead of the western column. McClintock swung out to open up the track, but it looked for a while as though he would have to fire almost down the throat. *Darter* pulled parallel to the target's course, getting ready to fire both bow and stern tubes. Then the enemy zigged by individual ship movements, and that made the setup much better. McClintock fired six forward tubes at the leading cruiser, then swung hard left and fired the stern tubes at the next in line. The first torpedoes hit with terrific explosions while McClintock was aiming the second salvo. When the last torpedo was fired McClintock whipped the scope around to have a look at the first target, while *Darter* headed down to deep submergence with empty tubes. The enemy cruiser was so close it filled the entire field of the periscope, a mass of flames and smoke, bright orange flames shooting out along the main deck, she was going down, water level with number one turret, there were hits on the second target. Then four destroyers arrived overhead, milling around confused by explosions and the racket, their depth charges wild.

Dace was still making her approach. As she sweated down toward her target she heard *Darter's* torpedoes hit. Through the periscope, Claggett saw a great pall of smoke over the western column but he had his hands too full to enjoy the spectacle. Claggett identified the leading ship of the eastward column as an *Atago*-class cruiser. Two ships behind was what looked like a battleship. Claggett was in a dilemma. Should he let the cruiser go by and try for the big one, or take the bird in hand. *Dace* had fired all her after torpedoes in previous attacks and had only her forward tubes loaded—a circumstance that increased the probability that an unfortunate enemy course change would let them all get away. Claggett decided to shoot the moon and try for the big one.

At 0654, twenty minutes after *Darter's* attack, *Dace* let go a six-torpedo salvo at the biggest ship in sight. Two minutes later the first of four torpedoes hit with a tremendous explosion. This was followed by breaking-up noises so terrific that Claggett had *Dace's* compartments checked for damage and the diving officer recommended that "we get the hell out here" because it sounded as though the enemy were sinking on top of them. Four destroyers came up and delivered an accurate depth-charge attack which *Dace* evaded at deep submergence. It was several hours before either *Dace* or *Darter* could get a look through the periscope.

Kurita had been coming up Palawan Passage on a steady course during the night. At dawn he increased speed to eighteen knots and started zigzagging. Suddenly *Atago* (Kurita's flagship) was hit with four torpedoes. Immediately afterward two torpedoes hit *Takao*, the second ship in the western column. *Atago* sank nineteen minutes later. As she went down *Maya*, third ship in the eastern column, was hit with four torpedoes and sank in four minutes. Destroyers picked up survivors and two destroyers were ordered to screen the crippled *Takao*. The rest of the fleet continued on, apprehensive of additional submarine traps.

Loss of Darter

About 0920 that morning, when *Darter* was able to raise her periscope after torpedoing two of Kurita's cruisers, she saw the heavy cruiser *Takao*, twelve thousand yards away, dead in the water. Two Japanese destroyers were standing by her and four planes were overhead. Mc-Clintock closed to attack but each time he closed the range to seven thousand or eight thousand yards the listening destroyers located the submarine and charged down at him. *Darter* had only Mark 23 torpedoes, with no slow-speed long-range setting, and she therefore had to fire from inside a range of four thousand yards. She did not have enough torpedoes remaining to attack both the destroyers and the cruiser.

When the pressure of the Japanese destroyers' counterattack eased on

Dace she came up to periscope depth to find only an empty sea in sight. It was four o'clock that afternoon before the damaged *Takao* came within range of Claggett's periscope vision. He then decided on a night submerged attack.

After dark both submarines surfaced. McClintock informed Claggett that *Darter* would make a surface attack from the southwest. If *Darter* drew off the destroyers *Dace* would come in from the northeast and complete her attack. McClintock was well aware of the navigational hazards in these dangerous waters. *Darter* had been unable to fix her position for twenty-four hours, and her dead reckoning was inaccurate from the uncertain surface and submerged Palawan currents. About eleven o'clock *Takao* got under way at speeds varying from six to ten knots. *Darter* went to seventeen knots to make an end around and attack from ahead, setting her course to pass Bombay Shoal by a margin of seven miles. Five minutes after one o'clock *Darter* hit the reef, full speed, with a tremendous crash, and almost immediately it was apparent that her situation was hopeless.

Informed of *Darter's* plight, Claggett abandoned the attack on *Takao* and brought *Dace* to *Darter's* aid. By six o'clock in the morning *Darter's* confidential papers had been destroyed, the crew transferred to *Dace* in rubber boats, and demolition charges set. When these failed to destroy the submarine, *Dace* fired torpedoes at her sister, but *Darter* was so high up on the reef that the torpedoes exploded against the reef. Dace then pumped thirty rounds of four-inch shells into the stranded submarine with little apparent effect. A Japanese plane came over, driving *Dace* down, and dropped two bombs at *Darter*, but unfortunately they missed. *Dace* sent a message requesting assistance in the destruction of *Darter*, and later that night left the area en route to Fremantle, with both submarine crews on board.

Angler *and* Guitarro

Kurita's apprehension about additional submarine traps was justified. That morning (23 October) *Bream* (Chapple) encountered the heavy cruiser *Aoba*, waiting to rendezvous with a fast transport force off Manila, en route to Ormoc on Leyte. Chapple hit *Aoba* with two torpedoes which did not sink the cruiser, but left it inoperative to be towed in to Manila. Near the north end of Palawan Channel *Angler* (Hess) was patrolling. She had intercepted *Darter's* contact reports and immediately moved in to cover the exits from Palawan Passage. *Guitarro* (Haskins) was covering Mindoro Strait, a little farther north.

Kurita had been picked up by the destroyer *Kishinami* after his flagship sank. For fear of submarines he remained in the destroyer rather than risk transfer to an adequate flagship until four o'clock that afternoon. He then transferred his flag to the battleship *Yamato*. Before eight o'clock that night (23 October) *Angler* had radar contact with *Yamato* at thirty-one thousand yards, but Hess was unable to close to attack range with the speeding Japanese task force.

With straining engines, *Angler* built up to 18.7 knots into the sea and trailed, sending contact reports to Christie and trying to raise *Bream* and *Guitarro*, which might be in position to intercept. About ten o'clock *Angler* ran into a tempting convoy, but the Japanese fleet was still uncommitted to a route past Mindoro, and Hess decided it was more important to trail the Japanese fleet than to sink a couple of *marus*. He evaded the convoy, losing ten miles in his stern chase to do so.

At two o'clock in the morning Kurita was definitely headed down Mindoro Strait toward Sibuyan Sea. When Hess tried to clear a contact report with this information the Japanese radio came on the air with intense interference and false call-ups and receipts. Shortly afterward *Angler's* radioman heard *Guitarro* get off her report with essentially the same information, and in less than an hour heard it rebroadcast to Kinkaid and Halsey from an Australian shore station. Far astern in the wake of the Japanese fleet, *Angler* and *Guitarro* turned back to cover their patrol areas.

On 23 October U.S. submarines knocked four Japanese heavy cruisers out of the order of battle for Leyte Gulf. The sudden loss of Kurita's flagship *Atago* disrupted command relations and communications of the Center Force on the eve of battle. Half of the flag communicators were picked up by one of the destroyers escorting *Takao* and hence were out of the battle. Of probable equal importance to the reduction of Japanese strength was the contact reports by *Darter*, *Dace*, *Angler*, and *Guitarro* revealing Kurita's progress toward the Sibuyan Sea. These reports alerted Kinkaid and Halsey that the Japanese Navy was coming out in force and gave them ample time to prepare to meet this threat.

Battle for Leyte Gulf

At 0812 on the morning of 24 October, planes from the Third Fleet carriers sighted Kurita's Center Force as it rounded the southern end of Mindoro. An hour later carrier planes spotted Nishimura's Southern Force in the Sulu Sea. Shima's Second Striking Force, trailing the Southern Force en route to Surigao Strait, was discovered by Fifth Army Air Force planes about noon. Carrier planes struck both Kurita's force and

Nishimura's force but concentrated on the Center Force as potentially the most dangerous. The giant battleship *Musashi* and one destroyer were sunk in the Sibuyan Sea. One heavy cruiser was so badly damaged it had to head back, and lesser damages were inflicted on two battleships and a light cruiser of the Center Force. One of the battleships and a destroyer of the Southern Force were also damaged by bomb hits. Japanese shore-based planes from Luzon attacked the Third Fleet, and the carrier *Princeton* was hit by a well-placed bomb. An inferno of flame and explosion swept the ship and she was abandoned and sunk by American forces later in the day.

Nishimura, with the Southern Force, continued on and entered Surigao Strait that night. The Seventh Fleet's bombardment and support forces under Oldendorf were drawn up to receive him. Nishimura's forces were annihilated. Shima, who followed the Southern Force into the Strait, retreated hastily to save his heavy cruisers and destroyers from the same fate.

Ozawa, with the Japanese carrier diversion force, had arrived off northern Luzon that morning without having been sighted. Shortly before noon on 24 October Ozawa's planes made an ineffective attack on the American carriers and then landed on Luzon. It was not until late afternoon that Halsey's search planes found Ozawa's carriers. Misled into believing that Kurita's Center Force had been knocked out, Halsey then turned all his attention to Ozawa's Diversion Force, just as the Japanese intended him to do. The Third Fleet turned north at eight o'clock that night to strike Ozawa, leaving San Bernardino Strait unguarded. No U.S. submarine was picketing San Bernardino as *Flying Fish* had done before the Battle of the Philippine Sea. San Bernardino was in a Blind Bombing Zone.

The Battle of Cape Engaño

At eight o'clock the next morning Mitscher's planes made their first strike on Ozawa's carriers. This was followed by wave after wave of carrier planes, sinking or crippling all four Japanese carriers. In the midst of this battle Halsey received a surprising message from Kinkaid that Kurita's still-powerful Center Force was loose off Samar heading for Leyte Gulf. Absorbed in destroying Ozawa, Halsey delayed until 1115 before sending his battleships and one carrier group south in response to Kinkaid's desperate call for help. Mitscher with two carrier groups continued attacking the Japanese task force. Cruisers and destroyers were sent north to sink the cripples. However, *Ise* and *Hyuga*, three light cruisers, and five destroyers escaped and retreated to the northward.

Lockwood's Submarines

Two wolf packs of Lockwood's submarines (*Haddock, Tuna,* and *Halibut* under Commander J. P. Roach, and *Pintado, Jallao,* and *Atule* under Commander B. A. Clarey) were crossing the Philippine Sea en route to patrol in Convoy College. These submarines were routed north of 20°30′ N, the boundary line of an Air Surface Zone into which submarines were not permitted to enter without special permission. When Lockwood learned from Cincpac dispatches that a battle off Cape Engaño was probable, he requested permission from Nimitz to send his submarines south into the prohibited zone. This permission Nimitz refused for fear of complicating the already complicated situation confronting Halsey. Mitscher, however, remembered previous cooperation between his carriers and submarines, and sent a dispatch inviting Lockwood to send his submarines south to help out. Unfortunately, in the heat of battle, with urgent messages cluttering up the ionosphere, this message did not get through in time for submarines to take advantage of it.

Early on the morning of 25 October Lockwood informed his submarines that a carrier battle east of Luzon was imminent. He disposed all six submarines on a scouting line just outside the Air Surface Zone, with fifteen miles between units, to intercept any cripples that might escape from the battle. His dispositions were excellent and timely. The submarines were near enough to the battle to hear distant explosions and to listen in on the voice radio circuits of the pilots going in for the last strike.

About half an hour before sunset *Halibut* (Galantin) sighted *Ise* headed north at thirty-one thousand yards. Galantin dove to attack. As *Halibut* came in she also sighted the light cruiser *Oyodo* accompanying the carrier-battleships. At 1844 Galantin fired six torpedoes at *Ise* and heard five explosions. When *Halibut* surfaced an hour later in the moonlight Galantin observed the bottom of a capsized ship still above the surface. Despite this evidence of a sinking both *Ise* and *Oyodo* escaped and what, if anything, was sunk by *Halibut* remains a mystery. *Haddock* (Roach) sighted both *Ise* and *Hyuga* and pursued all night but was unable to get within torpedo range.

About eight o'clock that evening *Jallao* (Icenhower) had radar contact with a northbound ship at twenty-seven thousand yards. *Pintado* (Clarey), to the westward, almost simultaneously picked up contact with the same ship. *Jallao* attacked at 2300 with seven torpedoes and *Pintado* was close enough to see that ship go down. This was the light cruiser *Tama,* the last ship to be sunk in the Battle of Cape Engaño.

Ise, Hyuga, Oyodo, Isuzu, and five destroyers escaped. They were sighted again by a wolf pack consisting of *Trigger*, *Sterlet*, and *Salmon* as the refugees entered the East China Sea. None of the submarines were able to get close enough to attack.

The Battle off Samar

In the meantime, Kurita in the Sibuyan Sea rallied the Center Force, and shortly after five o'clock in the afternoon of 24 October headed for San Bernardino. In this restricted strait, and off its exit into the Pacific, he expected to again encounter U.S. submarines but none were there to meet him. From these waters submarines had been excluded in order to give a clear field to carrier- and shore-based air and surface forces. But no U.S. force of any kind was in the vicinity of San Bernardino. The first U.S. intimation that Kurita had gained the Pacific was at 0607 on the morning of 25 October. An anti-submarine patrol plane from an escort carrier encountered four Japanese battleships, eight cruisers, and a large number of destroyers, almost within gun range of a task group of Seventh Fleet escort carriers. Sixteen escort carriers organized into three groups (Taffy 1, Taffy 2, and Taffy 3) were attached to the Seventh Fleet to provide search, air cover, and air support for the Amphibious Force in Leyte Gulf. Kurita had run right into Taffy 3, the northernmost group.

The thin-skinned eighteen-knot escort carriers were practically without gunpower, too slow to run, too weak to fight. They were escorted by destroyers and destroyer escorts and except for their air groups were nearly defenseless before the massive gunpower of Kurita's fast, heavy ships (including the monstrous 18-inch guns of *Yamato*). A desperate action followed as Taffy 3 retreated to avoid destruction from the Japanese big guns. The air forces of all three escort carrier groups assaulted the Japanese as the northernmost carrier came under gunfire. The destroyers and destroyer escorts charged in against heavy odds and, in some of the most gallant actions in the history of the U. S. Navy, fought desperately to turn aside the pursuit. Despite overwhelming Japanese strength in this one-sided action, the Japanese received more damage than they inflicted. One American escort carrier, two destroyers, and a destroyer escort went down under Japanese gunfire but three Japanese heavy cruisers were sunk. Kurita broke off the action shortly after nine o'clock and by noon was en route back to San Bernardino. He retired through the strait that night, losing only one trailing destroyer to Halsey's battleships as they dashed up, too late.

Even while the escort carriers of the northern group were battling for their lives against Kurita's Center Force, suicide planes from Davao were striking Taffy 1, the southern group, with the first planned *kamikaze* attack of the war. Before the day was over another escort carrier had been sunk and seven more damaged by suicide attack. These wide-ranging battles brought the hard-fighting escort carriers into contact with Japanese submarines.

Japanese Submarines at Leyte

When Toyoda issued the Sho-1 alert on 17 October, several Japanese submarines were south of Okinawa, still searching for Halsey. All other available submarines were ordered to sortie out Bungo Suido as soon as possible. *I-44* suffered a mechanical derangement and had to return. The rest were organized into two groups (Ko and Otsu) and directed to form the familiar double scouting line about five hundred miles east of the Philippines. Before this order could be carried out the dispositions were changed to a checkerboard pattern of squares, sixty miles on a side, laid out east of the Philippines. Three RO-boats and eight I-class submarines were disposed like chessmen in these squares. It is probable that most submarines did not reach these stations either, before the next change of orders. In any event they were poorly located and apparently no Japanese submarine sighted any of the great American armada approaching Leyte Gulf.

Miwa ordered his submarines to close in as soon as he learned of the expected fleet action east of the Philippines. On the night of 23 October he directed his eleven submarines to mass in an area from Samar to Surigao Strait, approximately sixty miles off the coast. Each submarine was ordered to fight heroically in all-out action and to push home an assult on an enemy ship at any cost. In their new location there was more action.

The three RO-boats were stationed too far north, but the eight I-class submarines were right in the waters through which the Battle off Samar raged on the twenty-fifth. *I-56* reported sinking a transport on the night of the twenty-fourth. The next day she reported sinking a carrier and a destroyer. At about eight o'clock that morning the escort carrier *Santee* of Taffy 1 was hit by a *kamikaze* plane. *Santee* had just brought the fire from the *kamikaze* hit under control when she was hit on the starboard side by a submarine torpedo. *Santee* did not sink. She controlled her flooding and a few hours later was making full speed. There were no torpedo hits to correspond to transport and destroyer sinkings reported by *I-56*. About eight-thirty that night a destroyer escort in the screen of Taffy 1 sighted a periscope and attacked with hedgehogs unsuccessfully. When the destroyer retired the Japanese submarine surfaced and *I-56* found an unexploded hedgehog on her deck; a piece of ordnance that aroused intense interest in Japan.

I-26 reported sighting four aircraft carriers on 25 October, and this may have been Taffy 1 after *I-56* attacked that group. The next morning Taffy 1 was passing through the same area again and destroyer escort *Richard M. Rowell* made sound contact with a submerged submarine. *Rowell* sighted the periscope half an hour later and attacked with hedge-hogs which exploded deep. This probably was the end of *I-26*. The Japanese credit *I-26* with sinking a cruiser on 31 October, on evidence of a report of a shore-based plane, but no cruiser was sunk, and the contact report on 25 October was the last directly heard from *I-26*.

I-46 reported sighting a convoy on 26 October, and that was the last ever heard from her. *I-56* reported sinking three transports on 27 October, but as in the successes she reported three days earlier there were no corresponding transports sunk. Although her accomplishments were far less than her claims *I-56*, must have been nearly out of torpedoes. Miwa ordered her to return to Japan. Her recovery of the unexploded hedgehog possibly had some bearing on her early return.

After the Battle off Samar, the remnant of the Japanese fleet retreated, pursued by carrier planes which finished off some of the cripples. On 27 October Toyoda directed Miwa to send part of his submarines to Lamon Bay on Luzon to intercept U.S. carriers attacking northern Luzon air bases, and to dispose the remainder off Leyte to intercept U.S. reinforcements. *RO-112* and *RO-109* departed from the Bungo in late October and these two submarines were ordered to join the other three RO-boats spread out in a thin line off Lamon Bay.

Although the Japanese charts show several I-boats off Leyte Gulf at the end of October it is probable that no more than three ever arrived there. The carriers of the Third Fleet, in addition to the pursuit of the retiring Japanese, were required to supply air cover for Leyte until Fifth Army Air Force could move up and take over. While one of the carrier groups was maneuvering off Leyte on 28 October carrying out this mission, a destroyer in the screen had sound contact with a submarine. The task force cleared the area at high speed, while destroyers *Gridley* and *Helm* developed the contact. Under depth-charge attack splinters of deck planks and human remains came to the surface. This was the end of *I-54*.

At half-past two on the dark and rainy morning of 29 October the destroyer escort *Eversole* was running out to rejoin her escort carrier group when her sonar operator picked up sound contact close by. Almost immediately *Eversole* was hit by two torpedoes and she went down. A tremendous explosion after she sank killed many of the men swimming in the water. The destroyer escort *Bull* was an hour behind her on the same course and rescued the survivors. While rescue work was in progress the destroyer escort *Whitehurst* was detached from the screen of a nearby tanker to assist. *Whitehurst* made sonar contact about fifty miles from where *Eversole* sank, and attacked with hedgehogs. Several violent explosions followed the attack. This was *I-45*, who had not long survived her success in sinking a destroyer escort.

On 3 November *I-41* reported sinking an aircraft carrier of the *Essex* class. *Reno* was torpedoed by a Japanese submarine on the moonlit night of 3 November, off San Bernardino Strait, and had to be towed back to Ulithi. This was probably the work of *I-41*, which had mistaken the light cruiser for a carrier in the moonlight, although the assigned station of *I-41* was far to the south off Mindanao. *I-41* made a later report of contact with a task force, after which she was heard from no more.

On 5 November *I-38* was ordered to make a reconnaissance of Ngulu, southeast of Ulithi, and report not later than 13 November. En route she reported contact with a task force and then disappeared forever. On 8 November Miwa ordered most of his submarines home, leaving only *RO-109* and *RO-112* north of Samar, and as he thought four I-class submarines off Leyte; but as noted two of these had been sunk and one had departed to reconnoiter Ngulu, leaving only *I-53* on guard.

Summary of Japanese Submarine Results at Leyte

The five RO-boats that were deployed east of the Philippines during the Leyte campaign made no contacts, no attacks, no successes, and all of them returned safely to port. Eight I-class submarines were more successful in making contact. They sank one destroyer escort and damaged one escort carrier and a light cruiser, rather meager accomplishment in comparison to the successes reported. Of the eight I-class submarines involved, moreover, six were lost. Miwa's morale may have been sustained by the exaggerated reports of accomplishment, and the number of submarines lost was less than the slaughter of the Marianas campaign. In percentage, however, these losses were brutal, and it must have done much to convince the Japanese that conventional submarine warfare, for them, was unprofitable. This plus the success and popularity of the Air Force's new *kamikaze* attack directed increased attention to the suicide weapons the submariners had been working on for some time.

I-12 *and* U-168

There were, however, two disquieting incidents in October that gave The U.S. anti-submarine warfare forces cause for concern. In late September Combined Fleet ordered Miwa to employ *I-12* to interrupt surface transportation on the U. S. West Coast and in the Hawaiian waters. On 4 October *I-12* left the Inland Sea and came through the Sea of Japan and Tsugaru Strait to head directly for the U. S. West Coast. She kept careful radio silence while proceeding along this unusual route, and nothing was known of her operation until she torpedoed a ship between Hawaii and San Francisco on 29 October, and shelled the lifeboats after the ship sank. This news caused consternation to American anti-submarine forces. The eastern Pacific had been so long free from submarine war that this attack seemed almost unfair, just at the time when every ship was needed for the stretched-out line of logistics and all the escorts were busy in the western Pacific.

Up until this point of the war, the Indian Ocean had been divided between German submarines and Japanese submarines on a geographical basis. The Germans used the Japanese submarine base at Penang for their submarines but otherwise they stayed on their side of the line and rarely came north of the Malay Barrier. On 6 October, however, the Dutch submarine *Zwaardvisch* sank the German submarine *U-168* in the Java Sea and brought back the German captain and navigator to prove it. Whether this presaged that the Germans were about to take a hand in the Pacific war was a moot question. *Zwaardvisch* topped off this very successful patrol by sinking the minelayer *Itsutshima* on 17 October.

U.S. Submarine Losses

Escolar (Millican), on her first patrol, led *Croaker* and *Perch* in a wolf pack into the Yellow Sea early in October. Finding few targets, Millican informed *Perch* by dispatch on 17 October that he was heading for the vicinity of Nagasaki. *Escolar* was never heard from again. There were minefields in her area and minefields in the area toward which she was headed. The locations of these minefields were known. Millican had been properly briefed and *Escolar's* projected operation as reported to *Perch* would not carry her into any known minefields. However, there is no other explanation of the loss of *Escolar,* and it is generally assumed that she hit a mine. In point of fact nothing is really known of her end.

Shark II (Blakely) also led a wolf pack on her last patrol. *Seadragon* and *Blackfish* followed her into Convoy College in early October. On 24 October *Shark* still had her full load of torpedoes. *Seadragon* received a message from Blakely on that day. *Shark* had radar contact with a single freighter and was going into attack. Nothing more was ever heard from *Shark.* The Japanese recorded a depth-charge attack which brought to the surface bubbles and heavy oil, clothing, and cork in *Shark's* approximate position on 24 October. Several U.S. submarines were attacked that day in that area but all the others survived. It is most probable that this attack was the cause of *Shark's* loss. Eight Japanese *marus* also went down that day in the same vicinity.

Three weeks later Commander Naval Unit China reported that a ship carrying eighteen hundred American prisoners of war from Manila to Japan had been sunk by an American submarine on 24 October. Five of the prisoners survived and reached China. It is possible that the lone freighter that *Shark* pursued was the prison ship and that *Shark* sank it. It is also possible that *Shark* may have been attacked while attempting to rescue prisoners; but all of it is conjecture.

There is no conjecture about the loss of *Tang*. On her fifth patrol O'Kane took *Tang* between the southern end of the long Nansei Shoto minefields and the northern end of Formosa into Formosa Strait. He was then in a position to get first pickings on the southbound traffic to the Philippines before it matriculated in Convoy College or encountered Christie's hard-driving submarines farther south. As was expected O'Kane found many targets in these restricted, shallow, dangerous waters. On 11 October *Tang* encountered a convoy north of Formosa and made two torpedo attacks, sinking two rather small *marus* (one of which the Japanese credited to a mine).

The next contact was far inside the Strait on 23 October. O'Kane took his submarine on the surface at night into the middle of a convoy of five *marus*, and fired all the torpedoes in *Tang's* tubes in a succession of brilliant attacks. The records of this attack from the Japanese side are confused but at least one *maru* was sunk, two others were heavily damaged, and the fate of another is unknown. Twenty-four hours later *Tang* found a southbound convoy of tankers and transports, heavily loaded. O'Kane again maneuvered into the middle of the convoy and started firing torpedoes. Two big tankers were sunk. The escorts charged in, shooting at *Tang*, illuminated against a background of burning tankers. O'Kane retaliated with torpedoes and saw one escort explode and sink. With only two torpedoes left, O'Kane maneuvered at full speed, avoiding attempts to ram him, until he had a setup on a damaged transport.

The first torpedo ran hot and straight. When the last torpedo left the tube a cheer came up from below. *Tang* could then set course for home with empty tubes and racks and a quick and brilliantly successful patrol behind her. But it was not to be. On the bridge, O'Kane saw *Tang's* last torpedo broach, porpoise, and circle back toward the submarine. He rang up full speed and threw the rudder over but the submarine did not have the agility to dodge her own torpedo. *Tang's* last torpedo hit her in her own stern. There was a violent explosion and the ship went down stern first with the after compartments flooded.

Nine men on the bridge, including O'Kane, were thrown into the water. Only three of them were still alive at dawn. One officer escaped from the conning tower as the submarine went down. *Tang* came to rest on the bottom at 180 feet, and the survivors gathered in the forward torpedo room. There they burned secret papers and waited for the departure of the Japanese patrols topside. Electrical fires ignited in the forward battery and became so hot the paint melted off the torpedo room bulkhead. Thirteen men escaped from the torpedo room through the escape trunk with Momsen lungs. Only five of them survived. Nine of *Tang's* crew were picked up by one of the Japanese destroyer escorts. All of them survived the beatings by their captors and the abuse of Japan's prison camps, although O'Kane was in bad shape when he was finally rescued at the end of the war.

October was a climactic month for naval war in the Pacific, and submarines were as deeply involved as any other element of naval power. The accomplishments of American submarines were equally great but, in October, more American submarines were lost than in any other month of the war. This increase in losses, however, was not due directly to any sudden increase in the efficiency of Japanese anti-submarine warfare. One submarine was destroyed by her own friends, one was sunk by her own torpedo, and one was lost by stranding. Only two of the five were sunk by enemy action. It was by the narrowest of margins, however, that *Salmon* saved herself from becoming a third victim of Japanese anti-submarine forces.

Salmon's *Escape*

Sterlet, Trigger, and *Salmon,* operating as a wolf pack, were south of Kyushu on 30 October. *Trigger* (Harlfinger) torpedoed a 10,000-ton tanker (*Korei Maru*) but did not sink it. About eight o'clock on the night of the thirtieth *Salmon* (Nauman) caught up with the tanker, guarded by four escorts, and got two more torpedoes into her. The tanker sank later, but all four escorts turned on *Salmon* and delivered an accurate pattern of depth charges. *Salmon* was badly hurt, and went down out of control to over five hundred feet. There the diving officer checked her with a 20° up angle, and slowly worked up to 150 feet, but *Salmon's* leaks were so serious that he could not hold her. Nauman decided to take his chances on the surface.

Salmon came up with a 15° list, and many leaks, and lay on the surface practically helpless. An escort vessel was only seven thousand yards away but for some reason did not attack. This gave *Salmon* time to correct her list, plug her leaks, get the engines ready, and bring up every gun she could muster for her last-ditch defense. The escort made a couple of passes, firing and then retiring, to hold the submarine at bay until the other escorts could join her. This must have been *Coast Defense Vessel No. 22,* for that 750-ton frigate was damaged by a submarine in that vicinity that night. *Salmon* abided these cat-and-mouse tactics until the other frigates started closing, and then Nauman took the offensive. He charged right at *No. 22,* passing on opposite and parallel courses at a range of fifty yards and let her have it with everything on board that would shoot. This knocked *No. 22* out of the battle. *Salmon* then ducked into a rain squall and put her tormentors astern, while her engines turned up full power. Audacity saved her from an almost hopeless situation, and she proved again the military maxim—when in doubt, attack.

Trigger, Silversides, and *Sterlet* joined *Salmon* that night to run interference for her, as she made her way south on the surface. Saipan sent out air cover to help, and *Salmon* made it safely into Saipan. When she reached a navy yard to repair her damage, however, a survey board found her damaged beyond economical repair and she never went to sea on a war patrol again.

XXIV

NOVEMBER–DECEMBER 1944

Continued Battle for Leyte

The naval Battle for Leyte Gulf in October knocked out the Japanese surface Navy as an offensive force. Japanese Imperial General Headquarters, however, decided to make Leyte the decisive battleground for the Philippines, and fierce battles in and around and over Leyte raged all during November and December. Prevented by weather and terrain from completing the necessary airfields, the U. S. Fifth Army Air Force was slow in providing air support. The Japanese staged in air replacements from Formosa and Kyushu and virtually regained control of the air. A new Tokyo Express ran from Luzon to Ormoc, on the west coast of Leyte, and poured in forty-five thousand Japanese reinforcements and ten thousand tons of supplies to contest MacArthur's possession of Leyte.

Kamikaze attacks were serious problems for both the Seventh Fleet and the carriers of the Third Fleet. During the last three days of October and the month of November nine of the Third Fleet's fast carriers were damaged by suicide planes. One Seventh Fleet destroyer and two smaller vessels were sunk by *kamikazes* and thirteen other ships, ranging in size from battleships to destroyers, were damaged. Third Fleet carrier task forces struck airfields on Luzon through which Japanese planes were staging and this brought about some relief. Carrier planes also attacked convoys making runs to Ormoc, and bombed shipping at Manila with devastating effect, but they were unable to stop the flow of supplies and reinforcements to Leyte. After *I-41* torpedoed *Reno*, on 3 November, neither American nor Japanese submarines took significant part in the battle in the Leyte area.

Japanese Submarines in the Philippines

About 1 November *RO-41* and *RO-43* were ordered to patrol the entrance to San Bernardino Strait to report and attack any American surface forces that might pass through to interfere with the Ormoc transportation operation. They made no contacts. On 8 November these two submarines were recalled to Japan along with most of the other Japanese submarines in the Philippines, leaving only three or four remaining in Leyte waters. The remaining ones were recalled the next week.

Miwa then sent the newly built *RO-49* and *RO-50* to the Philippines and stationed them east of Luzon to attack American carriers making strikes on Luzon airfields. *RO-50* reported sinking a carrier and a destroyer 150 miles northeast of Lamon Bay on 25 November. The Third Fleet had four carriers damaged by *kamikaze* air attack that day but any submarine attacks made by *RO-50* went unnoticed. *RO-49* and *RO-50* remained on patrol until early December, when they were relieved by *RO-43* and *RO-112*.

Conventional Japanese submarines did not take a direct part in the Ormoc transportation runs. Special transportation submarines built and operated by the Japanese Army may have done so. Army submarines were in the Philippines but there is little information on their activity. They were not capable of offensive operations.

Midget submarines, of the type used at Pearl Harbor, were also in the Philippines. These midgets were originally designed to be carried to the battle area on the backs of conventional submarines; or as at Midway in seaplane carriers. Despite many romantic Japanese accounts of their exploits, midgets were not very successful. Ten midgets had been brought to the Philippines in surface ships in 1944 to operate from shore bases at Davao, Zamboanga, and Cebu in defense of the Philippines. Only those at Cebu ever saw action.

The Japanese submarine base at Cebu was destroyed by carrier raids in mid-September, but by 1 November the base was able to support the operation of the six Cebu midgets, plus a pair from Zamboanga that moved up to Cebu later in November. These midgets made patrols into Ormoc Bay, but were ineffective because of the length of time required to make the run from Cebu. After four to seven days at sea the crews of the midgets were so exhausted they were not capable of aggressive offensive operations.

On 8 December a midget reported sinking a destroyer in Ormoc Bay, and another reported sinking two transports on 18 December but there is no confirmation of any of these sinkings. The operations of the midgets possibly accounts for submarine contacts reported in Ormoc Bay, where U.S. destroyers reported sinking an I-class submarine on 28 November. As far as is known, no conventional Japanese submarines were in the area. One of the midgets was lost by stranding in December.

U.S. Submarines in November

In the waters around Leyte there were no opportunities for U.S. submarines during November, except in the narrow, crowded, hotly contested Ormoc Bay, where the presence of friendly submarines would have been a serious embarrassment to the air and surface forces. The central Philippines remained designated as an Air Surface Zone, from which all U.S. submarines were excluded. Submarine operations at a distance, however, had important effects on the Philippine campaign. Christie's submarines were busy in the South China Sea, where they had a variety of missions to perform, providing lifeguard services for carrier strikes on Manila and supplying guerrilla forces on Luzon and Mindoro, as well as carrying out their primary mission of sinking Japanese ships.

Ray

One of the submarines that performed a variety of missions in the Manila area in November was *Ray* (Kinsella). *Ray* worked as a pack with *Bream* and *Guitarro* when not otherwise engaged on special missions. By the first of November *Ray* had rescued one of the Third Fleet pilots from a carrier plane shot down over Manila Bay. She had also landed men and materials for the guerrillas on Mindoro and in exchange received two additional passengers. One was a carrier pilot who had been shot down over Manila, fallen into the hands of guerrillas, and had been transported to Mindoro. The other was a guerrilla leader, Maximo Kalaw, with a Japanese price on his head, and too hot for Mindoro to hold. Kalaw had been Dean of Liberal Arts of the University of the Philippines before the war. When he arrived on board *Ray*, his sole possessions were the faded denim jodhpurs and the khaki shirt he wore, but his spirit was undaunted still.

Ray's passengers quite naturally hoped for a short submarine tour of duty and Kalaw expected to be dropped off in northern Australia from where he hoped to reach MacArthur's headquarters. But *Ray* was not one of the submarines shuttling back and forth in the regular Philippine trade. She was primarily on a combat mission, slated for a two-month patrol, after which she was scheduled to proceed to Pearl Harbor for a navy yard overhaul. *Ray's* passengers had no choice but to go where *Ray* went.

On 1 November *Ray* sank a small cargo vessel off Mindoro. She then joined up with her packmates, and three days later the pack sank an

8500-ton transport north of Manila. Two days later, on 6 November, the pack encountered a northbound convoy hugging the Luzon coast, and in it recognized a damaged heavy cruiser. This was *Kumano,* which had been damaged in the Battle off Samar, patched up at Manila, and with great good fortune had started out for Japan just before the Third Fleet planes clobbered Manila Harbor on 5 November.

Four submarines attacked the convoy and all four picked *Kumano* as their target; but this heavy cruiser was hard to sink. She was the survivor of famous Cruiser Division Seven (*Kumano, Suzuya, Mogami,* and *Mikuma*), and like every one of that division she absorbed a terrific amount of punishment. *Guitarro* fired nine torpedoes and observed three hits, but failed to stop *Kumano. Bream* fired four more and claimed two hits. *Raton's* salvo of six torpedoes ran right over *Ray,* while *Ray* was busy making her own approach. *Raton* claimed four hits in the cruiser. *Ray* fired a salvo of four and went deep. When next Kinsella observed *Kumano,* the cruiser had her bow blown off, stopped dead in the water, but still afloat.

Kinsella determined to finish off this almost unsinkable ship. Even though *Kumano* had probably received only a fraction of the torpedo hits claimed, she still displayed phenomenal resilience and damage control. The escorts were cluttered around her seaward side depending on the proximity of shallow water to protect the cruiser from shoreward. Kinsella, observing a small bay indenting the rugged Luzon coast, decided to dive under and come up on the shoreward side to hit *Kumano* from an unprotected angle. He went down to three hundred feet where the chart showed plenty of water; but the chart had not anticipated maneuvers of this kind. Three hundred feet deep *Ray* hit a coral pinnacle, which wiped off her sound heads, and sprang a leak in the torpedo room.

Dean Kalaw was billeted in the torpedo room, into which the water spurted with the force of a fire nozzle's jet. Jocular torpedomen working to check the flood told the dean not to worry; if they failed to stop the leak, Uncle Sam had generously provided a seven-million-dollar steel coffin for them all. But the little guerrilla was their match. He appreciated the honor, he responded, but he had been promised a funeral with four white horses and he was determined to live until the horses were provided.

Kumano was taken in tow and beached, where carrier planes found her later in the month and finished the destruction of the Japanese cruiser. *Ray* repaired her own damages and sank a *kaibokan* on 14 November before she left the Philippines en route to Hawaii. At Pearl Harbor intelligence officers welcomed Kalaw with open arms. Mindoro was a hot spot just then and firsthand information of conditions on that island were golden assets.

In November Christie's submarines sank seventeen *marus* and escorts off Manila, with eight or ten additional sinkings scattered throughout the rest of the South China Sea. On 25 November *Cavalla* (Kossler) made a night surface attack off the west coast of Borneo on a ship Kossler identified as a heavy cruiser, but which was actually the destroyer *Shimotsuki*. Two torpedoes hit *Shimotsuki* and the destroyer went down in a few minutes. Most of the ships sunk in the South China Sea were in some way connected with Japanese defense of the Philippines. While submarines thus harassed any Japanese ship that put to sea, carrier planes sowed Manila Bay with Japanese wrecks and sunken ships; and surface forces, carrier planes, and Army Air were all taking a heavy toll of combat ships and *marus* engaged in the Ormoc run.

Lockwood's Submarines

North of Luzon, and south of Formosa in Convoy College, there was another zone of danger for Japanese ships. Clarey's wolf pack (*Pintado, Jallao,* and *Atule*) proceeded to Convoy College after the Battle of Cape Engaño. *Pintado* (Clarey) fired six well-aimed torpedoes at an aircraft carrier. An escorting destroyer (*Akikaze*) steamed directly into the path of the torpedoes intended for the carrier and took two hits. The destroyer went down with a spectacular explosion but the carrier escaped. *Atule* (Maurer) had a very successful patrol. On the night of 1 November, in poor visibility, she made a surface attack on a large *maru,* northbound at high speed with three escorts. Maurer identified his target as a 10,000-tonner, and claimed two hits. This was an underestimate. The 16,975-ton *Asama Maru* was hit by *Atule's* torpedoes and sank. Before the patrol was over Maurer sank two escorts and another *maru* of 7000 tons.

Such success was unusual for Convoy College in November. A four-submarine wolf pack under command of F. W. Fenno sank only one escort and a small *maru* in a patrol that lasted through November and most of December. In another wolf pack of three submarines, commanded by L. P. Ramage, only *Pomfret* (J. B. Hess) had any success. *Pomfret* sank two good-size *marus* and a small naval auxiliary.

Roach's wolf pack (*Haddock, Halibut,* and *Tuna*) also entered Convoy College right after their participation in the Battle of Cape Engaño. They were in Luzon Strait most of the month of November, and each submarine made one or two attacks but they sank no ships. The Japanese anti-submarine forces were making desperate efforts to maintain communication between Formosa and Luzon, and by concentrating in the area probably made it easier for submarines elsewhere. With increased numbers of surface escorts and with radar planes at night and

MAD planes in the daytime, the Japanese made it difficult for U.S. submarines to conduct effective search operations and often forced attacking submarines to fire torpedoes from unfavorable bearings and at long ranges. MAD planes were less successful than they thought they were in sinking submarines but they were nevertheless a force to reckon with, as proved by *Halibut's* experience.

Halibut *and the MAD Plane*

Early on the morning of 14 November *Halibut* (Galantin) began having a series of air contacts which she evaded by maneuvers and short dives. At dawn she submerged and patrolled along the traffic route. Shortly before noon she heard pinging and half an hour later Galantin sighted the masts of a four-ship convoy with three surface escorts. He did not detect any air cover. Galantin closed at high submerged speed to reach a position from which he fired four electric torpedoes at long range. The convoy zigged during the torpedo run, and *Halibut* swung around to fire the stern tubes.

About that time a loud buzzing sound was heard overhead. The men in the battery compartments later described the noise as resembling fast screws, or a torpedo, or a low-flying plane, increasing in loudness and then decreasing for about forty seconds. After it passed and faded out the fourth time there was a loud explosion to port. *Halibut* went deep. Five minutes later there were three heavy explosions. Twenty minutes after that there were several very close blockbuster explosions, shaking the submarine violently, and forcing her down to 420 feet. *Halibut* was in serious trouble.

In the forward torpedo room all the torpedoes and their skids jumped up about a foot and slammed down hard. All the sea valves spun open, and the escape trunk sprung leaks. Every man was thrown violently into the bilges. In the forward battery compartment the high-pressure air line to Number One air bank was broken. The rush and roar of high-pressure air added to the confusion of lockers broken open and their contents spilled, and ruptured food containers and broken bottles in sudden disorder. Someone smelled chlorine gas. The occupants hastily secured and abandoned the compartment. The air bank bled down, creating a fifty-pound pressure in the compartment. It was some time before the pressure could be equalized enough to force open the closed watertight doors to send help to the forward torpedo room. Fortunately the Japanese were satisfied with their work and shoved off.

When *Halibut* surfaced after sunset Galantin found the hull so badly damaged that he terminated the patrol. *Pintado* escorted the damaged submarine back to Saipan. *Halibut* finally made it to the navy yard where her hull was found to be so badly strained and distorted that she was judged beyond economical repair. *Halibut* was retired from active service. Only the rugged integrity of her hull construction saved her and her crew.

Galantin suggested that the Japanese were using a new weapon. When they reached Saipan, however, he compared notes with Clarey in *Pintado*, which had approached the same convoy. *Pintado* had been unable to close to torpedo range, but Clarey had observed three planes flying in continuous circles ahead of and over the convoy. Galantin therefore concluded that *Halibut* had been sighted and attacked by the planes of an intensive air cover which he had not detected. Clarey's description fits very well with Japanese accounts of their tactics with MAD planes, and there is little doubt that *Halibut* had been picked up by their magnetic airborne detectors.

Spadefish *and* Shinyo

The best submarine results were scored in the East China Sea during November. One wolf pack in the southern end of the Yellow Sea and the northern end of the East China Sea, consisting of *Queenfish, Picuda,* and *Barb,* was under command of C. E. Loughlin, who also commanded *Queenfish.* Another pack, in the adjacent area to the south, consisted of *Spadefish, Sunfish,* and *Peto* and was commanded by G. W. Underwood, who also commanded *Spadefish.* In these areas the two wolf packs had first pick of Manila-bound convoys originating in Japan or in Manchuria.

The Japanese 23rd Infantry Division, embarked in nine transports, with five *kaibokans* and the carrier *Shinyo* to guard them, were being transported from Manchuria to the Philippines. The *kaibokans* at last had radar, but they had not yet had sufficient experience to be proficient in its use. *Shinyo* was a 17,000-ton converted aircraft carrier, on her first escort assignment after a long period in the navy yard. Her captain vowed before sailing that he would take revenge on U.S. submarines for sinking *Taiyo* and *Unyo* in Luzon Strait.

On 15 November *Queenfish* attacked and sank one of the transports out of the convoy. Loughlin's whole wolf pack closed in and pursued. *Picuda* (Shepard) sank one transport and damaged another on the night of 17 November. The pursuit brought Loughlin's pack down into Underwood's territory. *Spadefish* picked up the convoy's smoke and ran to get ahead of the transports.

Underwood elected to attack at night on the surface and let the convoy steam directly over *Spadefish* while she bided her time. At dusk the submarine came up to periscope depth and saw five *marus* and an escort carrier shepherded by six destroyers. The smoke of a burning ship was on the horizon. Through the water *Spadefish* could hear the repeated boom of depth charges intended for *Picuda*. *Sunfish* (Shelby) came in on the radio and informed Underwood that *Sunfish* was going in to attack.

Spadefish picked the escort carrier for her target and Underwood took his time to work into ideal position. The first approach was spoiled by a last-minute zigzag. *Spadefish* could detect the *kaibokan's* radar frequency but the Japanese escorts had not located the submarine, so Underwood withdrew and started another approach. In his own good time he fired six torpedoes and saw four hits. *Shinyo* burst into flame and went down by the stern. Her cargo of planes, intended for the Philippine *kamikaze* trade, slid over the side as *Shinyo's* angle increased, and finally the big ship came to rest with her stern on the bottom in twenty-three fathoms and her bow pointed to the sky.

While the carrier was sinking, *Spadefish* speeded ahead to gain position for another attack. An efficient escort detected the approaching submarine and opened up with 20-mm. and 40-mm. interspersed with a few larger caliber shells. Underwood was reluctant to dive and surrender the initiative in such shallow water. *Spadefish* played the old desperate game of "chasing splashes" while her engines strained to outrun the pursuing escort. Seizing a favorable opportunity during his dodging retreat, Underwood fired the stern tubes at the convoy and heard two torpedo hits. When the range had opened out to twenty-five hundred yards the discouraged Japanese escort dropped a few depth charges and fell back to the remnant of the convoy.

Four *marus* and *Shinyo* were torpedoed and sunk on 17 November in that locality, and another *maru* was severely damaged. This must have severely curtailed the 23rd Division's participation in the Philippine campaign. During the month of November twenty Japanese ships were sunk by submarines in the northern end of Tung Hai, despite the minefields, and the air cover, and the new radar on the escorts.

Sealion *and* Kongo

While this was going on in the northern end of Tung Hai, *Sealion* (Reich) was in the southern end, trying to outwit the Japanese system of making short daylight runs, and holing up in shallow East China Sea ports at night. On the morning of 21 November, shortly after midnight, *Sealion* was on the surface very close to where the Strait of Formosa broadens out into the East China Sea. Radar reported a contact at such extreme range that Reich at first believed the radar was bouncing radar waves off Formosa. It was shortly apparent, however, that a group of big ships was coming up along the coast, and a few minutes later Reich identified the target as two battleships and two cruisers, escorted by several destroyers, making sixteen knots on a steady northeasterly course. *Sealion* got off a contact report to Lockwood immediately.

Reich decided to remain on the surface. The possibility of *Sealion* being picked up by Japanese radar was a serious risk, but on the other hand *Sealion* needed all the surface speed she could command to close in to attack distance. An hour later *Sealion* was on the starboard beam of the task force making full power into a heavy sea, and gaining bearing very slowly. As *Sealion* pulled slowly ahead the radio watch reported that they could hear their contact report on the battleships being rebroadcast from Pearl Harbor for the benefit of submarines up north.

It was nearly three o'clock in the morning before Reich could turn in for attack. Then things happened fast. At a range of three thousand yards *Sealion* fired six electric torpedoes from the bow tubes at the nearest battleship, then turned on her heel and fired three more from the stern tubes at the second battleship in column. Shortly after the stern tube fish were swimming the bow tube salvo hit. A minute later there was at least one hit in the second target. A great burst of flame lit up the sky.

Japanese destroyers, completely unable to locate the submarine, dashed off in every direction and dropped a number of face-saving depth charges. *Sealion* stayed on the surface and pulled out to reload her tubes. Despite the hits, the task force seemed to be in no distress. The battleships increased speed to eighteen knots. By the time the torpedo reload was completed *Sealion* was out at eight thousand yards to the west of the battleships.

The sea and wind had built up, and when Reich went to flank speed, trying to draw ahead, green seas swept over the bridge. *Sealion's* laboring engines threatened to drive her under, but the heavy Japanese ships, relatively unaffected by the weather, pulled steadily ahead. Then one group of Japanese ships seemed unable to keep up the pace. They dropped back from their fleeing consorts and shortly *Sealion's* plotting party reported that the slow group was making only twelve knots. Reich turned in to attack the target he could reach, while the others steamed off over the horizon.

Just as *Sealion* was again in attack position there was a tremendous flash that lit up the sky, followed by a terrific explosion whose concussion could be clearly felt in *Sealion's* conning tower. The trailing battleship had blown up. It disappeared from the radar screen.

It was *Kongo*. She had been one of the fast battleships of Battleship Division Three. In the early part of the war this battleship division had usually accompanied the Kido Butai on its far-flung depredations. *Kongo* had fought in many important battles of the war, the last one being the battle off Samar. She was the only battleship to be sunk by a submarine during the war in the Pacific. *Haruna,* her sister ship and the only remaining survivor of the famous Battleship Division Three, had been the second battleship in the formation attacked by *Sealion.* The torpedoes aimed at *Haruna* had hit *Urakaze,* one of the screening destroyers. *Urakaze* was already at the bottom of Tung Hai when *Kongo* blew up.

Archerfish *and* Shinano

Although *Kongo* was one of the big submarine prizes of the war, *Archerfish,* up off the south coast of Honshu, found a bigger one. The Japanese built two super battleships, *Yamato* and *Musashi,* both commissioned early in the war. There was a third ship of this class being built, but after the Battle of Midway, when Japan desperately needed carriers, this third ship was named *Shinano* and converted to an aircraft carrier while she was on the building ways. On 24 November B-29s flying out of Saipan and Guam bombed Japan in the first of the great air raids destined to reduce Tokyo to a shambles. The Japanese Navy decided to move *Shinano* out of Tokyo Bay and take her to the Inland Sea. In haste she sailed with an untrained crew and with many navy yard workmen still aboard her.

Archerfish (Enright) was off Tokyo during the Army Air Force air raids to act as lifeguard. Early on the morning of 28 November Enright received word from Lockwood that the B-29 air raid scheduled for that day had been postponed. *Archerfish* spent the day on periscope patrol off Inamba Island, about a hundred miles south of Tokyo. About ten o'clock that night she had radar contact with a big ship coming down the coast at twenty knots. Within an hour Enright identified his target as an aircraft carrier.

The moon was nearly full but overcast cut down the visibility to fifteen thousand yards. Twenty knots was better speed than *Archerfish* was built for, and when Enright found himself out on the target's beam at fifteen thousand yards the situation looked hopeless. Plot estimated the base course as 210 degrees and the target was zigzagging along with short legs and frequent small course changes. Enright held *Archerfish's* nose down steady on the base course and ignored the target's zigs, scratching to make every turn of the screws count. The distance the carrier lost on the zigzags kept the submarine in the race, but it still looked hopeless. *Archerfish* was like a thoroughbred coming down the stretch, pulling her heart out, but everything she had to give was not enough, and she kept falling back.

In the engine room the enginemen watched and listened, metabolized in tune with the ambient symphony of power, wondering where the first break would come—a sticking valve, an overheated bearing, a lubrication oil leak—something would surely have to give if they kept up that speed too long. But they held on, torn between anxiety for their overloaded machinery and pride in engines that were "singin' like the mornin' stars for joy that they are made."

About three o'clock in the morning, after nearly five hours of this, the carrier suddenly made a radical zig toward the submarine, and *Archerfish* found herself out on the target's bow in attack position. Then things happened fast. At 0317 Enright fired a salvo of six torpedoes and saw the first one hit in the carrier's stern. As *Archerfish* went down deep, to avoid the counterattack, her crew heard four timed hits before the destroyers were in position to drop depth charges.

Shinano actually received three torpedo hits and these she should have carried off with relatively little difficulty. *Musashi*, which had the same hull design, took nineteen torpedoes and twenty-two bombs before she sank in the Sibuyan Sea. But everything went wrong with *Shinano's* damage control. Her crew was green and the ship was new. The navy yard workers panicked. A few hours after *Archerfish's* torpedoes hit, the big carrier sank. *Shinano* was the biggest ship ever sunk by a submarine.

Burt's Brooms

Ever since Halsey had been told about the crucifixion of captured fliers from the Doolittle raid, he had resolved to visit Tokyo with a carrier task force in retaliation. The Third Fleet was scheduled to strike Japan in November, but the conquest of the Philippines was behind schedule and Task Force 38 was required to provide air cover over Leyte and air strikes on Luzon and Ormoc. The carrier strike on Tokyo had to be postponed.

In planning for a carrier strike on Tokyo Lockwood had suggested that submarines do something about the cordon of picket boats that ringed Japan. In the Doolittle raid these pickets had first spotted the carriers and raised the alarm. If the Third Fleet hoped to make an undetected approach something would have to be done to neutralize the pickets. Lockwood proposed a submarine sweep that would destroy by gunfire the pickets in the path of the carriers. This would also temporarily eliminate the pickets as a Japanese early air raid warning of B-29 strikes headed for Tokyo.

Seven submarines (*Ronquil, Burrfish, Sterlet, Silversides, Trigger, Tambor,* and *Saury*) were organized as a submarine anti-picket boat sweep, under command of "Burt" Klakring, who shared Lockwood's enthusiasm and confidence in the submarine deck gun. The Third Fleet strike was called off but it was decided to try out the anti-picket boat sweep anyway.

The operation could hardly be called a success, considering the amount of effort involved. Two picket boats, each of less than 100 tons' displacement, were sunk and one was damaged. Accurate gunfire from a submarine's deck required a relatively calm sea, and at that time of the year in these latitudes wind and seas were rarely light. Wooden picket boats were hard to sink by gunfire, as many submariners discovered. The Japanese responded to the raid by rushing additional patrol craft and air search planes into the area and there were probably more pickets in the area after the sweep than there were when it started.

November Submarine Losses

Albacore (Rimmer), one of the distinguished veterans of the Pacific war, sailed from Pearl Harbor on 24 October on her eleventh patrol. She topped off with fuel at Midway and departed for her patrol area northeast of Honshu and south of Hokkaido, on 28 October, and was never heard from again. In her previous ten patrols she had sunk ten Japanese ships, one of them the big aircraft carrier *Taiho* at the Battle of the Philippine Sea.

The Japanese had planted several defensive minefields early in the war off the northeast Honshu coast and off Tsugaru Strait, and from time to time they had augmented the early fields with fresh sowings. Intelligence of the areas "closed to navigation" was fairly complete and reliable when *Albacore* sailed, and Rimmer had all the latest information. Because of the mine danger *Albacore* was directed to stay outside the one hundred-fathom curve. One hundred fathoms was considered, by the U. S. Navy, to be the maximum depth at which the moored mines used by the Japanese would be effective. Intelligence did not know then that the Japanese sometimes mined waters up to one thousand fathoms deep, nor did they have information of the exact location of mine lines within the larger areas outlined as dangerous to navigation by Japanese notices to mariners.

Although moored mines in deep water certainly had low efficiency, *Albacore* was unfortunate enough to hit one of these nodding sleepers. A Japanese patrol vessel witnessed an underwater explosion inside one of their minefields just outside the hundred-fathom curve near Esan Saki on the south coast of Hokkaido, on 7 November. After the explosion much heavy oil, bedding, and other debris came to the surface, almost certainly marking the end of *Albacore*. Rimmer, relying on his instructions to stay in waters over one hundred fathoms deep, had evidently cut across the deep end of a dangerous area with disastrous consequences.

Growler

The hour of *Growler's* end is also known. *Growler* too was on her eleventh patrol, and in her previous ten she too had sunk ten Japanese ships. She was commanded by Commander T. B. Oakley, who also led a wolf pack which included *Hake* and *Hardhead*. These three submarines were patrolling in the South China Sea west of Mindoro. *Growler* had contact with an enemy convoy before dawn on the morning of 8 November. Oakley quickly assigned all three submarines to attack sectors, and these veterans closed in on the Japanese convoy.

Hake heard two distant explosions, and *Hardhead* heard an explosion, which sounded like a torpedo hit in *Growler's* sector. At the same time the convoy zigged away from *Growler's* position. Both *Hardhead* and *Hake* were expertly worked over in depth-charge attacks by the escorts. After the convoy had passed they surfaced but were unable to contact *Growler*. She had most probably been sunk in the initial depth-charge attack heard by the other submarines.

Scamp

The fate of *Scamp* (Hollingsworth) is in considerable doubt. *Scamp* topped off at Midway on 21 October and departed en route to the Bonin Islands on her eighth patrol. On 8 November her area was shifted to the northward and she was told to stay north of the 28th parallel during the forthcoming B-29 air raids. Hollingsworth acknowledged this message on 9 November and reported that he had as yet made no contacts during the patrol. This was the last message received from *Scamp*. On 14 November she was ordered to lifeguard duty in the area off Inubo Saki, east of Tokyo. A number of other messages were addressed to her in the next fortnight but none required an acknowledgment. On 29 November, some fifteen days after *Scamp* had been directed to proceed to Inubo Saki, Joint Intelligence Center discovered evidence that a new minefield had been laid in that area.

A major operation sometimes brought fifty tons of captured documents to Jicpoa, where two hundred translators worked at a steady grind to translate the most urgent material. Red-bordered "Notices to Mariners" had high priority, but the ordinary unbordered ones usually contained trivia that could be safely deferred. For some reason the Japanese issued an unclassified notice of a restricted area off Inubo Saki. Because it had no red border this did not receive priority treatment and its translation was delayed. When it was translated the Submarine Force was notified immediately but it was too late. Urgent messages sent to *Scamp* were unanswered. It was an obvious conclusion that she had hit a mine.

The effect of this on the translators was electric. The thought that a submarine had been blasted into oblivion, with seventy men trapped three hundred feet below the surface in flooded compartments, while information which could have saved them was within reach of a translator's hand, was horrifying. It tied knots in the guts of every translator whenever he saw an untranslated notice to mariners. After the war it was learned that there were at least three depth-charge attacks which the Japanese rated as kills, in positions where *Scamp* may have been. It is more probable that one of these destroyed *Scamp* rather than the unlocated minefield.

Japanese Kaiten *Operations*

After the power of the Kido Butai was broken at the Battle of Midway a small group of junior Japanese submarine officers began to advocate the use of suicide torpedoes. It is probable that the whole movement was inspired by the unusual posthumous advancement and deification of the nine who died in the midget submarine attacks on Pearl Harbor, an ironic outcome of emotional evaluation and misguided propaganda for an operation which was, in fact, a disastrous failure. When seaplane carriers failed to bring this allegedly decisive weapon into action at the Battle of Midway, radical young officers became obsessed with devising a scheme which would insure the effective use of some similiar weapon in future operations.

They modified oxygen-charged Long Lance torpedoes by inserting a pilot compartment between the oxygen flask and the torpedo warhead. Such a torpedo, they reasoned, guided by a death-defying zealot, could not fail to hit its target. It could make forty knots, and if necesary pursue and overtake the fastest ship afloat. It could carry an explosive warhead big enough to sink the largest ship. Evasive tactics by the target would be unavailing, for the torpedo steersman would continue to direct the torpedo until it exploded against the target—carrying ship, torpedo, and pilot to destruction in one glorious cataclysmic holocaust.

High Japanese Navy brass was cool to this proposition. Miwa in particular found the suicide principle repugnant. Upon his insistence the device was modified so that the pilot could be released and ejected from the torpedo in the last five hundred feet of its run. Senior officers did not pay much attention to young fanatics while Japanese submarines continued to operate with reasonable success, and so long as there was a possibility of the great fleet victory of their dreams. When the Marianas campaign shattered the Japanese submarine force, and the destruction of the carrier forces dimmed hopes for a fleet victory, even the high brass considered weapons of desperation. The suicide torpedo was no more fantastic than other measures that were adopted.

During the summer of 1944 young men began to train with these weapons at Otsujima in the Inland Sea. Volunteers included young officers and petty officers. Although officers and enlisted men became drawn to each other in this desperate venture, and some of the artificial barriers between ranks broke down, it is a strange fact that the training of these men, who had literally dedicated their lives, still included the brutality and beatings characteristic of Japanese naval and military indoctrination. The suicide torpedoes were called *kaitens,* a word compounded from Japanese *kanji* meaning "sky" and "change" but carrying with it untranslatable connotations of a mystic power that would turn the course of the war toward victory.

Each pilot was convinced that when his opportunity came to ride a *kaiten* in battle and die, he would carry with him into oblivion an American carrier or a battleship—a firm conviction essential to the vitality of the project. None could contemplate death for a lesser objective. The mathematics of *kaiten* pilots was simple; one hundred *kaitens* and one hundred American capital ships would be sunk, and Japan would again have command of the sea.

In the fall of 1944 the *kaiten* project was handicapped by lack of submarines to carry *kaitens*. Too many Japanese submarines had been sunk. Submarines assigned to *kaiten* operation had to be modified to carry the weapon on deck and access hatches installed so that *kaitens* could be manned while the submarine was submerged. The first planned *kaiten* operation in early November was deferred because it was decided to use the full strength of the submarine force in the central Philippines.

Training was handicapped by lack of *kaitens* until mass production could increase their number. Mass production was handicapped by lack of steel and fuel and supplies and lubricants. So many ships had been sunk that Japanese industry was grinding to a halt. There was a shortage of skilled torpedo technicians, because so many torpedomen had gone down with sunken submarines. There was no time to train more technicians. There was a shortage of everything but volunteers to man the *kaitens*. Fifteen *kaiten* pilots were killed in training accidents, for the *kaiten* was not an easy weapon to manage, and at no time in training or in battle was there any further reference to Miwa's escape hatch.

On 7 November Miwa presided at a ceremony at Otsujima initiating the Kikusui (floating chrysanthemum) Special Attack Force which

would make the first *kaiten* attack. He told all the assembled trainees of
the glories of Admiral Onishi's *kamikaze* corps of suicide airplane pilots
in the Philippines, and pointed to *I-36*, *I-37*, and *I-47*, anchored in the
bay, ready to carry the Kikusui *kaitens* to their destiny. The twelve
pilots of the Kikusui unit were all young officers, including Lieutenant
Nishima, co-inventor of the *kaiten*, and to each of these at the ceremony's climax Miwa presented the symbolic short *hara-kiri* sword. Next
morning the three submarines sailed on their mission.

Simultaneous attacks on 20 November were planned for Kossol anchorage at Palau, and at Ulithi and Ngulu in the Carolines. *I-38* had
been pulled off patrol east of Leyte in early November to reconnoiter
Ngulu atoll, but on 12 November she encountered the destroyer *Nicholas* and was sunk with all hands. She never made her reconnaissance
report, so both *I-36* (Teremoto) and *I-47* (Orita) were assigned to Ulithi
and *I-37* (Kamimoto) was sent to Kossol anchorage.

I-37 did not arrive at her destination either. She was sighted the day
before the attack was scheduled and two destroyer escorts, *Conklin* and
McCoy Reynolds, were sent out from Kossol anchorage to conduct
hunter-killer operations. That afternoon they established sonar contact
and attacked with hedgehogs. After several attacks they scored a hit
which resulted in a tremendous explosion. *I-37* was destroyed with all
her *kaitens*.

The destroyer escorts never realized that they were engaged with a
special antagonist armed with suicide torpedoes. In submarine warfare
fanatic courage was not enough. Ordinary courage was expected of submariners but in addition, skill, training, and intelligence were essential
—not only at the point of contact, but in the building yards, the manu-
facturing plants, and the research laboratories. Fanatic courage *I-37*
had in superabundance, but her enemies had better electronic weapons
and the skilled men to use them.

On 16 November Combined Fleet reported that their radio intelligence unit had indication that the U.S. fleet had left Ulithi on the
fifteenth, but Miwa decided to continue with the attack. The next day,
an air reconnaissance from Truk confirmed that there were many ships
still present at Ulithi, including battleships and aircraft carriers. *I-36* and
I-47 arrived at Ulithi on 19 November and made a submarine reconnaissance of their own to plot out the location of major targets. The scheduled hour of the attack was early morning. Both submarines submerged
about midnight on the nineteenth and approached their launching positions submerged. *I-47* released all four of her *kaitens* at about half past
three in the morning. *I-36* released one *kaiten* about an hour and a half
later. The remaining three developed mechanical defects and were sunk
after the crews were removed.

About an hour after release of the last *kaiten* a loud explosion was heard in the direction of the anchorage. Orita in *I-47* made periscope observations and sighted a great pillar of fire and smoke inside the atoll at the northern anchorage. An hour and a half later other explosions could be heard inside Ulithi atoll.

I-36 and *I-47* returned to Kure on 30 November. A special meeting of over two hundred people, including Japan's leading experts, was held on board Sixth Fleet's flagship to evaluate results. Orita and Teremoto recounted the events of the attack with much emotion and described what they had heard and seen after the *kaitens* were launched. A Sixth Fleet Staff officer, weighing this evidence together with the attack plan, and aerial photographs taken in the pre-attack reconnaissance, evaluated the results. It was decided that the eccentric and revered Lieutenant Nishima sank an aircraft carrier and that the other four *kaitens* each sank a battleship. The meeting broke up in wild enthusiasm and the *kaiten* efforts were redoubled.

The actual results of the Kikusui Operation were much less. Early on the morning of 20 November the destroyer *Case* rammed and sank an object identified as a midget submarine outside the entrance channel to Ulithi. Marine Corps planes depth-charged another. At least one *kaiten* succeeded in penetrating to the fleet anchorage. It hit the fleet oiler *Mississinewa* with all the horrible fireworks a tanker loaded with aviation gasoline displayed when torpedoed. The oiler sank at her anchorage with the loss of fifty men, a serious loss but far short of what the Japanese thought they had achieved.

Other Japanese Submarine Activity

Other Japanese submarine activity in November and December was limited. The October threat to American communications in the Eastern Pacific was short-lived. *I-12* continued to operate in the Eastern Pacific after her October success in sinking a ship en route from California to Hawaii, to the consternation of traffic and routing officers who had grown rusty from lack of practice in handling such problems. The Japanese kept track of the operations of *I-12* by analysis of American radio traffic, and it is not surprising that they credited their submarine with sinking several ships in November and December, for there were the usual number of false sightings and attacks on phantoms. On 13 November U. S. Coast Guard cutter *Rockford* and the minelayer *Ardent* caught up with the real *I-12* and sank her. U.S. records give another identity to the submarine sunk by this pair but it could only have been *I-12*. She was the only Japanese submarine in that part of the Pacific. After *I-12* was sunk actual Japanese submarine attacks ceased in the Eastern Pacific, although the ghost of *I-12* was active into January.

German and Japanese Submarines in Malaya

The Philippine campaign had the indirect effect of ending the operations of Japanese submarines in the Indian Ocean. The two remaining I-class submarines operating in the Indian Ocean were recalled to take part in the defense of the Philippines, leaving only *RO-113* and *RO-115*. These two submarines shifted their base from Penang to Surabaya.

Six German submarines remained. On 23 September the British submarine *Trenchant* (Hezlet) sank *U-859* off Penang. British and Dutch submarines in Malacca Strait made the approach to Penang so hazardous that the Germans shifted their base to Batavia. This move did little to improve their safety. *U-537* ventured too far to the eastward in Java Sea and encountered *Flounder* (Stevens) north of Bali on 9 November. Stevens fired four torpedoes at the German submarine and at least one hit. *U-537* went down so fast there were no survivors.

Japanese Submarine Supply Service

Seven *I-361* class submarines were engaged in the futile business of transportation to cut-off Japanese island bases in the Marshalls and the Carolines. As these bases had been left far behind in the advance of military operations, transportation operations were nearly as safe as they were useless. *I-365*, however, was unfortunate. She left Japan on a transportation run to Truk and after completing her mission commenced her return journey on 16 November. On 29 November, off Honshu, when she was nearly home safe, she ran through the patrol area of *Scabbardfish*.

Scabbardfish (Gunn) was on lifeguard duty southeast of Tokyo Bay early on the morning of 29 November when through the high periscope Gunn sighted an approaching submarine. *Scabbardfish* ran ahead full speed on the surface to gain position ahead. She was forced down by a plane but was able to finish the approach submerged. *Scabbardfish* fired two torpedoes from the stern tubes and one hit *I-365* in the forward battery compartment. The Japanese submarine went down with horrible breaking-up noises and long screams of compressed air escaping from collapsed compartments, as she reached crushing depth. Gunn surfaced later and picked up a Japanese survivor who identified the sunken submarine as *I-365*. The Japanese Navy did not know what happened to her until after the end of the war.

December Operations in the Philippines

It had originally been planned to land on Mindoro on 5 December and establish an advance air base to provide protection for the big movement to Lingayen Gulf later in the month. These operations had to be postponed because of the stubborn Japanese resistance on Leyte and because the Fifth Army Air Force was unable to move up sufficient force to cover this forward thrust. The advances to Mindoro, through the restricted waters of the Philippines, leaving important Japanese bases in Cebu, Negros, Panay, and Mindanao on the flanks of the route, was a daring and dangerous move.

The landing on Mindoro took place on 15 December. The amphibious forces, support forces, and later the resupply convoys approached Mindoro through the Mindanao Sea, the Sulu Sea, and Mindoro Channel. Attacks by *kamikaze* planes increased in number and effectiveness. In the month of December thirteen ships were sunk and nine damaged by suicide planes. An escort carrier task force operated in the Sulu Sea to provide air support up to D-day at Mindoro. The Third Fleet struck Luzon airfields on 14, 15, and 16 December. On 17 and 18 December the Third Fleet encountered a typhoon which did more damage than some of its major battles. Two destroyers and one destroyer escort were sunk and twenty-one ships were damaged by the high winds and turbulent seas.

On 26 December a Japanese task force consisting of the heavy cruiser *Ashigara*, a light cruiser, and six destroyers struck Mindoro beachheads. The Japanese approach was undetected until within 180 miles of San José, and they were therefore opposed only by Army Air Force planes on Mindoro, plus a few Navy planes that could be rushed in from Leyte, and the PT boats based on Mindoro. The Japanese bombardment caused only superficial damage. Every one of the Japanese ships was damaged by bombs and one destroyer was sunk by a PT boat torpedo. Submarines patrolling in the South China Sea made no contact with this force, either coming or going.

Maru *Sinkings in December*

U.S. submarine dispositions in December followed the November pattern, but the results obtained in the war against Japanese commerce were far different. In November, fifty-seven Japanese *marus* had been sunk by submarines. In December, with approximately the same number of submarines at sea, the *maru* sinkings dropped off to twenty-one. The locations of these sinkings were scattered through the long length of the narrowing Japanese Empire. Generally the ships sunk were small, and only a few submarines could report results comparable with those of the preceding month of the expiring third year of the war.

Sea Devil (Styles) encountered a rare eleven-ship convoy west of Kyushu on 2 December. Styles sank two big ships out of the convoy, but his adventure with *Redfish* and an aircraft carrier a week later overshadowed the success.

Farther south at the beginning of December, a wolf pack consisting of *Trepang* (Davenport), *Razorback* (Brown), and *Segundo* (Fulp) arrived in Convoy College. Davenport was pack commander. He watched several Japanese planes making very low circuitous searches ahead of a convoy and correctly deduced that they were searching for submerged submarines with some new type of submarine detector. These MAD-equipped planes were unsuccessful in locating any of the three submarines submerged along the convoy's route, but their busy searches confined the submarines to cautious periscope exposures which resulted in a wide zigzag of the convoy going undetected. Only *Razorback* succeeded in making an attack and she had to fire at such long range that she scored no hits. The convoy escaped unharmed.

On December 6, however, *Trepang* made contact with a seven-ship convoy at night, and Davenport called in the other two members of the pack to help. *Trepang* sank four ships out of the convoy. *Segundo* torpedoed another which was finished off later by *Razorback*. *Trepang* was out of torpedoes after this night action and was ordered to return to Pearl Harbor.

Southwest Pacific Submarines

Progress of the war brought about a number of changes in operating conditions for Fremantle-based submarines. Sulu Sea was declared an Air Surface Zone and Sibutu Passage was thus closed to submarines. At the end of December areas off Luzon were also declared Air Surface Zones. On 30 December Rear Admiral Ralph Christie was ordered to become Commandant Puget Sound Navy Yard at Bremerton, Washington. Rear Admiral James Fife relieved him as Commander Submarines Southwest Pacific. By that time submarine operating areas in the South China Sea were crowded along the Indo-China coast. In desperate attempts to import oil, Japan sent tanker convoys north along this coast and this occasionally brought to a few U.S. submarines opportunities comparable to the old days.

Flasher (Grider) came up from Fremantle to patrol off Camranh Bay as a member of a wolf pack consisting of *Hawkbill, Becuna,* and *Flasher.* On 4 December *Hawkbill* sighted a tanker convoy and passed on the contact report to *Flasher.* This enabled *Flasher* to achieve a position ahead of the tankers, despite reduced visibility in stormy weather. In two brilliant attacks Grider sank the destroyer *Kishinami* and the 10,000-ton tanker *Hakko Maru.*

Later in the month, on 21 December, *Flasher* encountered another northbound convoy of five tankers, hugging the coast of Indo-China. A destroyer and three other escorts were grouped on the seaward flank. *Flasher* made a long end run and gained position ahead about one o'clock on the morning of 22 December, but the escorts were alert and thwarted the submarine's approach. Grider then took advantage of an indentation of the coastline to run around the bow of the convoy and attack from shoreward. Shortly after five o'clock in the morning he fired three torpedoes at the leading tanker, then shifted fire to the second ship and fired the remaining three bow tubes. The bow tubes empty, *Flasher* swung ship and fired the stern tubes at the third tanker. As the stern tube torpedoes left the tubes the first tanker blew up, brilliantly illuminating the whole ocean. Three big 10,000-ton tankers sank in the holocaust that followed—a rare triple of three tankers sunk in a single submarine attack.

Japanese Combat Ships vs. Submarines in December

Ships of the Japanese Navy were not as fortunate as the *marus* in the last month of 1944. *Pipefish* sank *Coast Defense Vessel No. 64* off Hainan Island on 3 December. *Pintado* sank two landing vessels southeast of Formosa ten day later. *Blenny* sank a frigate and *Hawkbill* sank the destroyer *Momo* near Manila on 15 December. *Tilefish* sank the torpedo boat *Chidori* south of Kyushu on the twenty-second, and *Razorback* finished up her Convoy College patrol by sinking the destroyer *Kuretake* on the eve of the submarine's departure for Pearl Harbor. These together with the destroyer sunk by *Flasher* early in the month made quite a hole in the dwindling number of Japanese escort vessels.

Redfish *and the Aircraft Carrier*

On 8 December *Redfish* (McGregor) was southwest of Nagasaki, rounding the northern flank of the great Nansei Shoto mine barrier, en route to patrol an area in the southern half of the East China Sea. Half a dozen U.S. submarines were within a radius of a hundred miles of this crossroads between minefields Oikawa had laid to keep submarines out of Tung Hai. When *Redfish* surfaced that evening she exchanged radar signals with *Sea Devil* and then set course to the southwest to proceed on mission assigned, but the night was young and *Redfish* and *Sea Devil* had work to do before it was over.

About eight o'clock *Redfish* picked up radar contact at thirty-one thousand yards with a group of ships headed eastward. She sent out a contact report to all submarines in the vicinity and began tracking. The "convoy" was making nineteen knots, and McGregor tried to cut across its wide zigzags to gain position ahead. When the enemy zigged the wrong way *Redfish* lost contact. She sent out information on the enemy's last position, course, and speed to *Sea Owl*, *Sea Poacher*, *Piranha*, *Sea Devil*, *Sunfish*, and *Plaice*, hoping that some of them would be in position to head them off. Shortly after ten o'clock *Redfish* again exchanged radar signals with *Sea Devil*, which was also in pursuit of the "convoy." A half hour later *Redfish* picked up radar contact again and continued dodging after the Japanese ships.

About one o'clock in the morning the moon rose, and in the uncertain moonlight McGregor saw that he was chasing a battleship, a large air-craft carrier, and three destroyers. The Japanese task force pulled steadily ahead and it seemed certain that it would win its race for safety. Suddenly there was a loud explosion in the task force. The carrier slowed down and dropped behind its consorts. *Sea Devil* had made the first attack and put a torpedo in the carrier. *Redfish* closed in fast and fired six torpedoes from a range of twenty-nine hundred yards. At least one hit and there was a series of many explosions impossible to identify. The carrier zigzagged wildly and destroyers gathered around to guard her. An hour later *Redfish* gained position to fire stern tubes and scored another hit, but the carrier continued on at twelve knots.

McGregor picked up a garbled message from *Plaice* (Stevens) report-ing that she had made two attacks. Lockwood later clarified that *Plaice* had been unable to close the carrier but had fired torpedoes at the escorting destroyers. The carrier was *Junyo*. She made it in to port but never went to sea again. The destroyer *Maki* was also heavily damaged that night.

Redfish continued on to her assigned area. A hurricane raged in Tung Hai, with seas so high it was doubtful that torpedoes would have held their course at normal depths. Targets were scarce, but floating mines, broken loose from Japanese minefields by the storm, were plentiful. Fortunately the weather moderated by 19 December.

Early that afternoon *Redfish* was spotted by a low-flying Japanese plane, which dropped one depth charge fairly close. Information on the submarine's position apparently did not get through to Japanese routing officers. Three hours later McGregor sighted masts on the horizon. The masts developed into destroyers and behind the destroyers came an aircraft carrier making eighteen knots on a southerly course.

Seven minutes later, without changing course once during the approach, *Redfish* reached almost ideal position and fired her four remaining bow torpedoes. Two torpedoes hit the carrier. The big Japanese ship took a 20-degree list and belched smoke and flame. The starboard escorting destroyer passed right astern of *Redfish* and McGregor, presented with a beautiful target, fired the stern tubes at the escort. The agile destroyer turned away and all the torpedoes missed. *Redfish* then had no torpedoes in the tubes and a burning carrier within range. As soon as the sweating torpedomen in the after room had one electric torpedo in the tubes McGregor fired. It hit with a thunderous explosion and the carrier went down.

The carrier was *Unryu*, loaded with suicide boats en route to the Philippines. The Japanese destroyer *Hinoki* claimed that she sank the attacking submarine. This was so close to the truth that *Redfish* would be the last to scoff at the claim.

As *Redfish* withdrew at periscope depth, McGregor maneuvered to get a shot at one of the destroyers. Suddenly *Hinoki* made contact and charged. *Redfish* went deep but on the way down seven well-placed depth charges exploded alongside the starboard bow. The steering gear and the bow planes were jammed. The pressure hull was cracked in the forward torpedo room. There were numerous leaks and other casualties. *Redfish* was forced to the bottom at 232 feet, and listened while *Hinoki* searched for the submarine to finish her off. Well after dark *Redfish* surfaced. The destroyers were still in sight and within gun range. *Redfish* withdrew at full speed. She still had a long and perilous journey around the minefields, harried by Japanese air and surface patrols, before she gained the comparative safety of the broad Pacific. It was Christmas Day before her weary crew could relax with the assurance they would reach home.

Damaged Submarines

In December no U.S. submarine was lost, but two others besides *Redfish* had very close calls. On 13 December *Bergall* (Hyde) was patrolling in the South China Sea. About half an hour before sunset Hyde sighted the masts of a ship at thirty-five thousand yards. He decided to make an end around run and seek a position to make a night attack. The targets were approaching Royalist Shoal off the south coast of Indo-China and the water was shallow—eleven to fourteen fathoms with several spots of only six fathoms. A submerged attack or submerged evasion after an attack would be very difficult. The night was clear and the sea was glassy, but there was no moon.

Bergall picked up radar contact after dark at twenty-six thousand yards. About half an hour later at seventeen thousand yards Hyde could dimly see the ships and identified them as a large warship and one escort. It was in fact the heavy cruiser *Myoko* and an escort, a very dangerous target under the circumstances. Either of the Japanese ships could outgun or outrun *Bergall,* and the water was too shallow to take a submarine below periscope depth. Hyde came on in, intent on getting off his attack before the submarine was sighted. At thirty-three hundred yards he picked a moment when the cruiser and the escort were overlapping and fired his bow tubes.

Two minutes after the last torpedo was off there was a terrific explosion and the whole target was enveloped in flame. Flames shot up to 750 feet and the big ship appeared to break in two. *Bergall* opened out the range to ten thousand yards and reloaded tubes. The escort made no move to interfere with the submarine. Hyde concluded that the escort too had been hit, and he decided to come back in to make sure of both ships.

When the range came down to nine thousand yards there was flash of gunfire from the escort. A two-gun salvo landed, one shell in *Bergall's* wake and the other a direct hit on the forward torpedo loading hatch. *Bergall* turned tail and got out of there at full speed, pursued by remarkably well-placed salvos until she was out of range. *Myoko* was heavily damaged but did not sink. She made it into Singapore where she stayed until the end of the war.

When *Bergall* got out from under the guns, Hyde took stock of his situation. The damage control party smothered electrical fires and repaired broken air lines. Ingenious repairs were made to plug the hole and keep the surface seas out of the torpedo room, but *Bergall* could not dive. She was two thousand miles from Exmouth Gulf, the nearest base where emergency repairs could be made. The first fourteen hundred miles of her journey was through enemy-controlled waters, through Karimata Strait, the Java Sea, and narrow Lombok Strait, flanked by Japanese air bases and patrolled by Japanese ships, before she could cross the Malay Barrier to the comparative safety of the Indian Ocean.

Hyde decided he could make it. On 15 December *Bergall* rendezvoused with *Angler* and transferred to her one officer and fifty-four men, leaving on board eight officers and twenty-one men to work the damaged submarine. Angler followed in *Bergall's* wake to rescue the salvage crew in case of necessity. On 20 December the pair of them arrived safely in Exmouth Gulf.

While this was going on in the Java Sea *Dragonet* (Lewis) was also making a long and perilous run to safety. *Dragonet* had been patrolling in the Kurile Islands. On 15 December she was within sight of Matsuwa To, near where *Herring* had been sunk by shore battery fire the previous June. *Dragonet* was patrolling at one hundred feet with frequent rises to periscope depth for a look around. The chart showed over four hundred feet of water. As the submarine headed back to depth after one periscope exposure she hit a pinnacle of rock.

The torpedo room flooded and had to be abandoned. The crew managed to put pressure on the torpedo room through the salvage air line and blow some of the water out. *Dragonet* surfaced with a heavy list, and was clearly visible within range of the guns of Matsuwa To. With great good fortune she cleared the range before the Japanese battery opened fire, and with good seamanship she finally made it through a heavy storm all the way to Midway and safety.

XXV

JANUARY–MARCH 1945

Lingayen Landings

On New Year's Day 1945, the bombardment and fire support groups of the Seventh Fleet rendezvoused at Leyte to form cruising dispositions for their passage through the Philippine Islands to Lingayen. The slow-speed minesweepers and the hydrographic group sortied first, on 2 January. Oldendorf's main force followed, passing through Surigao Strait into the Sulu Sea where it formed around two groups of escort carriers for air protection. Attack groups and reinforcement groups trailed in massive formations. The Seventh Fleet anticipated an attack by the remnants of the Japanese surface Navy, but the remaining heavy ships of Japan were in no condition or position to oppose this great armada en route to liberate Luzon.

The main opposition to the approach and attack on Lingayen came from *kamikazes,* and these increased both in numbers and effectiveness beyond anything that had ever been encountered before. By the time the landings were made, on 9 January, forty ships of the Seventh Fleet had been sunk or damaged in suicide attacks by Japanese planes.

Third Fleet Operations

On 3 and 4 January, in foul weather that prevented accurate observation of results, Task Force 38 struck Japanese airfields in Formosa and the Ryukyus. On 6 and 7 January carrier planes hit Luzon airfields. Although carrier strikes undoubtedly reduced the number of *kamikazes,* many suicide planes succeeded in taking off from Philippine fields. After fueling on the eighth, the Third Fleet ended its direct support of the Lingayen landing by a strike on Formosa on 9 January.

On the night of 9–10 January, Halsey took the Third Fleet through Luzon Strait into the South China Sea. The Third Fleet moved rapidly south to a striking position off Indo-China, hoping to catch the Japanese battleships *Ise* and *Hyuga* at Camranh Bay. *Ise* and *Hyuga* were not there but the Japanese were taken completely by surprise. Carrier strikes on Camranh Bay, and all up and down the Indo-China coast, made a clean sweep of Japanese shipping at sea and in port. In a single day twenty-two escort vessels were sunk or damaged. These were mostly *kaibokans* or smaller, but included the light cruiser *Kashii*. Thirty-two *marus* were sunk that day, including twelve tankers. Japanese commerce with Singapore and Malaya was completely disrupted and never recovered.

For the Third Fleet's sweep of the South China Sea, Southwest Pacific submarines had arranged special lifeguard services. *Angler* was stationed off Tizard Reef. *Kraken* was south of Hainan. *Rock* was thirty miles off Camranh Bay. On this assignment *Rock* had one very bad hour when the destroyer *English* mistook the submarine, on its assigned lifeguard station, for an unidentified sailboat making fourteen knots into the wind. The destroyer opened accurate fire at ninety-three hundred yards. *Rock* gave up attempts to establish her identity and dove for safety.

The Third Fleet hit Hainan and Hong Kong and passed out into the Pacific through Luzon Strait on 21 January. The next day the carriers struck airfields and shipping in the Ryukyus and completed important photographic reconnaissance of Okinawa, before returning to Ulithi on 23 January. In the month of January seventy-two *marus*, including forty tankers, were sunk by air attack, mostly by Third Fleet carrier strikes. On 26 January at Ulithi, Halsey passed over tactical command to Spruance. The Third Fleet became the Fifth Fleet and thereafter directed its attention northward.

Submarines in the South China Sea

The Celebes Sea and the Sulu Sea were Air Surface Zones, and the route through Lombok and Karimata Straits was the only available approach for American submarines to their operating areas off the Indo-China coast. British and Dutch submarines based on Fremantle patrolled the Java Sea and the South China Sea below 3° South, and these submarines also used Lombok Strait to reach their areas.

Fife was apprehensive of Japanese attempts to close these narrow passages, either by minefields in shallow Karimata or by rigorous anti-submarine patrol in Lombok. To avoid drawing attention to their use of this route, Fremantle-based submarines were forbidden to make attacks within 120 miles of Lombok, or to attack any target smaller than a heavy cruiser in Karimata.

Fortunately the Japanese never seriously challenged submarines' use of these passages, except for one ineffective effort to mine the deep, swift water of Lombok in 1943, when for a couple of months submarines were routed through Ombai Strait. Small Japanese surface vessels patrolled Lombok. Submarines normally ran through Lombok only at night on the surface and used radar and high surface speed to avoid patrols. In 1944 a battery of 6-inch guns was installed by the Japanese in an attempt to control the straits. This gave the submarines trouble on moonlit nights. Early in 1945 Army planes bombed the shore guns and the Japanese radar station at Lombok, with extensive damage to installations. The northern entrance to Lombok was sometimes patrolled by Japanese radar planes at night, but these usually could be avoided by alert submarines.

Loss of Barbel

In the latter part of January *Barbel* (Raguet) joined a wolf pack with *Perch, Tuna,* and *Gabilan* to cover the western approaches to Balabac and the southern entrance to Palawan Passage. On 3 February *Barbel* sent a message to several submarines in her vicinity reporting numerous airplane contacts. *Barbel* had been attacked from the air three times but escaped without damage. Raguet promised to transmit the next night and give further information on Japanese air patrols. On 6 February *Tuna* reported that she had been unable to contact *Barbel.* Japanese records show that on 4 February, off northwest Borneo, a plane attacked a submarine and scored a direct hit near the bridge. This probably was the attack which destroyed *Barbel.*

Japanese Tanker Movements

At the beginning of the year the Japanese had 1,927,000 gross tons of dry cargo vessels afloat, barely enough to import sufficient food from China and Manchuria to feed Japan. In January the Japanese Grand Escort Force abandoned all organized attempts to import dry cargo raw material from Southeast Asia. Except for tankers, traffic through the South China Sea dried up rapidly. The Japanese were so desperate for oil that they continued to try to push tankers through by *kamikaze* tactics, despite ruinous losses.

Besugo (Wogan) sank a 10,000-ton tanker on 6 January off the Malay coast. The same day *Sea Robin* (Stimson) sank another tanker off Hainan. For some time after the Third Fleet's strike of 12 January there were very few tankers left in the South China Sea. *Boarfish* (Gross) sank two large cargo ships on the last day of January off Indo-China. In February *Pampanito* (Summers), *Guavina* (Lockwood), *Hawkbill*

(Scanland), *Becuna* (Sturr), and *Blenny* (Hazzard) worked the Indo-China coast, and between them sank seven Japanese tankers. On 4 March *Baya* (Jarvis) sank a 5000-ton tanker and the next day *Bashaw* (Simpson) sank the 10,000-ton *Ryoei Maru*. On 20 March *Blenny* sank a tanker convoy of three small ships. *Bluegill* (Barr) sank a 5500-ton tanker on 28 March. That was the last big tanker to be sunk by submarines.

Japanese Combat Ships in the South China Sea

While the Third Fleet searched for *Ise* and *Hyuga,* these two Japanese battleships were anchored in Lingga Roads near Singapore. In February the Japanese decided to move the big ships north, with a cargo of oil in drums. They were sighted early in their voyage by H.M.S. *Tantalus* (MacKenzie) on 11 February, but the British submarine was forced down by screening aircraft and was unable to close to torpedo range. With the information that a Japanese task force was coming north Fife alerted all his submarines in the South China Sea.

Blackfin sighted the Japanese battleships on 12 February and trailed for two hours but was finally left astern. *Charr* sighted them the same day but the task force's seventeen-knot speed prevented the submarine from making an end around run and she lost contact. The next day *Blower* (Campbell) fired six torpedoes at one of the big ships and claimed two hits. *Bergall* (Hyde) succeeded in getting in to 4800 yards and from that long range fired six torpedoes. Hyde believed he made one hit. There is nothing in the Japanese records or in the subsequent movements of these ships to indicate that they received any damage in these attacks.

Lockwood followed the progress of the Japanese task force through Southwest Pacific areas by plotting intercepted contact reports from submarines and planes. Eleven of his submarines, in Convoy College and the East China Sea, were alerted and stationed along the projected route of the northbound Japanese. *Ise* and *Hyuga* steamed past these eager submarines without a scratch and eventually arrived at Kure, much to the chagrin of the whole submarine force.

Smaller Japanese combat vessels were not so fortunate. On 24 January *Blackfin* (Kitch) attacked a tanker with a destroyer escort off the Malay coast. The tanker (*Sarawak Maru*) was badly damaged but made it as far as Hong Kong where two months later she was sunk by a mine. *Shigure* (the escort), which had survived some desperate battles, was squarely hit by one of *Blackfin's* torpedoes and sank immediately. On 20 February *Pargo* (Bell) attacked the destroyer *Nokaze* off the coast of Indo-China. The first torpedo hit under the destroyer's bridge and *Nokaze* blew up with a spectacular eruption. *Nokaze* was the last Japanese destroyer to be sunk by a U.S. submarine. *Hammerhead* (Smith) sank the *kaibokan Yaku* on 23 February, and *Hoe* (Refo) sank *Shonan,* another *kaibokan,* two days later. Eight smaller escort vessels were sunk by submarines in the South China Sea in the first three months of 1945.

Smaller Marus

Japanese ships of all kinds in the South China Sea became fewer and smaller as the Philippine campaign progressed. Most Japanese traffic in the East Indies and Malaya was carried on by small coasters operating close inshore. British submarines were very adept in the use of their deck guns to break up this commerce. The shallow water of the Gulf of Siam was believed to be mined and had been avoided by U.S. submarines. In March H.M.S. *Tradewind* made a successful patrol of the Gulf. After that both British and American submarines regularly patrolled these shallow waters.

In February Subic Bay was occupied by the U. S. Army and soon thereafter submarine refueling facilities became available there. This greatly eased the logistic problem for all Allied submarines. It permitted submarines en route between Fremantle and their South China Sea areas to spend a few days on patrol in the Java Sea. *Sea Robin* (Stimson), patrolling there on the night of 4 March, picked up a convoy of three small cargo ships with three escorts. The convoy was making eight knots, and at night on the surface the submarine could run around them at will. The moon was bright but the sky was cloudy. The visibility changed rapidly and unpredictably so Stimson decided to make a submerged radar approach.

Sea Robin had a new ST radar, with radar and periscope combined in one instrument. Radar superiority and superior surface speed gave Stimson complete initiative. He ran out to eleven thousand yards and submerged to fifty-five feet. As the convoy came by he picked out the biggest ship and fired three torpedoes. The target exploded so violently that bits of wreckage fell in the sea around the submarine. An hour later, when *Sea Robin* surfaced, the convoy had passed by, leaving a trailing escort to fend off another attack. With his radar and high speed Stimson had no difficulty running around the protecting escort and reaching a new attack position ahead. In the next attack both of the remaining small freighters were sunk, wiping out the entire convoy.

Submarine Blockade

Radar and high surface speed gave submarine warfare a new potential. Essentially submarine war had been a war of attrition, based on the well-substantiated theory that if submarines continued to sink ships faster than the Japanese could build them, there would eventually come a day when the Japanese Empire would collapse for want of ships to maintain communications between its sea-divided parts. For three years submarines exacted a disintegrating toll of Japanese commerce until there was no longer sufficient dry cargo ships to import raw materials essential to Japan's war economy.

Fast-stepping, well-screened task forces still had an excellent chance of evading even well-placed submarine lines. Once *Ise* and *Hyuga* got by there was no hope of submarines running up ahead again for another try. A submarine had to be fortunate to make her initial contact on such a force sharp on the enemy's bow, or she was unable to attack. In attacking slower merchant ships, radar and high surface speed gave a submarine the ability to observe without being observed, while she used her speed to select her own time and place to attack.

The air forces, operating out of the Philippines, crowded Japanese shipping into a narrow lane skirting the western shores of the South China Sea. In this narrow lane submarines, with good engines and good radar, could impose an effective blockade against the tankers Japan tried to push through. Despite the heavy losses of tankers in January, the Japanese still had 618,000 gross tons of tankers afloat on 1 March, as compared with the maximum tonnage of 873,000 tons she had available at any time during the war.

There was plenty of oil in Japanese-held areas of the East Indies and there were tankers enough afloat to move it, yet Japan was desperate for oil. Even *kamikaze* planes and *kaitens* required fuel. A nation and a people determined to commit suicide needed fuel to do it effectively. The Japanese fermented sweet potatoes for alcohol for airplane fuel and distilled the roots of pine trees for oil, but they could not get tankers through the blockade. Japanese tankers headed for Japan despaired of ever reaching there, and in March the Grand Escort Force gave up all organized attempts to import oil from Southeast Asia. After that tankers were rare targets for submarines in the South China Sea.

Japanese Submarines in the Philippines

Japanese submarines did their best to interfere with the Luzon campaign but, during the month of December, there was only one RO-boat off the east coast and another off the west coast of Luzon. When Halsey appeared off Formosa on 2 January three submarines were sent out to get him but they were unable to locate the Third Fleet. By 5 January it was apparent to the Japanese that the expected invasion of Luzon was under way. Miwa tried to maintain a concentration of submarines northwest of Luzon to oppose this operation, but nearly all the larger I-class submarines were tied up in preparation for *kaiten* installations. There were eight RO-boats available in the Sixth Fleet and these were reinforced by ordering *RO-113* and *RO-115* (the last two Japanese submarines in the Indian Ocean) to the Manila area. They left for the Philippines about 26 January. The nearest base for repairs and replenishment was in the homeland, and with only ten RO-boats available the Japanese were able to maintain only three submarines in the Luzon area during most of January.

On 12 January *RO-49* claimed to have sunk an *Idaho*-class battleship west of Luzon. On 30 January *RO-46* reported sinking a tanker and two transports. The attack transport *Cavalier* was torpedoed by a submarine off the west coast of Luzon early on 30 January. She was not sunk but had to be towed to Leyte. The other reported attacks are unaccounted for.

By the end of January the Japanese Air Force was about washed up in the Philippines, and it was decided to pull back and operate from Formosan bases. Four submarines (*RO-46, RO-112, RO-113,* and *RO-115*) were ordered to transport plane crews from Batulinao, in northern Luzon, to Takao, in Formosa, in connection with this pullback. For Japanese submarines, this was a disastrous operation.

On 2 February *RO-115* was given orders to leave her patrol area off Manila and proceed to Takao to take part in transportation operations. She never made it. She was destroyed en route. *RO-46* did make one trip, successfully disembarked her passengers at Takao on 12 February, and then departed for the homeland. *RO-112* left Takao for Batulinao on 8 February and *RO-113* followed in her wake two days later. Neither of them arrived. Transport submarine *I-372* left Yokosuka for Takao on 8 February, but after three submarines had disappeared in this operation it was decided that submarine transportation operations on this run were too costly. The operation was canceled and *I-372* returned to Kure to be modified to carry *kaitens*.

Batfish *and the Takao Transportation Operation*

Batfish (Fyfe) was solely responsible for breaking up the Japanese Takao operation. *Batfish* was on patrol in Luzon Strait. On the night of 9 February she picked up radar contact at eleven thousand yards and closed her invisible target to eighteen hundred yards. She then fired four electric torpedoes and they all missed. The target apparently was unaware of the attack and continued on the surface until the range came down to one thousand yards. Lookouts in *Batfish* then sighted a Japanese submarine. Three torpedoes were fired and at least one hit. This was probably the reason *RO-115* never reached Takao.

The next night a similar situation arose. *Batfish* picked up radar transmissions like those she had detected the previous night coming from the Japanese submarine. This was a ticklish situation, feeling for an opening in the dark, each submarine probing with its radar, with the probability that the first one to get in its thrust would be the only survivor. Feeling his way in, Fyfe made visual contact, but before torpedoes could be fired the Japanese submarine dove. Half an hour later *Batfish's* soundman heard noises resembling the sound of a submarine blowing ballast tanks to surface. A pip popped up on the radar screen at eighty-six-hundred yards. Fyfe closed on the surface and fired four torpedoes. There was a heavy explosion, marking the end of *RO-112*.

Two days later, on 12 February, *Batfish* was still on guard at the same old stand when the familiar pattern was repeated. A Japanese submarine was located by radar at 0155 in the morning and Fyfe approached with radar to guide him. When the range closed to seven thousand yards the Japanese evidently picked up *Batfish's* radar transmission and dove. Fyfe then ran out ahead along the projected track of his enemy and waited. An hour later the Japanese submarine reappeared on *Batfish's* radar screen. Submerged until only the radar mast was above the surface, Fyfe came in to attack position and fired torpedoes. There was a loud explosion. The next morning *Batfish* recovered navigational equipment and books from the debris on the surface. Like the others, *RO-113* had been sunk with no survivors. Singlehanded, *Batfish* had broken up the Philippine–Formosa submarine transportation operation and emerged the victor in three successive lethal duels.

End of Japanese Submarine Operations in the Philippines

RO-55 also disappeared in early February, somewhere west of Luzon. She was scheduled to arrive on patrol in the Mindoro-Manila area on 5 February. On 2 February she reported engaging enemy aircraft. This was her last report. She was probably the victim of destroyer escort *Thomason's* successful hedgehog attack of 7 February.

After this there were only two conventional Japanese submarines remaining in the Philippines. *RO-50* on the east coast reported sinking a transport three hundred miles southeast of Surigao on 10 February. *LST-577* was damaged by a submarine torpedo at that time and had to be sunk later by U.S. forces as unsalvageable. *RO-109* reported torpedoing an aircraft carrier, a cruiser, and a destroyer sixty miles west of Lingayen, but these attacks can not be matched with any U.S. reports of action.

It was planned to send *RO-43* to Cebu with torpedoes and supplies for the midget submarines there, about 14 February, but when it became apparent that things were about to happen in the Ryukyus and the Bonins, this operation was called off. All conventional submarines were shortly thereafter recalled from the Philippines to prepare for the defense of the inner perimeter. This left only midget submarines in the Philippines.

Midget Submarine Operations

The Cebu midgets remained active until U.S. forces landed on that island. The constant heavy American surface traffic between Leyte and Lingayen through Surigao Strait and the Mindanao Sea provided an almost ideal setup for the operation of Japanese midget submarines. These two-man, battery-powered submarines ran down from Cebu, sometimes in groups of three, to an advanced base at Dumaguete near the southern tip of Negros. There they lay in wait until coastwatchers sent them information of a convoy or a task force coming through Surigao Strait. Without having to exhaust their batteries in high-speed running the midgets could then maneuver into a position on their target's track as U.S. ships came through the Mindanao Sea.

The midgets reported many great successes. On 3 January they claimed sinking a destroyer and two transports. Two days later they reported sinking a destroyer and another unidentified warship in the Mindanao Sea. One of the midgets on this operation failed to return, but it was credited with sinking a cruiser. The U.S. cruiser *Boise* had been target for the midget submarine attack that day. On 5 January, coming through the Mindanao Sea, *Phoenix* spotted torpedoes headed for *Boise* and signaled an alarm. *Boise* maneuvered at high speed and avoided the torpedoes completely. The destroyer *Taylor* made contact, rammed, depth-charged, and sank a midget submarine in retaliation. This was the only midget attack of the month in which U.S. and Japanese accounts can be coordinated.

During February the Cebu midgets claimed sinking a destroyer and a cruiser, and in March they claimed three transports but none of these attacks can be substantiated. On 26 March U. S. Army forces landed on Cebu. The Japanese record that the five remaining midget submarines scuttled and personnel joined the base defense forces. During the landings on Cebu destroyers *Conyngham*, *Flusser*, and *Newman* and *PC-1133* encountered midget submarines. *Newman* claimed sinking one by gunfire. This ended the operation of Japanese midget submarines in the Philippines. Despite their exaggerated claims the Cebu midgets failed to sink a single ship.

Kaitens

Many of the larger Japanese submarines (I-class) had been converted to carry *kaitens*. Good progress had been made in production of piloted torpedoes and in training *kaiten* pilots to attack anchored targets. By the middle of January the Japanese were ready to launch another *kaiten* attack. Encouraged by the illusion of success in attacking Ulithi, Miwa organized the Kongo Unit of *kaitens* and planned simultaneous attacks on several U.S. bases supporting the Philippine invasion.

In late December five I-class submarines left Japan, loaded with suicide torpedoes, to take position off widely dispersed U.S. bases for a planned attack on 12 January. By 10 January all of the selected bases had been scouted by Air Force reconnaissance planes launched from Japanese bypassed islands. The presence of suitable targets was thus assured, and orders were issued to carry out the surprise attacks planned as Operation Kongo.

I-56 (Morinaga) was prevented from approaching Seeadler Harbor in the Admiralties by an alert anti-submarine patrol and well-placed anti-submarine nets. After making several futile attempts she was recalled on 16 January. *I-47* (Orita) released four human torpedoes at Hollandia on 12 January as planned. As Orita retired on the surface he saw large fires in the harbor and heard, on the radio, submarine warnings being broadcast. *I-53* (Toyomasu) at Kossol Passage in Palau released four *kaitens*. One blew up shortly after launching. Another developed mechanical defects and had to be sunk after the pilot was removed. Toyomasu heard great explosions in Kossol Passage and reported that the remaining two *kaitens* were successful.

I-36 (Teremoto) attacked Ulithi with four human torpedoes. One of the *kaitens*, intended for the ammunition ship *Mazama*, exploded forty yards short of its target. What happened to the others is unknown. *I-36*, hearing the explosion, reported that all her human torpedoes succeeded. They were credited with sinking four ships, including a battleship and a fleet tanker. *I-48* (Toyama) was scheduled for a follow-up attack on Ulithi on 20 January but nothing was heard from her after she left Kure. Air reconnaissance of Ulithi on 20 January revealed a sunken tanker in the central anchorage where *I-48* was scheduled to attack. It was therefore concluded that Toyama had completed his attack before *I-48* was destroyed. In fact Toyama had been spotted off Ulithi and attacked unsuccessfully by a patrol plane on 22 January. The hunter-killer team of *Conklin*, *Corbesier*, and *Raby* followed up the attack and sank *I-48* with all her *kaitens* still on board.

An attack on Guam on 12 January was delivered by four *kaitens*. They were released by *I-58* commanded by Mochitsura Hashimoto, who has since published an excellent account of his experiences as a Japanese submarine commander. *I-58* left Kure on 29 December, after an inspiring address by Admiral Miwa, and an emotional send-off by cheering crowds as *I-58* got under way with her four *kaiten* pilots, seated on their *kaitens* on deck, wearing white *haitchi machis* bound around their heads and brandishing their *samurai* swords.

Arriving in the Marianas on 6 January they had a long wait while avoiding American patrols. The weather was fine, clear and calm, and morale was high. Closing to launching position on the surface on the night of 11 January, Hashimoto felt sorry for the human torpedo pilots because no battleships or aircraft carrier had been reported in Apra Harbor by the latest air reconnaissance. In *I-58* two of the *kaitens* could be entered only from the deck while the submarine was on the surface, and as there were indications that *I-58* had been discovered this had to be done some hours before the scheduled attack, to permit the submarine to make a submerged approach.

Two pilots for these *kaitens* came up on deck in the bright, soft, tropic night and looked around them for the last time. One of the doomed young men wanted to identify the strange constellations new to him in these romantic low latitudes and inquired, "Captain where is the Southern Cross?" It had not yet risen and for him would never rise. A short time later he shook hands firmly with Hashimoto and went down on deck to crawl into the cramped *kaiten* cockpit for the last few hours of his life. At three o'clock in the morning all four *kaitens* were released. They were expected to arrive at their target about four-thirty. As that hour approached a plane came over and forced Hashimoto to submerge again, so he was unable to observe the results of the attack.

No ships were sunk in the Kongo operation but the Japanese assessed the results as eighteen vessels sunk, including one converted aircraft carrier, nine large transports, one oil tanker, one cruiser, and six other large ships including aircraft carriers, battleships, and transports. Such optimistic estimates can only be the result of inexcusably poor staff work.

It can be expected that a commanding officer who sends men to certain death will grasp at any straw to convince himself that success justified the sacrifice, so it is understandable that *kaiten*-carrying submarines would overestimate results. The *kaiten* pilots themselves never brought back accounts of their experiences. The compulsion to blow himself and his craft to Kingdom Come in frustration must have been overwhelming for a *kaiten* pilot who had missed his target, and the explosion would be interpreted as success by the listening mother ship.

Midgets, like those at Cebu, were also prone to inaccurate observations. Their operators were distracted by a multitude of duties and their short periscopes were blinded by even moderate seas. Even in the largest submarines, essential maneuvers to evade counterattacks took precedence over observation of results; the ocean was full of furious explosions after any attacks and in the dark of night confusion was normal. The tendency to hear explosions at the expected time, and to see things that did not happen, even to the point of hallucination, is common to all men. Exaggerations were greater in attacks involving brief observation and split-second decisions, such as air attacks and submarine attacks usually were, but the discrepancies between different accounts of surface actions, especially at night, were also often fantastic. No man who has not been under very great pressure in combat can assume he would be a more accurate observer.

There was a rough relationship between the course of the war and the proportion of imagined to real accomplishments. In defeat the number of wild reports of fictitious results ran high. There was no relationship between ability and tendency to hallucination. Some of the most successful commanders, on both sides, brought back some of the most dramatic reports of things that did not happen. For all this a responsible staff must be prepared, and organized, to weigh evidence and make objective appraisals.

One has only to glance at the index of I-class and RO-class submarines (where * indicates lost submarines) to appreciate the disastrous losses suffered by the Japanese submarine force. Losses of this magnitude are fatal to efficiency. It is remarkable that they did not also destroy the morale of the Japanese submarine force. The courage, loyalty, and stoic discipline of the Japanese submariners demands the respect of everyone who has gone down to the sea in submarines, but the blind self-deception that sustained the futile *kaiten* operation is impossible to justify. Objectivity would have been difficult to achieve under the great emotional stress of defeat. High moral courage was required to acknowledge that brave men had sacrificed their lives with wrong tactics and inadequate weapons. But the failure of the high Japanese command to face up to this painful task amounts to betrayal of those who so eagerly set out to die.

Japanese Submarine Transportation Operations

During all these desperate actions, eight *I-361*-class Japanese submarines were engaged in communication between Japan and the cut off islands in the Central Pacific. Most of this work was unremarkable. *I-362* disappeared while en route from Yokosuka to Woleai in January. Her loss remains unexplained. *I-371* was lost returning to Japan from Truk. The Japanese were also unaware of what happened to her. *Lagarto*

(Latta) torpedoed a Japanese submarine off Kyushu on 24 February. This was undoubtedly *I-371*, which went down without a trace and with no survivors.

HA-106, first of her class, became operational in January. These 325-ton submarines of the HA-class were designed primarily to transport aviation gasoline, but when *HA-106* was completed she was first assigned to the Grand Escort Force. There she assisted in training anti-submarine forces. There is no record of her acting as a convoy escort or, in fact, of the Japanese ever deliberately using submarines in anti-submarine work other than in training.

By March the situation in Japan had become so acute that the Japanese gave up all organized attempts to supply the South Sea Islands. The Seventh Submarine Squadron that had been engaged in that business was deactivated. Most of the *I-361*-class submarines were converted to carry *kaitens*. Two submarines of that class were modified to carry gasoline, and together with three new HA-class submarines were assigned to bring in fuel oil from Singapore and the East Indies.

Lockwood's Submarines

Pickings for U.S. submarines were slim in the East China Sea, the Yellow Sea, and the waters around Japan. There were many submarines available in 1945 to patrol all these areas. The few targets encountered were hunted down by young submarine skippers, seeking the bubble reputation even in the cannon's mouth, and occasionally a wolf pack would still find a fat convoy.

A wolf pack consisting of *Queenfish* (Loughlin), *Picuda* (Shepard), and *Barb* (Fluckey) entered East China Sea early in January to patrol the coast of China from Wenchow south to where a blind bombing zone and Japanese minefields together closed Formosa Strait to submarine operations. Loughlin commanded the pack. For the first few days they encountered only a plethora of floating mines broken loose from Japanese minefields, but on 7 January *Barb* made contact with a convoy. Unable to close to torpedo range before the convoy reached Formosa, *Barb* succeeded in coaching *Picuda* into attack position. *Picuda* heavily damaged the 10,000-ton tanker *Munakata Maru*, which was sunk later that month in an air attack on Keelung.

The next night *Barb* again made contact with a convoy and successfully coached both her packmates into contact. The submarines pursued the convoy deep into the blind bombing zone, making a series of night attacks in which all three submarines participated. They reported that only one ship from the eight-ship convoy escaped.

The appraisal of the results of that attack are in confusion. Fluckey noted from the large volume of high-angle fire from the convoy that the Japanese appeared to believe they were under air attack. The Japanese attribute one of the ships sunk that night to air attack. They also report that the 9500-ton *Hawaii Maru* went down that night in Formosa Strait, although the same ship was reported sunk by a submarine south of Kyushu the month before. The Joint Army-Navy Assessment Board, after the war, credited *Barb* with sinking three ships, and *Barb* and *Picuda* together with sinking another. The Japanese record three ships sunk in Formosa Strait that night and four more damaged, so the submarine estimate may be as good as any.

Commander Naval Group China had a system to supply information of Japanese ship movements to submarines operating off the China coast. Coastwatchers and China Air Force reported that convoys were moving along the coast, although submarines could not find them. Fluckey believed the Japanese ships were frequenting very shallow inshore water during the daytime and holing up in Chinese ports at night. When Naval Groups China reported that a convoy was moving north, Fluckey decided to take *Barb* in to ferret the *marus* out of their holes.

On the afternoon of 22 January he approached the coast on the surface and mingled with the ever-present fleet of Chinese junks, depending on the junks to avoid mined water. After dark the junks were invisible at ranges over one thousand yards and *Barb* felt her way through the silent ghostly consorts by radar as she approached Namkwan Harbor. Radar discovered a great convoy of ships anchored in the outer harbor.

The Japanese were anchored twenty miles inside the twenty-fathom curve. Their southern flank was protected by a group of small islands. To the north was an area marked "unexplored" and "rocks awash." Three radar-equipped escorts picketed the convoy, and defensive minefields, if any, were unlocated. Leaving the junk fleet behind, *Barb* crossed the ten-fathom curve and headed in. *Barb* was buttoned up and prepared for any eventuality. The executive officer manned the bridge. The commanding officer was in the control room where he could see the radar screen. Fluckey considered ordering the crew into life jackets, a move which would save lives if they hit a mine, but with the crew already keyed up to high tension he decided against it. The control room was as silent as a cathedral, with only an occasional intoned report "single ping sounding, six fathoms."

At thirty-two hundred yards *Barb* fired the bow tubes into the dense mass of targets. Right full rudder. All ahead standard. Single ping sounding five fathoms. As she headed out Fluckey fired the stern tubes at a ship near the head of the column. All ahead flank. The commanding officer manned the bridge. Torpedoes started exploding. Ships blew up by induced explosions. Gunfire erupted from the Japanese ships. *Barb* hightailed it for deep water, weaving through the junks like a broken field runner on a football field. Fluckey was sure of at least four ships sunk, but only one (the 5200-ton *Taikyo Maru*) can be identified as sunk that night.

Most of the other ships sunk by Lockwood's submarines during January and February were smaller, but *Aspro* teamed up with Navy carrier planes to sink the 8000-ton aircraft ferry *Shinshu Maru* southwest of Formosa on 5 January. *Balao* sank a 5000-ton tanker southwest of Korea on the seventh. *Silversides* sank a 4500-ton freighter south of Kyushu on the twenty-fifth. On the twenty-ninth *Picuda* ended her patrol in Formosa Strait by sinking the 5500-ton *Clyde Maru*.

Spadefish (Underwood) led *Atule, Pompon,* and *Jallao* as a wolf pack deep into the Yellow Sea. *Atule* sank a 6880-ton freighter on 24 January. On the twenty-eighth *Spadefish* sank the *kaibokan Kume* and the 9200-ton converted seaplane tender *Sanuki Maru*. On 4 February *Spadefish* sank the 4273-ton *Tairai Maru*. Two days later she sank a much smaller ship within fifteen miles of Port Arthur. The other two submarines of the pack came home empty-handed. Moreover, *Tairai Maru* was the largest Japanese ship sunk by Lockwood's submarines in February. Four small escort vessels were sunk, but both escorts and *marus* were running smaller. In February submarines in all areas sank twenty *marus,* and these added up to only about 55,000 tons.

Reconnaissance

In preparing plans for new operations knowledge of future beachheads was essential. *Spearfish* made a notable reconnaissance of Iwo Jima. The water off that little-known island was deep right up to the shoreline in places. *Spearfish* lay a few hundred yards off Suribachi for hours with a few inches of periscope exposed while she took detailed pictures of the rugged mountain that would later guide the Marines in their assault. *Spearfish* encountered little interference from the Japanese in performing her mission, but *Swordfish* was not so fortunate.

Loss of Swordfish

In late December *Swordfish* (Montross) was sent to reconnoiter Okinawa. The Fifth Amphibious Force requested that a beach reconnaissance party be embarked to explore the extensive Okinawan offshore reefs, and the unknown beaches, but Spruance vetoed the request. He recognized the value of the intelligence to be gained but weighed it against the real danger that the submarine or the reconnaissance party might be lost in such a risky venture under circumstances that might compromise the location of planned landings. Counting the risk greater than the probable gain, Spruance directed that *Swordfish's* reconnaissance be restricted to the usual photographic and observation mission.

On 2 January *Swordfish* was directed to delay her arrival off Okinawa until after the January carrier strike on the Ryukyus. She acknowledged the receipt of the order on 3 January. This was the last message received from her. On 7 January she was directed to proceed with her mission. *Kete*, who was on patrol in the vicinity, reported making a radar contact with a U.S. submarine on 12 January. She believed this to be *Swordfish*. A few hours later *Kete* heard a heavy depth-charge attack from the direction of the radar contact. Probably this was *Swordfish's* last battle, although there is no record of a corresponding Japanese depth-charge attack. The submarine's reconnaissance mission may have taken her into freshly laid inshore minefields, planted to defend Okinawan beach approaches, and one of these may have accounted for *Swordfish*.

Guardfish *and* Extractor

Later in the month there was another tragedy involving a submarine. On 23 January *Guardfish* (Hammond) was north of Guam returning from patrol. She made radar contact on an unidentified vessel. *Guardfish* was in a Joint Zone, requiring positive identification of the target before attack. Hammond therefore sent a message to Submarine Headquarters reporting his contact. The Submarine Force replied that no other U.S. submarine was in Hammond's vicinity but that any surface ship should be presumed to be a friend. The operations officer at Guam reported to the Submarine Force that there were no friendly surface forces in the area either. *Guardfish* continued tracking and a few minutes before sunrise, in the uncertain light of dawn through a periscope, identified the target as an I-class Japanese submarine. She fired four torpedoes, two of which hit. As the ship went down it was evident that this was no submarine. *Guardfish* surfaced and picked up seventy-three survivors of U.S.S. *Extractor*, a small salvage vessel. Six of *Extractor's* crew went down with the ship.

This tragedy resulted from a series of errors, the ultimate one being the erroneous identification of *Extractor* as a submarine. The day before, *Extractor* had been directed to reverse course and return to port. She had received this message in such garbled form that she was unable to decipher it, and rather than break radio silence to ask for a repeat, she had continued on her course. The port director's plot, based on the assumption that *Extractor* had reversed course as directed, showed no ship in *Guardfish's* locality. The plotting officer was unable to imagine that there had been any deviation from plan. It might have happened anywhere that routine peformance of duty was all that was expected. If this accident had initiated a tightening up of the system of keeping track of ships in that area, it might have prevented a far greater tragedy a few months later.

Preparation for Iwo Jima

The release of the Fifth Fleet from the Philippines operation freed Nimitz's hands for the next operation. On 2 January he established his headquarters on Guam. Lockwood followed him and set up operational submarine headquarters in U.S.S. *Holland* in Apra Harbor on 24 January. General LeMay took over the 21st Bomber Command at Guam on 20 January and prepared for massive bombing attacks on Japanese cities. To support the B-29 bomber operations, it was soon apparent that Iwo Jima had to be taken. In Japanese possession the ugly little island was a staging base for Japanese air attacks on the B-29 bases in the Marianas. In U.S. possession it would provide emergency landing fields for the big bombers between their bases and their targets.

The importance of Iwo Jima was more apparent to the Japanese than it was to the Americans. The Japanese did everything within their power to hold it. For fear of submarines, Japanese transports unloaded at Chichi Jima and transferred Iwo-bound troops and supplies to small craft. This was not wholly effective. Submarines and surface task forces together exacted a steady toll of ships plying between the Bonins and Japan, drowning at least fifteen hundred troops and destroying much badly needed equipment. Despite all efforts to soften it up, however, the conquest of Iwo Jima proved to be a very costly one.

Carrier Raids on Tokyo

On 10 February the Japanese Combined Fleet Staff made an estimate of the situation. They predicted that carrier task forces would raid Japan after the middle of February, that the Bonin Islands would be invaded in late February, and the Nansei Shoto invaded in March. On 13 February Japanese radio intelligence warned that an American carrier task force had left the Marianas, and that the next offensive was very close.

The Fifth Fleet did sortie from Ulithi on 10 February and hit Tokyo with a series of air raids on 16 and 17 February. Despite the accurate prophecy of the Combined Fleet estimate, U.S. carrier task forces made an undetected approach on Tokyo. Profiting by the experience of the previous picket sweep, more elaborate provisions were made to clear the pickets from the carriers' path. One group of submarines (Latta's Lancers) made a diversionary sweep and sank two pickets by noisy gunfire. This action was intended to draw pickets away from the carriers' track while another group of submarines (Mac's Mops), under command of Captain B. F. McMahon, swept ahead of the carriers. Mac's Mops carried a new weapon, a small acoustic torpedo designed to sink a picket boat so quickly it would be unable to report the submarine contact.

Spruance did not depend upon the Japanese reacting as predicted. The airways ahead of the carriers were swept by B-29s and Navy Liberators. A scouting line of four destroyers patrolled ahead in advance of an intensive inner anti-submarine patrol of carrier planes just ahead of the carriers. These precautions and thick weather most of the way brought the carriers to their launching position undetected. Mac's Mops made no contacts. After their sweep was concluded they took up position for lifeguard duties during the carrier strike.

Pomfret *as Lifeguard*

Pomfret (J. B. Hess) was one of Mac's Mops assigned to lifeguard station outside Sagami Nada, the outer bay of Tokyo's approaches. About noon on 17 February Hess received a message that a fighter plane was down in the middle of the bay. The plane had been hit by Japanese anti-aircraft fire about twenty miles west of Tokyo but it had been able to stay in the air until the pilot could ditch in the water, uncomfortably close to land. The pilot was in a life raft about five miles from Suno Saki, where shore batteries were suspected, drifting toward the center of Sagami Nada where Hess had been informed there was a large area "restricted to navigation"—mined; and not more than five minutes' flight from several Japanese airfields.

The fighter group stood by their stricken comrade. They provided fighter cover for *Pomfret* in her two-hour surface run up the bay, and flew over the life raft to mark the submarine's objective. One by one, however, they had to retire because of trouble or lack of fuel, until only one plane was over *Pomfret* when she finally picked up Ensign Buchanan of U.S.S. *Cabot*. The last plane then departed, because of low fuel, and *Pomfret* followed her retiring air cover at a submarine's best approximate air speed. Although the Japanese must have been listening to the radio conversation between the planes and the submarine, *Pomfret* made it safely out without incident. This rescue was the subject of one of Ernie Pyle's newspaper columns under the heading, "Even if You Was Shot Down in Tokyo Harbor, the Navy Would Be in to Get You," but because of censorship *Pomfret* was not identified as the rescue ship.

Japanese Submarines at Iwo Jima

D-day on Iwo Jima was 19 February. The Marines landed without much interference from the Japanese Navy, but on shore they had a bloody battle with the well-dug-in Japanese Army. Japan had no surface vessels to throw into the battle of Iwo Jima. The distance to Japanese airfields was too great for an intensive *kamikaze* attack, although air attacks sank the escort carrier *Bismarck Sea* and damaged several other vessels. Iwo Jima was well located for an effective Japanese submarine defense and Miwa did his best.

When the Fifth Fleet planes attacked Tokyo, Miwa made a rapid change of his plans for submarine operations. Believing that a full-scale operation was in prospect for the Ryukyus he ordered *RO-43* to sortie for that area. Two RO-boats en route to the Philippines and two others on patrol off Luzon were ordered to Okinawa. Of these RO-55 (unknown to Miwa) had already been sunk. Shortly after these orders were issued it was clear that Iwo Jima was the objective of the next American offensive. Accordingly *RO-43* was ordered to proceed to the Bonins. The remaining submarines were directed to return to Japan. *RO-43* changed course for Iwo Jima, and was never heard from again. She was sunk by planes from the escort carrier *Anzio* on 26 February near the Volcano Islands.

Miwa then organized a new *kaiten* operation (Chihaya Unit) consisting of *I-368*, *I-370*, and *I-44*. They sortied from the Inland Sea between 20 and 22 February. Nothing was ever heard again from *I-368* or *I-370*. The Japanese assumed that they had been lost in gallant attacks on heavy units of the U.S. fleet. *I-368* was in fact a second victim of planes from escort carrier *Anzio* on 26 February, and *I-370* was sunk by destroyer escort *Finnegan* the same day. Neither submarine made an observed attack.

On 1 March *I-44* reported that she had been attacked by anti-submarine forces fifty miles from Iwo Jima and prevented from carrying out her mission. She was directed to return again to attack, but on 6 March she was recalled to Japan and the commanding officer was relieved of his command.

On 28 February Miwa organized another *kaiten* unit (Shimbu Unit) consisting of *I-58* and *I-36*, each carrying four human torpedoes. By 6 March, however, the Combined Fleet Staff had written off Iwo Jima as a loss, and directed Miwa to cease submarine operations there. *I-36* was recalled and *I-58* was directed to take station for the forthcoming "Tan" Operation. These orders reached *I-58* after she had started her final run in to Iwo Jima to attack anchored targets with her *kaitens*. Reluctantly

Hashimoto broke off the approach, recalled his suicide torpedo pilots from their tombs, jettisoned the *kaitens*, and headed for Okino Daito Shima.

The new task for *I-58* was to act as a radio beacon for bombers taking off from Japan to attack Ulithi. This was a one-way bombing attack for Japanese planes which did not have sufficient range to attack Ulithi and return to their Japanese bases. Light planes from Truk made a reconnaissance of Ulithi and found a carrier task force anchored there. On 10 March twenty-four medium bombers took off from Kanoya airfields for Ulithi. *I-58* successfully carried out her mission as radio beacon. The bombers made their attack and damaged the aircraft carrier *Randolf*. They crash-landed near Minami Daito Shima on their return and the submarine *HA-106* rescued some of the flight personnel.

Japanese Submarines off Okinawa

On the basis of radio intelligence information that the U.S. fleet had left Ulithi to attack the Ryukyus, *RO-41, RO-49, RO-56,* and *I-8* were sent to patrol southeast of Okinawa on 20 March. None of these submarines ever returned to Japan. *RO-41* made a radio report of the enemy situation on 22 March and was missing thereafter. The destroyer *Haggard* made radar contact on a surfaced submarine that night. The submarine promptly submerged and *Haggard* attacked with depth charges which brought *RO-41* to the surface. The destroyer opened fire on the moonlit target and rammed. *RO-41* went down with all hands.

On the night of 31 March the destroyer *Stockton* made radar contact on a surfaced submarine at 12,800 yards. The destroyer *Morrison* joined *Stockton* in a depth-charge attack which brought *I-8* to the surface. The destroyers pounded the stricken submarine with gunfire for half an hour before the shattered hull sank. In the morning the destroyers found a huge amount of oil and debris on the surface, together with the bodies of two Japanese sailors. One survivor was still swimming and was rescued. The commanding officer, Shigero Shinohara, and another survivor apparently succeeded in reaching Okinawa and eventually made their way back to Japan.

RO-49 lasted five days longer. The destroyer *Hudson* sank her in a depth-charge attack on the morning of 5 April. The destroyers *Monssen* and *Mertz* sank *RO-56*, the remaining submarine of the group, in a depth-charge attack on the morning of 9 April. A Japanese submarine torpedo passed ahead of the cruiser *Wichita* on 26 March and another missed *St. Louis* the same day. *Pensacola* avoided two Japanese submarine torpedoes on 27 March. Otherwise there is no evidence that anything was accomplished by the sacrifice of these four submarines.

The Okinawa Campaign

After Iwo Jima was secured on 16 March, the undivided attention of the Fifth Fleet was directed to the Okinawa campaign. U.S. submarine dispositions required little special adjustment for this operation. A few submarines were patrolling in the Kuriles and the Sea of Okhotsk and a few more were off northeast Honshu, but the bulk of Lockwood's submarines were either on lifeguard duty south of Japan, or patrolling the Yellow Sea and the East China Sea where they covered any possible route of any Japanese task force approaching Okinawa from Japan. Instructions were issued that, during the operation, contact reports on any previously unreported Japanese fleet units approaching Nansei Shoto would take precedence over attack. Two submarines were specifically assigned to guard Bungo Suido, and one was stationed off Kii Suido.

The opportunity for submarine attacks in March in the East China Sea was little better than in February. On the night of 19 March *Balao* (Worthington) attacked a four-ship convoy which was running south along the ten-fathom curve off the China coast. The 10,000-ton *Hakozaki Maru* was sunk in this attack and another 6000-ton *maru* was heavily damaged. These were the only large *marus* torpedoed in the East China Sea or the Yellow Sea in March.

Loss of Kete and Trigger

Kete (Ackerman) went out on her second patrol in the East China Sea in March. Her mission was to provide rescue service for carrier air strikes and to make special weather reports, in addition to carrying out a normal patrol. On 10 March she had a battle with a convoy and sank two 2500-ton *marus* and an escort vessel. Four days later she reported that she missed a cable layer with four torpedoes. As *Kete* then had only three torpedoes left she was directed to leave her area on 20 March and return to Midway. On 20 March, south of Kyushu in Nansei Shoto, she made a special weather report. That was the last message from her. Her loss is still a mystery.

The veteran *Trigger* (Connole) was lost shortly thereafter in the same general locality. She also had been directed to perform rescue services and conduct a normal patrol in the East China Sea to the eastward of the mine barrier. On 18 March she sank a 1000-ton *maru* just east of the restricted area. On 26 March she was directed to join *Sea Dog* and *Threadfin* in a coordinated attack group south of Kyushu. The 1500-ton repair ship *Odate* was sunk on 27 March and has been credited to *Trig-*

ger. Sea Dog was unable to establish communication with *Trigger* on 28 March and nothing was ever heard from her thereafter. Shortly after *Trigger* sent her last message *Threadfin* sank an escort vessel south of Kyushu and received a severe depth-charging in retaliation. *Threadfin* reported that there were many heavy depth charges to the eastward of her after the attack. The Japanese report a series of depth-charge attacks that brought up large quantities of oil. It is believed that *Trigger* was lost in this action.

XXVI

APRIL–JUNE 1945

At the end of the war President Truman charged the U. S. Strategic Bombing Survey with the conduct of a study of the effects of air attacks. The Survey interrogated many different sources in an effort to judge Japanese opinion. One report, by the combined faculty of the Tokyo Imperial University (The Effect of Urban Area Bombing on Japanese Wartime Economy) made the following initial statement:

"Before the first heavy strategic air raids started the munitions production of Japan had already been thrown into a desperate condition by the effective ocean blockade of the Allied forces, especially the United States submarine activity."

In the spring of 1945 the U. S. Submarine Force was a force in search of a new mission. Japanese overseas commerce was prostrate and Japanese economy could no longer support offensive war. Japan had lost the war but ending it was another matter. Many times Japanese irrevocably lost a battle, only to stage a great suicidal *banzai* charge at the end of it. The Japanese nation was still controlled by a military hierarchy imbued with the tradition of death before surrender, and there was no way out except to continue the war to its bitter end.

Lifeguard Submarines

B-29 bombing of the industrial cities of Japan began in November 1944, and reached a climax in the March 9–10 fire raid on Tokyo which burned to death 83,793 persons and rendered more than a million homeless. These raids brought home to the Japanese people the facts of defeat that had been concealed from the general public. For these raids, and for the carrier raids on Japanese airfields which preceded the Iwo Jima and Okinawa operations, submarines provided air rescue services, which occupied a part of the time of practically every submarine sent to patrol around Japan in 1945.

During big raids, assigned submarines operated on the surface at specified stations near the coast of Japan, standing by to search for and rescue downed aviators who were reported to them, generally by Dumbo (air-sea rescue planes) or by Commander Submarines Pacific headquarters on Guam. When not engaged in lifeguarding, these submarines carried on normal offensive patrols. At first B-29s made few calls on submarines for rescue service. To the crews of these big planes the small gray ships, wallowing in a strange sea, offered little more security than a badly damaged plane. They would keep the plane in the air as long as possible rather than ditch in the vicinity of a rescue submarine. The first submarine rescue of seven B-29 airmen was made by *Spearfish* (Cole) on 19 December 1944 near the Bonins, and it was not until 31 March that *Ronquil* (Lander) rescued seven more.

Experienced submariners rated air-sea rescue work as more dangerous than offensive patrols. Statistics did not bear them out, but lifeguarding required submarines to operate on the surface in dangerous locations under circumstances which often brought unwelcome Japanese attention. On 27, 29, and 30 April *Gato* (Holden), working with Dumbo planes, rescued a total of ten B-29 airmen who had parachuted from three crashed planes. Some of these rescues took place only five miles off the Japanese coast where, as Holden ironically remarked, "Kyushu is nicely visible for navigational purposes." Radar planes dogged *Gato's* wake by night, maneuvering to silhouette the submarine against the moon. In the daytime float Zero fighters attacked at every opportunity.

When Dumbo reported a life raft in the water shortly after dawn on the twenty-ninth, Holden blew all ballast dry, manned the bridge guns, and headed for the life raft at four-engine speed determined to stay on the surface until the rescue was effected. A Zero fighter attacked and *Gato* took it under fire with the bridge 20-mm. and 40-mm.—a procedure not recommended for a submarine except in dire emergency. The Zero scored two near-misses with its bombs and turned back to strafe, forcing *Gato* to submerge. Holden would not be driven off, however, and finally made the rescue of the airman late in the afternoon. As information of such rescues spread among the Army Air Force the lifeguard service became more popular. In May, June, and July, a total of 247 airmen were picked up out of the water by submarines. Of these, 131 were from B-29 bombers.

Loss of Snook

So far as is known, no U.S. submarine was lost while actually engaged in lifeguard work. There is some doubt about *Snook* (Walling). She disappeared sometime after she was last heard from in Convoy College, on 8 April. On 12 April *Snook* was ordered to lifeguard a

British carrier strike on Sakishima Gunto, about two hundred miles northeast of northern Formosa. Snook was not required to acknowledge that message and nothing was heard from her after her last message on 8 April, when she was several hundred miles from the assigned lifeguard station.

On 20 April the commander of the British carrier force reported that there was a plane down near *Snook's* station. *Snook* was ordered to search the area but she did not acknowledge receipt of those orders. *Bang* was sent in and rescued the British aviators. *Bang* saw nothing of *Snook* during this operation. It is possible that *Snook* was sunk while on this lifeguard mission, but it is more probable that she was sunk in Luzon Strait much earlier. No known Japanese attack accounts for her disappearance.

Okinawa Landing

On 1 April Marines and Army forces supported by heavy naval gunfire and air attacks landed on Okinawa. The landing had been preceded for several days by carrier strikes on Japanese airfields on Okinawa and Kyushu, bombardments by battleships, cruisers, and destroyers, and preliminary landings in Kerama Retto. The main landing was practically unopposed at the beachhead, the Japanese forces being well dug into prepared defense lines some distance back from the beaches. For the first few days U.S. naval support forces and transports were attacked only by local forces and by sporadic suicide plane attacks, but everybody knew that the storm was coming.

By 6 April Toyoda was ready for the major counterattack. A total of 355 suicide planes took off from Kyushu airfields to attack the U.S. fleet at Okinawa. Additional *kamikazes* and regular bombers and torpedo planes took off from Formosa. This huge mass suicide attack was intended to coordinate with the final attack of the remnant of the Japanese surface Navy and with a *kaiten* attack by the Japanese submarine force.

The great battleship *Yamato*, with the light cruiser *Yahagi* and eight destroyers, sortied through Bungo Suido on the night of 6 April. Their mission was to penetrate to the Okinawan anchorage and destroy what remained of the U.S. fleet after the *kamikaze* attacks. The oil shortage in Japan was then so critical that *Yamato* carried only enough fuel to get her to Okinawa and not enough to bring her back. The Grand Escort Force begrudged her even that, for they were of the opinion that their precious oil might better be expended in escorting food convoys from China rather than throwing it away in the grandstand play of the big battleship's *banzai* charge.

Threadfin *and* Hackleback *Make Contact*

U.S. submarines had been disposed about Japan with the objective of detecting such movements of major Japanese task forces. Off Bungo Suido a wolf pack of three submarines patrolled, with the primary mission of detecting any task force sortie. The pack operated under the restriction that a contact report on any major Japanese force must be cleared before a submarine was free to attack.

On the afternoon of 6 April *Threadfin* (Foote) watched several Japanese planes patrolling Bungo Suido. Two escort vessels then made an anti-submarine sweep, pinging as they came. Foote, who had torpedoed one escort vessel off Kyushu the week before, prepared his tubes to take on this pair, but the anti-submarine sweepers changed course 120 degrees and followed the one-hundred-fathom curve south, outside torpedo range. Two minesweepers swept a channel down Bungo West Channel. *Threadfin* took up a position five thousand yards from the swept channel and waited. At seven-forty it was fairly dark and *Threadfin* surfaced. Four minutes later the pips of four ships appeared on her radar screen.

The pips resolved into two big ships and at least four smaller ones. *Threadfin* was in a good position to attack, but Foote had specific orders to make a contact report first, and unless he opened out the range on the destroyers he was nearly sure to be discovered before he could clear a radio message. The Japanese task force was making twenty-five knots. *Threadfin* blew all ballast dry and pushed her engines well over full power while radiomen worked desperately to get off the contact report before the Japanese got by. In the ten minutes this required the battleship was out of range of *Threadfin's* torpedoes. Foote followed in the task force's wake, hoping that *Silversides* or *Hackleback* would slow the Japanese down, but the last opportunity for a submarine to fire torpedoes at a Japanese capital ship had been sacrificed to make a contact report.

Hackleback (Janney) made radar contact with *Yamato* and made additional contact reports but was unable to get in to torpedo range. Three hours later, with Spruance informed of the Japanese sortie, Lockwood removed the report-before-attack restriction, but no other submarine sighted the Japanese task force. The next evening *Threadfin* received news that *Yamato, Yahagi*, and four Japanese destroyers had been sunk by carrier air attack of Task Force 58 in the East China Sea. *Sea Devil* searched the battle area and picked up three Marine flyers from U.S.S. *Essex*. This ended U.S. submarine participation in the last big naval battle of the war.

Japanese Submarines at Okinawa

Between 29 March and 6 April four Japanese submarines (*I-44, I-47, I-56,* and *I-58*) departed for Okinawa, each carrying six *kaitens. I-47* (Orita) was first to sortie. She got no farther than southern Kyushu when she was attacked first by carrier planes and later by destroyers. Leaking great quantities of oil, she returned to Kure for repairs despite the practically mutinous protests of the *kaiten* pilots. *I-44* and *I-56* set out on 3 April, and the Japanese never heard from them again. *I-56* was sunk in a prolonged depth-charge attack by several destroyers on 18 April. *I-44* was sunk by carrier planes on 29 April. Notwithstanding optimistic Japanese estimates to the contrary, neither submarine made a successful attack.

I-58 (Hashimoto) came down through the East China Sea to the latitude of Okinawa. On 7 April Hashimoto received a message that his submarine would be joined in attacks on Okinawan anchorages by the battleship *Yamato. Yamato* had, in fact, been sunk by the time this message was received. The next day *I-58* was ordered to go in and fight to the death. *I-58* had an efficient radar and as she attempted to carry out these orders she had radar contact with many planes. In the next seven days she was approached by aircraft and forced to submerge over fifty times. The longest time she was permitted to remain on the surface was four hours. Alert radar saved *I-58* from being bombed, but the submarine was so thoroughly interdicted that it could not charge batteries sufficiently to make a long submerged run into Okinawan anchorages. On 14 April Hashimoto was ordered to take *I-58* out into the Pacific. To carry out these orders he had to dive under the Japanese East China Sea mine barrier and then run down along the Chinese coast nearly to Formosa before he could emerge from Tung Hai. After a month at sea, with no maintenance, the *kaitens* became inoperable and *I-58* returned to Japan on 29 April.

There were only three medium Japanese submarines equipped with conventional torpedoes ready for operation when Okinawa was invaded. The experiences of the *kaiten*-carrying submarines demonstrated the futility of attempting to penetrate into Okinawan anchorages. The three RO-boats were ordered to operate on American lines of communication at a radius of two hundred miles from Okinawa. They did not fare much better than the *kaiten* carriers. *RO-46* was sent to the vicinity of Kita Daito Shima and was last heard from on 17 April. *RO-109* was stationed two hundred miles south of Okinawa and there she was sunk on 25 April by the high-speed transport *Horace A. Bass*. *RO-50* made contact with a carrier task force but was unable to attack. She returned safely to Japan on 4 May.

Temmu Kaiten *Unit*

I-36 and *I-53*, equipped to carry *kaitens*, had not been ready for the precious sortie. They were joined by *I-47*, after her damage was repaired, to form the Temmu *Kaiten* Unit. Previously all *kaiten* attacks had been attempted on anchored ships, but the Japanese Submarine Force became convinced that U.S. fleet anchorages were too well guarded for this kind of attack to be successful. They advocated *kaiten* attacks against cruising ships at sea. Combined Fleet Staff argued that the *kaiten* pilots had insufficient experience to attempt attacks on ships under way and that in any moderate sea the short periscope of a *kaiten* would be blinded so the pilot would be unable to guide his mount. After the flat failure of the *kaiten* attack on Okinawan anchorages, however, it was decided to send the Temmu Unit to operate in the Philippine Sea to attack ships under way. Before they could leave *I-53* hit one of the many mines sown by B-29 bombers in the Inland Sea. She had to be sent to the navy yard for repairs. Advantage was taken of her repair period to install in *I-53* the first Japanese snorkel.

I-36 (Sugamasa) departed on 22 April to operate between Saipan and Okinawa. On 27 April Sugamasa reported that he had released four *kaitens* at a big convoy of over thirty ships, and ten minutes later heard four big explosions. The Japanese credited *I-36* with sinking three transports on the evidence. On 27 April *Ringness*, escorting landing vessels from Saipan to Okinawa, reported seeing a midget submarine explode, but none of *Ringness'* convoy was damaged. *I-36* returned to Kure on 1 May, but her *kaitens* had succeeded only in destroying themselves and killing their pilots.

I-47 (Orita), with six *kaitens* on board, operated between Okinawa and Ulithi. On the night of 1 May Orita fired four conventional torpedoes at a large convoy and claimed three hits. The next day he launched two *kaitens* with two transports and two escorts as targets. After twenty-five minutes there were two big explosions. Another *kaiten* was then launched to attack the escorts. After forty-nine minutes the sound of a distant explosion convinced the crew of *I-47* that their *kaiten* pilot had overtaken and blown up a fleeing destroyer. On 6 May *I-47* made contact with a cruiser. The sea was high and periscope visibility from a *kaiten* would be practically zero, but yielding to the clamor of the *kaiten* pilot to be sent to the attack, Orita released one *kaiten*. Telephone communication between the mother submarine and the two remaining *kaitens* had broken down, and as it was impossible to give their pilots essential attack instructions, these two *kaitens* were not released. Their pilots, who had twice been sent into their tombs to await orders to be released to certain death, were recalled into *I-47* to live with their memories. One of them (Yutaka Yokota) survived the war to write his memoirs as a *kaiten* pilot.

I-47 returned in triumph on 12 May. It was known that her *kaiten* pilots had been determined to blow themselves up if their attacks failed, yet the sound of explosions were taken as certain evidence of success, rather than as equally good evidence of the pilots' suicide in despair and frustration after discovering too late that Combined Fleet Staff had been right in its estimate of *kaiten* effectiveness in the open sea. *I-47* had, in fact, made no hits and caused no damage to her enemies.

Continuing Kaiten *Attacks*

Stimulated by their illusion of success, the Japanese Submarine Force continued with *kaiten* attacks on ships under way. They were handicapped by lack of *kaiten*-carrying submarines and by other difficulties. B-29 bombers had sowed the Inland Sea so thick with mines that training exercises were hazardous. *RO-64* hit a mine and sank in Hiroshima Bay while on training exercises on 12 April. *I-366* and *I-367* were scheduled for the next *kaiten* operation. On the eve of her scheduled departure *I-366* was damaged by a magnetic mine and had to be sent to the navy yard for repairs. *I-367* departed alone with five *kaitens* on 5 May. On 27 May, east of Okinawa, *I-367* released two *kaitens* and heard two explosions. She was credited with sinking a U.S. destroyer. This she did not do but she succeeded in returning safely on 4 June.

In late May *I-361* and *I-363* went out with *kaitens*. *I-361* was sunk by planes from U.S.S. *Anzio* on 30 May. *I-363* succeeded only in returning safely. *I-165*, a superannuated submarine modified to carry two *kaitens*, went to sea on 16 June. Japanese radio intelligence attributed great success to her. She did not return. *I-165* was sunk by shore-based U. S. Navy planes on 27 June. None of these *kaiten* operations accomplished anything.

I-36 (Sugamasa), which had made several *kaiten* patrols, went to sea with five *kaitens* in early June. On 28 June Sugamasa released one *kaiten* to attack a cargo ship which was, in fact, the supply ship

U.S.S. *Antares*. *Antares* first sighted the periscope of *I-36* and then saw a "midget submarine" in her wake. The supply ship commenced radical maneuvers and opened fire at the *kaiten*. The *kaiten* seemed to be making about twenty knots and the pilot was having difficulty controlling his craft in *Antares'* wake. One of *Antares'* 3-inch guns scored a hit and the *kaiten* disappeared. A large submarine (*I-36*) broached and was fired on by *Antares'* 5-inch gun. The big submarine was then attacked by escorting destroyers while the supply ship took evasive action.

The destroyer counterattack very nearly finished *I-36*. The Japanese submarine was severely damaged and leaking badly. Sugamasa could hear two destroyers hunting above him. In desperation he released two *kaitens* to attack the destroyers. An explosion convinced him that one *kaiten* had been successful. No U.S. destroyer was hit, but the *kaiten* might have confused the destroyer's sonar operator, for *I-36* then successfully evaded. The crew of *I-36*, weeping with emotion, credited their *kaitens* with sinking one destroyer and drawing off the attack of another to save the Japanese submarine by their sacrifices. *I-36* was still not safe. A patrol plane bombed her the next day and ruptured a fuel tank. As she limped home through Bungo on 5 July an American submarine missed her with a salvo of torpedoes.

Other Japanese Submarine Operations

On 10 May Vice Admiral Tadashige Daigo relieved Miwa as Commander-in-Chief of the Sixth Fleet.

I-372 made a trip to Wake in early April, arriving about the sixteenth. U.S. submarine *Sea Owl* (Bennett), returning from patrol in Convoy College, had picked this time to look in at Wake. Early on the morning of the sixteenth *Sea Owl* had radar contact with a submerging submarine. Correctly deducing that he had a supply submarine to deal with, Bennett stalked his quarry off the anchorage until the morning of 18 April. Then he caught *I-372* at anchor and unloading. Bennett fired four torpedoes and watched one of them hit the Japanese submarine between the conning tower and the stern. The target disappeared in a cloud of smoke. *I-372* had not been sunk, however. Probably *Sea Owl's* torpedo had hit the reef or some other obstruction. *I-372* finished unloading the next day and embarked sixty evacuees whom she delivered at Yokosuka on 29 April.

I-369 made a trip to Truk during the same period. Along the way she sighted many American ships, but *I-369* had been built as a transportation submarine and carried no torpedo tubes. *I-351*, designed and built as a tanker, made a trip to Singapore about 1 May, and returned to Japan with a cargo of precious aviation gasoline.

HA-101, -102, -103, -104, and *-105* were also engaged in short transportation runs. These small submarines were without torpedo tubes. Unlike the *I-361* class the HA-class submarines were too small to carry *kaitens. HA-103* and *-105,* in May and June, engaged in picket duty off south Honshu to warn of approaching enemy carriers or large land-based aircraft strikes.

Southwest Pacific Submarines

The invasion of Okinawa sharply divided the Empire of Japan and between its two main segments there was very little communication. In the South China Sea, north of Saigon, there was practically no Japanese traffic moving; but the Japanese attempted to hold together the Dutch East Indies and Malaya by sea communications. For carrying cargo they depended mainly on luggers and small coasters, cruising as much as possible in shallow water, but they had a few larger ships. At Singapore there were several cruisers (two of them disabled) and a number of smaller combat ships. When the situation became desperate the Japanese used these combat ships as transports.

British and Dutch submarines, out of Trincomalee, still operated in Malacca Strait and on the west coast of Malaya. These smaller submarines were better suited to the new operating condition in Java Sea and the Gulf of Siam than they were for long-range patrol. In April additional British and Dutch submarines were transferred from Trincomalee to Fremantle to operate under Fife's command. At the end of the war there were twenty-one British and four Dutch submarines with the Southwest Pacific command.

In April Fife began to roll up the rear areas and move to Subic Bay, Luzon. The British depot ship *Maidstone,* on which British submarines based, left Fremantle for Subic on 20 April. Fife's whole operational headquarters was shifted to Subic on 15 May. Lockwood assumed administrative command over the Southwest Pacific submarines in April, but this made little difference in operations, for Fife retained full operational control. The Convoy College area, between Formosa and Luzon, was placed in Fife's operations area to facilitate communication between lifeguard submarines and Army planes flying out out of Clark Field to bomb China and Formosa. As employment opportunities for the big American fleet submarines declined in the South China Sea, some of them were shifted to the Central Pacific.

Shallow Water Operations

U.S. submarines under Fife's command had to be content with smaller-size targets and learn to pursue them into shallow water, not always with happy results. On 14 March *Bream,* operating in the Java Sea, discovered two Japanese ships anchored in shallow water close to shore. *Bream* (McCallum) had taken with her on that patrol a party of Australian commandoes skilled in the use of limpet mines. On a dark night McCallum launched a small boat with two commando officers armed with limpet mines to sink the anchored ships. *Bream* never saw the commandoes again. After this tragic occurrence the use of limpet mines was unpopular with U.S. submarines.

Both U.S. and British submarines laid magnetic mines in shallow waters, and Allied Air Forces laid mines by air drop. On 13 June *Bergall,* while searching the shallow water of the Gulf of Siam, ran into an Allied minefield. The submarine was fortunate to escape with minor damage when she set off a magnetic mine. These mines had been laid by U.S. and R.A.F. planes and properly reported, but the Seventh Fleet Staff had neglected to pass on the information to Fife's command. For the most part the shallow water of the Gulf of Siam was hunted at night by submarines running on the surface, like torpedo boats, to pursue and sink their targets, and trusting to their speed and gunpower to hold off small escort vessels until the submarines reached the safety of deep water. It was a risky business for small gain.

Charr, Gabilan, *and* Isuzu

In early April the Japanese pressed the light cruiser *Isuzu* into service as a transport. On 4 April *Isuzu,* with four small escorts, encountered a wolf pack consisting of *Besugo* (Miller), *Gabilan* (Parham), and *Charr* (Boyle) off the Paternosters, north of Soembawa. None of the submarines were able to get in an attack and planes forced them down when they attempted to pursue. At night *Besugo* followed the Japanese force into the dangerous waters of Sape Strait to sink *Minesweeper No. 12,* one of the escorts.

Two nights later *Charr* and *Gabilan* made contact with *Isuzu* again, and with exchange of information by radio both submarines succeeded in getting into attack position. The radio traffic also attracted the British submarine *Spark* to the scene. *Gabilan* made a surface attack at night and damaged the cruiser. *Charr* dove at dawn and made a submerged attack which sank *Isuzu*. *Spark* was standing by to pick up the ball if *Charr* fumbled, and she witnessed the sinking. This was the ninth and last Japanese light cruiser to be sunk by U.S. submarines.

Marus *and Escorts in the Southwest Pacific*

Hardhead (Greenup) sank the 6886-ton *Araosan Maru* on 6 April and *Hammerhead* (Smith) sank the 5973-ton *Tottori Maru* on 15 May. The Japanese record that a submarine sank the 5819-ton *Hokushin Maru* on 30 June. A number of smaller *marus* and seven small escort vessels were also sunk, but not enough to balance the loss of one U.S. fleet submarine.

Loss *of* Lagarto

Lagarto, under the command of the veteran skipper Latta, teamed up with *Baya* to hunt for small *marus* in the Gulf of Siam. On 2 May *Baya* picked up contact with a small tanker, an auxiliary and two escorts, and by radio brought *Lagarto* into contact also. *Baya* came in to attack but was driven off by the gunfire of alert radar-equipped escorts.

Early the next morning *Lagarto* and *Baya* rendezvoused and agreed on a plan of attack for the next afternoon. Although the two submarines exchanged several contact reports during the day, *Baya* was unable to make an attack until after midnight. Again the alert radar-equipped escort drove her off by gunfire. There were no further messages from *Lagarto* and no contact of any kind was ever made with her again.

The Japanese reported an attack made by the minesweeper *Hatsutaka* on a submerged submarine in thirty fathoms of water at a time and place corresponding with *Lagarto's* position. *Hatsutaka* was one of the radar-equipped escorts of the convoy. This is undoubtedly the attack that sank *Lagarto*. Twelve days later *Hawkbill* (Scanland) torpedoed and sank *Hatsutaka*.

British and Dutch Submarines

Dutch submarines were primarily concerned with special missions to the Dutch East Indies, but a Netherlands submarine sank a small tanker off the coast of Sumatra on 10 April. British submarines of Fife's command preyed on luggers and coasters carrying nickel ore and other raw material to Singapore, generally sinking these small ships by gunfire after providing for their crews to make it to the nearest land. This type of warfare sometimes resulted in lively gun battles with small Japanese escorts, and several special minelayers and submarine chasers were sunk by British submarines in such encounters. There were four Japanese heavy cruisers in the Singapore area, although two of these were so disabled they were believed incapable of operation. As the British submarines went about the methodical destruction of Japanese commerce they kept a hungry watch on these cruisers.

In early May *Haguro* and a destroyer slipped out of Singapore to run supplies to the Japanese Army in Burma. The British submarines *Statesman* (Bulkeley) and *Subtle* (Andrew), out of Trincomalee, were patrolling in Malacca Strait. They sighted the Japanese task force and fired torpedoes at the heavy cruiser but missed. Their contact report brought British surface forces out of Ceylon to intercept the Japanese on their return trip. *Haguro* was damaged by a bombing plane from an escort carrier on 16 May. That night she was intercepted by four British destroyers and in a stirring night action the Japanese heavy cruiser was sunk by the British destroyers.

Ashigara was then the only remaining Japanese heavy cruiser capable of operation. Commander A. R. Hezlet, commanding H.M.S. *Trenchant,* hoping for an opportunity to meet the only major Japanese ship left in the area, made a special study of Japanese heavy cruisers while *Trenchant* was refitting in Australia. In early June *Trenchant,* on patrol in the Java Sea, was ordered to move over to an area on the Malay coast. While en route she intercepted contact reports from U.S.S. *Blueback* and U.S.S. *Chub,* reporting that *Ashigara* had entered Batavia. Hezlet requested and received permission to patrol Banka Strait to intercept the cruiser on its return voyage to Singapore. En route to this new position *Trenchant* rendezvoused with H.M.S. *Stygian* (Clarabut). There was an Allied minefield at the northern entrance to Banka Strait. It was decided that *Trenchant* would take station on the inside of the minefield, with *Stygian* on the other side, to be sure of intercepting the cruiser if she ran through the Strait.

On 8 June *Blueback* reported that *Ashigara* left Batavia northbound. Shortly afterward Hezlet sighted a destroyer coming up the Strait and closed in, expecting the cruiser close behind the destroyer. Despite *Trenchant's* efforts to present a small silhouette, the Japanese destroyer sighted the submarine and opened fire, but the British submarine successfully evaded the Japanese destroyer and remained on the surface. The Japanese destroyer continued on its way. In the middle of the morning, as *Trenchant* was lying submerged in ambush in the narrow and shallow water of Banka Strait, Hezlet heard torpedo explosions as *Stygian* fired at the same destroyer and missed. A series of distant depth-charge explosions followed. While the Japanese destroyer was thus engaged with *Stygian*, Hezlet caught sight of the cruiser, coming northward up the Strait, hugging the Sumatra coast.

Trenchant fired eight torpedoes from her bow tubes at a range of forty-seven hundred yards with a track angle of 120 degrees. *Ashigara* saw their broad white wakes reaching out toward her. She increased speed and changed course, but *Ashigara* was so close inshore that she had to turn toward the torpedoes or run aground. Five torpedoes hit the cruiser and left it a broken wreck. *Trenchant* swung around and fired the stern tubes. *Ashigara,* despite her stricken condition, opened up accurate gunfire at the periscope, and somehow manage to move ahead to avoid the stern tube torpedoes. The Japanese destroyer came speeding over the horizon too late, and was just in time to help small boats and junks pick up survivors after the cruiser capsized and sank. *Ashigara* was the last major Japanese combat ship sunk by an Allied submarine.

German Submarines in the Java Sea

In early 1945 there were seven German submarines operating out of Batavia. The withdrawal of the last two Japanese RO-boats from the East Indies during the Lingayen campaign left the Germans alone in that part of the world. On 23 April *Besugo* (Miller), patrolling in the Java Sea, sighted a surfaced submarine, flying the Japanese flag, and further identified by a painted Japanese emblem on her conning tower. Miller fired six torpedoes and at least one hit. The enemy submarine sank so rapidly there was only one survivor. He proved to be the navigator who identified *Besugo's* victim as the German submarine *U-183.*

When Germany surrendered on 7 May, there were six submarines still under German control in the Far East. All six were seized by the Japanese. They were renamed *I-501* to *I-506*. None of them ever accomplished anything for the Japanese.

Awa Maru

The biggest *maru* sunk by U.S. submarines in April was the biggest blunder of the war for the U. S. Submarine Force. The 11,600-ton ship *Awa Maru* sailed as a cartel ship from Moji, Japan, to Singapore and return carrying Red Cross supplies to prisoners of war in Singapore. *Awa Maru* was guaranteed safe conduct by the United States for this voyage. All submarines had been given this information together with the details of her routing.

On 1 April *Queenfish* and *Sea Fox* were operating as a coordinate attack group in the northern end of Formosa Strait. There was a dense fog with visibility only a few hundred yards. About ten o'clock that night *Queenfish* (Loughlin) had radar contact with a single north-bound ship at seventeen thousand yards. Radar indicated that the target was a destroyer making sixteen to eighteen knots on a steady course. *Queenfish* closed to twelve hundred yards but still could not see the target. In view of the small indicated size of his target Lough-lin set his torpedoes to run at three feet depth and fired four torpe-does from the stern tubes. All four hit. The flash of the torpedo explo-sion could be seen but the ship was still not visible.

A few minutes later *Queenfish* stopped in the midst of a heavy oil slick and maneuvered to pick up survivors. There were fifteen or twenty men clinging to wreckage but only one man would come aboard. He identified *Queenfish's* victim as *Awa Maru*. The cartel ship was on schedule and approximately on course. She was not sounding fog signals but was properly lighted and identified although her iden-tification marks could not be seen in the fog. She had carried munitions and contraband on both legs of her voyage but there was nothing in the cartel agreement to forbid this. There was very little the Submarine Force could say in extenuation. The blame was broadly distributed, but by tradition the Commanding Officer bore the responsibility. Loughlin, one of the best submarine skippers in the business, was re-lieved of his command and court-martialed.

East China Sea and Yellow Sea

The invasion of Okinawa crowded the Japanese *marus* out of the East China Sea. After 1 April there were practically no Japanese ships in Tung Hai south of the Yangtze River mouth. *Sea Devil* (Styles) sank all three ships of a convoy in the southern part of the Yellow Sea on 2 April. One of these was the 6866-ton *Taijo Maru*, but for the most part the thirty-three *marus* sunk by submarines in April were much smaller and generally the hunting was very difficult.

Tirante

On 9 April *Tirante* (Street) sank a rare 5500-ton transport in the Yellow Sea. *Tirante* was near the end of a successful patrol with six torpedoes remaining. After ten days of uneventful patrol off Saishu To, Street decided to investigate a reported anchorage off the north-west side of that island. The water was under ten fathoms deep. *Ti-*

rante started in at midnight on the surface, approaching from the north-west to avoid the most probable mined area.

Two patrol boats off the harbor were successfully evaded. *Tirante* came on in and made a thorough radar search of the harbor. About four o'clock in the morning Street discovered a good-size ship and two smaller ones in the anchorage. *Tirante* fired three torpedoes at the large ship, and the target exploded in brilliant white flame. The illumination disclosed the two smaller ships to be frigates, but before the frigates could react to the unprecedented situation *Tirante* fired her three remaining torpedoes for hits on both Japanese escorts. Street then swung *Tirante* around and retreated. Behind him were three sunken ships, *Juzan Maru* and the frigates *Nomi* and *Coast Defense Vessel No. 31.*

On her next patrol *Tirante* was off the west coast of Kyushu on 11 June. Tragets were scarce and when Street sighted a good-size ship alongside dock at Ha Shima, he decided to go in and get it. Ha Shima was only eight miles from Nagasaki Harbor entrance. There were many small coasters and fishing boats in the vicinity, which Street took as reassurance of the absence of Japanese minefields. It was probable that the ships and the harbor would be defended by shore batteries, but Street expected that a submerged approach and torpedo attack would so surprise the defenders that *Tirante* would be able to surface and get out before a strong counterattack could be organized.

After a careful submerged approach avoiding the shoals and rocks, *Tirante* arrived at her desired position, one thousand yards off the dock in a Japanese harbor at forty-five minutes before high noon. On the after deck of the target Street could clearly see a 4.7-inch gun with the Navy crew standing by in white uniforms; an unexpected hazard. The first torpedo hit amidships. The gun crew, expecting an air attack, trained aft and pointed skyward. Street fired another torpedo, which missed to hit a mud bank. The gun crew spotted the submarine's radar antenna and opened fire. The third torpedo demolished the target and put the gun out of action. *Tirante* surfaced and headed out at flank speed. Automatic gunfire opened up from the beach, but it was sporadic and inaccurate. *Tirante* escaped without damage, leaving behind her the 2200-ton *Hakuju Maru* destroyed alongside the dock.

Northern Japan

Sea Dog (Hydeman), while on lifeguard for a carrier strike south of Tokyo, sank a 7000-ton *maru* on 16 April. *Sunfish* (Reed), *Cero* (Berthrong), *Bowfin* (Tyree), and *Tench* (Baskett) operated off northeast Honshu and in the bight between Honshu and Hokkaido where four

U.S. submarines had previously been lost in the minefields. In April, May, and June they sank thirteen *marus*, all of them small, except one 7000-tonner sunk by *Cero*. *Sterlet* (Lewis) sank two *marus* in the Sea of Okhotsk in May. Except for the Sea of Japan, submarines thus drew a tight ring around Japan. Inside this ring B-29 bombers laid mines in the Inland Sea and bombers battered Japanese ships in port so successfully that in May bombs and mines each sank more *marus* than did the submarines.

Into the Sea of Japan

The Sea of Japan was Japan's sole remaining safe route to the Asian mainland. It could be reached only through one of three narrow straits, all closely guarded and known to be mined. Until this stage of the war submarines had carefully avoided minefields, Allied or Japanese, whenever they could find out about them. The Joint Intelligence Center had been remarkably successful in locating the areas closed to Japanese navigation and U.S. submarines generally stayed out of such areas. When only a small proportion of Japanese traffic crossed the Sea of Japan submarines could afford this sensible practice, but the contraction of the Japanese Empire changed all this.

In 1943 submarines had entered the Sea of Japan through La Pérouse Strait in three separate raids, in the last of which *Wahoo* had been lost. In 1945 La Pérouse was known to be better defended than in 1943. Although La Pérouse was mined, it was believed that the mines were laid deep so that surface traffic could pass safely over them. This would make it comparatively easy for the Japanese to effectively close these straits with strong surface patrols that could force submarines to dive into the minefields. In addition, the direction of the prevailing current in La Pérouse made this route much better as an exit than as an entrance into the Sea of Japan. Narrow Tsugaru Kaikyo was next to impossible as a submarine route. This situation directed attention to Tsushima Kaikyo.

The mine section of the Joint Intelligence Center was very apprehensive of a plan to run through the minefields of Tsushima. The area restricted to navigation was accurately known and well verified by ship sightings, but nothing was known of the exact location of the mine lines or the nature of the mines within the area. However, the University of California Division of War Research had developed a new FM sonar capable of detecting individual mines at a range of seven hundred yards. Sonar also detected schools of fish, kelp, and thermal patches, but a trained sonar man could usually tell the difference by the tone of the sonar return. A true mine returned a clear, bell-like tone quite aptly dubbed "Hell's Bells."

The new sonar was installed in a number of submarines and an intensive training program undertaken under Lockwood's personal direction. When he was satisfied that his submarines could locate and avoid a mine in submerged maneuvers Lockwood organized a group of nine submarines known as Hydeman's Hellcats, commanded by Commander E. T. Hydeman, commanding officer of *Sea Dog*. Their mission was to run under Tsushima minefield and destroy Japanese traffic in the Sea of Japan. Before they shoved off from Guam Lockwood asked Nimitz for permission to personally command the Hellcats in this operation, a request which Nimitz summarily refused.

The Hellcats left Guam on 27 May. En route to the East China Sea *Tinosa* picked up ten survivors of a crashed B-29 south of Kyushu. When the aviators learned of *Tinosa's* destination they were unanimous in their desire to be put safely back into their rubber boats. Fortunately *Tinosa* was able to transfer her reluctant passengers to *Scabbardfish* before the Hellcats reached Tsushima.

The west channel of Tsushima had been selected for the entry. *Sea Dog* (Hydeman), *Crevalle* (Steinmetz), and *Spadefish* (Germershausen) made the run on 3–4 June. The next night *Tunny* (Pierce), *Skate* (Lynch), and *Bonefish* (Edge) came up to the scratch line.

The night was clear and the sea flat calm. The submarines were in column three miles apart. Their course had been selected to be parallel with the prevailing current so that a slow-speed submerged submarine would not crab down onto the mine cables. No patrol boats were encountered. The submarines ran up to the southern boundary of the restricted area and dove for the eighteen-hour submerged run through the minefield.

Unknown to the Joint Intelligence Center the Japanese had reinforced this minefield only the month before. On its route through the restricted area, each submarine would cross four mine lines. The first two were laid with mine case depth at thirteen meters and twenty-three meters, with mines seventy meters apart, designed to catch a submarine at periscope depth or running deep at one hundred feet. The remaining two lines were at three meters and five meters depth.

Skate dove at 0410 on 5 June. Lynch decided to take her through at 150 feet depth, a fortunate decision for if the mines watched at their set depth *Skate* would be safely below the depth of the mine cases—provided the submarine did not snag a cable and pull a mine down on her. An hour later sonar picked up echoes which the soundman identified as thermal patches. About nine o'clock in the morning sonar returned unmistakable echoes from a mine line four hundred yards ahead. The mines were spaced so close together it was impossible to maneuver to evade individual mines. *Skate* went down to 175 feet and ran slowly, silently, handsomely through. No sooner had she reached her depth than everyone on board heard a mine cable brush down the entire length of the submarine. Even those who were asleep were awakened. The ghostly scraping lasted just under a minute and *Skate* was clear, but it was a minute which no one in *Skate* has ever forgotten.

An hour and a half later *Skate* passed through a second line. After she was safely through Lynch decided to bring her up to periscope depth so he could establish his position by periscope bearing of objects on shore and thus exactly locate the mine lines. It was a dangerous maneuver but justified by the importance of the information. Back down to 150 feet *Skate* finished the course. *Flying Fish* (Risser), *Bowfin* (Tyree), and *Tinosa* (Latham) followed in her wake the next night. All nine submarines successfully ran through the minefields without a casualty.

The submarines then proceeded to their assigned areas in the Sea of Japan and remained concealed until 9 June. The sudden onslaught of nine submarines in the Sea of Japan on that date was devastating. In the next seventeen days the Hellcats sank twenty-seven *marus*. *Shoyo Maru,* the second ship sunk by *Sea Dog* on the evening of 9 June, got off a radio message before she went down, alerting the Grand Escort Force. The Japanese were slow to react. The next noon *I-122* was running out of Maizuru to her training area in the safe Sea of Japan, making fifteen knots through a glassy sea. *Skate* saw her approach. Lynch fired four torpedoes. The first one hit and so thoroughly disintegrated the Japanese submarine that the last two torpedoes in the salvo ran right through the debris without detonating.

On 24 June all submarines assembled south of La Pérouse for the run through the Strait together. *Bonefish* (Edge) was missing. She had been last heard from by *Tunny* on 18 June. At that time Edge intended to take *Bonefish* into Toyama Wan to search that broad bay for targets. The Japanese record that on 18 June, near the entrance to Toyama Wan, patrol craft made an anti-submarine attack which brought up a large pool of oil and debris. It undoubtedly marked the end of *Bonefish*.

Naval Intelligence had briefed the Hellcat submarines that La Pérouse was free of mines that would endanger submarines while on the surface, but that there were mines laid deep to trap submerged submarines; and possibly controlled mines at the narrow part of the Strait. Hydeman decided to take all submarines out on the surface, at night, in formation so their radars would reinforce one another. They would attempt to avoid all surface vessels, be prepared to shoot it out against small Japanese patrol craft if necessary, and pray that they would encounter no large Japanese surface vessels that would force the submarines to dive into the minefields.

At midnight, on the twenty-fourth, eight submarines surfaced, formed two columns, and set course for La Pérouse at eighteen knots. *Sea Dog* lead one column, but when her radar failed she surrendered that post of honor to *Crevalle*, and fell in astern of the column. There was a beautiful woolly fog that reduced visibility at times to less than three hundred yards. Radar made one contact which developed into a vessel carrying full running lights, coming up the Strait; probably a Russian. All submarines came through unchallenged.

At 0520 the transit of La Pérouse Strait was completed. The formation broke up. *Tunny* remained on patrol of the Sea of Okhotsk near La Pérouse, attempting to make contact with *Bonefish*. Nothing was ever heard of *Bonefish* again.

XXVII

JULY–AUGUST 1945

End of the Okinawa Campaign

Halsey relieved Spruance on 27 May and the Third Fleet took over the conduct of the war at sea with very little change in strategy or tactics. There was no substitute for victory to end the war, very little latitude for strategic choice of the road to peace, and little to encourage hope that a defeated Japan would stop fighting without being overwhelmed by invasion.

The last *kikusui* (mass suicide plane) attack of the Okinawa campaign took off from Kyushu with forty-five planes on 21–22 June, bringing the total to 1900 suicide attacks during the Okinawa campaign. On 2 July the Okinawa operation was officially declared over. Thirty U.S. naval vessels had been sunk and 568 damaged, mostly by *kamikaze* plane attacks. The U. S. Navy lost 4900 men killed in action and 4824 were wounded. The assault forces of the Tenth Army (Army, Navy, and Marines) lost 7613 men killed, 31,807 wounded in action, and 26,000 in non-battle casualties. The defense of Okinawa was a futile operation for the Japanese. It did nothing but delay inevitable defeat, and the casualties of the defenders were many times those of the assault forces. Approximately 80,000 Japanese Army troops were on Okinawa and not many of them survived. There were few survivors among the *kamikaze* pilots, or in the naval vessels expended in futile sacrifice. Casualties were heavy in the Okinawa local defense forces. The total Japanese casualties have been estimated at 110,000.

Third Fleet Hits Japan

When the Okinawa campaign ended the Third Fleet proceeded with preparation for the invasion of Japan. Task Force 38 sortied from Leyte on 1 July. On 10 July Halsey hit Tokyo with a carrier strike, caught the

Japanese Air Forces by surprise, and destroyed a large number of planes on the ground. Four days later the fast carriers struck northern Honshu and Hokkaido. Battleships, cruisers, and destroyers moved in and bombarded the Japanese homeland for the first time. On 17 July American and British forces launched another strike on the Tokyo area. From then on British and American naval forces ranged up and down Japan, seeking out airfields, naval vessels, and defense installations to blast with air attacks or bombardment.

Between 16 and 23 July a task force of cruisers and destroyers roamed the East China Sea and the Yellow Sea to attack Japanese shipping. They found very few Japanese ships in an area already swept clean by submarines. After the task force retired, submarines sank only one small *maru* in the Yellow Sea before the war ended.

Submarine Patrols

Several submarines ran under the Tsushima minefield in July and August to operate in the Sea of Japan. Even in the Sea of Japan targets were small and hard to find. It was the best remaining operation area for submarines, yet only eight *marus* and two escort vessels were sunk there during July and August. Of these *Sennet* (Clark) sank four small *marus* late in July. *Jallao* (Icenhower) sank the 5795-ton *Teihoku Maru* on 11 August, the only sizable ship to be sunk by a submarine during the period. *Torsk* (Lewellen) sank a small *maru* and two *kaibokans* just before the war ended. The war ended with five U.S. submarines behind the Tsushima minefields, contending with both technical and diplomatic problems to continue operating in the Sea of Japan.

Barb *in the Sea of Okhotsk*

The activities of the Third Fleet drastically reduced the sea traffic along Japan's Pacific coast. Only two escort vessels and one small *maru* were sunk by submarines off northeast Honshu. *Barb* (Fluckey), operating off Hokkaido and Karafuto in the Sea of Okhotsk, exemplified the difficulties submarines encountered seeking worthwhile employment.

Barb sank a small *maru* near the southern tip of Karafuto on 5 July. Two weeks later she sank a *kaibokan* near the same spot. For the remainder of her patrol she was unable to find targets worthy of torpedo fire. Anticipating this she had brought with her on patrol a 5-inch rocket launcher. With gunfire and rockets she bombarded the shores of Karafuto and northern Hokkaido. On the night of 23–24 July *Barb* landed an eight-man landing party in a rubber boat. Her commandoes placed demolition charges on a busy Japanese railroad track, and after many adventures all hands returned to the ship. Just as their boats arrived back at *Barb,* with the successful landing party intact, a train hit the charges and blew up with a spectacular explosion. This was probably the first landing on Japan. It is doubtful that all this hectic submarine activity had much adverse effect on the Japanese will to continue the war.

Lifeguards

The Third Fleet's attacks on the coast of Japan added to the volume of the lifeguard business. It also added to its hazards. The Third Fleet was never completely successful in distinguishing friend from foe, as their surface ships nervously cruised the coastal waters of Japan, where submarines had operated since the war began.

On 18 July when the Third Fleet carriers struck Tokyo, *Gabilan* (Parham) was lifeguarding at the entrance to Sagami Nada. *Gabilan* had been there since the first of the month, working in close cooperation with Dumbo planes and protective fighter cover from either Army or Navy planes. *Gabilan* had on board fifteen airmen, one Army and fourteen from the carriers, whom she had rescued from hostile Japanese coastal waters. Both Army and Navy pilots were fully cognizant of air-submarine lifeguard procedures, and the teamwork was excellent. On several occasions fighter cover drove off Japanese opposition while *Gabilan* ran deep into Sagami Nada to make rescues from under the noses of the Japanese.

At the end of the air strike on the eighteenth Halsey decided to make an anti-shipping sweep of Sagami Nada, with cruisers and destroyers. When Lockwood learned of this he reminded the Third Fleet that the lifeguard submarine was in the path of the sweep, and at the same time ordered *Gabilan* to clear out as soon as possible.

Gabilan retreated at full speed as soon as she received Lockwood's message, but Parham's plot indicated that it would be impossible to keep outside radar range of surface forces. Two hours later he made radar contact with the Third Fleet task group at sixteen thousand to twenty-eight thousand yards. Two destroyers headed toward *Gabilan.* Despite every effort the submarine made to establish her identity, the destroyers opened up with rapid fire and straddled her on the first salvo. Ten full salvos fell around *Gabilan* before Parham could get her under, but fortunately there were no hits.

Only six days later *Toro* (Grant), off Shikoku, had a similiar experience. *Toro* had been pulled off her assigned station by an attempt to make a rescue on the night of 24 July, when she learned by intercepted radio messages that she was in the path of a cruiser and destroyer shipping sweep. Grant sent an urgent message to Lockwood, who tried to inform Third Fleet forces in time. A destroyer discovered *Toro* on the surface at seventy-four hundred yards and opened fire, straddling her on the first salvo. Grant went deep, fearing that the destroyer would follow up with hedgehogs. Fortunately the destroyer assessed the contact as a picket boat which she had miraculously sunk with one salvo. After a half hour's search for survivors the victorious destroyer cleared the area.

Despite such misadventures with surface vessels, the submarines maintained their lifeguard stations. The day after *Toro* was attacked by a U.S. destroyer that submarine rescued three Royal Navy aviators. Experience developed mutual confidence and teamwork between the submarines and the airmen. On 26 July *Whale* (Carde) picked a Navy plane pilot out of the ocean near Bungo Suido. This pilot had remained guarding his crashed wingman until his own plane was out of gas, secure in the knowledge that a submarine would come by to pick him up.

The Japanese learned that submarines and fighter planes could team up efficiently to fight for a rescue. On 3 August *Aspro* (Ashley), with Army planes for air cover, fought their way into Sagami Nada against the determined opposition of several Japanese fighter planes. *Aspro's* two-hour progress up the bay on the surface was accompanied by a running dogfight between the Army planes and the Japanese fighters. One U. S. Army plane and three Japanese planes were shot down in aerial combat. *Aspro* crash-dove twice as Japanese bombs made near-misses on the submarine. Japanese planes strafed the downed aviator waiting for rescue. Although there were bullet holes in the boat fore and aft, and Captain E. H. Miles was grazed by machine-gun fire, he was still in good condition when *Aspro* pulled him aboard and retreated to safer and deeper waters.

Minefield Reconnaissance

In preparation for the Third Fleet's shore bombardment, submarines performed an unusual service. It was well known that the inshore waters of Japan were protected by defensive minefields. These mines were planned to inhibit the operation of American submarines but they were equally dangerous to any unwary surface forces that entered the area. In planning shore bombardments by the Third Fleet Halsey took advantage of the ability of the submarines' new FM sonar to locate mines. He requested that submarines make a sonar sweep for mines inside the one-hundred-fathom curve in four areas he had selected for bombardment.

Runner (Bass) and *Redfin* (Miller) made the reconnaissance. The reliable range for detecting mines with FM sonar was only about five hundred yards. This gave submarines scant room and time to maneuver after a mine was located. The first *Runner* had been lost with all hands by striking a mine she was not looking for off northeast Honshu, in an area close by to one which *Runner II* was assigned to search for mines. No one envied *Runner* or *Redfin* their assignment. *Redfin* reported one area free of mines and a possible minefield in the other. *Runner* discovered a possible minefield in the area north of Inubo Saki. As this was Third Fleet's area of first priority *Runner* was asked to go back in again and verify her information on that area.

In her second search *Runner* did not detect mines. It was therefore considered that the first contacts had been kelp, or fish or transient thermal patches, and that the area was actually free of mines. On the night of 14–15 July a task force of U.S. and British battleships moved into the searched area, bombarded major industrial plants at Hatachi, and retired without striking any mines. It is possible, however, that *Runner's* first report of mines was accurate. In May 1943 the Japanese had planted two hundred mines in the northern end of the area searched by *Runner*, and the mines that had not broken loose in storms and stress in the intervening two years were still there.

Radar Pickets

Lockwood's submarines were also preparing for another new kind of reconnaissance. During the *kamikaze* attacks on Okinawa the U. S. Navy developed a defense of deploying destroyers from thirty to one hundred miles from Okinawa to act as radar warning pickets for approaching *kamikaze* attacks. These pickets were effective but at a terrific cost to the destroyers that manned the radar picket line. On their exposed stations the destroyer pickets absorbed the shock of the first wave of each mass *kamikaze* attack. With courage and tenacity never exceeded in any war on land or sea they stuck to their posts. Their losses were so harrowing that it was dreadful to contemplate what the next campaign would be like when the war moved closer to the *kamikaze* bases and Japanese fanatics were mustered in full strength to defend the homeland.

In this dilemma submarines prepared to take over a part of the job of radar pickets. To do the job effectively submarines had to be modified and more radar apparatus installed. One periscope had to be removed to make way for another vertical antenna and other extensive alterations made. *Finback* was outfitted and successfully tested. Twenty-four other submarines were similiarly modified to take over the job of radar pickets during the invasion of Japan. Fortunately they were never called on for that duty.

Southwest Pacific Submarines

In the Southwest Pacific Fife vigorously searched for profitable employment of the British, Dutch, and American submarines of his command, but most of the remaining Japanese ships were small and gun-shy. U.S. submarines sank four escort vessels and British submarines sank one in the month of July. Small coasters often proceeded under escort of submarine chasers in traffic between the islands of the East Indies. Submarines attacked these convoys, sometimes fighting gun duels with the escorts to get at the convoys. H.M.S. *Tiptoe* (Jay) and H.M.S. *Trump* (Catlow) made a notably successful cooperative patrol in Sunda Strait destroying this kind of coastal traffic.

Blenny (Hazzard) used various weapons including boarding parties with demolition charges to sink a total of sixty-three small vessels supplying Singapore. *Bugara* (Schade) carried out a similiar patrol in the Gulf of Siam and rivaled *Blenny's* record. The total tonnage sunk was insignificant, but the combined effort of British and American submarines disrupted the supply lines to Singapore, which still figured in the Japanese scheme of defense. This unconventional warfare led to many unconventional situations.

Unescorted small coasters were boarded and searched before they were destroyed. The fanatic Japanese members of the crews generally went over the side at the approach of the submarines, but the native crews were put in lifeboats, given food and water and their personal belongings, and released where they could get ashore and take to the hills. It was rumored that the Japanese at Singapore executed any native crews that lost a ship. It was apparent that the Chinese and native crews did not serve their Japanese masters with enthusiasm.

On 1 August *Cod* (Westbrook) intercepted a large three-masted junk and put a six-man boarding party aboard. The junk was loaded with contraband, but before the boarding party could be returned to *Cod,* a Japanese fighter plane came over and strafed both the submarine and the junk. *Cod* dove for safety with machine gun slugs spattering her bridge and superstructure. Before the plane retired a Japanese escort came by, preventing *Cod* from surfacing, and it was several hours before the submarine could return to pick up the boarding party. The junk had then disappeared.

There were four submarines in the vicinity, and when *Cod* broadcast a report of her trouble and a description of the junk they all joined in the search for the marooned submariners. After the second day the search seemed hopeless, but about noon on 3 August *Blenny* sighted a junk that matched the description. After a short chase *Blenny* came alongside to find the entire boarding party safe and being well treated by the Chinese crew. The junk was released with presents of canned goods and fresh bread, and *Cod's* boarding party was returned to the jubilant submarine.

Bugara (Schade), in the Gulf of Siam, encountered a new 150-ton schooner anchored in deep water. As Schade approached he noted seven large Malay canoes close by. It developed that the schooner was a Japanese vessel with a Chinese crew carrying rice to Singapore. When *Bugara* chanced upon her the schooner was under attack by Malay pirates, who had already killed two of the Chinese crew. Schade took off the crew and their lifeboats and sank the Japanese ship. He then dispersed the Malay pirates by gunfire before releasing the Chinese, who felt they had a far better deal with the submarine than they would have had with the pirates.

British Midgets

In July the British submarine tender *Bonaventure* arrived in the Philippines with several XE-type midget submarines aboard. These midgets weighed thirty-five tons each. They had a surface speed of six knots and a submerged speed of five knots and carried a crew of five officers and men, two of whom were divers. They were designed to enter enemy harbors where their divers could be released from the submerged submarines to place time fuse explosive charges under anchored ships.

XE-4 (Lieutenant M. H. Shean) was towed by H.M.S. *Spearhead* from Brunei, Borneo to a position fourteen miles from Cape San Jacques in Indo-China, and released before dawn on 31 July. Operating submerged and dragging a grapnel, *XE-4* located the Singapore–Saigon cable. While lying on the bottom, she then sent out a diver who cut out a piece of the cable and brought it back to *XE-4*. Two hours later the same midget located the Saigon–Hong Kong cable and cut it also. The next morning before dawn *XE-4* successfully rendezvoused with *Spearhead* and was towed back to Brunei. *XE-5*, towed by H.M.S. *Selene*, was not so fortunate. *XE-5* was released on 2 August near Hong Kong, but in a three-day search was unable to get hold of the Hong Kong–Singapore cable, probably because the cable was buried deep in the mud beyond reach of the grapnel.

The major operation of the British midgets was much more daring. *XE-1* (Lieutenant J. E. Smart), towed by H.M.S. *Spark*, and *XE-3* (Lieutenant I. E. Fraser), towed by H.M.S. *Stygian*, set out to penetrate into the harbor of Singapore and complete the destruction of the two damaged heavy cruisers located there. *Takao* (torpedoed by *Darter* on 23 October) and *Myoko* (torpedoed by *Bergall* on 13 December) had both been at Singapore since reaching that port in badly damaged condition. Both cruisers had been repeatedly photographed from the air and located at anchorages in shallow water behind torpedo nets. The Japanese cruisers were both believed to be unable to operate, but as long as they were afloat they were a potential menace to Allied operations in the Southwest Pacific. Where they lay, they were safe from attack by conventional submarines.

An attack on Japanese ships deep inside Singapore harbor by midget submarines appeared to be a suicide mission to experienced American submariners, but the British went right ahead with their plans. *Stygian* slipped the tow of *XE-3* about thirty miles east of Singapore near Horsburg Light shortly before midnight on 30 July. Fraser, in his bizarre craft, ran for twenty-five miles up the channel toward Singapore in the bright moonlight. About four-thirty in the morning he dove to avoid approaching Japanese ships, and continued the remainder of the journey submerged.

About ten-thirty in the morning *XE-3* arrived at the boom gate and found it open but guarded by an armed trawler. The midget passed through the gate without incident. Two hours later they sighted *Takao* as she lay heavily camouflaged against a land background. In the flat calm sea Fraser navigated mostly by fathometer with sparing periscope exposure. On his last look through the periscope he spotted a Japanese motor cutter, loaded to the gunwales with a Japanese Navy liberty party, only twenty-five yards from the scope. *XE-3* then went to deep submergence of twenty-two feet and bumped her way along the bottom of Johore Strait approaching the anchored Japanese cruiser. At 1442 the British midget brought up with a resounding thump against the side of *Takao*.

Fraser then had a very difficult time maneuvering alongside the cruiser, seeking a position from which a diver could drag limpet mines into position. He was apprehensive that any moment they would be discovered. Finally at 1532 the diver (Leading Seaman Magennis) crawled out of the submarine dragging six limpet mines into position underneath the cruiser. Like the first submarine attack in history, when Bushnell in the American submarine *Turtle* failed to attach a mine to the British ship *Eagle* in New York Harbor in 1776, Magennis was nearly thwarted by the bottom condition of his target. *Takao's* bottom was so fouled that the limpet magnets would not stick to her hull. Magennis ingeniously solved his problem by placing limpets on either side of the cruiser's keel and tying them together with their holdfasts.

When the limpets were in place and the diver successfully recovered, *XE-3* slipped her saddle charges. The starboard charge stuck, and the nearly exhausted Magennis volunteered to go out again and release it. After several minutes of hard and noisy labor with a heavy spanner he forced out the release pin and returned again to the comparative safety of a midget submarine under the bottom of a Japanese cruiser in Singapore Harbor. *XE-3* then struggled out from under *Takao* and worked her difficult way back out through the gate and up the channel to rendezvous with *Stygian* in the early hours of the next morning.

XE-1 (Smart) followed *XE-3* into Singapore Harbor but arrived too late to hunt for and find *Myoko* and get back out the gate before the hour set for the charges to go off. Smart therefore decided to attack *Takao* also. Despite the mines with which *XE-3* had then fouled *Takao's* anchorage, Smart succeeded. He maneuvered his craft alongside the Japanese cruiser and dropped saddle charges under the overhang of *Takao's* hull. *XE-1* also succeeded in getting back out the gate. Smart rendezvoused with H.M.S. *Spark* the following night.

As the midgets withdrew up the channel, and before they were picked up by their mother submarines, they witnessed a tremendous explosion behind Singapore Island, and hopefully marked it as the Japanese cruiser blowing up. Air photographs taken later failed to show much damage to *Takao* in the plan view. The British submarine Squadron Commander therefore concluded that the explosion seen by the returning midgets was a coincidence. This was too pessimistic an evaluation. Japanese records show "medium damage" to *Takao* on the night of 30 July in Singapore Harbor. The Japanese cruiser had her bottom blown out and rested securely on her shattered bottom for the remainder of the war. The British midgets achieved the success they so richly earned.

Loss of Bullhead

The last American submarine to be lost during the war was the first to be lost in Lombok Strait. Through the greater part of the war American, British, and Dutch submarines ran through Lombok coming and going between their patrol areas and Fremantle. It was good luck as well as good seamanship, good submarine operation, and good management that only one submarine paid the penalty for navigating the narrow, swift waters of this passage, against the persistent opposition of Japanese antisubmarine forces.

Bullhead (Holt) left Fremantle 31 July to operate in the Java Sea. U.S. submarines *Capitaine* and *Puffer* and British submarines *Taciturn* and *Thorough* were also assigned to patrol the Java Sea in August. *Capitaine*, the U.S. pack commander, did not arrive on station until 12 August. Three days later she reported that she had been unable to contact *Bullhead*.

The Japanese report that one of their planes attacked a submarine close by the coast of Bali on 6 August and claimed two direct hits. This was probably the fatal attack on *Bullhead*. The submarine's radar may have been temporarily blacked out by the high mountains of Bali, allowing the Japanese plane to make an undetected approach. It was a particularly sad loss, unknown until the war was over. *Bullhead* was the fifty-second U.S. submarine to be lost during the war—fifty of them in the Pacific and Southwest Pacific areas.

Japanese Plans to Attack the Panama Canal

Frustrated in submarine attacks on American task forces, the Japanese devised new and novel plans for submarine operations which would circumvent American anti-submarine defenses. Five large submarines were under construction, designed to carry special seaplanes. *I-13* and *I-14* (2650 tons) could each carry two seaplanes. The huge snorkel-equipped *I-400* class of submarines (3450 tons), with a cruising range of forty thousand miles, could each carry three seaplanes. By the middle of May *I-13*, *I-14*, *I-400*, and *I-401* were ready for operation.

A new type of seaplane torpedo bomber had been specially designed for these submarine aircraft carriers. It was planned to send all four submarines as a task force to launch ten planes in a suicide strike off Panama and destroy Gatun locks with bombs and torpedoes. By the first of June, however, the projected operation was in trouble.

I-400 alone required sixteen hundred tons of oil for the operation. There was only a total of two thousand tons available at Kure. *I-401* left Kure in the middle of May for Dairen, Manchuria, where oil was available. Almost immediately she struck a magnetic mine and had to return to Kure for repairs. *I-400* was substituted and successfully brought back a cargo of precious oil. However, the menace of magnetic mines made the Inland Sea out of the question for training with the seaplanes, and the whole operation had to be moved to the Sea of Japan. When *I-122* was torpedoed by *Skate* in the Sea of Japan on 10 June it was apparent that even that was no longer a safe training ground for Japanese submarines. There was literally no place to hide.

In the meantime trouble with the new seaplane developed. In late June two of the special seaplanes crashed in joint training exercises. B-29 air raids disrupted the production schedules of all aircraft factories, and it was impossible to deliver replacements or spare parts. The plan to attack Panama was abandoned. The Japanese submarine force hoped to substitute a plan to bombard San Francisco, but this plan also had to be given up. It was finally decided to send *I-13* and *I-14* to Truk with special reconnaissance planes, and from there to reconnoiter Ulithi. *I-400* and *I-401* would follow, and when reconnaissance had established the pres-

ence of a carrier task force inside Ulithi atoll, the six torpedo-bomber seaplanes of these monstrous Japanese submarines would attack the American anchorage.

I-13 departed from Ominato on 5 July to carry reconnaissance planes
to Truk. She was due at Truk on 20 July but she was never heard from
again by the Japanese. American records credit aircraft from the escort
carrier *Anzio* and the destroyer escort *Lawrence C. Taylor* with sinking
I-13 east of Honshu on 16 July. *Taylor* brought up convincing wreckage
with a hedgehog attack, but *I-13* should have been nearing Truk by 16
July, and there appears to be little chance that she was still off Honshu.
It can only be concluded that *I-13* is one of the many submarines about
whose end there will always be a mystery.

I-14 arrived at Truk with reconnaissance planes on 4 August. An attack on Ulithi was planned for 17 August. *I-400* and *I-401* left Ominato
on 26 July for their part in the operation. When hostilities ended both
the big submarines were southeast of Truk. The operation was canceled
and the submarines returned to Yokosuka where they surrendered.

Captain T. Ariizumi in *I-401* commanded the operation. He was one
of the few Japanese submariners wanted by Allied authorities for war
crimes. While in command of *I-8* in the Indian Ocean Ariizumi had ordered the execution of ninety-eight survivors of the Dutch merchantman
Tjisalak. After torpedoing the American freighter *Jean Nicolet* (also in
the Indian Ocean) the crew of *I-8* tortured and murdered sixty members
of the freighter's crew. Ariizumi solved the problem by committing suicide as *I-401* entered Tokyo Bay on her way to surrender at Yokosuka.

Kaiten *Operations*

Six Japanese submarines were organized as the "Tamon Unit" for
kaiten operations in July and August. Three of these submarines were
sent to the vicinity of Okinawa. *I-47* and *I-367* departed on 19 July for an
area three hundred to four hundred miles east of Okinawa. Although
Japanese records indicate that these submarines made no attacks, the
U.S. attack transport *Marathon* was damaged by a piloted torpedo in
that area on 21 July. Both *I-47* and *I-367* returned to port in August. On
6 August the first atomic bomb fell on Hiroshima. On 8 August *I-363* departed for the Okinawa area. The following day Russia declared war on
Japan. *I-363* was then ordered to return and operate in the Sea of Japan.
She made no attacks.

Three other submarines of the Tamon Unit were sent to the southern
part of the Philippine Sea. There they found better hunting. There had
been no Japanese submarine activity south of Formosa in the previous

few months, and American anti-submarine activity from Saipan south had relaxed. Convoys were being escorted, but individual combat ships were sailing singly, without escort, and at speeds (less than sixteen knots) set to save fuel rather than diminish submarine hazard. The Joint Intelligence Center had ceased publication of a weekly submarine situation chart in April. The Japanese submarine situation was well in hand. Shipping control was a routine duty.

Escort carrier hunter-killer groups had been very efficient against Japanese submarines, but none was then in the Philippine Sea. *Tulagi* was in dry dock. The *Anzio* group, that had sunk four Japanese submarines in the Philippine Sea, was operating east of the Marianas. The Japanese submarine force had been defeated but it was too dangerous to ignore.

I-53 (Ota) was the first of the Tamon submarines to make contact. On 24 July Ota sighted a convoy which he identified as fifteen transports escorted by three destroyers. It was actually a convoy of seven LSTs and a reefer escorted by *Underhill* (*DE-682*), five patrol craft, and three submarine chasers. *I-53* released two *kaitens* and claimed sinking two transports.

Underhill (Newcomb), in advance of the convoy, had discovered a floating mine about the time the Japanese submarine released the *kaitens*. Newcomb advised the convoy to change course while he destroyed the mine by gunfire. While he was so engaged sound picked up a contact, and *Underhill* called for one of the PCs for assistance. *PC-804* also established sound contact and dropped depth charges. A few seconds later *Underhill* sighted a periscope and laid down a shallow pattern of depth charges, which brought oil and debris to the surface. Newcomb reported that his DE had sunk a midget submarine. Almost immediately another midget was sighted by *PC-804*. *Underhill* charged in to ram the midget. A violent explosion followed, throwing flame and debris a thousand feet in the air. The entire forward end of *Underhill* disappeared, together with her captain and 111 members of her crew. A total of 116 survivors were rescued from the after end before it was sunk by gunfire from the patrol craft. These were the explosions evaluated by Ota as the sinking of two transports.

Shortly after midnight on 3–4 August, *I-53* released two *kaitens* while she was under attack by four patrol craft about four hundred miles east of Formosa. Ota reported hearing heavy explosions about three hours later. In the meantime *I-58* (Hashimoto) was patrolling along the Guam–Leyte route. On 28 July Hashimoto released two *kaitens* to attack a tanker and a destroyer. Although *I-58* heard an explosion which was hopefully evaluated as one tanker sunk, these attacks apparently went completely unnoticed by any American ship.

The next night, 29 July, about an hour before midnight, *I-58* surfaced in the moonlight and almost immediately made contact with an approaching ship about ten thousand meters away. *I-58* quickly submerged again. As the ship came closer on a steady course almost directly toward the Japanese submarine, Hashimoto identified his target as a battleship of the *Idaho* class. *Kaiten* pilots clamored for release, but under the conditions of changing visibility in the moonlight Hashimoto had greater confidence in his conventional torpedoes than in the bizarre suicidal *kaitens*. There was no accurate means for *I-58* to estimate the range, and this made target speed difficult to determine. Hashimoto esimated twenty knots. From a range of fifteen hundred meters he fired six torpedoes in a broad spread and observed three hits.

I-58's target was the heavy cruiser *Indianapolis*. En route from Guam to Leyte, the veteran cruiser had been routed on a direct course at 15.7 knots. Despite her lack of underwater sound apparatus, which made her dependent upon escorts for listening, she had been sent out without escorts. There were four reports of recent submarine contacts along her route (all of them were false). Shortly after sunset *Indianapolis* ceased zigzagging. This presented Hashimoto with a very elementary fire control problem; but it is doubtful, with the slow speed the cruiser was making, the absence of escorts, and the geometry of the situation created by the Japanese submarine's chance contact, that zigzagging would have made any difference to a submarine commander of Hashimoto's experience and competence.

Indianapolis was hit with two torpedoes and sank about fifteen minutes later. Her distress messages were never received. Hashimoto's message reporting his success was intercepted by U.S. radio intelligence and partially decoded some sixteen hours later to inform Cincpac headquarters at Guam that a Japanese submarine reported sinking something approximately at *Indianapolis'* predicted position. Nevertheless, search and rescue operations for the survivors did not start until a routine search plane out of Peleliu sighted men in the water some eighty-four hours after the ship sank. Of the 1199 men on board *Indianapolis* only 316 survived, and more than half of the 883 that perished died during the long exposure in the water waiting for rescue.

About 0815 on the morning of 10 August Hashimoto released two *kaitens* to attack a convoy about 260 miles northeast of the northern point of Luzon. *I-58* claimed two ships sunk, but there were no American records of this attack. Two days later, on 12 August, about 1800, Hashimoto released his last two *kaitens* to attack a ship which he identified as a 15,000-ton seaplane tender. This was most probably the landing ship dock *Oak Hill*, escorted by the destroyer escort *Thomas F. Nickel,* en route from Okinawa to Leyte. *Oak Hill* sighted a periscope feather about sunset. *Nickel* (Farmer) turned in to attack. Recognizing a *kaiten,*

Farmer profited by *Underhill's* experience and made a zigzag approach rather than come charging in to ram. Shortly after this contact the crew of *Nickel* heard a scraping noise alongside, which they believed to be a piloted torpedo in a very near miss. A *kaiten* broke water a few minutes later about twenty-five hundred yards away and exploded.

Another periscope was then reported by *Oak Hill*. Again *Nickel* avoided ramming tactics but dropped a pattern of shallow depth charges just ahead of the piloted torpedo. A heavy underwater blast resulted which *Nickel* assessed as another *kaiten* destroyed. Hearing these explosions Hashimoto in *I-58* believed his *kaitens* had sunk a seaplane tender.

I-366, the third unit of the southern section of the Tamon Unit, reported that she released three *kaitens* to attack a convoy five hundred miles north of Palau on the evening of 11 August. She claimed three ships sunk but again there are no corresponding American records of the attack.

The Tamon Unit was by far the most successful of the Japanese *kaiten* operations, measured by actual rather than mythical results, although even in the Tamon Operation the most spectacular success was scored by conventional rather than suicide torpedoes. The loss of *Indianapolis* with 883 lives, and of *Underhill* with 112 dead brought the total of Americans killed in the Tamon Operation to 995. All the *kaiten* operations of the Japanese submarine force cost them eight I-class submarines and a total of about nine hundred lives, but in the short space of six days *I-53* and *I-58* had evened the score.

End of the War Situation

Japanese propagandists preached the doctrine that the invaders were being enticed to land on Kyushu where *samurai* warriors could destroy the enemies of Japan "at one stroke." It was on Kyushu beachheads in A.D. 1280 that the great army and armada of Kublai Khan had been destroyed by fanatic Japanese defenders with the help of the legendary *kamikaze* typhoon. Twentieth-century fanatics preached that they could do it again. Propagandists succeeded not only in deceiving the rank and file but frequently in deceiving themselves, as they had with mythical air victories and illusionary successes of the *kaitens*. Many Japanese believe that the loss of Iwo Jima and Okinawa was part of a great strategy to lure the main strength of the invaders to Kyushu where it could be more effectively assailed by short-range *kamikaze* planes, midget submarines, *kaitens*, suicide boats, and other fantastic suicide weapons. The defense of Kyushu was planned accordingly.

On the walls of Japanese railroad stations and in other public places appeared the slogan "One hundred million Japanese die in honor." A total of 5350 *kamikaze* planes were ready and five thousand young Japanese men were trained to fly them. Several thousand planes that could be patched up to make a short non-return flight were under repair and in storage. A million Japanese Army troops were deployed in the homeland, and the remnants of the Kwantung Army were being pulled back from Manchuria as fast as possible.

A few Japanese, under the leadership of the Emperor, knew that Japan was defeated, and these devoted patriots attempted to negotiate a surrender that would avoid national suicide. The utmost secrecy was necessary to circumvent a rebellion of the Japanese Army that would attempt to overthrow any government that even considered surrender. In the ignorance of a Russian deal to declare war on Japan (in return for southern Karafuto and the Kurile Islands), the Japanese peace group tried to induce Russia to act as intermediary in peace negotiations. Under these circumstances the peace movement, in July, was making little real progress.

U.S. plans for Operation Olympic (the invasion of Kyushu) were initiated in January 1945, and by the end of the Okinawa campaign, plans were virtually complete. Based on January intelligence estimates it was planned to land in Kyushu at three separate beachheads about 1 November. Naval and military forces from all over the world were converging on the Philippines, Hawaii, and the Marianas for the great assault. Okinawa was being rapidly prepared as the advance base.

MacArthur estimated that the landing on Kyushu would cost fifty thousand American casualties and several times that number of Japanese casualties. In view of the losses in the much smaller Okinawa operations the estimators were certainly optimistic. Shortly after the Occupation MacArthur stated that if the Japanese Army had resorted to guerrilla warfare in the mountains it would have taken a million American troops ten years to master the situation. These dark estimates are all based on the optimistic assumption that Olympic would have been as successful as the other American amphibious operations of the war had been.

However, Japanese intelligence had picked the same three beachheads that the American planners had picked as the most probable landing points. Japanese defense concentrations in these areas were built up rapidly. Although modified American intelligence estimates reflected this buildup, there was never any indication that plans were being changed because of the changing situation. Under the complicated scheme of American command, with MacArthur in overall command, but with Nimitz in command during the amphibious phase, and Arnold with independent command of a strategic Air Force committed to win the war by strategic bombing, major changes in plans were difficult to achieve.

Amphibious operations generally plan to isolate an invasion area and then land with overwhelming superiority of force within the isolated area. On Kyushu, as postwar inspection confirmed, the defenders out-numbered the planned invasion force at the beachheads. This and the typhoon that hit the advance base at Okinawa like a *kamikaze* in November, and the strength and advantageous location of the suicide forces, make it quite probable that the first assault on Kyushu would have been repulsed. If plans had run their normal course and the atomic bombs had not been dropped, one of the bloodiest campaigns of history would probably have taken place, with cumulative casualties in the millions. Certainly the future of Japan, and of the world, would have been much grimmer.

Japanese Submarine Preparations

For *kamikaze* planes, for *kaitens*, and for suicide boats fuel was essential. After *I-351* completed her successful trip to Singapore in May, bringing back a cargo of gasoline, the Japanese drew up an ambitious plan to import two million gallons of gasoline from Singapore and Formosa with submarine tankers. Seven I-class and four HA-class submarines were assigned to this project, but most of them were never converted in time to take actual part in this new transportation proj-ect. *I-402* was converted from a submarine aircraft carrier to a sub-marine gasoline tanker, with a capacity of 182,000 gallons, but she was among those which never made a tanker trip. *I-372*, after her return from her hazardous trip to Wake, was converted at Yokosuka to carry gasoline. She was about ready to go when, on 18 July, planes from the Third Fleet in the raid on Yokosuka scored a near-miss on her. The midship gasoline tank section of *I-372* was ruptured and she sank.

I-351 left Sasebo for her second tanker trip in June and reached Singapore in July. On 11 July she left Singapore carrying 132,000 gal-lons of gasoline and was never heard from again by the Japanese. Three days after leaving Singapore *I-351* ran through the operating area of U.S.S. *Blower*. At 0223 in the morning of 15 July *Blower* fired torpedoes at an unidentified ship and missed. She quickly passed on a contact report to *Bluefish* in the adjacent area. *Bluefish* (Forbes) closed to investigate and identified a Japanese submarine on the sur-face. Forbes fired a spread that scored two torpedo hits. The Japanese submarine burst into flames and sank. The next morning *Bluefish* rescued three survivors who identified *Bluefish's* target as *I-351*.

Spikefish *and* I-373

On 9 August *I-373* left Sasebo and ran down through the East China Sea on her first tanker run to pick up a cargo from Formosa. The Japanese knew only that she did not arrive at her destination. *I-373* was sunk by U.S. submarine *Spikefish* on 14 August.

Spikefish (Managhan) had been on patrol in the Yellow Sea and the East China Sea for approximately forty unexciting days. Most of the time she had spent on lifeguard station with no calls for her service. In the first month of her patrol the most exciting incidents were sinking floating mines with rifle fire. Then on 6 August, without warning, she suddenly made contact with a large task force in the middle of the East China Sea. As the submarine closed to investigate, Managhan was unable to exchange satisfactory recognition signals. When *Spikefish* was too close to get off the task force's track Managhan recognized U.S. destroyer types. This was a U.S. carrier task force en route to strike Japanese shipping at Tinghai, China. *Spikefish* went deep and ran silent while the task force passed close by with destroyers running directly overhead with screw noises in every direction. It was a very harrowing experience. It put Managhan on notice that anything might happen.

On the evening of 13 August, therefore, Managhan was very wary when *Spikefish* made radar contact and closed to identify a large submarine on the surface zigzagging at ten knots on a southwesterly course. *Spikefish* tracked her adversary and sent a contact report to Lockwood. In the meantime the other submarine detected *Spikefish*. It suddenly made a large zig to a northeasterly course and dove. Lockwood radioed that there were no U.S. submarines in the area and that the contact must be Japanese.

A guessing game for very large stakes then ensued. Managhan guessed that the last course change of the Japanese submarine was a deception course. Reasoning that if he were in the Japanese submariner's shoes he would reverse course after he had submerged, Managhan ran south to regain contact. His reasoning proved correct. About midnight he had contact on the same target at eighty-six hundred yards. Still apprehensive, he tracked his quarry until dawn. Lockwood sent him another message to assure him that there were no friendly surface forces in the area. Before dawn *Spikefish* submerged out ahead on her target track. The first light revealed a submarine that was definitely Japanese.

Spikefish fired six torpedoes, two of which hit. The Japanese submarine disappeared in a pall of smoke. An hour later Managhan surfaced and ran through a heavy oil slick and large accumulations of debris. Five men, feigning death, could not be induced to come aboard. With difficulty *Spikefish* fished one uncooperative prisoner over the fantail. He identified the target as *I-382*. Whether this was a mistake in translation or a crude attempt at deception is unknown. It was definitely *I-373*, the 127th and last Japanese submarine to be lost during the war. It was a senseless Japanese sacrifice. *I-373* had sailed from Sasebo two days after the first atomic bomb fell on Hiroshima.

High Underwater Speed Submarines

The syndrome of order-counterorder-disorder, symptomatic of defeat, afflicted all Japanese submarine operations as the end of the war approached. Three new snorkel-equipped high underwater speed submarines of the *I-200* class, and ten smaller *HA-200* class, also designed for high underwater speed, joined the Japanese submarine force in 1945. Trouble developed with the snorkels and modifications were undertaken at Maizuru. Other mechanical difficulties delayed the assignment of high underwater speed submarines to war operations. It was finally decided to reserve them all for the anticipated Armageddon when the American invasion armada approached the sacred soil of Japan.

Shore-Based Midgets and Kaitens

Japan had stockpiled one hundred *kaitens* and four hundred two-man midgets to sally forth from shore bases and attack approaching ships of the expected invasion force. Two thousand small motor boats, each carrying a 550-pound explosive charge in its bow, were also secreted along the shore and in the harbors of southern Japan. *HA-109* and *HA-111* were assigned as tenders for the midget submarines, but the two HA-boats were frequently called out to patrol Bungo Suido in addition to their tender duties.

Practically cut off from communication with the rest of Japan, the *kaiten* pilots at Otsujima continued their intensive training for suicide. Five superannuated submarines (*I-156, -157, -158, -159,* and *-162*) were fitted out to carry *kaitens* and transport piloted torpedoes to selected shore bases along the invasion coast. *I-157* made three trips, carrying her capacity of two *kaitens* each, but the rest were diverted again before they could carry out their assignment. It was decided early in July to train the crews of these five old submarines to launch *kaitens* in combat operations so they could join the rest of the Japanese Navy in its final "*banzai* charge." *I-156* and *I-162* cruised to Dairen to obtain fuel for these training exercises. *I-159* made the last sortie of a *kaiten*-carrying submarine. She was in the Sea of Japan, and the others of her group were training in the Inland Sea when the war ended.

End of the War for U.S. Submarines

At Guam, anticipating Russia's entry into the war on or about 15 August, Lockwood received orders to prepare plans for coordinating U.S. submarine operation with the Russians. This was a ticklish situation. Five U.S. submarines were in the Sea of Japan, where they could be expected to encounter any Russian offensive against Japan almost as soon as it was initiated. Experience had already indicated that detailed information of Russian ship movements was hard to obtain.

On 5 August Lockwood was informed that the carrier strike on Kyushu scheduled for 7 August had been canceled, and that all submarines were to be pulled back at least one hundred miles from Kyushu's coastline. This was the submarine command's first intimation that anything unusual was afoot. The first atomic bomb was dropped on Hiroshima on 6 August. There was still no assurance that the end of the war was near. The second bomb was dropped on Nagasaki on 9 August and Russia declared war the same day. On 14 August *Torsk*, in the Sea of Japan, sank two *kaibokans* (*Coast Defense Vessels No. 13* and *No. 47*). These were the last Japanese ships to be sunk by a U.S. submarine.

Japan Surrenders

When the first atomic bomb fell on Hiroshima it was apparent that further Japanese resistance was national suicide. The nature of an atomic bomb was known to esoteric Japanese. They were working hard to develop one of their own and the dream of destroying their enemies "at one stroke" with an atomic bomb had replaced the hope of a victorious fleet engagement as a miraculous means to win the war. Yet even with the catastrophic appearance of the ultimate weapon in the hands of their enemy, the Japanese Supreme Council for the Direction of the War and the Japanese Cabinet could not agree to sue for peace. They met again with the Emperor as the Imperial Council, after the second bomb had dropped on Nagasaki, and over the protests of Generals Anami and Umezu and Admiral Toyoda, decided to accept the Potsdam declaration. A rebellion to rescue the Emperor from his "evil advisers" and suppress his peace message to the Japanese people flared briefly in the Army, but was quickly defeated. Hostilities ended on 15 August.

The Japanese have an epigram to the effect that brilliant strategy may win renown but the side that makes fewer mistakes will win the war. Neither side lacked courage, endurance, devotion, or skill, and the mistakes were plentiful in both American and Japanese submarine warfare. In the final analysis, however, the fatal Japanese mistake was the initial decision to start the war. For the deliberate resort to war as an instrument to support their national policy of expansion, the Japanese earned and deserved the defeat that was eventually administered.

Bibliography

GENERAL NARRATIVE OF THE WAR

The principle source of the general narrative of the war is derived from Morison, Samuel Eliot, *History of United States Naval Operations in World War II*. Boston: Little, Brown and Company, 1947–62.

This fifteen-volume history is unequaled for accuracy, thoroughness, and readability.

Other U.S. publications used as sources of the general narrative of the war are:

Bryan, J., III, *Admiral Halsey's Story*. New York: McGraw-Hill Book Co., 1947.

Compton, Karl, *If the Atomic Bomb Had Not Been Used. The Atlantic Monthly*, December 1946.

Karig, Walter, *Battle Report* (five volumes). New York: Rinehart & Company, 1944–52.

King, E. J. and Whitehall, William, *Fleet Admiral King—A Naval Record*. New York: W. W. Norton & Company, 1952.

Leahy, William D., *I Was There*. New York: McGraw-Hill Book Co., 1950.

Morison, Samuel Eliot, *Strategy and Compromise*. Boston: Little, Brown and Company, 1958.

Newcomb, Richard F., *Abandon Ship!* New York: Henry Holt & Co., 1958.

Potter, E. B. and Fredland, J. R., *The United States and World Sea Power*. Englewood Cliffs, N.J.: Prentice-Hall, 1955.

Tuleja, Thaddeus, *Climax at Midway*. New York: W. W. Norton & Company, 1960.

U.S. SUBMARINE OPERATIONS

Principle source of information on U.S. submarine operations is Commander Submarines Pacific, *History of Submarine Operations in World War II*, 1946 and *History of Submarine Commands in World War II*, 1946. Roscoe, Theodore, *United States Submarine Operations in World War II*, U. S. Naval Institute, 1949, has drawn heavily on the same sources and is more readily available, more efficiently arranged, and generally more readable. Primary source of much of the basic information is the individual submarine patrol reports. Lockwood, Charles A., *Sink 'em All*, New York: E. P. Dutton & Co., 1951, has the best information on submarine command decisions.

Many excellent individual accounts of submarine operations have been published, including:

Barnes, Robert H., *United States Submarines*. New Haven, Conn.: H. F. Morse Associates, 1946.

Beach, Edward L., *Submarine!* New York: Henry Holt & Co., 1952.

Frank, Gerold and Horan, James D., *U.S.S. SEAWOLF*. New York: G. P. Putnam's Sons, 1945.

Grider, George, *War Fish*. Boston: Little, Brown and Company, 1958.

Pratt, Fletcher, *The Torpedoes that Failed. The Atlantic Monthly*, July 1950.

Sterling, Forest J., *Wake of the Wahoo*. Philadelphia: Chilton Company, 1960.

Trumbull, Robert, *SILVERSIDES*. New York: Henry Holt & Company, 1945.

BRITISH AND DUTCH SUBMARINE OPERATIONS

Kroese, A., *The Dutch Navy at War*. London: George Allen & Unwin, 1945.

Lipscomb, F. W., *The British Submarine*. New York: The Macmillan Company, 1954.

Roskill, Stephen W., *The War at Sea 1939–1945* (three volumes). H. M. Stationery Office, 1954–61.

Young, Edward, *Undersea Patrol*. New York: McGraw-Hill Book Co., 1953.

JAPANESE SUBMARINE OPERATIONS

The principle source of information on Japanese Submarine Operations is a series of monographs prepared by Tatsuwaka Shibuyo, for Japanese Research Division, Military History Section, General Headquarters, Far East Command, 1954, as follows:

Outline of Submarine Operations in First Phase Operation. Japanese Monograph 102.

Submarine Operations in Second Phase Operation, Part 1 and Part 2. Japanese Monographs 110 and 111.*

Submarine Operations in Third Phase Operation, Parts 1, 2, 3, 4, 5. Japanese Monographs 163,* 171,* and 184 (three parts). (Monographs marked * have not been translated into English.)

The Imperial Japanese Navy in World War II, Military History Section, General Headquarters, Far East Command, 1952, is the best source of information on Japanese ships sunk and damaged. Both this publication and the submarine operations monographs listed above are frequently in disagreement with U.S. sources, particularly in regard to identification of Japanese submarine losses.

ADDITIONAL SOURCES FOR JAPANESE OPERATIONS

Fuchida, Mitsuo and Okumiya, Masatake, *Midway, The Battle that Doomed Japan*. Annapolis: U. S. Naval Institute, 1955.

Hashimoto, Mochitsura, *Sunk*. New York: Henry Holt & Co., 1954.

Hayashi, Saburo and Coox, Alvin, *Kogun*. Quantico, Va.: Marine Corps Association, 1959.

Ito, Masanori and Pineau, Roger, *The End of the Imperial Japanese Navy*. London: George Weidenfeld & Nicolson, 1963.

Kuwahara, Yasuo and Alfred, Gordon T., *Kamikaze*. New York: Ballantine Books, 1957.

Lord Russel of Liverpool, *The Knights of Bushido*. New York: E. P. Dutton & Co., 1958.

Okumiya, Masatake and Horikoshi, Jiro, *Zero!* New York: E. P. Dutton & Co., 1956.

Operational History of Naval Communications, December 1941–August 1945, prepared by Military History Section, Headquarters Army Forces, Far East, Japanese Monograph 118.

Shizuo Fukue, *Japanese Naval Vessels at the End of the War*. Administrative Division, Second Demobilization Bureau.

Yokota, Yutaka, *The Kaiten Weapon*. New York: Ballantine Books, 1962.

ANTI-SUBMARINE OPERATIONS

Hara, Tameichi, *Japanese Destroyer Captain*. New York: Ballantine Books, 1961.

Roscoe, Theodore, *United States Destroyer Operations in World War II*. Annapolis: U. S. Naval Institute, 1953.

MINE WARFARE

Lott, Arnold, *Most Dangerous Sea*. Annapolis: U. S. Naval Institute, 1959.

U. S. NAVY AND STRATEGIC BOMBING SURVEY PUBLICATIONS

Campaigns of the Pacific War, U. S. Strategic Bombing Survey, Pacific, 1946.

Effects of Air Attack on Japanese Urban Economy, Summary Report, U. S. Strategic Bombing Survey, 1946.

Interrogations of Japanese Officials (two volumes), U. S. Strategic Bombing Survey, Pacific, 1946.

Japanese Merchant Shipbuilding, U. S. Strategic Bombing Survey, 1947.

Japanese Naval and Merchant Shipping Losses During World War II from

All Causes, Joint Army-Navy Assessment Committee, U. S. Government Printing Office, 1947.

Japanese Naval Shipbuilding, U. S. Strategic Bombing Survey, 1946.

United States Navy Chronology, World War II, Naval History Division, Office of Chief of Naval Operations, U. S. Government Printing Office, 1955.

United States Submarine Losses, World War II, Naval History Division, Office of Chief of Naval Operations, U. S. Government Printing Office, 1963.

War against Japanese Transportation, U. S. Strategic Bombing Survey, 1947.

U. S. NAVAL INSTITUTE *PROCEEDINGS* (in chronological order)

Layton, Edwin T., *Rendezvous in Reverse,* May 1952.

Oi, Atushi, *Why Japan's Anti-Submarine Warfare Failed,* June 1952.

Fukaya, Hajime, *Three Japanese Submarine Developments,* August 1952.

Fukudome, Shigeri, *Strategic Aspects of the Battle off Formosa,* December 1952.

Pineau, Roger, *Spirit of the Divine Wind,* November 1958.

Torisa, Kennosuke and Chihaya, Masataka, *Japanese Submarine Tactics,* February 1961.

Fujita, Nobuo and Harrington, Joseph D., *I Bombed the USA,* June 1961.

Saville, Allison, *German Submarines in the Far East,* August 1961.

Herzog, Bodo and Saville, Allison, *Top Submarines in Two World Wars,* September 1961.

Yokota, Yutaka and Harrington, Joseph D., *Japan's Human Torpedo,* January 1962.

Lowry, George, *L-16 Mystery No Longer,* January 1963.

Nigel, J. G., *British Submarines in World War II,* March 1963.

Tanabe, Y., *I Sank the Yorktown at Midway,* May 1963.

Lemieux, C. N., *L-16 Sinking, "No Mistake Just Dirty Work,"* June 1963.

INDEX AND GLOSSARY

*—submarine lost; ↓—ship sunk by submarine; c.o.—commanding officer. *See* p. xi, "Special Procedures Used in the Index and Glossary."

ABDA, Amer., Br., Du., Aust. alliance, 72
Abe, Koso, 166
Abele, Mannert, L., c.o. *Grunion*, 154
Abemama, Gilbert Is., 263, 266–67, 280
Ackerman, Edward, c.o. *Kete*, 442
ACM, auxiliary minelayer
Adak, Aleutian Is., 164, 216
Advance Expeditionary Force, Japanese submarine task force, 52, 133, 162, 175, 375
AE, ammunition ship
↓ *Agano* (CL), ↓ by *Skate*, 294
A-Go Operation, Japanese counter-attack, 323, 329, 332, 350
AH, hospital ship
Ainsworth, Walden L., task force comdr., 217, 218
Air Flotilla 901, Japanese anti-submarine task group, 276, 328, 357, 378, 382
Airsols, Aircraft Solomon Islands, allied air task force, 256, 283, 294
AK, cargo ship
Akagi (CV), 56, 132; sunk, 141
↓ *Akigumo* (DD), ↓ by *Redfin*, 317
↓ *Akikaze* (DD), ↓ by *Pintado*, 401
Albacore (SS-218), ↓ *Tenryu*, 190; ↓ *Oshio*, 205, 258; ↓ *Sazanami*, 284; ↓ *Taiho* 340–41; *by mine, 408
Aleutians, 110, 132, 152, 164, 226, 232
Alhena (AK-26), torpedoed by *I-4*, 168
Alston, Agustus, c.o. *Pickerel*, 221
AM, AMc, minesweeper, coastal minesweeper
Amatsukaze (DD), 75, 82; torp. by *Redfin*, 286
Amberjack (SS-219), 176; *by *Hiyodori*, 204
Ambruster, Stephen H., c.o. *Tambor*, 156
Anderson, William L., c.o. *Thresher*, 107
Andrew, B. J. (Br.), c.o. *Subtle*, 455
Andrews, Charles H., c.o. *Gurnard*, 257, 321
Angle on the bow, angle between target's course and line of sight to the submarine, 11
Angler (SS-240), 353, 385, 420–23
Antares (AKS-3), 450
Anti-submarine warfare, Japanese, 54, 98, 108, 195, 273; improvements, 314, 328, 357, 401
Anti-submarine warfare, U.S., 51, 330, 392, 474

Anzio (CVE-57), *RO-43, *I-368, 440; *I-361, 450, 473–74
AD, tanker
Aoba (CA), 383, 385
AP transports, APD-high speed, APV-aircraft transports
Apogon (SS-308), 263, 303, 355
↓ *Arare* (DD), ↓ by *Growler*, 355
↓ *Arcata* (U. S. Army transport), ↓ by *I-7*, 154
Archerfish (SS-311), 306; ↓ CDV No. 24, 345; ↓ *Shinano* (CV), 406
Ardent (AM-340), *I-12, 413
Argonaut (APS-1), 37, 39, 51, 59, 164; *by surface escorts, 195
Ariizumi, Tatsunosuke, c.o. *I-8*; c.o. *I-401*, 473
Arunta (DD) (Aust.), *RO-33, 162
AS, submarine tender
↓ *Asahi* (AR), ↓ by *Salmon*, 126
↓ *Asakaze*(DD), ↓ by *Haddo*, 361
↓ *Asama Maru*, 303; ↓ by *Atule*, 401
↓ *Asanagi* (DD), ↓ by *Pollock*, 335
↓ *Ashigara* (CA), 415; ↓ by *Trenchant*, 455
↓ *Ashizuri* (AD), ↓ by *Puffer*, 334
Ashley, James H., c.o. *Seadragon*, 381; c.o. *Aspro*, 466
Asiatic Submarines, 46, 49, 63, 68, 72, 86
Aspro (SS-309), 294; ↓ *I-43*, 297, 322, 436, 466
↓ *Atago* (CA), ↓ by *Darter*, 384
Atomic bomb, 478, 481
Attu, Aleutian Is., 137, 148, 202, 216, 226
Atule (SS-403), 388; ↓ *Asama Maru*, 401, 436
Austin, Marshall H., c.o. *Redfin*, 317, 336
Awa Maru, cartel ship, 456

B-29 attacks, 406, 419, 438, 444, 459
Bach Kolling, J. W. (Du.), c.o. *O-19*, 73
Bacon, Barton E., c.o. *Pickerel*, 73
Balabac Strait, between Borneo and Palawan, 62, 322, 358, 382, 424
Balao (SS-285), 299, 436, 442
Balikpapan, eastern Borneo, 73, 75
Bang (SS-385), 325, 340, 344, 345, 355, 446
↓ *Bangkok Maru* (XCL), ↓ by *Pollock*, 230
Bangust (DE-739), *RO-42, 333
Banister, Alan B., c.o. *Sawfish*, 349
Barb (SS-220), 247, 324, 345, 363; ↓ *Unyo*, 367, 403, 434–35; ↓ CDV 112, 464
Barbel (SS-316), 362; *by aircraft, 424
Barr, Eric L., c.o. *Bluegill*, 318, 425

Bashaw (SS-241), 306, 425
Baskett, Thomas S., c.o. *Tautog*, 324; c.o. *Tench*, 458
Bass, Raymond H., c.o. *Plunger*, 228, 239, 245; c.o. *Runner*, 466
Batfish (SS-310), ↓ *Samidare*, 368, 382; ↓ *RO-112*, ↓ *RO-113*, ↓ *RO-115*, 428
Bawean Island, north of Surabaya, 80
Baya (SS-318), 425, 454
BB, battleship
Bear Pit, submarine operating area, 372, 374, 375
Beckley, (Br.), c.o. *Templar*, 285
Becuna (SS-319), 417, 425
Beeman, Arthur C., CPhM., 204
Bell, David B., c.o. *Pargo*, 425
Bennett, Carter L., c.o. *Permit*, 289; c.o. *Sea Owl*, 451
Bennington, L. W. A., (Br.), c.o. *Tally Ho*, 285
Benson, Roy S., c.o. *Trigger*, 191, 195, 215, 231
Benten Bana, cape on northeast Honshu, 172
Bergall (SS-320), torp. *Myoko*, 419, 425, 453
Berthrong, Raymond, c.o. *Cero*, 458
Besuga (SS-321), torp. *Suzutsuki*, 378, 380, 426; ↓ *Minesweeper No. 12*, 453; ↓ *U-183*, 456
Biak, northwest New Guinea, 323, 332
Billfish (SS-286), 259
Bismarck Sea, 209; battle of, 213, 258
Blackfin (SS-322), ↓ *Shigure*, 425
Blackfish (SS-221), 284, 306, 391, 393
Blair, Leon N., Blair's Blasters, 326
Blakely, Edward N., c.o. *Shark*, 326, 393
Blanchard, James W., c.o. *Albacore*, 284, 341
Blenny (SS-324), 417, 424, 468
Blower (SS-325), 425, 478
Blueback (SS-326), 455
Bluefish (SS-222), ↓ *Sanae*, 259, 322, 358; ↓ *I-351*, 478
Bluegill (SS-242), ↓ *Yubari*, 318, 425
Boarfish (SS-327), 424
Bole, John A., c.o. *Amberjack*, 176, 204
Bombardment by Japanese submarines, 16, 59, 95–96, 145, 148, 175, 206
Bombardment by U.S. submarines, 80, 165, 240, 267, 464
Bombay Shoal, Palawan Passage, 385
Bonaventure (AS) (Br.), 469
Bonefish (SS-223), 245, 259; ↓ *Inazuma*, 323, 460; *by surface vessels, 461
Bonin Islands, Ogasawara Gunto, 352, 362, 438
Bonin, Robert A., c.o. *Gudgeon*, 316
Bontier, Albert M., c.o. *Seawolf*, 370, 376
Bougainville, Solomon Is., 162, 243, 280
Bourland, Joseph H., c.o. *Runner*, 232
Bowfin (SS-287), 245, 259, 286, 311, 458, 461

Boyle, Francis D., c.o. *Charr*, 453
↓ *Brazil Maru*, ↓ by *Greenling*, 156
Bream (SS-243), 385, 399, 453
Bridson, G. (N.Z.), c.o. *Kiwi*, 206
Brindupke, Charles F., c.o. *Tullibee*, 306
Brinker, Robert M., c.o. *Grayling*, 245
Brisbane submarines, U.S. submarine base east Australia, Task Force No. 72, 102; Christie, 110, 112, 114, 125, 156, 169, 176; Fife, 184, 205, 212, 214, 217; declines, 257, 284, 298; Haines, 304
Broach, John C., c.o. *Hake*, 299, 332
Brockman, William H., c.o. *Nautilus*, 138–42, 149, 165
Brown, Charles D., c.o. *Razorback*, 416
Brown, Francis E., c.o. S-39, 158; c.o. S-44, 270
Brown, George E., acting c.o. *Sculpin*, 265
Brunei, northwest Borneo, 380, 382
Bruton, Henry C., c.o. *Greenling*, 117, 128, 156
Buchanan (DD-484), *RO-37*, 284
Bugara (SS-331), 468, 469
Buin, Bougainville, 179, 183, 221, 268
Buka, Solomon Is., 213, 256
Bulkeley, R. G., (Br.), c.o. *Statesman*, 455
Bullhead (SS-332), *by aircraft, 471
Buna, eastern New Guinea, 155, 160, 185, 192
Burden R. Hastings (DE-19), *RO-44*, 346
Bureau of Ordnance, Navy Department, 33, 40, 68, 87, 114, 150, 237, 245, 246, 286
Burlingame, Creed C., c.o. *Silversides*, 129
Burrfish (SS-312), 294, 371, 407
Bushido, Code of Chivalry in feudal Japan, 44
Bussemaker, A. J., (Du.), c.o. *O-16*, 70

CA, heavy cruiser
Cachalot (SS-170), 51, 90
Callaghan, Daniel J., task force comdr., 179
Campbell, Jack G., c.o. S-28, 356
Campbell, James H., c.o. *Blower*, 425
Camranh Bay, Indo-China, 49, 77, 79, 95, 423
Canopus (AS-9), 33, 49, 64, 69
Cape Bojeador, northwest Luzon, 359
Cape Bolinao, west Luzon, 23, 33
Cape Calavite, northwest Mindoro, 359
Cape Engaño, northeast Luzon, battle of, 388
Cape Esperance, Guadalcanal, battle of, 173, 183, 208
Cape Gloucester, west New Guinea, 280

Capelin (SS-289), *missing after 17 Nov. '43, 270

Cape St. George, New Ireland, battle of, 256

Capitaine (SS-336), 471

Carde, Freeland H., c.o. *Whale*, 466

Carlson's Raiders, 164, 265

Carpender, Arthur S., Comdr. Southwest Pacific Force Sept. '42–Feb. '43; Comdr. Seventh Fleet Feb. '43–Nov. '43, 212

Casco (APV-12), torp. by *RO-61*, 164, 241

Case (DD-370), 413

Cassedy, Hiram, c.o. *Searaven*, 109

Catchpole Operation, Eniwetok Feb. '44, 293

Catlow, A. A., (Br.), c.o. *Trump*, 468

Cavalla (SS-244), 338; ↓ *Shokaku*, 343, 352; ↓ *Shimotsuki*, 401

Cebu, P. I., Midget submarine base, 388, 398, 429

Cero (SS-225), 261, 458

Chandler (DMS-9), *I-185*, 347

Chappell, Lucius H., c.o. *Sculpin*, 73

Chapple, Wreford G., c.o. *S-38*, 19–33, 69; c.o. *Permit*, 239, 371; c.o. *Bream*, 385

Charr (SS-328), 425; ↓ *Isuzu*, 453

Charrette (DD-581), *I-175*, 296

Chester (CA-27), torp. by *I-176*, 175

Chicago (CA-29), 130; sunk, 206

↓ *Chidori* (TB), ↓ by *Tilefish*, 417

Chitose (CV), 161, 323

Chiyoda (AV), 132

Christie, Ralph W., comdr. submarines at Brisbane Apr. '42–Dec. '42, 110, 111, 125, 126, 184; Comsubsowespac Mar. '43–Dec. '44, 195, 212, 238, 260, 286, 324, 334, 353, 358, 376, 381, 416

Christmas Island, South of Java, 103, 202

Chub (SS-329), 455

↓ *Chuyo* (CVE), ↓ by *Sailfish*, 277

Cincaf, C-in-C Asiatic Fleet, Hart, until 6 Feb. '42, 45, 68, 72

Cincpac, C-in-C Pacific Fleet, 45; Nimitz, 31 Dec. '41–2 Sept. '45, 62, 111, 115, 135, 236, 316, 330, 388

Cincpoa, C-in-C Pacific Ocean Area, Nimitz, 8 May '42–2 Sept. '45, 111

Cincsowespac, C-in-C Southwest Pacific Area, MacArthur, 18 Apr. '42–2 Sept. '45, 111

Cisco (SS-290), *missing after 19 Sept. '43, 245

CL, light cruiser

Claggett, Bladen D., c.o. *Dace*, 294, 304, 382

Clarabut, (Br.), c.o. *Stygian*, 455

Clarey, Bernard A., 176; c.o. *Pintado*, 326, 362, 388, 401, 403

Clark, Albert H., c.o. *Trout*, 303

Clark, Charles R., c.o. *Sennet*, 464

Clark, James S., c.o. *Golet*, 345

Clementson, Merrill K., c.o. *Snapper*, 249

Close, Robert H., c.o. *Pilotfish*, 326

CM, minelayer

Coast Defense Vessels (DE) Japanese escort vessels about 800 tons, identified only by number, 23 were sunk by submarines. ↓ *No. 13*, by *Torsk*, 481; *No. 22*, damaged by *Salmon*, 395; ↓ *No. 24*, by *Archerfish*, 345; ↓ *No. 28*, by *Blenny*, 417; ↓ *No. 31*, by *Tirante*, 458; ↓ *No. 47*, by *Torsk*, 481; ↓ *No. 64*, by *Pipefish*, 417; ↓ *No. 112*, by *Barb*, 464

Coastwatchers, 156, 159, 202, 243, 325, 358; Japanese, 430; naval group China, 435

Cod (SS-224), 299, 358, 468

Coe, James W., c.o. *S-39*, 102; c.o. *Skipjack*, 125; c.o. *Cisco*, 245

Cole, Cyrus C., c.o. *Balao*, 299, 445

Combined Fleet, Japanese main battle fleet, Yamamoto, until 18 Apr. '43, 92, 106, 108, 131, 160, 195, 220; Koga, 18 Apr. '43–31 Mar. '44, 221, 231, 248, 304, 306; Toyoda, after 5 May '44, 308, 320, 328, 357, 392, 437, 449

Command changes, U.S., 45, 125, 184, 193, 212, 416

Commander, U. S. Fifth Fleet, Spruance, 5 Aug. '43–2 Sept. '45

Commander, U. S. Seventh Fleet, Carpender, 19 Feb. '43–Nov. '43; Kinkaid, Nov. '43–Sept. '45

Commander U. S. Third Fleet, Halsey, 15 Mar. '43–2 Sept. '45

Comsopac, Commander South Pacific, Ghormley, June '42–Oct. '42, 111; Halsey, Oct. '42–Mar. '43, 174, 184, 205; Newton, June '44–Mar. '45

Comsubaf, Commander Submarines Asiatic Fleet, Wilkes, Dec. '41–Feb. '42, 22, 49, 68, 72, 81

Comsubpac, Commander Submarines Pacific, Withers, Dec. '41–May '42, 50, 62, 91, 105, 111, 114, 118; English, May '42–Jan. '43, 125, 135, 150, 190; Brown, Jan. '43–Feb. '43; Lockwood, Feb. '43–Sept. '45, 193, 212, 236, 246, 281, 301, 316, 336, 372, 455

Comsubsowespac, Commander Submarines Southwest Pacific (comdr. submarines at Fremantle and also administrative command of submarines at Brisbane), Wilkes, Feb. '42–May '42; Lockwood, May '42–Feb. '43; McCann, Feb. '43–Mar. '43; Christie, Mar. '43–Dec. '44; Fife, Dec. '44–Aug. '45, 125, 186, 193, 222, 312, 416. *See also* Brisbane, Fremantle

Condor, (AMc-14), 56

Conklin (DE-439), *I-37, 412; *I-48, 431

Connaway, Fred, c.o. *Sculpin*, 264–65

Connole, David R., c.o. *Trigger*, 442

Convoy College, Luzon Strait's area, 352, 354, 358, 363, 381, 393, 401, 416, 445, 452. *See also* Devil's Sea

Convoys, Japanese, Matsu (Pine), 302, 304, 314; Take (Bamboo), 317; No. 3530, 327; Hi-71, 360, 363

Conyngham (DD-371), 430

Coordinated attack group, 261. *See* Wolf Pack

Coral Sea, 108; battle of, 113

Corbesier (DE-438), *I-48, 431

Corregidor, at entrance to Manila Bay, 19, 69, 85, 87, 109, 114

↓ *Corvina* (SS-226), 263; ↓ *by I-176, 270

Coumou, H. C. J. (Du.), c.o. K-12, 70

Coye, John S., c.o. *Silversides*, 257, 326

Craig, Edward C., 43

Craig, John R., c.o. *Grampus*, 213

Crevalle (SS-291), 260, 322, 353, 460

Croaker (SS-246), ↓ *Nagara*, 362, 393

Cromwell, John P., wolf pack comdr., 264–65

Crowley, John D., c.o. *Flier*, 358

Cutter, Slade D., c.o. *Seahorse*, 314, 338

Cuttlefish (SS-171), 51, 90, 117, 133, 136–37, 147

CV, aircraft carrier; CVL, light aircraft carrier; CVE, escort aircraft carrier

Cynthia Olsen, merchant vessel, sunk by I-26, 57

Dace (SS-247), 294, 304, 316, 382; ↓ *Maya*, 384

Daigo, Tadashige, Comdr. Sixth Fleet after 10 May '45, 451

Dairen, Manchuria, 215, 472, 480

Darter (SS-229), 294; torp. *Takao*, ↓ *Atago*, 384; *stranded, 385

Darwin, northwest Aust., 69, 74, 76, 77, 95, 312

Daspit, Lawrence R., c.o. *Tinosa*, 240–42, 247

Davao, Mindanao, 63, 73, 375

Davenport, Roy M., c.o. *Trepang*, 416

David W. Taylor (DD-551), *I-10, 347

Davis, James W., c.o. *Raton*, 257, 324

DD, destroyer

DE, escort destroyer, frigate kaibokan

Dealey, Samuel D., c.o. *Harder*, 307, 309, 315, 334, 361

Decoy ships, Q-ships, 288, 382

↓ *Delhi Maru* (XPG), ↓ *by Swordfish*, 288

Dempsey, James C., c.o. S-37, 76; c.o. *Cod*, 299

DeTar, John L., c.o. *Tuna*, 105

Devil's Sea, Convoy College, 352, 369

Diego Suarez, Madagascar, 108

Diversion Attack Force, Japanese task force, 350, 387

DM, light minelayer, usually old DD

Dodge, Harry B., c.o. *Seal*, 289

Dolphin (SS-169), 51, 62, 89, 90

Donaho, Glynn R., c.o. *Picuda*, 363

Doolittle J. H., Colonel, Tokyo raid, 107, 127, 191

Doorman, Karel (Du.), Rear Admiral, 76, 77, 80

Dornin, Robert E., 2, 5; c.o. *Trigger*, 249

Dragonet (SS-293), 420

Drum (SS-228), 119; ↓ *Mizuho*, 120, 133; torp. *Ryuho*, 190, 210

Dry, Melvin H., c.o. *Searaven*, 289, 294

Dumaguete, South Negros, P.I., 430

Dumbo, air-sea rescue plane, 445, 465

Dutch Harbor, Aleutian Is., 50, 110, 126, 130, 153, 177, 226, 240

Dykers, Thomas M., c.o. *Jack*, 300, 320

Eastern Solomons, battle of, 161

Eaton (DD-510), *RO-101, 244

Ebert, Walter G., c.o. *Scamp*, 235, 284

Edge, Lawrence L., c.o. *Bonefish*, 460, 461

Edsall (DD-219), *I-124, 95

Ellet (DD-398), *RO-35 or I-20, 243

Ellice Islands, between Gilberts and Fiji, 251, 298

Empress Augusta Bay, Bougainville, 236; battle of, 255

England (DE-635), *I-16, *RO-104, *RO-105, *RO-106, *RO-108, *RO-116, 330–31

English (DD-696), 423

English, Robert H., Comsubpac May '42–Jan. '43, 125, 135, 137, 149, 150, 193

Eniwetok, northwest Marshalls, 202, 254, 289, 293, 298, 333, 346

Enright, Joseph F., c.o. *Archerfish*, 406

Enterprise (CV-6), ↓ *I-70, 58, 92; Doolittle raid, 107, 111, 134, 138, 161, 175, 344

↓ *Erimo* (AD) ↓ *by S-39*, 102

Escolar (SS-294), *missing after 17 Oct. '44, 393

Espiritu Santo, New Hebrides, 161, 168, 174, 243

Eta Jima, Japanese Naval Academy, 44, 53

Euryale (AS-22), 312

↓ *Eversole* (DE-404), ↓ *by I-45*, 391

Exmouth Gulf, western Australia, 259, 420

↓ *Extractor* (ARS-16), ↓ *by Guardfish*, 437

Fair (DE-35), *I-175, 296

Farmer, Claude S., c.o. *Thomas F. Nickel*, 475

Fenno, Frank W., c.o. *Trout,* 85; wolf, pack, 401

Ferrall, William E., c.o. *Seadragon,* 73, 154, 183

Fife, James, 69, comdr. Brisbane Dec. '41–Mar. '42, 184, 193, 212, 214, 257, 304; Comsubsowespac Dec. '44–Aug. '45, 416, 423, 452, 468

Fifth Air Force, U. S., 213, 254, 255, 258, 299, 322, 332, 370, 385, 397

Fifth Fleet, U. S., Spruance, Aug. '43–Sept. '45, 212, 293, 333, 341, 344, 372, 423, 442

Finback (SS-230), 165, 245, 340, 344, 467

Finnegan (DE-307), *I-370,* 440

Finschhafen, New Guinea, 110, 242, 254

First Phase, Japanese war plans, 52, 96, 101, 104, 106, 111

First Striking Force, Japanese task force, 379

Fitzgerald, John A., c.o. *Grenadier,* 223

Flasher (SS-240), ↓ *Tahure,* 317; ↓ *Oi,* 353; ↓ *Kishinami,* 416

Fleet Submarine, submarines with sufficient speed and endurance to operate with the battle fleet. American fleet submarines were named after fish. 2, 38

Fletcher (DD-445), *I-18,* 209

Fletcher, Frank J., U.S. task force comdr., 90, 112, 157, 161, 162

Flier (SS-250), *mined, 358

Flintlock Operation, Kwajalein, 282, 289

Flounder (SS-251), ↓ *U-537,* 414

Fluckey, Eugene B., c.o. *Barb,* 324, 363, 434, 464

Flusser (DD-368), 430

Flying Fish (SS-229), 221, 337, 461

Foley, Robert J., c.o. *Gato,* 275, 294, 299

Foote, John J., c.o. *Threadfin,* 447

Forager Operation, Marianas

Forbes, George W., c.o. *Bluefish,* 478

Formosa, Taiwan, 371, 377, 422

Francis M. Robinson (DE-220), *RO-501,* 349

Fraser, I. E. (Br.), c.o. *XE-3,* 469

Frazier (DD-607), *I-9, 232; *I-35, 268

Fremantle, U.S. submarine base southwest Australia, 101, 102, 109. *See* Southwest Pacific Submarines

French Frigate Shoal, northwest Hawaii, 99, 108, 131

Fujita, Nobuo, 169

Fulp, James D., c.o. *Segundo,* 416

↓ *Fuyo* (DD), ↓ by *Puffer,* 281

Fyfe, John K., c.o. *Batfish,* 368, 382, 428

Gabilan (SS-252), 380, 423; torp. *Isuzu,* 453; lifeguard, 465

Galantin, Ignatius J., c.o. *Halibut,* 271, 314, 388, 401

Gallaher, Antone R., c.o. *Bang,* 325

Galvanic Operation, Gilbert Islands, 263

Gamble (DM-15), *I-123, 162

Gar (SS-206), 90, 105, 117, 177, 307, 372

Garrison, Malcom E., c.o. *Sand Lance,* 302, 304, 326

Gato (SS-212), 120, 243, 275, 294, 299, 372; lifeguard, 445

George (DE-697), 330

Germany, Japanese communications with, 108, 175, 349

Germershausen, William J., c.o. *Spadefish,* 460

Gilbert Islands, 90, 164, 250, 256; Operation Galvanic, 263

Gilmer (APD-11), *I-16, 348

Gilmore (DE-18), *I-180, 317

Gilmore, Howard W., c.o. *Growler,* 152, 203

Glenn, Paul E., c.o. *S-42,* 370

Golet (SS-361), *by surface vessel, 345

Gona, New Guinea 155

Goodenough I., southeast of New Guinea, 176

Grampus, 90, *missing after 12 Feb. '43, 213

Grand Escort Force, anti-submarine task force, Oikawa, Nov. '43–Aug. '44, 273, 276, 300, 302, 304, 311, 320, 326, 328; Nomura, after Aug. '44, 357, 368, 378, 423, 427, 436, 466, 461

Grant, James D., c.o. *Greenling,* 310, 371; c.o. *Toro,* 465

Grayback (SS-208), 90, 202, 213, 261; ↓ *Numukaze* 280; *by surface vessel, 303

Grayling (SS-209), 90, 91, 93, 147, 222; *missing after 19 Aug. '43, 245

Greenling (SS-213), 117, 128; ↓ *Brazil Maru,* 158, 202, 210, 214, 243, 371

Greenup, Francis A., c.o. *Hardhead,* 454

Greenwich Island, Kapingamaringi, between Solomons and Carolines, 176

Grenadier (SS-210), 90, 119; ↓ *Taiyo Maru,* 121, 150, 177; *by aircraft, 223

Grenfell, Elton W., c.o. *Gudgeon,* 1–18, 61, 93

Grider, George W., c.o. *Flasher,* 416

Gridley (DD-380), *I-54, 391

Griffin (AS-13), 110

Griffith, Walter T., c.o. *Bowfin,* 259

Gross, Royce L., c.o. *Halibut,* 191; c.o. *Seawolf,* 261; c.o. *Boarfish,* 424

Grouper (SS-214), 138, 202, 243, 245

Growler (SS-215), 149; ↓ *Arare,* 152, 163; damaged, 203, 255, 337, 345, 355, 363; ↓ *Shikinami,* ↓ *Hirato,* 366; *by surface vessels, 409

Gruner, William P., c.o. *Skate,* 294

Grunion (SS-216), ↓ *Subchasers No. 25* and 27; *missing after 30 July '42, 154

Guadalcanal, Solomon Is., 113, 155; Marines land, 156, 159, 167; battle of

Cape Esperance, 173, 177; battle of, 179; battle of Tassafaronga, 182; evacuation, 192, 206

Guam, Marianas Is., 304, 348, 351, 432, 438, 481

Guardfish (SS-217), 170; ↓ Patrol Boat No. 1, ↓ Hakaze, 196, 210, 243, 284; ↓ Umikaze, 289, 355; ↓ U.S.S. Extractor, 437

Guavina (SS-362), 424

*Gudgeon (SS-211), first patrol, 1–18; ↓ I-73, 18, 37, 38, 51, 61, 88, 90, 93, 96, 156, 176, 202, 215; ↓ Kamakura Maru, 223; *missing after 4 Apr. '44, 316

Guest (DD-472), *I-171, 284

Guitarro (SS-363), ↓ Kusagaki, 358, 360, 385, 399

Gunn, Frederick A., c.o. Scabbardfish, 414

Guns, S-boat guns, 21, 39; Triton, 127; Greenling, 128; Silversides, 129; Wahoo, 201, 216; Plunger, 229; British, 426, 468; Burt's Brooms, 407; Mac's Mops, 439

Gurnard (SS-254), 258; convoy Bamboo No. 1, 321; ↓ Tatekawa Maru, 323

HA, romaji for the third kana in the Japanese katakana syllabary. See Kana

HA class submarines, small Japanese submarines 320–370 tons, 375; HA-101, -102, -103, -104, -105, 452; HA-106, 434, 441; HA-107, -108, -109, 480; HA-111, 480; HA-200 class high-speed submarines, HA-201, -202, -203, -204, -205, -207, -208, -209, -210, 480

Hackleback (SS-295), 447

Haddo (SS-225), ↓ Sado, ↓ Asakaze, 361

Haddock (SS-231), 163; torp. Unyo, 286, 303, 388, 401

Hagberg, Oscar E., c.o. Albacore, 258

Haggard (DD-555), *RO-41, 441

Haggard (Br.), c.o. Truant, 78

Hailstone Operation, Truk, 293

Haines, John M., 165; Comtaskfor 72 (Brisbane) Mar. '44–Dec. '44, 304, 316

↓ Hakaze (DD), ↓ by Guardfish, 197

Hake (SS-256), 299; ↓ Kazagumo, 332, 361, 409

Halibut (SS-232), 191; torp. Junyo, 271, 286; ↓ Kamone, 314, 388; damaged by MAD planes, 401

Halmahera Island, 322, 370

Halsey, William F., task force comdr., 90, 92, 107, 134; Comsopac Oct. '42–Mar. '43, 174, 184, 212, 255, 330; Com. Third Fleet, Mar. '43–Sept. '45, 372, 374, 377, 380, 388, 407, 423, 463, 466

↓ Hammann (DD-412), ↓ by I-168, 145

Hammerhead (SS-364), 355; ↓ Yaku, 425, 454

Hammond, Douglas T., c.o. Guardfish, 437

Hara, Tameichi, c.o. Amatsukaze, 75, 82

Harada, c.o. I-17, 243

Harbin, Earl C., CMM, S-38, 31, 33

Harbin, Mike, gun's crew Silversides, 129

*Harder (SS-257), 307; lifeguard, 309; ↓ Ikazuchi, 315; ↓ Minazuki, ↓ Hayanami, ↓ Tanikaze, 334; ↓ Matsuwa, ↓ Hiburi, 361; *by surface vessels, 361

Hardhead (SS-365), ↓ Natori, 362, 409, 454

Harlfinger, Frederick J., c.o. Trigger, 314, 395

Harral, Brooks J., c.o. Ray, 323

Hart, Thomas C., C-in-C Asiatic Fleet until 4 Feb. '42, 19, 69, 72, 87

Hartman, Irwin S., c.o. S-41, 227

Haruna (BB), 64, 174, 344, 405

↓ Harusame (DD), ↓ by Wahoo, 198; sunk by bombers, 332

Hashimoto, Mochitsura, c.o. I-58, 432, 440, 448, 474

Haskins, Enrique D., c.o. Guitarro, 361, 385

Hatsukaze (DD), 82

↓ Hatsutaka (DM), *Lagarto, ↓ by Hawkbill, 454

Hawkbill (SS-366), ↓ Momo, 417, 424; ↓ Hatsutaka, 454

Hawes, Richard E., c.o. Pidgeon, 65

↓ Hayanami (DD), ↓ by Harder, 335

Hayasaki (AK), 203

Hazzard, William H., 76, c.o. Blenny, 424, 468

Heian Maru (AS), Sixth Fleet Flagship, sunk at Truk, 297

Helm (DD-388), *I-54, 391

Henderson, Charles M., c.o. Bluefish, 359

Henderson Field, Guadalcanal, 159, 161, 167, 174

↓ Henley (DD-391), ↓ by Japanese submarine, 254

Hensel, Karl G., c.o. Swordfish, 287

*Herring (SS-233), 292; ↓ Ishibaki, *by shore battery, 324

Hess, Franklin G., c.o. Angler, 353, 385

Hess, John B., c.o. Pomfret, 401, 439

Hezlet, A. R. (Br.), c.o. Trenchant, 414, 455

↓ Hiburi (DE), 360, ↓ by Harder, 361

↓ Hinode Maru No. 20 (AMC), ↓ by U.S. submarines, 365

↓ Hirato (DE), ↓ by Growler, 366

Hiryu (CV), 56, 61, 132, 142–43

Hiyo (CV), torp. by Trigger, 231, 344

↓ Hiyodori (TB), *Amberjack, 204; ↓ by Gunnel, 17 Nov. '44

Hoe (SS-258), 359, ↓ Shonan, 425

Hogan, Thomas W., c.o. *Bonefish*, 259, 323

↓ *Hokaze* (DD), ↓ by *Paddle*, 354

Holden, Richard, c.o. *Gato*, 445

Holland (AS-3), 49, 64, 69, 76, 438

Hollandia, north New Guinea, 304, 318, 431

Hollingsworth, John C., c.o. *Scamp*, 315, 409

Holt, Edward R., c.o. *Bullhead*, 471

Horace A. Bass (APD-124), *RO-109, 449

Hornet (CV-8), 107, 111, 134, 138, 168, 175

Hosogawa, Boshiro, comdr., Japanese Northern Force

Hottel, Martin P., c.o. *Cuttlefish*, 133, 137

Houston (CA-30), 76, 77, 80

Hudson (DD-475), *I-171, 284; *RO-49, 441

Hull, Jesse S., c.o. *Finback*, 164

Hurd, Kenneth C., c.o. *Seal*, 69, 79, 189

Hurt, David A., c.o. *Perch*, 81–85

Hyde, John M., c.o. *Bergall*, 419, 425

Hydeman, Earl T., c.o. *Sea Dog*, 458, 460

Hyuga (BB), 387, 423, 425

I, romaji for the first kana in the Japanese katakana syllabary. *See* Kana

I-class submarines, Japanese fleet submarines, 1000–3430 tons, 44

*I-1, 101, 176; *by *Kiwi* and *Moa*, 206

*I-2, 101, 174, 233; *by *Saufley*, 317

*I-3, 101; *by PT-59, 183

↓ *I-4, 101; torp. *Alhena*, 168; ↓ *by *Seadragon*, 184

*I-5, 101; *by *Wyman*, 348

*I-6, 58; torp. *Saratoga*, 95, 101, 217; *by *William C. Miller* and *Gilmer*, 348

*I-7, 59, 101; ↓ *Arcarta*, 154, 175; *by *Monaghan*, 233

*I-8, 206, 349; *by *Stockton* and *Morrison*, 441, 473

*I-9, 95, 99, 181, 220; *by *Frazier*, 323

*I-10, 107, 131, 333; *by *David W. Taylor* and *Riddle*, 347

*I-11, 168; *missing after 11 Jan. '44, 296

*I-12, 392; *by *Rockford* and *Ardent*, 413

*I-13, 472; *missing after 5 July '45, 473

I-14, 472

*I-15, 99; torp. *North Carolina*; ↓ *O'Brien*, 168; *by *Southard* or planes, 180 (*See* I-172)

*I-16, 54, 59, 107, 131, 180; *by *England*, 330

*I-17, 96, 162, 180; *by *Tui* and planes, 243

*I-18, 54, 96, 107, 131; *by *Fletcher* and planes, 208

*I-19, 99, 130; ↓ *Wasp*, 168, 181, 268; *by *Radford*, 268

*I-20, 54, 107, 131, 180; *by *Ellet* and *Saufley*, 243

*I-21, 109, 130, 148, 175, 181, 206; probably *by planes, missing after 27 Nov. '43, 268

*I-22, 54, 59, 108, 113, 130; *missing after 5 Oct. '42, 175

*I-23, 90; *missing after 14 Feb. '42, 96, 99

*I-24, 54, 96, 108, 113, 130, 148, 175, 180; *by PC-487, 232

*I-25, 95, 96, 101, 130, 148, 164; bombs Oregon, ↓ L-16, 169; *by *Patterson*, 243

*I-26, ↓ *Cynthia Olsen*, 58, 99, 158; torp. *Saratoga*, 162, 175, 180; ↓ *Juneau*, 181, 217, 348; *by *Richard M. Rowell*, 391

*I-27, 107, 130; *by *Paladin* and *Petard*, 285

↓ *I-28, 108, 113; ↓ *by *Tautog*, 116

↓ *I-29, 108, 113; ↓ *by *Sawfish*, 349, 367

*I-30, to Germany, 107; *by mine, 176, 349

*I-31, 181; *missing after 13 May '43, 226

*I-32, *by *Manlove* and PC-1135, 310

*I-33, *by training accident, 349

↓ *I-34, 227; ↓ *by *Taurus*, 268, 349

*I-35, 227; *by *Frazier* and *Meade*, 268

I-36, 254, 348, 412, 431, 440, 449

*I-37, *by *Conklin* and *McCoy Reynolds*, 412

*I-38, 310, 333, 347, 392; *by *Nicholas*, 412

*I-39, probably *by *Boyd*, missing after 25 Nov. '43, 268

*I-40, *missing after 22 Nov. '43, 268

*I-41, 348; torp. *Reno*, 392; probably *by *Anzio*, missing after 3 Nov. '44, 392

↓ *I-42, ↓ *by *Tunny*, 308

↓ *I-43, ↓ *by *Aspro*, 297

*I-44, 331, 390, 440; *by carrier planes, 448

*I-45, 348; ↓ *Eversole*, 391; *by *Whitehurst*, 392

*I-46, probably *by *Helm*, missing after 29 Oct. '44, 391

I-47, 412, 431, 448, 449, 473

*I-48, *by *Conklin*, *Corbesier*, and *Raby*, 431

*I-52, *sunk in Atlantic, 349

I-53 through I-75 were renumbered by adding 100 to their numbers on 20 May '42. *See* I-153 through I-175 for consolidated index. New I-52 through I-58 were built after 20 May '42

I-53, 392, 431; mined, 449; ↓ *Underhill*, 474

I-54, 348; *by *Helm* and *Gridley*, 391

I-55, 348; *by *Wyman*, 348

I-56, torp. *Santee*, 390, 431; *by U.S. destroyers, 448

I-58, kaitens, 432, 440, 448; ↓ *Indianapolis*, 474

I-121, 64, 95, 108, 131, 145, 162

↓ *I-122*, 95, 131, 180; ↓ *by *Skate*, 461

I-123, 62, 95, 131; *by *Gamble*, 162

I-124, 62; *by Aust. minesweepers *Deloraine*, *Lithgow*, and *Katoomba*, 95

Submarines *I-153* through *I-175* were numbered *I-53* through *I-75* until 20 May '42

I-153, as *I-53*, 95, 101

I-154, as *I-54*, 101

I-155, as *I-55*, 95, 101

I-156, as *I-56*, 95; as *I-156*, 480

I-157, as *I-57*, 95; as *I-157*, 233, 480

I-158, as *I-58*, 63, 95; as *I-158*, 480

I-159, as *I-59*, 95; as *I-159*, 480

I-160, as *I-60*, *by *Jupiter*, 95

I-162, as *I-62*, 95; as *I-162*, 480

↓ *I-164*, as *I-64*, 95; as *I-164*, ↓ *by *Triton*, 119

I-165, as *I-65*, 63, 95; as *I-165*, 207; *by planes, 450

↓ *I-166*, as *I-66*, 70, 95; as *I-166*, 206; ↓ *by *Telemachus*, 349

↓ *I-168*, 133, 144, 145; ↓ *Yorktown*, ↓ *Hammann*, 146; ↓ *by *Scamp*, 235

I-169, as *I-69*, 58, 96; as *I-169*, 276; *by Truk air raid, 317

I-170, as *I-70*, *by *Enterprise*, 58

I-171, as *I-71*, 57; as *I-171*, 131; *by *Guest* and *Hudson*, 284

I-172, as *I-72*, 57; as *I-172*, *by *Southard* or planes, 181

↓ *I-173*, as *I-73*, ↓ *by *Gudgeon*, 18, 96

I-174, 131, 243, 268; *by *MacDonough* and *Stephen Potter*, 317

I-175, 131, 185; ↓ *Liscomb Bay*, 265; *by *Charrette* and *Fair*, 296

I-176, torp. *Chester*, 175, 217; ↓ *Corvina*, 270, 276; *by U.S. destroyers, 330

I-177, 243, 257, 283, 317; *by *Samuel S. Miles*, 375

I-178, *by SC-669, 235

I-179, *by accident, 14 July '43

I-180, *by Gilmore, 317

I-181, *by U.S. destroyers, 284

I-182, *missing after 22 Aug. '43, 244

↓ *I-183*, ↓ *by *Pogy*, 313

I-184, *by carrier planes, 347

I-185, 333, *by *Newcomb* and *Chandler*, 347

I-200 class, high-speed submarines, *I-201*, -202, -203, 480

↓ *I-351*, submarine tanker 2650 tons, 451; ↓ *by *Bluefish*, 478

I-361 to -373 class, transportation submarines without torpedo tubes, 1470 to 1660 tons, 374, 413, 433

I-361, *by *Anzio*, 450

I-362, *missing after Jan. '45, 433

I-363, 450, 473

↓ *I-364*, ↓ *by *Sea Devil*, 375

↓ *I-365*, ↓ *by *Scabbardfish*, 414

I-366, 450, 476

I-367, 450, 473

I-368, *by *Anzio*, 440

I-369, 451

I-370, *by *Finnegan*, 440

↓ *I-371*, ↓ *by *Lagarto*, 433

I-372, 428, 451; *by carrier planes, 478

↓ *I-373*, ↓ *by *Spikefish*, 479

I-400 class, large plane carriers, 3430 tons, 485

I-400, -401, 472

I-402, 478

I-500 class, ex-German, *I-501* to -506, 456

Icefish (SS-367), 381

Icenhower, Joseph B., c.o. *Jallao*, 388, 464

↓ *Ikazuchi* (DD), ↓ by *Harder*, 315

↓ *Iki* (DE), ↓ by *Raton*, 324

↓ *Inazuma* (DD), ↓ by *Bonefish*, 323

↓ *Indianapolis* (CA-35), ↓ by *I-58*, 475

Indispensable Reef, south of Rennell I., 180

Indispensable Strait, between Santa Isabel and Florida Is., 159, 180

Ironbottom Sound, between Savo and Guadalcanal, 175, 177, 182, 206

Irvin, William D., c.o. *Nautilus*, 263, 266

Ise (BB), 387, 423, 425

↓ *Ishigaki* (DE), ↓ by *Herring*, 325

Ishikawa, Nobuo, c.o. *I-15*, 168

↓ *Isonami* (DD), ↓ by *Tautog*, 222

↓ *Isuzu* (CL), 232, 280, 388; ↓ by *Charr* and *Gabilan*, 453

↓ *Itsutshima* (CM), ↓ by *Zwaardvisch*, 393

Iwo Jima, Volcano Islands, 345, 436, 438, 440

Jack (SS-259), 300, 320

Jacobs, Tyrrell Dwight, c.o. *Sargo*, 63–68

Jallao (SS-368), ↓ *Tama*, 388, 401, 436, 464

Jaluit, Marshall Is., 89, 229, 263, 283

Janney, Frederick E., c.o. *Hackleback*, 447

Japan, Sea of, 237; La Pérouse, 239, 245, 269; Tsushima, 459, 464, 481

Jarman, L. J. (Du.), c.o. *K-16*, 70

Jarvis, Benjamin C., c.o. *Baya*, 425

Jay, R. L. (Br.), c.o. *Tiptoe*, 468

Jensen, Marvin J., c.o. *Puffer*, 274

Joint Intelligence Center (JICPOA), 239, 263, 282, 291, 345, 409, 459, 474

Jones, J. L. Capt., USMC, 267

Jukes, Herbert L., c.o. S-27, 149

↓ *Juneau* (*CL-52*), ↓ by *I-26*, 181

Junyo (CVE), 175; torp. by *Halibut*, 271; torp. by *Sea Devil* and *Redfish*, 418

Jupiter (DD) (Br.), *I-60*, 95

K class submarines. See also Submarines, Dutch

K-7, *air raid on Surabaya, 77

K-10, *scuttled, 79

K-11, 69

K-12, 69

K-13, 69; *scuttled, 79

K-14, 70, 352

K-15, 352

K-16, ↓ *Sagiri*, *by surface ships, 70

K-17, *missing after 16 Dec. '41, 70

K-18, 75; *scuttled, 79

Kaga (CV), 56, 102, 105, 132, 141; *Nautilus* torp., 143

Kaibokan, coast defense vessel, escort vessel, anti-submarine ship about 800 tons, 248, 273, 276, 357

Kaiten, suicide piloted torpedo, Kikusui, 411–12; Kongo, 431; Chihaya, Shimbu, 440; 446; Temmu, 449–51; Tamon, 473; Kyushu, 478

Kajioka, S., convoy commander, 319

↓ *Kako* (CA), ↓ by S-44, 158

Kalaw, Maximo M., Philippine guerrilla, 399

↓ *Kamakura Maru* (AP), ↓ by *Gudgeon*, 223

Kamikaze, suicide bombers, 389, 397, 422, 440, 446, 466, 478

Kamimoto, Nobuo, c.o. *I-37*, 412

↓ *Kamogawa Maru* (APV), ↓ by *Sailfish*, 102

↓ *Kamone* (ACM), ↓ by *Halibut*, 314

Kana, Japanese phonetic syllabary of, 48; characters, 302

Kanji, Chinese ideographs used in Japanese writing, 348, 411

↓ *Karatsu* (PG) (ex U.S.S. *Luzon*), ↓ by *Narwhal*, 299

Karimata Strait, between Borneo and Sumatra, 77, 353, 359, 420, 423

Kasuga Maru, see *Taiyo*, 120

Kasumi (DD), 153

Katoomba (PG) (Aust.), *I-124*, 95, 158

Katori (CL), Flagship of Sixth Fleet until Jan. '44, 58, 90, 290; sunk, 296

↓ *Katsuragi Maru* (APV), ↓ by *Sturgeon*, 176

Kavieng, New Ireland, 110, 176, 280

↓ *Kazagumo* (DD), ↓ by *Hake*, 332

Keating, Robert A., c.o. *Barbel*, 362

Kefauver, Russell, c.o. *Tambor*, 300

Kehl, George W., c.o. *Archerfish*, 307

Keithly, Roger M., 219; c.o. *Tilefish*, 417

Kema, northeast Celebes, 73, 74

Kendari, southeast Celebes, 75, 77, 104

Kennedy, Marvin G., c.o. *Wahoo*, 183, 201

Kenney, George C., Comdr. Gen. Allied Air Forces Southwest Pacific, 213, 217, 221

Kete (SS-369), 437; *missing after 20 Mar. '45, 442

Kido Butai, Striking Force, 8, 56, 77, 90, 92, 100, 104, 107, 111, 131–41

Kimmel, Husband E., Cincpac, 61, 62

Kimmel, Manning, c.o. *Robalo*, 356

Kinashi, Takaichi, c.o. *I-19*, 168

King II Operation, Leyte, 382

King (Br.), c.o. *Telemachus*, 349

King, Ernest J., Cominch, 45, 151, 305

King, Robert I., c.o. *Redfin*, 286

Kingfish (SS-234), 191

Kinkaid, Thomas C., Comdr. Seventh Fleet Nov. '43–Sept. '45, 323, 379

Kinsella, William T., c.o. *Ray*, 360, 399

Kirk, Oliver G., c.o. S-42, 126; c.o. *Lapon*, 239

Kirkpatrick, Charles C., c.o. *Triton*, 118, 122, 127, 152, 164

↓ *Kishinami* (DD), 302, 306; ↓ by *Flasher*, 416

Kiska, Aleutian Is., 137, 148, 152, 168, 177, 206, 216, 226, 227; evacuation of, 24

Kitagami, torp. by *Templar*, 285

Kitch, William L., c.o. *Blackfin*, 425

Kiwi (PG) (N.Z.), *I-1*, 206

Klakring, Thomas B., c.o. *Guardfish*, 170, 195; Burt's Brooms, 407

Koga, Mineichi, C-in-C Combined Fleet 18 Apr. '43–31 Mar. '44, 221, 227, 231, 236, 248, 254; leaves Truk, 294, 306; death of, 308

Kolombangara, Solomon Is., 205; battle of, 234

Komandorski Is., Bering Sea, battle of, 216

Komatsu, Teruhisa, Comdr. Sixth Fleet, Mar. '42–Nov. '43, 181

Kon Plan, plan to reinforce Biak, 332, 336, 338

Kondo, Nobutake, Comdr. Second Fleet, 132, 144

↓ *Kongo* (BB), 174, ↓ by *Sealion*, 405

↓ *Konron Maru*, train ferry, ↓ by *Wahoo*, 269

Kossler, Herman J., c.o. *Cavalla*, 338, 352, 401

Kossol Passage, anchorage northern Palau, 412, 431

Kraken (SS-370), 423

Kula Gulf, Solomon Is., 213; battle of, 234, 251
↓ *Kuma* (CL), ↓ by *Tally Ho*, 285
Kumano (CA), torp., 400
↓ *Kume* (DE), ↓ by *Spadefish*, 436
Kuop atoll, south of Truk, 115, 219, 319
↓ *Kuretake* (DD), ↓ by *Razorback*, 417
Kurita, Takeo, 255, Comdr. First Striking Force, 379, 382, 389
↓ *Kusagaki* (DE), ↓ by *Guitarro*, 358
Kusaie, southwest Marshalls, 283, 289
Kuykendall, C. W., *Tullibee*, 307
Kwajalein, Marshall Is., 56, 58, 60, 89, 90, 120, 154, 263, 267, 279; Flintlock Operation, 282, 289, 291
Kyushu, Japan, 13, 476; Operation Olympic, 477

L class submarines, *see* Russian submarines
L-15, 169
↓ **L-16*, ↓ *by *I-25*, 169
Lae, New Guinea, 110, 206, 217, 243
↓ **Lagarto* (SS-371), ↓ *I-371*, 433; *by *Hatsutaka*, 454
Lahaina, Maui, Hawaiian Is., 51, 53, 57
↓ *Lahaina* (freighter), ↓ by Japanese submarine, 59
Lake, Richard C., c.o. *Albacore*, 190, 205
Lander, Robert B., c.o. *Ronquil*, 445
Landsdowne (DD-486), 168
La Pérouse Strait, Soya Kaikyo, between Hokkaido and Sakhalin, 211, 239, 269, 459, 461
Lapon (SS-260), 239, 324
Latham, Richard C., c.o. *Tinosa*, 461
Latta, Frank D., c.o. *Narwhal*, 239, 299, 370; c.o. *Lagarto*, 434; Latta's Lancers, 439, 454
Laughon, Willard R., c.o. *Rasher*, 334
Lautrup, George W., c.o. *Gar*, 307
Lawrence C. Taylor (DE-415), 473
Layton, Edwin T., Cincpac staff, 100
Leary, Herbert F., comdr. Southwest Pacific Force Apr. '42–Sept. '42, 111
Lee, John E., c.o. *Croaker*, 362
Lent, Willis A., c.o. *Triton*, 60; c.o. *Grenadier*, 121
Lewellen, Bafford E., c.o. *Pollack*, 228; c.o. *Torsk*, 464
Lewis, Hugh H., c.o. *Sterlet*, 459
Lexington (CV-2), 90, 91, 96, 99, 110, 112, 113
Lexington (CV-16), 254, 280
Leyte, Philippine Is., 63, 370, 374; King II Oper., 382; Battle for Leyte Gulf, 386, 390, 422
Lifeguards, Japanese, 53, 99; U.S. at Marcus, 251; Wake, 252; Galvanic, 263, 268; Flintlock, 283, 289, 295;

Palau, 307, 308; Woleai, 309; Saipan, 314; Truk, 318, 378; *Pomfret*, 439, 444; for B-29s, 445, Third Fleet, 465
Lingayen Gulf, Luzon, 22–32, 68; landing, 422
Lingga Roads, southeast of Singapore, 380, 425
↓ *Liscome Bay* (CVE-56), ↓ by *I-175*, 268, 297
Litchfield (DD-336), 3, 51
Lockwood, Charles A., Comsubsowespac 125, 150; Comsubpac, 195, 212, 218, 225, 236, 240, 246, 252, 265, 282, 290, 293, 316, 338, 367, 368, 372, 380, 388, 407, 425, 438, 446, 465, 481
Lockwood, Ralph H., c.o. *Guavina*, 424
Logistics, 56, 88, 94, 106, 197, 312, 357, 440
Lombok Strait, between Bali and Lombok, 78, 102, 103, 259, 353, 420, 423, 471
Loomis, Sam C., c.o. *Stingray*, 370
Loughlin, Charles E., c.o. *Queenfish*, 363, 403, 434, 457
Lowrance, Vernon L., c.o. *Kingfish*, 191; c.o. *Sea Dog*
LSD, Landing Ship Dock; LST, Landing Ship Tank
↓ *LST-342*, ↓ by Japanese sub, 235
↓ *LST-577*, ↓ by *RO-50*, 429
Linga, Guadalcanal, 177
Luzon Strait, Convoy College, Devil's Sea, 325, 337, 345, 351
Lynch, Richard B., 263, c.o. *Seawolf*, 371; c.o. *Skate*, 460

MacArthur, Douglas, C-in-C Southwest Pacific Area, 68, 72, 86; Cincsowespac, 111, 167, 184, 212, 234, 258, 280, 283, 302, 304, 318, 332, 370, 371, 379, 477
MacDonough (DD-351), 163; **I-174*, 317
MacKenzie, George K., c.o. *Triton*, 214
MacKenzie, Rufus (Br.), c.o. *Tantulus*, 425
MacMillan, Duncan C., c.o. *Thresher*, 355
MAD, Magnetic Airborne Detector, 282, 357, 364, 401, 416
Magennis, J. J. (Br.), 470
Mahan, Alfred T., 53
Maidstone (AS) (Br.), 353, 452
Majuro, Marshall Is., 283, 291, 312, 333, 347
Makassar City, southwest Celebes, 74, 76, 77, 185
Makassar Strait, between Borneo and Celebes, 73, 76, 259
Makin, Gilbert Is., 164, 263, 265
Malacca Strait, between Malay and Sumatra, 268, 285, 349, 414, 455
Maloelap, Marshall Is., 89, 263

Managhan, Robert R., c.o. *Spikefish*, 479

Manila, Luzon, P.I., 19, 49, 64, 69, 374

↓ *Manini* (freighter), ↓ by Japanese submarine, 59

Manlove (*DE-36*), *I-32, 310

Manus, Admiralty Is., 298

Marcus Island, 92, 251

Mare Island, Navy yard in San Francisco Bay, 27, 48, 51

Marshall, Elliott E., c.o. *Capelin*, 270

Maru, appended to name of Japanese non-naval vessels, hence a Japanese merchant vessel. In practice many converted auxiliary ships continued to append Maru to their names, 18

↓ *Matsukaze* (DD), ↓ by *Swordfish*, 345

↓ *Matsuwa* (DE), 324, 360; ↓ by *Harder*, 361

Matsuwa To, Kurile Is., 239, 325, 421

Maurer, John H., c.o. *Atule*, 401

Maxson, Willis E., 252

↓ *Maya* (CA), 277, 344; ↓ by *Dace*, 384

Mazama (AE), kaiten attack, 431

McCallum, James L. P., c.o. *Bream*, 453

McClintock, David H., c.o. *Darter*, 382

McClusky, Clarence W., 141, 144

McCoy Reynolds (*DE-440*), *I-37, 412

McGregor, Donald, c.o. *Gar*, 117

McGregor, Louis D., c.o. *Redfish*, 363, 417

McGuire, James T., 229

McKinney, Eugene B., c.o. *Salmon*, 102, 103, 125; c.o. *Skate*, 252, 280

McKnight, John R., c.o. S-36, 74

McMahon, Bernard F., c.o. *Drum*, 190; Mac's Mops, 439

McMaster, Fitzhugh, c.o. *Hardhead*, 362

McMorris, Charles H., task force comdr., 216, 226

Meade (*DD-602*), *I-35, 268

↓ *Meiyo Maru* (AP), ↓ by S-38, 157

Melvin (*DD-680*), *RO-36, 333; *RO-114, 346

Menado, northeast Celebes, 73, 75

Metcalf, Ralph M., c.o. *Pogy*, 301, 313

Mertz (*DD-691*), *RO-56, 441

↓ *Michel* (XCL) (GER.), ↓ by *Tarpon*, 272

Michishio (DD), 78, torp. by *Trigger*, 290

Midget submarines (Br.), 469

Midget submarines, Japanese, 44, 54, 56, 130, 132, 180, 234, 364, 398, 430, 480

Midway, 16, 50, 59, 96; battle of, 107, 125, 132–47, 239, 269, 325

Mikuma (CA), 145

↓ *Mikura* (DE), 360; ↓ by *Threadfin*, 443

Mili atoll, Marshall Is., 263, 283

Miller, Charles K., c.o. *Redfin*, 466

Miller, Herman E., c.o. *Besuga*, 453, 456

Millican, William J., c.o. *Thresher*, 154; c.o. *Escolar*, 393

Milne Bay, southeast New Guinea, battle of, 167, 258

↓ *Minazuki* (DD), ↓ by *Harder*, 334

Mines, Japanese, 172, 215, 222, 232, 246; East China Sea, 276, 291, 325, 345, 393, 407, 409, 417, 459, 466

Mines, U.S., 58, 100, 177, 191, 223, 307, 450, 453, 472

Minesweepers, auxiliary (AMC) Japanese, 174–300 tons. 3 sunk by submarines. ↓ *No. 105*, by *Trenchant* (Br.), 455

Minesweepers, fleet (AM) Japanese, 492–615 tons, identified by number only. 11 sunk by submarines. ↓ *No. 12*, by *Besuga*, 453

Mingo (*SS-261*), ↓ *Tamanami*, 354

↓ *Mississinewa* (*AD-39*), ↓ by *I-47*, 413

Mitcher, Marc A., task force comdr., 290, 387, 388

Miwa, Shigeyoshi, comdr. Sixth Fleet, 13 July '44–10 May '45, 348, 349, 375, 378, 390, 391; kaitens, 410–11, 427, 431, 432, 440, 451

↓ *Mizuho* (AV), ↓ by *Drum*, 120

Moa (PG) (N.Z.), *I-1, 206

Mogami (CA), 145

Molucca Passage, east of Celebes, 73, 75, 77

Molumphy, George G., c.o. *Shipjack*, 289

↓ *Momo* (DD), ↓ by *Hawkbill*, 417

Momsen, Charles B., comdr. wolf pack, 261

Monaghan (*DD-354*), sinks midget, 57; *I-7, 233

Monroe, Henry S., c.o. *Ronquil*, 362

Monssen (*DD-798*), *RO-56, 441

Montross, Keats E., c.o. *Swordfish*, 436

Moore, John A., c.o. *Grayback*, 303

Moore, John R., c.o. S-44, 126, 157; c.o. *Sailfish*, 184

Moore, Raymond J., c.o. *Stingray*, 73

Morinaga, Masahiko, c.o. *I-56*, 431

Morotai, island north of Halmahera, 370, 374, 375

Morrison (*DD-560*), *I-8, 441

Morton, Dudley W., c.o. *Wahoo*, 198, 215, 245, 269

Moseley, Stanley P., c.o. *Pollack*, 61, 88, 119, 133

Munda, New Georgia, 202, 206, 212, 234

Munson, Henry G., c.o. S-38, 80, 157; c.o. *Rasher*, 359

Murphy, Charlton, c.o. *Sturgeon*, 345

Murphy, John W., c.o. *Tambor*, 60, 144

Musashi (BB), 294; torp. by *Tunny*, 308, 332, 336, 387

Muskallunge (SS-262), 339
Mustin (DD-413), 168
Mutsuki (DD), 161
↓*Mutsure* (DE), ↓by *Snapper*, 249
Myoko (CA), torp. by *Bergall*, 420, 469

↓*Nagara* (CL), 279; ↓by *Croaker*, 362
Nagumo, Chuichi, comdr. Kido Butai, 56, 77, 104, 132, 138, 143, 175
Naka (CL), torp. by *Seawolf*, 104
Na Line, Japanese submarine line, 329
Nanpo Shoto, islands south of Japan, 11
Nansei Shoto, islands southwest of Japan, 105, 325, 345, 417
Narwhal (SS-167), 37, 39, 51, 90, 105, 226, 239, 257; supply runs, 299, 345, 370, 376
↓*Natori* (CL), ↓by *Hardhead*, 362
↓*Natsushio* (DD), ↓by S-37, 76
Nauman, Harley K., c.o. *Salmon*, 395
Nauru, west of Gilberts, 250
Nautilus (SS-168), 37, 39, 51; at Midway, 138–42; ↓*Yamakaze*, 149, 164, 202, 226, 257, 263, 266–67; supply runs, 345, 370
Naval Group China, 394, 435
↓*Neches* (AD-5), ↓by Japanese submarine, 90
Nelson, William T., c.o. *Peto*, 257
↓*Nenohi* (DD), ↓by *Triton*, 152
Newcomb, R. M., c.o. *Underhill*, 474
Newman (DE-205), 430
Ngulu, southeast of Ulithi, 392, 412
Nicholas (DD-449), *I-38, 412
Nichols, Richard E., c.o. *Bashaw*, 306
Nimitz, Chester W., C-in-C Pacific Ocean Area, Cincpac, after 31 Dec. '41, 61, 62, 111, 134, 147, 184, 209, 212, 236, 237, 250, 254, 282, 302, 332, 371, 373, 438, 477
Nimitz, Chester W., Jr., c.o. *Haddo*, 361
Nishima, Sekio, 412, 413
Nichimura, Shoji, task force comdr., 104, 380, 387
Nishino, c.o. I-17, 96
Nisshin (AV), 132
↓*Nokaze* (DD), ↓by *Pargo*, 425
↓*Nomi* (DE), ↓by *Tirante*, 458
Nomura, Naokuni, comdr. Grand Escort Force after 3 Aug. '44, 357
North Carolina (BB-55), torp. by I-15, 168
Nouméa, New Caledonia, 181, 184
Nowell, Byron H., c.o. *Paddle*, 354
↓*Numakaze* (DD), ↓by *Grayback*, 280

O class submarines, Dutch submarines
*O-16, *by British mine, 69–70
*O-19, 70, 73; *stranded, July '45
*O-20, *by surface ships, 70
Oak Hill (LSD-7), 475
Oakley, Thomas B., c.o. *Growler*, 363, 366, 409

O'Bannon (DD-454), *RO-34, 218
Obiga, c.o. I-15, 243
↓*O'Brien* (DD-415), ↓by I-15, 168
↓*Odate* (AR), ↓by *Trigger*, 442
↓*Oi* (CL), ↓by *Flasher*, 353
Oikawa, Koshiro, comdr. Grand Escort Force Nov. '43–Aug. '44, 273, 276, 291, 325, 357
O'Kane, Richard H., 198; c.o. *Tang*, 294, 304, 306, 318, 345, 394
↓*Okikaze* (DD), ↓by *Trigger*, 195
Okinawa, Ryukyu Is., 344, 362, 377, 423, 436; Operation Iceberg, 442, 448
↓*Okinoshima* (CM), ↓by S-42, 126
↓*Okitsu Maru* (AV), ↓by *Skipjack*, 290
Oldendorf, Jesse B., task force comdr., 387, 422
Olsen, Eliot, c.o. *Grayling*, 91
Olympic Operation, Kyushu, 477
Ominato, northern Honshu, 133, 473
O'Regan, William V., wolf pack comdr., 355
Orita, Zenji, c.o. I-47, 412, 431, 448, 449
Ormoc Bay, Leyte, 385, 397, 398
↓*Oshio* (DD), ↓by *Albacore*, 215
Ota, Saichi, c.o. I-53, 474
Otsujima, kaiten base, 411, 480
Otus (AS-20), 49, 64, 69, 76
Ozawa, Jisaburo, task force comdr., 77, 323, 341, 351, 379, 387

Paddle (SS-263), 263, 266; ↓*Hokaze*, 354, 370
Palau Is., 105, 188, 236, 306, 371, 375
Palawan Channel, between Palawan, P.I. and Dangerous Ground, 322, 380, 382
Pampanito (SS-383), 363, 366, 424
Parche (SS-384), 325, 355
Pargo (SS-264), 322; ↓*Nokaze*, 425
Parham, William B., c.o. *Gabilan*, 453, 465
Parks, Lewis S., wolf pack comdr., 355
Patrol vessels (PG) Japanese, 750–1000 tons. Identified by number only. 5 sunk by submarines; ↓*No. 1*, by *Guardfish*, 196; ↓*No. 2*, by *Stubborn*, 468
Patterson (DD-392), *I-25, 243
PC, submarine chasers, PC-487, *I-24, 232; PC-804, 474; PC-1133, 430; PC-1135, *I-32, 310
Pearl Harbor, attacked, 1, 52–53, 57; I-7 reconn., 59; I-9 reconn., 95; second bombing, 99; I-36 reconn., 254
Peleliu, Palau Is., 307, 371, 373, 375
Penang, western Malay, 108, 285, 414
Pennsylvania (BB-38), 227
Perch (SS-176), *by Japanese DD, 81–85
Perch (SS-313), 393, 424

Perkins, William B., c.o. *Burrfish*, 294, 371

Permit (SS-174), 73, 86, 215, 239, 289, 294, 371

Peterson, George E., wolf pack, 325

Peterson, Richard W., c.o. *Icefish*, 381

Peto (SS-265), 257, 403

PF, Frigate; PG, gunboat

Phelps (DD-360), *RO-40*, 297

Philippine Sea, battle of, 336–44, 350, 473

Pickerel (SS-177), 73, 75; ↓ *SC No. 13*, 221; *missing after 7 Apr. '43, 221

Picuda (SS-382), ↓ *Yunagi*, 363, 403, 434, 436

Pieczentkowski, Herman A., c.o. *Sturgeon*, 176

Pierce, George E., c.o. *Tunny*, 363, 460

Pierce, John R., c.o. *Argonaut*, 165, 195

Pigeon (ASR-9), 63

Pike (SS-173), 73, 79

Pilotfish (SS-386), 326

Pintado (SS-387), 326, 362, 388; ↓ *Akikaze*, 401, 402, 417

Pipefish (SS-388), 338; ↓ *C.D.V. No. 64*, 417

Piranha (SS-389), 355, 417

Plaice (SS-390), 417

Plunger (SS-179), 51, 61, 88, 155, 228, 239, 245, 263, 266, 279

Pogy (SS-266), 221; ↓ *Minekaze*, 301; ↓ *I-183*, 313, 325

Pollack (SS-180), 51, 61, 88, 90, 105, 119, 133, 238; ↓ *Bangkok Maru*, 230, 266, 314; ↓ *Asanagi*, 325

Pomfret (SS-391), 401; lifeguard, 439

Pompanito (SS-383), 307

Pompano (SS-187), 51, 62, 202; *by mine, 246

Pompon (SS-267), 436

Ponape, Caroline Is., 89, 289, 318

Porpoise (SS-172), 49, 75

Porpoise (SS) (Br.), *missing in Malacca Strait after 19 Jan. '45

Port Moresby, southeast New Guinea, 111, 112, 155, 160, 167, 182

↓ *Porter* (DD-356), ↓ by Japanese submarine, 175

Porter, George E., c.o. *Bluefish*, 259

Post, William S., c.o. *Gudgeon*, 223

Pownall, Charles A., task force comdr., 251, 279

Prince of Wales (BB) (Br.), 20, 63, 64, 70

Prison ships, 366, 370, 394

↓ *Prusa* (freighter), ↓ by Japanese submarine, 59

PT, motor torpedo boats, PT-59, *I-3, 183; PT-122, 184; PT-150, PT-152, *RO-103, 218; ↓ PT-164, ↓ PT-173, ↓ by Japanese submarine, 235

Puffer (SS-263), 274; ↓ *Fuyo*, 281, 323, 334, 471

Q-ships, decoy ships, 288, 382

Queenfish (SS-393), 363, 366, 403, 434; ↓ *Awa Maru*, 457

Rabaul, northern New Britain, 90, 91, 96, 110, 197, 214, 247, 256

Raby (DE-698), 330; *I-48, 431

Radar, Japanese, 44, 195, 233, 269, 273, 341, 363, 403

Radar, U.S., 7, 10, 20, 40, 153; SD, 167, 170; SJ, 185, 191, 233, 249; ST, 426; radar pickets, 467

Radford (DD-446), *I-19, 268

Rainer, Gordon B., c.o. *Dolphin*, 89

Rakuyo Maru, prison ship, 366

Ramage, Lawson P., c.o. *Trout*, 198; c.o. *Parche*, 325, 355; wolf pack, 401

Raquet, Conde L., c.o. *Barbel*, 424

Rasher (SS-269), ↓ *Shioya*, 334; ↓ *Taiyo*, 358–59

Raton (SS-270), 257; ↓ *Iki*, 324, 359, 400

Ray (SS-271), 322, 360; torp. *Kumano*, 399

Razorback (SS-394), 416; ↓ *Kuretake*, 417

Reconnaissance, Japanese, 57, 95, 181, 254, 296, 310, 333

Reconnaissance, U.S., 50, 89, 198, 243, 250, 262, 289, 371, 436, 466

Redfin (SS-272), torp. *Amatsukaze*, 286; ↓ *Akigumo*, 317, 336, 358; mine reconn., 466

Redfish (SS-395), 363, 417; torp. *Junyo*, 418; ↓ *Unryu*, 419

Reed, John W., c.o. *Sunfish*, 458

Refo, Miles P., c.o. *Hoe*, 425

Reich, Eli T., c.o. *Sealion*, 345, 363, 404

Reid (DD-369), *RO-61, 164

Rendova, south of New Georgia, 202, 234

Reno (CL-96), torp. by *I-41*, 392

Repulse (CC) (Br.), 20, 63, 64, 70

Rhymes, Cassius D., 66, 67; c.o. *Chub*, 455

Rice, Robert H., c.o. *Drum*, 120, 210

Richard M. Rowell (DE-403), *Seawolf* 376; * I-26, 391

Riddle (DE-185), *I-10, 347

Rimmer, Hugh R., c.o. *Albacore*, 408

Ringgold (DD-189), 266

Ringness (APD-100), 449

Risser, Robert D., c.o. *Flying Fish*, 337, 461

RO, romaji for the second kana of the katakana syllabary. *See* Kana

RO class submarines, Japanese medium submarines, 525–998 tons, 44, 53

*RO-33, 95, 101, 113, 159; *by Arunta, 162

*RO-34, 95, 101, 113; *by O'Bannon and Strong, 218

*RO-35, *by Ellet or Saufley, 243

*RO-36, *by Melvin, 333

*RO-37, *by Buchanan, 284

*RO-38, *missing after 19 Nov. '43 (possibly *by Cotten), 268

*RO-39, *by Walker, 291, 296

*RO-40, *by Phelps and Sage, 297

*RO-41, ↓ Shelton, 375–76, 397; *by Haggard, 441

*RO-42, *by Bangust, 333

*RO-43, 375, 397, 429; *by Anzio, 440

*RO-44, 297, 333; *by Burden R. Hastings, 346

*RO-45, 314; *missing after 30 Apr. '44, 317

*RO-46, 375, 376; torp. Cavalier, 428; *missing after 17 Apr. '45, 448

*RO-47, *missing after 2 Oct. '44 (possibly *by McCoy Reynolds), 376

*RO-48, *by William C. Miller, 348

*RO-49, 398, 428; *by Hudson, 441

RO-50, 398; ↓ LST-577, 429, 449

*RO-55, *by Thomason, 429, 440

*RO-56, *by Monssen and Mertz, 441

*RO-60, *stranded, 59

*RO-61, 148, torp. Casco; *by planes and Reid, 164

RO-62, 59, 148, 164

RO-63, 59, 148, 168

*RO-64, 59, 148, 164, 168; *by mine, 450

*RO-65, *by air raid, 168

*RO-66, *by collision, 59

*RO-67, 168; *by mine

RO-68, 59, 148

*RO-100, *by mine, 268

*RO-101, *by Eaton, 244

*RO-102, *by PT-150 and PT-152, 218

*RO-103, ↓ Aludra, ↓ Deimos, ↓ LST-342, *missing after 24 July '43, 235

*RO-104, 255; *by England, 330

*RO-105, 255; *by England, 330

*RO-106, *by England, 330

*RO-107, *missing after 4 July '43 (possibly *by Taylor), 242

*RO-108, *by England, 330

*RO-109, 331, 391, 429; *by Horace A. Bass, 449

*RO-110, *by Aust. and Indian escorts, 285

*RO-111, *by Taylor, 333

↓ *RO-112, 331, 391, 397, 428; ↓ *by Batfish, 429

↓ *RO-113, 414, 428; ↓ *by Batfish, 429

*RO-114, *by Wadleigh and Melvin, 346

↓ *RO-115, 347, 414; ↓ *by Batfish, 428

*RO-116, *by England, 330

*RO-117, *by planes, 347

RO-500 class, German submarines built for Japan

RO-500, 359

*RO-501, *by Francis M. Robinson, 349

Roach, John P., c.o. Haddock, 286, 388, 401

*Robalo (SS-273), *by mine, 356

Rock (SS-274), 349, 355, 423

Rockford (PF-48), *I-12, 413

Ronquil (SS-396), 362, 380, 407, 445

Rooney, Roderick C., c.o. Corvina, 270

Ruble, Harold E., c.o. Piranha, 355

*Runner (SS-275), 225; *by mine, 232

Runner (SS-446), mine reconn., 466

Russia, 169, 211, 240, 462, 481

Russian submarines, L class

Ryuho (CVL), torp. by Drum, 191

Ryujo (CV), 104, 161, 191

S class submarine—American coast defense submarines, 800–850 tons, 19, 20, 37

S-18 (SS-123), 50, 110, 202

S-23 (SS-128), 50, 110

*S-26 (SS-131), *by collision, 92

*S-27 (SS-132), *stranded, 149

*S-28 (SS-133), *operational casualty, 356

S-30 (SS-135), 227

S-31 (SS-136), 177

S-34 (SS-139), S-35 (SS-140), 110

*S-36 (SS-141), 49; *stranded, 74

S-37 (SS-142), 72; ↓ Natsushio, 76, 80, 155

S-38 (SS-143), at Lingayen, 19–33, 69, 80, 102, 110; ↓ Meiyo Maru, 157

*S-39 (SS-144), 49, 86; ↓ Erimo, 102; *stranded, 158

S-40 (SS-145), 22, 69

S-41 (SS-146), 72, 227

S-42 (SS-153), 110; ↓ Okinoshima, 126, 370

S-43 (SS-154), 110

*S-44 (SS-155), 110, 113; ↓ Shoei Maru, 126; ↓ Kako 157; *by surface ship, 270

S-45 (SS-156), S-46 (SS-157), 110

S-47 (SS-158), 110, 113, 169, 370

Saddle Islands, off Yangtze River, 225

↓ Sado (DE), 300, 360; ↓ by Haddo, 361

Sagami Nada, bay south of Tokyo, 439, 465, 466

Sage (AM-11), *RO-40, 297

↓ Sagiri (DD), ↓ by K-16, 70

Sailfish (SS-192), ↓ Kamogawa Maru, 102, 114, 184; ↓ Chuyo, 277

St. George Channel, between New Britain and New Ireland, 110, 113, 169, 284

Saipan, 303, 309, 314, 328, 331; Operation Forager, 333, 348, 352
Sakamaki, Kazuo, c.o. midget, 57
Sakamoto, Kiichi, c.o. *I-1*, 207
Salamaua, New Guinea, 110, 192, 206
Salmon (SS-182), 22, 69, 102, 103; ↓ *Asahi*, 126, 231, 389; damaged, 395
Samar, P.I., battle of, 390
↓ *Samidare* (DD), 318; ↓ by *Batfish*, 368
Samuel S. Miles (DE-183), *I-177*, 376
Samurai, feudal warrior, 71, 221, 432
↓ *Sanae* (DD), ↓ by *Bluefish*, 259
San Bernardino Strait, between Luzon and Samar, 337, 372, 380, 387, 389, 397
Sand Lance (SS-381), 302; ↓ *Tatsuta*, 304, 326
Santa Cruz Is., 155, 174
Santee (CVE-29), torp. by *I-56*, 390
↓ *Sanuki Maru* (AV), ↓ by *Spadefish*, 436
↓ *Sanyo Maru* (AV), 65; ↓ by *Cabrilla*
Saratoga (CV-3), torp. by *I-6*, 90, 95, 111; torp. by *I-26*, 163
Sargo (SS-188), 65–68, 85
Saufley (DD-465), *RO-35 or I-20*, 244; *I-2*, 317
Saury (SS-189), 22, 69, 407
Savo Island, battle of, 156
Sawfish (SS-276), 210, 269; ↓ *I-29*, 349, 355
Sayre, Francis B., 85–86
↓ *Sazanami* (DD), ↓ by *Albacore*, 284
SC, submarine chaser, auxiliary
Scabbardfish (SS-397), ↓ *I-365*, 414, 460
Scamp (SS-277), ↓ *I-168*, 235, 284, 315; *missing after 9 Nov. '44, 409
Scanland, Francis W., c.o. *Hawkbill*, 425, 454
Schacht, Kenneth G., *Perch*, 84
Schade, Arnold F., c.o. *Growler*, 203, 339; c.o. *Bugara*, 468, 469
Schmidt, Maximilian G., c.o. *Scorpion*, 291
Scorpion (SS-278), 221, 225; *missing after 6 Jan. '44, 291
Scott, John A., c.o. *Tunny*, 219, 307
Scott, Norman, task force comdr., 173, 179
Sculpin (SS-191), 73, 176, 243, 264; *by *Yamagumo*, 264
Sea Devil (SS-400), ↓ *I-364*, 375, 416; torp. *Junyo*, 418, 447, 457
Sea Dog (SS-401), 442, 458; in Japan Sea, 460
Seadragon (SS-191), 49, 63, 73, 85, 154; ↓ *I-4*, 183, 381, 393
Sea Fox (SS-402), 457
Seahorse (SS-304), 314, 338, 345, 355, 372

Seal (SS-183), 69, 79, 102, 189, 263, 266, 268, 279, 283, 289, 310
Sealion (SS-195), 49; *by air raid, 63
Sealion (SS-315), 345, 363, 366; ↓ *Kongo* ↓ *Urakaze*, 404
Sea Owl (SS-405), 418, 451
Seaplanes, Japanese, 44, 53, 59, 99, 131, 180, 254, 472
Sea Poacher (SS-406), 418
Searaven (SS-196), 109, 202, 264, 266, 283, 289, 294, 295, 303
Sea Robin (SS-407), 424, 426
Seawolf (SS-197), 65, 78, 85, 103; torp. *Naka*, 104, 185–88, 260, 370, 371; *by own forces, 376
Second Fleet, Japanese, 22, 101, 107, 160, 255, 267
Second Striking Force, Japanese, 377, 378, 380
Seeadler Harbor, Admiralty Is., 312, 316, 431
Segundo (SS-398), 416
Selby, Frank G., c.o. *Puffer*, 323, 334
Selene (SS) (Br.), 469
Sellars, Robert F., c.o. *Blackfish*, 306
Sennet (SS-408), 464
Seventh Fleet, Allied naval forces in southwest Pacific, Asiatic Fleet became Naval Forces Southwest Pacific 4 Feb. '42, which became Southwest Pacific Force 20 Apr. '42, which became Seventh Fleet 19 Feb. '43. Carpender, Feb. '43–Nov. '43, 212; Kinkaid, Nov. '43–Sept. '45, 323, 379, 387, 389, 397, 422
Shad (SS-235), 261
Shane, Louis, c.o. *Shark*, 75
Shark (SS-174), 69; *missing after 7 Feb. '42, 75
Shark (SS-314), 326, 381; *missing after 24 Oct. '44, 393
Sharp, George A., c.o. *Nautilus*, 370
Shean, M. H. (Br.), c.o. *XE-4*, 469
Shelby, Edward E., c.o. *Sunfish*, 289, 294, 303, 404
↓ *Shelton* (DD-407), ↓ by *RO-41*, 376
Shepard, Evan T., c.o. *Picuda*, 403, 434
Sherman, Frederick C., task force comdr., 256, 280, 293
↓ *Shigure*, ↓ by *Blackfin*, 425
↓ *Shikinami* (DD), ↓ by *Growler*, 366
Shimizu, Mitsuyoshi, comdr., Sixth Fleet until Mar. '42, 58
↓ *Shimotsuki* (DD), ↓ by *Cavalla*, 401
↓ *Shinano* (CV), ↓ by *Archerfish*, 406
Shinohara, Shigero, c.o. *I-8*, 441
↓ *Shinsho Maru* (AR), ↓ by *Thresher*, 154
↓ *Shinsho Maru* (APV), ↓ by *Aspro*, 436
↓ *Shinyo* (Jinyo) (CVE), ↓ by *Spadefish*, 403
↓ *Shinyo Maru*, prison ship, ↓ by *Paddle*, 370

↓*Shioya* (AO), ↓by *Rasher*, 334

↓*Shirakumo* (DD), ↓by *Tautog*, 306

Shiranui (DD), torp. by *Growler*, 153

↓*Shirataka* (CM), 320; ↓by *Sealion*, 365

Shiratsuyu (DD), 337

↓*Shiriya* (AD), ↓by *Trigger*, 250

Sho Plan, Japanese plan, 375, 377

↓*Shoei Maru* (AR), ↓by *S-44*, 126

↓*Shokaku* (CV), 56, 92, 104, 107, 111, 113; pursuit of, 115–18, 161; ↓by *Cavalla*, 343

↓*Shonan* (DE), ↓by *Hoe*, 425

Shortland Is., southeast of Bougainville, 161, 204

Sibutu Passage, through Sulu Arch., 259, 323, 335, 416

Sibuyan Sea, P.I., 380, 387

Sieglaff, William B., c.o. *Tautog*, 222, 225, 305

Silversides (SS-236), 129, 133, 136, 155, 225, 244, 257, 326, 396, 407, 436, 447

Simpson, H. S., c.o. *Bashaw*, 425

Simpson Harbor, Rabaul, 197, 256

Sixth Fleet, Japanese Submarine Force, see also Advance Expeditionary Force; Shimizu until Mar. '42, 52, 53, 58; Komatsu, Mar. '42–Nov. '43, 181; Takagi, Nov. '43–July '44, 269, 297, 331, 333; Miwa, July '44–May '45, 348, 350, 357, 374, 413, 428; Daigo after May '45, 451

Skate (SS-305), lifeguard 252; torp. *Yamato*, 280; ↓*Agano*, 294; ↓*Usagumo*, 352, 460; ↓*I-122*, 461

Skipjack, 125, 177; ↓*Okitsu Maru*, ↓*Suzukaze*, 289, 303

Smart, J. E. (Br.), 469

Smith, Chester C., c.o. *Swordfish*, 64, 74

Smith, Frank M., c.o. *Hammerhead*, 425, 454

Snapper (SS-185), 214; ↓*Mutsure*, 249

Snook (SS-279), 225, 251; *missing after 8 Apr. '45, 445

Snorkel, 39, 449, 480

Solomon Islands, 108, 161, 192, 206, 214, 244, 255, 280

Soryu (CV), 56, 61, 132, 141

Sound, sonar, 6, 10, 13, 47, 79, 459, 466

Southard (DMS-10), *I-15 or I-172, 180

Southwest Pacific Submarines (Submarines Asiatic Fleet until Feb. '42). Fremantle-based, Seventh Fleet submarines; Wilkes, Feb. '42–May '42, 46, 86, 109; Lockwood, May '42–Feb. '43, 125, 154; McCann, Feb. '43–Mar '43; Christie, Mar. '43–Dec. '44, 193, 214, 222, 238, 244, 257, 258, 286, 334, 382, 416; Fife, Dec. '44–Aug. '45, 451, 468

Soya Kaikyo, see La Pérouse Strait

Spadefish (SS-411), 359, 363; ↓*Shinyo*, 403; ↓*Kume*, ↓*Sanuki Maru*, 436, 460

Spark (SS) (Br.), 453, 469

Spearfish (SS-190), 72, 114, 263, 283, 436, 445

Spearhead (SS) (Br.), 469

Spikefish (SS-404), ↓*I-373*, 479

Spruance, Raymond A., task force comdr., 134, 147; Comdr. Fifth Fleet, 212, 293, 296, 307, 333, 351, 372, 423, 436, 463

Staley, Joseph J., c.o. *Mingo*, 354

Statesman (SS) (Br.), 455

Steelhead (SS-280), 225, 251, 355

Steinmetz, Everett H., c.o. *Crevalle*, 460

Sterlet (SS-392), 378, 389, 395, 407, 459

Steven Potter (DD-538), *I-174, 317

Stevens, Clyde B., c.o. *Plaice*, 418

Stevens, James E., c.o. *Flounder*, 414

Stevenson, Harry C., c.o. *Aspro* after 15 Jan. '44, 294, 297

Stevenson, William A., c.o. *S-30*, 227; c.o. *Aspro* until 15 Jan. '44

Stimson, Paul C., c.o. *Sea Robin*, 424, 426

Stingray (SS-186), 22, 69, 73, 225, 340, 370

Stockton (DD-646), *I-8, 451

Stone, Lowell T., c.o. *Lapon*, 324

Stonehenge (SS) (Br.), *missing after 23 Mar. '44 in Malacca Strait

Stovall, William S., c.o. *Gudgeon*, 156; c.o. *Darter*, 294

Stratagem (SS) (Br.), *by surface ship 22 Nov. '44 in Malacca Strait

Strategic Bombing Survey, U. S., 444

Strategy, Japanese submarines, 46, 52–54, 96, 163, 193, 331, 350

Strategy, U.S. submarines, 46, 50–51, 86–87, 92–95, 136, 193, 282, 310, 337, 348

Street, George L., c.o. *Tirante*, 457

Strong (DD-467), *RO-34, 218

Sturgeon (SS-187), 73, 75, 87, 109, 154; ↓*Katsuragi Maru*, 176; torp. *Suzutzuki*, 286, 345, 362

Sturr, Henry D., c.o. *Becuna*, 425

Stygian (SS) Br.), 455, 469

Styles, Ralph E., c.o. *Sea Devil*, 375, 416, 457

Subic Bay, Luzon, 23, 49, 426

Submarines, American, S class, coastal; fleet submarines, transoceanic, named after fish, 37–40, 169, 176

Submarines, British, British submarines in Far East had names beginning with S or T (except *Porpoise*), 49, 79, 223, 285, 352, 414, 423, 426, 452, 454, 468

Submarines, Dutch, K and O class plus *Zwaardvisch*, 49, 69, 75, 78, 223, 352, 414, 423, 426, 452, 454, 468

Submarines, German, U class, 285, 393, 414, 456

Submarines, Japanese, I, RO and HA class, 44, 95, 107, 130, 159, 168, 175, 180, 206, 217, 226, 235, 268, 296, 310, 346, 374, 390, 397, 413, 427, 448, 478

Submarines Pacific Fleet. *See* Subpac

Submarines, Russian L class, 169

Submarine Chasers (PC), Japanese, 300–400 tons. Identified by number only. 8 sunk by submarines. ↓ *No. 13*, by *Pickerel*, 221, *No. 18*, 204; ↓ *No. 25*, ↓ *No. 27*, by *Grunion*, 154

Submarine Chasers Auxiliary (SC), 100 tons, 10 sunk by submarines. *No. 39*, 360

Subpac, Submarines Pacific Fleet, 45, 93, 105, 114, 209, 301, 336, 351, 388

Subtle (SS) (Br.), 455

Sugamasa, Tetsuaki, c.o. *I-36*, 449, 450

Summers, Paul E., c.o. *Pampanito*, 307, 363, 424

Sunfish (SS-281), 190, 283, 289, 294, 303, 352, 403, 418, 458

Supply Service, Submarine, Japanese, 181, 206, 227

Supply Service, Submarine, U.S., 85, 109, 257, 299, 375

Surabaya (Soerabaja), Java, 49, 68, 69, 77, 79, 81, 223, 414

Surf (SS) (Br.), 353

Surigao Strait, between Leyte and Mindanao, 337, 362, 372, 380; battle of, 386

Suwannee (CVE-27), *I-184, 347

↓ *Suzukaze* (DD), 102; ↓ by *Skipjack*, 290

Suzuki, Suguru, 99

Suzutsuki (DD), torp. by *Sturgeon*, 286; torp. by *Besugo*, 378

Swinburne, Edwin R., wolf pack, 363

Swordfish (SS-193), 64, 68, 69, 74, 86; ↓ *Delhi Maru*, 287; ↓ *Matsukaze*, 345; *missing after 3 Jan. '45, 436

Tabata, Tadashi, c.o. *I-175*, 268

Taciturn (SS) (Br.), 471

Tagami, Meiji, c.o. *I-25*, 95, 169

↓ *Tahure* (PG) (Fr.), ↓ by *Flasher*, 317

↓ *Taiho* (CV), ↓ by *Albacore*, 342

↓ *Taiyo* (CVE) (*Kasuga Maru*), 121, 354; ↓ by *Rasher*, 360

Takagi, Takeo, 113; Comdr. Sixth Fleet, Nov. '43–July '44, 269, 297, 310, 331, 333, 346, 348

Takao, Formosa, 49, 357, 428

Takao (CA), torp. by *Darter*, 384; British midgets, 469

↓ *Takasaki* (AD), ↓ by *Puffer*, 334

Tally Ho (SS) (Br.), ↓ *Kuma*, ↓ *UIT-23*, 285

↓ *Tama* (CL), ↓ by *Jallao*, 388

↓ *Tamanami* (DD), ↓ by *Mingo*, 354

Tambor (SS-198), 51, 60–61, 110, 144, 156, 177, 190, 202, 300, 407

Tanabe, Yahachi, c.o. *I-168*, 145; c.o. *I-176*, 217

Tanaka, Raizo, 182

Tang (SS-306), 294, 295, 303, 306; lifeguard, 318, 345; *by own torpedo, 394

↓ *Tanikaze* (DD), ↓ by *Harder*, 335

Tan Operation, bombing Ulithi, 440

Tantalus (SS) (Br.), 353, 425

Tarakan, eastern Borneo, 72, 75; oil, 334

Tarawa, Gilbert Is., 166, 230, 263, 265, 280

Tarpon (SS-175), 74, 209; ↓ *Michel*, 271, 283

Task Force 71, Fremantle-based submarines, 212

Task Force 72, Brisbane-based submarines, 212

Tassafaronga, near Lunga Point, Guadalcanal, battle of, 182

↓ *Tatsuta* (CL), 190; ↓ by *Sand Lance*, 304

Taurus (SS) (Br.) ↓ *I-34*, 268, 349

Tautog (SS-199), 51, 62, 115; ↓ *I-28*, 116, 177, 202; ↓ *Isonami*, 222, 225; ↓ *Shirakumo*, 305, 317, 324

Tawi Tawi, western Sulu Arch., 299, 323, 334

Taylor (DD-461), *RO-111*, 333, 430

Taylor, Arthur H., c.o. *Haddock*, 163

TBT, Target Bearing Transmitter, 48

TDC, Torpedo Data Computer, to solve torpedo fire control problems, 5, 12, 13, 20, 40

Telemachus (SS) (Br.), ↓ *I-166*, 349

Templar (SS) (Br.), torp. *Kitagami*, 285

Tench (SS-417), 458

Ten-Go Operation, Japanese air offensive

↓ *Tenryu* (CL), ↓ by *Albacore*, 190

Teremoto, Iwao, c.o. *I-36*, 412, 431

Theobald, Robert A., Comdr. North Pacific, 135, 137

Third Fleet, Halsey, 15 Mar. '43–3 Sept. '45, 212; plans, 372, 377, 379; battle for Leyte Gulf, 386, 391, 398, 415, 422; South China sweep, 422; Japan, 463, 466

Thomas F. Nickel (DE-587), 475

Thomas, Willis M., c.o. *Pompano*, 246

Thomason (DE-203), *RO-55*, 429

Thorough (SS) (Br.), 471

Threadfin (SS-410), 442, 447

Thresher (SS-200), 3, 51, 58, 62, 107; ↓ *Shinsho Maru*, 154, 177, 202, 263, 266, 355

Tilefish (SS-307), 349, 355; ↓ *Chidori*, 417

Tinian, Marianas Is., 304, 348, 351

Tinosa (SS-283), 240–42, 246, 325, 345, 460

Tiptoe (SS) (Br.), 468

Tirante (SS-420), ↓ *Nomi*, ↓ *CDV No. 31*, 457

Titus, Jack C., c.o. *Narwhal*, 370

Tjilatjap, southern Java, 76, 101

Toagel Mlungui, west passage Palau, 188, 308

Tokyo carrier air raids, 107, 438, 463

Tokyo Express, destroyer transports to Guadalcanal, 162, 167, 173, 179, 181; in reverse, 206; to Ormoc, 397

Tomioka, Sadatoshi, 106

Tonan Maru No. 2, 176, 300, 362

Tonan Maru No. 3, 240–42, 300

Tonnage, gross registered, is a measure of the capacity of a ship. It is the total enclosed space in cubic feet, divided by 100. Displacement tonnage, used to indicate size of naval vessels, is the weight of water displaced at standard loading expressed in long tons, 210

Toro (SS-422), 465

Torpedoes, Japanese, 43, 80, 173, 175, 183, 357

Torpedoes, U.S., 6, 21, 33, 40–43, 64, 65–68, 76, 86, 94, 108, 114, 126, 150, 156, 171, 185, 199, 216, 219, 232, 237, 240–42, 244, 247, 257, 269, 279, 281, 286, 311

Torpedo Data Computer, see TDC

Torpedo Junction, between Espiritu Santo and Solomons, 174, 175, 180

Torsk (SS-423), ↓ *CDV No. 13* and *No. 47*, 464, 481

Toyama, Zenshin, c.o. *I-48*, 431

Toyoda, Soemu, C-in-C Combined Fleet after 5 May '44, 308, 323, 329, 332, 347, 357, 378, 380, 390, 446, 482

Toyomasu, Seihachi, c.o. *I-53*, 431

Track angle, angle between target's course and track of approaching torpedo, 14

Tradewind (SS) (Br.), 426

Transports, fast (APD), Japanese, 1500–1900 tons. 4 sunk by submarines. ↓ *No. 12*, by *Pintado*, 417

Transports, special (LSV), Japanese, 1000 tons. 6 sunk by submarines. ↓ *No. 104*, by *Pintado*, 417; ↓ *No. 129*, by *Cod*, 358

Treasury Islands, southeast of Bougainville, 243

Trenchant (SS) (Br.), ↓ *U-859*, 414; ↓ *Ashigara*, 455

Trepang (SS-412), 416

Triebel, Charles O., c.o. *Snook*, 225, 251

Trigger (SS-237), 190; ↓ *Okikaze*, 195, 210, 214, 227; torp. *Hiyo*, 231; ↓ *Shiriya*, 249; torp. *Michishio*, ↓ *Yasukuni Maru*, 290, 314, 389, 395, 407; *missing after 25 Mar. '45, 442

Trincomalee, Ceylon, 79, 104, 285, 452

Triton (SS-201), 51, 60, 61, 90, 91, 94,

118; ↓ *I-64*, 119, 122, 127, 135; ↓ *Nenohi*, 152; 164, 210; *by destroyers, 214

Trout (SS-202), 51, 59, 85, 91, 147, 179, 198, 225; *by surface vessels, 303

Truant (SS) (Br.), 78, 109

Truk, Caroline Is., 89, 91, 101, 110, 115, 155, 167, 218, 236, 255, 263, 289; Hailstone Operation, 293, 318, 331, 472

Trump (SS) (Br.), 468

Trusty (SS) (Br.), 78

Tsushima Strait, 211, 269; minefields, 459 464

Tui (PG) (N.Z.), *I-17*, 243

Tulagi, Florida Is., Solomons, 113, 155, 177, 258, 284

Tullibee (SS-284), 286; *by own torpedo, 306

Tuna (SS-203), 51, 90, 105, 214, 258, 388, 401, 424

Tung Hai (East China Sea), 122, 225, 404, 418

Tunny (SS-283), 215, 219; ↓ *I-42*, torp. *Musashi*, 308, 363, 460

Turner, Richmond K., comdr. Fifth Amphib. Force, 168, 179, 227, 263

Tyree, Alexander K., c.o. *Bowfin*, 458, 461

U class submarines, German submarines

↓ *U-168* (SS) (Ger.), ↓ *by Zwaardvisch*, 393

↓ *U-183* (SS) (Ger.), ↓ *by Besugo*, 456

↓ *U-537* (SS) (Ger.), ↓ *by Flounder*, 414

↓ *U-859* (SS) (Ger.), ↓ *by Trenchant*, 414

↓ *UIT-23* (SS) (Ger.) (Ex It.), ↓ *by Tally Ho*, 285

Uchino, c.o. *I-8*, 349

Ulithi, Caroline Is., 371, 373, 377, 412, 431, 441

↓ *Umikaze* (DD), ↓ by *Guardfish*, 290

↓ *Underhill* (DE-682), ↓ by *I-53*, 474

Underwood, Gordon W., c.o. *Spadefish*, 363, 403, 436

↓ *Unryu* (CV), ↓ by *Redfish*, 419

↓ *Unyo* (CVE), 277; torp. by *Haddock*, 287, 303; ↓ by *Barb*, 367

↓ *Urakaze* (DD), 277, 343; ↓ by *Sealion*, 405

↓ *Usagumo* (DD), ↓ by *Skate*, 352

Van Well Groeneveld, C. A. J., (Du.), c.o. *K-14*, 70

Vella Lavella, Solomon Is., 204, 242, 255

Vella Gulf, Solomon Is., battle of, 242

Vladivostok, 169, 211

Voge, Richard G., c.o. *Sailfish*, 102; operation officer Subpac, 282, 312, 316, 326, 352

Wadleigh (*DD-689*), **RO-114*, 346
**Wahoo* (*SS-238*), 183; ↓*Harusame*, 198, 199–202, 215, 221; ↓*Konron Maru*, *missing after 9 Oct. '43, 269
Wake Island, 50, 60, 61, 90, 91, 252, 451
Walker, Francis D., c.o. *Crevalle*, 322, 353
Walker (*DD-517*), **RO-39*, 291
Walling, John F., c.o. *Snook*, 445
Ward (*APD-16*), sinks midget, 52, 57
Ward, Norville G., c.o. *Guardfish*, 284, 289, 355
Ward, Robert E. M., c.o. *Sailfish*, 278
Warder, Frederick B., c.o. *Seawolf*, 65, 78, 102, 103, 185; wolf pack, 262
Washington (*BB-56*), 173, 175
↓*Wasp* (*CV-7*), ↓by *I-19*, 168, 268
Weiss, Donald F., c.o. *Tinosa*, 325, 345
Westbrook, Edwin M., c.o. *Cod*, 468
Wewak, northern New Guinea, 198
Whale (*SS-239*), 177, 466
Whelchel, David L., c.o. *Steelhead*, 355
Whitaker, Reuben T., c.o. *Flasher*, 317, 353
White, David C., c.o. *Plunger*, 61, 88
Whitehurst (*DE-634*), **I-45*, 391
Wilkes, John, Comsubaf until Feb. '42, Comsubsowespac Feb. '42–May '42, 22, 49, 68, 69, 72, 81, 87, 101, 102, 111, 114, 125
Wilkins, Charles W., c.o. *Narwhal*, 105; comdr. wolf pack, 372
William C. Miller (*DE-259*), **I-6*, **RO-48*, 348
Willingham, Joseph H., c.o. *Tautog*, 115–16
Wingfield, W. R. G. (Br.), c.o. *Taurus*, 268, 349
Withers, Thomas, Comsubpac until Mar. '42, 50, 93, 105, 111, 114, 125
Wolf packs, coordinated attack groups, 261, 264, 312, 325
Wogan, Thomas L., c.o. *Tarpon*, 209, 271; c.o. *Besugo*, 378, 380, 426
Woleai Is., western Carolines, 309, 371
Worthington, Robert K. R., c.o. *Balao*, 442

Wotje, Marshall Is., 89, 100, 279, 283, 290, 310
Wright, Carleton H., task force comdr., 182
Wright, William L., c.o. *Sturgeon*, 73, 87, 154
Wyman (*DE-38*), **I-5*, **I-55*, 348

XE-1, -3, -4, -5, British midgets, 469–70
XCL, armed merchant cruiser
XPG, auxiliary patrol vessel

↓*Yaku* (DE), ↓by *Hammerhead*, 425
Yamaguchi, Tamori, Com. Cargo Div., 2, 142, 221
Yamagumo (DD), **Sculpin*, 264
↓*Yamakaze* (DD), ↓by *Nautilus*, 149
Yamamoto, Isoroku, C-in-C Combined Fleet until 18 Apr. '43, 52, 92, 104, 106, 111, 132, 136, 145, 160, 167, 181, 217, 218; death of, 220
Yamato (BB), 132, 254; torp. by *Skate*, 280, 336, 386, 446, 448
Yap, Caroline Is., 89, 309, 371, 372
↓*Yasukuni Maru* (AS), ↓by *Trigger*, 290
Yokosuka, naval base in Tokyo Bay, 56, 105, 231
Yokota, Minoru, c.o. *I-26*, 167
Yokota, Yutaka, kaiten pilot, 450
↓*Yorktown* (*CV-5*), 90, 110, 112, 113, 134, 142–46; ↓by *I-168*, 146
Yorktown (*CV-10*), 296
↓*Yoshida Maru No. 1* (AP), ↓by *Jack*, 320
Young, Lloyd V., c.o. *S-47*, 370
↓*Yubari* (CL), 61, ↓by *Bluegill*, 317
Yukikaze (DD), 323
↓*Yunagi* (DD), 360, ↓by *Picuda*, 363

Zabriske, David, c.o. *Herring*, 324
Zone classification, 258, 313, 380, 388, 416, 423
Zuikaku, 56, 92, 104, 107, 111, 113, 120
Zwaardvisch (SS) (Du.), ↓**U-168*, ↓*Itsutshima*, 393

ALASKA

BERING SEA

Unimak
Unimak Pass
Dutch Hbr.
Unalaska
Umnak

Atka
Adak
Amchitka

Attu
Agattu
Kiska

ALEUTIAN ISLANDS

50°N

160°W

180°

A

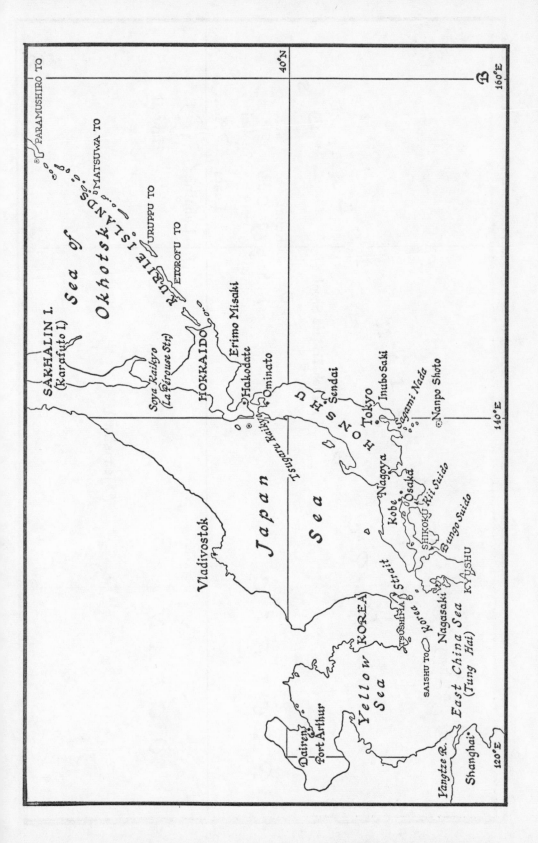

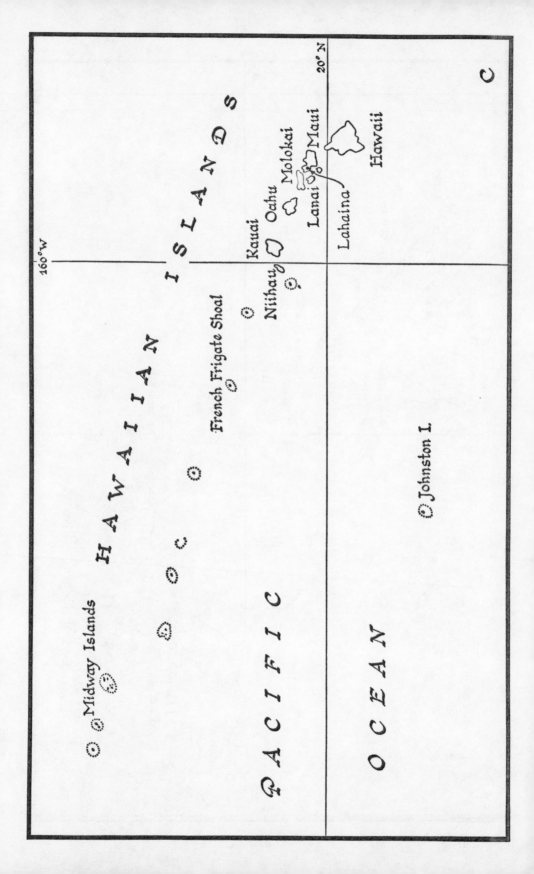

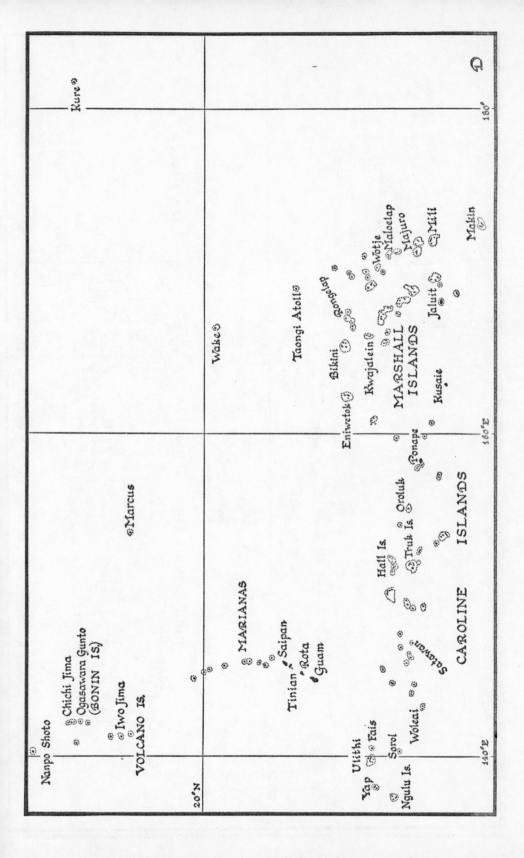

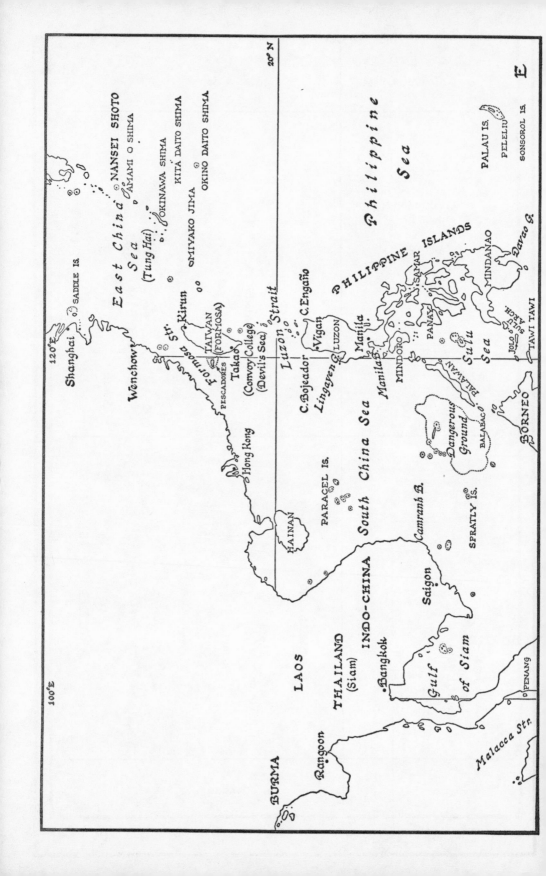

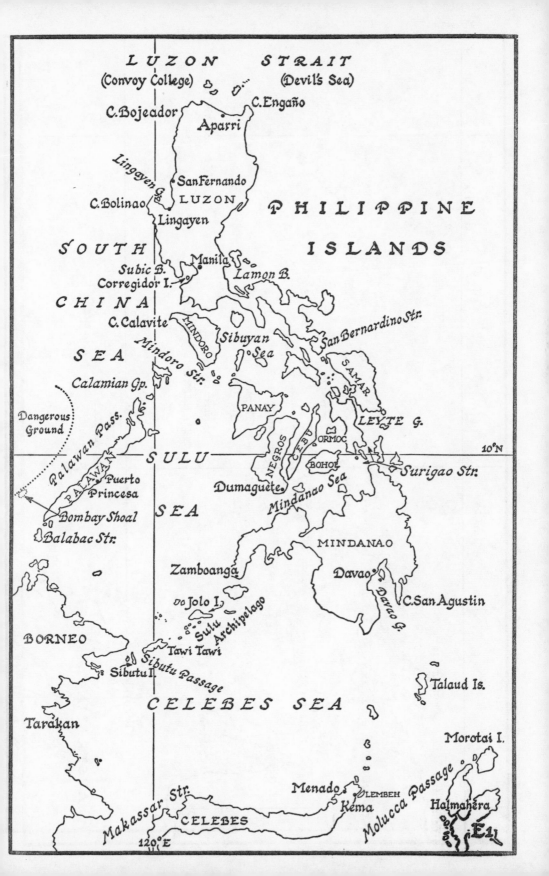

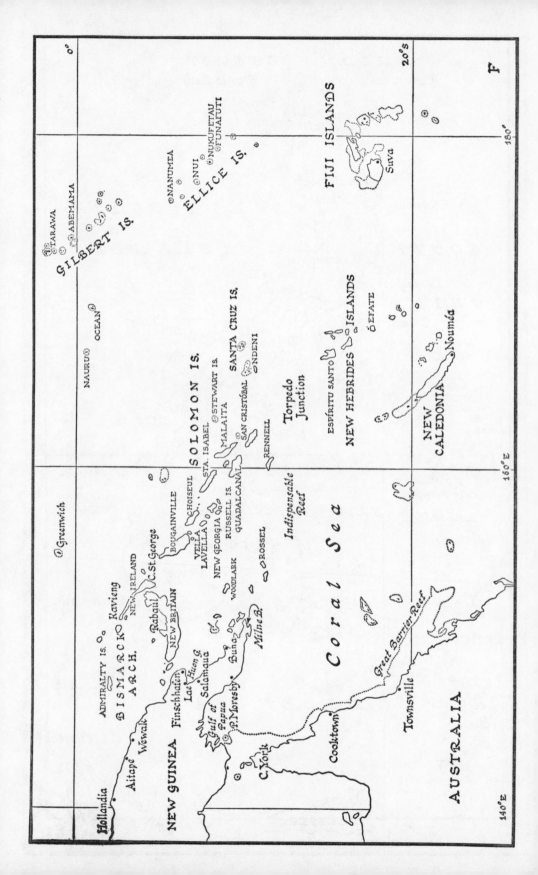

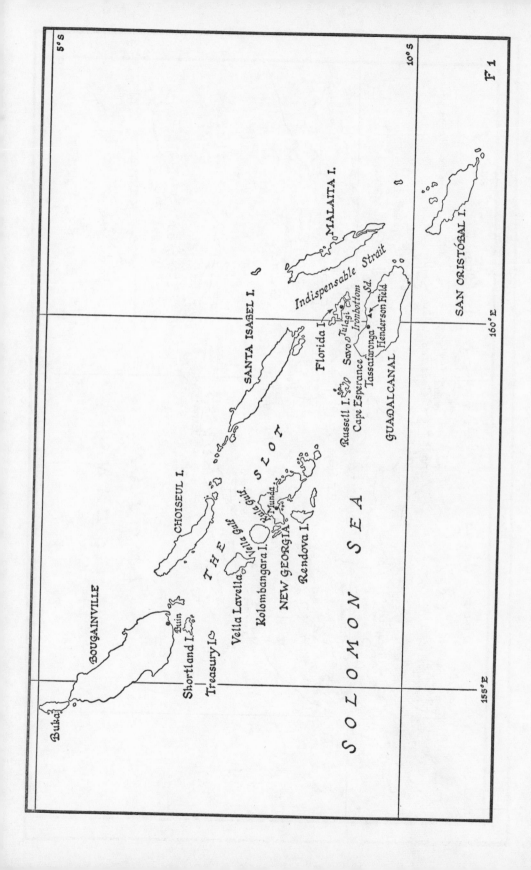

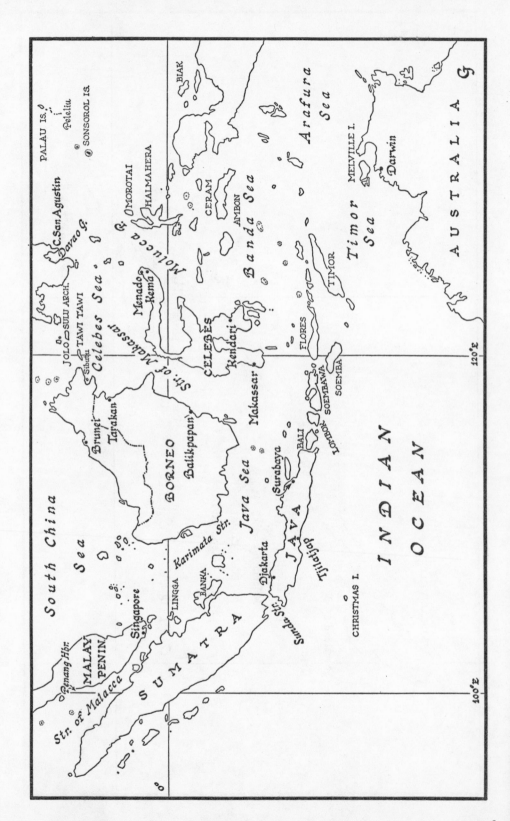

ASIA
Sea of Okhotsk
Kamchatka
KURIL IS.
Sea of Japan
JAPAN
Yellow Sea
East China Sea
Nansei Shoto
Nanpo Shoto
B
RYUKYU IS.
Okinawa
BONIN IS.
VOLCANO IS.
Marcus I.
FORMOSA
Luzon Strait
E1
Philippine Sea
PHILIPPINE IS.
MARIANAS IS.
Saipan
Guam
Eniwetok
Ulithi
South China Sea
Palau
Sulu Sea
Truk
MALAYA
Malacca Str.
E
CAROLINE IS.
Celebes Sea
Molucca Sea
Morotai
SUMATRA
Karimata Str.
Biak
Hollandia
BORNEO
Makassar Str.
NEW GUINEA
Rabaul
NEW BRITAIN
SOLOMON I
Java Sea
JAVA
PAPUA
F1
Lombok
Darwin
Coral Sea
INDIAN OCEAN
G
NEW HEBRID
Nouméa
Exmouth Gulf
AUSTRALIA
Brisbane
Fremantle
100°
120°
140°
160°